STANDARD ATOMIC WEIGHTS OF THE ELEMENTS 2001 Based on relative atomic mass of $^{12}C = 12$, where ^{12}C is a neutral atom in its nuclear and electronic ground state.[†]

Name	Symbol	Atomic Number	Atomic Weight	Name	Symbol	Atomic Number	Atomic Weight
Actinium*	Ac	89	(227)	Molybdenum	Mo	42	95.94(1)
Aluminum	Al	13	26.981538(2)	Neodymium	Nd	60	144.24(3)
Americium*	Am	95	(243)	Neon	Ne	10	20.1797(6)
Antimony	Sb	51	121.760(1)	Neptunium*	Np	93	(237)
Argon	Ar	18	39.948(1)	Nickel	Ni	28	58.6934(2)
Arsenic	As	33	74.92160(2)	Niobium	Nb	41	92.90638(2)
Astatine*	At	85	(210)	Nitrogen	N	7	14.0067(2)
Barium	Ba	56	137.327(7)	Nobelium*	No	102	(259)
Berkelium*	Bk	97	(247)	Osmium	Os	76	190.23(3)
Beryllium	Be	4	9.012182(3)	Oxygen	O	8	15.9994(3)
Bismuth	Bi	83	208.98038(2)	Palladium	Pd	46	106.42(1)
Bohrium	Bh	107	(264)	Phosphorus	P	15	30.973761(2)
Boron	B	5	10.811(7)	Platinum	Pt	78	195.078(2)
Bromine	Br	35	79.904(1)	Plutonium*	Pu	94	(244)
Cadmium	Cd	48	112.411(8)	Polonium*	Po	84	(209)
Cesium	Cs	55	132.90545(2)	Potassium	K	19	39.0983(1)
Calcium	Ca	20	40.078(4)	Praseodymium	Pr	59	140.90765(2)
Californium*	Cf	98	(251)	Promethium*	Pm	61	(145)
Carbon	C	6	12.0107(8)	Protactinium*	Pa	91	231.03588(2)
Cerium	Ce	58	140.116(1)	Radium*	Ra	88	(226)
Chlorine	Cl	17	35.453(2)	Radon*	Rn	86	(222)
Chromium	Cr	24	51.9961(6)	Rhenium	Re	75	186.207(1)
Cobalt	Co	27	58.933200(9)	Rhodium	Rh	45	102.90550(2)
Copper	Cu	29	63.546(3)	Roentgenium	Rg	111	(272)
Curium*	Cm	96	(247)	Rubidium	Rb	37	85.4678(3)
Darmstadtium	Ds	110	(271)	Ruthenium	Ru	44	101.07(2)
Dubnium	Db	105	(262)	Rutherfordium	Rf	104	(261)
Dysprosium	Dy	66	162.500(1)	Samarium	Sm	62	150.36(3)
Einsteinium*	Es	99	(252)	Scandium	Sc	21	44.955910(8)
Erbium	Er	68	167.259(3)	Seaborgium	Sg	106	(266)
Europium	Eu	63	151.964(1)	Selenium	Se	34	78.96(3)
Fermium*	Fm	100	(257)	Silicon	Si	14	28.0855(3)
Fluorine	F	9	18.9984032(5)	Silver	Ag	47	107.8682(2)
Francium*	Fr	87	(223)	Sodium	Na	11	22.989770(2)
Gadolinium	Gd	64	157.25(3)	Strontium	Sr	38	87.62(1)
Gallium	Ga	31	69.723(1)	Sulfur	S	16	32.065(5)
Germanium	Ge	32	72.64(1)	Tantalum	Ta	73	180.9479(1)
Gold	Au	79	196.96655(2)	Technetium*	Tc	43	(98)
Hafnium	Hf	72	178.49(2)	Tellurium	Te	52	127.60(3)
Hassium	Hs	108	(277)	Terbium	Tb	65	158.92534(2)
Helium	He	2	4.002602(2)	Thallium	Tl	81	204.3833(2)
Holmium	Ho	67	164.93032(2)	Thorium*	Th	90	232.0381(1)
Hydrogen	H	1	1.00794(7)	Thulium	Tm	69	168.93421(2)
Indium	In	49	114.818(3)	Tin	Sn	50	118.710(7)
Iodine	I	53	126.90447(3)	Titanium	Ti	22	47.867(1)
Iridium	Ir	77	192.217(3)	Tungsten	W	74	183.84(1)
Iron	Fe	26	55.845(2)	Ununbium	Uub	112	(285)
Krypton	Kr	36	83.798(2)	Ununhexium	Uuh	116	(292)
Lanthanum	La	57	138.9055(2)	Ununpentium	Uup	115	(228)
Lawrencium*	Lr	103	(262)	Ununquadium	Uuq	114	(289)
Lead	Pb	82	207.2(1)	Ununtrium	Uut	113	(284)
Lithium	Li	3	6.941(2)	Uranium*	U	92	238.02891(3)
Lutetium	Lu	71	174.967(1)	Vanadium	V	23	50.9415(1)
Magnesium	Mg	12	24.3050(6)	Xenon	Xe	54	131.293(6)
Manganese	Mn	25	54.938049(9)	Ytterbium	Yb	70	173.04(3)
Meitnerium	Mt	109	(268)	Yttrium	Y	39	88.90585(2)
Mendelevium*	Md	101	(258)	Zinc	Zn	30	65.409(4)
Mercury	Hg	80	200.59(2)	Zirconium	Zr	40	91.224(2)

[†]The atomic weights of many elements can vary depending on the origin and treatment of the sample. This is particularly true for Li; commercially available lithium-containing materials have Li atomic weights in the range of 6.939 and 6.996. The uncertainties in atomic weight values are given in parentheses following the last significant figure to which they are attributed.

*Elements with no stable nuclide; the value given in parentheses is the atomic mass number of the isotope of longest known half-life. However, three such elements (Th, Pa, and U) have a characteristic terrestrial isotopic composition, and the atomic weight is tabulated for these. **http://www.chem.qmw.ac.uk/iupac/AtWt/**

Fundamentals of Chemistry: CHEM 10050 – with Solutions Manual

Kent State University

Eighth Edition

Frederick A. Bettelheim

William H. Brown
Beloit College

Mary K. Campbell
Mount Holyoke College

Shawn O. Farrell
Olympic Training Center

Courtney A. Farrell

Mark S. Erickson
Hartwick College

THOMSON

BROOKS/COLE

Australia · Canada · Mexico · Singapore · Spain · United Kingdom · United States

Fundamentals of Chemistry: CHEM 10050 - with Solutions Manual
Bettelheim / Brown / Campbell / Farrell / Farrell / Erickson

Executive Editors:
Michele Baird, Maureen Staudt &
Michael Stranz

Project Development Manager:
Linda de Stefano

Marketing Coordinators:
Lindsay Annett and Sara Mercurio

Production/Manufacturing Supervisor:
Donna M. Brown

Pre-Media Services Supervisor:
Dan Plofchan

Rights and Permissions Specialists:
Kalina Hintz and Bahman Naraghi

Cover Image
Getty Images*

Fundamentals of Chemistry: CHEM 10050 - with Solutions Manual   / Bettelheim / Brown / Campbell / Farrell /Farrell / Erickson

ISBN 0-495-25793-1

International Divisions List

Asia (Including India):
Thomson Learning
(a division of Thomson Asia Pte Ltd)
5 Shenton Way #01-01
UIC Building
Singapore 068808
Tel: (65) 6410-1200
Fax: (65) 6410-1208

Australia/New Zealand:
Thomson Learning Australia
102 Dodds Street
Southbank, Victoria 3006
Australia

Latin America:
Thomson Learning
Seneca 53
Colonia Polano
11560 Mexico, D.F., Mexico
Tel (525) 281-2906
Fax (525) 281-2656

Canada:
Thomson Nelson
1120 Birchmount Road
Toronto, Ontario
Canada M1K 5G4
Tel (416) 752-9100
Fax (416) 752-8102

UK/Europe/Middle East/Africa:
Thomson Learning
High Holborn House
50-51 Bedford Row
London, WC1R 4LS
United Kingdom
Tel 44 (020) 7067-2500
Fax 44 (020) 7067-2600

Spain (Includes Portugal):
Thomson Paraninfo
Calle Magallanes 25
28015 Madrid
España
Tel 34 (0)91 446-3350
Fax 34 (0)91 445-6218

Contents

Matter, Energy, and Measurement

James Balog/Stone/Getty Images

A woman climbing a frozen waterfall in British Columbia.

GOB
Chemistry ⚛ Now™

Look for this logo in the text and go to GOB ChemistryNow at **http://now.brookscole.com/gob8** or on the CD to view tutorials and simulations, develop problem-solving skills, and test your conceptual understanding with unique interactive resources.

1.1 Why Do We Call Chemistry the Study of Matter?

The world around us is made of chemicals. Our food, our clothing, the buildings in which we live are all made of chemicals. Our bodies are made of chemicals, too. To understand the human body, its diseases, and its cures, we must know all we can about those chemicals. There was a time—only a few hundred years ago—when physicians were powerless to treat many diseases. Cancer, tuberculosis, smallpox, typhus, plague, and many other sicknesses struck people seemingly at random. Doctors, who had no idea what caused any of these diseases, could do little or nothing about them. Doctors treated them with magic as well as by such measures as bleeding, laxatives, hot plasters, and pills made from powdered stag horn, saffron, or gold. None of these treatments was effective, and the doctors, because they came into direct contact with highly contagious diseases, died at a much higher rate than the general public.

A woman being bled by a leech on her left forearm; a bottle of leeches is on the table. From a 1639 woodcut.

Courtesy of the National Library of Medicine

Medicine has made great strides since those times. We live much longer, and many once-feared diseases have been essentially eliminated or are curable. Smallpox has been eradicated, and polio, typhus, bubonic plague, diphtheria, and other diseases that once killed millions no longer pose a serious problem, at least not in the developed countries.

How has this medical progress come about? The answer is that diseases could not be cured until they were understood, and this understanding has emerged through greater knowledge of how the body functions. It is progress in our understanding of the principles of biology, chemistry, and physics that has led to these advances in medicine. Because so much of modern medicine depends on chemistry, it is essential that students who intend to enter the health professions have some understanding of basic chemistry. This book was written to help you achieve that goal. Even if you choose a different profession, you will find that the chemistry you learn in this course will greatly enrich your life.

The universe consists of matter, energy, and empty space. **Matter** is anything that has mass and takes up space. **Chemistry** is the science that deals with matter: the structure and properties of matter and the transformations from one form of matter to another. We will discuss energy in Section 1.8.

It has long been known that matter can change, or be made to change, from one form to another. In a **chemical change,** more commonly called a **chemical reaction,** substances are used up (disappear) and others are formed to take their places. An example is the burning of the mixture of hydrocarbons usually called "bottled gas." In this mixture of hydrocarbons, the main component is propane. When this chemical change takes place, propane and oxygen from the air are converted to carbon dioxide and water. Figure 1.1 shows another chemical change.

Matter also undergoes other kinds of changes, called **physical changes.** These changes differ from chemical reactions in that the identities of the substances do not change. Most physical changes involve changes of state—for example, the melting of solids and the boiling of liquids. Water remains water whether it is in the liquid state or in the form of ice or steam. The conversion from one state to another is a physical—not a chemical—change. Another important type of physical change involves making or separating mixtures. Dissolving sugar in water is a physical change.

When we talk about the **chemical properties** of a substance, we mean the chemical reactions that it undergoes. **Physical properties** are all properties that do not involve chemical reactions. For example, density, color, melting point, and physical state (liquid, solid, gas) are all physical properties.

GOB
Chemistry Now™
Click *Chemistry Interactive* to see an example of a **chemical change in action**

(a)   (b)   (c)

Charles D. Winters

GOB
Chemistry✦Now™

Active Figure 1.1   A chemical reaction. (*a*) Bromine, an orange-brown liquid, and aluminum metal. (*b*) These two substances react so vigorously that the aluminum becomes molten and glows white hot at the bottom of the beaker. The yellow vapor consists of vaporized bromine and some of the product of the reaction, white aluminum bromide. (*c*) Once the reaction is complete, the beaker is coated with aluminum bromide and the products of its reaction with atmospheric moisture. (*Note:* This reaction is dangerous! Under no circumstances should it be done except under properly supervised conditions.) **See a simulation based on this figure, and take a short quiz on the concepts at http://now.brookscole.com/gob8 or on the CD.**

1.2 | What Is the Scientific Method?

Scientists learn by using a tool called the **scientific method.** The heart of the scientific method is the testing of theories. It was not always so, however. Before about 1600, philosophers often believed statements just because they sounded right. For example, the great philosopher Aristotle (384–322 BCE) believed that if you took the gold out of a mine it would grow back. He believed this idea because it fitted in with a more general picture that he had about the workings of nature. In ancient times, most thinkers behaved in this way. If a statement sounded right, they believed it without testing it.

About 1600 CE, the scientific method came into use. Let us look at an example to see how the scientific method operates. The Greek physician Galen (200–130 BCE) recognized that the blood on the left side of the heart somehow gets to the right side. This is a fact. A **fact** is a statement based on direct experience. It is a consistent and reproducible observation. Having observed this fact, Galen then proposed a hypothesis to explain it. A **hypothesis** is a statement that is proposed, without actual proof, to explain the facts and their relationship. Because Galen could not actually see how the blood got from the left side to the right side of the heart, he came up with the hypothesis that tiny holes must be present in the muscular wall that separates the two halves.

Up to this point, a modern scientist and an ancient philosopher would behave the same way. Each would offer a hypothesis to explain the facts. From this point on, however, their methods would differ. To Galen, his explanation sounded right and that was enough to make him believe it, even though he couldn't see any holes. His hypothesis was, in fact, believed by virtually all physicians for more than 1000 years. When we use the scientific method, however, we do not believe a hypothesis just because it sounds right. We test it, using the most rigorous testing we can imagine.

Courtesy of the National Library of Medicine

Galen.

Hypothesis A statement that is proposed, without actual proof, to explain a set of facts and their relationship

William Harvey (1578–1657) tested Galen's hypothesis by dissecting human and animal hearts and blood vessels. He discovered that one-way valves separate the upper chambers of the heart from the lower chambers. He also discovered that the heart is a pump that, by contracting and expanding, pushes the blood out. Harvey's teacher, Fabricius (1537–1619), had previously observed that one-way valves exist in the veins, so that blood in the veins can travel only toward the heart and not the other way.

Harvey put these facts together to come up with a new hypothesis: Blood is pumped by the heart and circulates throughout the body. This was a better hypothesis than Galen's because it fitted the facts more closely. Even so, it was still a hypothesis and, according to the scientific method, had to be tested further. One important test took place in 1661, four years after Harvey died. Harvey had predicted that because there had to be a way for the blood to get from the arteries to the veins, tiny blood vessels must connect them. In 1661 the Italian anatomist Malpighi (1628–1694), using the newly invented microscope, found these tiny vessels, which are now called capillaries.

Theory The formulation of an apparent relationship among certain observed phenomena, which has been verified. A theory explains many interrelated facts and can be used to make predictions about natural phenomena. Examples are Newton's theory of gravitation and the kinetic molecular theory of gases, which we will encounter in Section 6.6. This type of theory is also subject to testing and will be discarded or modified if it is contradicted by new facts.

Malpighi's discovery supported the blood circulation hypothesis by fulfilling Harvey's prediction. When a hypothesis passes the tests, we have more confidence in it and call it a theory. A **theory** is the formulation of an apparent relationship among certain observed phenomena, which has been verified to some extent. In this sense, a theory is the same as a hypothesis except that we have a stronger belief in it because more evidence supports it. No matter how much confidence we have in a theory, however, if we discover new facts that conflict with it or if it does not pass newly devised tests, the theory must be altered or rejected. In the history of science, many firmly established theories have eventually been thrown out because they could not pass new tests.

The scientific method is thus very simple. We don't accept a hypothesis or a theory just because it sounds right. We devise tests, and only if the hypothesis or theory passes the tests do we accept it. The enormous progress made since 1600 in chemistry, biology, and the other sciences is a testimony to the value of the scientific method.

You may get the impression from the preceding discussion that science progresses in one direction: facts first, hypothesis second, theory last. Real life is not so simple, however. Hypotheses and theories call the attention of scientists to discover new facts. An example of this scenario is the discovery of the element germanium. In 1871, Mendeleev's Periodic Table—a graphic description of elements organized by properties—predicted the existence of a new element whose properties would be similar to those of silicon. Mendeleev called this element eka-silicon. In 1886, it was discovered in Germany (hence the name), and its properties were truly similar to those predicted by theory.

On the other hand, many scientific discoveries result from **serendipity,** or chance observation. An example of serendipity occurred in 1926, when James Sumner of Cornell University left an enzyme preparation of jack bean urease in a refrigerator over the weekend. Upon his return, he found that his solution contained crystals that turned out to be a protein. This chance discovery led to the hypothesis that all enzymes are proteins. Of course, serendipity is not enough to move science forward. Scientists must have the creativity and insight to recognize the significance of their observations. Sumner fought for more than 15 years for his hypothesis to gain acceptance because people believed that only small molecules can form crystals. Eventually his view won out, and he was awarded a Nobel Prize in chemistry in 1946.

1.3 | How Do Scientists Report Numbers?

Scientists often have to deal with numbers that are very large or very small. For example, an ordinary copper penny (dating from before 1982, when pennies in the United States were still made of copper) contains approximately

$$29,500,000,000,000,000,000,000 \text{ atoms of copper}$$

and a single copper atom weighs

$$0.000000000000000000000000023 \text{ pound}$$

which is equal to

$$0.0000000000000000000000104 \text{ gram}$$

Many years ago, an easy way to handle such large and small numbers was devised. This method, which is called **exponential notation,** is based on powers of 10. In exponential notation, the number of copper atoms in a penny is written

$$2.95 \times 10^{22}$$

and the weight of a single copper atom is written

$$2.3 \times 10^{-25} \text{ pound}$$

which is equal to

$$1.04 \times 10^{-22} \text{ grams}$$

The origin of this shorthand form can be seen in the following examples:

$$100 = 1 \times 10 \times 10 = 1 \times 10^2$$

$$1000 = 1 \times 10 \times 10 \times 10 = 1 \times 10^3$$

What we have just said in the form of an equation is "100 is a one with two zeroes after the one, and 1000 is a one with three zeroes after the one." We can also write

$$1/100 = 1/10 \times 1/10 = 1 \times 10^{-2}$$

$$1/1000 = 1/10 \times 1/10 \times 1/10 = 1 \times 10^{-3}$$

where negative exponents denote numbers less than 1. The exponent in a very large or very small number lets us keep track of the number of zeros. That number can become unwieldy with very large or very small quantities, and it is easy to lose track of a zero. Exponential notation helps us deal with this possible source of mathematical error.

When it comes to measurements, not all the numbers you can generate in your calculator or computer are of equal importance. Only the number of digits that are known with certainty are significant. Suppose that you measured the weight of an object as 3.4 g on a balance that you can read to the nearest 0.1 g. You can report the weight as 3.4 g but not as 3.40 or 3.400 g because you do not know the added zeros with certainty. This becomes even more important when you do calculations using a calculator. For example, you might measure a cube with a ruler and find that each side is 2.9 cm. If you are asked to calculate the volume, you multiply $2.9 \times 2.9 \times 2.9$. The calculator will then give you an answer that is 23.389 cm^3. However, your initial measurements were only good to a tenth of a centimeter, so your final answer cannot be good to a thousandth of a centimeter. As a scientist, it is important to report data that have the correct number of **significant figures.** A detailed account of using significant figures is presented in Appendix II. A discussion of accuracy, precision, and significant figures can be found in laboratory manuals [see Bettelheim and Landesberg, *Laboratory Experiments,* sixth edition (Experiment 2)].

EXAMPLE 1.1

Multiply:

(a) $(4.73 \times 10^5)(1.37 \times 10^2)$ (b) $(2.7 \times 10^{-4})(5.9 \times 10^8)$

Divide:

(c) $\dfrac{7.08 \times 10^{-8}}{300}$ (d) $\dfrac{5.8 \times 10^{-6}}{6.6 \times 10^{-8}}$ (e) $\dfrac{7.05 \times 10^{-3}}{4.51 \times 10^5}$

Solution

The way to do calculations of this sort is to use a button on scientific calculators that automatically uses exponential notation. The button is usually labeled "E."

(a) Enter 4.73E5, press the multiplication key, enter 1.37E2, and press the "=" key. The answer is 6.48×10^7. The calculator will display this number as 6.48E7. This answer makes sense. We add exponents when we multiply, and the sum of these two exponents is correct $(5 + 2 = 7)$. We also multiply the numbers, 4.73×1.37. This is approximately $4 \times 1.5 = 6$, so 6.48 is also reasonable.

(b) Here we have to deal with a negative exponent, so we use the "+/-" key. Enter 2.7E+/-4, press the multiplication key, enter 5.9E8, and press the "=" key. The calculator will display the answer as 1.593E5. To have the correct number of significant figures, we should report our answer as 1.6E5. This answer makes sense because 2.7 is a little less than 3, and 5.9 is a little less than 6, so we predict a number slightly less than 18; also the algebraic sum of the exponents $(-4 + 8)$ is equal to 4. This gives 16×10^4. In scientific notation, we normally prefer to report numbers between 1 and 10, so we rewrite our answer as 1.6×10^5. We made the first number 10 times smaller, so we increased the exponent by 1 to reflect that change.

(c) Enter 7.08E+/-8, press the division key, enter 300, and press the "=" key. The answer is 2.36×10^{-10}. The calculator will display this number as 2.36E − 10. We subtract exponents when we divide, and we can also write 300 as 3.00×10^2.

(d) Enter 5.8E+/-6, press the division key, enter 6.6E+/-8, and press the "=" key. The calculator will display the answer as 87.878787878788. We report this answer as 88 to get the right number of significant figures. This answer makes sense. When we divide 5.8 by 6.6, we get a number slightly less than 1. When we subtract the exponents algebraically $(-6 - [-8])$, we get 2. This means that the answer is slightly less than 1×10^2, or slightly less than 100.

(e) Enter 7.05E+/-3, press the division key, enter 4.51E5, and press the "=" key. The calculator displays the answer as 1.5632E-8, which, to the correct number of significant figures, is 1.56×10^{-8}. The algebraic subtraction of exponents is $-3 - 5 = -8$.

Problem 1.1

Multiply:

(a) $(6.49 \times 10^7)(7.22 \times 10^{-3})$ (b) $(3.4 \times 10^{-5})(8.2 \times 10^{-11})$

Divide:

(a) $\dfrac{6.02 \times 10^{23}}{3.10 \times 10^5}$ (b) $\dfrac{3.14}{2.30 \times 10^{-5}}$

1.4 | How Do We Make Measurements?

In our daily lives we are constantly making measurements. We measure ingredients for recipes, driving distances, gallons of gasoline, weights of fruits and vegetables, and the timing of TV programs. Doctors and nurses measure pulse rates, blood pressures, temperatures, and drug dosages. Chemistry, like other sciences, is based on measurements.

A measurement consists of two parts: a number and a unit. A number without a unit is usually meaningless. If you were told that a person's weight is 57, the information would be of very little use. Is it 57 pounds, which would indicate that the person is very likely a child or a midget, or 57 kilograms, which is the weight of an average woman or a small man? Or is it perhaps some other unit? Because so many units exist, a number by itself is not enough; the unit must also be stated.

In the United States, most measurements are made with the English system of units: pounds, miles, gallons, and so on. In most other parts of the world, however, few people could tell you what a pound or an inch is. Most countries use the **metric system,** a system that originated in France about 1800 and that has since spread throughout the world. Even in the United States, metric measurements are slowly being introduced (Figure 1.2). For

The label on this bottle of water shows the metric size (one liter) and the eqivalent in quarts.

Metric system A system of units of measurement in which the divisions to subunits are made by a power of 10

Figure 1.2 Road sign in Massachusetts showing metric equivalents of mileage.

Table 1.1	Base Units in the Metric System
Length	meter (m)
Volume	liter (L)
Mass	gram (g)
Time	second (s)
Temperature	°Celsius (°C)
Energy	calorie (cal)
Amount of substance	mole (mol)

GOB
Chemistry⚛Now™

Click *Mastering the Essentials* to practice using the **Metric System**

example, many soft drinks and most alcoholic beverages now come in metric sizes. Scientists in the United States have been using metric units all along.

Around 1960, international scientific organizations adopted another system, called the **International System of Units** (abbreviated **SI**). The SI is based on the metric system and uses some of the metric units. The main difference is that the SI is more restrictive: It discourages the use of certain metric units and favors others. Although the SI has advantages over the older metric system, it also has significant disadvantages. For this reason U.S. chemists have been very slow to adopt it. At this time, approximately 40 years after its introduction, not many U.S. chemists use the entire SI, although some of its preferred units are gaining ground.

In this book we will use the metric system (Table 1.1). Occasionally we will mention the preferred SI unit.

A. Length

The key to the metric system (and the SI) is that there is one base unit for each kind of measurement and that other units are related to the base unit only by powers of 10. As an example, let us look at measurements of length. In the English system we have the inch, the foot, the yard, and the mile (not to mention such older units as the league, furlong, ell, and rod). If you want to convert one unit to another unit, you must memorize or look up these conversion factors:

$$5280 \text{ feet} = 1 \text{ mile}$$

$$1760 \text{ yards} = 1 \text{ mile}$$

$$3 \text{ feet} = 1 \text{ yard}$$

$$12 \text{ inches} = 1 \text{ foot}$$

All this is unnecessary in the metric system (and the SI). In both systems the base unit of length is the **meter (m).** To convert to larger or smaller units we do not use arbitrary numbers like 12, 3, and 1760, but only 10, 100, 1/100, 1/10, or other powers of 10. This means that *to convert from one metric or SI unit to another, we only have to move the decimal point.* Furthermore, the other units are named by putting prefixes in front of "meter," and *these prefixes are the same throughout the metric system and the SI.* Table 1.2 lists the most important of these prefixes. If we put some of these prefixes in front of "meter," we have

$$1 \text{ kilometer (km)} = 1000 \text{ meters (m)}$$

$$1 \text{ centimeter (cm)} = 0.01 \text{ meter}$$

$$1 \text{ nanometer (nm)} = 10^{-9} \text{ meter}$$

Table 1.2	The Most Common Metric Prefixes	
Prefix	Symbol	Value
giga	G	$10^9 = 1,000,000,000$ (one billion)
mega	M	$10^6 = 1,000,000$ (one million)
kilo	k	$10^3 = 1000$ (one thousand)
deci	d	$10^{-1} = 0.1$ (one-tenth)
centi	c	$10^{-2} = 0.01$ (one-hundredth)
milli	m	$10^{-3} = 0.001$ (one-thousandth)
micro	μ	$10^{-6} = 0.000001$ (one-millionth)
nano	n	$10^{-9} = 0.000000001$ (one-billionth)

Table 1.3	Some Conversion Factors Between the English and Metric Systems	
Length	**Mass**	**Volume**
1 in. = 2.54 cm	1 oz = 28.35 g	1 qt = 0.946 L
1 m = 39.37 in	1 lb = 453.6 g	1 gal = 3.785 L
1 mile = 1.609 km	1 kg = 2.205 lb	1 L = 33.81 fl oz
	1 g = 15.43 grains	1 fl oz = 29.57 mL
		1 L = 1.057 qt

For people who have grown up using English units, it is helpful to have some idea of the size of metric units. Table 1.3 shows some conversion factors.

Some of these conversions are difficult enough that you will probably not remember them and must, therefore, look them up when you need them. Some are easier. For example, a meter is about the same as a yard. A kilogram is a little over two pounds. There are almost four liters in a gallon. These conversions may be important to you someday. For example, if you rent a car in Europe, the price of gas listed on the sign at the gas station will be in Euros per liter. When you realize that you are spending a dollar per liter and you know that there are almost four liters to a gallon, you will realize why so many people take the bus or a train instead.

B. Volume

Volume is space. The volume of a liquid, solid, or gas is the space occupied by that substance. The base unit of volume in the metric system is the **liter (L).** This unit is a little larger than a quart (Table 1.3). The only other common metric unit for volume is the milliliter (mL), which is equal to 10^{-3} L.

$$1 \text{ mL} = 0.001 \text{ L}$$

$$1000 \text{ mL} = 1 \text{ L}$$

One milliliter is exactly equal to one cubic centimeter (cc or cm^3):

$$1 \text{ mL} = 1 \text{ cc}$$

Thus there are 1000 cc in 1 L.

C. Mass

Mass is the quantity of matter in an object. The base unit of mass in the metric system is the **gram (g).** As always in the metric system, larger and smaller units are indicated by prefixes. The ones in common use are

$$1 \text{ kilogram (kg)} = 1000 \text{ g}$$

$$1 \text{ milligram (mg)} = 0.001 \text{ g}$$

The gram is a small unit; there are 453.6 g in one pound (Table 1.3).

We use a device called a balance to measure mass. Figure 1.3 shows two types of laboratory balances.

There is a fundamental difference between mass and weight. Mass is independent of location. The mass of a stone, for example, is the same whether we measure it at sea level, on top of a mountain, or in the depths of a mine. In contrast, weight is not independent of location. **Weight** is the

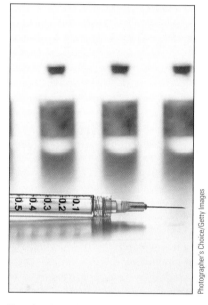

Hypodermic syringe. Note that the volumes are indicated in mL.

Figure 1.3 Two laboratory balances.

Courtesy of Brinkmann Instruments, Co.

force a mass experiences under the pull of gravity. This point was dramatically demonstrated when the astronauts walked on the surface of the Moon. The Moon, being a smaller body than the Earth, exerts a weaker gravitational pull. Consequently, even though the astronauts wore space suits and equipment that would be heavy on Earth, they felt lighter on the Moon and could execute great leaps and bounces during their walks.

Although mass and weight are different concepts, they are related to each other by the force of gravity. We frequently use the words interchangeably because we weigh objects by comparing their masses to standard refer-

---

 CHEMICAL CONNECTIONS 1A

Drug Dosage and Body Mass

In many cases, drug dosages are prescribed on the basis of body mass. For example, the recommended dosage of a drug may be 3 mg of drug for each kilogram of body weight. In this case, a 50 kg (110 lb) woman would receive 150 mg and an 82 kg (180 lb) man would get 246 mg. This adjustment is especially important for children, because a dose suitable for an adult will generally be too much for a child, who has much less body mass. For this reason, manufacturers package and sell smaller doses of certain drugs, such as aspirin, for children.

Drug dosage may also vary with age. Occasionally, when an elderly patient has an impaired kidney or liver function, the clearance of a drug from the body is delayed, and the drug may stay in the body longer than is normal. This persistence can cause dizziness, vertigo, and migraine-like headaches, resulting in falls and broken bones. Such delayed clearance must be monitored, and the drug dosage adjusted accordingly.

Children's

Dosing Chart

Weight (lb)	Age (yr)	Dose (tsp)
under 24 lb	under 2 yr	ask a doctor
24-35 lb	2-3 yr	1 tsp
36-47 lb	4-5 yr	1 1/2 tsp
48-59 lb	6-8 yr	2 tsp
60-71 lb	9-10 yr	2 1/2 tsp
72-95 lb	11 yr	3 tsp

Grape Flavored Liquid
for ages 2-11 years

4 FL OZ (120 mL)

Charles D. Winters

This package of Advil has a chart showing the proper doses for children of a given weight.

ence masses (weights) on a balance, and the gravitational pull is the same on the unknown object and on the standard masses. Because the force of gravity is essentially constant, mass is always directly proportional to weight.

D. Time

Time is the one quantity for which the units are the same in all systems: English, metric, and SI. The base unit is the **second (s):**

$$60 \text{ s} = 1 \text{ min}$$

$$60 \text{ min} = 1 \text{ h}$$

E. Temperature

Most people in the United States are familiar with the Fahrenheit scale of temperature. The metric system uses the centigrade, or **Celsius,** scale. In this scale, the boiling point of water is set at 100°C and the freezing point at 0°C. We can convert from one scale to the other by using the following formulas:

$$°F = \frac{9}{5} °C + 32$$

$$°C = \frac{5}{9} (°F - 32)$$

The 32 in these equations is a defined number and is, therefore, treated as if it had an infinite number of zeros following the decimal point. (See Appendix II.)

EXAMPLE 1.2

Normal body temperature is 98.6°F. Convert this temperature to Celsius.

Solution

$$°C = \frac{5}{9} (98.6 - 32) = \frac{5}{9} (66.6) = 37.0°C$$

Problem 1.2

Convert:
(a) 64.0°C to Fahrenheit   (b) 47°F to Celsius

Figure 1.4 shows the relationship between the Fahrenheit and Celsius scales.

A third temperature scale is the **Kelvin (K)** scale, also called the absolute scale. The size of a Kelvin degree is the same as that of a Celsius degree; the only difference is the zero point. The temperature −273°C is taken as the zero point on the Kelvin scale. This makes conversions between Kelvin and Celsius very easy. To go from Celsius to Kelvin, just *add* 273; to go from Kelvin to Celsius, *subtract* 273:

$$K = °C + 273$$

$$°C = K - 273$$

Figure 1.4 also shows the relationship between the Kelvin and Celsius scales. Note that we don't use the degree symbol in the Kelvin scale: 100°C equals 373 K, not 373°K.

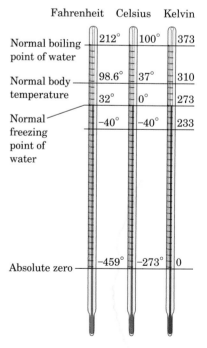

Figure 1.4 Three temperature scales.

Why was $-273°C$ chosen as the zero point on the Kelvin scale? The reason is that $-273°C$, *or 0 K, is the lowest possible temperature.* Because of this, 0 K is called **absolute zero.** Temperature reflects how fast molecules move. The more slowly they move, the colder it gets. At absolute zero, molecules stop moving altogether. Therefore, the temperature cannot get any lower. For some purposes it is convenient to have a scale that begins at the lowest possible temperature; the Kelvin scale fulfills this need. The Kelvin is the SI unit.

It is very important to have a "gut feeling" about the relative sizes of the units in the metric system. Often, while doing calculations, the only thing that might offer a clue that you have made an error is your understanding of the sizes of the units. For example, if you are calculating the amount of a chemical that is dissolved in water and you come up with an answer of 254 kg/mL, does your answer make sense? If you have no intuitive feeling about the size of a kilogram or a milliliter, you will not know. If you realize that a milliliter is about the volume of a thimble and that a standard bag of sugar might weigh 2 kg, then you will realize that there is no way to pack 254 kg into a thimble of water, and you will know that you made a mistake.

1.5 | What Is a Handy Way to Convert from One Unit to Another?

Factor-label method A procedure in which the equations are set up so that all the unwanted units cancel and only the desired units remain

Conversion factor A ratio of two different units

We frequently need to convert a measurement from one unit to another. The best and most foolproof way to do this is the **factor-label method.** In this method we follow the rule that *when multiplying numbers we also multiply units, and when dividing numbers we also divide units.*

For conversions between one unit and another, it is always possible to set up two fractions, called **conversion factors.** Suppose we wish to convert the weight of an object from 381 grams to pounds. We are converting the units, but we are not changing the object itself. We want a ratio that reflects the change in units. In Table 1.3, we see that there are 453.6 grams in 1 pound. That is, the amount of matter in 453.6 grams is the same as the amount in 1 pound. In that sense, it is a one-to-one ratio, even though the units are not numerically the same. The conversion factors between grams and pounds therefore are

$$\frac{1 \text{ lb}}{453.6 \text{ g}} \quad \text{and} \quad \frac{453.6 \text{ g}}{1 \text{ lb}}$$

To convert 381 grams to pounds, we must multiply by the proper conversion factor—but which one? Let us try both and see what happens.

First let us multiply by 1 lb/453.6 g:

$$381 \text{ g} \times \frac{1 \text{ lb}}{453.6 \text{ g}} = 0.840 \text{ lb}$$

Following the procedure of multiplying and dividing units when we multiply and divide numbers, we find that dividing grams by grams cancels out the grams. We are left with pounds, which is the answer we want. Thus 1 lb/453.6 g is the correct conversion factor because it converts grams to pounds.

Suppose we had done it the other way, multiplying by 453.6 g/1 lb:

$$381 \text{ g} \times \frac{453.6 \text{ g}}{1 \text{ lb}} = 173,000 \frac{\text{g}^2}{\text{lb}}$$

When we multiply grams by grams, we get g^2 (grams squared). Dividing by pounds gives g^2/lb. This is not the unit we want, so we used the incorrect conversion factor.

HOW TO...

Do Unit Conversions by the Factor-Label Method

One of the most useful ways of approaching conversions is to ask three questions:

- What information am I given? This is the starting point.
- What do I want to know? This is the answer that you want to find.
- What is the connection between the first two? This is the conversion factor. Of course, more than one conversion factor may be needed for some problems.

Let's look at how to apply these principles to a conversion from pounds to kilograms. Suppose we want to know the weight in kilograms of a woman who weighs 125 lb. We see in Table 1.3 that there are 2.205 lb in 1 kg. Note that we are starting out with pounds and we want an answer in kilograms.

$$125 \text{ lb} \times \frac{1 \text{ kg}}{2.205 \text{ lb}} = 56.7 \text{ kg}$$

- The weight in pounds is the starting point. We were given that information.
- We wanted to know the weight in kilograms. That was the desired answer, and we found the number of kilograms.
- The connection between the two is the conversion factor in which the unit of the desired answer is in the numerator of the fraction, rather than the denominator. It is not simply a mechanical procedure to set up the equation so that units cancel; it is a first step to understanding the underlying reasoning behind the factor-label method. If you set up the equation to give the desired unit as the answer, you have made the connection properly.

If you apply this kind of reasoning, you can always pick the right conversion factor. Given the choice between

$$\frac{2.205 \text{ lb}}{1 \text{ kg}} \quad \text{and} \quad \frac{1 \text{ kg}}{2.205 \text{ lb}}$$

you know that the second conversion factor will give an answer in kilograms, so you use it. When you check the answer, you see that it is reasonable. You expect a number that is about one half of 125, which is 62.5. The actual answer, 56.7, is close to that value. The number of pounds and the number of kilograms are not the same, but they represent the same weight. That fact makes the use of conversion factors logically valid; the factor-label method uses the connection to obtain a numerical answer.

The advantage of the factor-label method is that it lets us know when we have made an incorrect calculation. *If the units of the answer are not the ones we are looking for, the calculation must be wrong.* Incidentally, this principle works not only in unit conversions but in all problems where we make calculations using measured numbers.

The factor-label method gives the correct mathematical solution for a problem. However, it is a mechanical technique and does not require you to think through the problem. Thus it may not provide a deeper understanding. For this reason and also to check your answer (because it is easy to make mistakes in arithmetic—for example, by punching the wrong numbers into a calculator), you should always ask yourself if the answer you have obtained is reasonable. For example, the question might ask the mass of a single oxygen atom. If your answer comes out 8.5×10^6 g, it is not reasonable. A single atom cannot weigh more than you do! In such a case, you have obviously made a mistake and should take another look to see where you went wrong. Of course, everyone makes mistakes at times, but if you check you can at least determine whether your answer is reasonable. If it is not, you will immediately know that you have made a mistake and can then correct it.

Checking whether an answer is reasonable gives you a deeper understanding of the problem because it forces you to think through the relationship between the question and the answer. The concepts and the mathematical relationships in these problems go hand in hand. Mastery of the mathematical skills makes the concepts clearer, and insight into the concepts suggests ways to approach the mathematics. We will now give a few examples of unit conversions and then test the answers to see whether they are reasonable. To save space, we will practice this technique mostly in this chapter, but you should use a similar approach in all later chapters.

In unit conversion problems, you should always check two things. First, the numeric factor by which you multiply tells you whether the answer will be larger or smaller than the number being converted. Second, the factor tells you how much greater or smaller than the number you start with your answer should be. For example, if 100 kg is converted to pounds and there are 2.205 lb in 1 kg, then an answer of about 200 is reasonable—but an answer of 0.2 or 2000 is not.

EXAMPLE 1.3

The distance between Rome and Milan (the largest cities in Italy) is 358 miles. How many kilometers separate the two?

Solution
We want to convert miles to kilometers. Table 1.3 shows that 1 mi = 1.609 km. From this we get two conversion factors:

$$\frac{1 \text{ mi}}{1.609 \text{ km}} \quad \text{and} \quad \frac{1.609 \text{ km}}{1 \text{ mi}}$$

Which should we use? We use the one that gives the answer in kilometers:

$$358 \text{ mi} \times \text{conversion factor} = ? \text{ km}$$

This means that the miles must cancel, so the conversion factor 1.609 km/ 1 mi is appropriate.

$$358 \text{ mi} \times \frac{1.609 \text{ km}}{1 \text{ mi}} = 576 \text{ km}$$

Is this answer reasonable? We want to convert a given distance in miles to the same distance in kilometers. The conversion factor in Table 1.3 tells us that in a given distance the number of kilometers is larger than the number of miles. How much larger? The actual number is 1.609, which is approximately 1.5 times larger. Thus we expect that the answer in kilometers will be about 1.5 times greater than the number given in miles. The number given in miles is 358, which, *for the purpose of checking whether our answer is reasonable,* we can round off to, say, 400. Multiplying this number by 1.5 gives an approximate answer of 600 km. Our actual answer, 576 km, was of the same order of magnitude as the estimated answer, so we can say that it is reasonable. If the estimated answer had been 6 km, or 60 km, or 6000 km, we would suspect that we had made a mistake in calculating the actual answer.

Problem 1.3

How many kilograms are in 241 lb? Check your answer to see if it is reasonable.

EXAMPLE 1.4

The label on a container of olive oil says 1.844 gal. How many milliliters does the container hold?

Solution

Table 1.3 shows no factor for converting gallons to milliliters, but it does show that 1 gal = 3.785 L. Because we know that 1000 mL = 1 L, we can solve this problem by multiplying by two conversion factors, making certain that all units cancel except milliliters:

$$1.844 \text{ gal} \times \frac{3.785 \text{ L}}{1 \text{ gal}} \times \frac{1000 \text{ mL}}{1 \text{ L}} = 6980 \text{ mL}$$

Is this answer reasonable? The conversion factor in Table 1.3 tells us that there are more liters in a given volume than gallons. How much more? Approximately four times more. We also know that any volume in milliliters is 1000 times larger than the same volume in liters. Thus we expect that the volume expressed in milliliters will be 4 × 1000, or 4000, times more than the volume given in gallons. The estimated volume in milliliters will be approximately 1.8 × 4000, or 7000 mL. But we also expect that the actual answer should be somewhat less than the estimated figure because we overestimated the conversion factor (4 rather than 3.785). Thus the answer, 6980 mL, is quite reasonable. Note that the answer is given to four significant figures.

Problem 1.4

Calculate the number of kilometers in 8.55 miles. Check your answer to see whether it is reasonable.

EXAMPLE 1.5

The maximum speed limit on many roads in the United States is 65 mi/h. How many meters per second (m/s) is this speed?

Solution

Here we have essentially a double conversion problem: We must convert miles to meters and hours to seconds. We use as many conversion factors as necessary, always making sure that we use them in such a way that the proper units cancel:

$$65 \frac{\text{mi}}{\text{h}} \times \frac{1.609 \text{ km}}{1 \text{ mi}} \times \frac{1000 \text{ m}}{1 \text{ km}} \times \frac{1 \text{ h}}{60 \text{ min}} \times \frac{1 \text{ min}}{60 \text{ s}} = 29 \frac{\text{m}}{\text{s}}$$

Estimating the answer is a good thing to do when working any mathematical problem, not just unit conversions.

GOB
Chemistry·⚛·Now™

Click *Coached Problems* to practice doing unit conversions by the **Factor-Label Method**

Is this answer reasonable? To estimate the 65 mi/h speed in meters per second, we must first establish the relationship between miles and meters. As in Example 1.3, we know that there are more kilometers than miles in a given distance. How much more? As there are approximately 1.5 km in 1 mi, there must be approximately 1500 times more meters. We also know that in 1 hour there are $60 \times 60 = 3600$ seconds. The ratio of meters to seconds will be approximately 1500/3600, which is about one half. Therefore, we estimate that the speed in meters per second will be about one half of that in miles per hour or 32 m/s. Once again, the actual answer, 29 m/s, is not far from the estimate of 32 m/s, so the answer is reasonable.

As shown in these examples, when canceling units we do not cancel the numbers. The numbers are multiplied and divided in the ordinary way.

Problem 1.5

Convert the speed of sound, 332 m/s to mi/h. Check your answer to see whether it is reasonable.

1.6 | What Are the States of Matter?

Matter can exist in three states: gas, liquid, and solid. **Gases** have no definite shape or volume. They expand to fill whatever container they are put into. On the other hand, they are highly compressible and can be forced into small containers. **Liquids** also have no definite shape, but they do have a definite volume that remains the same when they are poured from one container to another. Liquids are only slightly compressible. **Solids** have definite shapes and definite volumes. They are essentially incompressible.

Whether a substance is a gas, a liquid, or a solid depends on its temperature and pressure. On a cold winter day, a puddle of liquid water turns to ice; it becomes a solid. If we heat water in an open pot at sea level, the liquid boils at 100°C; it becomes a gas—we call it steam. If we heated the same pot of water on top of Mount Everest, it would boil at about 70°C due to the reduced atmospheric pressure. Most substances can exist in the three states: They are gases at high temperature, liquids at a lower temperature, and solids when their temperature becomes low enough. Figure 1.5 shows a single substance in the three different states.

(a)

(b)

(c)

Charles D. Winters

Figure 1.5 The three states of matter for bromine: (*a*) bromine as a solid, (*b*) bromine as a liquid, and (*c*) bromine as a gas.

The chemical identity of a substance does not change when it is converted from one state to another. Water is still water whether it is in the form of ice, steam, or liquid water. We discuss the three states of matter, and the changes between one state and another, at greater length in Chapter 6.

1.7 | What Are Density and Specific Gravity?

A. Density

One of the many pollution problems that the world faces is the spillage of petroleum into the oceans from oil tankers or from offshore drilling. When oil spills into the ocean, it floats on top of the water. The oil doesn't sink because it is not soluble in water and because water has a higher density than oil. When two liquids are mixed (assuming that one does not dissolve in the other), the one of lower density floats on top (Figure 1.6).

The **density** of any substance is defined as its *mass per unit volume*. Not only do all liquids have a density, but so do all solids and gases. Density is calculated by dividing the mass of a substance by its volume:

$$d = \frac{m}{V} \quad d = \text{density}, \quad m = \text{mass}, \quad V = \text{volume}$$

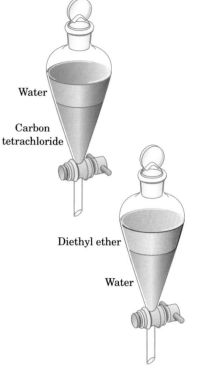

Water

Carbon tetrachloride

Diethyl ether

Water

Figure 1.6   Two separatory funnels containing water and another liquid. The density of carbon tetrachloride is 2.961 g/mL, that of water is 1.00 g/mL, and that of diethyl ether is 0.713 g/mL. In each case the liquid with the lower density is on top.

EXAMPLE 1.6

If 73.2 mL of a liquid has a mass of 61.5 g, what is its density in g/mL?

Solution

$$d = \frac{m}{V} = \frac{61.5 \text{ g}}{73.2 \text{ mL}} = 0.840 \ \frac{\text{g}}{\text{mL}}$$

Problem 1.6

The density of titanium is 4.54 g/mL. What is the mass, in grams, of 17.3 mL of titanium? Check your answer to see whether it is reasonable.

EXAMPLE 1.7

The density of iron is 7.86 g/cm³. What is the volume in milliliters of an irregularly shaped piece of iron that has a mass of 524 g?

Solution
Here we are given the mass and the density. In this type of problem, it is useful to derive a conversion factor from the density. Since 1 cm³ is exactly 1 mL, we know that the density is 7.86 g/mL. This means that 1 mL of iron has a mass of 7.86 g. From this we can get two conversion factors:

$$\frac{1 \text{ mL}}{7.86 \text{ g}} \quad \text{and} \quad \frac{7.86 \text{ g}}{1 \text{ mL}}$$

The spillage of more than 10 million gallons of petroleum in Prince William Sound, Alaska, in March 1989 caused a great deal of environmental damage.

Ken Graham/Stone/Getty Images

As usual, we multiply the mass by whichever conversion factor results in the cancellation of all but the correct unit:

$$524 \text{ g} \times \frac{1 \text{ mL}}{7.86 \text{ g}} = 66.7 \text{ mL}$$

Is this answer reasonable? The density of 7.86 g/mL tells us that the volume in milliliters of any piece of iron is always less than its mass in grams. How much less? Approximately eight times less. Thus we expect the volume to be approximately 500/8 = 63 mL. As the actual answer is 66.7 mL, it is reasonable.

Problem 1.7

An unknown substance has a mass of 56.8 g and occupies a volume of 23.4 mL. What is its density in g/mL? Check your answer to see whether it is reasonable.

The density of any liquid or solid is a physical property that is constant, which means that it always has the same value at a given temperature. We use physical properties to help identify a substance. For example, the density of chloroform (a liquid formerly used as an inhalation anesthetic) is 1.483 g/mL at 20°C. If we want to find out if an unknown liquid is chloroform, one thing we might do is measure its density at 20°C. If the density is, say, 1.355 g/mL, we know the liquid isn't chloroform. If the density is 1.483 g/mL, we cannot be sure the liquid is chloroform, because other liquids might also have this density, but we can then measure other physical properties (the boiling point, for example). If all the physical properties we measure match those of chloroform, we can be reasonably sure the liquid is chloroform.

We have said that the density of a pure liquid or solid is a constant at a given temperature. Density does change when the temperature changes. Almost always, density decreases with increasing temperature. This is true because mass does not change when a substance is heated, but volume almost always increases because atoms and molecules tend to get farther apart as the temperature increases. Since $d = m/V$, if m stays the same and V gets larger, d must get smaller.

The most common liquid, water, provides a partial exception to this rule. As the temperature increases from 4°C to 100°C, the density of water does decrease, but from 0°C to 4°C, the density increases. That is, water has its maximum density at 4°C. This anomaly and its consequences are due to the unique structure of water and will be discussed in Chemical Connections 6E.

B. Specific Gravity

Because density is equal to mass divided by volume, it always has units, most commonly g/mL or g/cc or (g/L for gases). **Specific gravity** is numerically the same as density, but it has no units (it is dimensionless). The reason is that specific gravity is defined as a comparison of the density of a substance with the density of water, which is taken as a standard. For example, the density of copper at 20°C is 8.92 g/mL. The density of water at the same temperature is 1.00 g/mL. Therefore, copper is 8.92 times as dense as water, and its specific gravity at 20°C is 8.92. Because water is taken as the standard and because the density of water is 1.00 g/mL at 20°C, the specific gravity of any substance is always numerically equal to its density, provided that the density is measured in g/mL or g/cc.

Specific gravity is often measured by a hydrometer. This simple device consists of a weighted glass bulb that is inserted into a liquid and allowed to float. The stem of the hydrometer has markings, and the specific gravity is read where the meniscus (the curved surface of the liquid) hits the marking. The specific gravity of the acid in your car battery and that of a urine sample in a clinical laboratory are measured by hydrometers. A hydrometer measuring a urine sample is also called urinometer (Figure 1.7). Normal urine can vary in specific gravity from about 1.010 to 1.030. Patients with diabetes mellitus have an abnormally high specific gravity of their urine samples, while those with some forms of kidney disease have an abnormally low specific gravity.

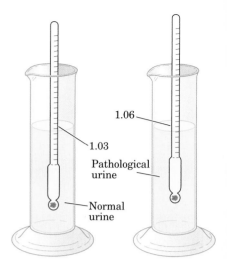

Figure 1.7 Urinometer.

EXAMPLE 1.8

The density of ethanol at 20°C is 0.789 g/mL. What is its specific gravity?

Solution

$$\text{Specific gravity} = \frac{0.789 \text{ g/mL}}{1.00 \text{ g/mL}} = 0.789$$

Problem 1.8

The specific gravity of a urine sample is 1.016. What is its density, in g/mL?

1.8 | How Do We Describe the Various Forms of Energy?

Energy is defined as the capacity to do work. It can be described as being either kinetic energy or potential energy.

Kinetic energy (KE) is the energy of motion. Any object that is moving possesses kinetic energy. We can calculate how much energy by the formula $KE = 1/2 mv^2$, where m is the mass of the object and v is its velocity. This means that kinetic energy increases (1) when an object moves faster and (2) when a heavier object is moving. When a truck and a bicycle are moving at the same velocity, the truck has more kinetic energy.

Potential energy is stored energy. The potential energy possessed by an object arises from its capacity to move or to cause motion. For example, body weight in the up position on a seesaw contains potential energy—it is capable of doing work. If given a slight push, it will move down. The potential energy of the body in the up position is converted to the kinetic energy of the body in the down position moving to the up position. Work is done against gravity in the process. Figure 1.8 shows another way in which potential energy is converted to kinetic energy.

An important principle in nature is that things have a tendency to seek their lowest possible potential energy. We all know that water always flows downhill and not uphill.

Several forms of energy exist. The most important are (1) mechanical energy, light, heat, and electrical energy, which are examples of kinetic energy possessed by all moving objects, whether elephants or molecules or electrons; and (2) chemical energy and nuclear energy, which are examples of potential energy or stored energy. In chemistry the most important form

Potential energy is stored in this drawn bow and becomes kinetic energy in the arrow when released.

Figure 1.8 The water held back by the dam possesses potential energy, which is converted to kinetic energy when the water is released.

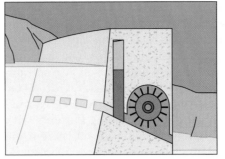
Potential energy ready to do work

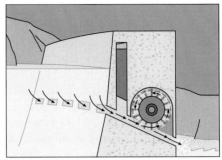
Kinetic energy doing work

An example of energy conversion. Light energy from the sun is converted to electrical energy by solar cells. The electricity runs a refrigerator on the back of the camel, keeping the vaccines cool so that they can be delivered to remote locations.

of potential energy is chemical energy—the energy stored within chemical substances and given off when they take part in a chemical reaction. For example, a log possesses chemical energy. When the log is ignited in a fireplace, the chemical energy (potential) of the wood is turned into energy in the form of heat and light. Specifically, the potential energy has been transformed into thermal energy (heat makes molecules move faster) and the radiant energy of light.

The various forms of energy can be converted from one to another. In fact, we make such conversions all the time. A power plant operates either on the chemical energy derived from burning fuel or on nuclear energy. This energy is converted to heat, which is converted to the electricity that is sent over transmission wires into houses and factories. Here we convert the electricity to light, heat (in an electrical heater, for example), or mechanical energy (in the motors of refrigerators, vacuum cleaners, and other devices).

Although one form of energy can be converted to another, the *total amount* of energy in any system does not change. *Energy can be neither created nor destroyed.* This statement is called the **law of conservation of energy.***

1.9 | How Do We Describe Heat and the Ways in Which It Is Transferred?

A. Heat and Temperature

One form of energy that is particularly important in chemistry is **heat.** This is the form of energy that most frequently accompanies chemical reactions. Heat is not the same as temperature, however. Heat is a form of energy, but temperature is not.

The difference between heat and temperature can be seen in the following example. If we have two beakers, one containing 100 mL of water and the other containing 1 L of water at the same temperature, the heat content of the water in the larger beaker is ten times that of the water in the smaller beaker, even though the temperature is the same in both. If you were to dip your hand accidentally into a liter of boiling water, you would be much more severely burned than if only one drop fell on your hand. Even though the water is at the same temperature in both cases, the liter of boiling water has much more heat.

---

*This statement is not completely true. As discussed in Sections 3.8 and 3.9, it is possible to convert matter to energy, and vice versa. Therefore, a more correct statement would be *matter-energy can be neither created nor destroyed.* However, the law of conservation of energy is valid for most purposes and is highly useful.

CHEMICAL CONNECTIONS 1B

Hypothermia and Hyperthermia

The human body cannot tolerate temperatures that are too low. A person outside in very cold weather (say, −20°F [−29°C]) who is not protected by heavy clothing will eventually freeze to death because the body loses heat. Normal body temperature is 37°C. When the outside temperature is lower than that, heat flows out of the body. When the air temperature is moderate (10°C to 25°C), this poses no problem and is, in fact, necessary because the body produces more heat than it needs and must lose some. At extremely low temperatures, however, too much heat is lost and

body temperature drops, a condition called **hypothermia.** A drop in body temperature of 1 or 2°C causes shivering, which is the body's attempt to increase its temperature by the heat generated through muscular action. An even greater drop results in unconsciousness and eventually death.

The opposite condition is **hyperthermia.** It can be caused either by high outside temperatures or by the body itself when an individual develops a high fever. A sustained body temperature as high as 41.7°C (107°F) is usually fatal.

As we saw in Section 1.4, temperature is measured in degrees. Heat can be measured in various units, the most common of which is the **calorie,** which is defined as the amount of heat necessary to raise the temperature of 1 g of liquid water by 1°C. This is a small unit, and chemists more often use the kilocalorie (kcal):

$$1 \text{ kcal} = 1000 \text{ cal}$$

Nutritionists use the word "Calorie" (with a capital "C") to mean the same thing as "kilocalorie"; that is, 1 Cal = 1000 cal = 1 kcal. The calorie is not part of the SI. The official SI unit for heat is the **joule (J),** which is about one-fourth as big as the calorie:

$$1 \text{ cal} = 4.184 \text{ J}$$

B. Specific Heat

As we noted, it takes 1 cal to raise the temperature of 1 g of liquid water by 1°C. **Specific heat (SH)** is the amount of heat necessary to raise the temperature of 1 g of any substance by 1°C. Each substance has its own specific heat, which is a physical property of that substance, like density or melting point. Table 1.4 lists specific heats for a few common substances. For example, the specific heat of iron is 0.11 cal/g · °C. Therefore, if we had 1 g of iron at 20°C, it would require only 0.11 cal to increase the temperature to 21°C. Under the same conditions, aluminum would require twice as much heat. Thus cooking in an aluminum pan of the same weight as an iron pan would require more heat than cooking in the iron pan. Note from Table 1.4 that ice and steam do not have the same specific heat as liquid water.

Table 1.4   Specific Heats for Some Common Substances

Substance	Specific Heat (cal/g · °C)	Substance	Specific Heat (cal/g · °C)
Water	1.00	Wood (typical)	0.42
Ice	0.48	Glass (typical)	0.22
Steam	0.48	Rock (typical)	0.20
Iron	0.11	Ethanol	0.59
Aluminum	0.22	Methanol	0.61
Copper	0.092	Ether	0.56
Lead	0.038	Carbon tetrachloride	0.21

CHEMICAL CONNECTIONS 1C

Cold Compresses, Waterbeds, and Lakes

The high specific heat of water is useful in cold compresses and makes them last a long time. For example, consider two patients with cold compresses: one compress made by soaking a towel in water and the other made by soaking a towel in ethanol. Both are at 0°C. Each gram of water in the water compress requires 25 cal to make the temperature of the compress rise to 25°C (after which it must be changed). Because the specific heat of ethanol is 0.59 cal/g · °C (see Table 1.4), each gram of ethanol requires only 15 cal to reach 25°C. If the two patients give off heat at the same rate, the ethanol compress is less effective because it will reach 25°C a good deal sooner than the water compress and will need to be changed sooner.

The high specific heat of water also means that it takes a great deal of heat to increase its temperature. That is why it takes a long time to get a pot of water to boil. Anyone who has a waterbed (300 gallons) knows that it takes days for the heater to bring the bed up to the desired temperature. It is particularly annoying when an overnight guest tries to adjust the temperature of your waterbed because the guest will probably have left before the change is noticed, but then you will have to set it back to your favorite temperature. This same effect in reverse explains why the outside temperature can be below zero (°C) for weeks before a lake will freeze. Large bodies of water do not change temperature very quickly.

It is easy to make calculations involving specific heats. The equation is

$$\text{Amount of heat} = \text{specific heat} \times \text{mass} \times \text{change in temperature}$$

$$\text{Amount of heat} = \text{SH} \times m \times \Delta T$$

where ΔT is the change in temperature. We can also write this equation as

$$\text{Amount of heat} = \text{SH} \times m \times (T_2 - T_1)$$

where T_2 is the final temperature and T_1 is the initial temperature in °C.

EXAMPLE 1.9

How many calories are required to heat 352 g of water from 23°C to 95°C?

Solution

$$\text{Amount of heat} = \text{SH} \times m \times \Delta T$$

$$\text{Amount of heat} = \text{SH} \times m \times (T_2 - T_1)$$

$$= \frac{1.00 \text{ cal}}{\text{g} \cdot °\text{C}} \times 352 \text{ g} \times (95 - 23)°\text{C}$$

$$= 2.5 \times 10^4 \text{ cal}$$

Is this answer reasonable? Each gram of water requires one calorie to raise its temperature by one degree. We have approximately 350 g of water. To raise its temperature by one degree would therefore require approximately 350 calories. But we are raising the temperature not by one degree but by approximately 70 degrees (from 23 to 95). Thus the total number of calories will be approximately $70 \times 350 = 24,500$ cal, which is close to the calculated answer. (Even though we were asked for the answer in calories, we should note that it will be more convenient to convert to 25 kcal. We are going to see that conversion from time to time.)

Problem 1.9

How many calories are required to heat 731 g of water from 8°C to 74°C? Check your answer to see whether it is reasonable.

EXAMPLE 1.10

If we add 450 cal of heat to 37 g of ethanol at 20°C, what is the final temperature?

Solution

The specific heat of ethanol is 0.59 cal/g·°C (see Table 1.4).

$$\text{Amount of heat} = \text{SH} \times m \times \Delta T$$

$$\text{Amount of heat} = \text{SH} \times m \times (T_2 - T_1)$$

$$450 \text{ cal} = 0.59 \text{ cal/g} \cdot °C \times 37 \text{ g} \times (T_2 - T_1)$$

We can show the units in fraction form by rewriting this equation.

$$450 \text{ cal} = 0.59 \frac{\text{cal}}{\text{g} \cdot °C} \times 37 \text{ g} \times (T_2 - T_1)$$

$$(T_2 - T_1) = \frac{\text{amount of heat}}{\text{SH} \times m}$$

$$(T_2 - T_1) = \frac{450 \text{ cal}}{\left[\dfrac{0.59 \text{ cal} \times 37 \text{ g}}{\text{g} \cdot °C}\right]} = \frac{21}{1/°C} = 21°C$$

(Note that we have the reciprocal of temperature in the denominator, which gives us temperature in the numerator. The answer has units of degrees Celsius.) Since the starting temperature is 20°C, the final temperature is 41°C.

Is this answer reasonable? The specific heat of ethanol is 0.59 cal/g·°C. This value is close to 0.5, meaning that about half a calorie will raise the temperature of 1 g by 1°C. However, 37 g of ethanol needs approximately 40 times as many calories for a rise, and $40 \times \frac{1}{2} = 20$ calories. We are adding 450 calories, which is about 20 times as much. Thus we expect the temperature to rise by about 20°C, from 20°C to 40°C. The actual answer, 41°C, is quite reasonable.

Problem 1.10

A 100 g piece of iron at 25°C is heated by adding 230 cal. What will be the final temperature? Check your answer to see whether it is reasonable.

EXAMPLE 1.11

We heat 50.0 g of an unknown substance by adding 205 cal, and its temperature rises by 7.0°C. What is its specific heat? Using Table 1.4, identify the substance.

Solution

$$SH = \frac{\text{Amount of heat}}{m \times (\Delta T)}$$

$$SH = \frac{\text{Amount of heat}}{m \times (T_2 - T_1)}$$

$$SH = \frac{205 \text{ cal}}{50.0 \text{ g} \times 7.0°C} = 0.59 \text{ cal/g} \cdot °C$$

The substance in Table 1.4 having a specific heat of 0.59 cal/g · °C is ethanol.

Is this answer reasonable? If we had water instead of an unknown substance with SH = 1 cal/g · °C, raising the temperature of 50.0 g by 7.0°C would require 50 × 7.0 = 350 cal. But we added only approximately 200 cal. Therefore, the SH of the unknown substance must be less than 1.0. How much less? Approximately 200/350 = 0.6. The actual answer, 0.59 cal/g · °C, is quite reasonable.

Problem 1.11

It required 88.2 cal to heat 13.4 g of an unknown substance from 23°C to 176°C. What is the specific heat of the unknown substance? Check your answer to see whether it is reasonable.

SUMMARY OF KEY QUESTIONS

SECTION 1.1 Why Do We Call Chemistry the Study of Matter?

- **Chemistry** is the science that deals with the structure of matter and the changes it can undergo. In a **chemical change** or **chemical reaction,** substances are used up and others are formed.
- Chemistry is also the study of energy changes during chemical reactions. In **physical changes** substances do not change their identity.

SECTION 1.2 What Is the Scientific Method?

- The **scientific method** is a tool used in science and medicine. The heart of the scientific method is the testing of **hypotheses** and **theories** by collecting facts.

SECTION 1.3 How Do Scientists Report Numbers?

- Because we frequently use very large or very small numbers, we use powers of 10 to express these numbers more conveniently, a method called **exponential notation.**
- With exponential notation, we no longer have to keep track of so many zeros, and we have the added con-

venience of being able to see which digits convey information (**significant figures**) and which merely indicate the position of the decimal point.

SECTION 1.4 How Do We Make Measurements?

- In chemistry we use the **metric system** for measurements.
- The base units are the meter for length, the liter for volume, the gram for mass, the second for time, and the calorie for heat. Other units are indicated by prefixes that represent powers of 10. Temperature is measured in degrees Celsius or in kelvins.

SECTION 1.5 What Is a Handy Way to Convert from One Unit to Another?

- Conversions from one unit to another are best done by the **factor-label method,** in which units are multiplied and divided.

SECTION 1.6 What Are the States of Matter?

- There are three states of matter: **solid, liquid, and gas.**

SECTION 1.7 What Are Density and Specific Gravity?

- **Density** is mass per unit volume. **Specific gravity** is density relative to water and thus has no units. Density usually decreases with increasing temperature.

SECTION 1.8 How Do We Describe the Various Forms of Energy?

- **Kinetic energy** is energy of motion; **potential energy** is stored energy. Energy can be neither created nor destroyed, but it can be converted from one form to another.

SECTION 1.9 How Do We Describe Heat and the Ways in Which It Is Transferred?

- **Heat** is a form of energy and is measured in calories. A calorie is the amount of heat necessary to raise the temperature of 1 g of liquid water by 1°C.
- Every substance has a **specific heat,** which is a physical constant. The specific heat is the number of calories required to raise the temperature of 1 g of a substance by 1°C.

PROBLEMS

GOB Chemistry· ·Now™

Assess your understanding of this chapter's topics with additional quizzing and conceptual-based problems at **http://now.brookscole.com/gob8** or on the CD.

A blue problem number indicates an applied problem.

■ denotes problems that are available on the GOB ChemistryNow website or CD and are assignable in OWL.

SECTION 1.1 Why Do We Call Chemistry the Study of Matter?

1.12 The life expectancy of a citizen in the United States is 76 years. Eighty years ago it was 56 years. In your opinion, what was the major contributor to this spectacular increase in life expectancy? Explain your answer.

1.13 Define the following terms:
(a) Matter   (b) Chemistry

SECTION 1.2 What Is the Scientific Method?

1.14 ■ In Table 1.4 you find four metals (iron, aluminum, copper, and lead) and three organic compounds (ethanol, methanol, and ether).What kind of hypothesis would you suggest about the specific heats of these chemicals?

1.15 ■ In a newspaper, you read that Dr. X claimed that he has found a new remedy to cure diabetes. The remedy is an extract of carrots. How would you classify this claim: (a) fact, (b) theory, (c) hypothesis, or (d) hoax? Explain your choice of answer.

1.16 ■ Classify each of the following as a chemical or physical change:
(a) Burning gasoline
(b) Making ice cubes
(c) Boiling oil
(d) Melting lead
(e) Rusting iron
(f) Making ammonia from nitrogen and hydrogen
(g) Digesting food

SECTION 1.3 How Do Scientists Report Numbers?

Exponential Notation

1.17 Write in exponential notation:
(a) 0.351   (b) 602.1   (c) 0.000128   (d) 628122

1.18 Write out in full:
(a) 4.03×10^5 (b) 3.2×10^3
(c) 7.13×10^{-5} (d) 5.55×10^{-10}

1.19 Multiply:
(a) $(2.16 \times 10^5)(3.08 \times 10^{12})$
(b) $(1.6 \times 10^{-8})(7.2 \times 10^8)$
(c) $(5.87 \times 10^{10})(6.62 \times 10^{-27})$
(d) $(5.2 \times 10^{-9})(6.8 \times 10^{-15})$

1.20 Divide:
(a) $\dfrac{6.02 \times 10^{23}}{2.87 \times 10^{10}}$ (b) $\dfrac{3.14}{2.93 \times 10^{-4}}$

(c) $\dfrac{5.86 \times 10^{-9}}{2.00 \times 10^3}$ (d) $\dfrac{7.8 \times 10^{-12}}{9.3 \times 10^{-14}}$

(e) $\dfrac{6.83 \times 10^{-12}}{5.02 \times 10^{14}}$

1.21 Add:
(a) $(7.9 \times 10^4) + (5.2 \times 10^4)$
(b) $(8.73 \times 10^4) + (6.7 \times 10^3)$
(c) $(3.63 \times 10^{-4}) + (4.776 \times 10^{-3})$

1.22 Subtract:
(a) $(8.50 \times 10^3) - (7.61 \times 10^2)$
(b) $(9.120 \times 10^{-2}) - 3.12 \times 10^{-3})$
(c) $(1.3045 \times 10^2) - (2.3 \times 10^{-1})$

1.23 ■ Solve:
$$\frac{(3.14 \times 10^3) \times (7.80 \times 10^5)}{(5.50 \times 10^2)}$$

1.24 ■ Solve:
$$\frac{(9.52 \times 10^4) \times (2.77 \times 10^{-5})}{(1.39 \times 10^7) \times (5.83 \times 10^2)}$$

Significant Figures

1.25 How many significant figures are in the following:
- (a) 0.012
- (b) 0.10203
- (c) 36.042
- (d) 8401.0
- (e) 32100
- (f) 0.0402
- (g) 0.000012

1.26 How many significant figures are in the following:
- (a) 5.71×10^{13}
- (b) 4.4×10^5
- (c) 3×10^{-6}
- (d) 4.000×10^{-11}
- (e) 5.5550×10^{-3}

1.27 Round off to two significant figures:
- (a) 91.621
- (b) 7.329
- (c) 0.677
- (d) 0.003249
- (e) 5.88

1.28 ■ Multiply these numbers, using the correct number of significant figures in your answer:
- (a) 3630.15×6.8
- (b) 512×0.0081
- (c) $5.79 \times 1.85825 \times 1.4381$

1.29 Divide these numbers, using the correct number of significant figures in your answer:
- (a) $\dfrac{3.185}{2.08}$
- (b) $\dfrac{6.5}{3.0012}$
- (c) $\dfrac{0.0035}{7.348}$

1.30 Add these groups of measured numbers using the correct number of significant figures in your answer:

- (a) 37.4083
      5.404
   10916.3
      3.94
      0.0006

- (b) 84
    8.215
    0.01
  151.7

- (c) 51.51
  100.27
   16.878
    3.6817

SECTION 1.4 How Do We Make Measurements?

1.31 In the SI system, the second is the base unit of time. We talk about atomic events that occur in picoseconds (10^{-12} s) or even in femtoseconds (10^{-15} s). But we don't talk about megaseconds or kiloseconds; the old standards of minutes, hours, and days prevail. How many minutes and hours are 20 kiloseconds?

1.32 ■ How many grams are in the following:
- (a) 1 kg
- (b) 1 mg

1.33 Estimate without actually calculating which one is the shorter distance:
- (a) 20 mm or 0.3 m
- (b) 1 inch or 30 mm
- (c) 2000 m or 1 mile

1.34 For each of these, tell which answer is closest:
- (a) A baseball bat has a length of 100 mm or 100 cm or 100 m
- (b) A glass of milk holds 23 cc or 230 mL or 23 L
- (c) A man weighs 75 mg or 75 g or 75 kg
- (d) A tablespoon contains 15 mL or 150 mL or 1.5 L
- (e) A paper clip weighs 50 mg or 50 g or 50 kg
- (f) Your hand has a width of 100 mm or 100 cm or 100 m
- (g) An audiocassette weighs 40 mg or 40 g or 40 kg

1.35 You are taken for a helicopter ride in Hawaii from Kona (sea level) to the top of the volcano Mauna Kea. Which property of your body would change during the helicopter ride:
- (a) height
- (b) weight
- (c) volume
- (d) mass

1.36 Convert to Celsius and to Kelvin:
- (a) 320°F
- (b) 212°F
- (c) 0°F
- (d) −250°F

1.37 Convert to Fahrenheit and to Kelvin:
- (a) 25°C
- (b) 40°C
- (c) 250°C
- (d) −273°C

SECTION 1.5 What Is a Handy Way to Convert from One Unit to Another?

1.38 Make the following conversions (conversion factors are given in Table 1.3):
- (a) 42.6 kg to lb
- (b) 1.62 lb to g
- (c) 34 in. to cm
- (d) 37.2 km to mi
- (e) 2.73 gal to L
- (f) 62 g to oz
- (g) 33.61 qt to L
- (h) 43.7 L to gal
- (i) 1.1 mi to km
- (j) 34.9 mL to fl oz

1.39 Make the following metric conversions:
- (a) 96.4 mL to L
- (b) 275 mm to cm
- (c) 45.7 kg to g
- (d) 475 cm to m
- (e) 21.64 cc to mL
- (f) 3.29 L to cc
- (g) 0.044 L to mL
- (h) 711 g to kg
- (i) 63.7 mL to cc
- (j) 0.073 kg to mg
- (k) 83.4 m to mm
- (l) 361 mg to g

1.40 You drive in Canada where the distances are marked in kilometers. The sign says you are 80 km from Ottawa. You are traveling at a speed of 75 mi/h. Would you reach Ottawa within one hour, after one hour, or later than that?

1.41 The speed limit in some European cities is 80 km/h. How many miles per hour is this?

1.42 Your car gets 25.00 miles on a gallon of gas. What would be your car's fuel efficiency in km/L?

SECTION 1.6 What Are the States of Matter?

1.43 Which states of matter have a definite volume?

1.44 Will most substances be solids, liquids, or gases at low temperatures?

1.45 ■ Does the chemical nature of a substance change when it melts from a solid to a liquid?

SECTION 1.7 What Are Density and Specific Gravity?

1.46 The volume of a rock weighing 1.075 kg is 334.5 mL. What is the density of the rock in g/mL? Express it to three significant figures.

1.47 The density of manganese is 7.21 g/mL, that of calcium chloride is 2.15 g/mL, and that of sodium acetate is 1.528 g/mL. You place these three solids in a liquid, in which they are not soluble. The liquid has a density of 2.15 g/mL. Which will sink to the bottom, which will stay on the top, and which will stay in the middle of the liquid?

1.48 The density of titanium is 4.54 g/mL. What is the volume, in milliliters, of 163 g of titanium?

1.49 A 335.0 cc sample of urine has a mass of 342.6 g. What is the density, in g/mL, to three decimal places?

1.50 The density of methanol at 20°C is 0.791 g/mL. What is the mass, in grams, of a 280 mL sample?

1.51 The density of dichloromethane, a liquid insoluble in water, is 1.33 g/cc. If dichloromethane and water are placed in a separatory funnel, which will be the upper layer?

1.52 A sample of 10.00 g of oxygen has a volume of 6702 mL. The same weight of carbon dioxide occupies 5058 mL.
 (a) What is the density of each gas in g/L?
 (b) Carbon dioxide is used as a fire extinguisher to cut off the fire's supply of oxygen. Do the densities of these two gases explain the fire-extinguishing ability of carbon dioxide?

1.53 Crystals of a material are suspended in the middle of a cup of water at 2°C. This means that the densities of the crystal and of the water are the same. How might you enable the crystals to rise to the surface of the water so that you can harvest them?

SECTION 1.8 How Do We Describe the Various Forms of Energy?

1.54 On many country roads you see telephones powered by a solar panel. What principle is at work in these devices?

1.55 While you drive your car, your battery is charged. How would you describe this process in terms of kinetic and potential energy?

SECTION 1.9 How Do We Describe Heat and the Ways in Which It Is Transferred?

1.56 ■ How many calories are required to heat the following (specific heats are given in Table 1.4)?
 (a) 52.7 g of aluminum from 100°C to 285°C
 (b) 93.6 g of methanol from −35°C to 55°C
 (c) 3.4 kg of lead from −33°C to 730°C
 (d) 71.4 g of ice from −77°C to −5°C

1.57 If 168 g of an unknown liquid requires 2750 cal of heat to raise its temperature from 26°C to 74°C, what is the specific heat of the liquid?

1.58 The specific heat of steam is 0.48 cal/g · °C. How many kilocalories are needed to raise the temperature of 10.5 kg steam from 120°C to 150°C?

Chemical Connections

1.59 (Chemical Connections 1A) If the recommended dose of a drug is 445 mg for a 180 lb man, what would be a suitable dose for a 135 lb man?

1.60 (Chemical Connections 1A) The average lethal dose of heroin is 1.52 mg/kg of body weight. Estimate how many grams of heroin would be lethal for a 200 lb man.

1.61 (Chemical Connections 1B) How does the body react to hypothermia?

1.62 (Chemical Connections 1B) Low temperatures often cause people to shiver. What is the function of this involuntary body action?

1.63 (Chemical Connections 1C) Which would make a more efficient cold compress, ethanol or methanol? (Refer to Table 1.4.)

Additional Problems

1.64 The meter is a measure of length. Tell what each of the following units measures:
 (a) cm^3 (b) mL   (c) kg   (d) cal
 (e) g/cc   (f) joule   (g) °C   (h) cm/s

1.65 A brain weighing 1.0 lb occupies a volume of 620 mL. What is the specific gravity of the brain?

1.66 ■ If the density of air is 1.25×10^{-3} g/cc, what is the mass in kilograms of the air in a room that is 5.3 m long, 4.2 m wide, and 2.0 m high?

1.67 Classify these as kinetic or potential energy:
 (a) Water held by a dam
 (b) A speeding train
 (c) A book on its edge before falling
 (d) A falling book
 (e) Electric current in a light bulb

1.68 The kinetic energy possessed by an object with a mass of 1 g moving with a velocity of 1 cm/s is called 1 erg. What is the kinetic energy, in ergs, of an athlete with a mass of 127 lb running at a velocity of 14.7 mi/h?

1.69 A European car advertises an efficiency of 22 km/L, while an American car claims an economy of 30 mi/gal. Which car is more efficient?

1.70 In Potsdam, New York, you can buy gas for US$2.02/gal. In Montreal, Canada, you pay US$0.60/L. (Currency conversions are outside the scope of this text, so you are not asked to do them here.) Which is the better buy? Is your calculation reasonable?

1.71 Shivering is the body's response to increase the body temperature. What kind of energy is generated by shivering?

1.72 When the astronauts walked on the Moon, they could make giant leaps in spite of their heavy gear.

(a) Why were their weights on the Moon so small?

(b) Were their masses different on the Moon than on the Earth?

1.73 Which of the following is the largest mass and which is the smallest?

(a) 41 g

(b) 3×10^3 mg

(c) 8.2×10^6 μg

(d) 4.1310×10^{-8} kg

1.74 Which quantity is bigger in each of the following pairs:

(a) 1 gigaton : 10 megaton

(b) 10 micrometer : 1 millimeter

(c) 10 centigram : 200 milligram

1.75 In Japan, high-speed "bullet trains" move with an average speed of 220 km/h. If Dallas and Los Angeles were connected by such a train, how long would it take to travel nonstop between these cities (a distance of 1490 miles)?

1.76 The specific heats of some elements at 25°C are as follows: aluminum = 0.215 cal/g · °C; carbon (graphite) = 0.170 cal/g · °C; iron = 0.107 cal/g · °C; mercury = 0.0331 cal/g · °C.

(a) Which element would require the smallest amount of heat to raise the temperature of 100 g of the element by 10°C?

(b) If the same amount of heat needed to raise the temperature of 1 g of aluminum by 25°C were applied to 1 g of mercury, by how many degrees would its temperature be raised?

(c) If a certain amount of heat is used to raise the temperature of 1.6 g of iron by 10°C, the temperature of 1 g of which element would also be raised by 10°C, using the same amount of heat?

1.77 Water that contains deuterium rather than ordinary hydrogen (see Chapter 3) is called heavy water. The specific heat of heavy water at 25°C is 4.217 J/g · °C. Which requires more energy to raise the temperature of 10.0 g by 10°C, water or heavy water?

1.78 One quart of milk costs 80 cents and one liter costs 86 cents. Which is the better buy?

1.79 Consider butter, density 0.860 g/mL, and sand, density 2.28 g/mL.

(a) If 1.00 mL of butter is thoroughly mixed with 1.00 mL of sand, what is the density of the mixture?

(b) What would be the density of the mixture if 1.00 g of the same butter were mixed with 1.00 g of the same sand?

1.80 Which speed is the fastest?

(a) 70 mi/h

(b) 140 km/h

(c) 4.5 km/s

(d) 48 mi/min

1.81 In calculating the specific heat of a substance, the following data are used: mass = 92.15 g; heat = 3.200 kcal; rise in temperature = 45°C. How many significant figures should you report in calculating the specific heat?

1.82 A solar cell generates 500 kilojoules of energy per hour. To keep a refrigerator at 4°C, one needs 250 kcal/h. Can the solar cell supply sufficient energy per hour to maintain the temperature of the refrigerator?

1.83 The specific heat of urea is 1.339 J/g · °C . If one adds 60.0 J of heat to 10.0 g of urea at 20°C, what would be the final temperature?

Special Categories

Three special categories of problems—Tying It Together, Looking Ahead, and Challenge Problems—will appear from time to time at the ends of chapters. Not every chapter will have these problems, but they will appear to make specific points.

Tying It Together

1.84 Heats of reaction are frequently measured by monitoring the change in temperature of a water bath in which the reaction mixture is immersed. A water bath used for this purpose contains 2.000 L of water. In the course of the reaction, the temperature of the water rose 4.85°C. How many calories were liberated by the reaction? (You will need to use what you know about unit conversions and apply that information to what you know about energy and heat.)

1.85 You have samples of urea (a solid at room temperature) and pure ethyl alcohol (a liquid at room temperature). Which technique or techniques would you use to measure the amount of each substance?

Looking Ahead

1.86 You have a sample of material used in folk medicine. Suggest the approach you would use to determine whether this material contains an effective substance for treating disease. If you do find a new and effective substance, can you think of a way to determine the amount present in your sample? (Pharmaceutical companies have used this approach to produce many common medications.)

1.87 Many substances that are involved in chemical reactions in the human body (and in all organisms) contain carbon, hydrogen, oxygen, and nitrogen arranged in specific patterns. Would you expect new medications to have features in common with these substances, or would you expect them to be drastically different? What are the reasons for your answer?

Challenge Problems

1.88 If 2 kg of a given reactant is consumed in the reaction described in Problem 1.84, how many calories are liberated for each kilogram?

1.89 You have a water sample that contains a contaminant you want to remove. You know that the contaminant is much more soluble in diethyl ether than it is in water. You have a separatory funnel available. Propose a way to remove the contaminant.

Atoms

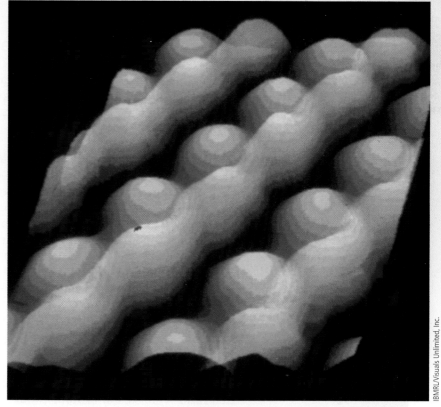

Image of atoms by SEM (scanning electron microscope).

IBMRL/Visuals Unlimited, Inc.

GOB
Chemistry·⚛·Now™
Look for this logo in the chapter and go to GOB ChemistryNow at **http://now.brookscole.com/gob8** or on the CD for tutorials simulations, and problems.

2.1 | What Is Matter Made Of?

This question was discussed for thousands of years, long before humans had any reasonable way of getting an answer. In ancient Greece, two schools of thought tried to answer this question. One group, led by a scholar named Democritus (about 460–370 BCE), believed that all matter is made of very small particles—much too small to see. Democritus called these particles atoms (Greek *atomos,* meaning "not to cut"). Some of his followers developed the idea that there were different kinds of atoms, with different properties, and that the properties of the atoms caused ordinary matter to have the properties we all know.

Not all ancient thinkers, however, accepted this idea. A second group, led by Zeno of Elea (born about 450 BCE), did not believe in atoms at all. They insisted that matter is infinitely divisible. If you took any object, such as a piece of wood or a crystal of table salt, you could cut it or otherwise divide it into two parts, divide each of these parts into two more parts, and continue the process forever. According to Zeno and his followers, you would never reach a particle of matter that could no longer be divided.

Today we know that Democritus was right and Zeno was wrong. Atoms are the basic units of matter. Of course, there is a great difference in the way we now look at this question. Today our ideas are based on evidence. Democritus had no evidence to prove that matter cannot be divided an infinite number of times, just as Zeno had no evidence to support his claim that matter can be divided infinitely. Both claims were based not on evidence but on visionary belief: one in unity, the other in diversity. In Section 2.3 we will discuss the evidence for the existence of atoms, but first we need to look at the diverse forms of matter.

2.2 | How Do We Classify Matter?

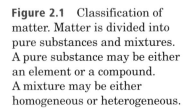

GOB
Chemistry・Now™

Click *Coached Problems* for an example of **Identifying Pure Substances and Mixtures**

Matter can be divided into two classes: pure substances and mixtures. Each class is then subdivided as shown in Figure 2.1.

A. Elements

An **element** is a substance (for example, carbon, hydrogen, and iron) that consists of identical atoms. At this time, 116 elements are known. Of these, 88 occur in nature; chemists and physicists have made the others. A list of the known elements appears on the inside back cover of this book, along with their symbols. Their symbols consist of one or two letters. Many symbols correspond directly to the name in English (for example, C for carbon, H for hydrogen, and Li for lithium), but a few are derived from the Latin or German names. Others are named for people who played significant roles in the development of science—in particular, atomic science (see Problem 2.11). Still other elements are named for geographic locations (see Problems 2.12).

B. Compounds

A **compound** is a pure substance made up of two or more elements in a fixed ratio by mass. For example, water is a compound made up of hydrogen and oxygen, and table salt is a compound made up of sodium and chlorine. There are an estimated 20 million known compounds, only a few of which we will meet in this book.

Figure 2.1 Classification of matter. Matter is divided into pure substances and mixtures. A pure substance may be either an element or a compound. A mixture may be either homogeneous or heterogeneous.

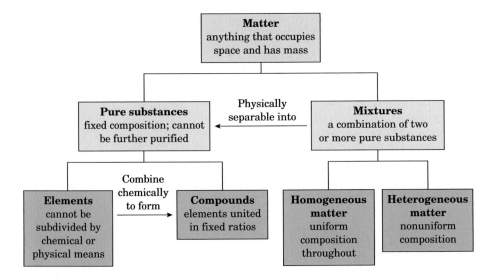

CHEMICAL CONNECTIONS 2A

Elements Necessary for Human Life

To the best of our knowledge, 20 of the 116 known elements are necessary for human life. The six most important of these—carbon, hydrogen, nitrogen, oxygen, phosphorus, and sulfur—are the subjects of organic chemistry and biochemistry (Chapters 10–31). Carbon, hydrogen, nitrogen, and oxygen are the "big four" in the human body. Seven other elements are also quite important, and our bodies use at least nine additional ones (trace elements) in very small quantities. The table lists these 20 major elements and their functions in the human body. Many of these elements are more fully discussed later in the book. For the average daily requirements for these elements, their sources in foods, and symptoms of their deficiencies, see Chapter 30.

Table 2A Elements and Their Functions in the Human Body

Element	Function	Element	Function
The Big Four		**The Trace Elements**	
Carbon (C) Hydrogen (H) Nitrogen (N) Oxygen (O)	The subject of Chapters 10–19 (organic chemistry) and 20–31 (biochemistry)	Chromium (Cr)	Increases effectiveness of insulin
		Cobalt (Co)	Part of vitamin B_{12}
The Next Seven		Copper (Cu)	Strengthens bones; assists in enzyme activity
Calcium (Ca)	Strengthens bones and teeth; aids in blood clotting	Fluorine (F)	Reduces the incidence of dental cavities
Phosphorus (P)	Present in phosphates of bone, in nucleic acids (DNA and RNA); and involved in energy transfer	Iodine (I)	An essential part of thyroid hormones
Potassium (K)	Helps regulate electrical balance of body fluids; essential for nerve conduction	Iron (Fe)	An essential part of some proteins, such as hemoglobin, myoglobin, cytochromes, and FeS proteins
Sulfur (S)	An essential component of proteins	Manganese (Mn)	Present in bone-forming enzymes; aids in fat and carbohydrate metabolism
Chlorine (Cl)	Necessary for normal growth and development		
Sodium (Na)	Helps regulate electrical balance in body fluids	Molybdenum (Mo)	Helps regulate electrical balance in body fluids
Magnesium (Mg)	Helps nerve and muscle action; present in bones	Zinc (Zn)	Necessary for the action of certain enzymes

A compound is characterized by its formula. The formula gives us the ratios of the compound's constituent elements and identifies each element by its atomic symbol. For example, in table salt the ratio of sodium atoms to chlorine atoms is 1 : 1. Given that Na is the symbol for sodium and Cl is the symbol for chlorine, the formula of table salt is NaCl. In water, the combining ratio is two hydrogen atoms to one oxygen atom. The symbol for hydrogen is H, that for oxygen is O, and the formula of water is H_2O. The subscripts following the atomic symbols indicate the ratio of the combining elements. The number 1 in these ratios is omitted from the subscript. It is understood that NaCl means a ratio of 1 : 1 and that H_2O represents a ratio of 2 : 1. You will find out more about the nature of combining elements in a compound and their names and formulas in Chapter 4.

Figure 2.2 shows four representations for a water molecule. We will have more to say about molecular models as we move through this book.

Figure 2.2 Four representations of a water molecule.

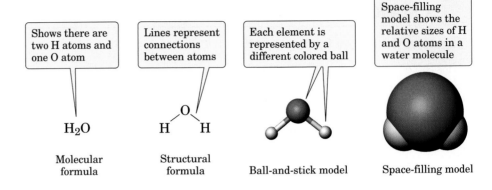

Shows there are two H atoms and one O atom

Lines represent connections between atoms

Each element is represented by a different colored ball

Space-filling model shows the relative sizes of H and O atoms in a water molecule

H_2O

H—O—H

Molecular formula   Structural formula   Ball-and-stick model   Space-filling model

---

EXAMPLE 2.1

(a) In the compound magnesium fluoride, magnesium (atomic symbol Mg) and fluorine (atomic symbol F) combine in a ratio of 1:2. Write the formula of magnesium fluoride.
(b) The formula of perchloric acid is $HClO_4$. What are the combining ratios of the elements in perchloric acid?

Solution
(a) The formula is MgF_2. We do not write a subscript of 1 after Mg.
(b) Both H and Cl have no subscripts, which means that hydrogen and chlorine have a combining ratio of 1:1. The subscript on oxygen is 4. Therefore, the combining ratios in $HClO_4$ are 1:1:4.

Problem 2.1

Write the formulas of compounds in which the combining ratios are as follows:
(a) Sodium:chlorine:oxygen, 1:1:3
(b) Aluminum (atomic symbol Al):fluorine (atomic symbol F), 1:3

C. Mixtures

A **mixture** is a combination of two or more pure substances. Most of the matter we encounter in our daily lives (including our own bodies) consists of mixtures rather than pure substances. For example, blood, butter, gasoline, soap, the metal in a wedding ring, the air we breathe, and the earth we walk on are all mixtures of pure substances. An important difference between a compound and a mixture is that the ratios by mass of the elements in a compound are fixed, whereas in a mixture the pure substances can be present in any mass ratio.

For some mixtures—blood, for example (Figure 2.3)—the texture of the mixture is even throughout. If you examine a mixture under magnification, however, you can see that it is composed of different substances.

Other mixtures are homogeneous throughout, and no amount of magnification will reveal the presence of different substances. The air we breathe, for example, is a mixture of gases, primarily nitrogen (78%) and oxygen (21%).

An important characteristic of a mixture is that it consists of two or more substances, each having different physical properties. If we know the physical properties of the individual substances, we can use appropriate physical means to separate the mixture into its component parts. Figure 2.4 shows one example of how a mixture can be separated.

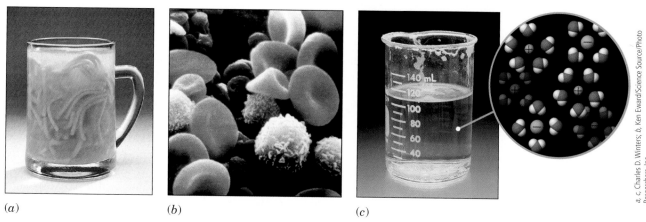

(a)   (b)   (c)

Figure 2.3   Mixtures. (a) A cup of noodle soup is a heterogeneous mixture. (b) A sample of blood may look homogeneous, but examination with an optical microscope shows that it is, in fact, a heterogeneous mixture of liquid and suspended particles (blood cells). (c) A homogeneous solution of salt, NaCl, in water. The models show that the salt solution contains Na^+ and Cl^- ions as separate particles in water, with each ion being surrounded by a shell of four or more water molecules. The particles in this solution cannot be seen with an optical microscope.

(a)   (b)   (c)

Figure 2.4   Separating a mixture of iron and sulfur. (a) The iron–sulfur mixture is stirred with a magnet, which attracts the iron filings. (b) Much of the iron is removed after the first stirring. (c) Stirring continues until no more iron filings can be removed.

2.3 | What Are the Postulates of Dalton's Atomic Theory?

Around 1805 an English chemist, John Dalton (1766–1844), put forth a scientific atomic theory. The major difference between Dalton's theory and that of Democritus (Section 2.1) is that Dalton based his theory on evidence rather than on a belief. First, let us state Dalton's theory, and then see what kind of evidence supported it.

1. All matter is made up of very tiny, indivisible particles, which Dalton called **atoms.**

2. All atoms of the same element have the same chemical properties. Conversely, atoms of different elements have different chemical properties.

3. Compounds are formed by the chemical combination of two or more different kinds of atoms.

4. A **molecule** is a tightly bound combination of two or more atoms that acts as a single unit.

Atom   The smallest particle of an element that retains the chemical properties of the element. The interaction among atoms accounts for the properties of matter.

A. Evidence for Dalton's Atomic Theory

The Law of Conservation of Mass

The great French chemist Antoine Laurent Lavoisier (1743–1794) discovered the **law of conservation of mass,** which states that matter can be neither created nor destroyed. Lavoisier proved this law by conducting many experiments in which he showed that the total mass of matter at the end of the experiment was exactly the same as that at the beginning. Dalton's theory explained this fact in the following way: If all matter consists of indestructible atoms, then any chemical reaction simply changes the attachments between atoms but does not destroy the atoms themselves.

In the following illustration, a carbon monoxide molecule reacts with a lead oxide molecule to give a carbon dioxide molecule and a lead atom. All of the original atoms are still present at the end; they have merely changed partners. Thus the total mass after this chemical change remains the same as it was before the change took place.

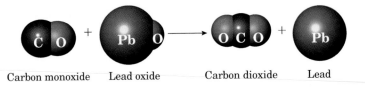

Carbon monoxide   Lead oxide   Carbon dioxide   Lead

GOB
Chemistry⚛Now™

Click *Chemistry Interactive* to see an example of **Chemical Change on the Nanoscale**

The Law of Constant Composition

Another French chemist, Joseph Proust (1754–1826), demonstrated the **law of constant composition,** which states that any compound is always made up of elements in the same proportion by mass. For example, if you decompose water, you will always get 8.0 g of oxygen for each 1.0 g of hydrogen. The mass ratio of oxygen to hydrogen in pure water is always 8.0 to 1.0, whether the water comes from the Atlantic Ocean or the Missouri River or is collected as rain, squeezed out of a watermelon, or distilled from urine. This fact was also evidence for Dalton's theory. If a water molecule consists of one atom of oxygen and two atoms of hydrogen, and if an oxygen atom has a mass 16 times that of a hydrogen atom, then the mass ratio of these two elements in water must always be 8.0 to 1.0. The two elements can never be found in water in any other mass ratio.

B. Monatomic, Diatomic, and Polyatomic Elements

Some elements—for example, helium and neon—consist of single atoms that are not connected to each other—that is, they are **monatomic elements.** In contrast, oxygen, in its most common form, contains two atoms in each molecule, connected to each other by a chemical bond. We write the formula for an oxygen molecule as O_2, with the subscript showing the number of atoms in the molecule. Six other elements also occur as diatomic molecules (that is, they contain two atoms of the same element per molecule): hydrogen (H_2), nitrogen (N_2), fluorine (F_2), chlorine (Cl_2), bromine (Br_2), and iodine (I_2). It is important to understand that, under normal conditions, free atoms of O, H, N, F, Cl, Br, and I do not exist. Rather, these seven elements occur only as **diatomic elements** (Figure 2.5).

Figure 2.5 Some diatomic, triatomic, and polyatomic elements. Hydrogen, nitrogen, oxygen, and chlorine are diatomic elements. Ozone, O_3, is a triatomic element. One form of sulfur, S_8, is a polyatomic element.

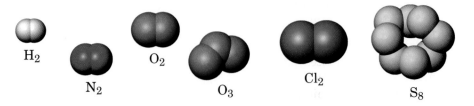

CHEMICAL CONNECTIONS 2B

Abundance of Elements in the Human Body and in the Earth's Crust

The table shows the abundances of the elements present in the human body. As you can see, oxygen is the most abundant element by mass, followed by carbon, hydrogen, and nitrogen. If we go by number of atoms, however, hydrogen is even more abundant in the human body than oxygen.

The table also shows the abundances of elements in the Earth's crust. Although 88 elements are found in the Earth's crust (we know very little about the interior of the Earth because we have not been able to penetrate into it very far), they are not present in anything close to equal amounts. In the Earth's crust as well as the human body, the most abundant element by mass is oxygen. But there the similarity ends. Silicon, aluminum, and iron, which are the second, third, and fourth most abundant elements in the Earth's crust, respectively, are not major elements in the body. While carbon is the second most abundant element by mass in the human body, it is present to the extent of only 0.08% in the Earth's crust.

Table 2B   The Relative Abundance of Elements in the Human Body and in the Earth's Crust, Including the Atmosphere and Oceans

| Element | Percentage in Human Body | | Percentage in Earth's Crust by Mass |
	By Number of Atoms	By Mass	
H	63.0	10.0	0.9
O	25.4	64.8	49.3
C	9.4	18.0	0.08
N	1.4	3.1	0.03
Ca	0.31	1.8	3.4
P	0.22	1.4	0.12
K	0.06	0.4	2.4
S	0.05	0.3	0.06
Cl	0.03	0.2	0.2
Na	0.03	0.1	2.7
Mg	0.01	0.04	1.9
Si	—	—	25.8
Al	—	—	7.6
Fe	—	—	4.7
Others	0.01	—	—

Some elements have even more atoms in each molecule. Ozone, O_3, has three oxygen atoms in each molecule. In one form of phosphorus, P_4, each molecule has four atoms. One form of sulfur, S_8, has eight atoms per molecule. Some elements have molecules that are much larger. For example, diamond has millions of carbon atoms all bonded together in a gigantic cluster. Diamond and S_8 are referred to as **polyatomic elements.**

2.4 | What Are Atoms Made Of?

A. Three Subatomic Particles

Today we know that matter is more complex than Dalton believed. A wealth of experimental evidence obtained over the last 100 years or so has convinced us that atoms are not indivisible but rather consist of even smaller particles called subatomic particles. Three subatomic particles make up all

There are many other subatomic particles but we will not deal with them in this book.

Table 2.1 Properties and Location within Atoms of Protons, Neutrons, and Electrons

Subatomic Particle	Charge	Mass (g)	Mass (amu)	Mass (amu); Rounded to One Significant Figure	Location in an Atom
Proton	+1	1.6726×10^{-24}	1.0073	1	In the nucleus
Electron	−1	9.1094×10^{-28}	5.4859×10^{-4}	0.0005	Outside the nucleus
Neutron	0	1.6749×10^{-24}	1.0087	1	In the nucleus

atoms: protons, electrons, and neutrons. Table 2.1 shows the charge, mass, and location of these particles in an atom.

A **proton** has a positive charge. By convention we say that the magnitude of the charge is +1. Thus one proton has a charge of +1, two protons have a charge of +2, and so forth. The mass of a proton is 1.6726×10^{-24} g, but this number is so small that it is more convenient to use another unit, called the **atomic mass unit (amu),** to describe its mass.

$$1 \text{ amu} = 1.6605 \times 10^{-24} \text{ g}$$

Thus a proton has a mass of 1.0073 amu. For most purposes in this book, it is sufficient to round this number to one significant figure and, therefore, we say that the mass of a proton is 1 amu.

An **electron** has a charge of −1, equal in magnitude to the charge on a proton, but opposite in sign. The mass of an electron is approximately 5.4859×10^{-4} amu or 1/1837 that of the proton. It takes approximately 1837 electrons to equal the mass of one proton.

Like charges repel, and unlike charges attract. Two protons repel each other just as two electrons also repel each other. A proton and an electron, however, attract each other.

> **Proton** A subatomic particle with a charge of +1 and a mass of approximately 1 amu; it is found in a nucleus.

> **Atomic mass unit (amu)** A unit of the scale of relative masses of atoms: 1 amu = 1.6605×10^{-24} g. By definition, 1 amu is 1/12 the mass of a carbon atom containing 6 protons and 6 neutrons.

> **Electron** A subatomic particle with a charge of −1 and a mass of approximately 0.0005 amu. It is found in the space surrounding a nucleus.

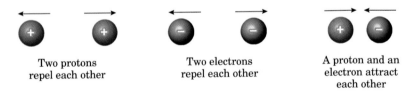

Two protons repel each other   Two electrons repel each other   A proton and an electron attract each other

> **Neutron** A subatomic particle with a mass of approximately 1 amu, and a charge of zero; it is found in the nucleus

A **neutron** has no charge. Therefore, neutrons neither attract nor repel each other or any other particle. The mass of a neutron is slightly greater than that of a proton: 1.6749×10^{-24} g or 1.0087 amu. Again, for our purposes, we round this number to 1 amu.

These three particles make up atoms, but where are they found? Protons and neutrons are found in a tight cluster in the center of an atom (Figure 2.6). This part of an atom is called the **nucleus.** We will discuss the nucleus in greater detail in Chapter 3. Electrons are found as a diffuse cloud outside the nucleus.

B. Mass Number

Each atom has a fixed number of protons, electrons, and neutrons. One way to describe an atom is by its **mass number,** which is the sum of the number of protons and neutrons in its nucleus. Note that an atom also contains electrons but because the mass of an electron is so small compared to that of protons and neutrons (Table 2.1), electrons are not counted in determining mass number.

$$\text{Mass number} = \text{the number of protons and neutrons in the nucleus of an atom.}$$

For example, an atom with 5 protons, 5 electrons, and 6 neutrons has a mass number of 11.

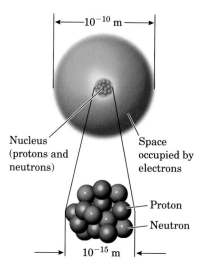

Figure 2.6 A typical atom. Protons and neutrons are found in the nucleus, and electrons are found as a cloud outside the nucleus. Notice how small the nucleus is compared to the size of an atom.

EXAMPLE 2.2

What is the mass number of an atom containing:
(a) 58 protons, 58 electrons, and 78 neutrons?
(b) 17 protons, 17 electrons, and 20 neutrons?

Solution
The mass number of an atom is the sum of the number of its protons and neutrons in its nucleus.
(a) The mass number is $58 + 78 = 136$.
(b) The mass number is $17 + 20 = 37$.

Problem 2.2

What is the mass number of an atom containing:
(a) 15 protons, 15 electrons, and 16 neutrons?
(b) 86 protons, 86 electrons, and 136 neutrons?

C. Atomic Number

The **atomic number** of an element is the number of protons in its nucleus.

$$\text{Atomic number} = \text{number of protons in the nucleus of an atom}$$

At the present time, 116 elements are known. These elements have atomic numbers from 1–116. The smallest atomic number belongs to the element hydrogen, which has only one proton, and the largest (so far) to the as-yet-unnamed heaviest known element, which contains 116 protons.

    If you know the atomic number and the mass number of an element, you can properly identify it. For example, the element with 6 protons, 6 electrons, and 6 neutrons has an atomic number of 6 and a mass number of 12. The element with atomic number 6 is carbon, C. Because its mass number is 12, we call this atomic nucleus carbon-12. Alternatively, we can write the symbol for this atomic nucleus as $^{12}_{6}\text{C}$. In this symbol, the mass number of the element is always written in the upper-left corner (as a superscript) of the symbol of the element, and the atomic number in the lower-left corner (as a subscript).

Atomic numbers for all the known elements are given in the atomic weight table on the inside back cover. They are also given in the Periodic Table on the inside front cover.

If you know the name of the element, you can look up its atomic number and atomic weight from the atomic weight table on the inside back cover. Conversely, if you know the atomic number of the element, you can look up its symbol from the Periodic Table on the inside front cover. The atomic number of each element is shown in red.

$$\text{Mass number (number of protons + neutrons)} \rightarrow {}^{12}_{6}\text{C}$$
$$\text{Atomic number (number of protons)} \rightarrow$$

EXAMPLE 2.3

Name the elements given in Example 2.2 and write the symbols for their atomic nuclei.

Solution

(a) This element has 58 protons. We see from the Periodic Table on the inside front cover of the text that the element of atomic number 58 is cerium, and its symbol is Ce. An atom of this element has 58 protons and 78 neutrons and, therefore, its mass number is 136. We call it cerium-136. Its symbol is $^{136}_{58}$Ce.

(b) This atom has 17 protons, making it a chlorine (Cl) atom. Because its mass number is 37, we call it chlorine-37. Its symbol is $^{37}_{17}$Cl.

Problem 2.3

Name the elements given in Problem 2.2. Write the symbols of their atomic nuclei.

EXAMPLE 2.4

A number of elements have an equal number of protons and neutrons in their nuclei. Among these are oxygen, nitrogen, and neon. What are the atomic numbers of these elements? How many protons and neutrons does an atom of each have? Write the name and the symbol of each of these atomic nuclei.

Solution

Atomic numbers for these elements are found in the list of elements on the inside back cover. This table shows that oxygen (O) has atomic number 8, nitrogen (N) has atomic number 7, and neon (Ne) has atomic number 10. This means that the oxygen has 8 protons and 8 neutrons. Its name is oxygen-16, and its symbol is $^{16}_{8}$O. Nitrogen has 7 protons and 7 neutrons, its name is nitrogen-14, and its symbol is $^{14}_{7}$N. Neon has 10 protons and 10 neutrons, its name is neon-20, and its symbol is $^{20}_{10}$Ne.

Problem 2.4

(a) What are the atomic numbers of mercury (Hg) and lead (Pb)?
(b) How many protons does an atom of each have?
(c) If both Hg and Pb have 120 neutrons in their nuclei, what is the mass number of each?
(d) Write the name and the symbol of each.

D. Isotopes

Although we can say that a carbon atom always has 6 protons and 6 electrons, we cannot say that a carbon atom must have any particular number of neutrons. Some of the carbon atoms found in nature have 6 neutrons; the mass number of these atoms is 12; they are written as carbon-12, and their symbol is $^{12}_{6}$C. Other carbon atoms have 6 protons and 7 neutrons and, therefore, a mass number of 13; they are written as carbon-13, and their symbol is $^{13}_{6}$C. Still other carbon atoms have 6 protons and 8 neutrons; they are written as carbon-14 or $^{14}_{6}$C. Atoms with the same number of protons but different numbers of neutrons are called **isotopes.** All isotopes of carbon contain 6 protons and 6 electrons (or they wouldn't be carbon). Each isotope, however, contains a different number of neutrons and, therefore, has a different mass number.

The fact that isotopes exist means that the second statement of Dalton's atomic theory (Section 2.3) is not correct.

The properties of isotopes of the same element are almost identical, and for most purposes we regard them as identical. They differ, however, in radioactivity properties, which we discuss in Chapter 3.

EXAMPLE 2.5

How many neutrons are in each isotope of oxygen? Write the symbol of each isotope.
(a) Oxygen-16   (b) Oxygen-17   (c) Oxygen-18

Solution

Each oxygen atom has 8 protons. The difference between the mass number and the number of protons gives the number of neutrons.
(a) Oxygen-16 has $16 - 8 = 8$ neutrons. Its symbol is $^{16}_{8}O$.
(b) Oxygen-17 has $17 - 8 = 9$ neutrons. Its symbol is $^{17}_{8}O$.
(c) Oxygen-18 has $18 - 8 = 10$ neutrons. Its symbol is $^{18}_{8}O$.

Problem 2.5

Two iodine isotopes are used in medical treatments: iodine-125 and iodine-131. How many neutrons are in each isotope? Write the symbol for each isotope.

Most elements are found on Earth as mixtures of isotopes, in a more or less constant ratio. For example, all naturally occurring samples of the element chlorine contain 75.77% chlorine-35 (18 neutrons) and 24.23% chlorine-37 (20 neutrons). Silicon exists in nature in a fixed ratio of three isotopes, with 14, 15, and 16 neutrons, respectively. For some elements, the ratio of isotopes may vary slightly from place to place but, for most purposes, we can ignore these slight variations. The atomic masses and isotopic abundances are determined using an instrument called a mass spectrometer.

E. Atomic Weight

The **atomic weight** of an element given in the Periodic Table is a weighted average of the masses (in amu) of its isotopes found on the Earth. As an example of the calculation of atomic weight, let us examine chlorine. As we have just seen, two isotopes of chlorine exist in nature, chlorine-35 and chlorine-37. The mass of a chlorine-35 atom is 34.97 amu, and the mass of a chlorine-37 atom is 36.97 amu. Note that the atomic weight of each chlorine isotope (its mass in amu) is very close to its mass number (the number of protons and neutrons in its nucleus). This statement holds true for the isotopes of chlorine and those of all elements, because protons and neutrons have a mass of approximately (but not exactly) 1 amu.

The atomic weight of chlorine is a weighted average of the masses of the two naturally occurring chlorine isotopes:

Atomic weight The weighted average of the masses of the naturally occurring isotopes of the element. The units of atomic weight are atomic mass units (amu).

GOB
Chemistry⋅Now™
Click *Coached Problems* to see an example of the **Average Atomic Mass from Isotopic Abundances**

$$\left(\frac{75.77}{100} \times 34.97 \text{ amu} \right) + \left(\frac{24.23}{100} \times 36.97 \text{ amu} \right) = 35.45 \text{ amu}$$

Chlorine-35 ↗   Chlorine-37 ↗

| 14 |
| **Cl** |
| 35.4527 |

Atomic weight in the Periodic Table is given to four decimal places

Some elements—for example, gold, fluorine, and aluminum—occur naturally as only one isotope. The atomic weights of these elements are close to whole numbers (gold, 196.97 amu; fluorine, 18.998 amu; aluminum, 26.98 amu). A table of atomic weights is found on the inside back cover of this book.

EXAMPLE 2.6

The natural abundances of the three stable isotopes of magnesium are 78.99% magnesium-24 (23.98 504 amu), 10.00% magnesium-25 (24.9858 amu), and 11.01% magnesium-26 (25.9829 amu). Calculate the atomic weight of magnesium and compare your value with that given in the Periodic Table.

Solution
To calculate the weighted average of the masses of the isotopes, multiply each atomic mass by its abundance and then add.

$$\left(\frac{78.99}{100} \times 23.99 \text{ amu}\right) + \left(\frac{10.00}{100} \times 24.986 \text{ amu}\right) + \left(\frac{11.01}{100} \times 25.983 \text{ amu}\right) =$$

$$18.95 \qquad + \qquad 2.499 \qquad + \qquad 2.861 \qquad = 24.31 \text{ amu}$$

The atomic weight of magnesium given in the Periodic Table to four decimal places is 24.3050.

Problem 2.6

The atomic weight of lithium is 6.941 amu. Lithium has only two naturally occurring isotopes: lithium-6 and lithium-7. Estimate which isotope is in greater natural abundance.

F. The Mass and Size of an Atom

A typical heavy atom (although not the heaviest) is lead-208, a lead atom with 82 protons, 82 electrons, and 126 neutrons. It has a mass of 3.5×10^{-22} g. You would need 1.3×10^{24} atoms of lead-208 to make 1 lb of lead—a very large number. There are approximately 6 billion people on Earth right now. If you divided 1 lb of these atoms among all the people on Earth, each person would get about 2.2×10^{14} atoms.

An atom of lead-208 has a diameter of about 3.5×10^{-10} m. If you could line them up with the atoms just touching, it would take 73 million lead atoms to make a line 1-inch long. Despite their tiny size, we can actually see atoms, in certain cases, by using a special instrument called a scanning tunneling microscope (Figure 2.7).

Virtually all of the mass of an atom is concentrated in its nucleus (because the nucleus contains the protons and neutrons). The nucleus of a lead-208 atom, for example, has a diameter of about 1.6×10^{-14} m. When you compare this with the diameter of a lead-208 atom, which is about 3.5×10^{-10} m, you see that the nucleus occupies only a tiny fraction of the total volume of the atom. If the nucleus of a lead-208 atom were the size of a baseball, then the entire atom would be much larger than a baseball stadium. In fact, it would be a sphere about one mile in diameter. Because a nucleus has such a relatively large mass concentrated in such a relatively small volume, a nucleus has a very high density. The density of a lead-208 nucleus, for example, is 1.8×10^{14} g/cm^3. Nothing in our daily life has a density anywhere near as high. If a paper clip had this density, it would weigh about 10 million (10^7) tons.

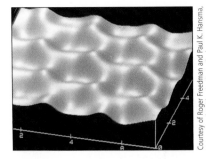

Figure 2.7 The surface of graphite is revealed with a scanning tunneling microscope. The contours represent the arrangement of individual carbon atoms on a crystal surface.

Courtesy of Roger Freedman and Paul K. Hansma, University of California–Santa Barbara

CHEMICAL CONNECTIONS 2C

Isotopic Abundances and Astrochemistry

The term **isotopic abundance** refers to the relative amounts of the isotopes of an element present in a sample of that element. When we speak of isotopic abundances and the atomic weights derived from them, we refer to isotopic abundances on Earth. For example, there are 11 known isotopes of chlorine, Cl, ranging from chlorine-31 to chlorine-41. Only two of these isotopes occur on Earth: chlorine-35 with an abundance of 75.77% and chlorine-37 with an abundance of 24.23%.

With the advance of space exploration, it has become evident that other parts of the solar system—the Sun, the Moon, planets, asteroids, comets, and stars, as well

Mars.

as intergalactic gases—may have different isotopic abundances. For example, the deuterium/hydrogen ratio ($^2H/^1H$) on Mars is five times larger than that on Earth. The $^{17}O/^{18}O$ ratio is also higher on Mars than on Earth. Such differences in isotopic abundances are used to establish theories about the origins and history of the solar system.

Furthermore, a comparison of isotopic abundances in certain meteorites found on Earth enables us to guess their origin. For example, it is now believed that certain meteorites that landed on Earth came from Mars. Scientists speculate that they were ejected from its surface when the Red Planet collided with some other large body—perhaps an asteroid.

2.5 | What Is the Periodic Table?

A. Origin of the Periodic Table

In the 1860s, a number of scientists—most notably the Russian Dmitri Mendeleev (1834–1907), then professor of chemistry at the University of St. Petersburg—produced one of the first periodic tables, the form of which we still use today. Mendeleev started by arranging the known elements in order of increasing atomic weight beginning with hydrogen. He soon discovered that when the elements are arranged according to increasing atomic weight, certain sets of properties recur periodically. Mendeleev then arranged those elements with recurring properties into **periods** (horizontal rows) by starting a new row each time he came to an element with properties similar to hydrogen. In this way, he discovered that lithium, sodium, potassium, and so forth each start new rows. All are metallic solids, all form ions with a charge of $+1$ (Li^+, Na^+, K^+, and so on), and all react with water to form metal hydroxides (LiOH, NaOH, KOH, and so on). Mendeleev also discovered that elements in other groups (vertical columns) share similar properties. For example, the elements fluorine (atomic number 9), chlorine (17), bromine (35), and iodine (53) all fall in the same column in the table. These elements, which are called **halogens,** are all colored substances, with color deepening as we go down the table (Figure 2.8). All form compounds with sodium that have the formula NaX (for example, NaCl and NaBr), but not NaX_2, Na_2X, Na_3X, or anything else. Only the elements in this column share this property.

At this point, we must say a word about the numbering of the columns of the Periodic Table. Mendeleev gave them numerals and added the letter A for some columns and B for others. This numbering pattern remains in common use in the United States today. An alternative pattern used internationally relies on the numbers 1 to 18, without added letters, going from left to right. Thus, in Mendeleev's numbering system, the halogens are in Group 7A;

Period of the Periodic Table
A horizontal row of the Periodic Table

Dmitri Mendeleev.

"X" is a commonly used symbol for a halogen.

Figure 2.8 Four halogens. Fluorine and chlorine are gases, bromine is a liquid, and iodine is a solid.

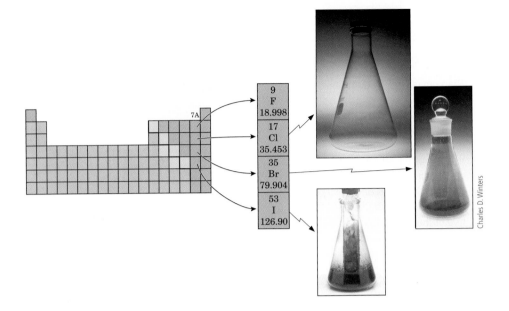

| 9
F
18.998 |
| 17
Cl
35.453 |
| 35
Br
79.904 |
| 53
I
126.90 |

Charles D. Winters

in the new international numbering system, they are in Group 17. Although this book uses the traditional numbering, both patterns are shown on the Periodic Table on the inside front cover.

If we look at the Periodic Table on the inside front cover of this book, we see that columns 1A and 2A extend above the rest, as does column 8A. The elements in columns 1A to 8A are called **main-group elements.** The elements in the B columns (Groups 3 to 12 in the new numbering system) are called **transition elements.** Notice that elements 58 to 71 and 90 to 103 are not included in the main body of the table but rather are shown separately at the bottom. These sets of elements, called **inner transition elements,** actually belong in the main body of the Periodic Table, between columns 3B and 4B (between La and Hf). As is customary, we put them outside the main body solely to make a more compact presentation. If you like, you may mentally take a pair of scissors, cut through the heavy line between columns 3B and 4B, move them apart, and insert the inner transition elements. You will now have a table with 32 columns.

Main-group element An element of any of the A groups of the Periodic Table

---

 CHEMICAL CONNECTIONS 2D

Strontium-90

Elements in the same column of the Periodic Table show similar properties. One important example is the similarity of strontium (Sr) and calcium (Ca) (strontium is just below calcium in Group 2A). Calcium is an important element for humans because our bones and teeth consist largely of calcium compounds. We need some of this mineral in our diet every day, and we get it mostly from milk, cheese, and other dairy products.

One of the products released by test nuclear explosions in the 1950s and 1960s was the isotope strontium-90. This isotope is radioactive, with a half-life of 28.1 years. (Half-life is discussed in Section 3.4.) Strontium-90 was present in the fallout from above-ground nuclear testing. It was carried all over the Earth by winds

and slowly settled to the ground, where it was eaten by cows and other animals. Strontium-90 got into milk and eventually into human bodies as well. If it were not so similar to calcium, our bodies would eliminate it within a few days. Because it is similar, however, some of the strontium-90 became deposited in bones and teeth (especially in children), subjecting all of us to a small amount of radioactivity for long periods of time.

A 1963 treaty between the United States and the former Soviet Union banned above-ground nuclear testing. Although a few other countries still conduct occasional above-ground tests, there is reason to hope that such testing will be completely halted in the near future.

B. Classification of the Elements

There are three classes of elements: metals, nonmetals, and metalloids. The majority of elements are **metals**—only 24 are not. Metals are solids (except for mercury, which is a liquid), shiny, conductors of electricity, ductile (they can be drawn into wires), and malleable (they can be hammered and rolled into sheets). They also form alloys, which are solutions of one or more metals dissolved in another metal. Brass, for example, is an alloy of copper and zinc. Bronze is an alloy of copper and tin, and pewter is an alloy of tin, antimony, and lead. In their chemical reactions, metals tend to give up electrons (Section 4.2). Figure 2.9 shows a form of the Periodic Table in which the elements are classified by type.

The second class of elements is the **nonmetals.** With the exception of hydrogen, the 18 nonmetals appear to the right side of the Periodic Table. With the exception of graphite, which is one form of carbon, they do not conduct electricity. At room temperature, nonmetals such as phosphorus and iodine are solids. Bromine is a liquid, and the elements of Group 8A (the noble gases)—helium through radon—are gases. In their chemical reactions, nonmetals tend to accept electrons (Section 4.2). Virtually all of the compounds we will encounter in our study of organic and biochemistry are built from just six nonmetals: H, C, N, O, P, and S.

Six elements are classified **metalloids:** boron, silicon, germanium, arsenic, antimony, and tellurium. These elements have some properties of metals and some properties of nonmetals. For example, some metalloids are shiny like metals, but do not conduct electricity. One of these metalloids, silicon, is a semiconductor—that is, it does not conduct electricity under a certain applied voltage, but becomes a conductor at higher applied voltages. This semiconductor property of silicon makes it a vital element for Silicon Valley–based companies and the entire electronics industry (Figure 2.10).

C. Examples of Periodicity in the Periodic Table

Not only do the elements in any particular column of the Periodic Table share similar properties, but the properties also vary in some fairly regular ways as we go up or down a column. For instance, Table 2.2 shows that the melting and boiling points of the **halogens** regularly increase as we go down the column.

Another example involves the Group 1A elements, also called the **alkali metals.** All alkali metals are soft enough to be cut with a knife, and their

Metal An element that is a solid (except for mercury, which is a liquid), shiny, conducts electricity, is ductile and malleable, and forms alloys.

Nonmetal An element that does not have the characteristic properties of a metal and tends to accept electrons

Although hydrogen (H) appears in Group 1A, it is not an alkali metal; it is a nonmetal. Hydrogen is placed in Group 1A because its s shell is the one being filled (Section 2.7).

Metalloid An element that displays some of the properties of metals and some of the properties of nonmetals

Halogen An element in Group 7A of the Periodic Table

Alkali metal An element in Group 1A of the Periodic Table

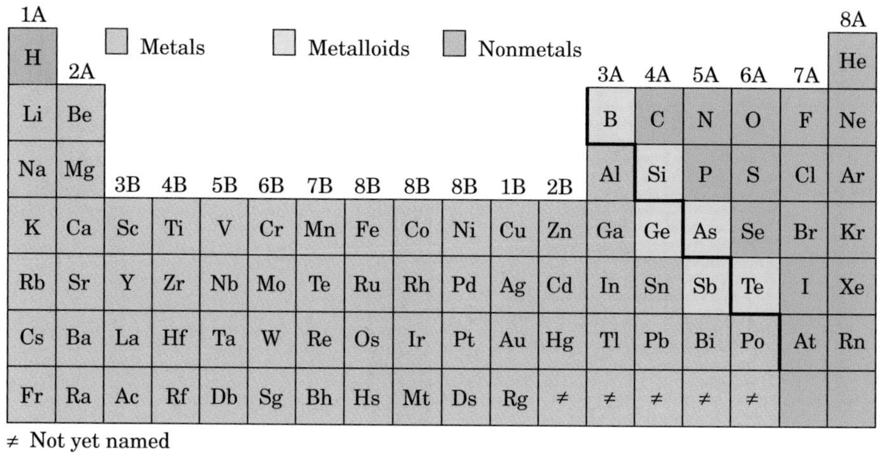

Figure 2.9 Classification of the elements.

1A																	8A
H	2A	Metals		Metalloids		Nonmetals						3A	4A	5A	6A	7A	He
Li	Be											B	C	N	O	F	Ne
Na	Mg	3B	4B	5B	6B	7B	8B	8B	8B	1B	2B	Al	Si	P	S	Cl	Ar
K	Ca	Sc	Ti	V	Cr	Mn	Fe	Co	Ni	Cu	Zn	Ga	Ge	As	Se	Br	Kr
Rb	Sr	Y	Zr	Nb	Mo	Te	Ru	Rh	Pd	Ag	Cd	In	Sn	Sb	Te	I	Xe
Cs	Ba	La	Hf	Ta	W	Re	Os	Ir	Pt	Au	Hg	Tl	Pb	Bi	Po	At	Rn
Fr	Ra	Ac	Rf	Db	Sg	Bh	Hs	Mt	Ds	Rg	≠	≠	≠	≠	≠		

≠ Not yet named

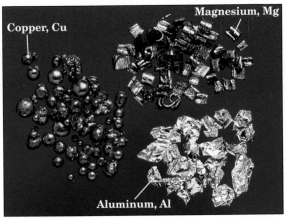

Copper, Cu

Magnesium, Mg

Aluminum, Al

(a) Metals

Bromine, Br$_2$ Iodine, I$_2$

(b) Nonmetals

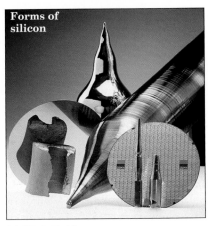

Forms of silicon

Charles D. Winters

(c) Metalloids

Figure 2.10 Representative elements. (a) Magnesium, aluminum, and copper are metals. All can be drawn into wires and conduct electricity. (b) Only 18 or so elements are classified as nonmetals. Shown here are liquid bromine and solid iodine. (c) Only six elements are generally classified as metalloids. This photograph is of solid silicon in various forms, including a wafer on which is printed electronic circuits.

Charles D. Winters

Sodium metal can be cut with a knife.

softness increases in going down the column. They have relatively low melting and boiling points, which decrease in going down the columns (Table 2.3).

All alkali metals react with water to form hydrogen gas, H$_2$, and a metal hydroxide with the formula MOH, where "M" stands for the alkali metal. The violence of their reaction with water increases in going down the column.

$$2Na + 2H_2O \longrightarrow 2NaOH + H_2$$

Sodium   Water   Sodium   Hydrogen
hydroxide   gas

They also form compounds with the halogens with the formula MX, where "X" stands for the halogen.

$$2Na + Cl_2 \longrightarrow 2NaCl$$

Sodium   Chlorine   Sodium
chloride

Table 2.2   Melting and Boiling Points of the Halogens (Group 7A Elements)

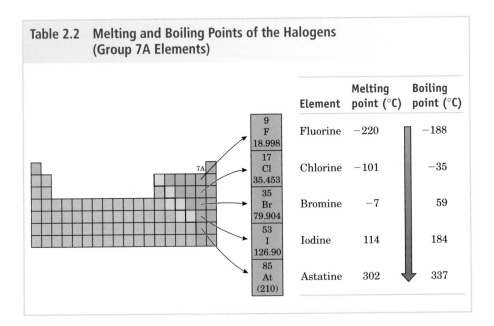

Element	Melting point (°C)	Boiling point (°C)
Fluorine	−220	−188
Chlorine	−101	−35
Bromine	−7	59
Iodine	114	184
Astatine	302	337

9
F
18.998

17
Cl
35.453

35
Br
79.904

53
I
126.90

85
At
(210)

Table 2.3 Melting and Boiling Points of the Alkali Metals (Group 1A Elements)

Element	Melting point (°C)	Boiling point (°C)
Lithium	180	1342
Sodium	98	883
Potassium	63	760
Rubidium	39	686
Cesium	28	669

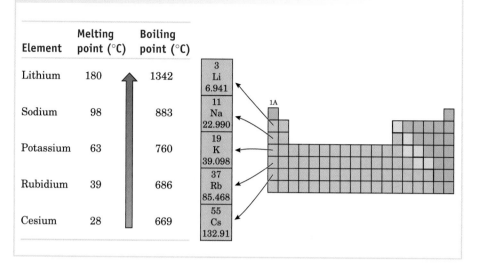

The elements in Group 8A, often called the **noble gases,** provide yet another example of how properties of elements change gradually within a column. Group 8A elements are gases under normal temperature and pressure, and they form either no compounds or very few compounds. Notice

^{GOB}
Chemistry Now™

Click *Chemistry Interactive* to see an example of **Chemical Periodicity**

CHEMICAL CONNECTIONS 2E

The Use of Metals as Historical Landmarks

The malleability of metals played an important role in the development of human society. In the Stone Age, tools were made from stone, which has no malleability. Then, about 11,000 BCE, it was discovered that the pure copper found on the surface of the Earth could be hammered into sheets, which made it suitable for use in vessels, utensils, and religious or artistic objects. This period became known as the Copper Age. Pure copper on the surface of the Earth, however, is scarce. Around 5000 BCE, humans found that copper could be obtained by putting malachite, $Cu_2CO_3(OH)_2$, a green copper-containing stone, into a fire. Malachite yielded pure copper at the relatively low temperature of 200°C.

Copper is a soft metal made of layers of large copper crystals. It can easily be drawn into wires because the layers of crystals can slip past one another. When hammered, the large crystals break into smaller ones with rough edges and the layers can no longer slide past one another. Therefore, hammered copper sheets are harder than drawn copper. Using this knowledge, the ancient profession of coppersmith was born, and beautiful plates, pots, and ornaments were produced.

Celtic shield.

Werner Forman/Art Resource, NY

Around 4000 BCE, it was discovered that an even greater hardness could be achieved by mixing molten copper with tin. The resulting alloy is called bronze. The Bronze Age was born somewhere in the Middle East and quickly spread to China and all over the world. Because hammered bronze takes an edge, knives and swords could be manufactured using it.

An even harder metal was soon to come. The first raw iron was found in meteorites. (The ancient Sumerian name of iron is "metal from heaven.") Around 2500 BCE, it was discovered that iron could be recovered from its ore by smelting. Smelting is the process of recovering a metal from its ore by heating the ore. Thus began the Iron Age. More advanced technology was needed for smelting iron ores because iron melts only at a high temperature (about 1500°C). For this reason, it took a longer time to perfect the smelting process and to learn how to manufacture steel, which is about 90–95% iron and 5–10% carbon. Steel objects appeared first in India around 100 BCE.

Modern historians look back at ancient cultures and use the discovery of a new metal as a landmark for that age.

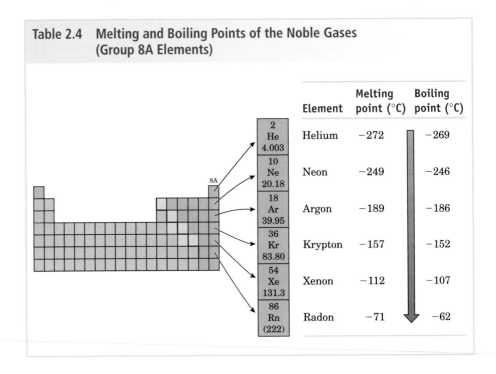

Table 2.4 Melting and Boiling Points of the Noble Gases (Group 8A Elements)

Element	Melting point (°C)	Boiling point (°C)
Helium	−272	−269
Neon	−249	−246
Argon	−189	−186
Krypton	−157	−152
Xenon	−112	−107
Radon	−71	−62

how close the melting and boiling points of the elements in this series are to one another (Table 2.4).

The Periodic Table is so useful that it hangs in nearly every chemistry classroom and chemical laboratory throughout the world. What makes it so useful is that it correlates a vast amount of data about the elements and their compounds and allows us to make many predictions about both chemical and physical properties. For example, if you were told that the boiling point of germane (GeH_4) is −88°C and that of methane (CH_4) is −164°C, could you predict the boiling point of silane (SiH_4)? The position of silicon in the table, between germanium and carbon, might lead you to a prediction of about −125°C. The actual boiling point of silane is −112°C, not far from this prediction.

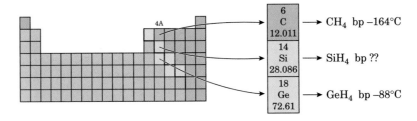

2.6 | How Are the Electrons in an Atom Arranged?

We have seen that the protons and neutrons of an atom are concentrated in the atom's very small nucleus, and that the electrons of an atom are located in the considerably larger space outside the nucleus. We can now ask how the electrons of an atom are arranged in this extranuclear space. Are they arranged randomly like seeds in a watermelon, or are they organized into layers like the layers of an onion?

Let us begin with hydrogen because it has only one electron and is the simplest atom. Before we do so, however, it is necessary to describe a dis-

Figure 2.11 An energy stairway. Unlike our stairways, the spaces between energy levels in an atom are not equal; they become smaller as they go up.

covery made in 1913 by the Danish physicist Niels Bohr. At the time, it was known that an electron is always moving around the nucleus and so possesses kinetic energy. Bohr discovered that only certain values are possible for this energy. This was a very surprising discovery. If you were told that you could drive your car at 23.4 mi/h or 28.9 mi/h or 34.2 mi/h, but never at any speed in between these values, you wouldn't believe it. Yet that is just what Bohr discovered about electrons in atoms. The lowest possible energy level is the **ground state.**

If an electron is to have more energy than it has in the ground state, only certain values are allowed; values in between are not permitted. Bohr was unable to explain why these energy levels of electrons exist in atoms, but the accumulated evidence forced him to the conclusion that they do. We say that the energy of electrons in atoms is quantized. We can liken quantization to walking up a flight of stairs (Figure 2.11). You can put your foot on any step, but you cannot stand any place between two steps.

Ground-state electron configuration The electron configuration of the lowest energy state of an atom

A. Electrons Are Distributed in Shells, Subshells, and Orbitals

One conclusion reached by Bohr is that electrons in atoms do not move freely in the space around the nucleus, but rather are confined to specific regions of space called **principal energy levels,** or more simply, **shells.** These shells are numbered 1, 2, 3, and 4, and so on from the inside out. Table 2.5 gives the number of electrons that each of the first four shells can hold.

Principal energy level An energy level containing orbitals of the same number (1, 2, 3, 4 and so forth)

Shell All orbitals of a principal energy level of an atom

Table 2.5	Distribution of Electrons in Shells	
Shell	**Number of Electrons Shell Can Hold**	**Relative Energies of Electrons in Each Shell**
4	32	Higher
3	18	↑
2	8	
1	2	Lower

Table 2.6 Distribution of Orbitals within Shells

Shell	Orbitals Contained in Each Shell	Maximum Number of Electrons Shell Can Hold
4	One 4s, three 4p, five 4d, and seven 4f orbitals	$2 + 6 + 10 + 14 = 32$
3	One 3s, three 3p, and five 3d orbitals	$2 + 6 + 10 = 18$
2	One 2s and three 2p orbitals	$2 + 6 = 8$
1	One 1s orbital	2

Electrons in the first shell are closest to the positively charged nucleus and are held most strongly by it; these electrons are said to be the lowest in energy (hardest to remove). Electrons in higher-numbered shells are farther from the nucleus and are held less strongly to it; these electrons are said to be higher in energy (easier to remove).

Shells are divided into **subshells** designated by the letters *s*, *p*, *d*, and *f*. Within these subshells, electrons are grouped in **orbitals.** An orbital is a region of space and can hold two electrons (Table 2.6). The second shell contains one *s* orbital and three *p* orbitals. All *p* orbitals come in sets of three and can hold six electrons. The third shell contains one *s* orbital, three *p* orbitals, and five *d* orbitals. All *d* orbitals come in sets of five and can hold ten electrons. All *f* orbitals come in sets of seven and can hold 14 electrons.

Subshell All of the orbitals of an atom having the same principal energy level and the same letter designation (either *s, p, d,* or *f*)

Orbital A region of space around a nucleus that can hold a maximum of two electrons

B. Orbitals Have Definite Shapes and Orientations in Space

All *s* orbitals have the shape of a sphere with the nucleus at the center of the sphere. Figure 2.12 shows the shapes of the 1*s* and 2*s* orbitals. Of the *s* orbitals, the 1*s* is the smallest sphere, the 2*s* is a larger sphere, and the 3*s* (not shown) is a still larger sphere. Figure 2.12 also shows the three-dimensional shapes of the three 2*p* orbitals. Each 2*p* orbital has the shape of a dumbbell with the nucleus at the midpoint of the dumbbell. The three 2*p* orbitals are at right angles to each other, with one orbital on the *x* axis, the second on the *y* axis, and the third on the *z* axis. The shapes of 3*p* orbitals are similar, but larger.

The *d* and *f* orbitals are less important to us, so we will not discuss their shapes.

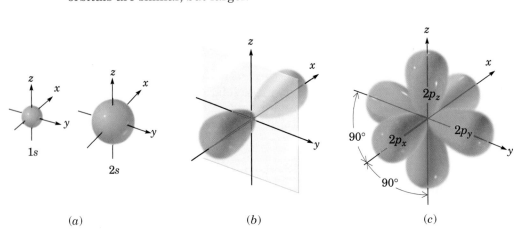

(a) (b) (c)

Figure 2.12 The 1*s*, 2*s*, and 2*p* orbitals. (*a*) A 1*s* orbital has the shape of a sphere, with the nucleus at the center of the sphere. A 2*s* orbital is a larger sphere than a 1*s* orbital, and a 3*s* orbital is larger still. (*b*) A 2*p* orbital has the shape of a dumbbell, with the nucleus at the midpoint of the dumbbell. (*c*) Each 2*p* orbital is perpendicular to the other two. The 3*p* orbitals are similar in shape but larger. To make it easier for you to see the two lobes of each 2*p* orbital, one lobe is colored red and the other is colored blue.

   Because the vast majority of organic molecules and biomolecules consist of the elements H, C, N, O, P, and S, which use only $1s$, $2s$, $2p$, $3s$, and $3p$ orbitals for bonding, we will concentrate on just these and other elements of the first, second, and third periods of the Periodic Table.

C. Electron Configurations of Atoms are Governed by Three Rules

The **electron configuration** of an atom is a description of the orbitals that its electrons occupy. The orbitals available to all atoms are the same—namely, $1s$, $2s$, $2p$, $3s$, $3p$, and so on. In the ground state of an atom, only the lowest-energy orbitals are occupied; all other orbitals are empty. We determine the ground-state electron configuration of an atom using the following rules:

Rule 1. Orbitals fill in the order of increasing energy from lowest to highest.

> **Example:** In this book we are concerned primarily with elements of the first, second, and third periods of the Periodic Table. Orbitals in these elements fill in the order $1s$, $2s$, $2p$, $3s$, and $3p$. Figure 2.13 shows the order of filling through the third period.

Rule 2. Each orbital can hold up to two electrons with spins paired.

> **Example:** With four electrons, the $1s$ and $2s$ orbitals are filled and we write them as $1s^2 2s^2$. With an additional six electrons, the three $2p$ orbitals are filled and we write them either in the expanded form of $2p_x^2 2p_y^2 2p_z^2$, or in the condensed form $2p^6$. Spin pairing means that the electrons spin in opposite directions (Figure 2.14).

Rule 3. When there is a set of orbitals of equal energy, each orbital becomes half-filled before any of them becomes completely filled.

> **Example:** After the $1s$ and $2s$ orbitals are filled, a fifth electron is put into the $2p_x$ orbital, a sixth into the $2p_y$ orbital, and a seventh into the $2p_z$ orbital. Only after each $2p$ orbital has one electron is a second added to any $2p$ orbital.

D. Showing Electron Configurations: Orbital Box Diagrams

To illustrate how these rules are used, let us write ground-state electron configurations for several of the elements in periods 1, 2, and 3. In the following **orbital box diagrams,** we use a box to represent an orbital, an arrow with its head up to represent a single electron, and a pair of arrows with heads in opposite directions to represent two electrons with paired spins. In addition, we show both expanded and condensed electron configurations. Table 2.7 gives the complete condensed ground-state electron configurations for elements 1 through 18.

Hydrogen (H)   The atomic number of hydrogen is 1, which means that it has a single electron. In the ground state, this electron is placed in the $1s$ orbital. Shown first is its orbital box diagram and then its electron configuration. The ground-state electron configuration of a hydrogen atom has one unpaired electron.

H (1)   [↑]   Electron configuration: $1s^1$
$1s$

There is one electron
in this orbital

Electron configuration A description of the orbitals of an atom or ion occupied by electrons

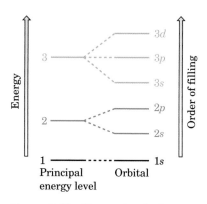

Figure 2.13   Energy levels for orbitals through the third shell.

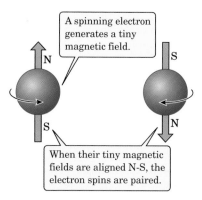

A spinning electron generates a tiny magnetic field.

When their tiny magnetic fields are aligned N-S, the electron spins are paired.

^{GOB}
Chemistry ⋅✦⋅ Now™
Active Figure 2.14   The pairing of electron spins. **See a simulation based on this figure, and take a short quiz on the concepts at http://www.now.brookscole.com/gob8 or on the CD.**

Table 2.7 Ground-State Electron Configurations of the First 18 Elements

	Orbital Box Diagram									Electron Configuration (Condensed)	Noble Gas Notation
	$1s$	$2s$	$2p_x$	$2p_y$	$2p_z$	$3s$	$3p_x$	$3p_y$	$3p_z$		
H (1)	↑									$1s^1$	
He (2)	↑↓									$1s^2$	
Li (3)	↑↓	↑								$1s^2\,2s^1$	[He] $2s^1$
Be (4)	↑↓	↑↓								$1s^2\,2s^2$	[He] $2s^2$
B (5)	↑↓	↑↓	↑							$1s^2\,2s^2\,2p^1$	[He] $2s^2\,2p^1$
C (6)	↑↓	↑↓	↑	↑						$1s^2\,2s^2\,2p^2$	[He] $2s^2\,2p^2$
N (7)	↑↓	↑↓	↑	↑	↑					$1s^2\,2s^2\,2p^3$	[He] $2s^2\,2p^3$
O (8)	↑↓	↑↓	↑↓	↑	↑					$1s^2\,2s^2\,2p^4$	[He] $2s^2\,2p^4$
F (9)	↑↓	↑↓	↑↓	↑↓	↑					$1s^2\,2s^2\,2p^5$	[He] $2s^2\,2p^5$
Ne (10)	↑↓	↑↓	↑↓	↑↓	↑↓					$1s^2\,2s^2\,2p^6$	[He] $2s^2\,2p^6$
Na (11)	↑↓	↑↓	↑↓	↑↓	↑↓	↑				$1s^2\,2s^2\,2p^6\,3s^1$	[Ne] $3s^1$
Mg (12)	↑↓	↑↓	↑↓	↑↓	↑↓	↑↓				$1s^2\,2s^2\,2p^6\,3s^2$	[Ne] $3s^2$
Al (13)	↑↓	↑↓	↑↓	↑↓	↑↓	↑↓	↑			$1s^2\,2s^2\,2p^6\,3s^2\,3p^1$	[Ne] $3s^2\,3p^1$
Si (14)	↑↓	↑↓	↑↓	↑↓	↑↓	↑↓	↑	↑		$1s^2\,2s^2\,2p^6\,3s^2\,3p^2$	[Ne] $3s^2\,3p^2$
P (15)	↑↓	↑↓	↑↓	↑↓	↑↓	↑↓	↑	↑	↑	$1s^2\,2s^2\,2p^6\,3s^2\,3p^3$	[Ne] $3s^2\,3p^3$
S (16)	↑↓	↑↓	↑↓	↑↓	↑↓	↑↓	↑↓	↑	↑	$1s^2\,2s^2\,2p^6\,3s^2\,3p^4$	[Ne] $3s^2\,3p^4$
Cl (17)	↑↓	↑↓	↑↓	↑↓	↑↓	↑↓	↑↓	↑↓	↑	$1s^2\,2s^2\,2p^6\,3s^2\,3p^5$	[Ne] $3s^2\,3p^5$
Ar (18)	↑↓	↑↓	↑↓	↑↓	↑↓	↑↓	↑↓	↑↓	↑↓	$1s^2\,2s^2\,2p^6\,3s^2\,3p^6$	[Ne] $3s^2\,3p^6$

Helium (He) The atomic number of helium is 2, which means that it has two electrons. In the ground state, both electrons are placed in the $1s$ orbital with paired spins, which fills the $1s$ orbital. All electrons in helium are paired.

This orbital is now filled with two electrons

He (2) ↑↓   Electron configuration: $1s^2$
        $1s$

Lithium (Li) Lithium, atomic number 3, has three electrons. In the ground state, two electrons are placed in the $1s$ orbital with paired spins, and the third electron is placed in the $2s$ orbital. The ground-state electron configuration of a lithium atom has one unpaired electron.

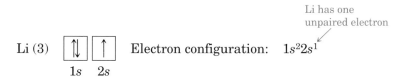

Li has one unpaired electron

Li (3)   Electron configuration: $1s^2 2s^1$

$1s$ $2s$

Carbon (C)   Carbon, atomic number 6, has six electrons. Two are placed in the $1s$ orbital with paired spins and two are placed in the $2s$ orbital with paired spins. The fifth and sixth electrons are placed one each in the $2p_x$ and $2p_y$ orbitals. The ground-state electron configuration of carbon has two unpaired electrons.

All orbitals of equal energy have at least one electron before any of them is filled

In a condensed electron configuration, orbitals of equal energy are grouped together

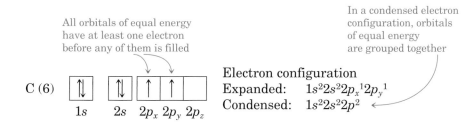

C (6)

$1s$ $2s$ $2p_x\ 2p_y\ 2p_z$

Electron configuration
Expanded: $1s^2 2s^2 2p_x{}^1 2p_y{}^1$
Condensed: $1s^2 2s^2 2p^2$

Oxygen (O)   Oxygen, atomic number 8, has eight electrons. The first four electrons fill the $1s$ and $2s$ orbitals. The next three electrons are placed in the $2p_x$, $2p_y$, and $2p_z$ orbitals so that each $2p$ orbital has one electron. The remaining electron now fills the $2p_x$ orbital. Oxygen has two unpaired electrons.

Oxygen has two unpaired electrons

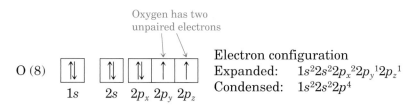

O (8)

$1s$ $2s$ $2p_x\ 2p_y\ 2p_z$

Electron configuration
Expanded: $1s^2 2s^2 2p_x{}^2 2p_y{}^1 2p_z{}^1$
Condensed: $1s^2 2s^2 2p^4$

Neon (Ne)   Neon, atomic number 10, has ten electrons, which completely fill all orbitals of the first and second shells. Neon has no unpaired electrons.

Ne (10)

$1s$ $2s$ $2p_x\ 2p_y\ 2p_z$

Electron configuration
Expanded: $1s^2 2s^2 2p_x{}^2 2p_y{}^2 2p_z{}^2$
Condensed: $1s^2 2s^2 2p^6$

Sodium (Na)   Sodium, atomic number 11, has 11 electrons. The first 10 fill the $1s$, $2s$, and $2p$ orbitals. The 11th electron is placed in the $3s$ orbital. Sodium has one unpaired electron.

Na (11)

$1s$ $2s$ $2p_x\ 2p_y\ 2p_z$ $3s$

Electron configuration
Expanded: $1s^2 2s^2 2p_x{}^2 2p_y{}^2 2p_z{}^2 3s^1$
Condensed: $1s^2 2s^2 2p^6 3s^1$

Phosphorus (P)   Phosphorus, atomic number 15, has 15 valence electrons. The first 12 fill the $1s$, $2s$, $2p$, and $3s$ orbitals. Electrons 13, 14, and 15 are placed one each in the $3p_x$, $3p_y$, and $3p_z$ orbitals. Phosphorus has three unpaired electrons.

P (15)

| $1s$ | $2s$ | $2p_x$ $2p_y$ $2p_z$ | $3s$ | $3p_x$ $3p_y$ $3p_z$ |

Electron configuration
Expanded: $1s^22s^22p_x{}^22p_y{}^22p_z{}^23s^23p_x{}^13p_y{}^13p_z{}^1$
Condensed: $1s^22s^22p^63s^23p^3$

E. Showing Electron Configurations: Noble Gas Notations

In an alternative way of writing electron configurations, we use the symbol of the noble gas immediately preceding the particular atom to indicate the electron configuration of all filled shells. The first shell of lithium, for example, is abbreviated [He] and the single electron in its $2s$ shell is indicated by $2s^1$. Thus the electron configuration of lithium is $[He]2s^1$.

F. Showing Electron Configurations: Lewis Dot Structures

When discussing the physical and chemical properties of an element, chemists often focus on the outermost shell of its electrons because electrons in this shell are the ones involved in the formation of chemical bonds (Chapter 4) and in chemical reactions (Chapter 5). Outer-shell electrons are called **valence electrons,** and the energy level in which they are found is called the **valence shell.** Carbon, for example, with a ground-state electron configuration of $1s^22s^22p^2$, has four valence (outer-shell) electrons.

To show the outermost electrons of an atom, we commonly use a representation called a **Lewis dot structure,** named after the American chemist Gilbert N. Lewis (1875–1946), who devised this notation. A Lewis structure shows the symbol of the element surrounded by a number of dots equal to the number of electrons in the outer shell of an atom of that element. In a Lewis structure, the atomic symbol represents the nucleus and all filled inner shells. Table 2.8 shows Lewis structures for the first 18 elements of the Periodic Table.

The noble gases helium and neon have filled valence shells. The valence shell of helium is filled with two electrons; that of neon is filled with eight electrons (Table 2.7). Neon and argon have in common an electron configuration in which the s and p orbitals of their valence shells are filled with eight electrons. The valence shells of all other elements shown in Table 2.8 contain fewer than eight electrons.

At this point, let us compare the Lewis structures given in Table 2.8 with the ground-state electron configurations given in Table 2.7. The Lewis structure of boron (B), for example, is shown in Table 2.8 with three valence

Valence electron An electron in the outermost occupied (valence) shell of an atom

Valence shell The outermost occupied shell of an atom

Lewis dot structure The symbol of the element surrounded by a number of dots equal to the number of electrons in the valence shell of an atom of that element

Table 2.8 Lewis Dot Structures for Elements 1–18 of the Periodic Table

1A	2A	3A	4A	5A	6A	7A	8A
H·							He:
Li·	Be:	B:	·C:	·N:	:O:	:F:	:Ne:
Na·	Mg:	Al:	·Si:	·P:	:S:	:Cl:	:Ar:

Each dot represents one valence electron.

electrons; these are the paired $2s$ electrons and the single $2p_x$ electron shown in Table 2.7. The Lewis structure of carbon (C) is shown in Table 2.8 with four valence electrons; these are the two paired $2s$ electrons and the unpaired $2p_x$ and $2p_y$ electrons shown in Table 2.7.

EXAMPLE 2.7

The Lewis dot structure for nitrogen shows five valence electrons. Write the expanded electron configuration for nitrogen and show to which orbitals its five valence electrons are assigned.

Solution
Nitrogen, atomic number 7, has the following ground-state electron configuration:

$$1s^2 2s^2 2p_x{}^1 2p_y{}^1 2p_z{}^1$$

The five valence electrons of the Lewis dot structure are the two paired electrons in the $2s$ orbital and the three unpaired electrons in the $2p_x$, $2p_y$, and $2p_z$ orbitals.

Problem 2.7
Write the Lewis dot structure for the element that has the following ground-state electron configuration. What is the name of this element?

$$1s^2 2s^2 2p_x{}^2 2p_y{}^2 2p_z{}^2 3s^2 3p_x{}^1$$

2.7 | How Are Electron Configuration and Position in the Periodic Table Related?

When Mendeleev published his first Periodic Table in 1869, he could not explain why it worked—that is, why elements with similar properties became aligned in the same column. Indeed, no one had a good explanation for this phenomenon. It was not until the discovery of electron configurations that chemists finally understood why the Periodic Table works. The answer is very simple: Elements in the same column have the same configuration of electrons in their outer shells. Figure 2.15 shows the relationship between shells (principal energy levels) and orbitals being filled.

All main-group elements have in common the fact that either their s or p orbitals are being filled. Notice that the $1s$ shell is filled with two electrons; there are only two elements in the first period. The $2s$ and $2p$ orbitals are filled with eight electrons; there are eight elements in period 2. Similarly, the $3s$ and $3p$ orbitals are filled with eight electrons; there are eight elements in period 3.

To create the elements of period 4, one $4s$, three $4p$, and five $3d$ orbitals are available. These orbitals can hold a total of 18 electrons; there are 18 elements in period 4. Similarly, there are 18 elements in period 5. Inner transition elements are created by filling f orbitals, which come in sets of seven and can hold a total of 14 electrons; there are 14 inner transition elements in the lanthanide series and 14 in the actinide series.

GOB
Chemistry‑⋆‑Now™

Click *Chemistry Interactive* to see an example of **Electron Configurations and Periodic Blocks**

Figure 2.15 Electron configuration and the Periodic Table.

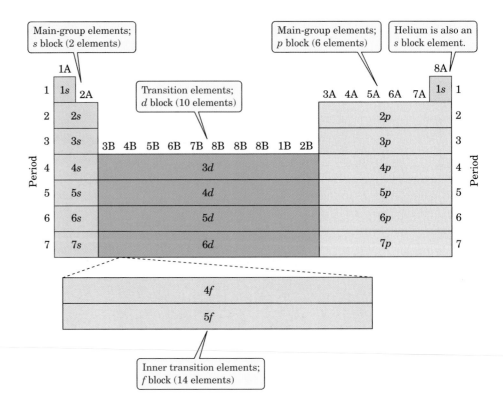

To see the similarities in electron configurations within the Periodic Table, let us look at the elements in column 1A. We already know the configurations for lithium, sodium, and potassium (Table 2.7). To this list we can add rubidium and cesium. All elements in column 1A have one electron in their valence shell (Table 2.9).

All Group 1A elements are metals, with the exception of hydrogen, which is a nonmetal. The properties of elements largely depend on the electron configuration of their outer shell. As a consequence, it is not surprising that Group 1A elements, all of which have the same outer-shell configuration, are metals (except for hydrogen) and have such similar physical and chemical properties.

Table 2.9 Noble Gas Notation and Lewis Dot Structures for the Alkali Metals (Group 1A Elements)

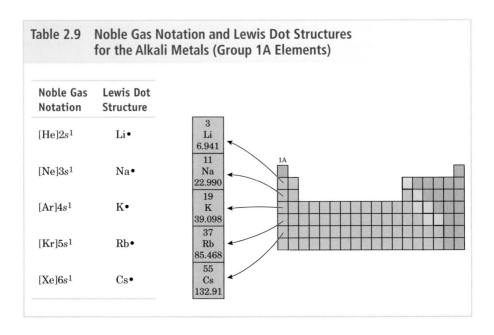

Noble Gas Notation	Lewis Dot Structure
$[He]2s^1$	Li•
$[Ne]3s^1$	Na•
$[Ar]4s^1$	K•
$[Kr]5s^1$	Rb•
$[Xe]6s^1$	Cs•

2.8 | What Are Periodic Properties?

As we have now seen, the Periodic Table was constructed on the basis of trends (periodicity) in chemical properties. With an understanding of electron configurations, chemists realized that the periodicity in chemical properties could be understood in terms of periodicity in electron configuration. As we noted in the opening of Section 2.7 "The Periodic Table works because elements in the same column have the same configuration of electrons in their outer shells." Thus, chemists could now explain why certain chemical and physical properties of elements changed in predictable ways in going down a column or going across a row of the Periodic Table. In this section, we will concentrate on the periodicity of one physical property (atomic size), and one chemical property (ionization energy) to illustrate how periodicity is related to position in the Periodic Table.

A. Atomic Size

The size of an atom is determined by the size of its outermost occupied orbital. The size of a sodium atom, for example, is the size of its singly-occupied $3s$ orbital. The size of a chlorine atom is determined by the size of its three $3p$ orbitals. The simplest way to determine the size of an atom is to determine the distance between atoms in a sample of the element. A chlorine molecule, for example, has a diameter of 198 pm (pm = picometer; 1 pm = 10^{-12} meter). The radius of a chlorine atom is thus 99 pm, which is one-half of the distance between the two chlorine atoms in Cl_2.

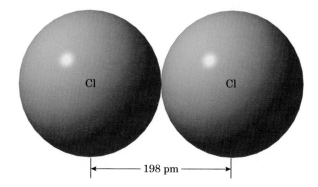

Similarly, the distance between carbon atoms in diamond is 154 pm, and so the radius of a carbon atom is 77 pm.

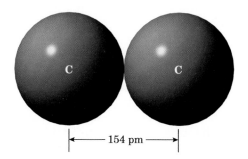

From measurements such as these we can assemble a set of atomic radii (Figure 2.16). From the information in this figure, we can see that for main group elements, (1) atomic radii increase in going down a group and (2) decrease in going across a period. Let us examine the correlation between each of these trends and electron configuration.

Figure 2.16 Atomic radii of main-group elements (in picometers, 1 pm = 10^{-12} m).

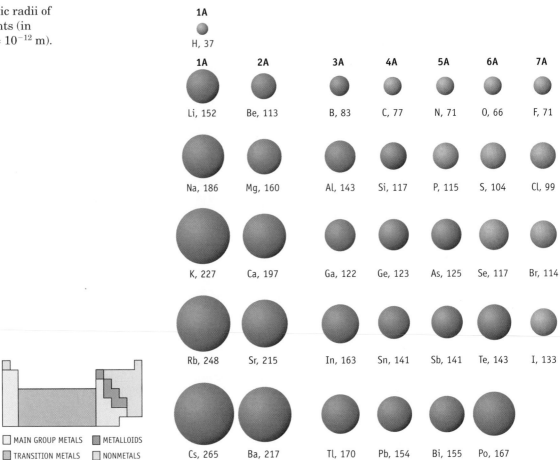

MAIN GROUP METALS METALLOIDS
TRANSITION METALS NONMETALS

1. The size of an atom is determined by its outermost electrons. In going down a column, the outermost electrons are assigned to higher and higher principal energy levels. The electrons of lower principal energy levels (those lying below the valence shell) must occupy some space, so the outer-shell electrons must be farther and farther from the nucleus, and therefore, the increase in size in going down a column is rationalized.

2. For elements in the same period, the principal energy level remains the same (for example, the valence electrons of all period 2 elements occupy the second principal energy level). But in going from one element to the next across a period, one more proton is added to the nucleus, thus increasing the nuclear charge by one unit for each step from left to right across the period. The result is the nucleus exerts an increasingly stronger pull on the valence electrons and atomic radii decreases.

B. Ionization Energy

Atoms are electrically neutral—the number of electrons outside the nucleus of an atom is equal to the number of protons inside the nucleus. Atoms do not normally lose or gain protons or neutrons, but they can lose or gain electrons. When a lithium atom, for example, loses one electron, it becomes a lithium **ion.** A lithium atom has three protons in its nucleus and three electrons outside the nucleus. When a lithium atom loses one of these electrons, it still has three protons in its nucleus (and, therefore, is still lithium), but now it has only two electrons outside the nucleus. The charge of two of the protons is cancelled by the two remaining electrons, but there is no third

Ion An atom with an unequal number of protons and electrons

electron to cancel the charge of the third proton. Therefore, a lithium ion has a charge of +1 and we write it as Li⁺. The ionization energy for a lithium atom in the gas phase is 0.52 kJ/mol.

$$\text{Li} \;+\; \text{energy} \longrightarrow \text{Li}^+ \;+\; \text{e}^-$$

Lithium   Ionization   Lithium   Electron
              energy   ion

Ionization energy is a measure of how difficult it is to remove the most loosely held electron from an atom in the gaseous state. The more difficult it is to remove the electron, the higher the ionization energy required to remove an electron from an atom. Ionization energies are always positive because energy must be supplied to overcome the attractive force between the electron and the positively charged nucleus. Figure 2.17 shows the ionization energies for the atoms of main-group elements 1 through 37 (hydrogen through rubidium).

As we see in this figure, ionization energy generally increases as we go up a column of the Periodic Table and, with a few exceptions, generally increases as we go from left to right across a row. For example, within the Group 1A metals, rubidium gives up its 5s electron most easily and lithium gives up its 2s electron least easily.

We explain this trend by saying that the 5s electron of rubidium is farther from the positively charged nucleus than is the 4s electron in potassium, which in turn is farther from the positively charged nucleus than is the 3s electron of sodium, and so forth. Furthermore, the 5s electron of rubidium is more "shielded" by inner-shell electrons from the attractive force of the positive nucleus than is the 4s electron of potassium, and so forth. The greater the shielding, the lower the ionization energy. Thus, going down a column of the Periodic Table, the shielding of an atom's outermost electrons increases, and the elements' ionization energies decrease.

We explain the increase in ionization energy across a row by the fact that the valence electrons across a row are in the same shell (principal energy level) and, therefore, are approximately the same distances from the nucleus. The number of protons in the nucleus, however, increases regularly across a row, which means that valence electrons experience an increasingly stronger pull by the nucleus, which makes them more difficult to remove. Thus ionization energy increases from left to right across a row of the periodic table.

Ionization energy The energy required to remove the most loosely held electron from an atom in the gas phase

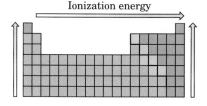

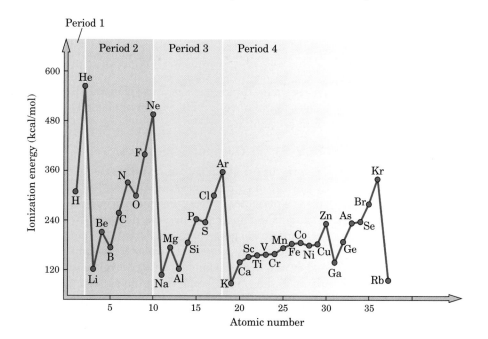

Figure 2.17 Ionization energy versus atomic number for elements 1–37.

SUMMARY OF KEY QUESTIONS

SECTION 2.1 What Is Matter Made Of?

- The Greek philosopher Democritus (circa 460–370 BCE) was the first person to propose an atomic theory of matter. He stated that all matter is made of very tiny particles, which he called atoms.

SECTION 2.2 How Do We Classify Matter?

- We classify matter as **elements, compounds,** or **mixtures.**

SECTION 2.3 What Are the Postulates of Dalton's Atomic Theory?

- (1) All matter is made up of atoms; (2) all atoms of a given element are identical and the atoms of any one element are different from those of any other element; (3) compounds are formed by the chemical combination of two or more different kinds of atoms; and (4) a molecule is a cluster of two or more atoms that acts as a single unit.
- Dalton's theory is based on the **law of conservation of mass** (matter can be neither created nor destroyed) and the **law of constant composition** (any compound is always made up of elements in the same proportion by mass).

SECTION 2.4 What Are Atoms Made Of?

- Atoms consist of protons and neutrons found inside the nucleus and electrons located outside it. An **electron** has a mass of approximately 0.0005 amu and a charge of -1. A **proton** has a mass of approximately 1 amu and a charge of $+1$. A **neutron** has a mass of approximately 1 amu and no charge.
- The **mass number** of an atom is the sum of the number of its protons and neutrons.
- The **atomic number** of an element is the number of protons in its nucleus.
- **Isotopes** are atoms with the same atomic number but different mass numbers; that is, they have the same number of protons in their nuclei but different numbers of neutrons.
- The **atomic weight** of an element is a weighted average of the masses (in amu) of the isotopes as they occur in nature.
- Atoms are very tiny, with a very small mass, almost all of which is concentrated in the nucleus. The nucleus is tiny, with an extremely high density.

SECTION 2.5 What Is the Periodic Table?

- The **Periodic Table** is an arrangement of elements into columns with similar properties, which gradually change as we move down a column.
- **Metals** are solids (except for mercury, which is a liquid), shiny, conductors of electricity, ductile, malleable, and form alloys, which are solutions of one or more metals dissolved in another metal. In their chemical reactions, metals tend to give up electrons.
- With the exception of hydrogen, the 18 **nonmetals** appear on the right side of the Periodic Table. With the exception of graphite, they do not conduct electricity. In their chemical reactions, nonmetals tend to accept electrons.
- Six elements are classified as **metalloids:** boron, silicon, germanium, arsenic, antimony, and tellurium. These elements have some properties of metals and some properties of nonmetals.

SECTION 2.6 How Are the Electrons in an Atom Arranged?

- Electrons in atoms exist in **principal energy levels** or **shells.**
- All principal energy levels except the first are divided into **subshells** designated by the letters *s, p, d,* and *f.* Within each subshell, electrons are grouped into **orbitals.** An orbital is a region of space that can hold two electrons with paired spins. All *s* orbitals are spherical and can hold two electrons. All *p* orbitals come in sets of three, and each is shaped like a dumbbell. A set of three *p* orbitals can hold six electrons.
- (1) Orbitals fill in order of increasing energy; (2) each orbital can hold a maximum of two electrons with paired spins; and (3) when filling orbitals of equivalent energy, each orbital adds one electron before any orbital adds a second electron.
- The electron configuration of an atom may be shown by an orbital notation, an orbital box diagram, or a noble gas notation.
- Electrons in the outermost or **valence shell** of an atom are called **valence electrons.** In a **Lewis dot structure** of an atom, the symbol of the element is surrounded by a number of dots equal to the number of its valence electrons.

SECTION 2.7 How Are Electron Configuration and Position in the Periodic Table Related?

- The Periodic Table works because elements in the same column have the same outer-shell electron configuration.

SECTION 2.8 What Are Periodic Properties?

- The **size of an atom (atomic radius)** is determined by the size of its outermost occupied orbital. Atomic size is a periodic property. For main group elements, (1) atomic size increases in going down a Group, and (2) decreases in going across a Period. In going down a column, the outermost electrons are assigned to higher and higher principal energy levels. For elements in the same Period, the principal energy level remains the same but from one element to the next, the nuclear charge increases by one unit (by one proton). As a result of this increase in nuclear charge across a Period, the nucleus exerts an increasingly stronger pull on the valence electrons and atomic size decreases.

• **Ionization energy** is the energy necessary to remove the most loosely held electron from an atom in the gas phase to form an **ion.** Ionization energy

increases from bottom to top within a column of the Periodic Table because the valence shell of the atom becomes closer to the positively charged nucleus. It increases from left to right within a row because the positive charge on the nucleus increases in this direction.

PROBLEMS

Chemistry⊷Now™

Assess your understanding of this chapter's topics with additional quizzing and conceptual-based problems at **http://now.brookscole.com/gob8** or on the CD.

A blue problem number indicates an applied problem.

■ denotes problems that are available on the GOB ChemistryNow website or CD and are assignable in OWL.

SECTION 2.1 What Is Matter Made Of?

2.8   In what way(s) was Democritus's atomic theory similar to Dalton's atomic theory?

SECTION 2.2 How Do We Classify Matter?

2.9   Classify each of the following as an element, a compound, or a mixture:
(a) Oxygen   (b) Table salt
(c) Sea water   (d) Wine
(e) Air   (f) Silver
(g) Diamond   (h) A pebble
(i) Gasoline   (j) Milk
(k) Carbon dioxide   (l) Bronze

2.10 ■ Name these elements (try not to look at a Periodic Table):
(a) O   (b) Pb   (c) Ca   (d) Na
(e) C   (f) Ti   (g) S   (h) Fe
(i) H   (j) K   (k) Ag   (l) Au

2.11 The elements game, Part I. Name and give the symbol of the element that is named for each person.
(a) Niels Bohr (1885–1962), Nobel Prize for physics in 1922
(b) Pierre and Marie Curie, Nobel Prize for chemistry in 1903
(c) Albert Einstein (1879–1955), Nobel Prize for physics in 1921
(d) Enrico Fermi (1901–1954), Nobel Prize for physics in 1938
(e) Ernest Lawrence (1901–1958), Nobel Prize for physics in 1939
(f) Lisa Meitner (1868–1968), codiscoverer of nuclear fission
(g) Dmitri Mendeleev (1834–1907), first person to formulate a workable Periodic Table

(h) Alfred Nobel (1833–1896), discoverer of dynamite
(i) Ernest Rutherford (1871–1937), Nobel Prize for chemistry in 1908
(j) Glen Seaborg (1912–1999), Nobel Prize for chemistry in 1951

2.12 The elements game, Part II. Name and give the symbol of the element that is named for each geographic location.
(a) The Americas
(b) Berkeley, California
(c) The state and University of California
(d) Dubna, location in Russia of the Joint Institute of Nuclear Research
(e) Europe
(f) France
(g) Gallia, Latin name for ancient France
(h) Germany
(i) Hafnia, Latin name for ancient Copenhagen
(j) Hesse, a German state
(k) Holmia, Latin name for ancient Stockholm
(l) Lutetia, Latin name for ancient Paris
(m) Magnesia, a district in Thessaly
(n) Poland, the native country of Marie Curie
(o) Rhenus, Latin name for the river Rhine
(p) Ruthenia, Latin name for ancient Russia
(q) Scandia, Latin name for ancient Scandinavia
(r) Strontian, a town in Scotland
(s) Ytterby, a village in Sweden (three elements)
(t) Thule, the earliest name for Scandinavia

2.13 The elements game, Part III. Give the names and symbols for the four elements named for planets.

2.14 ■ Write the formulas of compounds in which the combining ratios are as follows:
(a) Potassium : oxygen, 2 : 1
(b) Sodium : phosphorus : oxygen, 3 : 1 : 4
(c) Lithium : nitrogen : oxygen, 1 : 1 : 3

2.15 Write the formulas of compounds in which the combining ratios are as follows:
(a) Sodium : hydrogen : carbon : oxygen, 1 : 1 : 1 : 3
(b) Carbon : hydrogen : oxygen, 2 : 6 : 1
(c) Potassium : manganese : oxygen, 1 : 1 : 4

SECTION 2.3 What Are Postulates of Dalton's Atomic Theory?

2.16 How does Dalton's atomic theory explain the following:
(a) The law of conservation of mass?
(b) The law of constant composition?

2.17 When 2.16 g of mercury oxide is heated, it decomposes to yield 2.00 g of mercury and 0.16 g of oxygen. Which law is supported by this experiment?

2.18 The compound carbon monoxide contains 42.9% carbon and 57.1% oxygen. The compound carbon dioxide contains 27.3% carbon and 72.7% oxygen. Does this disprove Proust's law of constant composition?

2.19 ■ Calculate the percentage of hydrogen and oxygen in water, H_2O, and hydrogen peroxide, H_2O_2.

SECTION 2.4 What Are Atoms Made Of?

2.20 Where in an atom are these subatomic particles located?
(a) Protons   (b) Electrons   (c) Neutrons

2.21 It has been said that "the number of protons determines the identity of the element." Do you agree or disagree with this statement? Explain.

2.22 What is the mass number of an atom with
(a) 22 protons, 22 electrons, and 26 neutrons?
(b) 76 protons, 76 electrons, and 114 neutrons?
(c) 34 protons, 34 electrons, and 45 neutrons?
(d) 94 protons, 94 electrons, and 150 neutrons?

2.23 Name and give the symbol for each element in Problem 2.22.

2.24 Given the mass number and the number of neutrons, what is the name and symbol of each element?
(a) Mass number 45; 24 neutrons
(b) Mass number 48; 26 neutrons
(c) Mass number 107; 60 neutrons
(d) Mass number 246; 156 neutrons
(e) Mass number 36; 18 neutrons

2.25 If each of the atoms in Problem 2.24 acquired two more neutrons, what element would each then be?

2.26 How many neutrons are there in
(a) A carbon atom of mass number 13?
(b) A germanium atom of mass number 73?
(c) An osmium atom of mass number 188?
(d) A platinum atom of mass number 195?

2.27 ■ How many protons and how many neutrons does each of these isotopes of radon contain?
(a) Rn-210   (b) Rn-218   (c) Rn-222

2.28 ■ How many neutrons and protons are there in each isotope?
(a) ^{22}Ne (b) ^{104}Pd
(c) ^{35}Cl (d) Tellurium-128
(e) Lithium-7   (f) Uranium-238

2.29 Tin-118 is one of the isotopes of tin. Write the symbols for the isotopes of tin that contain two, three, and six more neutrons than tin-118.

2.30 What is the difference between atomic number and mass number?

2.31 Define:
(a) Ion   (b) Isotope

2.32 ■ There are only two naturally occurring isotopes of antimony: ^{121}Sb (120.90 amu) and ^{123}Sb (122.90 amu). The atomic weight of antimony given in the Periodic Table is 121.75. Which of its two naturally occurring isotopes has the greater natural abundance?

2.33 The two most abundant naturally occurring isotopes of carbon are carbon-12 (98.90%, 12.000 amu) and carbon-13 (1.10%, 13.003 amu). From these abundances, calculate the atomic weight of carbon and compare your calculated value with that given in the Periodic Table.

2.34 Another isotope of carbon, carbon-14, occurs in nature but in such small amounts relative to carbon-12 and carbon-13 that it does not contribute in a significant way to the atomic weight of carbon as recorded in the Periodic Table. Carbon-14 is invaluable in the science of radiocarbon dating (see Chemical Connections 3A). Give the number of protons, neutrons, and electrons in an atom of carbon-14.

2.35 The isotope carbon-11 does not occur in nature but has been made in the laboratory. This isotope is used in a medical imaging technique called positron emission tomography (PET, see Section 3.7A). Give the number of protons, neutrons, and electrons in an atom of carbon-11.

2.36 Other isotopes used in PET therapy are fluorine-18, nitrogen-13, and oxygen-15. None of these isotopes occurs in nature; all must be produced in the laboratory. Give the number of protons, neutrons, and electrons in an atom of each of these artificial isotopes.

2.37 Americium-241 is used in household smoke detectors. This element has 11 known isotopes, none of which occurs in nature, but must be made in the laboratory. Give the number of protons, neutrons, and electrons in an atom of americium-241.

2.38 In dating geological samples, scientists compare the ratio of rubidium-87 to strontium-87. Give the number of protons, neutrons, and electrons in an atom of each element.

SECTION 2.5 What Is the Periodic Table?

2.39 How many metals, metalloids, and nonmetals are there in the third period of the Periodic Table?

2.40 Which group(s) of the Periodic Table contain
(a) Only metals?   (b) Only metalloids?
(c) Only nonmetals?

2.41 Which period(s) in the Periodic Table contain more nonmetals than metals? Which contain more metals than nonmetals?

2.42   Using only the Periodic Table, group the following elements according to similar properties: As, I, Ne, F, Mg, K, Ca, Ba, Li, He, N, P.

2.43   Which of the following are transition elements?
(a) Pd   (b) K   (c) Co
(d) Ce   (e) Br   (f) Cr

2.44   Which element in each pair is more metallic?
(a) Silicon or aluminum
(b) Arsenic or phosphorus
(c) Gallium or germanium
(d) Gallium or aluminum

2.45   ■ Classify these elements as metals, nonmetals, or metalloids:
(a) Argon   (b) Boron   (c) Lead
(d) Arsenic   (e) Potassium   (f) Silicon
(g) Iodine   (h) Antimony   (i) Vanadium
(j) Sulfur   (k) Nitrogen

SECTION 2.6 How Are the Electrons in an Atom Arranged?

2.46   How many periods of the Periodic Table have two elements? How many have eight elements? How many have 18 elements? How many have 32 elements?

2.47   What is the correlation between the group number of the main-group elements (1A, 2A, . . . , 8A) and the number of valence electrons in an element in the group?

2.48   Given your answer to Problem 2.47, write the Lewis dot structures for each of the following elements using no information other than the number of the group in the Periodic Table to which the element belongs.
(a) Carbon (4A)   (b) Silicon (4A)
(c) Oxygen (6A)   (d) Sulfur (6A)
(e) Aluminum (3A)   (f) Bromine (7A)

2.49   ■ Write the condensed ground-state electron configuration for each of the following elements. The element's atomic number is given in parentheses.
(a) Li (3)   (b) Ne (10)   (c) Be (4)
(d) C (6)   (e) Mg (12)

2.50   Write the Lewis dot structure for each element in Problem 2.49.

2.51   ■ Write the condensed ground-state electron configuration for each of the following elements. The element's atomic number is given in parentheses.
(a) He (2)   (b) Na (11)   (c) Cl (17)
(d) P (15)   (e) H (1)

2.52   Write the Lewis dot structure for each element in Problem 2.51.

2.53   What is the same and what is different in the electron configurations of
(a) Na and Cs?   (b) O and Te?
(c) C and Ge?

2.54   Silicon, atomic number 14, is in Group 4A. How many orbitals are occupied by the valence electrons of Si in its ground state?

2.55   You are presented with a Lewis dot structure of element X as X$\colon$. To which two groups in the Periodic Table might this element belong?

2.56   The electron configurations for the elements with atomic numbers higher than 36 follow the same rules as given in the text for the first 36 elements. In fact, you can arrive at the correct order of filling of orbitals from Figure 2.15 by starting with H and reading the orbitals from left to right across the first row, then the second row, and so on. Write the condensed ground-state electron configuration for
(a) Rb   (b) Sr   (c) Br

SECTION 2.7 How Are Electron Configuration and Position in the Periodic Table Related?

2.57   Why do the elements in column 1A of the Periodic Table (the alkali metals) have similar but not identical properties?

SECTION 2.8 What Are Periodic Properties?

2.58   Account for the following observations.
(a) The atomic radius of an anion is always larger than the atoms from which it is derived. Examples: Cl 99 pm and Cl$^-$ 181 pm; O 73 pm and O^{2-} 140 pm.
(b) The atomic radius of a cation is always smaller than that of the atom from which it is derived. Examples: Li 152 pm and Li$^+$ 76 pm; Na 156 pm and Na$^+$ 98 pm.

2.59   ■ Using only the Periodic Table, arrange the elements in each set in order of increasing ionization energy:
(a) Li, Na, K   (b) C, N, Ne
(c) O, C, F   (d) Br, Cl, F

2.60   Account for the fact that the first ionization energy of oxygen is less than that of nitrogen.

2.61   Every atom except hydrogen has a series of ionization energies because they have more than one electron that can be removed. Following are the first three ionization energies for magnesium.

$$Mg(g) \longrightarrow Mg^+(g) + e^-(g) \qquad IE_1 = 738 \text{ kJ/mol}$$

$$Mg^+(g) \longrightarrow Mg^{2+}(g) + e^-(g) \qquad IE_2 = 1450 \text{ kJ/mol}$$

$$Mg^{2+}(g) \longrightarrow Mg^{3+}(g) + e^-(g) \qquad IE_3 = 7734 \text{ kJ/mol}$$

(a) Write the ground-state electron configuration for Mg, Mg$^+$, Mg^{2+}, and Mg^{3+}.
(b) Account for the large increase in ionization energy for the removal of the third electron compared with the ionization energies for removal of the first and second electrons.

Chemical Connections

2.62 (Chemical Connections 2A) Why does the body need sulfur, calcium, and iron?

2.63 (Chemical Connections 2B) Which are the two most abundant elements, by weight, in

(a) The Earth's crust?　　(b) The human body?

2.64 (Chemical Connections 2C) Consider the isotopic abundance of hydrogen on Mars. Would the atomic weight of hydrogen on Mars be greater than, the same as, or smaller than that on Earth?

2.65 (Chemical Connections 2D) Why is strontium-90 more dangerous to humans than most other radioactive isotopes that were present in the Chernobyl fallout?

2.66 (Chemical Connections 2E) Bronze is an alloy of which two metals?

2.67 (Chemical Connections 2E) Copper is a soft metal. How can one make it harder?

Additional Problems

2.68 Give the designations of all subshells in the

(a) 1 shell　　　　　　　(b) 2 shell

(c) 3 shell　　　　　　　(d) 4 shell

2.69 Tell whether metals or nonmetals are more likely to have each of the following characteristics:

(a) Conduct electricity and heat

(b) Accept electrons

(c) Be malleable

(d) Be a gas at room temperature

(e) Be a transition element

(f) Lose electrons

2.70 What is the outer-shell electron configuration of the elements in

(a) Group 3A?　　　　　(b) Group 7A?

(c) Group 5A?

2.71 ■ Determine the number of protons, electrons, and neutrons present in

(a) ^{32}P　　(b) ^{98}Mo　　(c) ^{44}Ca

(d) ^{3}H　　(e) ^{158}Gd　　(f) ^{212}Bi

2.72 What percentage of the mass of each element is contributed by neutrons?

(a) Carbon-12　　　　　(b) Calcium-40

(c) Iron-55　　　　　　(d) Bromine-79

(e) Platinum-195　　　(f) Uranium-238

2.73 Do isotopes of the heavy elements (for example, those from atomic number 37 to 53) contain more, the same, or fewer neutrons than protons?

2.74 ■ What is the symbol for each of the following elements? (Try not to look at a Periodic Table.)

(a) Phosphorus　　　　(b) Potassium

(c) Sodium　　　　　　(d) Nitrogen

(e) Bromine　　　　　　(f) Silver

(g) Calcium　　　　　　(h) Carbon

(i) Tin　　　　　　　　(j) Zinc

2.75 The natural abundance of boron isotopes is as follows: 19.9% boron-10 (10.013 amu) and 80.1% boron-11 (11.009 amu). Calculate the atomic weight of boron (watch the significant figures) and compare your calculated value with that given in the Periodic Table.

2.76 How many electrons are in the outer shell of each of the following elements?

(a) Si　　　(b) Br　　　(c) P

(d) K　　　(e) He　　　(f) Ca

(g) Kr　　　(h) Pb　　　(i) Se

(j) O

2.77 The mass of a proton is 1.67×10^{-24} g. The mass of a grain of salt is 1.0×10^{-2} g. How many protons would it take to have the same mass as a grain of salt?

2.78 (a) What are the charges of an electron, a proton, and a neutron?

(b) What are the masses (in amu, to one significant figure) of an electron, a proton, and a neutron?

2.79 ■ Rubidium has two natural isotopes: rubidium-85 and rubidium-87. What is the natural abundance of each isotope if the atomic weight of rubidium is 85.47?

2.80 What is the name of this element and how many protons and neutrons does it have in its nucleus: $^{131}_{54}$X?

2.81 Based on the data presented in Figure 2.16, which atom would have the highest ionization energy: I, Cs, Sn, or Xe?

2.82 Assume that a new element has been discovered with atomic number 117. Its chemical properties should be similar to those of At. Predict whether the new element's ionization energy will be greater than, the same as, or smaller than that of (a) At and (b) Ra.

Looking Ahead

2.83 Suppose that you face a problem similar to Mendeleev: You must predict the properties of an element not yet discovered. What will element 118 be like if and when enough of it is made for chemists to study its physical and chemical properties?

2.84 Compare the neutron to proton ratio for heavier and lighter elements. Does the value of this ratio generally increase, decrease, or remain the same as atomic number increases?

Nuclear Chemistry

NASA

The Sun's energy is the result of nuclear fusion.

GOB
Chemistry Now™
Look for this logo in the chapter and go to GOB ChemistryNow at
http://now.brookscole.com/gob8
or on the CD for tutorials, simulations, and problems.

3.1 | How Was Radioactivity Discovered?

Every so often, a scientist makes the kind of discovery that changes the future of the world in some significant way. In 1896 a French physicist, Henri Becquerel (1852–1908), made one of these discoveries. At the time, Becquerel was engaged in a study of phosphorescent materials. In his experiments, he exposed certain salts—among them uranium salts—to sunlight for several hours, whereupon they phosphoresced. He then placed the glowing salts on a photographic plate that had been wrapped in opaque paper. Becquerel observed that, by placing a coin or a metal cutout between the phosphorescing salts and the covered plate, he could create photographic images of the coin or metal cutout. He concluded that besides emitting visible light, the phosphorescent materials must be emitting something akin to Xrays, which William Röntgen had discovered just the previous year. What was even more surprising to Becquerel was that his uranium salts continued to emit this same type of penetrating radiation long after their phosphorescence has ceased. What he had discovered was a type of radiation that Marie Curie was to call radioactivity. For this discovery, Becquerel shared the 1903 Nobel Prize for physics with Pierre and Marie Curie.

In this chapter, we will study the major types of radioactivity, their origin in the nucleus, the uses of radioactivity in the health and biological sciences, and its use as a source of power and energy.

3.2 | What Is Radioactivity?

GOB
Chemistry·ᚲ·Now™
Click *Coached Problems* to see **Evidence of Subatomic Particles**

Early experiments identified three kinds of radiation, which were named alpha (α), beta (β), and gamma (γ) rays after the first three letters of the Greek alphabet. Each type of radiation behaves differently when it passes between electrically charged plates. When a radioactive material is placed in a lead container that has a small opening, the emitted radiation passes through the opening and then between charged plates (Figure 3.1). One ray (β) is deflected toward the positive plate, indicating that it consists of negatively charged particles. A second ray (α) is deflected toward the negative plate, indicating that it consists of positively charged particles. A third

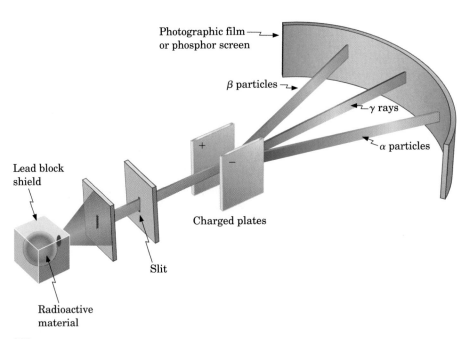

GOB
Chemistry·ᚲ·Now™
Active Figure 3.1 Electricity and radioactivity. Positively charged alpha (α) particles are attracted to the negative plate and negatively charged beta (β) particles are attracted to the positive plate. Gamma (γ) rays have no charge and are not deflected as they pass between the charged plates. Note that beta particles are deflected more than alpha particles. **See a simulation based on this figure, and take a short quiz on the concepts at http://www.now.brookscole.com/gob8 or on the CD.**

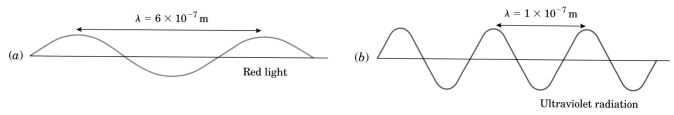

Figure 3.2   Two electromagnetic waves with different wavelengths.

ray (γ) passes between the charged plates without deflection, indicating that it has no charge.

Alpha particles are helium nuclei. Each contains two protons and two neutrons; each has an atomic number of 2 and a charge of +2.

Beta particles are electrons. Each has a charge of −1.

Gamma rays are high-energy electromagnetic radiation. They have no mass or charge.

Gamma rays are only one form of electromagnetic radiation. Many others exist, including visible light, radio waves, and cosmic rays. All consist of waves (Figure 3.2).

The only difference between one form of electromagnetic radiation and another is the **wavelength** (λ, Greek letter lambda), which is the distance from one wave crest to the next. The **frequency** (ν, Greek letter nu) of a radiation is the number of crests that pass a given point in one second. Mathematically wavelength and frequency are related by the following equation, where c is the speed of light (3.0×10^8 m/s):

$$\lambda = \frac{c}{\nu}$$

As you can see from this relationship, the lower the frequency (ν), the longer the wavelength (λ); conversely, the shorter the frequency, the longer the wavelength.

A direct relationship also exists between the frequency of electromagnetic and its energy: The higher the frequency, the higher its energy. Electromagnetic radiation comes in packets; the smallest units are called **photons.**

Figure 3.3 shows the wavelengths of various types of radiation of the electromagnetic spectrum. Gamma rays are electromagnetic radiation of very high frequency (and high energy). Humans cannot see them because our eyes are not sensitive to waves of this frequency, but they can be detected

The only radiation known to have an even higher frequency (and energy) than gamma rays is cosmic rays.

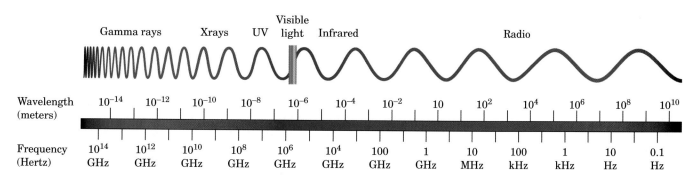

Figure 3.3   The electromagnetic spectrum.

Table 3.1 Particles and Rays Frequently Encountered in Radiation

Particle or Ray	Common Name of Radiation	Symbol	Charge	Atomic Mass Units	Penetrating Power[a]	Energy[b] Range
Proton	Proton beam	$_1^1\text{H}$	+1	1	1–3 cm	60 MeV
Electron	Beta particle	$_{+1}^0\text{e}$ or β	−1	$0.00055\left(\dfrac{1}{1835}\right)$	0–4 mm	1–3 MeV
Neutron	Neutron beam	$_0^1\text{n}$	0	1	—	—
Positron	—	$_{+1}^0\text{e}$ or β^+	+1	0.00055	—	—
Helium nucleus	Alpha particle	$_2^4\text{He}$ or α	+2	4	0.02–0.04 mm	3–9 MeV
Energetic radiation	{ Gamma ray	γ	0	0	1–20 cm	0.1–10 MeV
	{ X ray		0	0	0.01–1 cm	0.1–10 keV

[a]Distance at which half the radiation has been stopped in water.
[b]MeV = 1.602×10^{-13} J = 3.829×10^{-14} cal.

UV stands for ultraviolet and IR for infrared.

The electron-volt (eV) is a non-SI energy unit used frequently in nuclear chemistry.
1 eV = 1.60×10^{-19} J

by instruments (Section 3.5). Another kind of radiation, called Xrays, has frequencies (and energies) higher than those of visible light but less than those of gamma rays.

Materials that emit radiation (alpha, beta, or gamma) are called **radioactive.** Radioactivity comes from the atomic nucleus and not from the electron cloud. Table 3.1 summarizes the properties of the particles and rays that come out of radioactive nuclei, along with the properties of some other particles and rays. Note that Xrays are not considered to be a form of radioactivity, because they do not come out of the nucleus but are generated in other ways.

We have said that humans cannot see gamma rays. We cannot see alpha or beta particles either. Likewise, we cannot hear them, smell them, or feel them. They are undetectable by our senses. We can detect radioactivity only by instruments, as discussed in Section 3.5.

3.3 | What Happens When a Nucleus Emits Radioactivity?

As mentioned in Section 2.4D, different nuclei consist of different numbers of protons and neutrons. It is customary to indicate these numbers with subscripts and superscripts placed to the left of the atomic symbol. The atomic number (the number of protons in an atom of the element) is shown as a subscript and the mass number (the number of protons and neutrons) as a superscript. For example, here are the symbols and names for the three isotopes of hydrogen:

$_1^1\text{H}$	hydrogen-1	hydrogen	(not radioactive)
$_1^2\text{H}$	hydrogen-2	deuterium	(not radioactive)
$_1^3\text{H}$	hydrogen-3	tritium	(radioactive)

A. Radioactive and Stable Nuclei

Some isotopes are radioactive, whereas others are stable. Scientists have identified more than 300 naturally occurring isotopes. Of these, 264 are stable, meaning that the nuclei of these isotopes never give off any radioactivity. As far as we can tell, they will last forever. The remainder are

radioactive isotopes—they do give off radioactivity. Furthermore, scientists have made more than 1000 artificial isotopes in laboratories. All artificial isotopes are radioactive.

Isotopes in which the number of protons and neutrons are balanced seem to be stable. In the lighter elements, this balance occurs when the numbers of protons and neutrons are approximately equal. For example, $^{12}_{6}C$ is a stable nucleus (six protons and six neutrons), as are $^{16}_{8}O$ (eight protons and eight neutrons), and $^{20}_{10}Ne$ (ten protons and ten neutrons). Among the heavier elements, stability requires more neutrons than protons. Lead-206, one of the most stable isotopes of lead, contains 82 protons and 124 neutrons.

If there is a serious imbalance in the proton-to-neutron ratio (either too few or too many neutrons), a nucleus will undergo **nuclear reaction** to make the ratio more favorable and the nucleus more stable.

Radioactive isotope A radiation-emitting isotope of an element

The role of neutrons seems to be to provide binding energy to overcome the repulsion between protons.

Nuclear reaction A reaction that changes atomic nuclei of elements (usually to atomic nuclei of other elements)

B. Beta Emission

If a nucleus has more neutrons than it needs for stability, it can stabilize itself by converting a neutron to a proton and an electron.

$$\underset{\text{Neutron}}{^{1}_{0}n} \longrightarrow \underset{\text{Proton}}{^{1}_{1}H} + \underset{\text{Electron}}{^{0}_{-1}e}$$

The proton remains in the nucleus but the electron is emitted from it. The emitted electron is called a **beta particle,** and the process is called **beta emission.** Phosphorus-32, for example, is a beta emitter:

$$^{32}_{15}P \longrightarrow ^{32}_{16}S + ^{0}_{-1}e$$

A phosphorus-32 nucleus has 15 protons and 17 neutrons. The nucleus remaining after an electron has been emitted has 16 protons and 16 neutrons; its atomic number is increased by 1 but its mass number is unchanged. The new nucleus is, therefore, sulfur-32. Thus, when the unstable phosphorus-32 (15 protons and 17 neutrons) is converted to sulfur-32 (16 protons and 16 neutrons), nuclear stability is achieved

The changing of one element into another is called **transmutation.** It happens naturally every time an element gives off a beta particle. Every time a nucleus emits a beta particle, it is transformed into another nucleus with the same mass number but an atomic number one unit greater.

H O W T O . . .

Balance a Nuclear Equation

In writing nuclear equations, we consider only the nucleus and disregard the surrounding electrons. There are two simple rules for balancing nuclear equations:

1. The sum of the mass numbers (superscripts) on both sides of the equation must be equal.
2. The sum of the atomic numbers (subscripts) on both sides of the equation must be equal. For the purposes of determining atomic numbers in a nuclear equation, an electron emitted from the nucleus has an atomic number of -1.

To see how to apply these rules, let us look at the decay of phosphorus-32, a beta emitter.

$$^{32}_{15}\text{P} \longrightarrow {}^{32}_{16}\text{S} + {}^{0}_{-1}\text{e}$$

1. Mass number balance: The total mass number on each side of the equation is 32.
2. Atomic number balance: The atomic number on the left is 15. The sum of the atomic numbers on the right is $16 - 1 = 15$.

Thus, in the phosphorus-32 decay equation, mass numbers are balanced (32 and 32), atomic numbers are balanced (15 and 15), and, therefore, the nuclear equation is balanced.

EXAMPLE 3.1

Carbon-14, $^{14}_{6}\text{C}$, is a beta emitter. Write an equation for this nuclear reaction, and identify the product element.

$$^{14}_{6}\text{C} \longrightarrow ? + {}^{0}_{-1}\text{e}$$

Solution
The $^{14}_{6}\text{C}$ nucleus has six protons and eight neutrons. One of its neutrons is converted to a proton and an electron. The electron is emitted as a beta particle, but the proton remains in the nucleus. The nucleus now has seven protons and seven neutrons:

$$^{14}_{6}\text{C} \longrightarrow {}^{14}_{7}? + {}^{0}_{-1}\text{e}$$

The sum of the mass numbers on each side of the equation is 14, and the sum of the atomic numbers on each side is 6. When we look in the Periodic Table to find out which element has atomic number 7, we see that it is nitrogen. The product of this nuclear reaction is, therefore, nitrogen-14 and we can now write a complete equation.

$$^{14}_{6}\text{C} \longrightarrow {}^{14}_{7}\text{N} + {}^{0}_{-1}\text{e}$$

Problem 3.1
Iodine-139 is a beta emitter. Write an equation for this nuclear reaction, and identify the product.

C. Alpha Emission

For heavy elements, the loss of alpha (α) particles is an especially important stabilization process. For example,

$$^{238}_{92}\text{U} \longrightarrow {}^{234}_{90}\text{Th} + {}^{4}_{2}\text{He}$$

$$^{210}_{84}\text{Po} \longrightarrow {}^{206}_{82}\text{Pb} + {}^{4}_{2}\text{He} + \gamma$$

Note that the radioactive decay of polonium-210 emits both an α particle and gamma rays.

A general rule for alpha emission is this: The new nucleus always has a mass number four units lower and an atomic number two units lower than the original nucleus.

EXAMPLE 3.2

Polonium-218 is an alpha emitter. Write an equation for this nuclear reaction, and identify the product.

Solution
The atomic number of polonium is 84, so the partial equation is

$$^{218}_{84}\text{Po} \longrightarrow ? + {}^{4}_{2}\text{He}$$

The mass number of the new isotope is $218 - 4 = 214$. The atomic number of the new isotope is $84 - 2 = 82$. We can now write

$$^{218}_{84}\text{Po} \longrightarrow {}^{214}_{82}? + {}^{4}_{2}\text{He}$$

In the Periodic Table we find that the element with an atomic number of 82 is lead, Pb. Therefore, the product is $^{214}_{82}\text{Pb}$, and we can now write the complete equation:

$$^{218}_{84}\text{Po} \longrightarrow {}^{214}_{82}\text{Pb} + {}^{4}_{2}\text{He}$$

Problem 3.2
Thorium-223 is an alpha emitter. Write an equation for this nuclear reaction and identify the product.

D. Positron Emission

A positron is a particle that has the same mass as an electron, but a charge of $+1$ rather than -1. Its symbol is β^+ or $^{0}_{+1}\text{e}$. Positron emission is much rarer than alpha or beta emission. Because a positron has no appreciable mass, the nucleus is transmuted into another nucleus with the same mass number but an atomic number that is one unit less. Carbon-11, for example, is a positron emitter:

$$^{11}_{6}\text{C} \longrightarrow {}^{11}_{5}\text{B} + {}^{0}_{+1}\text{e}$$

In this balanced nuclear equation, the mass numbers on both the left and the right are 11. The atomic number on the left is 6; that on the right is also 6 $(5 + 1 = 6)$.

EXAMPLE 3.3

Nitrogen-13 is a positron emitter. Write an equation for this nuclear reaction, and identify the product.

Solution
We begin by writing a partial equation:

$$^{13}_{7}\text{N} \longrightarrow ? + {}^{0}_{+1}\text{e}$$

Because a positron has no appreciable mass, the mass number of the new isotope is still 13. The sum of the atomic numbers on each side must be 7, which means that the atomic number of the new isotope must be 6. In the Periodic Table we see that the element with atomic number 6 is carbon. Therefore, the new isotope formed in this nuclear reaction is carbon-13 and the balanced nuclear equation is

$$^{13}_{7}\text{N} \longrightarrow {}^{13}_{6}\text{C} + {}^{0}_{+1}\text{e}$$

Problem 3.3

Arsenic-74 is a positron emitter used in locating brain tumors. Write an equation for this nuclear reaction and identify the product.

E. Gamma Emission

Both alpha and beta emissions can be either "pure" or mixed with gamma rays.

Although rare, some nuclei are pure gamma emitters:

$$^{11}_{5}\text{B}^* \longrightarrow {}^{11}_{5}\text{B} + \gamma$$

Gamma emission often accompanies α and β emissions.
In this equation, $^{11}_{5}\text{B}^*$ symbolizes a boron nucleus in a high-energy (excited) state. In this case, no transmutation takes place. The boron is still boron, but its nucleus is in a lower-energy (more stable) state after the emission of excess energy in the form of gamma rays. When all excess energy has been emitted, the nucleus returns to its most stable, lowest-energy state.

F. Electron Capture

In electron capture (abbreviated E.C.), an extranuclear electron is captured by the nucleus and there reacts with a proton to form a neutron. Thus, the atomic number of the element is reduced by one, but the mass number is unchanged. Beryllium-7, for example, decays by electron capture to give lithium-7:

$$^{7}_{4}\text{Be} + {}^{0}_{-1}\text{e} \longrightarrow {}^{7}_{3}\text{Li}$$

EXAMPLE 3.4

Chromium-51, which is used to create images that show the size and shape of the spleen, decays by electron capture and gamma emission. Write an equation for this nuclear decay and identify the product.

Solution
We begin by writing a partial equation:

$$^{51}_{24}\text{Cr} + {}^{0}_{-1}\text{e} \longrightarrow ? + \gamma$$

There is no change in mass number, so the new nucleus has a mass number of 51. The new nucleus has 23 protons, one less than chromium-51. In the Periodic Table we see that the element with atomic number 23 is vanadium and, therefore, the new element formed is vanadium-51. We can now write the complete equation for this nuclear decay:

$$^{51}_{24}\text{Cr} + \ _{-1}^{0}\text{e} \longrightarrow \ ^{51}_{23}\text{V} + \gamma$$

Problem 3.4

Thallium-201, a radioisotope used to evaluate heart function in exercise stress tests, decays by electron capture and gamma emission. Write an equation for this nuclear decay and identify the product.

3.4 | What Is Nuclear Half-life?

Suppose we have 40 g of a radioactive isotope—say, $^{90}_{38}\text{Sr}$. Strontium-90 nuclei are unstable and decay by beta emission to yttrium-90:

$$^{90}_{38}\text{Sr} \longrightarrow \ ^{90}_{39}\text{Y} + \ _{-1}^{0}\beta$$

Our 40-g sample of strontium-90 contains about 2.7×10^{23} atoms. We know that these nuclei decay, but at what rate? Do all of the nuclei decay at the same time, or do they decay gradually over time? The answer is that they decay one at a time, at a fixed rate. For strontium-90, the decay rate is such that one half of our sample (about 1.35×10^{23} atoms) will have decayed by the end of 28.1 years. The time it takes for one half of any sample of radioactive material to decay is called the **half-life, $t_{1/2}$**.

It does not matter how big or small a sample is. For example, in the case of our 40 g of strontium-90, 20 g will be left at the end of 28.1 years (the rest will be converted to yttrium-90). It will then take another 28.1 years for half of the remainder to decay, so that at the end of that time we will have 10 g of strontium-90. If we wait for a third span of 28.1 years, then 5 g will be left. If we had begun with 100 g, then 50 g would be left after the first 28.1-year period.

Figure 3.4 shows the radioactive decay curve of iodine-131. Inspection of this graph shows that, at the end of 8 days, half of the original has disappeared. Thus the half-life of iodine-131 is 8 days. It would take a total of 16 days, or two half-lives, for three fourths of the original amount of iodine-131 to decay.

When a nucleus gives off radiation, it is said to *decay*.

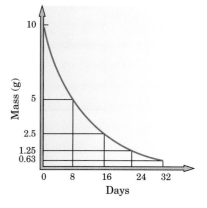

Figure 3.4 The decay curve of iodine-131.

EXAMPLE 3.5

If 10.0 mg of $^{131}_{53}\text{I}$ is administered to a patient, how much is left in the body after 32 days?

Solution

We know from Table 3.2 that $t_{1/2}$ of iodine-131 is eight days. We also know that 32 days corresponds to four half-lives. Thus 5.00 mg is left after one half-life; 2.50 mg after two half-lives; 1.25 mg after three half-lives; and 0.625 mg after four half-lives.

$$10.0 \text{ mg} \times \overbrace{\frac{1}{2} \times \frac{1}{2} \times \frac{1}{2} \times \frac{1}{2}}^{32 \text{ days (4 half-lives)}} = 0.625 \text{ mg}$$

> **Problem 3.5**
> Barium-122 has a half-life of 2 minutes. Suppose you obtained a sample weighing 10.0 g. It takes 10 minutes to set up the experiment in which barium-122 will be used. How many grams of barium-122 will be left when you begin the experiment?

In theory, it would take an infinite amount of time for all of a radioactive sample to disappear. In reality, most of the radioactivity disappears after five half-lives; by that time, only 3% of the original remains.

$$\overbrace{\frac{1}{2} \times \frac{1}{2} \times \frac{1}{2} \times \frac{1}{2} \times \frac{1}{2}}^{\text{5 half-lives}} \times 100 = 3.1\%$$

After ten half-lives, less than 0.1% of the activity remains.

The half-life of an isotope is independent of temperature and pressure—indeed, of all other conditions—and is a property of the particular isotope only. It does not depend on what kinds of atoms surround the particular nucleus (that is, what kind of molecule the nucleus is part of). We do not know any way to speed up radioactive decay or to slow it down.

Table 3.2 gives some half-lives. Even this brief sampling indicates the tremendous differences among half-lives. Some isotopes, such as technetium-99m, decay and disappear in a day; others, such as uranium-238, remain radioactive for billions of years. Very short-lived isotopes, especially the artificial heavy elements (Section 3.8) with atomic numbers greater than 100, have half-lives of the order of seconds.

The usefulness or inherent danger in radioactive isotopes is related to their half-lives. In assessing the long-range health effects of atomic-bomb

GOB
Chemistry•⚛•Now™
Click *Coached Problems* to see an example of **Radiochemical Dating**

Table 3.2 Half-lives of Some Radioactive Nuclei

Name	Symbol	Half-life	Radiation
Hydrogen-3 (tritium)	$^{3}_{1}\text{H}$	12.26 years	Beta
Carbon-14	$^{14}_{6}\text{C}$	5730 years	Beta
Phosphorus-28	$^{28}_{15}\text{P}$	0.28 second	Positrons
Phosphorus-32	$^{32}_{15}\text{P}$	14.3 days	Beta
Potassium-40	$^{40}_{19}\text{K}$	1.28×10^{9} years	Beta + gamma
Scandium-42	$^{42}_{21}\text{Sc}$	0.68 second	Positrons
Cobalt-60	$^{60}_{27}\text{Co}$	5.2 years	Gamma
Strontium-90	$^{90}_{38}\text{Sr}$	28.1 years	Beta
Technetium-99m	$^{99m}_{43}\text{Tc}$	6.0 hours	Gamma
Indium-116	$^{116}_{49}\text{In}$	14 seconds	Beta
Iodine-131	$^{131}_{53}\text{I}$	8 days	Beta + gamma
Mercury-197	$^{197}_{80}\text{Hg}$	65 hours	Gamma
Polonium-210	$^{210}_{84}\text{Po}$	138 days	Alpha
Radon-205	$^{205}_{86}\text{Rn}$	2.8 minutes	Alpha
Radon-222	$^{222}_{86}\text{Rn}$	3.8 days	Alpha
Uranium-238	$^{238}_{92}\text{U}$	4×10^{9} years	Alpha

CHEMICAL CONNECTIONS 3A

Radioactive Dating

Carbon-14, with a half-life of 5730 years, can be used to date archeological objects as old as 60,000 years. This dating technique relies on the principle that the carbon-12/carbon-14 ratio of an organism—whether plant or animal—remains constant during the lifetime of the organism. When the organism dies, the carbon-12 level remains constant (carbon-12 is not radioactive), but any carbon-14 present decays by beta emission to nitrogen-14.

$$^{14}_{6}C \longrightarrow \; ^{14}_{7}N \; + \; ^{\;0}_{-1}e$$

Using this fact, a scientist can calculate the changed carbon-12/carbon-14 ratio to determine the date of an artifact.

For example, in charcoal made from a tree that has recently died, the carbon-14 gives a radioactive count of 13.70 disintegrations/min per gram of carbon. In a piece of charcoal found in a cave in France near some ancient Cro-Magnon cave paintings, the carbon-14 count was 1.71 disintegrations/min for each gram of carbon. From this information, the cave paintings can be dated. After one half-life, the number of disintegrations/minute per gram is 6.85; after two half-lives, it is 3.42, and after three half-lives, it is 1.71. Therefore, three half-lives have passed since the paintings were created. Given that carbon-14 has a half-life of 5730 years, the paintings are about $3 \times 5730 = 17,190$ years old.

The famous Shroud of Turin, a piece of linen cloth with the image of a man's head on it, was believed by many to be the original cloth that was wrapped around the body of Jesus Christ after his death. However, radioactive dating showed, with 95% certainty, that the plants from which the linen was obtained were alive sometime between AD 1260 and 1380, proving that the cloth could

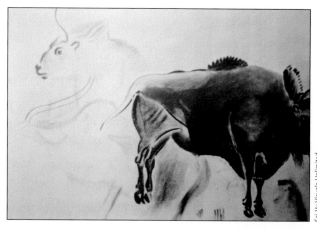

Cro-Magnon cave painting.

not have been the shroud of Christ. Note that it was not necessary to destroy the shroud to perform the tests. In fact, scientists in different laboratories used just a total of a few square centimeters of cloth from its edge.

Rock samples can be dated on the basis of their lead-206 and uranium-238 content. The assumption is that all of the lead-206 comes from the decay of uranium-238, which has a half-life of 4.5 billion years. One of the oldest rocks found on the earth is a granite outcrop in Greenland, dated at 3.7×10^9 years old.

On the basis of dating of meteorites, the estimated age of the solar system is 4.6×10^9 years.

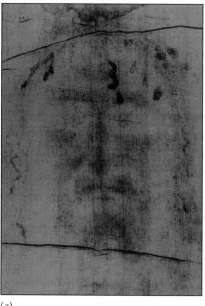

(a)

(b)

The Shroud of Turin (a) as it appears to the eye and (b) as a photographic image, which brings out the images more clearly.

A Geiger-Müller counter.

GOB
Chemistry⚛Now™

Click *Chemistry Interactive* to see the workings of a **Geiger-Müller Counter**

A television picture tube works on a similar principle.

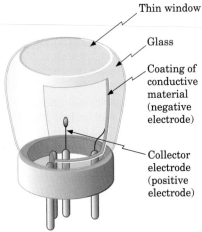

Thin window

Glass

Coating of conductive material (negative electrode)

Collector electrode (positive electrode)

Figure 3.5 A schematic drawing of a Geiger-Müller counter. The counter is made of a glass cylinder, the inner surface of which is coated with a material that conducts electricity. In the center is the collector electrode, made of tungsten wire. The collector electrode is positively charged to about 1200 volts. The space within the tube is filled with helium or argon gas at low pressure. A thin Mylar window at the end keeps the gas in, yet allows the ionizing radiation to pass through. When ionizing radiation enters the tube, it converts argon or helium atoms to positive ions, which go to the negative electrode. The current caused by these positive ions is amplified and used to operate the counter.

damage or of nuclear power plant accidents, like those at Three Mile Island, Pennsylvania, in 1979 and Chernobyl (in the former Soviet Union) in 1986 (Chemical Connections 3E), we can see that radioactive isotopes with long half-lives, such as $^{85}_{36}Kr$ ($t_{1/2} = 10$ years) or $^{60}_{27}Co$ ($t_{1/2} = 5.2$ years) are more important than short-lived ones. Conversely, when a radioactive isotope is used in medical imaging or therapy, short-lived isotopes are more useful because they disappear faster from the body—for example, $^{99m}_{43}Tc$, $^{32}_{15}P$, $^{131}_{53}I$, and $^{197}_{80}Hg$.

3.5 | How Do We Detect and Measure Nuclear Radiation?

As already noted, radioactivity is not detectable by our senses. We cannot see it, hear it, feel it, or smell it. Then how do we know it is there? Alpha, beta, gamma, positron, and Xrays all have a property we can use to detect them: When these rays interact with matter, they usually knock electrons out of the electron cloud surrounding an atomic nucleus, thereby creating positively charged ions from neutral atoms. For this reason, we call all of these rays **ionizing radiation.**

Ionizing radiation is characterized by two physical measurements: (1) its **intensity,** which is the number of particles or photons emerging per unit time, and (2) the **energy** of each particle or photon emitted.

A. Intensity

To measure intensity, we take advantage of the ionizing property of radiation. Instruments such as the **Geiger-Müller counter** (Figure 3.5) and the **proportional counter** contain a gas such as helium or argon. When a radioactive nucleus emits alpha or beta particles or gamma rays, these radiations ionize the gas, and the instrument registers this fact by indicating that an electric current is passing between two electrodes. In this way, the instrument counts particle after particle.

Other measuring devices, such as **scintillation counters,** have a material called a phosphor that emits a unit of light for each alpha or beta particle or gamma ray that strikes it. Once again, the particles are counted one by one. The quantitative measure of radiation intensity can be reported in counts/minute or counts/second.

A commonly used unit of radiation intensity is the **curie** (Ci), named in honor of Marie Curie, whose lifelong work with radioactive materials greatly helped expand our understanding of nuclear phenomena. One curie is defined as 3.7×10^{10} disintegrations per second (dps). This is radiation of very high intensity, the amount a person would get from 1 g of pure $^{286}_{88}Ra$. This intensity is too high for regular medical use, so the units most commonly used in the health sciences are small fractions of it. Another, albeit much smaller, unit of radiation activity (intensity) is the **becquerel** (Bq), which is the SI unit. One becquerel is one disintegration per second (dps).

$$1 \text{ becquerel (Bq)} = 1.0 \text{ dps}$$

$$1 \text{ curie (Ci)} = 3.7 \times 10^{10} \text{ dps}$$

$$1 \text{ millicurie (mCi)} = 3.7 \times 10^7 \text{ dps}$$

$$1 \text{ microcurie (}\mu\text{Ci)} = 3.7 \times 10^4 \text{ dps}$$

EXAMPLE 3.6

A radioactive isotope with an intensity (activity) of 100 mCi per vial is delivered to a hospital. The vial contains 10 mL of liquid. The instruction is to administer 2.5 mCi intravenously. How many milliliters of the liquid should be administered?

Solution

The intensity (activity) of a sample is directly proportional to the amount present, so

$$2.5 \ \cancel{mCi} \times \frac{10 \ mL}{100 \ \cancel{mCi}} = 0.25 \ mL$$

Problem 3.6

A radioactive isotope in a 9.0-mL vial has an intensity of 300 mCi. A patient is required to take 50 mCi intravenously. How much liquid should be used for the injection?

The intensity of any radiation decreases with the square of the distance from the source. If, for example, the distance from a radiation source doubles, then the intensity of the received radiation decreases by a factor of four.

$$\frac{I_1}{I_2} = \frac{d_2^2}{d_1^2}$$

EXAMPLE 3.7

If the intensity of radiation is 28 mCi at a distance of 1.0 m, what is the intensity at a distance of 2.0 m?

Solution

From the preceding equation we have

$$\frac{28 \ mCi}{I_2} = \frac{2.0^2}{1.0^2} = 4.0$$

$$I_2 = \frac{28 \ mCi}{4.0} = 7.0 \ mCi$$

Problem 3.7

If the intensity of radiation 1.0 cm from a source is 300 mCi, what is the intensity at 3.0 m?

B. Energy

The energies of different particles or photons vary. As shown in Table 3.1, each particle has a certain range of energy. For example, beta particles have an energy range of 1 to 3 MeV (mega-electron-volts). This range may overlap with the energy range of some other type of radiation—for example, gamma rays. The penetrating power of a radiation depends on its energy as well on the mass of its particles. Alpha particles are the most massive and the most highly

Figure 3.6 Penetration of radioactive emissions. Alpha particles, with a charge of +2 and a mass of 4 amu, interact strongly with matter but penetrate the least; they are stopped by several sheets of paper. Beta particles, with less mass and a lower charge than alpha particles, interact less strongly with matter; they easily penetrate paper but are stopped by a 0.5-cm sheet of lead. Gamma rays, with neither mass nor charge, have the greatest penetrating power. It takes 10 cm of lead to stop them.

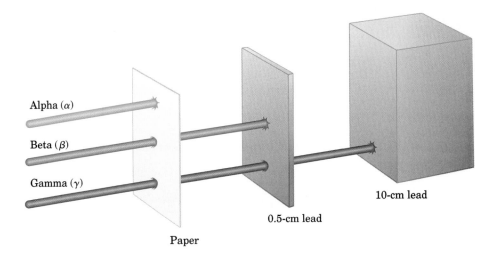

charged and, therefore, the least penetrating; they can be stopped by several sheets of ordinary paper, by ordinary clothing, and by the skin. Beta particles have less mass and lower charge than alpha particles and, consequently, have greater penetrating power. They can penetrate several millimeters of bone or tissue. Gamma radiation, which has neither mass nor charge, is the most penetrating of the three types of radiation. (Alpha particles, when in the body, are more damaging, however.) They can pass completely through the body. Several centimeters of lead or concrete are required to stop gamma rays (Figure 3.6).

One easy way to protect against ionizing radiation is to wear lead aprons, covering sensitive organs. This practice is followed routinely when diagnostic Xrays are taken. Another way to lessen the damage from ionizing radiation is to move farther away from the source.

3.6 | How Is Radiation Dosimetry Related to Human Health?

The term *activity of a radiation* is the same as *intensity of a radiation*

In studying the effect of radiation on the body, neither the energy of the radiation (in kcal/mol) nor its intensity (in Ci) alone or in combination is of particular importance. Rather, the critical question is what kind of effects such radiation produces in the body. Three different units are used to describe the effects of radiation on the body: roentgens, rads, and rems.

Roentgens (R) Roentgens are a measure of the energy delivered by a radiation source and are, therefore, a measure of exposure to a particular form of radiation. One roentgen is the amount of radiation that produces ions having 2.58×10^{-4} coulomb of ions per kilogram (a coulomb is a unit of electrical charge).

Rads The rad, which stands for *r*adiation *a*bsorbed *d*ose, is a measure of the radiation absorbed from a radiation source. The SI unit is the gray (Gy), where 1 Gy = 100 rad. Roentgens (delivered energy) do not take into account the effect of radiation on tissue and the fact that different tissues absorb different amounts of delivered radiation. Radiation damages body tissue by causing ionization; for such ionization to occur, the tissue must absorb the delivered energy. The relationship between the delivered dose in roentgens and the absorbed dose in rads can be illustrated as follows: Exposure to 1 roentgen yields 0.97 rad of absorbed radiation in water, 0.96 rad in muscle, and 0.93 rad in bone. This relationship holds for high-energy photons. For lower-energy photons, such as "soft" Xrays, each roentgen yields 3 rads of absorbed dose in bone. This principle underlies diagnostic Xrays, wherein soft tissue lets the radiation through to strike a photographic plate but bone absorbs the radiation and casts a shadow on the plate.

Rems   The rem, which stands for *r*oentgen *e*quivalent for *m*an, is a measure of the effect of the radiation when a person absorbs 1 roentgen. Other units are the **millirem** (mrem; 1 mrem = 1×10^{-3} rem) and the **sievert** (Sv; 1 Sv = 100 rem). The sievert is the SI unit. The rem is used because tissue damage from 1 rad of absorbed energy depends on the type of radiation. One rad from alpha rays, for example, causes ten times more damage than 1 rad from Xrays or gamma rays. Table 3.3 summarizes the various radiation units and what each measures.

Although alpha particles cause more damage than Xrays or gamma rays, they have a very low penetrating power (Table 3.1) and cannot pass through the skin. Consequently, they are not harmful to humans or animals as long as they do not enter the body. If they do get in, however, they can prove quite harmful. They can get inside, for example, if a person swallows or inhales a small particle of a substance that emits alpha particles. Beta particles are less damaging to tissue than alpha particles but penetrate farther and so are generally more harmful. Gamma rays, which can completely penetrate the skin, are by far the most dangerous and harmful form of radiation. Remember, of course, that α particles once in the body, as for example, alpha radiation from radon-222, are very damaging. Therefore, for comparison purposes and for determining exposure from all kinds of sources, the equivalent dose is an important measure. If an organ receives radiation from different sources, the total effect can be summed up in rems (or mrem or Sv). For example, 10 mrem of alpha particles and 15 mrem of gamma radiation give a total of 25 mrem absorbed equivalent dose. Table 3.4 shows the amount of radiation exposure that an average person obtains yearly from both natural and artificial sources.

The naturally occurring background radiation varies with the geological location. For example, a tenfold higher than average radiation has been detected at some phosphate mines. People who work in nuclear medicine are, of course, exposed to greater amounts. To ensure that exposures do not get too high, they wear radiation badges. A single whole-body irradiation of 25 rem is noticeable in the blood count, and 100 rem causes the typical symptoms of radiation sickness, which include nausea, vomiting, a decrease in the white blood cell count, and loss of hair. A dose of 400 rem causes death within one month in 50% of exposed persons, and 600 rem is almost invariably

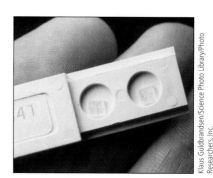

A radiation badge.

Klaus Guldbrandsen/Science Photo Library/Photo Researchers, Inc.

Table 3.3	Radiation Dosimetry		
Unit	What the Unit Measures	SI Unit	Other Units
Roentgen	The amount of radiation delivered from a radiation source	Roentgen (R)	
Rad	The ratio between radiation absorbed by a tissue and radiation delivered to the tissue	Gray (Gy)	1 rad = 0.01 Gy
Rem	The ratio between the tissue damage caused by a rad of radiation and the type of radiation	Sievert (Sv)	1 rem = 0.01 Sv

The Indoor Radon Problem

Most of our exposure to ionizing radiation comes from natural sources (Table 3.4), with radon gas being the main source. Radon has more than 20 isotopes, all of which are radioactive. The most important is radon-222, an alpha emitter. Radon-222 is a natural decay product of uranium-238, which is widely distributed in the Earth's crust.

Radon poses a particular health hazard among radioactive elements because it is a gas at normal temperatures and pressures. As a consequence, it can enter our lungs with the air we breathe and become trapped in the mucous lining of the lungs. Radon-222 has a half-life of 3.8 days. It decays naturally and produces, among other isotopes, two harmful alpha emitters: polonium-218 and polonium-214. These polonium isotopes are solids and do not leave the lungs with exhalation. In the long run, they can cause lung cancer.

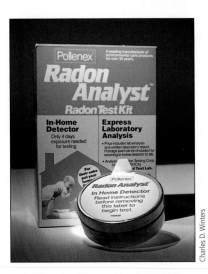

Testing devices are available to determine whether radon is building up in a home.

The U.S. Environmental Protection Agency has set a standard of 4 pCi/L (one picocurie, pCi, is 10^{-12} Ci) as a safe exposure level. A survey of single-family homes in the United States showed that 7% exceeded this level. Most radon seeps into dwellings through cracks in cement foundations and around pipes, then accumulates in basements. The remedy is to ventilate both basements and houses enough to reduce the radiation levels. In a notorious case, a group of houses in Grand Junction, Colorado was built from bricks made from uranium tailings. Obviously, the radiation levels in these buildings were unacceptably high. Because they could not be controlled, the buildings had to be destroyed. In our modern radiation-conscious age, more and more homebuyers choose to request a certification of radon levels before buying a house.

---

lethal within a short time. It should be noted that as much as 50,000 rem is needed to kill bacteria and as much as 10^6 rem to inactivate viruses.

Fortunately, most of us never get a single dose of more than a few rem and so never suffer from any form of radiation sickness. This does not mean, however, that small doses are totally harmless. The harm may arise in two ways:

1. Small doses of radioactivity over a period of years can cause cancer, especially blood cancers such as leukemia. Repeated exposure to sunlight also carries a risk of tissue damage. Most of the high-energy UV radiation of the sun is absorbed by the Earth's protective ozone layer in the stratosphere. In tanning, however, the repeated overexposure to UV radiation can cause skin cancer (see Chemical Connections 19D). No one knows how many cancers have resulted from this practice, because the doses are so small and continue for so many years that they cannot be measured accurately. Also, because so many other causes of cancer exist, it is often difficult or impossible to decide whether any particular case is caused by radiation.

2. If any form of radiation strikes an egg or sperm cell, it can cause a change in the genes (see Chemical Connections 25E). Such changes are called mutations. If an affected egg or sperm cell mates, grows, and becomes a new individual, that individual may have mutated characteristics, which are usually harmful and frequently lethal.

Because radiation carries so much potential for harm, it would be nice if we could totally escape it. But can we? Table 3.4 shows that this is impossible. Naturally occurring radiation, called **background radiation,** is present everywhere on Earth. This background radiation vastly outstrips the average radiation level from artificial sources (mostly diagnostic Xrays). If we eliminated all forms of artificial radiation, including medical uses, we would still be exposed to the background radiation.

Table 3.4 Average Exposure to Radiation from Common Sources

Source	Dose (mrem/year)
Naturally Occurring Radiation	
Cosmic rays	27
Terrestrial radiation (rocks, buildings)	28
Inside human body (K-40 and Ra-266 in the bones)	39
Radon in the air	200
Total	294
Artificial Radiation	
Medical Xrays[a]	39
Nuclear medicine	14
Consumer products	10
Nuclear power plants	0.5
All others	1.5
Total	65.0
Grand total	359[b]

[a]Individual medical precedures may expose certain parts of the body to much higher doses. For instance, one chest Xray gives 27 mrem and a diagnostic GI series gives 1970 mrem.

[b]The federal safety standard for allowable occupational exposure is about 5000 mrem/year. It has been suggested that this level be lowered to 4000 mrem/year or even lower to reduce the risk of cancer stemming from low levels of radiation.

SOURCE: *National Council on Radiation Protection and Measurements,* NCRP Report No. 93 (1993).

Cosmic rays High-energy particles, mainly protons, from outer space bombarding the Earth

3.7 | What Is Nuclear Medicine?

When we think of nuclear chemistry, our first thoughts may well be of nuclear power, atomic bombs, and weapons of mass destruction. True as this may be, it is also true that nuclear chemistry and the use of radioactive elements have become invaluable tools in all areas of science. Nowhere is this more important than in nuclear medicine—that is, in the use of radioactive isotopes as tools for both the diagnosis and the treatment of diseases. To describe the full range of medical uses of nuclear chemistry would take far more space than this text allows. Recognizing this fact, we have chosen several examples of each use to illustrate the range of applications of nuclear chemistry to the health sciences.

A. Medical Imaging

Medical imaging is the most widely used aspect of nuclear medicine. The goal of medical imaging is to create a picture of a target tissue. To create a useful image requires three things:

- A radioactive element administered in pure form or in a compound that becomes concentrated in the tissue to be imaged
- A method of detecting radiation from the radioactive source and recording its intensity and location
- A computer to process the intensity–location data and transform those data into a useful image

Chemically and metabolically, a radioactive isotope in the body behaves in exactly the same way as do the nonradioactive isotopes of the same element. In the simplest form of imaging, a radioactive isotope is injected

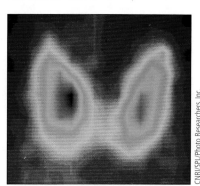

A scan of radiation released by radioactive iodine concentrated in thyroid tissue gives an image of the thyroid gland.

CNRI/SPL/Photo Researchers, Inc.

Table 3.5 Some Radioactive Isotopes Useful in Medical Imaging

	Isotope	Mode of Decay	Half-life	Use in Medical Imaging
$^{11}_{6}C$	Carbon-11	β^+, γ	20.3 m	Brain scan to trace glucose metabolism
$^{18}_{9}F$	Fluorine-18	β^+, γ	109 m	Brain scan to trace glucose metabolism
$^{32}_{15}P$	Phosphorus-32	β	14.3 d	Detect eye tumors
$^{51}_{24}Cr$	Chromium-51	E.C., γ	27.7 d	Diagnose albinism, image the spleen and gastrointestinal tract
$^{59}_{26}Fe$	Iron-59	β, γ	44.5 d	Bone marrow function, diagnose anemias
$^{67}_{31}Ga$	Gallium-67	E.C., γ	78.3 h	Whole-body scan for tumors
$^{75}_{34}Se$	Selenium-75	E.C., γ	118 d	Pancreas scan
$^{81m}_{36}Kr$	Krypton-81m	γ	13.3 s	Lung ventilation scan
$^{81}_{38}Sr$	Strontium-81	β	22.2 m	Scan for bone diseases, including cancer
$^{99m}_{43}Tc$	Technetium-99m	γ	6.01 h	Brain, liver, kidney, bone scans; diagnosis of damaged heart muscle
$^{131}_{53}I$	Iodine-131	β, γ	8.04 d	Diagnosis of thyroid malfunction
$^{197}_{80}Hg$	Mercury-197	E,C, γ	64.1 h	Kidney scan
$^{201}_{81}Tl$	Thallium-201	E,C, γ	3.05 d	Heart scan and exercise stress test

Normal

Meningioma (brain tumor)

"Brain death"

Scalp tumor

CRC Handbook in Clinical Laboratory Science

Figure 3.7 A comparison of dynamic scan patterns for normal and pathological brains. The studies were performed by injecting technetium-99m into blood vessels.

intravenously and a technician uses a detector to monitor how the radiation becomes distributed in the body of the patient. Table 3.5 lists some of the most important radioisotopes used in imaging and diagnosis.

The use of iodine-131, a beta and gamma emitter ($t_{1/2}$ = 8.0 days), to image and diagnose a malfunctioning thyroid gland is a good example. The thyroid gland in the neck produces a hormone, thyroxine, which controls the overall rate of metabolism (use of food) in the body. One molecule of thyroxine contains four iodine atoms. When radioactive iodine-131 is administered into the bloodstream, the thyroid gland takes it up and incorporates it into the thyroxine (Chemical Connections 13C). A normally functioning thyroid absorbs about 12% of the administered iodine within a few hours. An overactive thyroid (hyperthyroidism) absorbs and localizes iodine-131 in the gland faster, and an underactive thyroid (hypothyroidism) does so much more slowly than normal. By counting the gamma radiation emitted from the neck, then, one can determine the rate of uptake of iodine-131 into the thyroid gland and diagnose hyperthyroidism or hypothyroidism.

Most organ scans are similarly based on the preferential uptake of some radioactive isotopes by a particular organ (Figure 3.7).

Another important type of medical imaging is positron emission tomography (PET). This method is based on the property that certain isotopes (such as carbon-11 and fluorine-18) emit positrons (Section 3.3D). Fluorine-18 decays by positron emission to oxygen-18:

$$^{18}_{9}F \longrightarrow {}^{18}_{8}O + {}^{0}_{+1}e$$

Positrons have very short lives. When a positron collides with an electron, the two annihilate each other, resulting in two gamma rays.

$$\underset{\text{Positron}}{^{0}_{+1}e} + \underset{\text{Electron}}{^{0}_{-1}e} \longrightarrow 2\gamma$$

Because electrons are present in every atom, there are always lots of them around, so positrons generated in the body cannot live long.

A favorite tagged molecule for following the uptake and metabolism of glucose, $C_6H_{12}O_6$, is 18-fluorodeoxyglucose (FDG), a molecule of glucose in which one of glucose's six oxygen atoms is replaced by fluorine-18. When FDG is administered intravenously, the tagged glucose soon enters blood

CHEMICAL CONNECTIONS 3C

Magnetic Resonance Imaging

Magnetic resonance imaging (MRI) is probably the best known of the various medical imaging techniques. Like those techniques we have already discussed, MRI involves atomic nuclei; unlike the other techniques, it does not involve nuclear decay or the emission of particles or rays from the nucleus.

Nuclear magnetic resonance (NMR) was discovered in the 1950s. By the 1960s, it had become an invaluable analytical tool for chemists. By the early 1970s, it was realized that this technique could be used to image parts of the body and could serve as a valuable addition to diagnostic medicine. Because the term "nuclear magnetic resonance" sounds to many people as if the technique might involve radioactive material, health care personnel call the technique magnetic resonance imaging.

MRI is based on the following principles:

- The nuclei of certain elements behave as if they are tiny bar magnets; that is, they behave as if they have a north pole and a south pole.
- In the presence of a very strong external magnetic field, a majority of these tiny nuclear bar magnets become aligned with the external field; that is, they become aligned so that their north poles align with the south pole of the external field, and their south poles align with the north pole of the external field.
- If energy in the form of radio-frequency waves is focused on the aligned nuclei, their nuclear bar magnets flip so that they become aligned against the external field.
- Resonance occurs when the proper combination of external magnetic field and radio-frequency wave causes a nuclear bar magnet to flip from alignment with the external field to alignment against it.
- A computer records which radio-frequency waves cause the nuclear bar magnets to flip to alignment against the external field, along with their location in the body and, with these data, constructs a useful image.
- The body contains several nuclei that, in principle, could be used for MRI. Of these, hydrogen-1, most of which comes from water, fats, and membrane phospholipids, gives the most useful signals.

In MRI, the patient is placed in a magnetic field gradient that can be varied from one part of the body to another. Nuclei in the

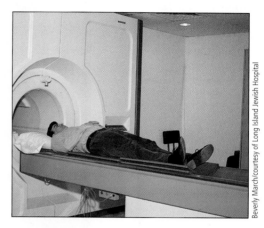

A medical MRI imager.

weaker magnetic field gradient absorb radiation at a lower radio frequency. Nuclei elsewhere, in the stronger magnetic field, absorb radiation at a higher radio frequency. Because a magnetic field gradient along a single axis images a plane, MRI techniques can create views of any part of the body in slice-like sections. Paul Lauterbur and Sir Peter Mansfield were awarded the 2003 Nobel Prize in physiology/medicine for their discoveries that led to the development of this imaging technique.

MRI is especially good for imaging soft tissues that contain many hydrogen atoms. Because bones contain few hydrogen atoms, they are almost transparent in this kind of imaging. Thus, the soft tissues with their different water content stand out in an MRI.

An important application of MRI is in the examination of the brain and spinal cord. White and gray matter, the two different layers of the brain, are easily distinguished by MRI. The resulting information is useful in the study of such diseases as multiple sclerosis.

Magnetic resonance imaging and Xray imaging are in many cases complementary. The hard, outer layer of bone is essentially invisible to MRI but shows up extremely well in Xray images, whereas soft tissue is nearly transparent to Xrays, but shows up well in MRI.

and from there moves to the brain. Detectors for the gamma rays can pick up the signals that come from the areas where the tagged glucose accumulates. In this way, one can see which areas of the brain are involved when we process, for example, visual information (Figure 3.8). PET scans can diagnose early stages of epilepsy and other diseases that involve abnormal glucose metabolism, such as schizophrenia.

Because tumors have high metabolic rates, PET scans using FDG are becoming increasingly preferred as the diagnostic choice for their detection and localization. FDG/PET has been used in the diagnosis of malignant melanoma, malignant lymphoma, and ovarian cancer, among other conditions.

Figure 3.8 Positron emission tomography brain scans. The upper scans show that 18-fluorodeoxyglucose can cross the blood–brain barrier. The lower scans show that visual stimulation increases the blood flow to and the glucose concentration in certain areas of the brain. These areas are shown in red.

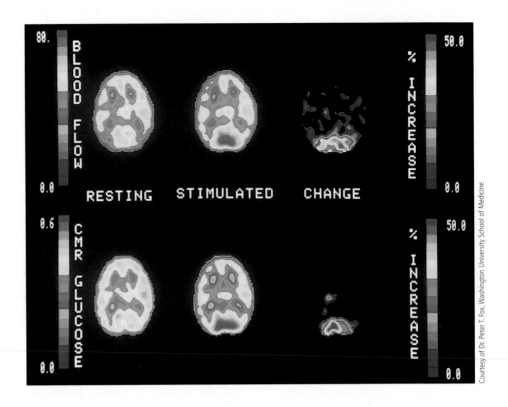

Another important use of radioactive isotopes is to learn what happens to ingested material. The foods and drugs swallowed or otherwise taken in by the body are transformed, decomposed, and excreted. To understand the pharmacology of a drug, it is important to know how these processes occur. For example, a certain drug may be effective in treating certain bacterial infections. Before beginning a clinical trial of the drug, its manufacturer must prove that the drug is not harmful to humans. In a typical case, the drug is first tested in animal studies. It is synthesized, and some radioactive isotope, such as hydrogen-3, carbon-14, or phosphorus-32, is incorporated into its structure. The drug is administered to the test animals, and after a certain period the animals are sacrificed. The fate of the drug is then determined by isolating from the body any radioactive compounds formed.

One typical pharmacological experiment studied the effects of tetracycline. This powerful antibiotic tends to accumulate in bones and is not given to pregnant women because it is transferred to the bones of the fetus. A particular tetracycline was tagged with radioactive hydrogen-3, and its uptake in rat bones was monitored in the presence and the absence of a sulfa drug. With the aid of a scintillation counter, researchers measured the radiation intensity of the maternal and fetal bones. They found that the sulfa drug helped to minimize this undesirable side effect of tetracycline—namely, its accumulation in the fetal bones.

The metabolic fate of essential chemicals in the body can also be followed with radioactive tracers. The use of radioactive isotopes has illuminated a number of normal and pathological body functions as well.

B. Radiation Therapy

The main use of radioactive isotopes in therapy is the selective destruction of pathological cells and tissues. Recall that radiation, whether from gamma rays, Xrays, or other sources, is detrimental to cells. Ionizing radia-

CHEMICAL CONNECTIONS 3D

How Radiation Damages Tissues: Free Radicals

As mentioned earlier, high-energy radiation damages tissue by causing ionization. That is, the radiation knocks electrons out of the molecules that make up the tissue (generally one electron per molecule), thereby forming unstable ions. For example, the interaction of high-energy radiation with water forms an unstable cation.

$$\text{Energy} + H_2O \longrightarrow H_2O^+ + e^-$$

$$H_2O^+ \longrightarrow H^+ + \cdot OH$$

Hydroxyl radical

The positive charge on the cation means that one of the electrons normally present in the water molecule, either from a covalent bond or from an unshared pair, is missing in this cation; it has been knocked out. Once formed, the H_2O^+ cation is unstable and decomposes or H^+ and a hydroxyl radical:

The unpaired electron is on oxygen

$$[\text{H}-\overset{\cdot}{\underset{\cdot\cdot}{\text{O}}}-\text{H}]^+$$

It is instructive to consider the hydroxide ion and the hydroxyl radical.

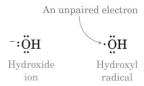

An unpaired electron

Hydroxide ion   Hydroxyl radical

Whereas the oxygen atom in the hydroxide ion, OH⁻, has a complete octet—it is surrounded by three unshared pairs of electrons and one shared—the oxygen atom in the hydroxyl radical is surrounded by only seven valence electrons,—two unshared pairs, one shared pair and one unpaired electron. Compounds that have unpaired electrons are called **free radicals**, or more simply, just **radicals**.

The fact that the oxygen atom of the ·OH radical has an incomplete octet makes the radical extremely reactive. It rapidly interacts with other molecules, causing chemical reactions that damage tissues. These reactions may have especially serious consequences if they occur inside cell nuclei and damage genetic material. In addition, they affect rapidly dividing cells more than they do stationary cells. Thus the damage is greater to embryonic cells, cells of the bone marrow, the intestines, and cells in the lymph. Symptoms of radiation sickness include nausea, vomiting, a decrease in the white blood cell count, and loss of hair.

---

tion damages cells, especially those that divide rapidly. This damage may be great enough to destroy diseased cells or to sufficiently alter the genes in them so that multiplication of the cells slows down.

In therapy applications, cancerous cells are the main targets for such ionizing radiation. Radiation is typically used when a cancer is highly localized; however, it may also be employed when the cancerous cells spread and are in a metastatic state. In addition, it is used for preventive purposes, to eliminate any possible remaining cancerous cells after surgery has been performed. The idea, of course, is to kill cancerous cells but not normal ones. Therefore, radiation such as high-energy Xrays or gamma rays from a cobalt-60 source is focused at a small part of the body where cancerous cells are suspected to reside. Besides Xrays and gamma rays from cobalt-60, other ionizing radiation is used to treat inoperable tumors. Proton beams from cyclotrons, for instance, have been used to treat ocular melanoma and tumors of the skull base and spine.

Despite this pinpointing technique, the radiation inevitably kills normal cells along with their cancerous counterparts. Because the radiation is most effective against rapidly dividing cancer cells, rather than normal cells, and because the radiation is aimed at a specific location, the damage to healthy tissues is minimized.

Another way to localize radiation damage in therapy is to use specific radioactive isotopes. In the case of thyroid cancer, large doses of iodine-131 are administered, which are taken up by the gland. The isotope, which has high radioactivity, kills all the cells of the gland (cancerous as well as normal ones), but does not appreciably damage other organs.

A metastatic state exists when the cancerous cells break off from their primary site(s) and begin moving to other parts of the body.

Another radioisotope, iodine-125, is used in the treatment of prostate cancer. Seeds of iodine-125, a gamma emitter, are implanted in the cancerous area of the prostate gland while being imaged with ultrasound. The seeds deliver 160 Gy (16,000 rad) over their lifetime.

A newer form of treatment of prostate cancer with great potential relies on actinium-225, an alpha emitter. As discussed in Section 3.6, alpha particles cause more damage to the tissues than any other form of radiation, but they have low penetrating power. Researchers have developed a very clever way to deliver actinium-225 to the cancerous region of the prostate gland without damaging healthy tissues. The cancer has a high concentration of prostate-specific antigen (PSA) on its surface. A monoclonal antibody (Section 30.4) hones in on the PSA and interacts with it. A single actinium-225 atom attached to such a monoclonal antibody can deliver the desired radiation, thereby destroying the cancer. Actinium-225 is especially effective because it has a half-life of ten days and it decays to three nuclides, themselves alpha emitters. In clinical trials, a single injection of antibody with an intensity in the kBq range (nanocuries) led to tumor regression without toxicity.

3.8 | What Is Nuclear Fusion?

An estimated 98% of all matter in the universe is made up of hydrogen and helium. The "big bang" theory of the formation of the universe postulates that our universe started with an explosion (big bang) in which matter was formed out of energy and that, at the beginning, only the lightest element, hydrogen, was in existence. Later, as the universe expanded, stars were born when the hydrogen clouds collapsed under gravitational forces. In the cores of these stars, hydrogen nuclei fused together to form helium.

The fusion of two hydrogen nuclei into a helium nucleus liberates a very large amount of energy in the form of photons, largely by the following reaction:

$$\underset{\substack{\text{Hydrogen-2}\\\text{(Deuterium)}}}{^{2}_{1}\text{H}} \quad + \quad \underset{\substack{\text{Hydrogen-3}\\\text{(Tritium)}}}{^{3}_{1}\text{H}} \quad \longrightarrow \quad ^{4}_{2}\text{He} + ^{1}_{0}\text{n} + 5.3 \times 10^{8} \text{ kcal/mol He}$$

Nuclear fusion Joining together atomic nuclei to form a nucleus heavier than the starting nuclei.

The reactions occurring in the Sun are essentially the same as those in hydrogen bombs.

This process, called **fusion,** is how the Sun makes its energy. Uncontrolled fusion is employed in the "hydrogen bomb." If we can ever achieve a controlled version of this fusion reaction (which is unlikely to happen in the near term), we should be able to solve our energy problems.

As we have just seen, the fusion of deuterium and tritium nuclei to form a helium nucleus gives off a very large amount of energy. What is the source of this energy? When we compare the masses of the reactants and the products we see that there is a loss of $5.0301 - 5.0113 = 0.0188$ g for each mole of helium formed:

$$^{2}_{1}\text{H} \quad + \quad ^{3}_{1}\text{H} \longrightarrow ^{4}_{2}\text{He} \quad + \quad ^{1}_{0}\text{n}$$

$$\text{2.01410 g} \quad \text{3.0161 g} \quad \text{4.0026 g} \quad \text{1.0087 g}$$

$$\text{5.0301 g} \qquad\qquad \text{5.0113 g}$$

When the deuterium and tritium nuclei are converted to helium and a neutron, the extra mass has to go somewhere. But where? The answer is that the missing mass is converted to energy. We even know, from the equation developed by Albert Einstein (1879–1955), how much energy we can get from the conversion of any amount of mass:

$$E = mc^2$$

This equation says that the mass (m), in kilograms, that is lost multiplied by the square of the velocity of light (c^2, where $c = 3.0 \times 10^8$ m/s), in meters squared per second squared (m^2/s^2), is equal to the amount of energy created (E), in joules. For example, 1 g of matter completely converted to energy would produce 8.8×10^{13} J, which is enough energy to boil 34,000,000 L of water initially at 20°C. This is equivalent to the amount of water in an Olympic-size swimming pool. As you can see, we get a tremendous amount of energy from a little bit of mass.

All of the **transuranium elements** (elements with atomic numbers greater than 92) are artificial and have been prepared by a fusion process in which heavy nuclei are bombarded with light ones. Many, as their names indicate, were first prepared at the Lawrence Laboratory of the University of California, Berkeley, by Glenn Seaborg (1912–1999; Nobel laureate in chemistry, 1951) and his colleagues:

$$^{244}_{96}\text{Cm} + {}^{4}_{2}\text{He} \longrightarrow {}^{245}_{97}\text{Bk} + {}^{1}_{1}\text{H} + 2\,{}^{1}_{0}\text{n}$$

$$^{238}_{92}\text{U} + {}^{12}_{6}\text{C} \longrightarrow {}^{246}_{98}\text{Cf} + 4\,{}^{1}_{0}\text{n}$$

$$^{252}_{98}\text{Cf} + {}^{10}_{5}\text{B} \longrightarrow {}^{257}_{103}\text{Lr} + 5\,{}^{1}_{0}\text{n}$$

These transuranium elements are unstable, and most have very short half-lives. For example, the half-life of lawrencium-257 is 0.65 second. Many of the new superheavy elements have been obtained by bombarding lead isotopes with calcium-48 or nickel-64. So far, the creation of elements 110, 111, and 112–116 has been reported, even though their detection was based on the observation of the decay of a single atom.

3.9 | What Is Nuclear Fission and How Is It Related to Atomic Energy?

In the 1930s, Enrico Fermi (1901–1954) and his colleagues in Rome, and Otto Hahn (1879–1968), Lisa Meitner (1878–1968), and Fritz Strassman (1902–1980) in Germany tried to produce new transuranium elements by bombarding uranium-235 with neutrons. To their surprise, they found that, rather than fusion, they obtained **nuclear fission** (fragmentation of large nuclei into smaller pieces):

$$^{235}_{92}\text{U} + {}^{1}_{0}\text{n} \longrightarrow {}^{141}_{56}\text{Ba} + {}^{92}_{36}\text{Kr} + 3\,{}^{1}_{0}\text{n} + \gamma + \text{energy}$$

In this reaction, a uranium-235 nucleus first absorbs a neutron to become uranium-236 and then breaks into two smaller nuclei. The most important product of this nuclear decay is energy, which results because the products have less mass than the starting materials. This form of energy, called **atomic energy,** has been used for both war (in the atomic bomb) and peace.

Nuclear power plant in Salem, New Jersey.

Figure 3.9 A chain reaction begins when a neutron collides with a nucleus of uranium-235.

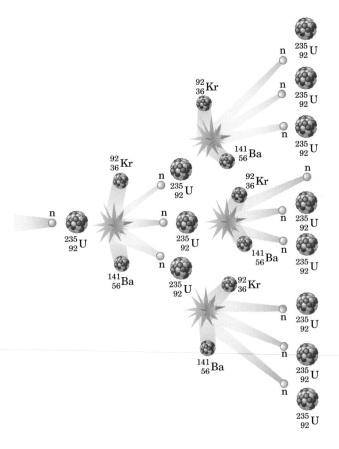

With uranium-235, each fission produces three neutrons, which in turn can generate more fissions by colliding with other uranium-235 nuclei. If even one of these neutrons produces a new fission, the process becomes a self-propagating **chain reaction** (Figure 3.9) that continues at a constant rate. If all three neutrons are allowed to produce new fission, the rate of the reaction increases constantly and eventually culminates in a nuclear explosion. In nuclear plants, the rate of reaction can be controlled by inserting boron control rods to absorb neutrons.

In nuclear power plants, the energy produced by fission is sent to heat exchangers and used to generate steam, which drives a turbine to produce electricity. Today, more than 15% of the electrical energy in the United States is supplied by such plants. The opposition to nuclear plants is based on safety considerations and on the unsolved problems of waste disposal. Although nuclear plants in general have good safety records, accidents such as those at Chernobyl (see Chemical Connections 3E) and Three Mile Island have caused concern.

Waste disposal is a long-range problem. The fission products of nuclear reactors are highly radioactive themselves, with long half-lives. Spent fuel contains these high-level fission products as nuclear wastes, together with uranium and plutonium that can be recovered and reused as mixed oxide (MOX) fuel. Reprocessing is costly: Although done routinely in Europe and Russia, it is not practiced by nuclear plants in the United States for economic reasons. However, this situation may change because cleaner extraction processes have been developed that use supercritical carbon dioxide (Chemical Connections 6F), thereby eliminating the need to dispose of solvent.

The United States has about 50,000 metric tons of spent fuel, stored under water and in dry casks at power plants. The additional nuclear

CHEMICAL CONNECTIONS 3E

Radioactive Fallout from Nuclear Accidents

On April 26, 1986, an accident occurred at the nuclear reactor in the town of Chernobyl in the former Soviet Union. It was a clear reminder of the dangers involved in this industry and of the far-reaching contamination that such accidents can produce. In Sweden, more than 500 miles away from the accident, the radioactive cloud increased the background radiation from 4 to 15 times the normal level. The radioactive cloud reached England, about 1300 miles away, one week later. There, it increased the natural background radiation by 15%. The radioactivity from iodine-131 was measured at 400 Bq/L in milk and 200 Bq/kg in leafy vegetables. Even some 4000 miles away in Spokane, Washington, an iodine-131 activity of 242 Bq/L was found in rainwater, and smaller activities—1.03 Bq/L of ruthenium-103 and 0.66 Bq/L of cesium-137—were recorded as well. These levels are not harmful.

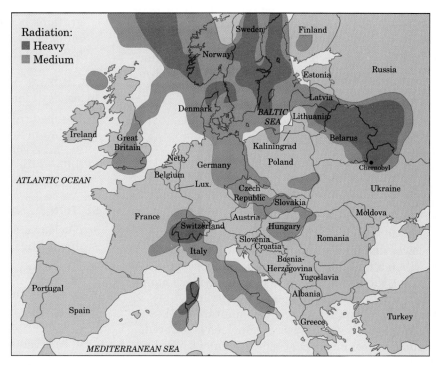

Map showing those areas most affected by the Chernobyl accident.

wastes from the nuclear weapons program, research reactors, and other sources are stored by the Department of Energy in three major sites. After 40 years, the level of radioactivity that the wastes had immediately after their removal from the reactor is reduced a thousandfold. Such nuclear waste is a good candidate for underground burial. Recently, the U.S. federal government gave its final approval to a plan to store nuclear waste in Yucca Mountain, Nevada.

Environmental concerns persist, however. The site cannot be guaranteed to stay dry for centuries. Moisture may corrode the steel cylinders and even the inner glass/ceramic cylinders surrounding the nuclear waste. Some fear that leaked materials from such storage tanks may escape if carbon-14 is oxidized to radioactive carbon dioxide or, less likely, that other radioactive nuclides may contaminate the groundwater, which lies far below the desert rock of Yucca Mountain.

To keep these problems in perspective, one must remember that most other ways of generating large amounts of electrical power have their own environmental problems. For example, burning coal or oil contributes to the accumulation of CO_2 in the atmosphere and to acid rain (see Chemical Connections 7A).

Closer to the source of the nuclear accident, in neighboring Poland, potassium iodide pills were given to children. This step was taken to prevent radioactive iodine-131 (which might come from contaminated food) from concentrating in their thyroid glands, which could lead to cancer. In the wake of the September 11, 2001, terrorist attacks, Massachusetts became the first state to authorize the storage of KI pills in case of nuclear-related terrorist activity.

Storage of nuclear wastes in a storage room carved out of an underground salt bed.

SUMMARY OF KEY QUESTIONS

SECTION 3.1 How Was Radioactivity Discovered?
- Henri Becquerel discovered radioactivity in 1896.

SECTION 3.2 What Is Radioactivity?
- The four major types of radioactivity are **alpha particles** (helium nuclei), **beta particles** (electrons), **gamma rays** (high-energy photons), and **positrons** (positively charged electrons).

SECTION 3.3 What Happens When a Nucleus Emits Radioactivity?
- When a nucleus emits a **beta particle,** the new element has the same mass number but an atomic number one unit greater.
- When a nucleus emits an **alpha particle,** the new element has an atomic number two units lower and a mass number four units smaller.
- When a nucleus emits a **positron** (positive electron), the new element has the same mass number but an atomic number one unit smaller.
- In **gamma emission,** no transmutation takes place; only the energy of the nucleus is lowered.
- In **electron capture,** the new element has the same mass number but an atomic number one unit smaller.

SECTION 3.4 What Is Nuclear Half-life?
- Each radioactive isotope decays at a fixed rate described by its **half-life,** which is the time required for half of the sample to decay.

SECTION 3.5 How Do We Detect and Measure Nuclear Radiation?
- Radiation is detected and counted by devices such as **Geiger-Müller counters.**

- The main unit of intensity of radiation is the **curie (Ci),** which is equal to 3.7×10^{10} disintegrations per second. Other common units are the millicurie (mCi), the microcurie (μCi), and the becquerel (Bq).

SECTION 3.6 How Is Radiation Dosimetry Related to Human Health?
- For medical purposes and to measure potential radiation damage, the absorbed dose is measured in **rads.** Different particles damage body tissues differently; the **rem** is a measure of relative damage caused by type of radiation.

SECTION 3.7 What Is Nuclear Medicine?
- Nuclear medicine is the use of radionuclei for diagnostic imaging and therapy.

SECTION 3.8 What Is Nuclear Fusion?
- **Nuclear fusion** is the combining (fusing) of two lighter nuclei to form a heavier nucleus. Helium is synthesized in the interiors of stars by fusion of hydrogen nuclei. The energy released in this process is the energy of our Sun.

SECTION 3.9 What Is Nuclear Fission and How Is It Related to Atomic Energy?
- **Nuclear fission** is the splitting of a heavier nucleus into two or more smaller nuclei. Nuclear fission releases large amounts of energy, which can be either controlled (nuclear reactors) or uncontrolled (nuclear weapons).

SUMMARY OF KEY REACTIONS

1. **Beta (β) emission (Section 3.3B)** When a nucleus decays by beta emission, the new element has the same mass number but an atomic number one unit greater.

$$^{32}_{15}\text{P} \longrightarrow \,^{32}_{16}\text{S} + \,^{0}_{-1}\text{e}$$

2. **Alpha (α) emission (Section 3.3C)** When a nucleus decays by alpha emission, the new nucleus has a mass number four units smaller and an atomic number two units smaller.

$$^{238}_{92}\text{U} \longrightarrow \,^{234}_{90}\text{Th} + \,^{4}_{2}\text{He}$$

3. **Positron (β^+) emission (Section 3.3D)** When a nucleus decays by positron emission, the new element has the

same mass number but an atomic number one unit smaller.

$$^{11}_{6}\text{C} \longrightarrow \,^{11}_{5}\text{B} + \,^{0}_{+1}\text{e}$$

4. **Gamma (γ) emission (Section 3.3E)** When a nucleus emits gamma radiation, there is no change in either mass number or atomic number of the nucleus.

$$^{11}_{5}\text{B}^* \longrightarrow \,^{11}_{5}\text{B} + \gamma$$

5. **Electron capture (Section 3.3F)** When a nucleus decays by electron capture, the product nucleus has the same mass number but an atomic number one unit smaller.

$$^{7}_{4}\text{Be} + \,^{0}_{-1}\text{e} \longrightarrow \,^{7}_{3}\text{Li}$$

6. **Nuclear fusion (Section 3.8)** In nuclear fusion, two or more nuclei react to form a larger nucleus. In the process, there is a slight decrease in mass; the sum of the masses of the fusion products is less than the sum of the masses of the starting nuclei. The lost mass appears as energy.

$$^2_1\text{H} + ^3_1\text{H} \longrightarrow ^4_2\text{He} + ^1_0\text{n} + 5.3 \times 10^8 \text{ kcal/mol He}$$

7. **Nuclear fission (Section 3.9)** In nuclear fission, a nucleus captures a neutron to form a nucleus with a mass number increased by one unit. The new nucleus then splits into two smaller nuclei.

$$^{235}_{92}\text{U} + ^1_0\text{n} \longrightarrow ^{141}_{56}\text{Ba} + ^{92}_{36}\text{Kr} + 3\,^1_0\text{n} + \gamma + \text{energy}$$

PROBLEMS

Chemistry Now™

Assess your understanding of this chapter's topics with additional quizzing and conceptual-based problems at **http://now.brookscole.com/gob8** or on the CD.

A blue problem number indicates an applied problem.

■ denotes problems that are available on the GOB ChemistryNow website or CD and are assignable in OWL.

SECTION 3.2 What Is Radioactivity?

3.8 What is the difference between an alpha particle and a proton?

3.9 Microwaves are a form of electromagnetic radiation that is used for the rapid heating of foods. What is the frequency of a microwave with a wavelength of 5.8 cm?

3.10 In each case, given the frequency, give the wavelength in centimeters or nanometers and tell what kind of radiation it is.
(a) 7.5×10^{14}/s
(b) 1.0×10^{10}/s
(c) 1.1×10^{15}/s
(d) 1.5×10^{18}/s

3.11 ■ Red light has a wavelength of 650 nm. What is its frequency?

3.12 ■ Which has the longest wavelength: (a) infrared, (b) ultraviolet, or (c) Xrays? Which has the highest energy?

3.13 ■ Write the symbol for a nucleus with the following components:
(a) 9 protons and 10 neutrons
(b) 15 protons and 17 neutrons
(c) 37 protons and 50 neutrons

3.14 In each pair, tell which isotope is more likely to be radioactive:
(a) Nitrogen-14 or nitrogen-13
(b) Phosphorus-31 or phosphorus-33
(c) Lithium-7 or lithium-9
(d) Calcium-39 or calcium-40

3.15 Which isotope of boron is the most stable: boron-8, boron-10, or boron-12?

3.16 Which isotope of oxygen is the most stable: oxygen-14, oxygen-16, or oxygen-18?

SECTION 3.3 What Happens When a Nucleus Emits Radioactivity?

3.17 Samarium-151 is a beta emitter. Write an equation for this nuclear reaction and identify the product nucleus.

3.18 ■ The following nuclei turn into new nuclei by emitting beta particles. Write an equation for each nuclear reaction and identify the product nucleus.
(a) $^{159}_{63}\text{Eu}$ (b) $^{141}_{56}\text{Ba}$ (c) $^{242}_{95}\text{Am}$

3.19 Chromium-51 is used in diagnosing the pathology of the spleen. The nucleus of this isotope captures an electron according to the following equation. What is the transmutation product?

$$^{51}_{24}\text{Cr} + ^{0}_{-1}\text{e} \longrightarrow ?$$

3.20 ■ The following nuclei decay by emitting alpha particles. Write an equation for each nuclear reaction and identify the product nucleus.
(a) $^{210}_{83}\text{Bi}$ (b) $^{238}_{94}\text{Pu}$ (c) $^{174}_{72}\text{Hf}$

3.21 Curium-248 was bombarded, yielding antimony-116 and cesium-160. What was the bombarding nucleus?

3.22 Phosphorus-29 is a positron emitter. Write an equation for this nuclear reaction and identify the product nucleus.

3.23 For each of the following, write a balanced nuclear equation and identify the radiation emitted.
(a) Beryllium-10 changes to boron-10
(b) Europium-151m changes to europium-151
(c) Thallium-195 changes to mercury-195
(d) Plutonium-239 changes to uranium-235

3.24 In the first three steps in the decay of uranium-238, the following isotopic species appear: uranium-238, thorium-234, protactinium-234, which then decays to uranium-234. What kind of emission occurs in each step?

3.25 What kind of emission does *not* result in transmutation?

3.26 ■ Complete the following nuclear reactions.

(a) $^{16}_{8}O + ^{16}_{8}O \longrightarrow ? + ^{4}_{2}He$

(b) $^{235}_{92}U + ^{1}_{0}n \longrightarrow ^{90}_{38}Sr + ? + 3\,^{1}_{0}n$

(c) $^{13}_{6}C + ^{4}_{2}He \longrightarrow ^{16}_{8}O + ?$

(d) $^{210}_{83}Bi \longrightarrow ? + ^{0}_{-1}e$

(e) $^{12}_{6}C + ^{1}_{1}H \longrightarrow ? + \gamma$

3.27 Americium-240 is made by bombarding plutonium-239 with α particles. In addition to americium-240, a proton and two neutrons are formed. Write a balanced equation for this nuclear reaction.

SECTION 3.4 What Is Nuclear Half-life?

3.28 Iodine-125 emits gamma rays and has a half-life of 60 days. If a 20-mg pellet of iodine-125 is implanted onto a prostate gland, how much iodine-125 remains there after one year?

3.29 Polonium-218, a decay product of radon-222 (see Chemical Connections 3B), has a half-life of 3 min. What percentage of the polonium-218 formed will remain in the lung 9 min after inhalation?

3.30 ■ A rock containing 1 mg plutonium-239/kg rock is found in a glacier. The half-life of plutonium-239 is 25,000 years. If this rock was deposited 100,000 years ago during an ice age, how much plutonium-239, per kilogram of rock, was in the rock at that time?

3.31 The element radium is extremely radioactive. If you converted a piece of radium metal to radium chloride (with the weight of the radium remaining the same), would it become less radioactive?

3.32 In what ways can we increase the rate of radioactive decay? Decrease it?

3.33 Suppose 50.0 mg of potassium-45, a beta emitter, was isolated in pure form. After one hour, only 3.1 mg of the radioactive material was left. What is the half-life of potassium-45?

3.34 A patient receives 200 mCi of iodine-131, which has a half-life of eight days.

(a) If 12% of this amount is taken up by the thyroid gland after two hours, what will be the activity of the thyroid after two hours, in millicuries and in counts per minute?

(b) After 24 days, how much activity will remain in the thyroid gland?

SECTION 3.5 How Do We Detect and Measure Nuclear Radiation?

3.35 If you work in a lab containing radioisotopes emitting all kinds of radiation, from which emission should you seek most protection?

3.36 What do Geiger-Müller counters measure: (a) the intensity or (b) the energy of radiation?

3.37 You work in a lab and it is known that radioactivity is being emitted with an intensity of 175 mCi at a distance of 1.0 m from the source. How far, in meters, from the source should you stand if you wish to be subjected to no more than 0.20 mCi?

SECTION 3.6 How Is Radiation Dosimetry Related to Human Health?

3.38 Does a curie (Ci) measure radiation intensity or energy?

3.39 What property is measured each term?

(a) Rad   (b) Rem   (c) Roentgen

(d) Curie   (e) Gray   (f) Becquerel

(g) Sievert

3.40 A radioactive isotope with an activity (intensity) of 80.0 mCi per vial is delivered to a hospital. The vial contains 7.0 cc of liquid. The instruction is to administer 7.2 mCi intravenously. How many cubic centimeters of liquid should be used for one injection?

3.41 Why does exposure of a hand to alpha rays not cause serious damage to the person, whereas entry of an alpha emitter into the lung as an aerosol produces very serious damage to the person's health?

3.42 A certain radioisotope has an intensity of 10^6 Bq at 1-cm distance from the source. What would be the intensity at 20 cm? Give your answer in both Bq and μCi units.

3.43 Assuming the same amount of effective radiation, in rads, from three sources, which would be the most damaging to the tissues: alpha particles, beta particles, or gamma rays?

3.44 In an accident involving radioactive exposure, person A received 3.0 Sv while person B received 0.50 mrem of exposure. Who was hurt more seriously?

SECTION 3.7 What Is Nuclear Medicine?

3.45 In 1986, the nuclear reactor in Chernobyl had an accident and spewed radioactive nuclei that were carried by the winds for hundreds of miles. Today, among the child survivors of the event, the most common damage is thyroid cancer. Which radioactive nucleus do you expect to be responsible for these cancers?

3.46 Cobalt-60, with a half-life of 5.26 years, is used in cancer therapy. The energy of the radiation from cobalt-62 is even higher (half-life = 14 minutes). Why isn't cobalt-60 also used for cancer therapy?

3.47 Match the radioactive isotope with its proper use:

_____ (a) Cobalt-60   1. Heart scan in exercise

_____ (b) Thallium-201   2. Measure water content of body

_____ (c) Tritium   3. Kidney scan

_____ (d) Mercury-197   4. Cancer therapy

SECTION 3.8 What Is Nuclear Fusion?

3.48 What is the product of the fusion of hydrogen-2 and hydrogen-3 nuclei?

3.49 Assuming that one proton and two neutrons will be produced in an alpha-bombardment fusion reaction, which target nucleus would you use to obtain berkelium-249?

3.50 Element 109 was first prepared in 1982. A single atom of this element ($^{266}_{109}$Mt), with a mass number of 266 was made by bombarding a bismuth-209 nucleus with an iron-58 nucleus. What other products, if any, must have been formed besides $^{266}_{109}$Mt?

3.51 A new element was formed when lead-208 was bombarded by krypton-86. One could detect four neutrons as the product of the fusion. Identify the new element.

SECTION 3.9 What Is Nuclear Fission and How Is It Related to Atomic Energy?

3.52 Boron-10 is used as control rods in nuclear reactors. This nucleus absorbs a neutron and then emits an alpha particle. Write an equation for each nuclear reaction and identify each product nucleus.

Chemical Connections

3.53 (Chemical Connections 3A) Why is it accurate to assume that the carbon-14 to carbon-12 ratio in a living plant remains constant over the lifetime of the plant?

3.54 (Chemical Connections 3A) In a recent archeological dig in the Amazon region of Brazil, charcoal paintings were found in a cave. The carbon-14 content of the charcoal was one-fourth of what is found in charcoal prepared from that year's tree harvest. How long ago was the cave settled?

3.55 (Chemical Connections 3A) Carbon-14 dating of the Shroud of Turin indicated that the plant from which the shroud was made was alive around AD 1350. To how many half-lives does this correspond?

3.56 (Chemical Connections 3A) The half-life of carbon-14 is 5730 years. The wrapping of an Egyptian mummy gave off 7.5 counts per minute per gram of carbon. A piece of linen purchased today would give an activity of 15 counts per minute per gram of carbon. How old is the mummy?

3.57 (Chemical Connections 3B) How does radon-222 produce polonium-218?

3.58 (Chemical Connections 3E) In a nuclear accident, one of the radioactive nuclei that concerns people is iodine-131. Iodine is easily vaporized, can be carried by the winds, and can cause radioactive fallout hundreds—even thousands—of miles away. Why is iodine-131 especially harmful?

Additional Problems

3.59 Phosphorus-32 ($t_{1/2}$ = 14.3 d) is used in the medical imaging and diagnosis of eye tumors. Suppose a patient is given 0.010 mg of this isotope. Prepare a graph showing the mass in milligrams remaining in the patient's body after one week. (Assume that none is excreted from the body.)

3.60 During the bombardment of argon-40 with protons, one neutron is emitted for each proton absorbed. What new element is formed?

3.61 Neon-19 and sodium-20 are positron emitters. What products result in each case?

3.62 The half-life of nitrogen-16 is 7 seconds. How long does it take for 100 mg of nitrogen-16 to be reduced to 6.25 mg?

3.63 Do the curie and the becquerel measure the same or different properties of radiation?

3.64 Selenium-75 has a half-life of 120.4 days, so it would take 602 days (five half-lives) to diminish to 3% of the original quantity. Yet this isotope is used for pancreatic scans without any fear that the radioactivity will cause undue harm to the patient. Suggest a possible explanation.

3.65 Use Table 3.4 to determine the percentage of annual radiation we receive from the following sources:

(a) Naturally occurring sources

(b) Diagnostic medical sources

(c) Nuclear power plants

3.66 $^{225}_{89}$Ac is an alpha emitter. In its decay process, it produces three more alpha emitters in succession. Identify each of the decay products.

3.67 Which radiation will cause more ionization, Xrays or radar?

3.68 You have an old wristwatch that still has radium paint on its dial. Measurement of the radioactivity of the watch shows a beta-ray count of 0.50 count/s. If 1.0 microcurie of radiation of this sort produces 1000 mrem/year, how much radiation, in millirems, do you expect from the wristwatch if you wear it for one year?

3.69 Americium-241, which is used in some smoke detectors, has a half-life of 432 years and is an alpha emitter. What is the decay product of americium-241, and approximately what percentage of the original americium-241 will be still around after 1000 years?

3.70 On rare occasions a nucleus, instead of emitting a beta particle, captures one. Berkelium-246 is such a nucleus. What is the product of this nuclear transmutation?

3.71 A patient is reported to have been irradiated by a dose of 1 sievert in a nuclear accident. Is he in mortal danger?

3.72 What is the ground state of a nucleus?

3.73 Explain the following:

(a) It is impossible to have a completely pure sample of any radioactive isotope.

(b) Beta emission of a radioactive isotope creates a new isotope with an atomic number one unit higher than that of the radioactive isotope.

3.74 Yttrium-90, which emits beta particles, is used in radiotherapy. What is the decay product of yttrium-90?

3.75 The half-lives of some oxygen isotopes are as follows:

Oxygen-14: 71 s   Oxygen-15: 124 s

Oxygen-19: 29 s   Oxygen-20: 14 s

Oxygen-16 is the stable, nonradioactive isotope. Do the half-lives indicate anything about the stability of the other oxygen isotopes?

3.76 $^{225}_{89}$Ac is effective in prostate cancer therapy when administered at kBq levels. If an antibody tagged with $^{225}_{89}$Ac has an intensity of 2 million Bq/mg and if a solution contains 5 mg/L tagged antibody, how many milliliters of the solution should you use for an injection to administer 1 kBq intensity?

3.77 When $^{208}_{82}$Pb is bombarded with $^{64}_{28}$Ni, a new element and six neutrons are produced. Identify the new element.

3.78 Americium-241, the isotope used in smoke detectors, has a half-life of 475 years, which is sufficiently long to allow for handling in large quantities. This isotope is prepared in the laboratory by bombarding plutonium-239 with neutrons. In this reaction, plutonium-239 absorbs two neutrons and then decays by emission of a β particle. Write an equation for this nuclear reaction and identify the isotope formed as an intermediate between plutonium-239 and americium-241.

3.79 Boron-10, an effective absorber of neutrons, is used in control rods of uranium-235 fission reactors to absorb neutrons and thereby control the rate of reaction. Boron-10 absorbs a neutron and then emits an α particle. Write a balanced equation for this nuclear reaction and identify the nucleus formed as an intermediate between boron-10 and the final nuclear product.

3.80 Tritium, $^{3}_{1}$H, is a beta emitter widely used as a radioactive tracer in chemical and biochemical research. Tritium is prepared by the bombardment of lithium-6 with neutrons. Complete the following nuclear equation:

$$^{6}_{3}\text{Li} + ^{1}_{0}\text{n} \longrightarrow ^{6}_{3}\text{He} + ?$$

Chemical Bonds

Sodium chloride crystal.

Charles D. Winters

4.1 | What Do We Need to Know Before We Begin?

In Chapter 2, we stated that compounds are tightly bound groups of atoms. In this chapter, we will see that the atoms in compounds are held together by powerful forces of attraction called chemical bonds. There are two main types: ionic bonds and covalent bonds. We begin by examining ionic bonds. To talk about ionic bonds, however, we must first discuss why atoms form the ions they do.

4.2 | What Is the Octet Rule?

In 1916, Gilbert N. Lewis (Section 2.6) devised a beautifully simple model that unified many of the observations about chemical bonding and chemical reactions. He pointed out that the lack of chemical reactivity of the noble gases (Group 8A) indicates a high degree of stability of their electron configurations: helium with a filled valence shell of two electrons ($1s^2$), neon with

GOB
Chemistry🔸Now™
Look for this logo in the chapter and go to GOB ChemistryNow at **http://now.brookscole.com/gob8** or on the CD for tutorials, simulations, and problems.

Noble Gas	Noble Gas Notation
He	$1s^2$
Ne	$[He]2s^22p^6$
Ar	$[Ne]3s^23p^6$
Kr	$[Ar]4s^24p^6$
Xe	$[Kr]5s^25p^6$

Octet rule When undergoing chemical reaction, atoms of Group 1A–7A elements tend to gain, lose, or share sufficient electrons to achieve an election configuration having eight valence electrons

Anion An ion with a negative electric charge

Cation An ion with a positive electric charge

GOB
Chemistry•⚛•Now™
Click *Chemistry Interactive* to see an example of **Ion Formation**

a filled valence shell of eight electrons ($2s^22p^6$), argon with a filled valence shell of eight electrons ($3s^23p^6$), and so forth.

The tendency to react in ways that achieve an outer shell of eight valence electrons is particularly common among Group 1A–7A elements and is given the special name of the **octet rule.** An atom with almost eight valence electrons tends to gain the needed electrons to have eight electrons in its valence shell and an electron configuration like that of the noble gas nearest to it in atomic number. In gaining electrons, the atom becomes a negatively charged ion called an **anion.** An atom with only one or two valence electrons tends to lose the number of electrons required to have an electron configuration like the noble gas nearest it in atomic number. In losing electrons, the atom becomes a positively charged ion called a **cation.** When an ion forms, the number of protons and neutrons in the nucleus of the atom remains unchanged; only the number of electrons in the valence shell of the atom changes.

EXAMPLE 4.1

Show how the following chemical changes obey the octet rule:
(a) A sodium atom loses an electron to form a sodium ion, Na^+.

$$Na \longrightarrow Na^+ + e^-$$

A sodium atom   A sodium ion   An electron

(b) A chlorine atom gains an electron to form a chloride ion, Cl^-.

$$Cl + e^- \longrightarrow Cl^-$$

A chlorine atom   An electron   A chloride ion

Solution
To see how each chemical change follows the octet rule, first write the condensed ground-state electron configuration (Section 2.6C) of the atom involved in the chemical change and the ion it forms, and then compare them.
(a) The condensed ground-state electron configurations for Na and Na^+ are

$$Na \text{ (11 electrons): } 1s^22s^22p^6\ 3s^1$$

$$Na^+ \text{ (10 electrons): } 1s^22s^22p^6$$

A sodium atom has one electron in its valence shell. The loss of this one valence electron changes the sodium atom to a sodium ion, Na^+, which has a complete octet of electrons in its valence shell and the same electron configuration as neon, the noble gas nearest to it in atomic number. We can write this chemical change using Lewis dot structures (Section 2.6F):

$$Na\cdot \longrightarrow Na^+ + e^-$$

(b) The condensed ground-state electron configurations for Cl and Cl^- are as:

$$Cl \text{ (17 electrons): } 1s^22s^22p^6\ 3s^23p^5$$

$$Cl^- \text{ (18 electrons): } 1s^22s^22p^6\ 3s^23p^6$$

A chlorine atom has seven electrons in its valence shell. The gain of one electron changes the chlorine atom to a chloride ion, Cl^-, which has a complete octet of electrons in its valence shell and the same electron configuration as argon, the noble gas nearest to it in atomic number. We can write this chemical change using Lewis dot structures:

$$:\ddot{Cl}\cdot + e^- \longrightarrow :\ddot{Cl}:^-$$

Problem 4.1

Show how the following chemical changes obey the octet rule:
(a) A magnesium atom forms a magnesium ion, Mg^{2+}
(b) A sulfur atom forms a sulfide ion, S^{2-}

The octet rule gives us a good way to understand why Group 1A–7A elements form the ions that they do. It is not perfect, however, for the following two reasons:

1. Ions of period 1 and 2 elements with charges greater than +2 are unstable. Boron, for example, has three valence electrons. If it lost these three electrons, it would become B^{3+} and have a complete outer shell like that of helium. It seems, however, that this is far too large a charge for an ion of this period 2 element; consequently, this ion is not found in stable compounds. By the same reasoning, carbon does not lose its four valence electrons to become C^{4+}, nor does it gain four valence electrons to become C^{4-}. Either of these changes would place too great a charge on this period 2 element.

2. The octet rule does not apply to Group 1B–7B elements (the transition elements), most of which form ions with two or more different positive charges. Copper, for example, can lose one valence electron to form Cu^+; alternatively, it can lose two valence electrons to form Cu^{2+}.

It is important to understand that there are enormous differences between the properties of an atom and those of its ion(s). Atoms and their ions are completely different chemical species and have completely different chemical and physical properties. Consider, for example, sodium and chlorine. Sodium is a soft metal made of sodium atoms that react violently with water. Chlorine atoms are very unstable and even more reactive than sodium atoms. Both sodium and chlorine are poisonous. NaCl, common table salt, is made up of sodium ions and chloride ions. These two ions are quite stable and unreactive. Neither sodium ions nor chloride ions react with water at all.

Because atoms and their ions are different chemical species, we must be careful to distinguish one from the other. Consider the drug commonly known as "lithium," which is used to treat manic depression. The element lithium, like sodium, is a soft metal that reacts with water. The drug used to treat manic depression is not lithium atoms, Li, but rather lithium ions, Li^+, usually given in the form of lithium carbonate, Li_2CO_3. Another example comes from the fluoridation of drinking water, and of toothpastes and dental gels. The element fluorine, F_2, is an extremely poisonous and corrosive gas; it is not what is used for this purpose. Instead, fluoridation uses fluoride ions, F^-, in the form of sodium fluoride, NaF, a compound that is unreactive and nonpoisonous in the concentrations used.

(*a*) Sodium chloride

(*b*) Sodium

(*c*) Chlorine

(*a*) The chemical compound sodium chloride (table salt) is composed of the elements (*b*) sodium and (*c*) chlorine in chemical combination; Salt is very different from the elements that constitute it.

4.3 | How Do We Name Anions and Cations?

Names for anions and cations are formed by using a system developed by the International Union of Pure and Applied Chemistry. We will refer to these names as "systematic" names. Of course, many ions have "common" names that were in use long before chemists undertook an effort to systematize their naming. In this and the following chapters, we will make every effort to use systematic names for ions, but where a long-standing common name remains in use, we will give it as well.

A. Naming Monatomic Cations

A monatomic (containing only one atom) cation forms when a metal loses one or more valence electrons. Elements of Groups 1A, 2A, and 3A form only one type of cation. For ions from these metals, the name of the cation is the name of the metal followed by the word "ion" (Table 4.1). There is no need to specify the charge on these cations, because only one charge is possible. For example, Na^+ is sodium ion and Ca^{2+} is calcium ion.

Most transition and inner transition elements form more than one type of cation and, therefore, the name of the cation must show its charge. To show the charge we write a Roman numeral immediately following (with no space) the name of the metal (Table 4.2). For example, Cu^+ is copper(I) ion and Cu^{2+} is copper(II) ion. Note that even though silver is a transition metal, it forms only Ag^+; therefore, there is no need to use a Roman numeral to show this ion's charge.

Copper(I) oxide and copper(II) oxide. The different copper ion charges result in different colors.

Table 4.1 Names of Cations from Some Metals That Form Only One Positive Ion

Group 1A		Group 2 A		Group 3 A	
Ion	Name	Ion	Name	Ion	Name
H^+	Hydrogen ion	Mg^{2+}	Magnesium ion	Al^{3+}	Aluminum ion
Li^+	Lithium ion	Ca^{2+}	Calcium ion		
Na^+	Sodium ion	Sr^{2+}	Strontium ion		
K^+	Potassium ion	Ba^{2+}	Barium ion		

Table 4.2 Names of Cations from Four Metals That Form Two Different Positive Ions

Ion	Systematic Name	Common Name	Origin of the Symbol of the Element or the Common Name of the Ion
Cu^+	Copper(I) ion	Cuprous ion	*Cupr-* from *cuprum,* the Latin name for copper
Cu^{2+}	Copper(II) ion	Cupric ion	
Fe^{2+}	Iron(II) ion	Ferrous ion	*Ferr-* from *ferrum,* the Latin name for iron
Fe^{3+}	Iron(III) ion	Ferric ion	
Hg^+	Mercury(I) ion	Mercurous ion	*Hg* from *hydrargyrum,* the Latin name for mercury
Hg^{2+}	Mercury(II) ion	Mercuric ion	
Sn^{2+}	Tin(II) ion	Stannous ion	*Sn* from *stannum,* the Latin name for tin
Sn^{4+}	Tin(IV) ion	Stannic ion	

In the older, common system for naming metal cations with two different charges, the suffix *-ous* is used to show the smaller charge and *-ic* is used to show the larger charge (Table 4.2).

B. Naming Monatomic Anions

A monatomic anion is named by adding *-ide* to the stem part of the name. Table 4.3 gives the names of the monatomic anions we deal with most often.

C. Naming Polyatomic Ions

A **polyatomic ion** contains more than one atom. Examples are the hydroxide ion, OH^-, and the phosphate ion, PO_4^{3-}. We will not be concerned with how these ions are formed, only that they exist and are present in the materials around us. While rules for naming polyatomic ions have been developed, the simplest thing to do is just to memorize them.

The preferred system for naming polyatomic ions that differ in the number of hydrogen atoms is to use the prefixes *di-, tri-,* and so forth, to show the presence of more than one hydrogen. For example, HPO_4^{2-} is hydrogen phosphate ion, and $H_2PO_4^-$ is dihydrogen phosphate ion. Table 4.4 lists some of the important polyatomic ions. Because several hydrogen-containing polyatomic anions have common names that are still widely used, you should memorize them as well. In these common names, the prefix *bi* is used to show the presence of one hydrogen.

Table 4.3 Names of the Most Common Monatomic Anions

Anion	Stem Name	Anion Name
F^-	*fluor*	Fluoride
Cl^-	*chlor*	Chloride
Br^-	*brom*	Bromide
I^-	*iod*	Iodide
O^{2-}	*ox*	Oxide
S^{2-}	*sulf*	Sulfide

GOB
Chemistry∙᚛∙Now™
Click *Coached Problems* to see an example of **Polyatomic Ions**

Table 4.4 Names of Common Polyatomic Ions

Polyatomic Ion	Name	Polyatomic Ion	Systematic Name
NH_4^+	Ammonium	HCO_3^-	Hydrogen carbonate (bicarbonate)*
OH^-	Hydroxide	SO_3^{2-}	Sulfite
NO_2^-	Nitrite	HSO_3^-	Hydrogen sulfite (bisulfite)
NO_3^-	Nitrate	SO_4^{2-}	Sulfate
CH_3COO^-	Acetate	HSO_4^-	Hydrogen sulfate (bisulfate)
CN^-	Cyanide	PO_4^{3-}	Phosphate
MnO_4^-	Permanganate	HPO_4^{2-}	Hydrogen phosphate
CrO_4^{2-}	Chromate	$H_2PO_4^-$	Dihydrogen phosphate
CO_3^{2-}	Carbonate		

* Common names, where still widely used, are given in parentheses.

CHEMICAL CONNECTIONS 4A

Coral Chemistry and Broken Bones

Bone is a highly structured matrix consisting of both inorganic and organic materials. The inorganic material is chiefly hydroxyapatite, $Ca_5(PO_4)_3OH$, which makes up about 70% of bone by dry weight. By comparison, the enamel of teeth consists almost entirely of hydroxyapatite. Chief among the organic components of bone are collagen fibers (proteins; see Chemical Connections 21F), which thread their way through the inorganic matrix, providing extra strength and allowing bone to flex under stress. Also weaving through the hydroxyapatite–collagen framework are blood vessels that supply nutrients.

A problem faced by orthopedic surgeons is how to repair bone damage. For a minor fracture, usually a few weeks in a cast suffice for the normal process of bone growth to repair the damaged area. For severe fractures, especially those involving bone loss, a bone graft may be needed. An alternative to a bone graft is an implant of synthetic bone material. One such material, called Pro Osteon, is derived by heating coral with ammonium hydrogen phosphate to form a hydroxyapatite similar to that of bone. Throughout the heating process, the porous structure of the coral, which resembles that of bone, is retained.

$$5CaCO_3 + 3(NH_4)_2HPO_4 \xrightarrow[\text{24–60 hours}]{200°C}$$
$$\underset{\text{Coral}}{}$$

$$\underset{\text{Hydroxyapatite}}{Ca_5(PO_4)_3OH} + 3(NH_4)_2CO_3 + 2H_2CO_3$$

The surgeon can shape a piece of this material to match the bone void, implant it, stabilize the area by inserting metal plates

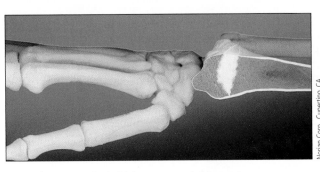

A wrist fracture repaired with bone cement (white area).

and/or screws, and let new bone tissue grow into the pores of the implant.

In an alternative process, a dry mixture of calcium dihydrogen phosphate monohydrate, $Ca(H_2PO_4)_2 \cdot H_2O$, calcium phosphate, $Ca_3(PO_4)_2$, and calcium carbonate, $CaCO_3$, is prepared. Just before the surgical implant occurs, these chemicals are mixed with a solution of sodium phosphate to form a paste that is then injected into the bony area to be repaired. In this way, the fractured bony area is held in the desired position by the synthetic material while the natural process of bone rebuilding replaces the implant with living bone tissue.

4.4 | What Are the Two Major Types of Chemical Bonds?

A. Ionic and Covalent Bonds

According to the Lewis model of chemical bonding, atoms bond together in such a way that each atom participating in a bond acquires a valence-shell electron configuration matching that of the noble gas nearest to it in atomic number. Atoms acquire completed valence shells in two ways:

1. An atom may lose or gain enough electrons to acquire a filled valence shell, becoming an ion as it does so (Section 4.2). An **ionic bond** results from the force of attraction between a cation and an anion.

2. An atom may share electrons with one or more other atoms to acquire a filled valence shell. A **covalent bond** results from the force of attraction between two atoms that share one or more pairs of electrons.

We can now ask how to determine whether two atoms in a compound are bonded by an ionic bond or a covalent bond. One way to do so is to con-

Ionic bond A chemical bond resulting from the attraction between a positive ion and a negative ion

Covalent bond A bond resulting from the sharing of electrons between two atoms

Norian Corp., Cupertino, CA

sider the relative positions of the two atoms in the Periodic Table. Ionic bonds usually form between a metal and a nonmetal. An example of an ionic bond is that formed between the metal sodium and the nonmetal chlorine in the compound sodium chloride, Na^+Cl^-. When two nonmetals or a metalloid and a nonmetal combine, the bond between them is usually covalent. Examples of compounds containing covalent bonds between nonmetals include Cl_2, H_2O, CH_4, and NH_3. Examples of compounds containing covalent bonds between a metalloid and a nonmetal include BF_3, $SiCl_4$, and AsH_3.

Another way to determine the bond type is to compare the electronegativities of the atoms involved, which is the subject of the next subsection.

B. Electronegativity and Chemical Bonds

Electronegativity is a measure of an atom's attraction for the electrons it shares in a chemical bond with another atom. The most widely used scale of electronegativities (Table 4.5) was devised by Linus Pauling in the 1930s. On the Pauling scale, fluorine, the most electronegative element, is assigned an electronegativity of 4.0, and all other elements are assigned values relative to fluorine.

As you study the electronegativity values in Table 4.5, note that they generally increase from left to right across a row of the Periodic Table and from bottom to top within a column. Values increase from left to right because of the increasing positive charge on the nucleus, which leads to a stronger attraction for electrons in the valence shell. Values increase going up a column because of the decreasing distance of the valence electrons from the nucleus, which leads to stronger attraction between a nucleus and its valence electrons.

You might compare these trends in electronegativity with the trends in ionization energy (Section 2.8). Each illustrates the periodic nature of elements within the Periodic Table. Ionization energy measures the amount of energy necessary to remove an electron from an atom. Electronegativity measures how tightly an atom holds the electrons that it shares with another atom. Notice that for periods within the Periodic Table, both electronegativity and ionization potential generally increase from left to right across a row of the Periodic Table from Columns 1A to 7A. In addition, both electronegativity and ionization potential increase in going up a column.

Electronegativity increases

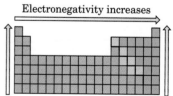

Table 4.5   Electronegativity Values of the Elements (Pauling Scale)

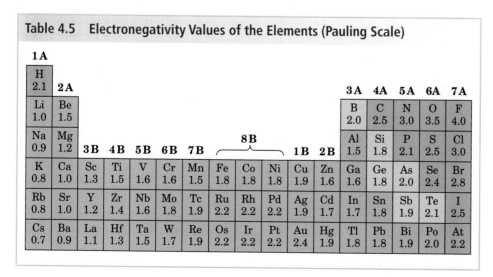

1A												3A	4A	5A	6A	7A
H 2.1	2A															
Li 1.0	Be 1.5											B 2.0	C 2.5	N 3.0	O 3.5	F 4.0
Na 0.9	Mg 1.2	3B	4B	5B	6B	7B	8B		1B	2B	Al 1.5	Si 1.8	P 2.1	S 2.5	Cl 3.0
K 0.8	Ca 1.0	Sc 1.3	Ti 1.5	V 1.6	Cr 1.6	Mn 1.5	Fe 1.8	Co 1.8	Ni 1.8	Cu 1.9	Zn 1.6	Ga 1.6	Ge 1.8	As 2.0	Se 2.4	Br 2.8
Rb 0.8	Sr 1.0	Y 1.2	Zr 1.4	Nb 1.6	Mo 1.8	Tc 1.9	Ru 2.2	Rh 2.2	Pd 2.2	Ag 1.9	Cd 1.7	In 1.7	Sn 1.8	Sb 1.9	Te 2.1	I 2.5
Cs 0.7	Ba 0.9	La 1.1	Hf 1.3	Ta 1.5	W 1.7	Re 1.9	Os 2.2	Ir 2.2	Pt 2.2	Au 2.4	Hg 1.9	Tl 1.8	Pb 1.8	Bi 1.9	Po 2.0	At 2.2

EXAMPLE 4.2

Judging from their relative positions in the Periodic Table, which element in each pair has the larger electronegativity?
(a) Lithium or carbon   (b) Nitrogen or oxygen
(c) Carbon or oxygen

Solution
The elements in each pair are in the second period of the Periodic Table. Within a period, electronegativity increases from left to right.
(a) C > Li   (b) O > N   (c) O > C

Problem 4.2

Judging from their relative positions in the Periodic Table, which element in each pair has the larger electronegativity?
(a) Lithium or potassium   (b) Nitrogen or phosphorus
(c) Carbon or silicon

4.5 | What Is an Ionic Bond and How Does One Form?

A. Forming Ionic Bonds

According to the Lewis model of bonding, an ionic bond forms by the transfer of one or more valence-shell electrons from an atom of lower electronegativity to the valence shell of an atom of higher electronegativity. The more electronegative atom gains one or more valence electrons and becomes an anion; the less electronegative atom loses one or more valence electrons and becomes a cation. The compound formed by the combination of positive and negative ions is called an **ionic compound.**

As a guideline, we say that this type of electron transfer to form an ionic compound is most likely to occur if the difference in electronegativity between two atoms is approximately 1.9 or greater. A bond is more likely to be covalent if this difference is less than 1.9. You should be aware that the value of 1.9 for the formation of an ionic bond is somewhat arbitrary. Some chemists prefer a slightly larger value, others a slightly smaller value. The essential point is that the value of 1.9 gives us a guidepost against which to decide if a bond is more likely to be ionic or more likely to be covalent. Section 4.7 discusses covalent bonding.

An example of an ionic compound is that formed between the metal sodium (electronegativity 0.9) and the nonmetal chlorine (electronegativity 3.0). The difference in electronegativity between these two elements is 2.1. In forming the ionic compound NaCl, the single $3s$ valence electron of a sodium atom is transferred to the partially filled valence shell of a chlorine atom.

$$\text{Na } (1s^2 2s^2 2p^6 3s^1) + \text{Cl } (1s^2 2s^2 2p^6 3s^2 3p^5) \longrightarrow \text{Na}^+ (1s^2 2s^2 2p^6) + \text{Cl}^- (1s^2 2s^2 2p^6 3s^2 3p^6)$$

Sodium atom   Chlorine atom   Sodium ion   Chloride ion

In the following equation, we use a single-headed curved arrow to show this transfer of one electron:

$$\text{Na} \cdot + \cdot \ddot{\text{Cl}} \colon \longrightarrow \text{Na}^+ \; \colon \ddot{\text{Cl}} \colon ^-$$

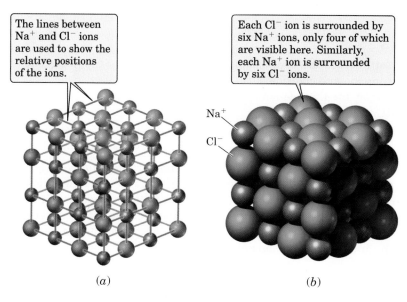

The lines between Na^+ and Cl^- ions are used to show the relative positions of the ions.

Each Cl^- ion is surrounded by six Na^+ ions, only four of which are visible here. Similarly, each Na^+ ion is surrounded by six Cl^- ions.

Na^+

Cl^-

Figure 4.1   The structure of a sodium chloride crystal. (*a*) Ball-and-stick models show the relative positions of the ions. (*b*) Space-filling models show the relative sizes of the ions.

(*a*)   (*b*)

The ionic bond in solid sodium chloride results from the force of attraction between positive sodium ions and negative chloride ions. In its solid (crystalline) form, sodium chloride consists of a three-dimensional array of Na^+ and Cl^- ions arranged as shown in Figure 4.1.

Although ionic compounds do not consist of molecules, they do have a definite ratio of one kind of ion to another; their formulas give this ratio. For example, NaCl represents the simplest ratio of sodium ions to chloride ions—namely, $1:1$.

B. Predicting Formulas of Ionic Compounds

Ions are charged particles, but the matter we see all around us and deal with every day is electrically neutral (uncharged). If ions are present in any sample of matter, the total number of positive charges must equal the total number of negative charges. Therefore, we cannot have a sample containing only Na^+ ions. Any sample that contains Na^+ ions must also contain negative ions, such as Cl^-, Br^-, or S^{2-}, and the sum of the positive charges must equal the sum of the negative charges.

EXAMPLE 4.3

Write the formulas for the ionic compounds formed from the following ions:
(a) Lithium ion and bromide ion
(b) Barium ion and iodide ion
(c) Aluminum ion and sulfide ion

Solution
(a) Table 4.1 shows that the charge on a lithium ion is $+1$, and Table 4.3 shows that the charge on a bromide ion is -1. The formula for lithium bromide is LiBr.
(b) The charge on a barium ion is $+2$ and the charge on an iodide ion is -1. Two I^- ions are required to balance the charge of one Ba^{2+} ion. The formula for barium iodide is BaI_2.
(c) The charge on an aluminum ion is $+3$, and the charge on a sulfide ion is -2. For the compound to have an overall charge of zero, the ions must combine in the ratio of two aluminum ions to three sulfur ions. The formula of aluminum sulfide is Al_2S_3.

Problem 4.3

Write the formulas for the ionic compounds formed from the following ions:
(a) Potassium ion and chloride ion
(b) Calcium ion and fluoride ion
(c) Iron(III) ion and oxide ion

Remember that the subscripts in the formulas for ionic compounds represent the ratio of the ions. Thus a crystal of BaI_2 has twice as many iodide ions as barium ions. For ionic compounds, when both charges are 2, as in the compound formed from Ba^{2+} and O^{2-}, we must "reduce to lowest terms." That is, barium oxide is BaO, not Ba_2O_2. The reason is that we are looking at ratios only, and the ratio of ions in barium oxide is $1:1$.

4.6 | How Do We Name Ionic Compounds?

To name an ionic compound, we give the name of the cation first followed by the name of the anion.

A. Binary Ionic Compounds of Metals That Form Only One Positive Ion

A **binary compound** contains only two elements. In a **binary ionic compound,** both of the elements are present as ions. The name of the compound consists of the name of the metal from which the cation (positive ion) was formed, followed by the name of the anion (negative ion). We ignore subscripts in naming binary ionic compounds. For example, $AlCl_3$ is named aluminum chloride. We know this compound contains three chloride ions because the positive and negative charges must match—that is, one Al^{3+} ion must combine with three Cl^- ions to balance the charges.

EXAMPLE 4.4

Name these binary ionic compounds:
(a) LiBr   (b) Ag_2S (c) NaBr

Solution
(a) Lithium bromide   (b) Silver sulfide   (c) Sodium bromide

Problem 4.4

Name these binary ionic compounds:
(a) MgO   (b) BaI_2 (c) KCl

EXAMPLE 4.5

Write the formulas for these binary ionic compounds:
(a) Barium hydride   (b) Sodium fluoride   (c) Calcium oxide

Solution
(a) BaH_2 (b) NaF   (c) CaO

Problem 4.5

Write the formulas for these binary ionic compounds:
(a) Magnesium chloride   (b) Aluminum oxide   (c) Lithium iodide

B. Binary Ionic Compounds of Metals That Form More Than One Positive Ion

Table 4.2 shows that many transition metals form more than one positive ion. For example, copper forms both Cu^+ and Cu^{2+} ions. For systematic names, we use Roman numerals in the name to show the charge. For common names we use the *-ous/-ic* system.

EXAMPLE 4.6

Give each binary compound a systematic name and a common name.
(a) CuO   (b) Cu_2O

Solution
Remember in answering part (b) that we ignore subscripts in naming binary ionic compounds. Therefore, the 2 in Cu_2O is not indicated. You know that two copper(I) ions are present because two positive charges are needed to balance the two negative charges on an O^{2-} ion.
(a) Systematic name: copper(II) oxide. Common name: cupric oxide.
(b) Systematic name: copper(I) oxide. Common name: cuprous oxide.

Problem 4.6

Give each binary compound a systematic name and a common name.
(a) FeO   (b) Fe_2O_3

C. Ionic Compounds That Contain Polyatomic Ions

To name ionic compounds containing polyatomic ions, name the positive ion first and then the negative ion, each as a separate word.

EXAMPLE 4.7

Name these ionic compounds, each of which contains a polyatomic ion:
(a) $NaNO_3$ (b) $CaCO_3$ (c) $(NH_4)_2SO_3$ (d) NaH_2PO_4

Solution
Recall that the name of the $H_2PO_4^-$ ion is dihydrogen phosphate.
(a) Sodium nitrate   (b) Calcium carbonate
(c) Ammonium sulfite   (d) Sodium dihydrogen phosphate

Problem 4.7

Name these ionic compounds, each of which contains a polyatomic ion:
(a) K_2HPO_4 (b) $Al_2(SO_4)_3$ (c) $FeCO_3$

CHEMICAL CONNECTIONS 4B

Ionic Compounds in Medicine

Many ionic compounds have medical uses, some of which are shown in the table.

Formula	Name	Medical Use
$AgNO_3$	Silver nitrate	Astringent (external)
$BaSO_4$	Barium sulfate	Radiopaque medium for Xray work
$CaSO_4$	Calcium sulfate	Plaster casts
$FeSO_4$	Iron(II) sulfate	To treat iron deficiency
$KMnO_4$	Potassium permanganate	Anti-infective (external)
KNO_3	Potassium nitrate (saltpeter)	Diuretic
Li_2CO_3	Lithium carbonate	To treat manic depression
$MgSO_4$	Magnesium sulfate (Epsom salts)	Cathartic
$NaHCO_3$	Sodium bicarbonate (baking soda)	Antacid
NaI	Sodium iodide	Iodine for thyroid hormones
NH_4Cl	Ammonium chloride	To acidify the digestive system
$(NH_4)_2CO_3$	Ammonium carbonate	Expectorant
SnF_2	Tin(II) fluoride	To strengthen teeth (external)
ZnO	Zinc oxide	Astringent (external)

Charles D. Winters

Drinking a "barium cocktail" containing barium sulfate makes the intestinal tract visible on an Xray.

4.7	What Is a Covalent Bond and How Does One Form?

A. Formation of a Covalent Bond

A covalent bond forms when electron pairs are shared between two atoms whose difference in electronegativity is less than 1.9. As we have already mentioned, the most common covalent bonds occur between two nonmetals or between a nonmetal and a metalloid.

According to the Lewis model, a pair of electrons in a covalent bond functions in two ways simultaneously: It is shared by two atoms and it fills the valence shell of each atom. The simplest example of a covalent bond is that in a hydrogen molecule, H_2. When two hydrogen atoms bond, the single electrons from each atom combine to form an electron pair. A bond formed by sharing a pair of electrons is called a **single bond** and is represented by a single line between the two atoms. The electron pair shared between the two hydrogen atoms in H_2 completes the valence shell of each hydrogen. Thus, in H_2, each hydrogen has two electrons in its valence shell and an electron configuration like that of helium, the noble gas nearest to it in atomic number.

The single line represents a shared pair of electrons

$$H\cdot + \cdot H \longrightarrow H\text{—}H$$

Table 4.6 Classification of Chemical Bonds		
Electronegativity Difference Between Bonded Atoms	Type of Bond	Most Likely to Form Between
Less than 0.5 0.5 to 1.9	Nonpolar covalent Polar covalent }	Two nonmetals or a nonmetal and a metalloid
Greater than 1.9	Ionic	A metal and a nonmetal

B. Nonpolar and Polar Covalent Bonds

Although all covalent bonds involve the sharing of electrons, they differ widely in the degree of sharing. We classify covalent bonds into two categories, **nonpolar covalent** and **polar covalent,** depending on the difference in electronegativity between the bonded atoms. In a nonpolar covalent bond, electrons are shared equally. In a polar covalent bond, they are shared unequally. It is important to realize that no sharp line divides these two categories, nor, for that matter, does a sharp line divide polar covalent bonds and ionic bonds. Nonetheless, the rule-of-thumb guidelines given in Table 4.6 will help you decide whether a given bond is more likely to be nonpolar covalent, polar covalent, or ionic.

An example of a polar covalent bond is that in H—Cl, in which the difference in electronegativity between the bonded atoms is 3.0 − 2.1 = 0.9. A covalent bond between carbon and hydrogen, for example, is classified as nonpolar covalent because the difference in electronegativity between these two atoms is only 2.5 − 2.1 = 0.4. You should be aware, however, that there is some slight polarity to a C—H bond but, because it is quite small, we arbitrarily say that a C—H bond is nonpolar.

Nonpolar covalent bond
A covalent bond between two atoms whose difference in electronegativity is less than 0.5

Polar covalent bond A covalent bond between two atoms whose difference in electronegativity is between 0.5 and 1.9

EXAMPLE 4.8

Classify each bond as nonpolar covalent, polar covalent, or ionic.
(a) O—H   (b) N—H   (c) Na—F
(d) C—Mg   (e) C—S

Solution

Bond	Difference in Electronegativity	Type of Bond
(a) O—H	3.5 − 2.1 = 1.4	Polar covalent
(b) N—H	3.0 − 2.1 = 0.9	Polar covalent
(c) Na—F	4.0 − 0.9 = 3.1	Ionic
(d) C—Mg	2.5 − 1.2 = 1.3	Polar covalent
(e) C—S	2.5 − 2.5 = 0	Nonpolar covalent

Problem 4.8

Classify each bond as nonpolar covalent, polar covalent, or ionic.
(a) S—H   (b) P—H   (c) C—F   (d) C—Cl

An important consequence of the unequal sharing of electrons in a polar covalent bond is that the more electronegative atom gains a greater fraction of the shared electrons and acquires a partial negative charge, indicated by the symbol δ− (read "delta minus"). The less electronegative atom has a lesser fraction of the shared electrons and acquires a partial positive charge, indicated by the symbol δ+ (read "delta plus"). This separation of charge produces a **dipole** (two poles). We commonly show the presence of a bond dipole by an arrow, with the head of the arrow near the negative end of the dipole and a cross on the tail of the arrow near the positive end (Figure 4.2).

We can also show the polarity of a covalent bond by an electron density model. In this type of molecular model, a blue color shows the presence of a δ+ charge and a red color shows the presence of a δ− charge. Figure 4.2 also shows an electron density model of HCl. The ball-and-stick model in the center shows the orientation of atoms in space. The transparent surface surrounding the ball-and-stick model shows the relative sizes of the atoms (equivalent to the size shown by a space-filling model). Colors on the surface show the distribution of electron density. We see by the blue color that hydrogen bears a δ+ charge and by the red color that chlorine bears a δ− charge.

Dipole A chemical species in which there is a separation of charge; there is a positive pole in one part of the species, and a negative pole in another part

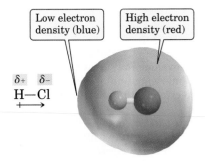

Figure 4.2 HCl is a polar covalent molecule. In the electron density model of HCl, red indicates a region of high electron density, and blue indicates a region of low electron density.

EXAMPLE 4.9

Using the symbols δ− and δ+, indicate the polarity in each polar covalent bond.
(a) C—O
(b) N—H
(c) C—Mg

Solution
For (a), carbon and oxygen are both in period 2 of the Periodic Table. Because oxygen is farther to the right than carbon, it is more electronegative than carbon. For (c), magnesium is a metal located to the far left in the Periodic Table and carbon is a nonmetal located to the right. All nonmetals, including hydrogen, have a greater electronegativity than do the metals in columns 1A and 2A. The electronegativity of each element is given below the symbol of the element.

$$
\begin{array}{ccc}
\overset{\delta+\quad\delta-}{(a)\ \ C-O} & \overset{\delta-\quad\delta+}{(b)\ \ N-H} & \overset{\delta-\quad\delta+}{(c)\ \ C-Mg} \\
2.5\ \ 3.5 & 3.0\ \ 2.1 & 2.5\ \ 1.2
\end{array}
$$

Problem 4.9
Using the symbols δ^- and δ^+, indicate the polarity in each polar covalent bond.
(a) C—N
(b) N—O
(c) C—Cl

C. Drawing Lewis Structures of Covalent Compounds

The ability to write Lewis structures for covalent molecules is a fundamental skill for the study of chemistry. The following How To box will help you with this task.

HOW TO ...

Draw Lewis Structures

GOB
Chemistry ·**·**·Now™
Click *Mastering the Essentials* to practice
How to Draw Lewis Structures

1. *Determine the number of valence electrons in the molecule.*
   Add up the number of valence electrons contributed by each atom. To determine the number of valence electrons, you simply need to know the number of each kind of atom in the molecule. You don't have to know anything about how the atoms are bonded to each other.

   Example: The Lewis structure for formaldehyde, CH_2O, must show 12 valence electrons:

   $$4 \text{ (from C)} + 2 \text{ (from the two H)} + 6 \text{ (from O)} = 12$$

2. *Determine the connectivity of the atoms (which atoms are bonded to each other) and connect bonded atoms by single bonds.*
   Drawing a Lewis structure is often the most challenging task. For some molecules we give you as examples or problems, we ask you to propose a connectivity. For most, however, we give you the experimentally determined connectivity and ask you to complete the Lewis structure.

   Example: The atoms in formaldehyde are bonded in the following order. Note that we do not attempt at this point to show bond angles or the three-dimensional shape of the molecule; we just show what is bonded to what.

   $$
   \begin{array}{c}
   O \\
   | \\
   H-C-H
   \end{array}
   $$

   This partial structure shows six valence electrons in the three single bonds. In it we have accounted for six of the 12 valence electrons.

3. *Arrange the remaining electrons so that each atom has a complete outer shell.*
   Each hydrogen atom must be surrounded by two electrons. Each carbon, nitrogen, oxygen, and halogen atom must be surrounded by eight valence electrons (to satisfy the octet rule). The remaining valence electrons may be shared between atoms in bonds or may be unshared pairs on a single atom. A pair of electrons involved in a covalent bond (**bonding electrons**) is shown as a single line; an unshared pair of electrons (**nonbonding electrons**) is shown as a pair of Lewis dots.

   By placing two pairs of bonding electrons between C and O, we give carbon a complete octet. By placing the remaining four electrons on oxygen as two Lewis dot pairs, we give oxygen eight valence electrons and a complete octet (octet rule). Note that we placed the two pairs of bonding electrons between C and O before we assigned the unshared pairs of electrons on the oxygen.

Bonding electrons Valence electrons involved in forming a covalent bond; that is, shared electrons

Nonbonding electrons Valence electrons not involved in forming covalent bonds; that is, unshared electrons

Single bond A bond formed by sharing one pair of electrons and represented by a single line between two atoms

Lewis Structure A formula for a molecule or ion showing all pairs of bonding electrons as single, double, or triple bonds, and all nonbonded electrons as pairs of Lewis dots

Structural formula A formula showing how atoms in a molecule or ion are bonded to each other; similar to a Lewis structure except that a structural formula typically shows only bonding pairs of electrons

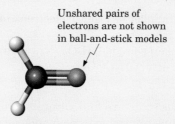

Unshared pairs of electrons are not shown in ball-and-stick models

Lewis structure

Ball-and-stick model of formaldehyde

As a check on this structure, verify (1) that each atom has a complete valence shell (which each does) and (2) that the Lewis structure has the correct number of valence electrons (12, which it does).

4. In a **double bond,** two atoms share two pairs of electrons; we represent a double bond by two lines between the bonded atoms. Double bonds are most common between atoms of C, N, O, and S. In the organic and biochemistry chapters in particular, we shall see many examples of $C=C$, $C=N$, and $C=O$ double bonds.

5. In a **triple bond,** two atoms share three pairs of electrons; we show a triple bond by three lines between the bonded atoms. Triple bonds are most common between atoms of C and N—for example, $C\equiv C$ and $C\equiv N$ triple bonds.

Double bond A bond formed by sharing two pairs of electrons and represented by two lines between the two bonded atoms

Triple bond A bond formed by sharing three pairs of electrons and represented by three lines between the two bonded atoms

---

Table 4.7   Lewis Structures for Several Small Molecules

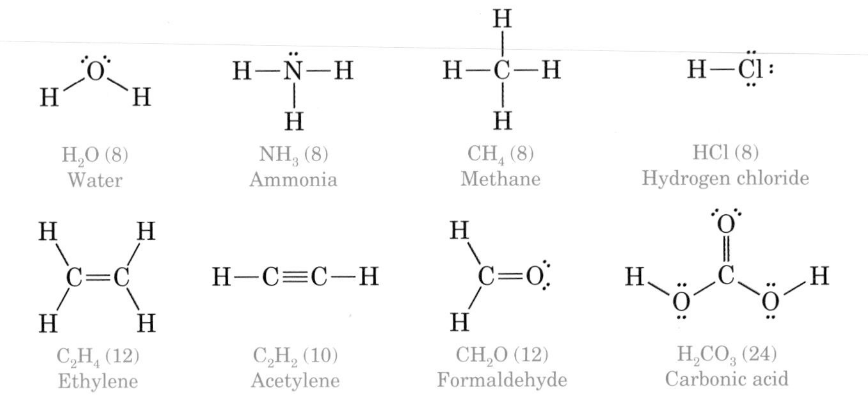

H_2O (8)
Water

NH_3 (8)
Ammonia

CH_4 (8)
Methane

HCl (8)
Hydrogen chloride

C_2H_4 (12)
Ethylene

C_2H_2 (10)
Acetylene

CH_2O (12)
Formaldehyde

H_2CO_3 (24)
Carbonic acid

The number of valence electrons in each molecule is given in parentheses after the molecular formula of the compound.

Table 4.7 gives Lewis structures and names for several small molecules. Notice that each hydrogen is surrounded by two valence electrons, and that each carbon, nitrogen, oxygen, and chlorine is surrounded by eight valence electrons. Furthermore, each carbon has four bonds, each nitrogen has three bonds and one unshared pair of electrons, each oxygen has two bonds and two unshared pairs of electrons, and chlorine (as well as other halogens) has one bond and three unshared pairs of electrons.

EXAMPLE 4.10

State the number of valence electrons in each molecule, and draw a Lewis structure for each:
(a) Hydrogen peroxide, H_2O_2 (b) Methanol, CH_3OH
(c) Acetic acid, CH_3COOH

Solution
(a) A Lewis structure for hydrogen peroxide, H_2O_2, must show six valence electrons from each oxygen and one from each hydrogen for a total of

12 + 2 = 14 valence electrons. We know that hydrogen forms only one covalent bond, so the connectivity of atoms must be as follows:

$$H—O—O—H$$

The three single bonds account for six valence electrons. The remaining eight valence electrons must be placed on the oxygen atoms to give each a complete octet:

H—Ö—Ö—H   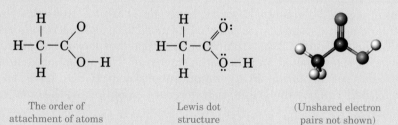   Ball-and-stick models show only nuclei and covalent bonds; they do not show unshared pairs of electrons

(b) A Lewis structure for methanol, CH_3OH, must show four valence electrons from carbon, one from each hydrogen, and six from oxygen for a total of 4 + 4 + 6 = 14 valence electrons. The connectivity of atoms in methanol is given on the left. The five single bonds in this partial structure account for ten valence electrons. The remaining four valence electrons must be placed on oxygen as two Lewis dot pairs to give it a complete octet.

$$\begin{array}{c} H \\ | \\ H—C—O—H \\ | \\ H \end{array} \qquad \begin{array}{c} H \\ | \\ H—C—Ö—H \\ | \\ H \end{array}$$

The order of   Lewis dot
attachment of atoms   structure

(c) A molecule of acetic acid, CH_3COOH, must contain four valence electrons from each carbon, six from each oxygen, and one from each hydrogen for a total of 8 + 12 + 4 = 24 valence electrons. The connectivity of atoms, shown on the left, contains seven single bonds, which accounts for 14 valence electrons. The remaining ten electrons must be added in such a way that each carbon and oxygen atom has a complete outer shell of eight electrons. This can be done in only one way, which creates a double bond between carbon and one of the oxygens.

$$\begin{array}{c} H \\ | \\ H—C—C \\ | \quad\ \diagdown \\ H \qquad O—H \end{array} \begin{array}{c} O \\ \end{array} \qquad \begin{array}{c} H \quad\ \ \ddot{O}: \\ | \quad\ \ \| \\ H—C—C \\ | \quad\ \ \diagdown \\ H \qquad \ddot{O}—H \end{array}$$

The order of   Lewis dot   (Unshared electron
attachment of atoms   structure   pairs not shown)

In this Lewis dot structure, each carbon has four bonds: One carbon has four single bonds, and the other carbon has two single bonds and one double bond. Each oxygen has two bonds and two unshared pairs of electrons: One oxygen has one double bond and two unshared pairs of electrons, and the other oxygen has two single bonds and two unshared pairs of electrons.

Problem 4.10

Draw a Lewis structure for each molecule. Each has only one possible order of attachment of its atoms, which is left for you to determine.
(a) Ethane, C_2H_6
(b) Chloromethane, CH_3Cl
(c) Hydrogen cyanide, HCN

EXAMPLE 4.11

Why does carbon have four bonds and no unshared pairs of electrons in covalent compounds?

Solution
When carbon has four bonds, it has a complete octet. An additional lone pair of electrons would place ten electrons in the valence shell of carbon and violate the octet rule.

Problem 4.11

Draw a Lewis structure of a covalent compound in which carbon has
(a) Four single bonds
(b) Two single bonds and one double bond
(c) Two double bonds
(d) One single bond and one triple bond

D. Exceptions to the Octet Rule

The Lewis model of covalent bonding focuses on valence electrons and the necessity for each atom other than hydrogen to have a completed valence shell containing eight electrons. Although most molecules formed by main-group elements (Groups 1A–7A) have structures that satisfy the octet rule, some important exceptions exist. One exception involves molecules that contain an atom with more than eight electrons in its valence shell. Atoms of period 2 elements use one 2s and three 2p orbitals for bonding; these four orbitals can contain only eight valence electrons—hence the octet rule. Atoms of period 3 elements, however, have one 3s orbital, three 3p orbitals, and five 3d orbitals; they can accommodate more than eight electrons in their valence shells (Section 2.6A). In phosphine, PH_3, phosphorus has eight electrons in its valence shell and obeys the octet rule. The phosphorus atoms in phosphorus pentachloride, PCl_5, and phosphoric acid, H_3PO_4, have ten electrons in their valence shells and, therefore, are exceptions to the octet rule.

8 electrons in the valence shell of P

10 electrons in the valence shell of P

10 electrons in the valence shell of P

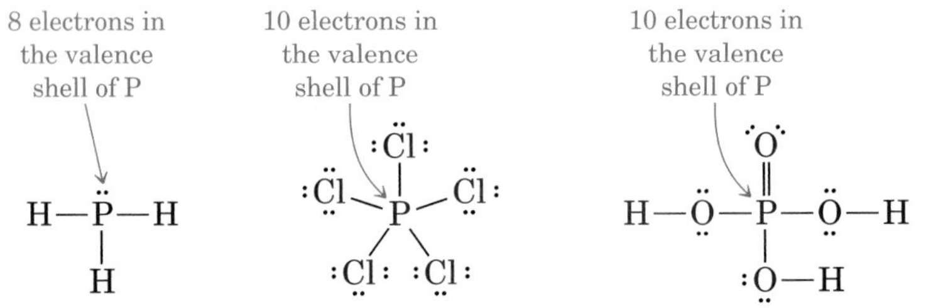

Phosphine   Phosphorus pentachloride   Phosphoric acid

Sulfur, another period 3 element, forms compounds in which it has 8, 10, and even 12 electrons in its valence shell. The sulfur atom in H_2S has 8 electrons in its valence shell and obeys the octet rule. The sulfur atoms in SO_2 and H_2SO_4 have 10 and 12 electrons in their valence shells and are exceptions to the octet rule.

8 electrons in the valence shell of sulfur

10 electrons in the valence shell of sulfur

12 electrons in the valence shell of sulfur

Hydrogen sulfide   Sulfur dioxide   Sulfuric acid

4.8 | How Do We Name Binary Covalent Compounds?

A **binary covalent compound** is a binary (two-element) compound in which all bonds are covalent. In naming a binary covalent compound:

1. First name the less electronegative element (see Table 4.5). Note that the less electronegative element is also generally written first in the formula.

2. Then name the more electronegative element. To name it, add *-ide* to the stem name of the element. Chlorine, for example, becomes chloride, and oxygen becomes oxide.

3. Use the prefixes *di-, tri-, tetra-,* and so on to show the number of atoms of each element. The prefix *mono-* is omitted when it refers to the first atom named, and it is rarely used with the second atom. An exception to this rule is CO, which is named carbon monoxide.

The name is then written as two words.

Name of the first element in the formula; use prefixes *di-* and so forth if necessary	Name of the second element; use prefixes *mono-* and so forth if necessary

EXAMPLE 4.12

Name these binary covalent compounds:
(a) NO   (b) SF_2 (c) N_2O

Solution
(a) Nitrogen oxide (more commonly called nitric oxide)
(b) Sulfur difluoride
(c) Dinitrogen oxide (more commonly called nitrous oxide or laughing gas)

Problem 4.12

Name these binary covalent compounds:
(a) NO_2 (b) PBr_3 (c) SCl_2 (d) BF_3

CHEMICAL CONNECTIONS 4C

Nitric Oxide: Air Pollutant and Biological Messenger

Nitric oxide, NO, is a colorless gas whose importance in the environment has been known for several decades, but whose biological importance is only now being fully recognized. This molecule has 11 valence electrons. Because its number of electrons is odd, it is not possible to draw a structure for NO that obeys the octet rule; there must be one unpaired electron, here shown on the less electronegative nitrogen atom:

An unpaired ⟶ electron $:\ddot{N}=\ddot{O}:$

Nitric oxide

The importance of NO in the environment arises from the fact that it forms as a by-product during the combustion of fossil fuels. Under the temperature conditions of the internal combustion engine and other combustion sources, nitrogen and oxygen of the air react to form small quantities of NO:

$$N_2 + O_2 \xrightarrow{\text{heat}} 2NO$$

Nitric oxide

When inhaled, NO passes from the lungs into the bloodstream. There it interacts with the iron in hemoglobin, decreasing its ability to carry oxygen.

What makes nitric oxide so hazardous in the environment is that it reacts almost immediately with oxygen to form NO_2. When dissolved in water, NO_2 reacts with water to form nitric acid, which is a major acidifying component of acid rain.

$$2NO + O_2 \longrightarrow 2NO_2$$

Nitric oxide   Nitrogen dioxide

$$NO_2 + H_2O \longrightarrow HNO_3$$

Nitrogen dioxide   Nitric acid

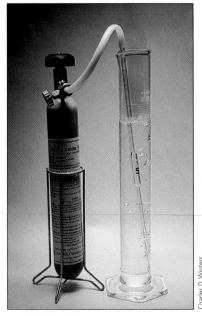

Colorless nitric oxide, NO, coming from the tank, bubbles through the water. When it reaches the air, it is oxidized to brown nitrogen dioxide, NO_2.

Imagine the surprise when it was discovered within the last two decades that this highly reactive, seemingly hazardous compound is synthesized in humans and plays a vital role as a signaling molecule in the cardiovascular system (Chemical Connections 24F).

4.9 | What Is Resonance?

As chemists developed a deeper understanding of covalent bonding in organic and inorganic compounds, it became obvious that, for a great many molecules and ions, no *single* Lewis structure provides a truly accurate representation. For example, Figure 4.3 shows three Lewis structures for the carbonate ion, CO_3^{2-}. In each structure, carbon is bonded to three oxygen

Figure 4.3 (a–c) Three Lewis structures for the carbonate ion.

(a)   (b)   (c)

atoms by a combination of one double bond and two single bonds. Each Lewis structure implies that one carbon-oxygen bond is different from the other two. However, this is not the case. It has been determined experimentally that all three carbon-oxygen bonds are identical.

The problem for chemists, then, is how to describe the structure of molecules and ions for which no single Lewis structure is adequate and yet still retain Lewis structures. As an answer to this problem, Linus Pauling proposed the theory of resonance.

A. Theory of Resonance

The theory of **resonance,** developed primarily by Pauling in the 1930s, provides an explanation. According to this theory, many molecules and ions are best described by writing two or more Lewis structures and considering the real molecule or ion to be a hybrid of these structures. Individual Lewis structures are called **contributing structures** (or sometimes **resonance structures** or **resonance contributors**). We show that the real molecule or ion is a **resonance hybrid** of the various contributing structures by interconnecting them with **double-headed arrows.** Do not confuse the double-headed arrow with the double arrow used to show chemical equilibrium. As we explain shortly, resonance structures are not in equilibrium with each other.

Figure 4.4 shows three contributing structures for the carbonate ion. These contributing structures are said to be equivalent; all three have identical patterns of covalent bonding.

Resonance A theory that many molecules and ions are best described as a hybrid of two or more Lewis contributing structures

Contributing structure Representations of a molecule or ion that differ only in the distribution of valence electrons

Resonance hybrid A molecule or ion described as a composite or hybrid of a number of contributing structures

Double-headed arrow A symbol used to show that the structures on either side of it are resonance contributing structures

HOW TO ...

Draw Curved Arrows and Push Electrons

Notice in Figure 4.4 that the only difference among contributing structures (a), (b), and (c) is the position of the valence electrons. To generate one resonance structure from another, chemists use a **curved arrow.** The arrow indicates where a pair of electrons originates (the tail of the arrow) and where it is repositioned in the next structure (the head of the arrow).

A curved arrow is nothing more than a bookkeeping symbol for keeping track of electron pairs or, as some call it, **electron pushing.** Do not be misled by its simplicity. Electron pushing will help you see the relationship among contributing structures.

Following are contributing structures for the nitrite and acetate ions. Curved arrows show how the contributing structures are interconverted. For each ion, the contributing structures are equivalent: They have the same bonding pattern.

Nitrite ion
(equivalent contributing structures)

Acetate ion
(equivalent contributing structures)

A common mistake is to use curved arrows to indicate the movement of atoms or positive charges. This is never correct. Curved arrows are used only to show the repositioning of electron pairs, when a new resonance hybrid is generated.

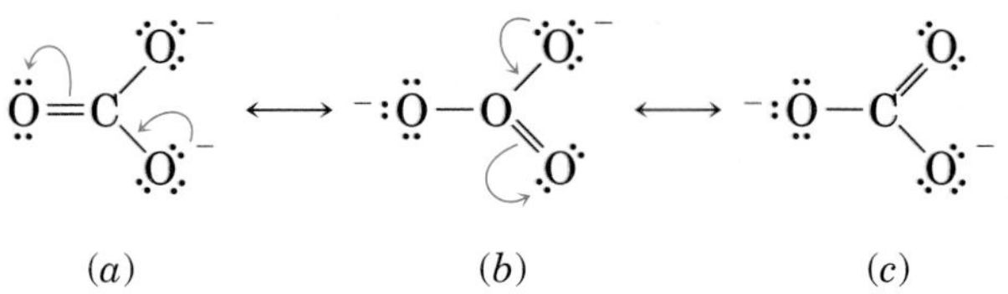

Figure 4.4 (*a–c*) The carbonate ion represented as a hybrid of three equivalent contributing structures. Curved arrows (in red) show how electron pairs are redistributed from one contributing structure to the next.

(*a*)   (*b*)   (*c*)

The use of the term "resonance" for this theory of covalent bonding might appear to suggest that bonds and electron pairs are constantly changing back and forth from one position to another over time. This notion is not at all correct. The carbonate ion, for example, has one—and only one—real structure. The problem is ours: How do we draw that one real structure? The resonance method offers a way to describe the real structure while simultaneously retaining Lewis structures with electron-pair bonds and showing all nonbonding pairs of electrons. Thus, although we realize that the carbonate ion is not accurately represented by any one contributing structure shown in Figure 4.4, we continue to represent it by one of these for convenience. We understand, of course, that we are referring to the resonance hybrid.

One consequence of resonance is that it is a stabilizing factor when it exists—that is, a resonance hybrid is more stable than chemists would estimate or calculate compared to any one of its contributing structures. We will see three particularly striking illustrations of the stability of resonance hybrids when we consider the unusual chemical properties of benzene and aromatic hydrocarbons in Chapter 13, the acidity of carboxylic acids in Chapter 18, and the geometry of the amide bonds in proteins in Chapter 19.

EXAMPLE 4.13

Draw the contributing structure indicated by the curved arrows. Be certain to show all valence electrons and all charges.

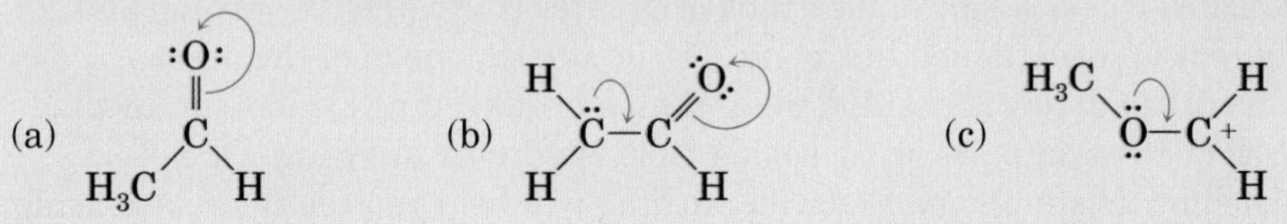

(a)   (b)   (c)

Solution

(a)   (b)   (c)

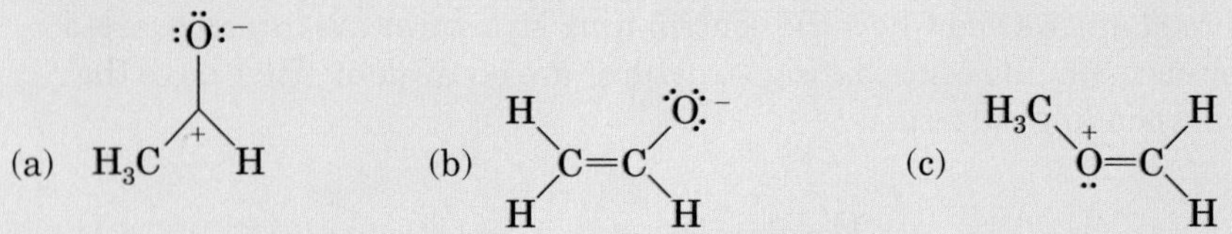

Problem 4.13

Draw the contributing structure indicated by the curved arrows. Be certain to show all valence electrons and all charges.

(a)   (b)   (c)

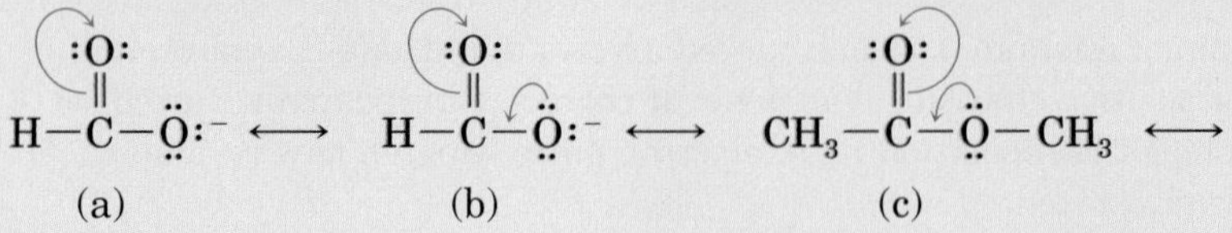

B. Writing Acceptable Contributing Structures

Certain rules must be followed to write acceptable contributing structures:

1. All contributing structures must have the same number of valence electrons.

2. All contributing structures must obey the rules of covalent bonding. In particular, no contributing structure may have more than two electrons in the valence shell of hydrogen or more than eight electrons in the valence shell of a second-period element. Third-period elements, such as phosphorus and sulfur, may have up to 12 electrons in their valence shells.

3. The positions of all nuclei must be the same in all resonance structures; that is, contributing structures must differ only in the distribution of valence electrons.

4. All contributing structures must have the same number of paired and unpaired electrons.

EXAMPLE 4.14

Which sets are valid pairs of contributing structures?

$$\text{(a)} \quad \underset{\substack{\|\\ \text{:O:}}}{\text{CH}_3-\text{C}-\text{CH}_3} \quad \text{and} \quad \underset{\substack{|\\ \text{:Ö:}^-\\ +}}{\text{CH}_3-\text{C}-\text{CH}_3}$$

$$\text{(b)} \quad \underset{\substack{\|\\ \text{:O:}}}{\text{CH}_3-\text{C}-\text{CH}_3} \quad \text{and} \quad \underset{\substack{|\\ \text{:Ö}-\text{H}}}{\text{CH}_2=\text{C}-\text{CH}_3}$$

Solution

(a) These are valid contributing structures. They differ only in the distribution of valence electrons.

(b) These are not valid contributing structures. They differ in the arrangement of their atoms.

Problem 4.14

Which sets are valid pairs of contributing structures?

(a) $\text{CH}_3-\text{C}\begin{smallmatrix}\nearrow \ddot{\text{O}} \\ \searrow \ddot{\text{O}}:^-\end{smallmatrix}$ and $\text{CH}_3-\overset{+}{\text{C}}\begin{smallmatrix}\nearrow \ddot{\text{O}}:^- \\ \searrow \ddot{\text{O}}:^-\end{smallmatrix}$

(b) $\text{CH}_3-\text{C}\begin{smallmatrix}\nearrow \ddot{\text{O}} \\ \searrow \ddot{\text{O}}:^-\end{smallmatrix}$ and $\text{CH}_3-\text{C}\begin{smallmatrix}\nearrow \ddot{\text{O}} \\ \searrow\!\!\searrow \ddot{\text{O}}\end{smallmatrix}$

A final note: Do not confuse resonance contributing structures with equilibration among different species. A molecule described as a resonance hybrid is not equilibrating among the individual electron configurations of the contributing structures. Rather, the molecule has only one structure, which is best described as a hybrid of its various contributing structures. The colors on the color wheel provide a good analogy. Purple is not a primary color; the primary colors of blue and red are mixed to make purple.

You can think of molecules represented by resonance hybrids as being purple. Purple is not sometimes blue and sometimes red: Purple is purple. In an analogous way, a molecule described as a resonance hybrid is not sometimes one contributing structure and sometimes another: It is a single structure all the time.

4.10 | How Do We Predict Bond Angles in Covalent Molecules?

In Section 4.7, we used a shared pair of electrons as the fundamental unit of covalent bonds and drew Lewis structures for several small molecules containing various combinations of single, double, and triple bonds (see, for example, Table 4.7). We can predict **bond angles** in these and other molecules by using the **valence-shell electron-pair repulsion (VSEPR) model.**

According to this model, the valence electrons of an atom may be involved in the formation of single, double, or triple bonds, or they may be unshared. Each combination creates a negatively charged region of electron density around the nucleus. Because like charges repel each other, the various regions of electron density around an atom spread out so that each is as far away as possible from the others.

You can demonstrate the bond angles predicted by this model in a very simple way. Imagine that a balloon represents a region of electron density. If two balloons are tied together by their ends, they assume the shapes shown in Figure 4.5. The point where they are tied together represents the atom about which you want to predict a bond angle, and the balloons represent regions of electron density about that atom.

We use the VSEPR model and the balloon model analogy in the following way to predict the shape of a molecule of methane, CH_4. The Lewis structure for CH_4 shows a carbon atom surrounded by four regions of electron density. Each region contains a pair of electrons forming a single covalent bond to a hydrogen atom. According to the VSEPR model, the four regions radiate from carbon so that they are as far away from one another as possible. The maximum separation occurs when the angle between any two regions of electron density is 109.5°. Therefore, we predict all H—C—H bond angles to be 109.5°, and the shape of the molecule to be **tetrahedral**

Bond angle The angle between two atoms bonded to a central atom

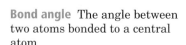
GOB
Chemistry⚛Now™
Click *Coached Problems* for an example of **Determining Molecular Shapes**

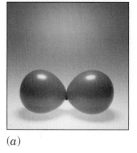
(*a*)

(*b*)

(*c*)

Charles D. Winters

GOB
Chemistry⚛Now™
Active Figure 4.5 Balloon models to predict bond angles. (*a*) Two balloons assume a linear shape with a bond angle of 180° about the tie point. (*b*) Three balloons assume a trigonal planar shape with bond angles of 120° about the tie point. (*c*) Four balloons assume a tetrahedral shape with bond angles of 109.5° about the tie point. **See a simulation based on this figure, and take a short quiz on the concepts at http://www.brookscole.com/gob8 or on the CD.**

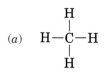

(a)

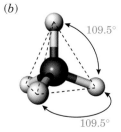

(b)
109.5°

109.5°

Figure 4.6 The shape of a methane molecule, CH_4. (*a*) Lewis structure and (*b*) ball-and-stick model. The hydrogens occupy the four corners of a regular tetrahedron, and all H—C—H bond angles are 109.5°.

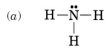

(a)

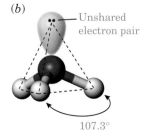

(b)
Unshared electron pair

107.3°

Figure 4.7 The shape of an ammonia molecule, NH_3. (*a*) Lewis structure and (*b*) ball-and-stick model. The H—N—H bond angles are 107.3°, slightly smaller than the H—C—H bond angles of methane.

(Figure 4.6). The H—C—H bond angles in methane have been measured experimentally and found to be 109.5°. Thus the bond angles and shape of methane predicted by the VSEPR model are identical to those observed experimentally.

We can predict the shape of an ammonia molecule, NH_3, in the same way. The Lewis structure of NH_3 shows nitrogen surrounded by four regions of electron density. Three regions contain single pairs of electrons that form covalent bonds with hydrogen atoms. The fourth region contains an unshared pair of electrons [Figure 4.7(a)]. Using the VSEPR model, we predict that the four regions are arranged in a tetrahedral manner and that the three H—N—H bond angles in this molecule are 109.5°. The observed bond angles are 107.3°. We can explain this small difference between the predicted and the observed angles by proposing that the unshared pair of electrons on nitrogen repels adjacent electron pairs more strongly than the bonding pairs repel one another.

The geometry of an ammonia molecule is described as **pyramidal;** that is, the molecule is shaped like a triangular-based pyramid with the three hydrogens located at the base and the single nitrogen located at the apex.

Figure 4.8 shows a Lewis structure and a ball-and-stick model of a water molecule. In H_2O, oxygen is surrounded by four regions of electron density. Two of these regions contain pairs of electrons used to form single covalent bonds to hydrogens; the remaining two regions contain unshared electron pairs. Using the VSEPR model, we predict that the four regions of electron density around oxygen are arranged in a tetrahedral manner and that the H—O—H bond angle is 109.5°. Experimental measurements show that the actual H—O—H bond angle in a water molecule is 104.5°, a value smaller than that predicted. We can explain this difference between the predicted and the observed bond angle by proposing, as we did for NH_3, that unshared pairs of electrons repel adjacent pairs more strongly than bonding pairs do. Note that the distortion from 109.5° is greater in H_2O, which has two unshared pairs of electrons, than it is in NH_3, which has only one unshared pair.

A general prediction emerges from this discussion. If a Lewis structure shows four regions of electron density around an atom, the VSEPR model predicts a tetrahedral distribution of electron density and bond angles of approximately 109.5°.

(a)

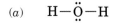

(b)
Unshared electron pairs

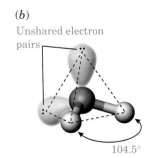

104.5°

Figure 4.8 The shape of a water molecule, H_2O. (*a*) Lewis structure and (*b*) ball-and-stick model.

Formaldehyde

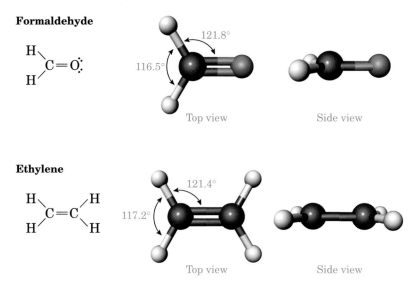

Figure 4.9 The shapes of formaldehyde, CH$_2$O, and ethylene, C$_2$H$_4$.

Ammonia gas is drilled into the soil of a farm field. Most of the ammonia manufactured in the world is used as fertilizer because ammonia supplies the nitrogen needed by green plants.

Arthur C. Smith III/Grant Heilman Photography

In many of the molecules we will encounter, an atom is surrounded by three regions of electron density. Figure 4.9 shows Lewis structures and ball-and-stick models for molecules of formaldehyde, CH$_2$O, and ethylene, C$_2$H$_4$.

In the VSEPR model, we treat a double bond as a single region of electron density. In formaldehyde, carbon is surrounded by three regions of electron density. Two regions contain single pairs of electrons, each of which forms a single bond to a hydrogen; the third region contains two pairs of electrons, which form a double bond to oxygen. In ethylene, each carbon atom is also surrounded by three regions of electron density; two contain single pairs of electrons, and the third contains two pairs of electrons.

Three regions of electron density about an atom are farthest apart when they lie in a plane and make angles of 120° with one another. Thus the predicted H—C—H and H—C—O bond angles in formaldehyde and the H—C—H and H—C—C bond angles in ethylene are all 120°. Furthermore, all atoms in each molecule lie in a plane. Thus, both formaldehyde and ethylene are planar molecules. The geometry about an atom surrounded by three regions of electron density, as in formaldehyde and ethylene, is described as **trigonal planar.**

In still other types of molecules, a central atom is surrounded by two regions of electron density. Figure 4.10 shows Lewis structures and ball-and-stick models of molecules of carbon dioxide, CO$_2$, and acetylene, C$_2$H$_2$.

In carbon dioxide, carbon is surrounded by two regions of electron density; each contains two pairs of electrons and forms a double bond to an

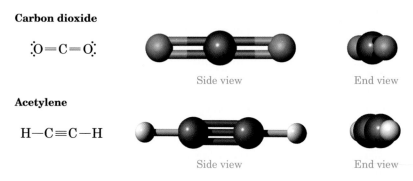

Figure 4.10 The shapes of carbon dioxide, CO$_2$, and acetylene, C$_2$H$_2$.

Table 4.8   Predicted Molecular Shapes (VSEPR model)

Regions of Electron Density Around Central Atom	Predicted Distribution of Electron Density	Predicted Bond Angles	Examples (Shape of the Molecule)
4	Tetrahedral	109.5°	Methane (tetrahedral) Ammonia (pyramidal) Water (bent)
3	Trigonal planar	120°	Ethylene (planar) Formaldehyde (planar)
2	Linear	180°	Carbon dioxide (linear) Acetylene (linear)

oxygen atom. In acetylene, each carbon is also surrounded by two regions of electron density; one contains a single pair of electrons and forms a single bond to a hydrogen atom, and the other contains three pairs of electrons and forms a triple bond to a carbon atom. In each case, the two regions of electron density are farthest apart if they form a straight line through the central atom and create an angle of 180°. Both carbon dioxide and acetylene are linear molecules.

Table 4.8 summarizes the predictions of the VSEPR model. In this table, three-dimensional shapes are shown using a solid wedge to represent a bond coming toward you, out of the plane of the paper. A broken wedge represents a bond going away from you, behind the plane of the paper. A single line represents a bond in the plane of the paper.

EXAMPLE 4.15

Predict all bond angles and the shape of each molecule:
(a) CH_3Cl (b) $CH_2=CHCl$

Solution
(a) The Lewis structure for CH_3Cl shows that carbon is surrounded by four regions of electron density. Therefore, we predict that the distribution of electron pairs about carbon is tetrahedral, all bond angles are 109.5°, and the shape of CH_3Cl is tetrahedral.

(b) In the Lewis structure for $CH_2=CHCl$, each carbon is surrounded by three regions of electron density. Therefore, we predict that all bond angles are 120° and that the molecule is planar. The bonding about each carbon is trigonal planar.

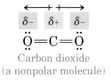

(Top view)   (Viewed along the C═C bond)

Problem 4.15

Predict all bond angles for these molecules:
(a) CH_3OH (b) CH_2Cl_2 (c) H_2CO_3 (carbonic acid)

4.11 | How Do We Determine if a Molecule Is Polar?

In Section 4.7B, we used the terms "polar" and "dipole" to describe a covalent bond in which one atom bears a partial positive charge and the other bears a partial negative charge. We also saw that we can use the difference in electronegativity between bonded atoms to determine the polarity of a covalent bond and the direction of its dipole. We can now combine our understanding of bond polarity and molecular geometry (Section 4.10) to predict the polarity of molecules. To discuss the physical and chemical properties of a molecule, it is essential to have an understanding of polarity. Many chemical reactions, for example, are driven by the interaction of the positive part of one molecule with the negative part of another molecule.

A molecule will be polar if (1) it has polar bonds and (2) its centers of partial positive charge and partial negative charge lie at different places within the molecule. Consider first carbon dioxide, CO_2, a molecule with two polar carbon-oxygen double bonds. The oxygen on the left pulls electrons of the O═C bond toward it, giving it a partial negative charge. Similarly, the oxygen on the right pulls electrons of the C═O bond toward it by the same amount, giving it the same partial negative charge as the oxygen on the left. Carbon bears a partial positive charge. We can show the polarity of these bonds by using the symbols $\delta+$ and $\delta-$. Alternatively, we can show that each carbon-oxygen bond has a dipole by using an arrow, where the head of the arrow points to the negative end of the dipole and the crossed tail is positioned at the positive end of the dipole. Because carbon dioxide is a linear molecule, its centers of negative and positive partial charge coincide. Therefore, CO_2 is a nonpolar molecule; that is, it has no dipole.

$$\overset{\displaystyle \longleftarrow +\ +\longrightarrow}{\underset{\substack{\ddot{\text{O}}=\text{C}=\ddot{\text{O}}}}{\delta-\quad \delta+\quad \delta-}}$$

Carbon dioxide
(a nonpolar molecule)

In a water molecule, each O—H bond is polar. Oxygen, the more electronegative atom, bears a partial negative charge and each hydrogen bears a partial positive charge. The center of partial positive charge in a water molecule is located halfway between the two hydrogen atoms, and the center of partial negative charge is on the oxygen atom. Thus a water molecule has polar bonds and, because of its geometry, is a polar molecule.

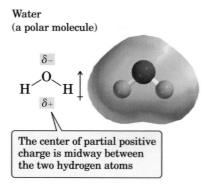

Water
(a polar molecule)

The center of partial positive charge is midway between the two hydrogen atoms

Ammonia has three polar N—H bonds. Because of its geometry, the centers of partial positive and partial negative charges are found at different places within the molecule. Thus ammonia has polar bonds and, because of its geometry, is a polar molecule.

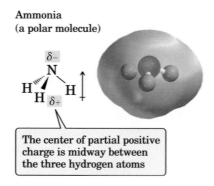

Ammonia
(a polar molecule)

The center of partial positive charge is midway between the three hydrogen atoms

EXAMPLE 4.16

Which of these molecules are polar? Show the direction of the molecular dipole by using an arrow with a crossed tail.
(a) CH_2Cl_2 (b) CH_2O (c) C_2H_2

Solution
Both dichloromethane, CH_2Cl_2, and formaldehyde, CH_2O, have polar bonds and, because of their geometry, are polar molecules. Because acetylene, C_2H_2, contains no polar bonds, it is a nonpolar molecule.

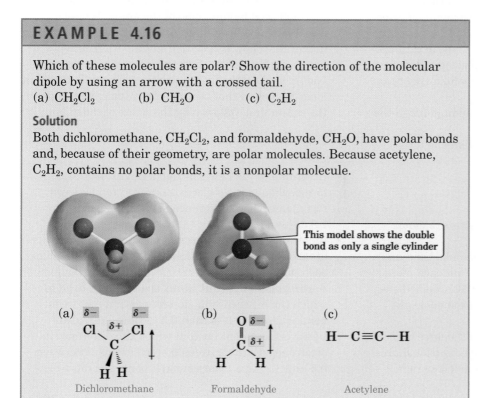

This model shows the double bond as only a single cylinder

(a)   Dichloromethane

(b)   Formaldehyde

(c) $H—C{\equiv}C—H$ Acetylene

Problem 4.16

Which of these molecules are polar? Show the direction of the molecular dipole by using an arrow with a crossed tail.
(a) CH_3Cl (b) HCN (c) C_2H_6

SUMMARY OF KEY QUESTIONS

SECTION 4.2 What Is the Octet Rule?

- The **octet rule** states that elements of Groups 1A–7A tend to gain or lose electrons so as to achieve an outer shell containing eight valence electrons.
- An atom with almost eight valence electrons tends to gain the needed electrons to have eight electrons in its valence shell—that is, to achieve the same electron configuration as the noble gas nearest to it in atomic number. In gaining electrons, the atom becomes a negatively charged ion called an **anion.**
- An atom with only one or two valence electrons tends to lose the number of electrons required to have eight valence electrons in its next lower shell—that is, to have the same electron configuration as the noble gas nearest it in atomic number. In losing electrons, the atom becomes a positively charged ion called a **cation.**

SECTION 4.3 How Do We Name Anions and Cations?

- For metals that form only one type of cation, the name of the cation is the name of the metal followed by the word "ion."
- For metals that form more than one type of cation, we show the charge on the ion by placing a Roman numeral in parentheses immediately following the name of the metal.
- A **monatomic anion** is named by adding -*ide* to the stem part of the name.
- A **polyatomic ion** contains more than one type of atom.

SECTION 4.4 What Are the Two Major Types of Chemical Bonds?

- The two major types of chemical bonds are ionic bonds and covalent bonds.
- According to the Lewis model of chemical bonding, atoms bond together in such a way that each atom participating in a bond acquires a valence-shell electron configuration matching that of the noble gas nearest to it in atomic number.
- **Electronegativity** is a measure of the force of attraction that an atom exerts on electrons it shares in a chemical bond. It increases from left to right

across a row and from bottom to top in a column of the Periodic Table.
- An **ionic bond** forms between two atoms if the difference in electronegativity between them is greater than 1.9.
- A **covalent bond** forms if the difference in electronegativity between the bonded atoms is 1.9 or less.

SECTION 4.5 What Is an Ionic Bond and How Does One Form?

- An **ionic bond** forms by the transfer of valence-shell electrons from an atom of lower electronegativity to the valence shell of an atom of higher electronegativity.
- In an ionic compound, the total number of positive charges must equal the total number of negative charges.

SECTION 4.6 How Do We Name Ionic Compounds?

- For a **binary ionic compound,** name the cation first, followed by the name of the anion. Where a metal ion may form different cations, use a Roman numeral to show its positive charge. Alternatively, use the suffix -*ous* to show the lower positive charge, and -*ic* to show the higher positive charge. To name an ionic compound that contains polyatomic ions, name the cation first, followed by the name of the anion.

SECTION 4.7 What Is a Covalent Bond and How Does One Form?

- According to the Lewis model, a **covalent bond** forms when pairs of electrons are shared between two atoms whose difference in electronegativity is 1.9 or less.
- A pair of electrons in a covalent bond is shared by two atoms and at the same time fills the valence shell of each atom.
- A **nonpolar covalent bond** is a covalent bond in which the difference in electronegativity between bonded atoms is less than 0.5. A **polar covalent bond** is a covalent bond in which the difference in electronegativity between bonded atoms is between 0.5 and 1.9. In a polar covalent bond, the more elec-

tronegative atom bears a partial negative charge (δ^-) and the less electronegative atom bears a partial positive charge (δ^+). This separation of charge produces a **dipole.**

- A **Lewis structure** for a covalent compound must show (1) the correct arrangement of atoms, (2) the correct number of valence electrons, (3) no more than two electrons in the outer shell of hydrogen, and (4) no more than eight electrons in the outer shell of any period 2 element.

- Exceptions to the octet rule include compounds of period 3 elements, such as phosphorus and sulfur, which may have as many as 10 and 12 electrons, respectively, in their valence shells.

SECTION 4.8 How Do We Name Binary Covalent Compounds?

- To name a **binary covalent compound,** name the less electronegative element first, followed by the name of the more electronegative element. The name of the more electronegative element is derived by adding *-ide* to the stem name of the element. Use the prefixes *di-, tri-, tetra-,* and so on to show the presence of two or more atoms of the same kind.

SECTION 4.9 What Is Resonance?

- According to the theory of resonance, a molecule or ion for which no single Lewis structure is adequate is best described by writing two or more **resonance contributing structures** and considering the real molecule or ion to be a hybrid of these contributing structures. To show how valence electrons are redistributed from one contributing structure to the next, we use curved arrows. A curved arrow extends from where the electrons are initially shown (on an atom or in a covalent bond) to their new location (on an adjacent atom or an adjacent covalent bond).

SECTION 4.10 How Do We Predict Bond Angles in Covalent Molecules?

- The **valence-shell electron-pair repulsion (VSEPR) model** predicts bond angles of 109.5° about atoms surrounded by four regions of electron density; angles of 120° about atoms surrounded by three regions of electron density; and angles of 180° about atoms surrounded by two regions of electron density.

SECTION 4.11 How Do We Determine if a Molecule Is Polar?

- A molecule is polar (has a dipole) if it has polar bonds and the centers of partial positive and partial negative charge do not coincide.

- If a molecule has polar bonds but the centers of partial positive and negative charges coincide, the molecule is nonpolar (it has no dipole).

PROBLEMS

GOB Chemistry ⬩Now™

Assess your understanding of this chapter's topics with additional quizzing and conceptual-based problems at **http://now.brookscole.com/gob8** or on the CD.

A blue problem number indicates an applied problem.

■ denotes problems that are available on the GOB ChemistryNow website or CD and are assignable in OWL.

SECTION 4.2 What Is the Octet Rule?

4.17 How many electrons must each atom gain or lose to acquire an electron configuration identical to the noble gas nearest to it in atomic number?
  (a) Li (b) Cl (c) P (d) Al
  (e) Sr (f) S (g) Si (h) O

4.18 Show how each chemical change obeys the octet rule.
  (a) Lithium forms Li^+
  (b) Oxygen forms O^{2-}

4.19 Show how each chemical change obeys the octet rule.
  (a) Hydrogen forms H^- (hydride ion)
  (b) Aluminum forms Al^{3+}

4.20 Write the formula for the most stable ion formed by each element.
  (a) Mg (b) F (c) Al
  (d) S (e) K (f) Br

4.21 Why is Li^- not a stable ion?

4.22 Predict which ions are stable:
  (a) I^- (b) Se^{2+} (c) Na^+
  (d) S^{2-} (e) Li^{2+} (f) Ba^{3+}

4.23 Predict which ions are stable:
  (a) Br^{2-} (b) C^{4-} (c) Ca^+
  (d) Ar^+ (e) Na^- (f) Cs^+

4.24 Why are carbon and silicon reluctant to form ionic bonds?

4.25 Table 4.2 shows the following ions of copper: Cu^+ and Cu^{2+}. Do these violate the octet rule? Explain.

SECTION 4.3 How Do We Name Anions and Cations?

4.26 ■ Name each polyatomic ion.
  (a) HCO_3^- (b) NO_2^- (c) SO_4^{2-}
  (d) HSO_4^- (e) $H_2PO_4^-$

SECTION 4.4 What Are the Two Major Types of Chemical Bonds?

4.27 Why does electronegativity generally increase in going up a column of the Periodic Table?

4.28 Why does electronegativity generally increase in going from left to right across a row of the Periodic Table?

4.29 Judging from their relative positions in the Periodic Table, which element in each pair has the larger electronegativity?
(a) F or Cl   (b) O or S   (c) C or N   (d) C or F

4.30 Toward which atom are the electrons shifted in a covalent bond between each of the following pairs:
(a) H and Cl   (b) N and O   (c) C and O
(d) Cl and Br   (e) C and S   (f) P and S
(g) H and O

4.31 Which of these bonds is the most polar? The least polar?
(a) C—N   (b) C—C (c) C—O

4.32 Classify each bond as nonpolar covalent, polar covalent, or ionic.
(a) C—Cl   (b) C—Li   (c) C—N

4.33 Classify each bond as nonpolar covalent, polar covalent, or ionic.
(a) C—Br   (b) S—Cl   (c) C—P

SECTION 4.5 What Is an Ionic Bond and How Does One Form?

4.34 Complete the chart by writing formulas for the compounds formed:

	Br⁻	ClO₄⁻	O²⁻	NO₃⁻	SO₄²⁻	PO₄³⁻	OH⁻
Li⁺							
Ca²⁺							
Co³⁺							
K⁺							
Cu²⁺							

4.35 ■ Write a formula for the ionic compound formed from each pair of elements.
(a) Sodium and bromine
(b) Sodium and oxygen
(c) Aluminum and chlorine
(d) Barium and chlorine
(e) Magnesium and oxygen

4.36 Although not a transition metal, lead can form Pb^{2+} and Pb^{4+} ions. Write the formula for the compound formed between each of these lead ions and the following anions:
(a) Chloride ion   (b) Hydroxide ion
(c) Oxide ion

4.37 Describe the structure of sodium chloride in the solid state.

4.38 What is the charge on each ion in these compounds?
(a) CaS   (b) MgF_2 (c) Cs_2O
(d) $ScCl_3$ (e) Al_2S_3

4.39 ■ Write the formula for the compound formed from the following pairs of ions:
(a) Iron(III) ion and hydroxide ion
(b) Barium ion and chloride ion
(c) Calcium ion and phosphate ion
(d) Sodium ion and permanganate ion

4.40 Write the formula for the ionic compound formed from the following pairs of ions:
(a) Iron(II) ion and chloride ion
(b) Calcium ion and hydroxide ion
(c) Ammonium ion and phosphate ion
(d) Tin(II) ion and fluoride ion

4.41 Which formulas are not correct? For each that is not correct, write the correct formula.
(a) Ammonium phosphate; $(NH_4)_2PO_4$
(b) Barium carbonate; Ba_2CO_3
(c) Aluminum sulfide; Al_2S_3
(d) Magnesium sulfide; MgS

4.42 Which formulas are not correct? For each that is not correct, write the correct formula.
(a) Calcium oxide; CaO_2
(b) Lithium oxide; LiO
(c) Sodium hydrogen phosphate; $NaHPO_4$
(d) Ammonium nitrate; NH_4NO_3

SECTION 4.6 How Do We Name Ionic Compounds?

4.43 Potassium chloride and potassium bicarbonate are used as potassium supplements. Write the formula of each compound.

4.44 Potassium nitrite has been used as a vasodilator and as an antidote for cyanide poisoning. Write the formula of this compound.

4.45 Name the polyatomic ion in each compound.
(a) Na_2SO_3 (b) KNO_3 (c) Cs_2CO_3
(d) NH_4OH (e) K_2HPO_4

4.46 Write the formulas for the ions present in each compound.
(a) NaBr   (b) $FeSO_3$
(c) $Mg_3(PO_4)_2$ (d) KH_2PO_4
(e) $NaHCO_3$ (f) $Ba(NO_3)_2$

4.47 Name these ionic compounds:
(a) NaF   (b) MgS
(c) Al_2O_3 (d) $BaCl_2$
(e) $Ca(HSO_3)_2$ (f) KI
(g) $Sr_3(PO_4)_2$ (h) $Fe(OH)_2$
(i) NaH_2PO_4 (j) $Pb(CH_3COO)_2$
(k) BaH_2 (l) $(NH_4)_2HPO_4$

4.48 ■ Write formulas for the following ionic compounds:
(a) Potassium bromide   (b) Calcium oxide
(c) Mercury(II) oxide   (d) Copper(II) phosphate
(e) Lithium sulfate   (f) Iron(III) sulfide

4.49 Write formulas for the following ionic compounds:
(a) Ammonium hydrogen sulfite
(b) Magnesium acetate
(c) Strontium dihydrogen phosphate
(d) Silver carbonate
(e) Strontium chloride
(f) Barium permanganate

SECTION 4.7 What Is a Covalent Bond and How Does One Form?

4.50 How many covalent bonds are normally formed by each element?
(a) N   (b) F   (c) C
(d) Br   (e) O

4.51 What is
(a) A single bond?
(b) A double bond?
(c) A triple bond?

4.52 In Section 2.3B, we saw that there are seven diatomic elements.
(a) Draw Lewis structures for each of these diatomic elements.
(b) Which diatomic elements are gases at room temperature? Which are liquids? Which are solids?

4.53 ■ Draw a Lewis structure for each covalent compound.
(a) CH_4 (b) C_2H_2 (c) C_2H_4
(d) BF_3 (e) CH_2O (f) C_2Cl_6

4.54 What is the difference between a molecular formula, a structural formula, and a Lewis structure?

4.55 ■ Write the total number of valence electrons in each molecule.
(a) NH_3 (b) C_3H_6 (c) $C_2H_4O_2$ (d) C_2H_6O
(e) CCl_4 (f) HNO_2 (g) CCl_2F_2 (h) O_2

4.56 ■ Draw a Lewis structure for each of the following molecules. In each case, the atoms can be connected in only one way.
(a) Br_2 (b) H_2S (c) N_2H_4 (d) N_2H_2
(e) CN^- (f) NH_4^+ (g) N_2 (h) O_2

4.57 What is the difference between (a) a bromine atom, (b) a bromine molecule, and (c) a bromide ion? Draw the Lewis structure for each.

4.58 Acetylene (C_2H_2), hydrogen cyanide (HCN), and nitrogen (N_2) each contain a triple bond. Draw a Lewis structure for each molecule.

4.59 Why can't hydrogen have more than two electrons in its valence shell?

4.60 Why can't second-row elements have more than eight electrons in their valence shells? That is, why does the octet rule work for second-row elements?

4.61 Why does nitrogen have three bonds and one unshared pair of electrons in covalent compounds?

4.62 Draw a Lewis structure of a covalent compound in which nitrogen has
(a) Three single bonds and one pair of electrons
(b) One single bond, one double bond, and one unshared pair of electrons
(c) One triple bond and one unshared pair of electrons

4.63 Why does oxygen have two bonds and two unshared pairs of electrons in covalent compounds?

4.64 Draw a Lewis structure of a covalent compound in which oxygen has
(a) Two single bonds and two unshared pairs of electrons
(b) One double bond and two unshared pairs of electrons

4.65 The ion O^{6+} has a complete outer shell. Why is this ion not stable?

4.66 Draw a Lewis structure for a molecule in which a carbon atom is bonded by a double bond to (a) another carbon atom, (b) an oxygen atom, and (c) a nitrogen atom.

4.67 Which of the following molecules have an atom that does not obey the octet rule (not all these are stable molecules)?
(a) BF_3 (b) CF_2 (c) BeF_2 (d) C_2H_4
(e) CH_3 (f) N_2 (g) NO

SECTION 4.8 How Do We Name Binary Covalent Compounds?

4.68 Name these binary covalent compounds.
(a) SO_2 (b) SO_3 (c) PCl_3 (d) CS_2

SECTION 4.9 What Is Resonance?

4.69 Write two acceptable contributing structures for the bicarbonate ion, HCO_3^- and show by the use of curved arrows how the first contributing structure is converted to the second.

4.70 Ozone, O_3, is an unstable blue gas with a characteristic pungent odor. In an ozone molecule, the connectivity of the atoms is O—O—O, and both O—O bonds are equivalent.
(a) How many valence electrons must be present in an acceptable Lewis structure for an ozone molecule?
(b) Write two equivalent resonance contributing structures for ozone. Be certain to show any positive or negative charges that may be present in your contributing structures. By *equivalent contributing structures*, we mean that each has the same pattern of bonding

(c) Show by the use of curved arrows how the first of your contributing structures may be converted to the second.

(d) Based on your contributing structures, predict the O—O—O bond angle in ozone.

(e) Explain why the following is not an acceptable contributing structure for an ozone molecule:

$$\ddot{O}=\ddot{O}=\ddot{O}$$

4.71 ■ Nitrous oxide, N_2O, laughing gas, is a colorless, nontoxic, tasteless, and odorless gas. It is used as an inhalation anesthetic in dental and other surgeries. Because nitrous oxide is soluble in vegetable oils (fats), it is used commercially as a propellant in whipped cream toppings.

Charles D. Winters

Nitrous oxide dissolves in fats. The gas is added under pressure to cans of whipped topping. When the valve is opened, the gas expands, thus expanding (whipping) the topping and forcing it out of the can.

(a) How many valence electrons are present in a molecule of N_2O?

(b) Write two equivalent contributing structures for this molecule. The connectivity in nitrous oxide is N—N—O.

(c) Explain why the following is not an acceptable contributing structure:

$$:N\equiv N=\ddot{O}$$

SECTION 4.10 How Do We Predict Bond Angles in Covalent Molecules?

4.72 State the shape of a molecule whose central atom is surrounded by
(a) Two regions of electron density
(b) Three regions of electron density
(c) Four regions of electron density

4.73 Hydrogen and oxygen combine in different ratios to form H_2O (water) and H_2O_2 (hydrogen peroxide).
(a) How many valence electrons are found in H_2O? In H_2O_2?
(b) Draw Lewis structures for each molecule in part (a). Be certain to show all valence electrons.
(c) Using the VSEPR model, predict the bond angles about the oxygen atom in water and about each oxygen atom in hydrogen peroxide.

4.74 Hydrogen and nitrogen combine in different ratios to form three compounds: NH_3 (ammonia), N_2H_4 (hydrazine), and N_2H_2 (diimide).
(a) How many valence electrons must the Lewis structure of each molecule show?
(b) Draw a Lewis structure for each molecule.
(c) Predict the bond angles about the nitrogen atom(s) in each molecule.

4.75 Predict the shape of each molecule.
(a) CH_4 (b) PH_3 (c) CHF_3 (d) SO_2
(e) SO_3 (f) CCl_2F_2 (g) NH_3 (h) PCl_3

4.76 Predict the shape of each ion.
(a) NO_2^- (b) NH_4^+ (c) CO_3^{2-}

SECTION 4.11 How Do We Determine if a Molecule Is Polar?

4.77 Both CO_2 and SO_2 have polar bonds. Account for the fact that CO_2 is nonpolar and SO_2 is polar.

4.78 Consider the molecule boron trifluoride, BF_3.
(a) Write a Lewis structure for BF_3.
(b) Predict the F—B—F bond angles using the VSEPR model.
(c) Does BF_3 have polar bonds? Is it a polar molecule?

4.79 Is it possible for a molecule to have polar bonds and yet have no dipole? Explain.

4.80 Is it possible for a molecule to have no polar bonds and yet have a dipole? Explain.

4.81 ■ In each case, tell whether the bond is ionic, polar covalent, or nonpolar covalent.
(a) Br_2 (b) BrCl   (c) HCl   (d) SrF_2
(e) SiH_4 (f) CO   (g) N_2 (h) CsCl

4.82 Account for the fact that chloromethane, CH_3Cl, which has only one polar C—Cl bond, is a polar molecule, but carbon tetrachloride, CCl_4, which has four polar C—Cl bonds, is a nonpolar molecule.

Chemical Connections

4.83 (Chemical Connections 4A) What are the three main inorganic components of one dry mixture currently used to create synthetic bone?

4.84 (Chemical Connections 4B) Why is sodium iodide often present in the table salt we buy at the grocery store?

4.85 (Chemical Connections 4B) What is a medical use of barium sulfate?

4.86 (Chemical Connections 4B) What is a medical use of potassium permanganate?

4.87 (Chemical Connections 4A) What is the main metal ion present in bone and tooth enamel?

4.88 (Chemical Connections 4C) In what way does the gas nitric oxide, NO, contribute to the acidity of acid rain?

Additional Problems

4.89 Explain why argon does not form either (a) ionic bonds or (b) covalent bonds.

4.90 Knowing what you do about covalent bonding in compounds of carbon, nitrogen, and oxygen, and given the fact that silicon is just below carbon in the Periodic Table, phosphorus is just below nitrogen, and sulfur is just below oxygen, predict the molecular formula for the compound formed by (a) silicon and chlorine, (b) phosphorus and hydrogen, and (c) sulfur and hydrogen.

4.91 ■ Use the valence-shell electron-pair repulsion model to predict the shape of a molecule in which a central atom is surrounded by five regions of electron density—as, for example, in phosphorus pentafluoride, PF_5. (*Hint:* Use molecular models or, if you do not have a set handy, use a marshmallow or gumdrop and toothpicks.)

4.92 Use the valence-shell electron-pair repulsion model to predict the shape of a molecule in which a central atom is surrounded by six regions of electron density—as, for example, in sulfur hexafluoride, SF_6.

4.93 Chlorine dioxide, ClO_2, is a yellow to reddish yellow gas at room temperature. This strong oxidizing agent is used for bleaching cellulose, paper pulp, and textiles, and for water purification. It was the gas used to kill anthrax spores in the anthrax-contaminated Hart Senate Office Building.
   (a) How many valence electrons are present in ClO_2?
   (b) Draw a Lewis structure for this molecule. (*Hint:* The order of attachment of atoms in this molecule is O—Cl—O. Chlorine is a period 3 element, and its valence shell may contain more than eight electrons.)

Reading Labels

4.94 Name and write the formula for the fluorine-containing compound present in fluoridated toothpastes and dental gels.

4.95 If you read the labels of sun-blocking lotions, you will find that a common UV-blocking agent is a compound containing zinc. Name and write the formula of this zinc-containing compound.

4.96 On packaged table salt, it is common to see a label stating that the salt "supplies iodide, a necessary nutrient." Name and write the formula of the iodine-containing compound found in iodized salt.

4.97 We are constantly warned about the dangers of "lead-based" paints. Name and write the formula for a lead-containing compound found in lead-based paints.

4.98 If you read the labels of several liquid and tablet antacid preparations, you will find that in many of them, the active ingredients are compounds containing hydroxide ions. Name and write formulas for these hydroxide ion–containing compounds.

4.99 Iron forms Fe^{2+} and Fe^{3+} ions. Which ion is found in the over-the-counter preparations intended to treat "iron-poor blood"?

4.100 Read the labels of several multivitamin/multimineral formulations. Among their components you will find a number of so-called trace minerals—minerals required in the diet of a healthy adult in amounts less than 100 mg per day, or present in the body in amounts less than 0.01 percent of total body weight. Following are 18 trace minerals. Name at least one form of each trace mineral present in multivitamin formulations.

   (a) Phosphorus   (b) Magnesium
   (c) Potassium   (d) Iron
   (e) Calcium   (f) Zinc
   (g) Manganese   (h) Titanium
   (i) Silicon   (j) Copper
   (k) Boron   (l) Molybdenum
   (m) Chromium   (n) Iodine
   (o) Selenium   (p) Vanadium
   (q) Nickel   (r) Tin

4.101 Write formulas for these compounds.
   (a) Calcium sulfite, which is used in preserving cider and other fruit juices
   (b) Calcium hydrogen sulfite, which is used in dilute aqueous solutions for washing casks in brewing to prevent souring and cloudiness of beer and to prevent secondary fermentation
   (c) Calcium hydroxide, which is used in mortar, plaster, cement, and other building and paving materials
   (d) Calcium hydrogen phosphate, which is used in animal feeds and as a mineral supplement in cereals and other foods

4.102 Many paint pigments contain transition metal compounds. Name the compounds in these pigments using a Roman numeral to show the charge on the metal ion.
   (a) Yellow, CdS (b) Green, Cr_2O_3
   (c) White, TiO_2 (d) Purple, $Mn_3(PO_4)_2$
   (e) Blue, Co_2O_3 (f) Ochre, Fe_2O_3

Looking Ahead

4.103 Perchloroethylene, which is a liquid at room temperature, is one of the most widely used solvents for commercial dry cleaning. It is sold for this purpose under several trade names, including Perclene. Does this molecule have polar bonds? Is it a polar molecule? Does it have a dipole?

$$\begin{array}{ccc} Cl & & Cl \\ & C{=}C & \\ Cl & & Cl \end{array}$$
Perchloroethylene

4.104 Vinyl chloride is the starting material for the production of poly(vinyl chloride), abbreviated PVC. Its recycling code is "V". The major use of PVC is for tubing in residential and commercial construction (Section 12.7).

$$\begin{array}{ccc} H & & Cl \\ & C{=}C & \\ H & & H \end{array}$$
Vinyl chloride

(a) Complete the Lewis structure for vinyl chloride by showing all unshared pairs of electrons.

(b) Predict the H—C—H, H—C—C, and Cl—C—H, bond angles in this molecule.

(c) Does vinyl chloride have polar bonds? Is it a polar molecule? Does it have a dipole?

4.105 Tetrafluoroethylene is the starting material for the production of poly(tetrafluoroethylene), a polymer that is widely used for the preparation of nonstick coatings on kitchenware (Section 12.7). The most widely known trade name for this product is Teflon.

$$\begin{array}{c} \text{F} \qquad\qquad \text{F} \\ \diagdown \qquad\quad \diagup \\ \text{C}{=}\text{C} \\ \diagup \qquad\quad \diagdown \\ \text{F} \qquad\qquad \text{F} \end{array}$$

Tetrafluoroethylene

(a) Complete the Lewis structure for tetrafluoroethylene by showing all unshared pairs of electrons.

(b) Predict the F—C—F and F—C—C bond angles in this molecule.

(c) Does tetrafluoroethylene have polar bonds? Is it a polar molecule? Does it have a dipole?

4.106 Some of the following structural formulas are incorrect because they contain one or more atoms that do not have their normal number of covalent bonds. Which structural formulas are incorrect, and which atom or atoms in each have the incorrect number of bonds?

(a)
$$\begin{array}{c} \quad\;\; \text{H} \;\; \text{H} \\ \quad\;\; | \quad\; | \\ \text{Cl}{-}\text{C}{=}\text{C}{-}\text{H} \\ \quad\;\; | \\ \quad\;\; \text{H} \end{array}$$

(b)
$$\begin{array}{c} \qquad\qquad \text{H} \qquad\qquad\;\; \text{H} \\ \qquad\qquad | \qquad\qquad\;\; | \\ \text{H}{-}\text{O}{-}\text{C}{-}\text{C}{-}\text{N}{-}\text{C}{-}\text{H} \\ \qquad\qquad | \quad\; | \quad\; | \quad\; | \\ \qquad\qquad \text{H} \;\; \text{H} \;\; \text{H} \;\; \text{H} \end{array}$$

(c)
$$\begin{array}{c} \qquad\; \text{H} \qquad\qquad \text{H} \\ \qquad\; | \qquad\qquad | \\ \text{H}{-}\text{C}{-}\text{N}{-}\text{C}{-}\text{C}{-}\text{O} \\ \qquad\; | \quad\; | \quad\; | \quad\; | \\ \qquad\; \text{H} \;\; \text{H} \;\; \text{H} \;\; \text{H} \end{array}$$

(d)
$$\begin{array}{c} \qquad\qquad\; \text{H} \qquad\qquad \text{H} \\ \qquad\qquad\; | \qquad\qquad | \\ \text{F}{=}\text{C}{-}\text{C}{-}\text{O}{-}\text{C}{-}\text{H} \\ \quad\; | \quad\; | \qquad\quad | \\ \text{H}{-}\text{O} \;\; \text{H} \qquad\;\; \text{H} \end{array}$$

(e)
$$\begin{array}{c} \qquad\qquad\qquad\qquad\qquad \text{H} \\ \qquad\qquad\qquad\qquad\qquad | \\ \text{H}{-}\text{C}{=}\text{C}{=}\text{C}{-}\text{O}{-}\text{C}{-}\text{H} \\ \quad\;\; | \qquad\;\; | \qquad\quad | \\ \quad\;\; \text{Br} \qquad \text{H} \qquad\quad \text{H} \end{array}$$

(f)
$$\begin{array}{c} \text{H}{-}\text{C}{\equiv}\text{C}{-}\text{C}{=}\text{C}{-}\text{H} \\ \qquad\qquad | \quad\; | \quad\; | \\ \qquad\qquad \text{H} \;\; \text{H} \;\; \text{H} \end{array}$$

Chemical Reactions

Fireworks are spectacular displays of chemical reactions.

Joseph Nettis/Photo Researchers, Inc.

GOB
Chemistry⊶Now™

Look for this logo in the chapter and go to GOB ChemistryNow at **http://now.brookscole.com/gob8** or on the CD for turtorials, simulations, and problems.

5.1 | What Are Chemical Reactions?

In Chapter 1, we learned that chemistry is mainly concerned with two things: the structure of matter and the transformations of one form of matter to another. In Chapters 2, 3, and 4, we discussed the first of these topics, and now we are ready to turn our attention to the second. In a chemical change, also called a **chemical reaction,** one or more **reactants** (starting materials) are converted into one or more **products.**

Chemical reactions occur all around us. They fuel and keep alive the cells of living tissues; they occur when we light a match, cook dinner, start a car, listen to a portable radio, or watch television. Most of the world's manufacturing processes involve chemical reactions; they include petroleum

A table of atomic weights is given on the inside back cover. Atomic weights can also be found in the Periodic Table on the inside front cover.

Table 5.1 Formula Weights for Two Ionic and Two Covalent Compounds

Ionic Compounds

Sodium chloride (NaCl)	23.0 amu Na + 35.5 amu Cl = 58.5 amu
Nickel(II) chloride hydrate $(NiCl_2 \cdot 6H_2O)$*	58.7 amu Ni + 2(35.5 amu Cl) + 12(1.0 amu H) + 6(16.0 amu O) = 237.7 amu

Covalent Compounds

Water (H_2O)	2(1.0 amu H) + 16.0 amu O = 18.0 amu
Aspirin $(C_9H_8O_4)$	9(12.0 amu C) + 8(1.0 amu H) + 4(16.0 amu O) = 180.0 amu

*Nickel(II) chloride crystallizes from an aqueous solution with six moles of water per mole of $NiCl_2$. The presence of water molecules in the crystal is indicated by the name "hydrate."

refining and food processing as well as the manufacture of drugs, plastics, synthetic fibers, explosives, and many other materials.

In this chapter we discuss four aspects of chemical reactions: (1) how to write and balance chemical equations, (2) mass relationships in chemical reactions, (3) types of chemical reactions, and (4) heat gains and losses.

5.2 | What Are Molecular Weights and Formula Weights, and How Do They Differ?

We begin our study of mass relationships with a discussion of formula weight. The **formula weight (FW)** of any substance is the sum of the atomic weights in atomic mass units (amu) of all the atoms in the compound's formula. The term "formula weight" can be used for both ionic and molecular compounds and tells nothing about whether the compound is ionic or molecular. Table 5.1 gives formula weights for two ionic compounds and two covalent compounds.

Another term, **molecular weight (MW),** is strictly correct only when used for covalent compounds. In this book, we use "formula weight" for both ionic and covalent compounds and "molecular weight" only for covalent compounds.

Molecular weight (MW) The sum of the atomic weights of all atoms in a molecular compound expressed in atomic mass units (amu)

EXAMPLE 5.1

What is the molecular weight of (a) glucose, $C_6H_{12}O_6$, and (b) urea, $(NH_2)_2CO$?

Solution

(a) Glucose, $C_6H_{12}O_8$

C	$6 \times 12.0 = 72.0$
H	$12 \times 1.0 = 12.0$
O	$6 \times 16.0 = 96.0$
	$C_6H_{12}O_6 = 180.0$ amu

(b) Urea, $(NH_2)_2CO$

N	$2 \times 14.0 = 28.0$
H	$4 \times 1.0 = 4.0$
C	$1 \times 12.0 = 16.0$
O	$1 \times 16.0 = 16.0$
	$(NH_2)_2CO = 60.0$ amu

Problem 5.1

What is (a) the molecular weight of ibuprofen, $C_{13}H_{18}O_2$, and (b) the formula weight of barium phosphate, $Ba_3(PO_4)_2$?

5.3 | What Is a Mole and How Do We Use It to Calculate Mass Relationships?

Atoms and molecules are so tiny (Section 2.4F) that chemists are seldom able to deal with them one at a time. When we weigh even a very small quantity of a compound, huge numbers of formula units (perhaps 10^{19}) are present. The formula unit may be atoms, molecules, or ions. To overcome this problem, chemists long ago defined a unit called the **mole (mol)**. A mole is the amount of substance that contains as many atoms, molecules, or ions as there are atoms in exactly 12 g of carbon-12. The important point here is that whether we are dealing with a mole of iron atoms, a mole of methane molecules, or a mole of sodium ions, a mole always contains the same number of formula units. We are used to scale-up factors in situations where there are large numbers of units involved in counting. We buy eggs by the dozen and pencils by the gross. Just as the dozen (12 units) is a useful scale-up factor for eggs, and the gross (144 units) is a useful scale-up factor for pencils, the mole is a useful scale-up factor for atoms and molecules. We will soon see that the number of units is much larger for a mole than for a dozen or a gross.

The number of formula units in a mole is called **Avogadro's number** after the Italian physicist, Amadeo Avogadro (1776–1856), who first proposed the concept of a mole, but was not able to determine the number experimentally. Note that Avogadro's number is not a defined value, but rather a value that must be determined experimentally. Its value is now known to nine significant figures.

Avogadro's number = $6.02214199 \times 10^{23}$ formula units per mole

For most calculations in this text, we round this number to three significant figures to 6.02×10^{23} formula units per mole.

A mole of hydrogen atoms is 6.02×10^{23} hydrogen atoms, a mole of sucrose (table sugar) molecules is 6.02×10^{23} sugar molecules, a mole of apples is 6.02×10^{23} apples, and a mole of sodium ions is 6.02×10^{23} sodium ions. Just as we call 12 of anything a dozen, 20 a score, and 144 a gross, we call 6.02×10^{23} of anything a mole.

The **molar mass** of any substance (the mass of one mole of any substance) is the formula weight of the substance expressed in grams. For instance, the formula weight of glucose, $C_6H_{12}O_6$ (Example 5.1) is 180 amu; therefore, 180 g of glucose is one mole of glucose. Likewise, the formula weight of urea, $(NH_2)_2CO$, is 60.0 amu and, therefore, 60.0 g of $(NH_2)_2CO$ is one mole of urea. For atoms, one mole is the atomic weight expressed in grams: 12.0 g of carbon is one mole of carbon atoms; 32.1 g of sulfur is one mole of sulfur atoms; and so on. As you see, the important point here is that to talk about the mass of a mole, we need to know the chemical formula of the substance we are considering. Figure 5.1 shows one-mole quantities of several compounds.

GOB
Chemistry ❖ Now™

Click *Chemistry Interactive* to explore more about **Moles**

Mole (mol) The formula weight of a substance expressed in grams

Avogadro's number 6.02×10^{23} formula units per mole; the amount of any substance that contains as many formula units as the number of atoms in 12 g of carbon-12.

One mole of pennies placed side by side would stretch for more than 1 million light-years, a distance far outside our solar system and even outside our own galaxy. Six moles of this text would weigh as much as the Earth.

Molar mass The mass of one mole of a substance expressed in grams; the formula weight of a compound expressed in grams

GOB
Chemistry ❖ Now™

Click *Coached Problems* for examples of **Determining Molar Mass**

Figure 5.1 One-mole quantities of (*a*) six metals and (*b*) four compounds. (*a*) Top row (left to right): Cu beads (63.5 g), Al foil (27.0 g), and Pb shot (207.2 g). Bottom row (left to right): S powder (32.1 g), Cr chunks (52.0 g), and Mg shavings (24.4 g). (*b*) H_2O (18.0 g); small beaker, NaCl (58.4 g); large beaker, aspirin, $C_9H_8O_4$, (180.2 g); green $NiCl_2 \cdot 6H_2O$ (237.7 g).

Charles D. Winters

(*a*)   (*b*)

Now that we know the relationship between moles and molar mass (g/mol), we can use molar mass as a conversion factor to convert from grams to moles, and from moles to grams. For this calculation, we use molar mass as a conversion factor.

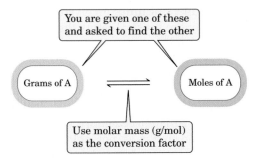

Suppose we want to know the number of moles of water in a graduated cylinder that contains 36.0 g of water. We know that the molar mass of water is 18.0 g/mol. If 18.0 g of water is one mole of water, then 36.0 g must be two moles of water.

$$36.0 \text{ g } H_2O \times \frac{1 \text{ mol } H_2O}{18.0 \text{ g } H_2O} = 2.00 \text{ mol } H_2O$$

Molar mass can also be used to convert from moles to grams. Suppose you have a beaker that contains 0.753 mol of sodium chloride and you are asked to calculate the number of grams of sodium chloride in the beaker. As a conversion factor, use the fact that the molar mass of NaCl is 58.5 g/mol.

$$0.753 \text{ mol NaCl} \times \frac{58.5 \text{ g NaCl}}{1 \text{ mol NaCl}} = 44.1 \text{ g NaCl}$$

This type of calculation can be performed for ionic compounds, such as NaF, as well as for molecular compounds, such as CO_2 and urea.

EXAMPLE 5.2

We have 27.5 g of sodium fluoride, NaF, the form of fluoride ions most commonly used in fluoride toothpastes. How many moles is this?

Solution

The formula weight of NaF = 23.0 + 19.0 = 42.0 amu. Thus each mole of NaF has a mass of 42.0 g, allowing us to use the conversion factor 1 mol NaF = 42.0 g NaF:

$$27.5 \text{ g NaF} \times \frac{1 \text{ mol NaF}}{42.0 \text{ g NaF}} = 0.655 \text{ mol NaF}$$

Problem 5.2

A person drinks 1500 g of water per day. How many moles is this?

EXAMPLE 5.3

We wish to weigh 3.41 mol of ethanol, C_2H_6O. How many grams is this?

Solution

The formula weight of C_2H_6O is 2(12.0) + 6(1.0) + 16.0 = 46.0 amu, so the conversion factor is 1 mol C_2H_6O = 46.0 g C_2H_6O.

$$3.41 \text{ mol } C_2H_6O \times \frac{46.0 \text{ g } C_2H_6O}{1.00 \text{ mol } C_2H_6O} = 157 \text{ g } C_2H_6O$$

Problem 5.3

We wish to weigh 2.84 mol of sodium sulfide, Na_2S. How many grams is this?

EXAMPLE 5.4

How many moles of nitrogen atoms and oxygen atoms are there in 21.4 mol of the explosive trinitrotoluene (TNT), $C_7H_5N_3O_6$?

Solution

The formula $C_7H_5N_3O_6$ tells us that each molecule of TNT contains three nitrogen atoms and six oxygen atoms. It also tells us that each mole of TNT contains three moles of N atoms and six moles of O atoms. Therefore, we have the following conversion factors: 1 mol TNT = 3 mol N atoms, and 1 mol TNT = 6 mol O atoms. The number of moles of N atoms in 21.4 mol of TNT is

$$21.4 \text{ mol TNT} \times \frac{3 \text{ mol N atoms}}{1 \text{ mol TNT}} = 64.2 \text{ mol N atoms}$$

The number of moles of O atoms in 21.4 mol of TNT is

$$21.4 \text{ mol TNT} \times \frac{6 \text{ mol O atoms}}{1 \text{ mol TNT}} = 128 \text{ mol O atoms}$$

Note that we give the answer to three significant figures because we were given the number of moles to three significant figures. The ratio of moles of O atoms to moles of TNT is an exact number.

Problem 5.4

How many moles of C atoms, H atoms, and O atoms are there in 2.5 mol of glucose, $C_6H_{12}O_6$?

EXAMPLE 5.5

How many moles of sodium ions, Na^+, are there in 5.63 g of sodium sulfate, Na_2SO_4?

Solution

First, we need to find out how many moles of Na_2SO_4 we have. The formula weight of Na_2SO_4 is $2(23.0) + 32.1 + 4(16.0) = 142.1$ amu. In the conversion of grams Na_2SO_4 to moles of Na_2SO_4, we can use the conversion factor 1 mol Na_2SO_4 = 142.1 g Na_2SO_4.

$$5.63 \text{ g } Na_2SO_4 \times \frac{1 \text{ mol } Na_2SO_4}{142.1 \text{ g } Na_2SO_4} = 0.0396 \text{ mol } Na_2SO_4$$

The formula Na_2SO_4 shows us that each mole of Na_2SO_4 contains two moles of Na^+ ions. Therefore, we use the conversion factor 1 mol Na_2SO_4 = 2 mol Na^+. The number of moles of Na^+ ions in 5.63 g of Na_2SO_4 is

$$0.0396 \text{ mol } Na_2SO_4 \times \frac{2 \text{ mol } Na^+}{1 \text{ mol } Na_2SO_4} = 0.0792 \text{ mol } Na^+$$

Problem 5.5

How many moles of copper(I) ions, Cu^+, are there in 0.062 g of copper(I) nitrate, $CuNO_3$?

EXAMPLE 5.6

An aspirin tablet, $C_9H_8O_4$, contains 0.360 g of aspirin. (The rest of it is starch or other fillers.) How many molecules of aspirin are present in this tablet?

Solution

The molecular weight of aspirin is $9(12.0) + 8(1.0) + 4(16.0) = 180.0$ amu. First we need to find out how many moles of aspirin are in 0.360 g:

$$0.360 \text{ g aspirin} \times \frac{1 \text{ mol aspirin}}{180.0 \text{ g aspirin}} = 0.00200 \text{ mol aspirin}$$

Each mole of aspirin contains 6.02×10^{23} molecules. Therefore, the number of molecules of aspirin in the tablet is

$$0.00200 \text{ mol} \times 6.02 \times 10^{23} \frac{\text{molecules}}{\text{mol}} = 1.20 \times 10^{21} \text{ molecules}$$

Problem 5.6

How many molecules of water, H_2O, are in a glass of water (235 g)?

5.4 | How Do We Balance Chemical Equations?

When propane, which is the major component in bottled gas or LP (lique-fied petroleum) gas, burns in air, it reacts with the oxygen in the air. These reactants are converted to the products carbon dioxide and water in a chemical reaction called **combustion.** We can write this chemical reaction in the form of a **chemical equation,** using chemical formulas for the reac-tants and products, and an arrow to indicate the direction in which the reaction proceeds. In addition, it is important to show the state of each reactant and product—that is, whether it is a gas, liquid, or solid. We use the symbol (g) for gas, (ℓ) for liquid, (s) for solid, and (aq) for a substance dissolved in water (aqueous). We place the appropriate symbol immedi-ately following each reactant and product. In our combustion equation, propane, oxygen, and carbon dioxide are gases, and the flame produced when propane burns is hot enough that the water forms as a gas (steam).

$$C_3H_8(g) + O_2(g) \longrightarrow CO_2(g) + H_2O(g)$$

Propane   Oxygen   Carbon   Water
                                dioxide

Combustion Burning in air

Chemical equation A representation using chemical formulas of the process that occurs when reactants are converted to products

The equation we have written is incomplete, however. While it tells us the formulas of the starting materials and products (which every chemical equation must do) and the physical state of each reactant and product, it does not give the amounts correctly. It is not balanced, which means that the number of atoms on the left side of the equation is not the same as the number of atoms on the right side. From the law of conservation of mass (Section 2.3A), we know that, in chemical reactions, atoms are never destroyed or created; they merely shift from one substance to another. Thus all the atoms present at the start of the reaction (on the left side of the equa-tion) must still be present at the end of the reaction (on the right side of the equation). The equation we have just written has three carbon atoms on the left side but only one on the right side.

Propane burning in air.

Charles D. Winters

EXAMPLE 5.7

Balance this equation:

$$Ca(OH)_2(s) + HCl(g) \longrightarrow CaCl_2(s) + H_2O(\ell)$$

Calcium   Hydrogen   Calcium
hydroxide   chloride   chloride

Solution
The calcium is already balanced—there is one Ca on each side. There is one Cl on the left and two on the right. To balance them, we add the coeffi-cient 2 in front of HCl:

$$Ca(OH)_2(s) + 2HCl(g) \longrightarrow CaCl_2(s) + H_2O(\ell)$$

Looking at hydrogens, we see that there are four hydrogens on the left but only two on the right. Placing the coefficient 2 in front of H_2O balances the hydrogens. It also balances the oxygens and completes the balancing of the equation:

$$Ca(OH)_2(s) + 2HCl(g) \longrightarrow CaCl_2(s) + 2H_2O(\ell)$$

Problem 5.7

Following is an unbalanced equation for photosynthesis, the process by which green plants convert carbon dioxide and water to glucose and oxygen. Balance this equation.

$$CO_2(g) + H_2O(\ell) \xrightarrow{\text{Photosynthesis}} C_6H_{12}O_6(aq) + O_2(g)$$
Glucose

EXAMPLE 5.8

Balance this equation for the combustion of butane, the fluid most commonly used in pocket lighters:

$$C_4H_{10}(\ell) + O_2(g) \longrightarrow CO_2(g) + H_2O(g)$$
Butane

Solution

The equation for the combustion of butane is very similar to the one we examined at the beginning of this section for the combustion of propane. Here we put a 4 in front of the CO_2 (because there are four carbons on the left) and a 5 in front of the H_2O (because there are ten hydrogens on the left):

$$C_4H_{10}(g) + O_2(g) \longrightarrow 4CO_2(g) + 5H_2O(g)$$

When we count the oxygens, we find 2 on the left and 13 on the right. We can balance their numbers by putting $\frac{13}{2}$ in front of the O_2.

$$C_4H_{10}(g) + \tfrac{13}{2}O_2(g) \longrightarrow 4CO_2(g) + 5H_2O(g)$$

Although chemists sometimes have good reason to write equations with fractional coefficients, it is common practice to use only whole-number coefficients. We accomplish this by multiplying everything by 2, which gives the balanced equation:

$$2C_4H_{10}(g) + 13O_2(g) \longrightarrow 8CO_2(g) + 10H_2O(g)$$

Problem 5.8

Balance this equation:

$$C_6H_{14}(g) + O_2(g) \longrightarrow CO_2(g) + H_2O(g)$$

A pocket lighter contains butane in both the liquid and the gaseous state.

Jeff J. Daly/Visuals Unlimited, Inc.

EXAMPLE 5.9

Balance this equation:

$$Na_2SO_3(aq) + H_3PO_4(aq) \longrightarrow H_2SO_3(aq) + Na_3PO_4(aq)$$
Sodium   Phosphoric   Sulfurous   Sodium
sulfite   acid   acid   phosphate

HOW TO ...

Balance a Chemical Equation

To balance an equation, we place numbers in front of the formulas until the number of each kind of atom in the products is the same as the number in the starting materials. These numbers are called **coefficients.** As an example, let us balance our propane equation:

$$C_3H_8(g) + O_2(g) \longrightarrow CO_2(g) + H_2O(g)$$

Propane   Oxygen   Carbon   Water
                  dioxide

To balance an equation:

1. Begin with atoms that appear in only one compound on the left and only one compound on the right. In the equation for the reaction of propane and oxygen, begin with either carbon or hydrogen.
2. If an atom occurs as a free element—as, for example, O_2 does in the reaction of propane with oxygen—balance this element last.
3. You can change only coefficients in balancing an equation; you cannot change chemical formulas. For example, if you have H_2O on the left side of an equation but need two oxygens, you can add the coefficient "2" to read $2H_2O$. You cannot, however, get two oxygens by changing the formula to H_2O_2. You can't do this because the reactant is water, H_2O, and not hydrogen peroxide, H_2O_2.

For the equation for the reaction of propane with oxygen, we can begin with carbon. Three carbon atoms appear on the left and one on the right. If we put a 3 in front of the CO_2 (indicating that three CO_2 molecules are formed), three carbons will appear on each side, and the carbons will be balanced:

Three C on each side

$$C_3H_8(g) + O_2(g) \longrightarrow 3CO_2(g) + H_2O(g)$$

Next we look at the hydrogens. There are eight on the left and two on the right. If we put a 4 in front of the H_2O, there will be eight hydrogens on each side and the hydrogens will be balanced:

Eight H on each side

$$C_3H_8(g) + O_2(g) \longrightarrow 3CO_2(g) + 4H_2O(g)$$

The only atom still unbalanced is oxygen. Notice that we saved this reactant for last (rule 2). There are two oxygen atoms on the left and ten on the right. If we put a 5 in front of the O_2 on the left, we both balance the oxygen atoms and arrive at the balanced equation:

Ten O on each side

$$C_3H_8(g) + 5O_2(g) \longrightarrow 3CO_2(g) + 4H_2O(g)$$

At this point, the equation ought to be balanced, but we should always check, just to make sure. In a balanced equation, there must be the same number of atoms of each element on both sides. A check of our work shows three C, ten O, and eight H atoms on each side. The equation is, indeed, balanced.

GOB
Chemistry Now™
Click *Chemistry Interactive* for more practice on **How to Balance Chemical Equations**

Solution

The key to balancing equations like this one is to realize that polyatomic ions such as SO_3^{2-} and PO_4^{3-} usually remain intact on both sides of the equation. We can begin by balancing the Na^+ ions. We put a 3 in front of Na_2SO_3 and a 2 in front of Na_3PO_4, giving us six Na^+ ions on each side:

Six Na on each side

$$3Na_2SO_3(aq) + H_3PO_4(aq) \longrightarrow H_2SO_3(aq) + 2Na_3PO_4(aq)$$

There are now three SO_3^{2-} units on the left and only one on the right, so we put a 3 in front of H_2SO_3:

Three SO_3^{2-} units on each side

$$3Na_2SO_3(aq) + H_3PO_4(aq) \longrightarrow 3H_2SO_3(aq) + 2Na_3PO_4(aq)$$

Now let's look at the PO_4^{3-} units. There are two PO_4^{3-} units on the right, but only one on the left. To balance them, we put a 2 in front of H_3PO_4. In doing so, we balance not only the PO_4^{3-} units but also the hydrogens, and arrive at the balanced equation:

Two PO_4^{3-} units on each side

$$3Na_2SO_3(aq) + 2H_3PO_4(aq) \longrightarrow 3H_2SO_3(aq) + 2Na_3PO_4(aq)$$

Problem 5.9

Balance this equation:

$$K_2C_2O_4(aq) + Ca_3(AsO_4)_2(s) \longrightarrow K_3AsO_4(aq) + CaC_2O_4(s)$$

| Potassium oxalate | Calcium arsenate | Potassium arsenate | Calcium oxalate |

One final point about balancing chemical equations. The following equation for the combustion of propane is correctly balanced:

$$C_3H_8(g) + 5O_2(g) \longrightarrow 3CO_2(g) + 4H_2O(g)$$

Propane

Would it be correct if we doubled all the coefficients?

$$2C_3H_8(g) + 10O_2(g) \longrightarrow 6CO_2(g) + 8H_2O(g)$$

Propane

This equation is mathematically and scientifically correct, but chemists do not normally write equations with coefficients that are all divisible by a common number. A correctly balanced equation is almost always written with the coefficients expressed as the lowest set of whole numbers.

5.5 | How Do We Calculate Mass Relationships in Chemical Reactions?

A. Stoichiometry

As we saw in Section 5.4, a balanced chemical equation tells us not only which substances react and which form, but also the molar ratios in which they react. For example, using the molar ratios in a balanced chemical equation, we can calculate the mass of starting materials we need to produce a particular mass of a product. The study of mass relationships in chemical reactions is called **stoichiometry.**

Let us look once again at the balanced equation for the burning of propane:

$$C_3H_8(g) + 5O_2(g) \longrightarrow 3CO_2(g) + 4H_2O(g)$$
Propane

This equation tells us not only that propane and oxygen are converted to carbon dioxide and water, but also that 1 mol of propane combines with 5 mol of oxygen to produce 3 mol of carbon dioxide and 4 mol of water; that is, we know the mole ratios involved. The same is true for any other balanced equation. This fact allows us to answer questions such as the following:

1. How many moles of any particular product are formed if we start with a given mass of a starting material?

2. How many grams (or moles) of one starting material are necessary to react completely with a given number of grams (or moles) of another starting material?

3. How many grams (or moles) of starting material are needed if we want to form a certain number of grams (or moles) of a certain product?

4. How many grams (or moles) of another product are obtained when a certain amount of main product is produced?

It might seem as if we have four different types of problems here. In fact, we can solve them all by the same very simple procedure summarized in the following diagram:

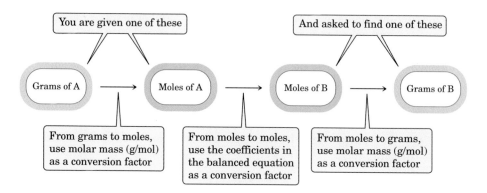

You will always need a conversion factor that relates moles to moles. You will need the conversion factors from grams to moles and from moles to grams according to the way the problem is asked; you may need one or both

GOB
Chemistry⚛Now™
Click *Chemistry Interactive* to explore
Weight Relations in Chemical Reactions

Stoichiometry The mass relationships in a chemical reaction

"Stoichiometry" comes from the Greek *stoicheion,* meaning "element," and *metron,* meaning "measure."

In Section 5.4, we saw that the coefficients in an equation represent numbers of molecules. Because moles are proportional to molecules (Section 5.3), the coefficients in an equation also represent numbers of moles.

in some problems and not in others. It is easy to weigh a given number of grams, but the molar ratio determines the amount of substance involved in a particular reaction.

EXAMPLE 5.10

Ammonia is produced on an industrial scale by the reaction of nitrogen gas with hydrogen gas (the Haber process) according to this balanced equation:

$$N_2(g) + 3H_2(g) \longrightarrow 2NH_3(g)$$

Ammonia

How many grams of N_2 are necessary to produce 7.50 g of NH_3?

Solution

Step 1 The coefficients in an equation refer to the relative numbers of moles, not grams. Therefore, we must first find out how many moles of NH_3 are in 7.50 g of NH_3. To convert grams of NH_3 to moles of NH_3, we use the conversion factor 1 mol NH_3 = 17.0 g NH_3. At this stage, we don't do the multiplication, but just leave the relationship set up:

$$7.50 \text{ g } NH_3 \times \frac{1 \text{ mol } NH_3}{17.0 \text{ g } NH_3} = \text{mol } NH_3$$

Step 2 Next we turn to the balanced equation, which shows us that 2 mol of NH_3 are produced from 1 mol of N_2. We multiply the number of moles of NH_3 by this conversion factor:

$$7.50 \text{ g } NH_3 \times \frac{1 \text{ mol } NH_3}{17.0 \text{ g } NH_3} \times \frac{1 \text{ mol } N_2}{2 \text{ mol } NH_3} = \text{mol } N_2$$

Step 3 To find the number of grams of N_2, we multiply by the conversion factor 28.0 g N_2 = 1 mol N_2. At this point, the conversion factors are set up properly and we have converted from grams of NH_3 to grams of N_2. Now we do the arithmetic and get an answer of 6.18 g N_2:

$$7.50 \text{ g } NH_3 \times \frac{1 \text{ mol } NH_3}{17.0 \text{ g } NH_3} \times \frac{1 \text{ mol } N_2}{2 \text{ mol } NH_3} \times \frac{28.0 \text{ g } N_2}{1 \text{ mol } N_2} = 6.18 \text{ g } N_2$$

In all such problems, we are given the mass (or number of moles) of one compound and asked to find the mass (or number of moles) of another compound. The two compounds can be on the same side of the equation or on opposite sides. We can do all such problems by the three steps we have just used.

Problem 5.10

Pure aluminum is prepared by the electrolysis of aluminum oxide according to this equation:

$$Al_2O_3(s) \xrightarrow{\text{Electrolysis}} Al(s) + O_2(g)$$

Aluminum
oxide

(a) Balance this equation.
(b) What mass of aluminum oxide is required to prepare 27 g (1 mol) of aluminum?

EXAMPLE 5.11

Silicon to be used in computer chips is manufactured by a process represented by the following reaction:

$$SiCl_4(s) + 2Mg(s) \longrightarrow Si(s) + 2MgCl_2(s)$$
Silicon   Magnesium
tetrachloride   chloride

A sample of 225 g of silicon tetrachloride, $SiCl_4$, is reacted with an excess (more than necessary) amount of Mg. How many moles of Si are produced?

Solution

We are given 225 g of $SiCl_4$ and asked for moles of Si. We must first convert grams of $SiCl_4$ to moles of $SiCl_4$. For this calculation we use the conversion factor 1 mol $SiCl_4$ = 170 g $SiCl_4$:

$$225 \text{ g } SiCl_4 \times \frac{1 \text{ mol } SiCl_4}{170 \text{ g } SiCl_4} = \text{mol } SiCl_4$$

Next we use the conversion factor 1 mol $SiCl_4$ = 1 mol Si, which we obtain from the balanced chemical equation. Now we do the arithmetic and obtain an answer of 1.32 mol Si:

$$225 \text{ g } SiCl_4 \times \frac{1 \text{ mol } SiCl_4}{170 \text{ g } SiCl_4} \times \frac{1 \text{ mole Si}}{1 \text{ mol } SiCl_4} = 1.32 \text{ mol Si}$$

Problem 5.11

In the industrial synthesis of acetic acid, methanol is reacted with carbon monoxide. How many moles of CO are required to produce 16.6 mol of acetic acid?

$$CH_3OH(g) + CO(g) \longrightarrow CH_3COOH(\ell)$$
Methanol Carbon   Acetic acid
     monoxide

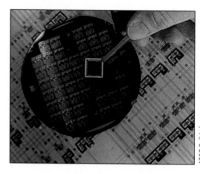

As microprocessor chips became increasingly smaller, the purity of the silicon becomes more important, because impurities can prevent the circuit from working properly.

EXAMPLE 5.12

When urea, $(NH_2)_2CO$, is acted on by the enzyme urease in the presence of water, ammonia and carbon dioxide are produced:

$$(NH_2)_2CO(aq) + H_2O(\ell) \xrightarrow{\text{Urease}} 2NH_3(aq) + CO_2(g)$$
Urea   Ammonia

If excess water is present (more than necessary for the reaction), how many grams each of CO_2 and NH_3 are produced from 0.83 mol of urea?

Solution
For grams of CO_2:
We are given moles of urea and asked for grams of CO_2. We first use the conversion factor 1 mol urea = 1 mol CO_2 to get the number of moles of CO_2 that will be formed:

$$0.83 \text{ mol urea} \times \frac{1 \text{ mol } CO_2}{1 \text{ mol urea}} = \text{mol } CO_2$$

Then we use the conversion factor 1 mol CO_2 = 44 g CO_2 to give us the answer:

$$0.83 \text{ mol urea} \times \frac{1 \text{ mol } CO_2}{1 \text{ mol urea}} \times \frac{44 \text{ g } CO_2}{1 \text{ mol } CO_2} = 37 \text{ g } CO_2$$

For grams of NH_3:
We follow the same procedure as for CO_2 but use different conversion factors:

$$0.83 \text{ mol urea} \times \frac{2 \text{ mol } NH_3}{1 \text{ mol urea}} \times \frac{17 \text{ g } NH_3}{1 \text{ mol } NH_3} = 28 \text{ g } NH_3$$

Problem 5.12

Ethanol is produced industrially by the reaction of ethylene with water in the presence of an acid catalyst. How many grams of ethanol are produced from 7.24 mol of ethylene? Assume that excess water is present.

$$\underset{\text{Ethylene}}{C_2H_4(g)} + H_2O(\ell) \xrightarrow{\text{Acid catalyst}} \underset{\text{Ethanol}}{CH_3CH_2OH(\ell)}$$

GOB
Chemistry·꘎·Now™

Click *Coached Problems* to practice working with **Limiting Reactants**

B. Limiting Reagents

Frequently reactants are mixed in molar proportions that differ from those that appear in a balanced equation. It often happens that one reactant is completely used up when other reactants have not been used up. At times, we deliberately choose to have an excess of one reagent over another. As an example, consider an experiment in which NO is prepared by mixing five moles of N_2 with one mole of O_2. Only one mole of N_2 will react, consuming the one mole of O_2. The oxygen is used up completely and four moles of nitrogen are left over. These mole relationships are summarized under the balanced equation:

	$N_2(g)$	+ $O_2(g)$	$\longrightarrow$ 2NO(g)
Before reaction (moles)	5.0	1.0	0
After reaction (moles)	4.0	0	2.0

Limiting reagent The reactant that is consumed, leaving an excess of another reagent or reagents unreacted

The **limiting reagent** is the reactant that is used up first. In this example, O_2 is the limiting reagent, because it governs how much NO can form. The other reagent, N_2, is in excess.

EXAMPLE 5.13

Suppose 12 g of C is mixed with 64 g of O_2, and the following reaction takes place:

$$C(s) + O_2(g) \longrightarrow CO_2(g)$$

(a) Which reactant is the limiting reagent, and which reactant is in excess?
(b) How many grams of CO_2 will be formed?

Solution

(a) We use the molar mass of each reactant to calculate the number of moles of each present before reaction.

$$12 \text{ g C} \times \frac{1 \text{ mol C}}{12 \text{ g C}} = 1 \text{ mol C}$$

$$64 \text{ g O}_2 \times \frac{1 \text{ mol O}_2}{32 \text{ g O}_2} = 2 \text{ mol O}_2$$

According to the balanced equation, reaction of one mole of C requires one mole of O_2. But two moles of O_2 are present at the start of the reaction. Therefore, C is the limiting reagent and O_2 is in excess.

(b) To calculate the number of grams of CO_2 formed, we use the conversion factor 1 mol CO_2 = 44 g CO_2.

$$12 \text{ g C} \times \frac{1 \text{ mol C}}{12 \text{ g C}} \times \frac{1 \text{ mol CO}_2}{1 \text{ mol C}} \times \frac{44 \text{ g CO}_2}{12 \text{ mol CO}_2} = 44 \text{ g CO}_2$$

We can summarize these numbers in the following table. Note that, as required by the law of conservation of mass, the sum of the masses of the material present after reaction is the same as the amount present before the reaction took place—namely, 76 g of material.

	C	+	O$_2$	⟶	CO$_2$
Before reaction	12 g		64 g		0
Before reaction	1.0 mol		2.0 mol		0
After reaction	0		1.0 mol		1.0 mol
After reaction	0		32 g		44 g

Problem 5.13

Assume that 6.0 g of C and 2.1 g H_2 are mixed and react to form methane according to the following balanced equation:

$$C(s) + 2H_2(g) \longrightarrow CH_4(g)$$
$$\text{Methane}$$

(a) Which reactant is the limiting reagent and which reactant is in excess?
(b) How many grams of CH_4 are produced in the reaction?

C. Percent Yield

When carrying out a chemical reaction, we often get less of a product than we might expect from the type of calculation we discussed in Section 5.5A. For example, suppose we react 32.0 g (1 mol) of CH_3OH with excess CO to form acetic acid:

$$CH_3OH + CO \longrightarrow CH_3COOH$$
$$\text{Methanol} \quad \text{Carbon} \quad \text{Acetic acid}$$
$$\text{monoxide}$$

If we calculate the expected yield based on the stoichiometry of the balanced equation, we find that we should get 1 mol (60.0 g) of acetic acid. Suppose, however, we get only 57.8 g of acetic acid. Does this result mean that the law

A reaction that does not give the main product is called a side reaction.

Occasionally, the percent yield is larger than 100%. For example, if a chemist fails to dry a product completely before weighing it, the product weighs more than it should because it also contains water. In such cases, the actual yield may be larger than expected and the percent yield may be greater than 100%.

of conservation of mass is being violated? No, it does not. We get less than 60.0 g of acetic acid either because some of the CH_3OH does not react or because some of it reacts in some other way, or perhaps because our laboratory technique is not perfect and we lose a little in transferring material from one container to another.

At this point, we need to define three terms, all of which relate to yield of product in a chemical reaction:

Actual yield The mass of product formed in a chemical reaction

Theoretical yield The mass of product that should form in a chemical reaction according to the stoichiometry of the balanced equation

Percent yield The actual yield divided by the theoretical yield times 100

$$\text{Percent yield} = \frac{\text{actual yield}}{\text{theoretical yield}} \times 100$$

We summarize the data for the preparation of acetic acid in the following table:

	CH$_3$OH	+	CO	$\longrightarrow$	CH$_3$COOH
Before reaction	32.0 g		Excess		0
Before reaction	1.00 mol		Excess		0
Theoretical yield					1.00 mol
Theoretical yield					60.0 g
Actual yield					57.8 g

We calculate the percent yield in this experiment as follows:

$$\text{Percent yield} = \frac{57.8 \text{ g acetic acid}}{60.0 \text{ g acetic acid}} \times 100 = 96.3\%$$

Why is it important to know the percent yield of a chemical reaction or a series of reactions? The most important reason often relates to cost. If the yield of commercial product is, say, only 10%, the chemists will probably be sent back to the lab to tweak the experimental conditions in an attempt to improve the yield. As an example, consider a reaction in which starting material A is converted first to compound B, then to compound C, and finally to compound D.

$$A \longrightarrow B \longrightarrow C \longrightarrow D$$

Suppose the yield is 50% at each step. In this case, the yield of compound D is 13% based on the mass of compound A. If, however, the yield at each step is 90%, the yield of compound D increases to 73%; and if the yield at each step is 99%, the yield of compound D is 97%. These numbers are summarized in the following table:

If the Percent Yield per Step Is	The Percent Yield of Compound D Is
50%	$0.50 \times 0.50 \times 0.50 \times 100 = 13\%$
90%	$0.90 \times 0.90 \times 0.90 \times 100 = 73\%$
99%	$0.99 \times 0.99 \times 0.99 \times 100 = 97\%$

EXAMPLE 5.14

In an experiment forming ethanol, the theoretical yield is 50.5 g. The actual yield is 46.8 g. What is the percent yield?

Solution

$$\text{Percent Yield} = \frac{46.8 \text{ g}}{50.5 \text{ g}} \times 100 = 92.7\%$$

Problem 5.14

In an experiment to prepare aspirin, the theoretical yield is 153.7 g. If the actual yield is 124.5 g, what is the percent yield?

5.6 | How Can We Predict if Ions in Aqueous Solution Will React with Each Other?

Many ionic compounds are soluble in water. As we saw in Section 4.5, ionic compounds always consist of both positive and negative ions. When they dissolve in water, the positive and negative ions become separated from each other by water molecules. We call such a separation a **dissociation.** For example,

$$NaCl(s) \xrightarrow{H_2O} Na^+(aq) + Cl^-(aq)$$

H$_2$O above the arrow means that the reaction takes place in water.

What happens when we mix **aqueous solutions** of two different ionic compounds? Does a reaction take place between the ions? The answer depends on the ions. If any of the negative and positive ions come together to form a water-insoluble compound, then a reaction takes place and a precipitate forms; otherwise, no reaction occurs.

Aqueous solution A solution in which the solvent is water

As an example, suppose we prepare one solution by dissolving sodium chloride, NaCl, in water and a second solution by dissolving silver nitrate, AgNO$_3$, in water.

$$\text{Solution 1} \quad NaCl(s) \xrightarrow{H_2O} Na^+(aq) + Cl^-(aq)$$
$$\text{Solution 2} \quad AgNO_3(s) \xrightarrow{H_2O} Ag^+(aq) + NO_3^-(aq)$$

If we now mix the two solutions, four ions are present in the solution: Ag$^+$, Na$^+$, Cl$^-$, and NO$_3^-$. Two of these ions, Ag$^+$ and Cl$^-$, react to form the compound AgCl (silver chloride), which is insoluble in water. A reaction therefore takes place, forming a white precipitate of AgCl that slowly sinks to the bottom of the container (Figure 5.2). We write this reaction as follows:

$$Ag^+(aq) + NO_3^-(aq) + Na^+(aq) + Cl^-(aq) \longrightarrow AgCl(s) + Na^+(aq) + NO_3^-(aq)$$

Silver ion   Nitrate ion   Sodium ion   Chloride ion   Silver chloride

Notice that the Na$^+$ and NO$_3^-$ ions do not participate in the reaction, but merely remain dissolved in the water. Ions that do not participate in a reaction are called **spectator ions**—certainly an appropriate name.

Spectator ion An ion that appears unchanged on both sides of a chemical equation

Figure 5.2 Adding Cl⁻ ions to a solution of Ag⁺ ions produces a white precipitate of silver chloride, AgCl.

Net ionic equation A chemical equation that does not contain spectator ions

ᴳᴼᴮ
Chemistry.⚛.Now™
Click *Coached Problems* to explore more about **Net Ionic Equations**

Figure 5.3 When aqueous solutions of $NaHCO_3$ and HCl are mixed, a reaction between HCO_3^- and H_3O^+ ions produces CO_2 gas, which can be seen as bubbles.

We can simplify the equation for the formation of silver chloride by omitting all spectator ions:

$$\text{Net ionic equation:} \quad \underset{\substack{\text{Silver} \\ \text{ion}}}{Ag^+(aq)} + \underset{\substack{\text{Chloride} \\ \text{ion}}}{Cl^-(aq)} \longrightarrow \underset{\substack{\text{Silver} \\ \text{chloride}}}{AgCl(s)}$$

This kind of equation that we write for ions in solution is called a **net ionic equation.** Like all other chemical equations, net ionic equations must be balanced. We balance them in the same way as we do other equations, except now we must make sure that charges balance as well as atoms.

Net ionic equations show only the ions that react—no spectator ions are shown. For example, the net ionic equation for the precipitation of arsenic(III) sulfide from aqueous solution is

$$\text{Net ionic equation:} \quad 2As^{3+}(aq) + 3S^{2-}(aq) \longrightarrow As_2S_3(s)$$

Not only are there two arsenic atoms and three sulfur atoms on each side, but the total charge on the left side is the same as the total charge on the right side; they are both zero.

In general, ions in solution react with each other only when one of these four things can happen:

1. Two ions form a solid that is insoluble in water. AgCl is one example, as shown in Figure 5.2.

2. Two ions form a gas that escapes from the reaction mixture as bubbles. An example is the reaction of sodium bicarbonate, $NaHCO_3$, with HCl to form gaseous carbon dioxide, CO_2 (Figure 5.3). The net ionic equation for this reaction is

$$\text{Net ionic equation:} \quad \underset{\substack{\text{Bicarbonate} \\ \text{ion}}}{HCO_3^-(aq)} + H_3O^+(aq) \longrightarrow \underset{\substack{\text{Carbon} \\ \text{dioxide}}}{CO_2(g)} + 2H_2O(\ell)$$

3. An acid neutralizes a base. Acid–base reactions are so important that we devote Chapter 9 to them.

4. One of the ions can oxidize another. We discuss this type of reaction in Section 5.7.

In many cases, no reaction takes place when we mix solutions of ionic compounds because none of these situations holds. For example, if we mix solutions of copper(II) nitrate, $Cu(NO_3)_2$, and potassium sulfate, K_2SO_4, we merely have a mixture containing Cu^{2+}, K^+, NO_3^-, and SO_4^{2-} ions dissolved in water. None of these ions reacts with the others; therefore, we see nothing happening (Figure 5.4).

Figure 5.4 (*a*) The beaker on the left contains a solution of potassium sulfate (colorless) and the beaker on the right contains a solution of copper(II) nitrate (blue). (*b*) When the two solutions are mixed, the blue color becomes lighter because the copper(II) nitrate is less concentrated, but nothing else happens.

(*a*)

(*b*)

CHEMICAL CONNECTIONS 5A

Solubility and Tooth Decay

The outermost protective layer of a tooth is the enamel, which is composed of approximately 95% hydroxyapatite, $Ca_{10}(PO_4)_6(OH)_2$, and 5% collagen (Chemical Connections 21G). Like most other phosphates and hydroxides, hydroxyapatite is insoluble in water. In acidic media, however, it dissolves to a slight extent, yielding Ca^{2+}, PO_4^{3-}, and OH^- ions. This loss of enamel creates pits and cavities in the tooth.

Acidity in the mouth is produced by bacterial fermentation of remnants of food, especially carbohydrates. Once pits and cavities

form in the enamel, bacteria can hide there and cause further damage in the underlying softer material called dentin. The fluoridation of water brings F^- ions to the hydroxyapatite. There, F^- ions take the place of OH^- ions, forming the considerably less acid-soluble fluoroapatite, $Ca_{10}(PO_4)_6F_2$. Fluoride-containing toothpastes enhance this exchange process and provide further protection against tooth decay.

EXAMPLE 5.15

When a solution of barium chloride, $BaCl_2$, is added to a solution of sodium sulfate, Na_2SO_4, a white precipitate of barium sulfate, $BaSO_4$, forms. Write the net ionic equation for this reaction.

Solution
Because both barium chloride and sodium sulfate are ionic compounds, each exists in water as its dissociated ions:

$$Ba^{2+}(aq) + 2Cl^-(aq) \quad \text{and} \quad 2Na^+(aq) + SO_4^{2-}(aq)$$

We are told that a precipitate of barium sulfate forms:

$$Ba^{2+}(aq) + 2Cl^-(aq) + 2Na^+(aq) + SO_4^{2-}(aq) \longrightarrow$$
$$\underset{\substack{\text{Barium} \\ \text{sulfate}}}{BaSO_4(s)} + 2Na^+(aq) + 2Cl^-(aq)$$

Because Na^+ and Cl^- ions appear on both sides of the equation (they are spectator ions), we cancel them and are left with the following net ionic equation:

$$\text{Net ionic equation:} \quad Ba^{2+}(aq) + SO_4^{2-}(aq) \longrightarrow BaSO_4(s)$$

Problem 5.15
When a solution of copper(II) chloride, $CuCl_2$, is added to a solution of potassium sulfide, K_2S, a black precipitate of copper(II) sulfide, CuS, forms. Write the net ionic equation for the reaction.

The mixing of solutions of barium chloride, $BaCl_2$, and sodium sulfate, Na_2SO_4, forms a white precipitate of barium sulfate, $BaSO_4$.

Charles D. Winters

Of the four ways for ions to react in water, one of the most common is the formation of an insoluble compound. We can predict when this result will happen if we know the solubilities of the ionic compounds. There is no simple way to remember which ionic solids are soluble in water and which are not, but we can make some useful generalizations.

1. All compounds containing Na^+, K^+, or NH_4^+ ions are soluble in water.

2. All nitrates (NO_3^-) and acetates (CH_3COO^-) are soluble in water.

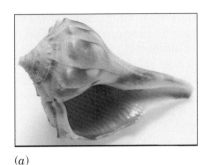

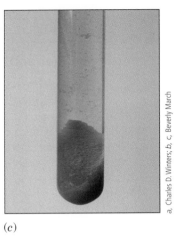

(*a*)   (*b*)   (*c*)

(*a*) Sea animals of the mollusk family often use insoluble $CaSO_4$ to construct their shells. Both (*b*) iron(III) hydroxide, $Fe(OH)_3$, and (*c*) copper(II) carbonate, $CuCO_3$, are insoluble in water.

3. Most chlorides (Cl^-) and sulfates (SO_4^{2-}) are soluble in water. Important exceptions include silver chloride ($AgCl$), lead(II) chloride ($PbCl_2$), mercury(I) chloride (Hg_2Cl_2), barium sulfate ($BaSO_4$), and lead sulfate ($PbSO_4$), which are insoluble in water.

4. Most carbonates (CO_3^{2-}), phosphates (PO_4^{3-}), sulfides (S^{2-}), and hydroxides (OH^-) are insoluble in water. Important exceptions include $LiOH$, $NaOH$, KOH, and aqueous NH_3, which are soluble in water.

5.7 | What Are Oxidation and Reduction, and Why Do They Always Occur Together?

One of the most important and most common types of reaction is oxidation–reduction. **Oxidation** is the loss of electrons. **Reduction** is the gain of electrons. An **oxidation–reduction reaction** (often called a **redox reaction**) involves the transfer of electrons from one species to another. An example is the oxidation of zinc by copper ions, the net ionic equation for which is

$$Zn(s) + Cu^{2+}(aq) \longrightarrow Zn^{2+}(aq) + Cu(s)$$

When we put a piece of zinc metal into a beaker containing copper(II) ions in aqueous solution, three things happen (Figure 5.5):

1. Some of the zinc metal dissolves and goes into solution as Zn^{2+}.

2. Copper metal is deposited on the zinc metal.

3. The blue color of the Cu^{2+} ions gradually disappears.

The zinc metal loses electrons to the copper ions:

$$Zn(s) \longrightarrow Zn^{2+}(aq) + \boxed{2e^-} \quad \textbf{Zn is oxidized}$$

At the same time, the Cu^{2+} ions gain electrons from the zinc. The copper ions are reduced:

$$Cu^{2+}(aq) + \boxed{2e^-} \longrightarrow Cu(s) \quad \textbf{Cu^{2+} is reduced}$$

Oxidation and reduction are not independent reactions. That is, a species cannot gain electrons from nowhere, nor can a species lose electrons

Oxidation The loss of electrons; the gain of oxygen atoms or the loss of hydrogen atoms

Reduction The gain of electrons; the loss of oxygen atoms or the gain of hydrogen atoms

Redox reaction An oxidation–reduction reaction

Negative ions such as Cl^- or NO_3^- are present to balance charges, but we do not show them because they are spectator ions.

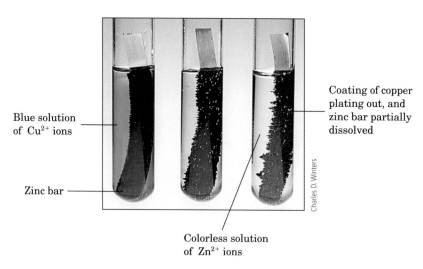

Blue solution of Cu^{2+} ions

Zinc bar

Coating of copper plating out, and zinc bar partially dissolved

Colorless solution of Zn^{2+} ions

Charles D. Winters

Figure 5.5   When a piece of zinc is added to a solution containing Cu^{2+} ions, the Zn is oxidized by Cu^{2+} ions, and the Cu^{2+} ions are reduced by the Zn.

to nothing. In other words, no oxidation can occur without an accompanying reduction, and vice versa. In the preceding reaction, Cu^{2+} is oxidizing Zn. We call Cu^{2+} an **oxidizing agent.** Similarly, Zn is reducing Cu^{2+}, and we call Zn a **reducing agent.**

We summarize these oxidation–reduction relationships for the reaction of zinc metal with Cu(II) ion in the following way:

Electrons flow from Zn to Cu^{2+}

$$Zn(s)   +   Cu^{2+}(aq) \longrightarrow Zn^{2+}(aq) + Cu(s)$$

Loses electrons; is oxidized

Gains electrons; is reduced

Gives electrons to Cu^{2+}; is the reducing agent

Takes electrons from Zn; is the oxidizing agent

> **Oxidizing agent** An entity that accepts electrons in an oxidation–reduction reaction
>
> **Reducing agent** An entity that donates electrons in an oxidation–reduction reaction

Although the definitions we have given for oxidation (loss of electrons) and reduction (gain of electrons) are easy to apply in many redox reactions, they are not so easy to apply in other cases. For example, another redox reaction is the combustion (burning) of methane, CH_4, in which CH_4 is oxidized to CO_2 while O_2 is reduced to CO_2 and H_2O:

$$CH_4(g) + O_2(g) \longrightarrow CO_2(g) + 2H_2O(g)$$
Methane

It is not easy to see the electron loss and gain in such a reaction, so chemists developed another definition of oxidation and reduction, one that is easier to apply in many cases, especially where organic compounds are involved:

Oxidation The gain of oxygen and/or the loss of hydrogen

Reduction The loss of oxygen and/or the gain of hydrogen

Applying these alternative definitions to the reaction of methane with oxygen, we find the following:

$$CH_4(g)   +   2O_2(g) \longrightarrow CO_2(g) + 2H_2O(g)$$

Gains O and loses H; is oxidized

Gains H; is reduced

Is the reducing agent

Is the oxidizing agent

In fact, this second definition is much older than the one involving electron transfer; it is the definition given by Lavoisier when he first discovered oxidation and reduction more than 200 years ago. Note that we could not apply this definition to our zinc-copper example.

EXAMPLE 5.16

In each equation, identify the substance that is oxidized, the substance that is reduced, the oxidizing agent, and the reducing agent.
(a) $Al(s) + Fe^{3+}(aq) \longrightarrow Al^{3+}(aq) + Fe(s)$

(b) $\underset{\text{Methanol}}{CH_3OH(g)} + O_2(g) \longrightarrow \underset{\text{Formic acid}}{HCOOH(g)} + H_2O(g)$

Solution

(a) $Al(s)$ loses three electrons in going to Al^{3+}; therefore, aluminum is oxidized. In the process of being oxidized, $Al(s)$ gives its electrons to Fe^{3+}, so $Al(s)$ is the reducing agent. Fe^{3+} gains three electrons in going to $Fe(s)$ and is reduced. In the process of being reduced, Fe^{3+} accepts three electrons from $Al(s)$, so Fe^{3+} is the oxidizing agent. To summarize:

Electrons flow
from Al to Fe^{3+}

$3e^-$

$\underset{\substack{\text{Loses electrons;} \\ \text{aluminum is oxidized} \\ \text{Gives electrons} \\ \text{to } Fe^{3+};\ Al \text{ is the} \\ \text{reducing agent}}}{Al(s)}$ + $\underset{\substack{\text{Gains electrons;} \\ \text{iron is reduced} \\ \text{Takes electrons} \\ \text{from Al; } Fe^{3+} \text{ is the} \\ \text{oxidizing agent}}}{Fe^{3+}(aq)} \longrightarrow Al^{3+}(aq) + Fe(s)$

(b) Because it is not easy to see the loss or gain of electrons in this example, we apply the second set of definitions. In converting CH_3OH to $HCOOH$, CH_3OH both gains oxygens and loses hydrogens; it is oxidized. In being converted to H_2O, O_2 gains hydrogens; it is reduced. The compound that is oxidized is the reducing agent; CH_3OH is the reducing agent. The compound that is reduced is the oxidizing agent; O_2 is the oxidizing agent. To summarize:

$\underset{\substack{\text{Is oxidized;} \\ \text{methanol is} \\ \text{the reducing} \\ \text{agent}}}{CH_3OH(g)} + \underset{\substack{\text{Is reduced;} \\ \text{oxygen is} \\ \text{the oxidizing} \\ \text{agent}}}{O_2(g)} \longrightarrow HCOOH(g) + H_2O(g)$

Problem 5.16

In each equation, identify the substance that is oxidized, the substance that is reduced, the oxidizing agent, and the reducing agent:
(a) $Ni^{2+}(aq) + Cr(s) \longrightarrow Ni(s) + Cr^{2+}(aq)$

(b) $\underset{\text{Formaldehyde}}{CH_2O(g)} + H_2(g) \longrightarrow \underset{\text{Methanol}}{CH_3OH(g)}$

Air pollution is caused by incomplete fuel combustion.

CHEMICAL CONNECTIONS 5B

Voltaic Cells

In Figure 5.5, we see that when a piece of zinc metal is put in a solution containing Cu^{2+} ions, zinc atoms give electrons to Cu^{2+} ions. We can change the experiment by putting the zinc metal in one beaker and the Cu^{2+} ions in another, and then connecting the two beakers by a length of wire and a salt bridge (see the accompanying figure). A reaction still takes place: Zinc atoms still give electrons to Cu^{2+} ions. Now, however, the electrons must flow through the wire to get from the Zn to the Cu^{2+}. This flow of electrons produces an electric current, and the electrons keep flowing until either the Zn or the Cu^{2+} is used up. In this way, the apparatus generates an electric current by using a redox reaction. We call this device a **voltaic cell** or, more commonly, a battery.

The electrons produced at the zinc end carry negative charges. This end of the battery is a negative electrode (the **anode**). The electrons released at the anode as zinc is oxidized go through an outside circuit and, in doing so, produce the battery's electric current. At the other end of the battery, at the positively charged electrode (the **cathode**), electrons are consumed as Cu^{2+} ions are reduced to copper metal.

To see why a salt bridge is necessary, we must look at the Cu^{2+} solution. Because we cannot have positive charges in any place without an equivalent number of negative charges, negative ions must be in the beaker as well—perhaps sulfate, nitrate, or some other anion. When electrons come over the wire, the Cu^{2+} is converted to Cu:

$$Cu^{2+}(aq) + 2e^- \longrightarrow Cu(s)$$

This reaction diminishes the number of Cu^{2+} ions, but the number of negative ions remains unchanged. The salt bridge is necessary to carry some of these negative ions to the other beaker, where they are needed to balance the Zn^{2+} ions being produced by the following reaction:

$$Zn(s) \longrightarrow Zn^{2+}(aq) + 2e^-$$

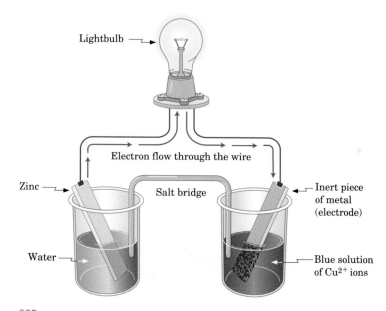

Active Figure Voltaic cell. **See a simulation based on this figure, and take a short quiz on the concepts at http://now.brookscole.com/gob8 or on the CD.**

We have said that redox reactions are extremely common. Here are some important categories:

1. **Combustion** All combustion (burning) reactions are redox reactions in which the compounds or mixtures that are burned are oxidized by oxygen, O_2. They include the burning of gasoline, diesel oil, fuel oil, natural gas, coal, wood, and paper. All these materials contain carbon, and all except coal also contain hydrogen. If the combustion is complete,

The rusting of iron and steel can be a serious problem in an industrial society.

These household bleaches are oxidizing agents.

carbon is oxidized to CO_2 and hydrogen is oxidized to H_2O. In an incomplete combustion, these elements are oxidized to other compounds, many of which cause air pollution. Unfortunately, much of today's combustion that takes place in gasoline and diesel engines and in furnaces is incomplete, so it contributes to air pollution. In the incomplete combustion of methane, for example, carbon is oxidized to carbon monoxide, CO, due to a lack of sufficient oxygen to complete its oxidation to CO_2:

$$2CH_4(g) + 3O_2(g) \longrightarrow 2CO(g) + 4H_2O(g)$$
Methane

2. **Respiration** Humans and animals get their energy by respiration. The oxygen in the air we breathe oxidizes carbon-containing compounds in our cells to produce CO_2 and H_2O. In fact, this oxidation reaction is really the same as combustion, although it takes place more slowly and at a much lower temperature. We discuss these reactions more fully in Chapter 27. The important product of these reactions is not CO_2 (which the body eliminates) or H_2O, but energy.

3. **Rusting** When iron or steel objects are left out in the open air, they eventually rust (steel is mostly iron but contains certain other elements, too). In rusting, iron is oxidized to a mixture of iron oxides. We can represent the main reaction by the following equation:

$$4Fe(s) + 3O_2(g) \longrightarrow 2Fe_2O_3(s)$$

4. **Bleaching** Most bleaching involves oxidation, and common bleaches are oxidizing agents. The colored compounds being bleached are usually organic compounds; oxidation converts them to colorless compounds.

5. **Batteries** A voltaic cell (Chemical Connections 5B) is a device in which electricity is generated from a chemical reaction. Such cells are often called batteries (Figure 5.6). We are all familiar with batteries in our cars and in such portable devices as radios, flashlights, cell phones, and computers. In all cases, the reaction taking place in the battery is a redox reaction.

(a)

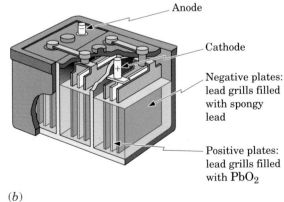

Anode

Cathode

Negative plates: lead grills filled with spongy lead

Positive plates: lead grills filled with PbO_2

(b)

Figure 5.6 (a) Dry cell batteries. (b) A lead storage battery.

CHEMICAL CONNECTIONS 5C

Oxidizing Antiseptics

An antiseptic is a compound that kills bacteria. Antiseptics are used to treat wounds—not to heal them any faster, but rather to prevent them from becoming infected by bacteria. Some antiseptics operate by oxidizing (and hence destroying) compounds essential to the normal functioning of the bacteria. One example is iodine, I_2, which was used as a household antiseptic for minor cuts and bruises for many years, not in the pure form but as a dilute solution in ethanol, called a tincture. Pure I_2 is a steel-gray solid that gives off a purple vapor when heated. In contrast, the tincture is a brown liquid. Another example of an oxidizing antiseptic is a dilute solution (commonly 3%) of hydrogen peroxide, H_2O_2, which is used as a mouth rinse to heal gum infections. Oxidizing antiseptics, however, are often regarded as too harsh. They not only kill bacteria but also harm skin and other normal tissues. For this reason, oxidizing antiseptics have largely been replaced by phenolic antiseptics (Section 13.5).

Disinfectants are also employed to kill bacteria, but they are used on inanimate objects rather than on living tissues. Many disinfectants are oxidizing agents. Two important examples are chlorine, Cl_2, a pale green gas, and ozone, O_3, a colorless gas. Both gases are

These tablets, which produce chlorine when mixed with water, are added to a swimming pool filter.

Yoav Levy/Phototake, NYC

added in small quantities to municipal water supplies to kill any harmful bacteria that may be present. Both gases must be handled carefully because they are very poisonous.

5.8 | What Is Heat of Reaction?

In almost all chemical reactions, not only are starting materials converted to products, but heat is also either given off or absorbed. For example, when one mole of carbon is oxidized by oxygen to produce one mole of CO_2, 94.0 kilocalories of heat is given off:

$$C(s) + O_2(g) \longrightarrow CO_2(g) + 94.0 \text{ kcal}$$

The heat given off or gained in a reaction is called the **heat of reaction.** A reaction that gives off heat is **exothermic;** a reaction that absorbs heat is **endothermic.** The amount of heat given off or absorbed is proportional to the amount of material. For example, when 2 mol of carbon is oxidized by oxygen to give carbon dioxide, $2 \times 94.0 = 188$ kcal of heat is given off.

The energy changes accompanying a chemical reaction are not limited to heat. In some reactions, such as in voltaic cells (Chemical Connections 5B), the energy given off takes the form of electricity. In other reactions, such as photosynthesis (the reaction whereby plants convert water and carbon dioxide to sugar and oxygen), the energy absorbed is in the form of light.

An example of an endothermic reaction is the decomposition of mercury(II) oxide:

$$\underset{\substack{\text{Mercury(II) oxide} \\ \text{(mercuric oxide)}}}{2HgO(s)} + 43.4 \text{ kcal} \longrightarrow 2Hg(\ell) + O_2(g)$$

This equation tells us that, if we want to decompose 2 mol of mercury(II) oxide into the elements $Hg(\ell)$ and $O_2(g)$, we must add 43.4 kcal of energy to HgO.

Heat of reaction The heat given off or absorbed in a chemical reaction

Exothermic reaction A chemical reaction that gives off heat

Endothermic reaction A chemical reaction that absorbs heat

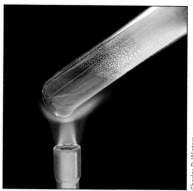

Mercury(II) oxide, a red compound, decomposes into two elements when heated: mercury (a metal) and oxygen (a nonmetal). Mercury vapor condenses on the cooler upper portion of the test tube.

Charles D. Winters

Incidentally, the law of conservation of energy tells us that the reverse reaction, the oxidation of mercury, must give off exactly the same amount of heat:

$$2Hg(\ell) + O_2(g) \longrightarrow 2HgO(s) + 43.4 \text{ kcal}$$

Especially important are the heats of reaction for combustion reactions. As we saw in Section 5.7, combustion reactions are the most important heat-producing reactions, because most of the energy required for modern society to function is derived from them. All combustions are exothermic. The heat given off in a combustion reaction is called the **heat of combustion.**

SUMMARY OF KEY QUESTIONS

SECTION 5.2 What Are Molecular Weights and Formula Weights, and How Do They Differ?

- The **formula weight** of a compound is the sum of the atomic weights of all atoms in the compound expressed in atomic mass units (amu). Formula weight applies to both ionic and molecular compounds.
- The term **molecular weight,** also expressed in amu, applies to only molecular compounds.

SECTION 5.3 What Is a Mole and How Do We Use It to Calculate Mass Relationships?

- A **mole (mol)** of any substance is defined as Avogadro's number (6.02×10^{23}) of formula units of the substance.
- The **molar mass** of a substance is its formula weight expressed in grams.

SECTION 5.4 How Do We Balance Chemical Equations?

- A **chemical equation** is an expression showing which reactants are converted to which products. A balanced chemical equation shows how many moles of each starting material are converted to how many moles of each product.

SECTION 5.5 How Do We Calculate Mass Relationships in Chemical Reactions?

- **Stoichiometry** is the study of the mass relationships in chemical reactions.
- The reagent that is used up first in a reaction is called the **limiting reagent.**
- The **percent yield** for a reaction equals the **actual yield** divided by the **theoretical yield** multiplied by 100.

SECTION 5.6 How Can We Predict if Ions in Aqueous Solution Will React with Each Other?

- When ions are mixed in aqueous solution, they are said to react with one another if (1) a precipitate forms, (2) a gas forms, (3) an acid neutralizes a base, or (4) an oxidation–reduction reaction takes place.
- Ions that do not react are called **spectator ions.**
- A **net ionic equation** shows only those ions that react. In a net ionic equation, both the charges and the number of atoms must be balanced.

SECTION 5.7 What Are Oxidation and Reduction, and Why Do They Always Occur Together?

- **Oxidation** is the loss of electrons; **reduction** is the gain of electrons. These two processes must take place together; you cannot have one without the other. The joint process is often called a redox reaction.
- Oxidation can also be defined as the gain of oxygens and/or the loss of hydrogens. Reduction can also be defined as the loss of oxygens and/or the gain of hydrogens.

SECTION 5.8 What Is Heat of Reaction?

- Almost all chemical reactions are accompanied by either a gain or a loss of heat. This heat is called the **heat of reaction.**
- Reactions that give off heat are **exothermic;** those that absorb heat are **endothermic.**
- The heat given off in a combustion reaction is called the **heat of combustion.**

PROBLEMS

SECTION 5.2 What Are Molecular Weights and Formula Weights, and How Do They Differ?

5.17 ■ Calculate the formula weight of
  (a) KCl
  (b) Na_3PO_4
  (c) $Fe(OH)_2$

5.18 Calculate the formula weight of
  (a) $NaAl(SO_3)_2$
  (b) $Al_2(SO_4)_3$
  (c) $(NH_4)_2CO_3$

5.19 Calculate the molecular weight of
  (a) Sucrose, $C_{12}H_{22}O_{11}$
  (b) Glycine, $C_2H_5NO_2$
  (c) DDT, $C_{14}H_9Cl_5$

SECTION 5.3 What Is a Mole and How Do We Use It to Calculate Mass Relationships?

5.20 ■ Calculate the number of moles in
  (a) 32 g of methane, CH_4
  (b) 345.6 g of nitric oxide, NO
  (c) 184.4 g of chlorine dioxide, ClO_2
  (d) 720 g of glycerin, $C_3H_8O_3$

5.21 ■ Calculate the number of grams in
  (a) 1.77 mol of nitrogen dioxide, NO_2
  (b) 0.84 mol of 2-propanol, C_3H_8O (rubbing alcohol)
  (c) 3.69 mol of uranium hexafluoride, UF_6
  (d) 0.348 mol of galactose, $C_6H_{12}O_6$
  (e) 4.9×10^{-2} mol of vitamin C, $C_6H_8O_6$

5.22 Calculate the number of moles of
  (a) O atoms in 18.1 mol of formaldehyde, CH_2O
  (b) Br atoms in 0.41 mol of bromoform, $CHBr_3$
  (c) O atoms in 3.5×10^3 mol of $Al_2(SO_4)_3$
  (d) Hg atoms in 87 g of HgO

5.23 Calculate the number of moles of
  (a) S^{2-} ions in 6.56 mol of Na_2S
  (b) Mg^{2+} ions in 8.320 mol of $Mg_3(PO_4)_2$
  (c) Acetate ion, CH_3COO^-, in 0.43 mol of $Ca(CH_3COO)_2$

5.24 Calculate the number of
  (a) Nitrogen atoms in 25.0 g of TNT, $C_7H_5N_3O_6$
  (b) Carbon atoms in 40.0 g of ethanol, C_2H_6O
  (c) Oxygen atoms in 500 mg of aspirin, $C_9H_8O_4$
  (d) Sodium atoms in 2.40 g of sodium dihydrogen phosphate, NaH_2PO_4

5.25 A single atom of cerium weighs just about twice as much as a single atom of gallium. What is the weight ratio of 25 atoms of cerium to 25 atoms of gallium?

5.26 What is the mass in grams of each number of molecules of formaldehyde, CH_2O?
  (a) 100 molecules   (b) 3000 molecules
  (c) 5.0×10^6 molecules   (d) 2.0×10^{24} molecules

5.27 How many molecules are in
  (a) 2.9 mol of TNT, $C_7H_5N_3O_6$
  (b) one drop (0.0500 g) of water
  (c) 3.1×10^{-1} g of aspirin, $C_9H_8O_4$

5.28 A typical deposit of cholesterol, $C_{27}H_{46}O$, in an artery might have a mass of 3.9 mg. How many molecules of cholesterol are in this mass?

5.29 The molecular weight of hemoglobin is about 68,000 amu. What is the mass in grams of a single molecule of hemoglobin?

SECTION 5.4 How Do We Balance Chemical Equations?

5.30 ■ Balance each equation.
  (a) $HI + NaOH \longrightarrow NaI + H_2O$
  (b) $Ba(NO_3)_2 + H_2S \longrightarrow BaS + HNO_3$
  (c) $CH_4 + O_2 \longrightarrow CO_2 + H_2O$
  (d) $C_4H_{10} + O_2 \longrightarrow CO_2 + H_2O$
  (e) $Fe + CO_2 \longrightarrow Fe_2O_3 + CO$

5.31 ■ Balance each equation.
  (a) $H_2 + I_2 \longrightarrow HI$
  (b) $Al + O_2 \longrightarrow Al_2O_3$
  (c) $Na + Cl_2 \longrightarrow NaCl$
  (d) $Al + HBr \longrightarrow AlBr_3 + H_2$
  (e) $P + O_2 \longrightarrow P_2O_5$

5.32 If you blow carbon dioxide gas into a solution of calcium hydroxide, a milky-white precipitate of calcium carbonate forms. Write a balanced equation for the formation of calcium carbonate in this reaction.

5.33 Calcium oxide is prepared by heating limestone (calcium carbonate, $CaCO_3$) to a high temperature, at which point it decomposes to calcium oxide and carbon dioxide. Write a balanced equation for this preparation of calcium oxide.

5.34 The brilliant white light in some fireworks displays is produced by burning magnesium in air. The magnesium reacts with oxygen in the air to form magnesium oxide. Write a balanced equation for this reaction.

5.35 The rusting of iron is a chemical reaction of iron with oxygen in the air to form iron(III) oxide. Write a balanced equation for this reaction.

5.36 When solid carbon burns in a limited supply of oxygen gas, carbon monoxide gas, CO, forms. This gas is deadly to humans because it combines with hemoglobin in the blood, making it impossible for the blood to transport oxygen. Write a balanced equation for the formation of carbon monoxide.

5.37 Solid ammonium carbonate, $(NH_4)_2CO_3$, decomposes at room temperature to ammonia, carbon dioxide, and water. Because of the ease of decomposition and the penetrating odor of ammonia, ammonium carbonate can be used as smelling salts. Write a balanced equation for this decomposition.

5.38 In the chemical test for arsenic, the gas arsine, AsH_3, is prepared. When arsine is decomposed by heating, arsenic metal deposits as a mirrorlike coating on the surface of a glass container, and hydrogen gas, H_2, is given off. Write a balanced equation for the decomposition of arsine.

5.39 When a piece of aluminum metal is dropped into hydrochloric acid, HCl, hydrogen is released as a gas, and a solution of aluminum chloride forms. Write a balanced equation for this reaction.

5.40 In the industrial chemical preparation of chlorine, Cl_2, an electric current is passed through an aqueous solution of sodium chloride to give $Cl_2(g)$ and $H_2(g)$. The other product of this reaction is sodium hydroxide. Write a balanced equation for this reaction.

SECTION 5.5 How Do We Calculate Mass Relationships in Chemical Reactions?

5.41 ■ For the reaction

$$2N_2(g) + 3O_2(g) \longrightarrow 2N_2O_3(g)$$

(a) How many moles of N_2 are required to react completely with 1 mole of O_2?

(b) How many moles of N_2O_3 are produced from the complete reaction of 1 mole of O_2?

(c) How many moles of O_2 are required to produce 8 moles of N_2O_3?

5.42 Magnesium reacts with sulfuric acid according to the following equation. How many moles of H_2 are produced by the complete reaction of 230 mg of Mg with sulfuric acid?

$$Mg(s) + H_2SO_4(aq) \longrightarrow MgSO_4(aq) + H_2(g)$$

5.43 ■ Chloroform, $CHCl_3$, is prepared industrially by the reaction of methane with chlorine. How many grams of Cl_2 are needed to produce 1.50 moles of chloroform?

$$CH_4(g) + 3Cl_2(g) \longrightarrow CHCl_3(\ell) + 3HCl(g)$$
$$\text{Methane} \qquad\qquad \text{Chloroform}$$

5.44 ■ At one time, acetaldehyde was prepared industrially by the reaction of ethylene with air in the presence of a copper catalyst. How many grams of acetaldehyde can be prepared from 81.7 g of ethylene?

$$C_2H_4(g) + O_2(g) \longrightarrow C_2H_4O(g)$$
$$\text{Ethylene} \qquad\qquad \text{Acetaldehyde}$$

5.45 Chlorine dioxide, ClO_2, is used for bleaching paper. It is also the gas used to kill the anthrax spores that contaminated the Hart Senate Office Building in 2001. Chlorine dioxide is prepared by treating sodium chlorite with chlorine gas.

$$NaClO_2(aq) + Cl_2(g) \longrightarrow ClO_2(g) + NaCl(aq)$$
$$\text{Sodium} \qquad\qquad\qquad \text{Chlorine}$$
$$\text{chlorite} \qquad\qquad\qquad \text{dioxide}$$

(a) Balance the equation for the preparation of chlorine dioxide.

(b) Calculate the weight of chlorine dioxide that can be prepared from 5.50 kg of sodium chlorite.

5.46 Ethanol, C_2H_6O, is added to gasoline to produce "gasohol," a fuel for automobile engines. How many grams of O_2 are required for complete combustion of 421 g of C_2H_6O?

$$C_2H_5OH(\ell) + 3O_2(g) \longrightarrow 2CO_2(g) + 3H_2O$$
$$\text{Ethanol}$$

5.47 In photosynthesis, green plants convert CO_2 and H_2O to glucose, $C_6H_{12}O_6$. How many grams of CO_2 are required to produce 5.1 g of glucose?

$$6CO_2(g) + 6H_2O(\ell) \xrightarrow{\text{Photosynthesis}} C_6H_{12}O_6(aq) + 6O_2(g)$$
$$\text{Glucose}$$

5.48 Iron ore is converted to iron by heating it with coal, C, and oxygen according to the following equation:

$$2Fe_2O_3(s) + 6C(s) + 3O_2(g) \longrightarrow 4Fe(s) + 6CO_2(g)$$

If the process is run until 3940 g of Fe is produced, how many grams of CO_2 will also be produced?

5.49 Given the reaction in Problem 5.48, how many grams of C are necessary to react completely with 0.58 g of Fe_2O_3?

5.50 ■ Aspirin is made by the reaction of salicylic acid with acetic anhydride. What is the theoretical yield of aspirin if 85.0 g of salicylic acid is treated with excess acetic anhydride?

$$C_7H_6O_3(s) + C_4H_6O_3(\ell) \longrightarrow C_9H_8O_4(s) + C_2H_4O_2(\ell)$$

| Salicylic acid | Acetic anhydride | Aspirin | Acetic acid |

5.51 Suppose that the yield of aspirin by the reaction shown in Problem 5.50 is 75%. How many grams of salicylic acid would be required to give an actual yield of 25.0 g of aspirin?

5.52 Benzene reacts with bromine to produce bromobenzene according to the following equation:

$$C_6H_6(\ell) + Br_2(\ell) \longrightarrow C_6H_5Br(\ell) + HBr(g)$$

| Benzene | Bromine | Bromobenzene | Hydrogen bromide |

If 60.0 g of benzene is mixed with 135 g of bromine,
(a) Which is the limiting reagent?
(b) How many grams of bromobenzene are formed in the reaction?

5.53 ■ Ethyl chloride is prepared by the reaction of chlorine with ethane according to the following balanced equation. When 5.6 g of ethane is reacted with excess chlorine, 8.2 g of ethyl chloride forms. Calculate the percent yield of ethyl chloride.

$$C_2H_6(g) + Cl_2(g) \longrightarrow C_2H_5Cl(\ell) + HCl(g)$$

| Ethane | | Ethyl chloride |

5.54 Diethyl ether is made from ethanol according to the following reaction:

$$2C_2H_5OH(\ell) \longrightarrow (C_2H_5)_2O(\ell) + H_2O(\ell)$$

| Ethanol | Diethyl ether |

In an experiment, starting with 517 g of ethanol gave 391 g of diethyl ether. What was the percent yield in this experiment?

SECTION 5.6 How Can We Predict if Ions in Aqueous Solution Will React with Each Other?

5.55 Define (a) spectator ion, (b) net ionic equation, and (c) aqueous solution.

5.56 Balance these net ionic equations.
(a) $Ag^+(aq) + Br^-(aq) \longrightarrow AgBr(s)$
(b) $Cd^{2+}(aq) + S^{2-}(aq) \longrightarrow CdS(s)$
(c) $Sc^{3+}(aq) + SO_4^{2-}(aq) \longrightarrow Sc_2(SO_4)_3(s)$
(d) $Sn^{2+}(aq) + Fe^{2+}(aq) \longrightarrow Sn(s) + Fe^{3+}(aq)$
(e) $K(s) + H_2O(\ell) \longrightarrow K^+(aq) + OH^-(aq) + H_2(g)$

5.57 In the equation

$$2Na^+(aq) + CO_3^{2-}(aq) + Sr^{2+}(aq) + 2Cl^-(aq) \longrightarrow SrCO_3(s) + 2Na^+(aq) + 2Cl^-(aq)$$

(a) Identify the spectator ions.
(b) Write the balanced net ionic equation.

5.58 Predict whether a precipitate will form when aqueous solutions of the following compounds are mixed. If a precipitate will form, write its formula, and write a net ionic equation for its formation. To make your predictions, use the solubility generalizations in Section 5.6.
(a) $CaCl_2(aq) + K_3PO_4(aq) \longrightarrow$
(b) $KCl(aq) + Na_2SO_4(aq) \longrightarrow$
(c) $(NH_4)_2CO_3(aq) + Ba(NO_3)_2(aq) \longrightarrow$
(d) $FeCl_2(aq) + KOH(aq) \longrightarrow$
(e) $Ba(NO_3)_2(aq) + NaOH(aq) \longrightarrow$
(f) $Na_2S(aq) + SbCl_3(aq) \longrightarrow$
(g) $Pb(NO_3)_2(aq) + K_2SO_4(aq) \longrightarrow$

5.59 ■ When a solution of ammonium chloride is added to a solution of lead(II) nitrate, $Pb(NO_3)_2$, a white precipitate, lead(II) chloride, forms. Write a balanced net ionic equation for this reaction. Both ammonium chloride and lead nitrate exist as dissociated ions in aqueous solution.

5.60 When a solution of hydrochloric acid, HCl, is added to a solution of sodium sulfite, Na_2SO_3, sulfur dioxide gas is released from the solution. Write a net ionic equation for this reaction. An aqueous solution of HCl contains H^+ and Cl^- ions, and Na_2SO_3 exists as dissociated ions in aqueous solution.

5.61 When a solution of sodium hydroxide is added to a solution of ammonium carbonate, H_2O is formed and ammonia gas, NH_3, is released when the solution is heated. Write a net ionic equation for this reaction. Both NaOH and $(NH_4)_2CO_3$ exist as dissociated ions in aqueous solution.

5.62 ■ Using the solubility generalizations given in Section 5.6, predict which of these ionic compounds are soluble in water.
(a) KCl   (b) NaOH   (c) $BaSO_4$
(d) Na_2SO_4 (e) Na_2CO_3 (f) $Fe(OH)_2$

5.63 ■ Using the solubility generalizations given in Section 5.6, predict which of these ionic compounds are soluble in water.
(a) $MgCl_2$ (b) $CaCO_3$ (c) Na_2SO_3
(d) NH_4NO_3 (e) $Pb(OH)_2$

SECTION 5.7 What Are Oxidation and Reduction, and Why Do They Always Occur Together?

5.64 Give two definitions of oxidation and two definitions of reduction.

5.65 Can reduction take place without oxidation? Explain.

5.66 ■ In the reaction

$$Pb(s) + 2Ag^+(aq) \longrightarrow Pb^{2}(aq) + 2Ag(s)$$

(a) Which species is oxidized and which species is reduced?

(b) Which species is the oxidizing agent and which species is the reducing agent?

5.67 In the reaction

$$C_7H_{12}(\ell) + 10O_2(g) \longrightarrow 7CO_2(g) + 6H_2O(\ell)$$

(a) Which species is oxidized and which species is reduced?

(b) Which species is the oxidizing agent and which is the reducing agent?

5.68 When a piece of sodium metal is added to water, hydrogen is evolved as a gas and a solution of sodium hydroxide is formed.

(a) Write a balanced equation for this reaction.

(b) What is oxidized in this reaction? What is reduced?

SECTION 5.8 What Is Heat of Reaction?

5.69 What is the difference between *exothermic* and *endothermic?*

5.70 Which of these reactions are exothermic and which are endothermic?

(a) $2NH_3(g) + 22.0 \text{ kcal} \longrightarrow N_2(g) + 3H_2(g)$

(b) $H_2(g) + F_2(g) \longrightarrow 2HF(g) + 124 \text{ kcal}$

(c) $C(s) + O_2(g) \longrightarrow CO_2(g) + 94.0 \text{ kcal}$

(d) $H_2(g) + CO_2(g) + 9.80 \text{ kcal} \longrightarrow H_2O(g) + CO(g)$

(e) $C_3H_8(g) + 5O_2(g) \longrightarrow$
$$3CO_2(g) + 4H_2O(g) + 531 \text{ kcal}$$

5.71 In the following reaction, 9.80 kcal is absorbed per mole of CO_2 undergoing reaction. How much heat is given off if two moles of water is reacted with two moles of carbon monoxide?

$$H_2(g) + CO_2(g) + 9.80 \text{ kcal} \longrightarrow H_2O(g) + CO(g)$$

5.72 Following is the equation for the combustion of acetone:

$$2C_3H_6O(\ell) + 8O_2(g) \longrightarrow 6CO_2(g) + 6H_2O(g) + 853.6 \text{ kcal}$$
Acetone

How much heat will be given off if 0.37 mol of acetone is burned completely?

5.73 The oxidation of glucose, $C_6H_{12}O_6$, to carbon dioxide and water is exothermic. The heat liberated is the same whether glucose is metabolized in the body or burned in air.

$$C_6H_{12}O_6 + 6O_2 \longrightarrow 6CO_2 + 6H_2O + 670 \text{ kcal/mol}$$
Glucose

Calculate the heat liberated when 15.0 g of glucose is metabolized to carbon dioxide and water in the body.

5.74 The heat of combustion of glucose, $C_6H_{12}O_6$, is 670 kcal/mol. The heat of combustion of ethanol, C_2H_6O, is 327 kcal/mol. The heat liberated by oxidation of each compound is the same whether it is burned in air or metabolized in the body. On a kcal/g basis, metabolism of which compound liberates more heat?

5.75 A plant requires approximately 4178 kcal for the production of 1.00 kg of starch (Section 19.6A) from carbon dioxide and water.

(a) Is the production of starch in a plant an exothermic process or an endothermic process?

(b) Calculate the energy in kilocalories required by a plant for the production of 6.32 g of starch.

5.76 To convert 1 mol of iron(III) oxide to its elements requires 196.5 kcal:

$$Fe_2O_3(s) + 196.5 \text{ kcal} \longrightarrow 2Fe(s) + \tfrac{3}{2}O_2(g)$$

How many grams of iron can be produced if 156.0 kcal of heat is absorbed by a large-enough sample of iron(III) oxide?

Chemical Connections

5.77 (Chemical Connections 5A) How does fluoride ion protect the enamel against tooth decay?

5.78 (Chemical Connections 5A) What kind of ions is hydroxyapatite made of?

5.79 (Chemical Connections 5B) A voltaic cell is represented by the following equation:

$$Fe(s) + Zn^{2+}(aq) \longrightarrow Fe^{2+}(aq) + Zn(s)$$

Which electrode is the anode and which electrode is the cathode?

5.80 (Chemical Connections 5C) Hydrogen peroxide is not only an antiseptic but also an oxidizing agent. The following equation shows the reaction of hydrogen peroxide with acetaldehyde to give acetic acid:

$$C_2H_4O(\ell) + H_2O_2(\ell) \longrightarrow C_2H_4O_2(\ell) + H_2O(\ell)$$
Acetaldehyde Hydrogen   Acetic   Water
              peroxide   acid

In this reaction, which species is oxidized and which species is reduced? Which species is the oxidizing agent and which species is the reducing agent?

Additional Problems

5.81 When gaseous dinitrogen pentoxide, N_2O_5, is bubbled into water, nitric acid, HNO_3, forms. Write a balanced equation for this reaction.

5.82 In a certain reaction, Cu^+ is converted to Cu^{2+}. Is Cu^+ ion oxidized or reduced in this reaction? Is Cu^+ ion an oxidizing agent or a reducing agent in this reaction?

5.83 Using the equation

$$Fe_2O_3(s) + 3CO(g) \longrightarrow 2Fe(s) + 3CO_2(g)$$

(a) Show that this is a redox reaction. Which species is oxidized and which is reduced?

(b) How many moles of Fe_2O_3 are required to produce 38.4 mol of Fe?

(c) How many grams of CO are required to produce 38.4 mol of Fe?

5.84 Explain this statement: Our modern civilization depends on the heat obtained from chemical reactions.

5.85 When an aqueous solution of Na_3PO_4 is added to an aqueous solution of $Cd(NO_3)_2$, a precipitate forms. Write a net ionic equation for this reaction and identify the spectator ions.

5.86 The active ingredient in an analgesic tablet is 488 mg of aspirin, $C_9H_8O_5$. How many moles of aspirin does the tablet contain?

5.87 Chlorophyll, the compound responsible for the green color of leaves and grasses, contains one atom of magnesium in each molecule. If the percentage by weight of magnesium in chlorophyll is 2.72%, what is the molecular weight of chlorophyll?

5.88 If 7.0 kg of N_2 is added to 11.0 kg of H_2 to form NH_3, which reactant is in excess?

$$N_2(g) + 3H_2(g) \longrightarrow 2NH_3(g)$$

5.89 Lead(II) nitrate and aluminum chloride react according to the following equation:

$$3Pb(NO_3)_2 + 2AlCl_3 \longrightarrow 3PbCl_2 + 2Al(NO_3)_3$$

In an experiment, 8.00 g of lead nitrate was reacted with 2.67 g of aluminum chloride, and 5.55 g of lead chloride was formed.

(a) Which reactant was the limiting reagent?

(b) What was the percent yield?

5.90 Assume that the average red blood cell has a mass of 2×10^{-8} g and that 20% of its mass is hemoglobin (a protein whose molar mass is 68,000). How many molecules of hemoglobin are present in one red blood cell?

5.91 Reaction of pentane, C_5H_{12}, with oxygen, O_2, gives carbon dioxide and water.

(a) Write a balanced equation for this reaction.

(b) In this reaction, what is oxidized and what is reduced?

(c) What is the oxidizing agent and what is the reducing agent?

5.92 Ammonia is prepared industrially by the reaction of nitrogen and hydrogen according to the following equation:

$$N_2(g) + 3H_2(g) \longrightarrow 2NH_3(g)$$
Ammonia

If 29.7 kg of N_2 is added to 3.31 kg of H_2,

(a) Which reactant is the limiting reagent?

(b) How many grams of the other reactant are left over?

(c) How many grams of NH_3 are formed if the reaction goes to completion?

Looking Ahead

5.93 The heat of combustion of methane, CH_4, the major component of natural gas, is 213 kcal/mol. The heat of combustion of propane, C_3H_8, the major component of LPG or bottled gas, is 530 kcal/mol.

(a) Write a balanced equation for the complete combustion of each fuel to CO_2 and H_2O.

(b) On a kcal/mol basis, which of these two fuels is the better source of heat energy?

(c) On a kcal/g basis, which of these two fuels is the better source of heat energy?

5.94 The two major sources of energy in our diets are fats and carbohydrates. Palmitic acid, one of the major components of both animal fats and vegetable oils, belongs to a group of compounds called fatty acids. The metabolism of fatty acids is responsible for releasing the energy from fats. The major carbohydrates in our diets are sucrose (table sugar; Section 20.4A) and starch (Section 20.5A). Both starch and sucrose are first converted in the body to glucose, and then glucose is metabolized to produce energy. The heat of combustion of palmitic acid is 2385 kcal/mol, and that of glucose is 670 kcal/mol. Following are equations for the metabolism of each body fuel:

$$C_{16}H_{32}O_2(aq) + O_2(g) \longrightarrow CO_2(g) + H_2O(\ell) + 2385 \text{ kcal/mol}$$
Palmitic acid
(256 g/mol)

$$C_6H_{12}O_6(aq) + O_2(g) \longrightarrow CO_2(g) + H_2O(\ell) + 670 \text{ kcal/mol}$$
Glucose
(180 g/mol)

(a) Balance the equation for the metabolism of each fuel.

(b) Calculate the heat of combustion of each in kcal/g.

(c) In terms of kcal/mol, which of the two is the better source of energy for the body?

(d) In terms of kcal/g, which of the two is the better source of energy for the body?

CHAPTER 6

Gases, Liquids, and Solids

Hot-air balloon, Utah.

Vince Streano/Corbis

GOB
Chemistry✦•Now™
Look for this logo in the chapter and go to GOB ChemistryNow at **http://now.brookscole.com/gob8** or on the CD for tutorials, simulations, and problems.

6.1 What Are the Three States of Matter?

Various forces hold matter together and cause it to take different forms. In an atomic nucleus, very strong forces of attraction keep the protons and neutrons together (Chapter 3). In an atom itself, there are attractions between the positive nucleus and the negative electrons that surround it. Within molecules, atoms are attracted to each other by covalent bonds, the arrangement of which causes the molecules to assume a particular shape. Within an ionic crystal, three-dimensional shapes arise because of electrostatic attractions between ions.

In addition to these forces, there are attractive forces between molecules. These forces, which are the subject of this chapter, are weaker than any of the forces already mentioned; nevertheless, they help to determine whether a particular compound is a solid, a liquid, or a gas at room temperature.

These attractive forces hold matter together; in effect, they counteract another form of energy—kinetic energy—that tends to lead to a number of different ways for molecules to arrange themselves. In the absence of attractive

CHEMICAL CONNECTIONS 6A

Entropy: A Measure of Dispersal of Energy

As noted earlier, the molecules of a gas move randomly. The higher the temperature, the faster they move. In general, random motion means that many more arrangements of molecules are possible. When the temperature decreases, the molecules slow down and fewer different arrangements are possible. When all the molecules of a system become motionless and line up perfectly, we achieve the greatest possible order. At this point, the substance is a solid. The measure of such order is called **entropy.** When the order is perfect, the entropy of the system is zero. When molecules rotate or move from one place to another, the disorder increases, as does the entropy. Thus, when a crystal melts, entropy increases; when a liquid vaporizes, it also increases. When the temperature of a gas, a liquid, a solid, or a mixture of these states increases, the entropy of the system increases because an increase in temperature always increases molecular motions. When we combine two pure substances and they mix, disorder increases and so does the entropy.

We learned about the absolute, or Kelvin, temperature scale in Section 1.4E. Absolute zero (0 K or −273°C) is the lowest possible temperature. Although scientists have not been able to reach absolute zero, they have been able to produce temperatures within

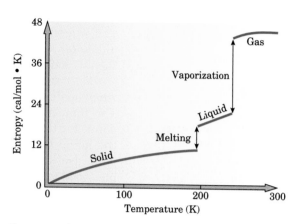

The entropy of ammonia, NH_3, as a function of absolute temperature.

a few billionths of a degree of it. At this low temperature, virtually all molecular motion ceases, almost perfect order reigns, and the entropy of the substance is nearly zero. In fact, a completely ordered pure crystalline solid at 0 K has an entropy of zero.

forces, the kinetic energy that particles possess keeps them constantly moving, mostly in random, disorganized ways. Kinetic energy increases with increasing temperature. Therefore, the higher the temperature, the greater the tendency of particles to have more possible arrangements. The total energy remains the same, but it is more widely dispersed. This dispersal of energy will have some important consequences, as we will see shortly.

The physical state of matter thus depends on a balance between the kinetic energy of particles, which tends to keep them apart, and the attractive forces between them, which tend to bring them together (Figure 6.1).

At high temperatures, molecules possess a high kinetic energy and move so fast that the attractive forces between them are too weak to hold them together. This situation is called the **gaseous state.** At lower temperatures, molecules move more slowly, to the point where the forces of attraction between them become important. When the temperature is low enough, a gas condenses to form a **liquid state.** Molecules in the liquid state still move past

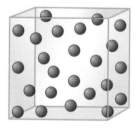

Gas

• Molecules far apart and disordered
• Negligible interactions between molecules

Liquid

• Intermediate situation

Solid

• Molecules close together and ordered
• Strong interactions between molecules

Figure 6.1 The three states of matter. A gas has no definite shape, and its volume is the volume of the container. A liquid has a definite volume but no definite shape. A solid has a definite shape and a definite volume.

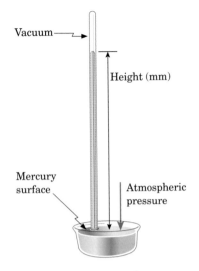

Figure 6.2 A mercury barometer.

Pressure The force per unit area exerted against a surface

1 atm = 760 mm Hg
     = 760 torr
     = 101,325 pascals
     = 29.92 in. Hg

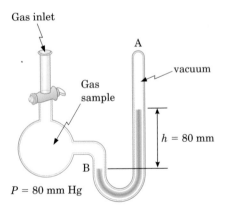

Figure 6.3 A mercury manometer.

each other, but they travel much more slowly than they do in the gaseous state. When the temperature is even lower, molecules no longer have enough velocity to move past each other. In the **solid state**, each molecule has a certain number of nearest neighbors, and these neighbors do not change.

The attractive forces between molecules are the same in all three states. The difference is that, in the gaseous state (and to a lesser degree in the liquid state), the kinetic energy of the molecules is great enough to overcome the attractive forces between them.

Most substances can exist in any of the three states. Typically a solid, when heated to a sufficiently high temperature, melts and becomes a liquid. The temperature at which this change takes place is called the melting point. Further heating causes the temperature to rise to the point at which the liquid boils and becomes a gas. This temperature is called the boiling point. Not all substances, however, can exist in all three states. For example, wood and paper cannot be melted. On heating, they either decompose or burn (depending on whether air is present), but they do not melt. Another example is sugar, which does not melt when heated but rather forms a dark substance called caramel.

6.2 | What Is Gas Pressure and How Do We Measure It?

On the earth we live under a blanket of air that presses down on us and on everything else around us. As we all know from weather reports, the **pressure** of the atmosphere varies from day to day.

A gas consists of molecules in rapid, random motion. The pressure a gas exerts on a surface, such as the walls of a container, results from the continual bombardment on the walls of the container by the rapidly moving gas molecules. We use an instrument called a **barometer** (Figure 6.2) to measure atmospheric pressure. A barometer consists of a long glass tube that is completely filled with mercury and then inverted into a pool of mercury in a dish. Because there is no air at the top of the mercury column in the tube (there is no way air could get in), no gas pressure is exerted on the mercury column. The entire atmosphere, however, exerts its pressure on the mercury in the open dish. The difference in the heights of the two mercury levels is the atmospheric pressure.

Pressure is most commonly measured in **millimeters of mercury (mm Hg)**. Pressure is also measured in **torr**, a unit named in honor of the Italian physicist and mathematician Evangelista Torricelli (1608–1647), who invented the barometer. At sea level, the average pressure of the atmosphere is 760 mm Hg. We use this number to define still another unit of pressure, the **atmosphere (atm).**

There are several other units with which to measure pressure. The SI unit is the pascal, and meteorologists report pressure in inches of mercury. In this book we use only mm Hg and atm.

A barometer is adequate for measuring the pressure of the atmosphere, but to measure the pressure of a gas in a container, we use a simpler instrument called a **manometer.** One form of manometer consists of a U-shaped tube containing mercury (Figure 6.3). Arm A has been evacuated, and sealed, and it has zero pressure. Arm B is connected to the container in which the gas sample is enclosed. The pressure of the gas depresses the level of the mercury in arm B. The difference between the two mercury levels gives the pressure directly in mm Hg. If more gas is added to the sample container, the mercury level in B will be pushed down and that in A will rise as the pressure in the bulb increases.

6.3 | What Are the Laws That Govern the Behavior of Gases?

By observing the behavior of gases under different sets of temperatures and pressures, scientists have established a number of relationships. In this section, we study three of the most important.

These gas laws we describe hold not only for pure gases but also for mixtures of gases.

A. Boyle's Law and the Pressure–Volume Relationship

Boyle's law states that for a fixed mass of gas at a constant temperature, the volume of the gas is inversely proportional to the pressure. If the pressure doubles, for example, the volume decreases by one half. This law can be stated mathematically in the following equation, where P_1 and V_1 are the initial pressure and volume, and P_2 and V_2 are the final pressure and volume:

$$PV = \text{constant} \quad \text{or} \quad P_1V_1 = P_2V_2$$

This relationship between pressure and volume accounts for what happens in the cylinder of a car engine (Figure 6.4).

GOB
Chemistry‑♦‑Now™
Click *Chemistry Interactive* for an interactive exploration of a **Boyle's Law** experiment

---

CHEMICAL CONNECTIONS 6B

Breathing and Boyle's Law

Under normal resting conditions, we breathe about 12 times per minute, each time inhaling and exhaling about 500 mL of air. When we inhale, we lower the diaphragm or raise the rib cage, either of which increases the volume of the chest cavity. In accord with Boyle's law, as the volume of the chest cavity increases, the pressure within it decreases and becomes lower than the outside pressure. As a result, air flows from the higher-pressure area outside the body into the lungs. While the difference in these two pressures is only about 3 mm Hg, it is enough to cause air to flow into the lungs. In exhaling, we reverse the process: We raise the diaphragm

or lower the rib cage. The resulting decrease in volume increases the pressure inside the chest cavity, causing air to flow out of the lungs.

In certain diseases the chest becomes paralyzed, and the affected person cannot move either the diaphragm or the rib cage. In such a case, a respirator is used to help the person breathe. The respirator first pushes down on the chest cavity and forces air out of the lungs. The pressure of the respirator is then lowered below atmospheric pressure, causing the rib cage to expand and draw air into the lungs.

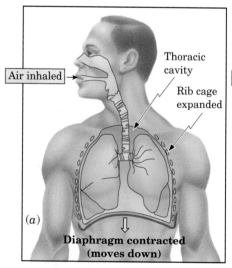

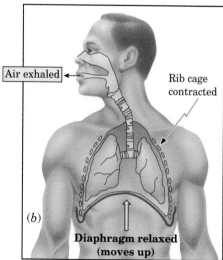

Schematic drawing of the chest cavity.

Figure 6.4 Boyle's law illustrated in an automobile cylinder. When the piston moves up, the volume occupied by the gas (a mixture of air and gasoline vapor) decreases and the pressure increases. The spark plug then ignites the compressed gasoline vapor.

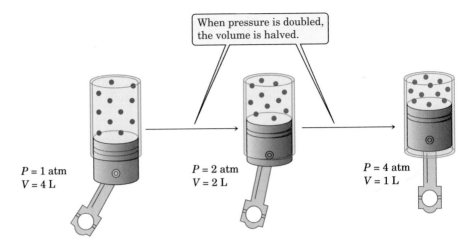

When pressure is doubled, the volume is halved.

$P = 1$ atm
$V = 4$ L

$P = 2$ atm
$V = 2$ L

$P = 4$ atm
$V = 1$ L

GOB
Chemistry ⚛ Now™

Click *Chemistry Interactive* for an interactive exploration of a **Charles's Law** experiment

When using the gas laws, temperature must be expressed in kelvins (K). The zero in this scale is the lowest possible temperature.

Greg Gawlowski/Dembinsky Photo Associates

Figure 6.5 Charles's law illustrated in a hot-air balloon. Because the balloon can stretch, the pressure inside it remains constant. When the air in the balloon is heated, its volume increases, expanding the balloon. As the air in the balloon expands, it becomes less dense than the surrounding air, providing the lift for the balloon. (Charles was one of the first balloonists.)

Combined gas law The pressure, volume, and temperature in kelvins of two samples of the same gas are related by the equation $P_1V_1/T_1 = P_2V_2/T_2$

B. Charles's Law and the Temperature–Volume Relationship

Charles's law states that the volume of a fixed mass of gas at a constant pressure is directly proportional to the temperature in kelvins (K). In other words, as long as the pressure on a gas remains constant, increasing the temperature of the gas causes an increase in the volume occupied by the gas. Charles's law can be stated mathematically this way:

$$\frac{V}{T} = \text{a constant} \qquad \text{or} \qquad \frac{V_1}{T_1} = \frac{V_2}{T_2}$$

This relationship between volume and temperature is the basis of the hot-air balloon operation (Figure 6.5).

C. Gay-Lussac's Law and the Temperature–Pressure Relationship

Gay-Lussac's law states that, for a fixed mass of a gas at constant volume, the pressure is directly proportional to the temperature in kelvins (K):

$$\frac{P}{T} = \text{a constant} \qquad \text{or} \qquad \frac{P_1}{T_1} = \frac{P_2}{T_2}$$

As the temperature of the gas increases, the pressure increases proportionately. Consider, for example, what happens inside an autoclave. Steam generated inside an autoclave at 1 atm pressure has a temperature of 100°C. As the steam is heated further, the pressure within the autoclave increases as well. A valve controls the pressure inside the autoclave; if the pressure exceeds the designated maximum, the valve opens, releasing the steam. At maximum pressure, the temperature may reach 120°C to 150°C. All microorganisms in the autoclave are destroyed at such high temperatures.

Table 6.1 shows mathematical expressions of these three laws.

The three gas laws can be combined and expressed by a mathematical equation called the **combined gas law:**

$$\frac{PV}{T} = \text{a constant} \qquad \text{or} \qquad \frac{P_1V_1}{T_1} = \frac{P_2V_2}{T_2}$$

Table 6.1	Mathematical Expressions of the Three Gas Laws for a Fixed Mass of Gas	
Name	**Expression**	**Constant**
Boyle's law	$P_1V_1 = P_2V_2$	T
Charles's law	$\dfrac{V_1}{T_1} = \dfrac{V_2}{T_2}$	P
Gay-Lussac's law	$\dfrac{P_1}{T_1} = \dfrac{P_2}{T_2}$	V

EXAMPLE 6.1

A gas occupies 3.00 L at 2.00 atm pressure. Calculate its volume when we increase the pressure to 10.15 atm at the same temperature.

Solution

First we identify the known quantities. Because T_1 and T_2 are the same in this example and consequently cancel each other, we don't need to know the temperature.

Initial: $P_1 = 2.00$ atm $V_1 = 3.00$ L

Final: $P_2 = 10.15$ atm $V_2 = ?$

We want the final volume, so we solve the combined gas law equation for V_2:

$$V_2 = \frac{P_1 V_1 \cancel{T_2}}{\cancel{T_1} P_2} = \frac{(2.00 \ \cancel{atm})(3.00 \ \text{L})}{10.15 \ \cancel{atm}} = 0.591 \ \text{L}$$

Problem 6.1

A gas occupies 3.8 L at 0.70 atm pressure. If we expand the volume at constant temperature to 6.5 L, what is the final pressure?

EXAMPLE 6.2

In an autoclave, steam at 100°C is generated at 1.00 atm. After the autoclave is closed, the steam is heated at constant volume until the pressure gauge indicates 1.13 atm. What is the final temperature in the autoclave?

Solution

All temperatures in gas law calculations must be in kelvins; therefore, we must convert the Celsius temperature to kelvins:

$$100°C = 100 + 273 = 373 \ \text{K}$$

We then identify the known quantities. Because V_1 and V_2 are the same in this example and consequently cancel each other, we don't need to know the volume of the autoclave.

Initial: $P_1 = 1.00$ atm $T_1 = 373$ K

Final: $P_2 = 1.13$ atm $T_2 = ?$

An autoclave used to sterilize hospital equipment.

Because we want a final temperature, we now solve the combined gas law equation for T_2:

$$T_2 = \frac{P_2 V_2 T_1}{P_1 V_1} = \frac{(1.13 \text{ atm})(373 \text{ K})}{1.00 \text{ atm}} = 421 \text{ K}$$

The final temperature is 421 K, or $421 - 273 = 148°C$.

Problem 6.2

A constant volume of oxygen gas, O_2, is heated from 120°C to 212°C. The final pressure is 20.3 atm. What was the initial pressure?

EXAMPLE 6.3

A gas in a flexible container has a volume of 0.50 L and a pressure of 1.0 atm at 393 K. When the gas is heated to 500 K, its volume expands to 3.0 L. What is the new pressure of the gas in the flexible container?

Solution
The known quantities are

Initial: $P_1 = 1.0 \text{ atm}$ $V_1 = 0.50 \text{ L}$ $T_1 = 393 \text{ K}$

Final: $P_2 = ?$ $V_2 = 3.0 \text{ L}$ $T_2 = 500 \text{ K}$

Solving the combined gas law for P_2, we find

$$P_2 = \frac{P_1 V_1 T_2}{T_1 V_2} = \frac{(1.0 \text{ atm})(0.50 \text{ L})(500 \text{ K})}{(3.0 \text{ L})(393 \text{ K})} = 0.21 \text{ atm}$$

Problem 6.3

A gas is expanded from an initial volume of 20.5 L at 0.92 atm at room temperature (23.0°C) to a final volume of 340.6 L. During the expansion the gas cools to 12.0°C. What is the new pressure?

6.4 | What Are Avogadro's Law and the Ideal Gas Law?

Avogadro's law Equal volumes of gases at the same temperature and pressure contain the same number of molecules

The relationship between the amount of gas present and its volume is described by **Avogadro's law,** which states that equal volumes of gases at the same temperature and pressure contain equal numbers of molecules. Thus, if the temperature, pressure, and volumes of two gases are the same, then the two gases contain the same number of molecules, regardless of their identity (Figure 6.6). Avogadro's law is valid for all gases, no matter what they are.

Standard temperature and pressure (STP) 0°C (273 K) and one atmosphere pressure

The actual temperature and pressure at which we compare two or more gases do not matter. It is convenient, however, to select one temperature and one pressure as standard, and chemists have chosen 1 atm as the standard pressure and 0°C (273 K) as the standard temperature. These conditions are called **standard temperature and pressure (STP).**

All gases at STP or any other combination of temperature and pressure contain the same number of molecules in any given volume. But how many is that? In Chapter 5 we saw that one mole contains 6.02×10^{23} formula units. What volume of a gas at STP contains one mole of molecules? This quantity has been measured experimentally and found to be 22.4 L. Thus one mole of any gas at STP occupies a volume of 22.4 L.

Avogadro's law allows us to write a gas law that is valid not only for any pressure, volume, and temperature, but also for any quantity of gas. This law, called **the ideal gas law,** is

$$PV = nRT$$

where P = pressure of the gas in atmospheres (atm)
   V = volume of the gas in liters (L)
   n = amount of the gas in moles (mol)
   T = temperature of the gas in kelvins (K)
   R = a constant for all gases, called the **ideal gas constant**

We can find the value of R by using the fact that one mole of any gas at STP occupies a volume of 22.4 L:

$$R = \frac{PV}{nT} = \frac{(1.00 \text{ atm})(22.4 \text{ L})}{(1.00 \text{ mol})(273 \text{ K})} = 0.0821 \frac{\text{L} \cdot \text{atm}}{\text{mol} \cdot \text{K}}$$

The ideal gas law holds for all ideal gases at any temperature, pressure, and volume. But the only gases we have around us in the real world are real gases. How valid is it to apply the ideal gas law to real gases? The answer is that, under most experimental conditions, real gases behave sufficiently like ideal gases that we can use the ideal gas law for them with little trouble. Thus, using $PV = nRT$, we can calculate any one quantity—P, V, T, or n—if we know the other three quantities.

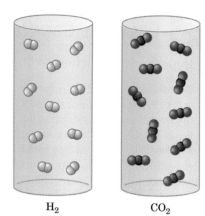

H_2 CO_2

T, P, and V
are equal in
both containers

Figure 6.6 Avogadro's law. Two tanks of gas of equal volume at the same temperature and pressure contain the same number of molecules.

Ideal gas law $PV = nRT$

Ideal Gas A gas whose physical properties are described accurately by the ideal gas law

Universal gas constant (R)
$0.0821 \text{ L} \cdot \text{atm} \cdot \text{mol}^{-1} \cdot \text{K}^{-1}$

Real gases behave most like ideal gases at low pressures (1 atm or less) and high temperatures (300 K or higher).

EXAMPLE 6.4

One mole of CH_4 gas occupies 20.0 L at 1.00 atm pressure. What is the temperature of the gas in kelvins?

Solution

Solve the ideal gas law for T and plug in the given values:

$$T = \frac{PV}{nR} = \frac{PV}{n} \times \frac{1}{R} = \frac{(1.00 \text{ atm})(20.0 \text{ L})}{(1.00 \text{ mol})} \times \frac{\text{mol} \cdot \text{K}}{0.0821 \text{ L} \cdot \text{atm}} = 244 \text{ K}$$

Note that we calculated the temperature for 1.00 mol of CH_4 gas under these conditions. The answer would be the same for 1.00 mol of CO_2, N_2, NH_3, or any other gas under these conditions. Note also that we have shown the gas constant separately to make it clear what is happening with the units attached to all quantities. We are going to do this throughout.

Problem 6.4

If 2.00 mol of NO gas occupies 10.0 L at 295 K, what is the pressure of the gas in atmospheres?

GOB
Chemistry ⚛ Now™

Click *Coached Problems* to see a simulation of the **Ideal Gas Law**

CHEMICAL CONNECTIONS 6C

Hyperbaric Medicine

Ordinary air contains 21% oxygen. Under certain conditions, the cells of tissues can become starved for oxygen (hypoxia), and quick oxygen delivery is needed. Increasing the percentage of oxygen in the air supplied to a patient is one way to remedy this situation, but sometimes even breathing pure (100%) oxygen may not be enough. For example, in carbon monoxide poisoning, hemoglobin, which normally carries most of the O_2 from the lungs to the tissues, binds CO and cannot take up any O_2 in the lungs. Without any help, tissues would soon become starved for oxygen and the patient would die. When oxygen is administered under a pressure of 2 to 3 atm, it dissolves in the plasma to such a degree that the tissues receive enough of it to recover without the help of the poisoned hemoglobin molecules. Other conditions for which hyperbaric medicine is used are treatment of gas gangrene, smoke inhalation, cyanide poisoning, skin grafts, thermal burns, and diabetic lesions.

Breathing pure oxygen for prolonged periods, however, is toxic. For example, if O_2 is administered at 2 atm for more than 6 hours, it may damage both lung tissue and the central nervous system. In addition, this treatment may cause nuclear cataract formation,

Hyperbaric oxygen chamber at Medical City Dallas Hospital.

necessitating postrecovery eye surgery. Therefore, recommended exposures of O_2 are 2 hours at 2 atm and 90 minutes at 3 atm. The benefits of hyperbaric medicine must be carefully weighed against these and other contraindications.

Molar volume. The cube has a volume of 22.4 liters, which is the volume of one mole of gas at STP.

EXAMPLE 6.5

If there is 5.0 g of CO_2 gas in a 10-L cylinder at 25°C, what is the gas pressure within the cylinder?

Solution
We are given the quantity of CO_2 in grams but, to use the ideal gas law, we must express the quantity in moles. Therefore, we must first convert grams of CO_2 to moles, and then use this value in the ideal gas law. To convert from grams to moles, we use the conversion factor 1 mol CO_2 = 44 g.

$$5.0 \text{ g } CO_2 \times \frac{1 \text{ mol } CO_2}{44 \text{ g } CO_2} = 0.11 \text{ mol } CO_2$$

We now use this value in the ideal gas equation to solve for the pressure of the gas.

$$P = \frac{nRT}{V}$$

$$= \frac{nT}{V} \times R = \frac{(0.11 \text{ mol } CO_2)(298 \text{ K})}{10 \text{ L}} \times \frac{0.0821 \text{ L} \cdot \text{atm}}{\text{mol} \cdot \text{K}} = 0.27 \text{ atm}$$

Problem 6.5

A certain quantity of neon gas is under 1.05 atm pressure at 303 K in a 10.0-L vessel. How many moles of neon are present?

EXAMPLE 6.6

If 3.3 g of a gas at 40°C and 1.15 atm pressure occupies a volume of 1.0 L, what is the mass of one mole of the gas?

Solution

This problem is more complicated than previous ones. We are given grams of gas and P, T, and V values. We are asked to calculate the mass of one mole of the gas (g/mol). We can solve this problem in two steps.

Step 1 Use the P, V, and T measurements and the ideal gas law to calculate the number of moles of gas present in the sample. To use the ideal gas law, we must first convert 40°C to kelvins: $40 + 273 = 313$ K.

$$n = \frac{PV}{RT} = \frac{PV}{T} \times \frac{1}{R} = \frac{(0.15 \text{ atm})(1.0 \text{ L})}{313 \text{ K}} \times \frac{\text{mol} \cdot \text{K}}{0.0821 \text{ L} \cdot \text{atm}} = 0.0448 \text{ mol}$$

Step 2 Calculate the mass of one mole of the gas by dividing grams by moles.

$$\text{Mass of one mole} = \frac{3.3 \text{ g}}{0.0448 \text{ mol}} = 74 \text{ g} \cdot \text{mol}^{-1}$$

Problem 6.6

An unknown amount of He gas occupies 30.5 L at 2.00 atm pressure and 300 K. What is the weight of the gas in the container?

6.5 | What Is Dalton's Law of Partial Pressures?

In a mixture of gases, each molecule acts independently of all the others, provided that the gases behave as ideal gases and do not react with each other. For this reason, the ideal gas law works for mixtures of gases as well as for pure gases. **Dalton's law of partial pressures** states that the total pressure, P_T, of a mixture of gases is the sum of the partial pressures of each individual gas:

$$P_T = P_1 + P_2 + P_3 + \cdots$$

A corollary to Dalton's law is that the **partial pressure** of a gas in a mixture is the pressure that the gas would exert if it were alone in the container. The equation holds separately for each gas in the mixture as well as for the mixture as a whole.

Partial pressure The pressure that a gas in a mixture of gases would exert if it were alone in the container

EXAMPLE 6.7

To a tank containing N_2 at 2.0 atm and O_2 at 1.0 atm, we add an unknown quantity of CO_2 until the total pressure within the tank is 4.6 atm. What is the partial pressure of the CO_2?

Solution

Dalton's law tells us that the addition of CO_2 does not affect the partial pressures of the N_2 or O_2 already present in the tank. The partial pressures of N_2 and O_2 remain at 2.0 atm and 1.0 atm, respectively, and their sum is 3.0 atm. If the new pressure is 4.6 atm, the partial pressure of the added CO_2 must be 1.6 atm. Thus, when the final pressure is 4.6 atm, the partial pressures are

$$4.6 \text{ atm} = 2.0 \text{ atm} + 1.0 \text{ atm} + 1.6 \text{ atm}$$

| Total pressure | Partial pressure of N_2 | Partial pressure of O_2 | Partial pressure of CO_2 |

Problem 6.7

A vessel under 2.015 atm pressure contains nitrogen, N_2, and water vapor, H_2O. The partial pressure of N_2 is 1.908 atm. What is the partial pressure of the water vapor?

6.6 | What Is the Kinetic Molecular Theory?

GOB
Chemistry﹣Now™

Click *Coached Problems* to see a simulation of the **Kinetic Molecular Theory**

To this point, we have studied the macroscopic properties of gases—namely, the various laws dealing with the relationships among temperature, pressure, volume, and number of molecules in a sample of gas. Now let us examine the behavior of gases at the molecular level and see how we can explain their behavior in terms of molecules and the interactions between them.

The relationship between the observed behavior of gases and the behavior of individual gas molecules within the gas can be explained by the **kinetic molecular theory,** which makes the following assumptions about the molecules of a gas:

1. Gases consist of particles, either atoms or molecules, constantly moving through space in straight lines, in random directions, and with various speeds. Because these particles move in random directions, different gases mix very readily.

2. The average kinetic energy of gas particles is proportional to the temperature in kelvins. The higher the temperature, the faster they move through space, and the greater their kinetic energy.

3. Molecules collide with each other, much as billiard balls do, bouncing off each other and changing direction. Each time they collide, they may exchange kinetic energies (one moves faster than before, the other slower), but the total kinetic energy of the gas sample remains the same.

4. Gas particles have no volume. Most of the volume taken up by a gas is empty space, which explains why gases can be compressed so easily.

5. There are no attractive forces between gas particles. They do not stick together after a collision occurs.

6. Molecules collide with the walls of the container, and these collisions constitute the pressure of the gas. The greater the number of collisions per unit time, the greater the pressure.

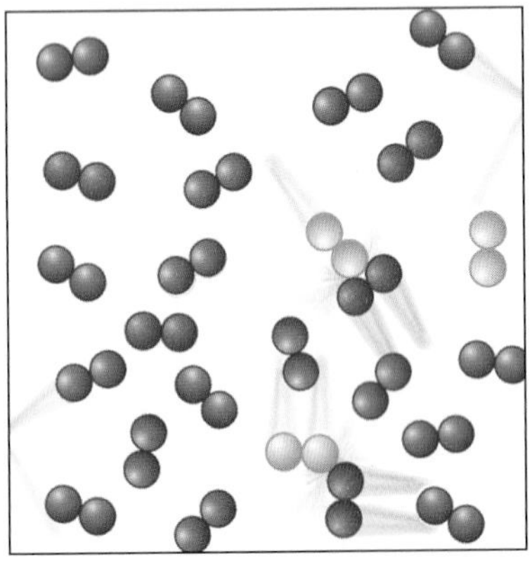

Figure 6.7 The kinetic molecular model of a gas. Molecules of nitrogen (blue) and oxygen (red) are in constant motion and collide with each other and with the walls of the container. Collisions with the walls of the container create the gas pressure. In air at STP, 6.02×10^{23} molecules undergo approximately 10 billion collisions per second.

These six assumptions of the kinetic molecular theory give us an idealized picture of the molecules of a gas and their interactions with one another (Figure 6.7). In real gases, however, forces of attraction between molecules do exist, and molecules do occupy some volume. Because of these factors, a gas described by these six assumptions of the kinetic molecular theory is called an **ideal gas.** In reality, there is no ideal gas; all gases are real. At STP, however, most real gases behave in much the same way that an ideal gas would, so we can safely use these assumptions.

6.7 | What Types of Attractive Forces Exist Between Molecules?

As noted in Section 6.1, the strength of the intermolecular forces (forces between molecules) in any sample of matter determines whether the sample is a gas, a liquid, or a solid under normal conditions of temperature and pressure. In general, the closer the molecules are to each other, the greater the effect of the intermolecular forces. When the temperature of a gas is high (room temperature or higher) and the pressure is low (1 atm or less), molecules of the gas are so far apart that we can effectively ignore attractions between them and treat the gas as ideal. When the temperature decreases, the pressure increases, or both, the distances between molecules decrease so that we can no longer ignore intermolecular forces. In fact, these forces become so important that they cause **condensation** (change from a gas to a liquid) and **solidification** (change from a liquid to a solid). Therefore, before discussing the structures and properties of liquids and solids, we must look at the nature of these intermolecular forces of attraction.

In this section, we discuss three types of intermolecular forces: London dispersion forces, dipole–dipole interactions, and hydrogen bonding. Table 6.2 shows the strengths of these three forces. Also shown for comparison are the strengths of ionic and covalent bonds, both of which are considerably stronger than the other three types of intermolecular forces. Although intermolecular forces are relatively weak compared to ionic and covalent bonds,

Condensation The change of a substance from the vapor or gaseous state to the liquid state

Table 6.2 Forces of Attraction Between Molecules and Ions

Attractive Force	Example	Typical Energy (kcal/mol)
Ionic bonds	$Na^+ \cdots Cl^-$, $Mg^{2+} \cdots O^{2-}$	170–970
Single, double, and triple covalent bonds	$C-C$ $C=C$ $C\equiv C$ $O-H$	80–95 175 230 90–120
Hydrogen bonding		2–10
Dipole-dipole interaction		1–6
London dispersion forces	$Ne \cdots Ne$	0.01–2.0

For purposes of comparison, the strengths of single, double, and triple covalent bonds are also given.

it is the former that determines many of the physical properties of molecules, such as melting point, boiling point, and viscosity. As we will see in Chapters 21–31, these forces are also extremely important in determining the three-dimensional shapes of biomolecules such as proteins and nucleic acids, and in deciding how these types of biomolecules recognize and interact with one another.

A. London Dispersion Forces

Attractive forces are present between all molecules, whether they are polar or nonpolar. If the temperature falls far enough, even nonpolar molecules such as He, Ne, H_2, and CH_4 can be liquefied. Neon, for example, is a gas at room temperature and atmospheric pressure. It can be liquefied if cooled to $-246°C$. The fact that these and other nonpolar gases can be liquefied means that some sort of interaction must occur between them to make them stick together in the liquid state. These weak attractive forces are called **London dispersion forces,** after the American chemist Fritz London (1900–1954), who was the first to explain them.

London dispersion forces have their origin in electrostatic interactions. To visualize the origin of these forces, it is necessary to think in terms of instantaneous distributions of electrons within an atom or molecule. Consider, for example, a sample of neon atoms, which can be liquefied if cooled to $-246°C$. Over time, the distribution of electron density in a neon atom is symmetrical, and a neon atom has no dipole; that is, it has no separation of positive and negative charges. However, at any given instant, the electron density in a neon atom may be shifted more toward one part of the atom than another, thus creating a temporary dipole (Figure 6.8). This temporary dipole, which lasts for only tiny fractions of a second, induces temporary dipoles in adjacent neon atoms. The attractions between these temporary induced dipoles are called London dispersion forces, and they make nonpolar molecules stick together to form the liquid state.

London dispersion forces exist between all molecules, but they are the only forces of attraction between nonpolar molecules. They range in strength from 0.01 to 2.0 kcal/mol depending on the mass, size, and shape of the interacting molecules. In general, their strength increases as the mass and number of electrons in a molecule increase. Even though London dispersion forces are very weak, they contribute significantly to the attractive forces between large molecules because they act over large surface areas.

London dispersion forces Extremely weak attractive forces between atoms or molecules caused by the electrostatic attraction between temporary induced dipoles

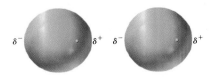

δ^- δ^+ δ^- δ^+

Figure 6.8 London dispersion forces. A temporary polarization of electron density in one neon atom creates positive and negative charges, which in turn induce temporary positive and negative charges in an adjacent atom. The intermolecular attractions between the temporary induced positive end of one dipole and the negative end of another temporary dipole are called London dispersion forces.

B. Dipole–Dipole Interactions

As mentioned in Section 4.11, many molecules are polar. The attraction between the positive end of one dipole and the negative end of another dipole is called a **dipole–dipole interaction.** These interactions can exist between two identical polar molecules or between two different polar molecules. To see the importance of dipole–dipole interactions, we can look at the differences in boiling points between nonpolar and polar molecules of comparable molecular weight. Butane, C_4H_{10}, with a molecular weight of 58 amu, is a nonpolar molecule with a boiling point of 0.5°C. Acetone, C_3H_6O, with the same molecular weight, has a boiling point of 58°C. Acetone is a polar molecule, and its molecules are held together in the liquid state by dipole–dipole attractions between the negative end of the C=O dipole of one acetone molecule and the positive end of the C=O dipole of another acetone molecule. Because it requires more energy to overcome the dipole–dipole

Dipole–dipole interaction The interaction between the positive end of a dipole of one molecule and the negative end of another dipole in the same or different molecule

interactions between acetone molecules than it does to overcome the considerably weaker London dispersion forces between butane molecules, acetone has a higher boiling point than butane.

$$CH_3-CH_2-CH_2-CH_3$$

Butane
(bp 0.5°C)

$$CH_3-\overset{\overset{\displaystyle O}{\|}}{\underset{\delta^+}{C}}-CH_3 \quad \delta^-$$

Acetone
(bp 58°C)

C. Hydrogen Bond

As we have just seen, the attraction between the positive end of one dipole and the negative end of another results in dipole–dipole attraction. When the positive end of one dipole is a hydrogen atom bonded to an O or N (atoms of high electronegativity; see Table 4.5) and the negative end of the other dipole is an O or N atom, the attractive interaction between dipoles is particularly strong and is given a special name: **hydrogen bond.** An example is the hydrogen bonding that occurs between molecules of water in both the liquid and solid states (Figure 6.9).

The strength of hydrogen bonding ranges from 2 to 10 kcal/mol. The strength in liquid water, for example, is approximately 5 kcal/mol. By comparison, the strength of the O—H covalent bond in water is approximately 119 kcal/mol. As can be seen by comparing these numbers, an O----H hydrogen bond is considerably weaker than an O—H covalent bond. Nonetheless, the presence of hydrogen bonds in liquid water has an important effect on the physical properties of water. Because of hydrogen bonding, extra energy is required to separate each water molecule from its neighbors—hence the relatively high boiling point of water. As we will see in later chapters, hydrogen bonds play an especially important role in biological molecules.

Hydrogen bonds are not restricted to water, however. They form between two molecules whenever one molecule has a hydrogen atom covalently bonded to O or N, and the other molecule has an O or N atom.

Hydrogen bond A noncovalent force of attraction between the partial positive charge on a hydrogen atom bonded to an atom of high electronegativity, most commonly oxygen or nitrogen, and the partial negative charge on a nearby oxygen or nitrogen

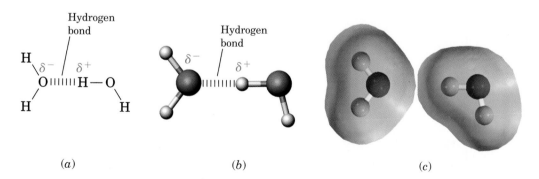

Figure 6.9   Two water molecules joined by a hydrogen bond (*a*) Structural formulas, (*b*) ball-and-stick models, and (*c*) electron density models.

EXAMPLE 6.8

Can a hydrogen bond form between
(a) Two molecules of methanol, CH_3OH?
(b) Two molecules of formaldehyde, CH_2O?
(c) One molecule of methanol, CH_3OH, and one of formaldehyde, CH_2O?

Solution
(a) Yes. Methanol is a polar molecule and has a hydrogen atom covalently bonded to an oxygen atom.

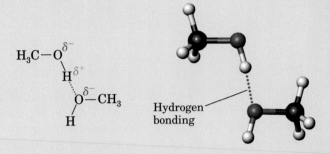

(b) No. Although formaldehyde is a polar molecule, it does not have a hydrogen covalently bonded to an oxygen or nitrogen atom. Its molecules, however, are attracted to each other by dipole–dipole interaction—that is, by the attraction between the negative end of the $C{=}O$ dipole of one molecule and the positive end of the $C{=}O$ dipole of another molecule.

(c) Yes. Methanol has a hydrogen atom bonded to an oxygen atom and formaldehyde has an oxygen atom.

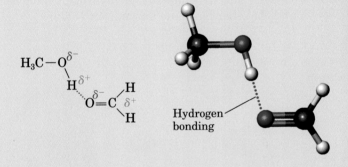

Problem 6.8

Will the molecules in each set form a hydrogen bond between them?
(a) A molecule of water and a molecule of methanol, CH_3OH
(b) Two molecules of methane, CH_4

6.8 | How Do We Describe the Behavior of Liquids at the Molecular Level?

We have seen that we can describe the behavior of gases under most circumstances by the ideal gas law, which assumes that there are no attractive forces between molecules. As pressure increases in a real gas, however, the molecules of a gas become squeezed into a smaller space, with the result that attractions between molecules become increasingly effective in causing molecules to stick together.

If the distances between molecules decrease so that they touch or almost touch each other, the gas condenses to a liquid. Unlike gases, liquids do not fill all the available space, but they do have a definite volume, irrespective of the container. Because gases have a lot of empty space between molecules, it is easy to compress them into a smaller volume. In contrast, there is very little empty space in liquids; consequently, liquids are difficult to compress. A great increase in pressure is needed to cause even a very small decrease in the volume of a liquid. Thus liquids, for all practical purposes, are incompressible. In addition, the density of liquids is much greater than that of gases because the same mass occupies a much smaller volume in liquid form than it does in gaseous form.

The brake system in a car is based on hydraulics. The force you exert with the brake pedal is transmitted to the brake via cylinders filled with liquid. This system works very well until an air leak occurs. Once air gets into the brake line, pushing the brake pedal compresses air instead of moving the brake pads.

The positions of molecules in the liquid state are random, and some irregular empty space is available into which molecules can slide. Molecules in the liquid state are, therefore, constantly changing their positions with respect to neighboring molecules. This property causes liquids to be fluid and explains why liquids have a constant volume but not a constant shape.

A. Surface Tension

Unlike gases, liquids have surface properties, one of which is **surface tension** (Figure 6.10). The surface tension of a liquid is directly related to the strength of the intermolecular attraction between its molecules. Water has a high surface tension because of strong hydrogen bonding among water molecules. As a result, a steel needle can easily be made to float on the surface of water. If, however, the same needle is pushed below the elastic skin into the interior of the liquid, it sinks to the bottom. Similarly, water bugs gliding on the surface of a pond appear to be walking on an elastic skin of water.

B. Vapor Pressure

An important property of liquids is their tendency to evaporate. A few hours after a heavy rain, for example, most of the puddles have dried up; the water has evaporated and gone into the air. The same thing occurs if we leave a container of water or any other liquid out in the open. Let us explore how this change occurs.

In any liquid, there is a distribution of velocities among its molecules. Some of the molecules have high kinetic energy and move rapidly. Others have low kinetic energy and move slowly. Whether fast or slow, a molecule in the interior of the liquid cannot go very far before it hits another molecule and has its speed and direction changed by the collision. A molecule at the

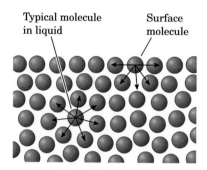

Typical molecule in liquid   Surface molecule

Figure 6.10 Surface tension. Molecules in the interior of a liquid have equal intermolecular attractions in every direction. Molecules at the surface (the liquid–gas interface), however, experience greater attractions toward the interior of the liquid than toward the gaseous state above it. Therefore, molecules on the surface are preferentially pulled toward the center of the liquid. This pull crowds the molecules on the surface, thereby creating a layer, like an elastic skin, that is tough to penetrate.

A water-strider standing on water. The surface tension of water supports it.

Hermann Eisenbeiss/Photo Researchers, Inc.

CHEMICAL CONNECTIONS 6D

Blood Pressure Measurement

Liquids, like gases, exert a pressure on the walls of their containers. Blood pressure, for example, results from pulsating blood pushing against the walls of the blood vessels. When the heart ventricles contract, pushing blood out into the arteries, the blood pressure is high (systolic pressure); when the ventricles relax, the blood pressure is lower (diastolic pressure). Blood pressure is usually expressed as a fraction showing systolic over diastolic pressure— for instance, 120/80. The normal range in young adults is 100 to 120 mm Hg systolic and 60 to 80 mm Hg diastolic. In older adults, the corresponding normal ranges are 115 to 135 and 75 to 85 mm Hg, respectively.

A sphygmomanometer—the instrument used to measure blood pressure—consists of a bulb, a cuff, a manometer, and a stethoscope. The cuff is wrapped around the upper arm and inflated by squeezing the bulb (figure, part *a*). The inflated cuff exerts a pressure on the arm, which is read on the manometer. When the cuff is sufficiently inflated, its pressure collapses the brachial artery, preventing pulsating blood from flowing to the lower arm. At this

pressure, no sound is heard in the stethoscope because the applied pressure in the cuff is greater than the blood pressure. Next, the cuff is slowly deflated, which decreases the pressure on the arm (figure, part *b*). The first faint tapping sound is heard when the pressure in the cuff just matches the systolic pressure as the ventricle contracts—that is, when the pressure in the cuff is low enough to allow pulsating blood to begin flowing into the lower arm. As the cuff pressure continues to decrease, the tapping first becomes louder and then begins to fade. At the point when the last faint tapping sound is heard, the cuff pressure matches the diastolic pressure when the ventricle is relaxed, thus allowing continuous blood flow into the lower arm. (figure, part *c*)

Digital blood pressure monitors are now available for home or office use. In these instruments, the stethoscope and the manometer are combined in a sensory device that records the systolic and diastolic blood pressures together with the pulse rate. The cuff and the inflation bulb are used the same way as in traditional sphygmomanometers.

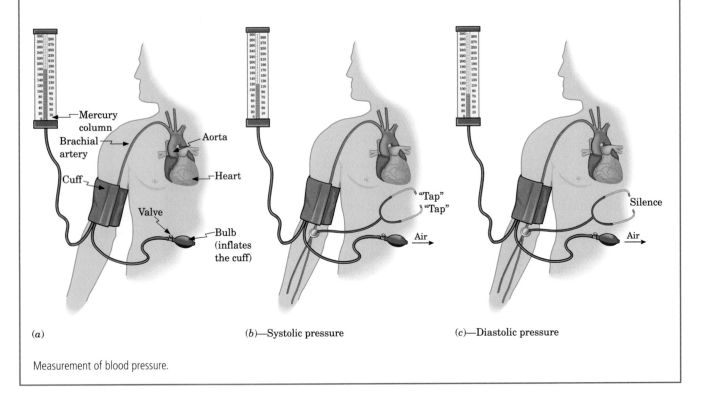

(*a*)   (*b*)—Systolic pressure   (*c*)—Diastolic pressure

Measurement of blood pressure.

surface, however, is in a different situation (Figure 6.11). If it is moving slowly (has a low kinetic energy), it cannot escape from the liquid because of the attractions of its neighboring molecules. If it is moving rapidly (has a high kinetic energy) and upward, however, it can escape from the liquid and enter the gaseous space above it.

In an open container, this process continues until all molecules have escaped. If the liquid is in a closed container, as in Figure 6.12, the molecules in the gaseous state cannot diffuse away (as they would do if the con-

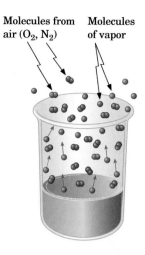

Molecules from
air (O$_2$, N$_2$)   Molecules
of vapor

Figure 6.11 Evaporation. Some
molecules at the surface of a
liquid are moving fast enough to
escape into the gaseous space.

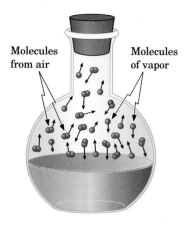

Molecules
from air   Molecules
of vapor

Figure 6.12 Evaporation
and condensation. In a closed
container, molecules of liquid
escape into the vapor phase,
and the liquid recaptures vapor
molecules.

tainer were open). Instead, they remain in the air space above the liquid,
where they move rapidly in straight lines until they strike something. Some
of these vapor molecules move downward, strike the surface of the liquid,
and are recaptured by it.

At this point we have reached an **equilibrium.** As long as the temperature does not change, the number of vapor molecules reentering the liquid
equals the number escaping from it. At equilibrium, the space above the liquid shown in Figure 6.12 contains both air and vapor molecules, and we can
measure the partial pressure of the vapor, called the **vapor pressure** of the
liquid. Note that we measure the partial pressure of a gas but call it the
vapor pressure of the liquid.

The vapor pressure of a liquid is a physical property of the liquid and a
function of temperature (Figure 6.13). As the temperature of a liquid
increases, the average kinetic energy of its molecules increases and the easier it becomes for molecules to escape from the liquid state to the gaseous
state. As the temperature of the liquid increases, its vapor pressure continues to increase until it equals the atmospheric pressure. At this point, bubbles of vapor form under the surface of the liquid, and then force their way
upward through the surface of the liquid, and the liquid boils.

The molecules that evaporate from a liquid surface are those that have
a higher kinetic energy. When they enter the gas phase, the molecules left
behind are those with a lower kinetic energy. Because the temperature of a
sample is proportional to the average kinetic energy of its molecules, the
temperature of the liquid drops as a result of evaporation. This evaporation
of the layer of water from your skin produces the cooling effect you feel
when you come out of a swimming pool and the layer of water evaporates
from your skin.

C. Boiling Point

The **boiling point** of a liquid is the temperature at which its vapor pressure is equal to the pressure of the atmosphere in contact with its surface.
The boiling point when the atmospheric pressure is 1 atm is called the

Vapor A gas

Equilibrium A condition in which
two opposing physical forces are
equal

Vapor pressure The pressure of a
gas in equilibrium with its liquid
form in a closed container

At equilibrium, the rate of
vaporization equals the rate
of liquefaction.

Boiling point The temperature
at which the vapor pressure of a
liquid is equal to the atmospheric
pressure

Figure 6.13 The change in vapor pressure with temperature for four liquids. The normal boiling point of a liquid is defined as the temperature at which its vapor pressure equals 760 mm Hg.

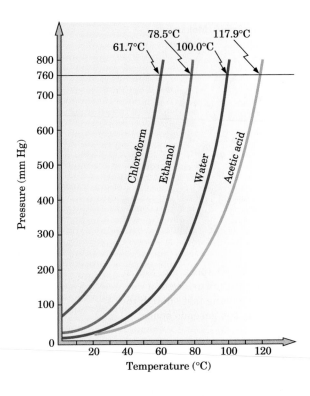

Normal boiling point The temperature at which a liquid boils under a pressure of 1 atm

normal boiling point. For example, 100°C is the normal boiling point of water because it is the temperature at which water boils at 1 atm pressure.

The use of a pressure cooker is an example of boiling water at higher temperatures. In this type of pot, food is cooked at, say, 2 atm, where the boiling point of water is 121°C. Because the food has been raised to a higher temperature, it cooks faster than it would in an open pot, in which boiling water cannot get hotter than 100°C. Conversely, at low pressures water boils at lower temperatures. For example, at the top of a mountain where the atmospheric pressure is less than 760 mm Hg, the boiling point of water might be 95°C.

D. Factors That Affect Boiling Point

As Figure 6.13 shows, different liquids have different normal boiling points. Table 6.3 gives molecular formulas, molecular weights, and normal boiling points for four liquids.

As you study the information in this table, note that chloroform, which has the largest molecular weight of the five compounds, has the lowest boiling point. Water, which has the lowest molecular weight, has the second

Table 6.3	Names, Molecular Formulas, Molecular Weights, and Normal Boiling Points for Hexane and the Four Liquids in Figure 6.13		
Name	**Molecular Formula**	**Molecular Weight (amu)**	**Boiling Point (°C)**
Chloroform	$CHCl_3$	120	62
Hexane	$CH_3CH_2CH_2CH_2CH_2CH_3$	86	69
Ethanol	CH_3CH_2OH	46	78
Water	H_2O	18	100
Acetic acid	CH_3COOH	60	118

highest boiling point. From a study of these and other compounds, chemists have determined that the boiling point of covalent compounds depends primarily on three factors:

1. **Intermolecular forces** Water (H_2O, MW 18) and methane (CH_4, MW 16) have about the same molecular weight. The normal boiling point of water is 100°C, while that of methane is −164°C. The difference in boiling points reflects the fact that CH_4 molecules in the liquid state must overcome only the weak London dispersion forces to escape to the vapor state (low boiling point). In contrast, water molecules, being hydrogen-bonded to each other, need more kinetic energy (and a higher boiling temperature) to escape into the vapor phase. Thus the difference in boiling points between these two compounds is due to the greater strength of hydrogen bonding compared with the much weaker London dispersion forces.

2. **Number of sites for intermolecular interaction (surface area)** Consider the boiling points of methane, CH_4 and hexane, C_6H_{14}. Both are nonpolar compounds with no possibility for hydrogen bonding or dipole–dipole interactions between their molecules. The only force of attraction between molecules of either compound is London dispersion forces. The normal boiling point of hexane is 69°C, and that of methane is −164°C. The difference in their boiling points reflects the fact that hexane has more electrons and a larger surface area than methane. Because of its larger surface area, there are more sites for London dispersion forces to arise between hexane molecules than in methane molecules and, therefore, hexane has the higher boiling point.

3. **Molecular shape** When molecules are similar in every way except shape, the strengths of their London dispersion forces determine their relative boiling points. Consider pentane, bp 36.1°C, and 2,2-dimethylpropane, bp 9.5°C (Figure 6.14).

Both compounds have the same molecular formula, C_5H_{12}, and the same molecular weight, but the boiling point of pentane is approximately 26° higher than that of 2,2-dimethylpropane. These differences in boiling point are related to molecular shape in the following way. The only forces of attraction between these nonpolar molecules are London dispersion forces. Pentane is a roughly linear molecule, whereas 2,2-dimethylpropane has a spherical shape and a smaller surface area than pentane. As surface area decreases, contact between adjacent molecules, the strength of London dispersion forces, and boiling points all decrease. Consequently, London dispersion forces between molecules of 2,2-dimethylpropane are less than those between molecules of pentane and, therefore, 2,2-dimethylpropane has a lower boiling point.

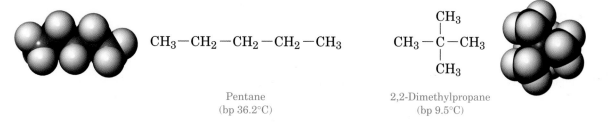

$$CH_3-CH_2-CH_2-CH_2-CH_3$$

Pentane
(bp 36.2°C)

$$CH_3-\overset{\overset{\displaystyle CH_3}{|}}{\underset{\underset{\displaystyle CH_3}{|}}{C}}-CH_3$$

2,2-Dimethylpropane
(bp 9.5°C)

Figure 6.14 Pentane and 2,2-dimethylpropane have the same molecular formula, C_5H_{12}, but quite different shapes.

CHEMICAL CONNECTIONS 6E

The Densities of Ice and Water

The hydrogen-bonded superstructure of ice contains empty spaces in the middle of each hexagon because the H_2O molecules in ice are not as closely packed as those in liquid water. For this reason, ice has a lower density (0.917 g/cm³) than does liquid water (1.00 g/cm³). As ice melts, some of the hydrogen bonds are broken and the hexagonal superstructure of ice collapses into the more densely packed organization of water. This change explains why ice floats on top of water instead of sinking to the bottom. Such behavior is highly unusual—most substances are denser in the solid state than they are in the liquid state. The lower density of ice keeps fish and microorganisms alive in many rivers and lakes that would freeze solid each winter if the ice sank to the bottom. The presence of ice on top insulates the remaining water and keeps it from freezing.

The fact that ice has a lower density than liquid water means that a given mass of ice takes up more space than the same mass of liquid water. This factor explains the damage done to biological tissues by freezing. When parts of the body (usually fingers, toes, nose, and ears) are subjected to extreme cold, they develop a condition called frostbite. The water in the cells freezes despite the blood's attempt to keep the temperature at 37°C. As liquid water freezes, it expands and in doing so ruptures the walls of cells containing it, causing damage. In some cases, frostbitten fingers or toes must be amputated.

Cold weather can damage plants in a similar way. Many plants are killed when the air temperature drops below the freezing point of water for several hours. Trees can survive cold winters because they have a low water content inside their trunks and branches.

Slow freezing is often more damaging to plant and animal tissues than quick freezing. In slow freezing, only a few crystals form, and these can grow to large sizes, rupturing cells. In quick freezing, such as can be achieved in liquid nitrogen (at a temperature of −196°C), many tiny crystals form. Because they do not grow much, tissue damage may be minimal.

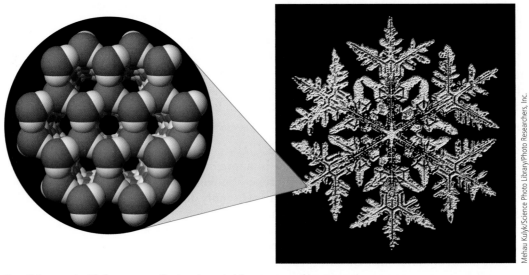

Mehau Kulyk/Science Photo Library/Photo Researchers, Inc.

Snowflakes are six-sided structures reflecting the underlying structure of ice.

6.9 | What Are the Characteristics of the Various Types of Solids?

Even in the solid state, molecules and ions do not stop moving completely. They vibrate around fixed points.

Crystallization The formation of a solid from a liquid

When liquids are cooled, their molecules come closer together and attractive forces between them become so strong that random motion stops, and a solid forms. Formation of a solid from a liquid is called solidification or, alternatively, **crystallization.**

All solids have a regular shape that, in many cases, is obvious to the eye (Figure 6.15). This regular shape often reflects the arrangement of the particles within the crystal. In table salt, for example, the Na^+ and Cl^- ions are arranged in a cubic system (Figure 4.1). Metals also consist of particles arranged in a regular crystal lattice (generally not cubic), but here the par-

Garnet

Sulfur

Quartz

Pyrite

Figure 6.15   Some crystals.

ticles are atoms rather than ions. Because the particles in a solid are almost always closer together than they are in the corresponding liquid, solids almost always have a higher density than liquids.

As can be seen in Figure 6.15, crystals have characteristic shapes and symmetries. We are familiar with the cubic nature of table salt and the hexagonal ice crystals in snowflakes. A less well-known fact is that some compounds have more than one type of solid state. The best-known example is the element carbon, which has five crystalline forms (Figure 6.16). Diamond occurs when solidification takes place under very high pressure (thousands of atmospheres). Another form of carbon is the graphite in a pencil. Carbon atoms are packed differently in high-density, hard diamonds than they are in low-density, soft graphite.

In a third form of carbon, each molecule contains 60 carbon atoms arranged in a structure having 12 pentagons and 20 hexagons as faces, resembling a soccer ball [Figure 6.16(c)]. Because the famous architect Buckminster Fuller (1895–1983) invented domes of a similar structure (he called them geodesic domes), the C-60 substance was named buckminster-fullerene, or "buckyball" for short. The discovery of buckyballs has generated a whole new area of carbon chemistry. Similar cage-like structures containing 72, 80, and even larger numbers of carbon have been synthesized. As a group, they are called fullerenes.

New variations on the fullerenes are nanotubes [(Figure 6.16(d)]. The *nano-* part of the name comes from the fact that the cross section of each

Richard E. Smalley (1943–), Robert F. Curl, Jr. (1933–), and Harold Kroto (1939–) were awarded the 1996 Nobel Prize in chemistry for the discovery of these compounds.

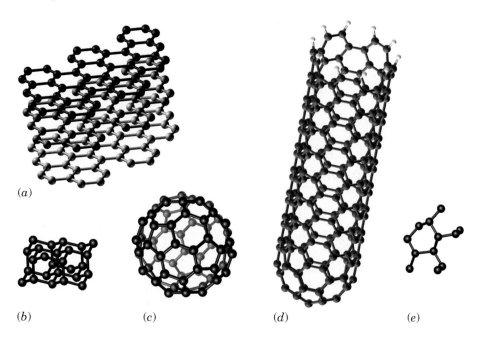

Figure 6.16   Solid forms of carbon: (*a*) graphite, (*b*) diamond, (*c*) "buckyball," (*d*) nanotube, and (*e*) soot.

(*a*)

(*b*)   (*c*)   (*d*)   (*e*)

Table 6.4 Types of Solids

Type	Made Up Of	Characteristics	Examples
Ionic	Ions in a crystal lattice	High melting point	$NaCl$, K_2SO_4
Molecular	Molecules in a crystal lattice	Low melting point	Ice, aspirin
Polymeric	Giant molecules; can be crystalline, semicrystalline, or amorphous	Low melting point or cannot be melted; soft or hard	Rubber, plastics, proteins
Network	A very large number of atoms connected by covalent bonds	Very hard; very high melting point or cannot be melted	Diamond, quartz
Amorphous	Randomly arranged atoms or molecules	Mostly soft, can be made to flow, but no melting point	Soot, tar, glass

tube is only nanometers in size (10^{-9} m). Nanotubes come in a variety of forms. Single-walled carbon nanotubes can vary in diameter from 1 to 3 nm and are about 20 mm long. These compounds have generated great industrial interest because of their optical and electronic properties. They may play a role in miniaturization of instruments, giving rise to a new generation of nanoscale devices.

Soot is the fifth form of solid carbon. This substance solidifies directly out of carbon vapor and is an **amorphous solid;** that is, its atoms have no set pattern and are arranged randomly [Figure 6.16(e)]. Another example of an amorphous solid is glass. In essence, glass is an immobilized liquid.

As we have now seen, some crystalline solids consist of orderly arrays of ions (ionic solids; Figure 4.1), and others consist of molecules (molecular solids). Ions are held in the crystal lattice by ionic bonds. Molecules are held only by intermolecular forces, which are much weaker than ionic bonds. Therefore, molecular solids generally have much lower melting points than do ionic solids.

Other types of solids exist as well. Some are extremely large molecules, with each molecule having as many as 10^{23} atoms, all connected by covalent bonds. In such a case, the entire crystal is one big molecule. We call such molecules **network solids** or network crystals. A good example is diamond [Figure 6.16(b)]. When you hold a diamond in your hand, you are holding a gigantic assembly of bonded atoms. Like ionic crystals, network solids have very high melting points—if they can be melted at all. In many cases they cannot be. Table 6.4 summarizes the various types of solids.

6.10 | What Is a Phase Change and What Energies Are Involved?

A. The Heating Curve for $H_2O(s)$ to $H_2O(g)$

Imagine the following experiment: We heat a piece of ice that is initially at $-20°C$. At first we don't see any difference in its physical state. The temperature of the ice increases, but its appearance does not change. At $0°C$, the ice begins to melt and liquid water appears. As we continue heating, more and more of the ice melts, but the temperature stays constant at $0°C$ until all the ice has melted and only liquid water remains. After all the ice has

Table 6.5   Energy Required to Heat 1.0 g of Solid Water at −20°C to 120°C

Physical Change	Energy (cal/g)	Basis for Calculation of Energy Required
Warming ice from −20°C to 0°C	9.6	Specific heat of ice = 0.48 cal/g·°C
Melting ice; temperature = 0°C	80	Heat of fusion of ice = 80 cal/g
Warming water from 0°C to 100°C	100	Specific heat of liquid water = 1.0 cal/g·°C
Boiling water; temperature = 100°C	540	Heat of vaporization = 540 cal/g
Warming steam from 100°C to 120°C	9.6	Specific heat of steam = 0.48 cal/g·°C

melted, the temperature of the water again increases as heat is added. At 100°C, the water boils. We continue heating as it continues to evaporate, but the temperature of the remaining liquid water does not change. Only after all the liquid water has changed to gaseous water (steam) does the temperature of the sample rise above 100°C.

These changes in state are called **phase changes. A phase** is any part of a system that looks uniform (homogeneous) throughout. Solid water (ice) is one phase, liquid water is another, and gaseous water is still another phase. Table 6.5 summarizes the energies for each step in the conversion of ice to steam.

Let us use the data in Table 6.5 to calculate the heat required to raise the temperature of 1.0 g of ice at −20°C to water vapor at 120°C. We begin with ice, whose specific heat is 0.48 cal/g·°C (Table 1.4). It requires 0.48 × 20 = 9.6 cal to raise the temperature of 1.0 g of ice from −20 to 0°C.

$$0.48 \, \frac{cal}{g \cdot °C} \times 1.0 \, g \times 20°C = 9.6 \, cal$$

After the ice reaches 0°C, additional heat causes a phase change: Solid water melts and becomes liquid water. The heat necessary to melt 1.0 g of any solid is called its **heat of fusion.** The heat of fusion of ice is 80 cal/g. Thus it requires 80 cal to melt 1.0 g of ice—that is, to change 1.0 g of ice at 0°C to liquid water at 0°C.

Only after the ice has completely melted does the temperature of the water rise again. The **specific heat** of liquid water is 1 cal/g·°C (Table 1.4). Thus it requires 100 cal to raise the temperature of 1.0 g of liquid water from 0° to 100°C. Contrast this with the 80 cal required to melt 1.0 g of ice.

When liquid water reaches 100°C, the normal boiling point of water, the temperature of the sample remains constant as another phase change takes place: Liquid water vaporizes to gaseous water. The amount of heat necessary to vaporize 1.0 g of a liquid at its normal boiling point is called its **heat of vaporization.** For water, this value is 540 cal/g. Once all of the liquid water has been vaporized, the temperature again rises as the water vapor (steam) is heated. The specific heat of steam is 0.48 cal/g (Table 1.4). Thus it requires 9.6 cal to heat one 1.0 g of steam from 100°C to 120°C. The data for heating 1.0 g of water from −20°C to 120°C can be shown in a graph called a **heating curve** (Figure 6.17).

An important aspect of these phase changes is that each one of them is reversible. If we start with liquid water at room temperature and cool it by immersing the container in a dry ice bath (−78°C), the reverse process is observed. The temperature drops until it reaches 0°C, and then ice begins to crystallize. During this phase change, the temperature of the sample stays constant but heat is given off. The amount of heat given off when 1.0 g of liquid water at 0°C freezes is exactly the same as the amount of heat absorbed when the 1.0 g of ice at 0°C melts.

Phase change A change from one physical state (gas, liquid, or solid) to another

The criterion of uniformity is the way it appears to our eyes and not as it is on the molecular level.

Vapors of gaseous CO_2 are cold enough to cause the moisture in the air above it to condense. The mixture of CO_2 vapors and condensed water vapor is heavier than air and slowly glides along the table or other surface on which the dry ice is placed.

Active Figure 6.17 The heating curve of ice. The graph shows the effect of adding heat to 1.0 g of ice initially at −20°C and raising its temperature to 120°C. **See a simulation based on this figure, and take a short quiz on the concepts at http://now.brookscole.com/gob8 or on the CD.**

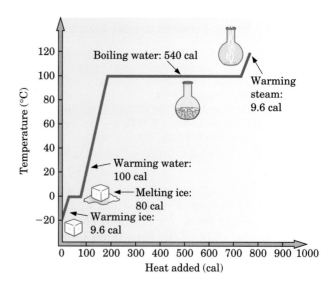

A transition from the solid state directly into the vapor state without going through the liquid state is called **sublimation.** Solids usually sublime only at reduced pressures (less than 1 atm). At high altitudes, where the atmospheric pressure is low, snow sublimes. Solid CO_2 (dry ice) sublimes at −78.5°C under 1 atm pressure. At 1 atm pressure, CO_2 can exist only as a solid or as a gas, never as a liquid.

These freeze-dried coffee crystals were prepared by subliming water from frozen coffee.

Charles D. Winters

EXAMPLE 6.9

The heat of fusion of ice is 80 cal/g. How many calories are required to melt 1.0 mol of ice?

Solution
One mole of H_2O has a mass of 18 g. We use the factor-label method to calculate the heat required to melt one mole of ice at 0°.

$$\frac{80 \text{ cal}}{\text{g ice}} \times 18 \text{ g ice} = 1.4 \times 10^3 \text{ cal} = 1.4 \text{ kcal}$$

Problem 6.9
What mass of water at 100°C can be vaporized by the addition of 45.0 kcal of heat?

EXAMPLE 6.10

What will be the final temperature if we add 1000 cal of heat to 10.0 g of ice at 0°C?

Solution
The first thing the added heat will do is to melt the ice. This phase change will use up 10.0 g × 80 cal/g = 800 cal. The remaining 200 cal will be used to heat the liquid water. The specific heat (SH; Section 1.9) of liquid water is 1.00 cal/g · °C (Table 1.4). The amount of heat required to bring about this change is given by the following equation:

$$\text{Amount of heat} = \text{SH} \times m \times (T_2 - T_1)$$

Solving this equation for $T_2 - T_1$ gives

$$T_2 - T_1 = \text{Amount of heat} \times \frac{1}{SH} \times \frac{1}{m}$$

$$T_2 - T_1 = 200 \ \text{cal} \times \frac{\text{g} \cdot °C}{1.00 \ \text{cal}} \times \frac{1}{10.0 \ \text{g}} = 20°C$$

Thus the temperature of the liquid water will rise by 20°C from 0°C, and it is now 20°C.

Problem 6.10

The specific heat of iron is 0.11 cal/g · °C (Table 1.4). The heat of fusion of iron—that is, the heat required to convert iron from a solid to a liquid at its melting point—is 63.7 cal/g. Iron melts at 1530°C. How much heat must be added to 1.0 g of iron at 25°C to completely melt it?

We can show all phase changes for any substance on a **phase diagram.** Figure 6.18 is a phase diagram for water. Temperature is plotted on the *x*-axis and pressure on the *y*-axis. Three areas with different colors are labeled solid, liquid, and vapor. Within these areas water exists either as ice or liquid water or water vapor. The line (A–B) separating the solid phase from the liquid phase contains all the freezing (melting) points of water—for example, 0°C at 1 atm and 0.005°C at 400 mm Hg.

At the melting point, the solid and liquid phases coexist. The line separating the liquid phase from the gas phase (A-C) contains all the boiling points of water—for example, 100°C at 760 mm Hg and 84°C at 400 mm Hg. At the boiling points, the liquid and gas phases coexist.

Finally, the line separating the solid phase from the gas phase (A-D) contains all the sublimation points. At the sublimation points, the solid and gas phases coexist.

At a unique point (A) on the phase diagram, called the **triple point,** all three phases coexist. The triple point for water occurs at 0.01°C and 4.58 mm Hg pressure.

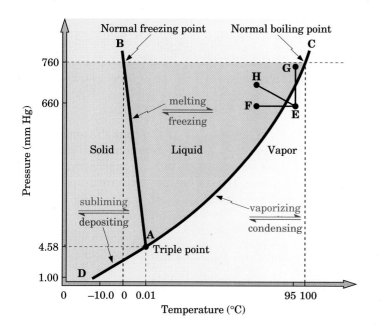

Figure 6.18   Phase diagram of water. Temperature and pressure scales are greatly reduced.

CHEMICAL CONNECTIONS 6F

Supercritical Carbon Dioxide

We are conditioned to think that a compound may exist in three phases: solid, liquid, or gas. Under certain pressures and temperatures, however, fewer phases may exist. A case in point is the plentiful nonpolar substance carbon dioxide. At room temperature and 1 atm pressure, CO_2 is a gas. Even when it is cooled to $-78°C$, it does not become a liquid but rather goes directly from a gas to a solid, which we call dry ice. At room temperature, a pressure of 60 atm is necessary to force molecules of CO_2 close enough together that they condense to a liquid.

Much more esoteric is the form of carbon dioxide called supercritical CO_2, which has some of the properties of a gas and some of the properties of a liquid. It has the density of a liquid but maintains its gas-like property of being able to flow with little viscosity or surface tension. What makes supercritical CO_2 particularly useful is that it is an excellent solvent for many organic materials. For example, supercritical CO_2 can extract caffeine from ground coffee beans and, after extraction when the pressure is released, it simply evaporates leaving no traces behind. Similar processes can be performed with organic solvents, but traces of solvent may be left behind in the decaffeinated coffee and may alter its taste.

To understand the supercritical state, it is necessary to think about the interactions of molecules in the gas and liquid states. In the gaseous state, molecules are far apart, there is very little interaction between them, and most of the volume occupied by the gas is empty space. In the liquid state, molecules are held close together by the attractive forces between their molecules, and there is very little empty space between them. The supercritical state is something between these two states. Molecules are close enough together to give the sample some of the properties of a liquid but at the same time far enough apart to give it some of the properties of a gas.

The critical temperature and pressure for carbon dioxide are 31°C and 73 atm. When supercritical CO_2 is cooled below the critical temperature and/or compressed, there is a phase transition and the gas and liquid coexist. At a critical temperature and pressure, the two phases merge. Above critical conditions, the supercritical fluid exists, which exhibits characteristics that are intermediate between those of a gas and those of a liquid.

A phase diagram illustrates how one may go from one phase to another. For example, suppose we have water vapor at 95°C and 660 mm Hg (E). We want to condense it to liquid water. We can decrease the temperature to 70°C without changing the pressure (moving horizontally from E to F). Alternatively, we can increase the pressure to 760 mm Hg without changing the temperature (moving vertically from E to G). Or we can change both temperature and pressure (moving from E to H). Any of these processes will condense the water vapor to liquid water, although the resulting liquids will be at different pressures and temperatures. The phase diagram allows us to visualize what will happen to the phase of a substance when we change the experimental conditions from one set of temperature and pressure to another set.

EXAMPLE 6.11

What will happen to ice at 0°C if the pressure decreases from 1 atm to 0.001 atm?

Solution
According to Figure 6.18, when the pressure decreases while the temperature remains constant, we move vertically from 1 atm to 0.001 atm (0.76 mm Hg). During this process we cross the boundary separating the solid phase from the vapor phase. Thus, when the pressure drops to 0.001 atm, ice sublimes and becomes vapor.

Problem 6.11

What will happen to water vapor if it is cooled from 100°C to −30°C while the pressure stays at 1 atm?

SUMMARY OF KEY QUESTIONS

SECTION 6.1 What Are the Three States of Matter?

- Matter can exist in three different states: gas, liquid, and solid.
- Attractive forces between molecules tend to hold matter together, whereas the kinetic energy of the molecules tends to disorganize matter.

SECTION 6.2 What Is Gas Pressure and How Do We Measure It?

- Gas pressure results from the bombardment of the gas particles on the walls of its container.
- The pressure of the atmosphere is measured with a barometer. Three common units of pressure are millimeters of mercury, torr, and atmospheres: 1 mm Hg = 1 torr and 760 mm Hg = 1 atm.

SECTION 6.3 What Are the Laws That Govern the Behavior of Gases?

- **Boyle's law** states that for a gas at constant temperature, the volume of the gas is inversely proportional to the pressure.
- **Charles's law** states that the volume of a gas at constant pressure is directly proportional to the temperature in kelvins.
- **Gay-Lussac's law** states that for gas at constant volume, the pressure is directly proportional to the temperature in kelvins.
- These laws are combined and expressed as the **combined gas law:**

$$\frac{P_1 V_1}{T_1} = \frac{P_2 V_2}{T_2}$$

SECTION 6.4 What Are Avogadro's Law and the Ideal Gas Law?

- **Avogadro's law** states that equal volumes of gases at the same temperature and pressure contain the same number of molecules.
- The ideal gas law, $PV = nRT$, incorporates Avogadro's law into the combined gas law.

SECTION 6.5 What Is Dalton's Law of Partial Pressures?

- **Dalton's law of partial pressures** states that the total pressure of a mixture of gases is the sum of the partial pressures of each individual gas.

SECTION 6.6 What Is the Kinetic Molecular Theory?

- The **kinetic molecular theory** explains the behavior of gases. Molecules in the gaseous state move rapidly and randomly, allowing a gas to fill all the available space of its container. Gas molecules have no volume and no forms of attraction between them. In their random motion, gas molecules collide with the walls of the container and thereby exert pressure.

SECTION 6.7 What Types of Attractive Forces Exist Between Molecules?

- **Intermolecular forces of attraction** are responsible for the condensation of gases into the liquid state and for the solidification of liquids to the solid state. In order of increasing strength, the intermolecular forces of attraction are **London dispersion forces, dipole–dipole attractions,** and **hydrogen bonds.**

SECTION 6.8 How Do We Describe the Behavior of Liquids at the Molecular Level?

- **Surface tension** is the energy of intermolecular attractive forces at the surface of a liquid.
- **Vapor pressure** is the pressure of a vapor (gas) above its liquid in a closed container. The vapor pressure of a liquid increases with increasing temperature.
- The **boiling point** of a liquid is the temperature at which its vapor pressure equals the atmospheric pressure. The boiling point of a liquid is determined by (1) the nature and strength of the intermolecular forces between its molecules, (2) the number of sites for intermolecular interaction, and (3) molecular shape.

SECTION 6.9 What Are the Characteristics of the Various Types of Solids?

- Solids crystallize in well-formed geometrical shapes that often reflect the patterns in which the atoms are arranged within the crystals.
- The **melting point** is the temperature at which a substance changes from the solid state to the liquid state.
- **Crystallization** is the formation of a solid from a liquid.

SECTION 6.10 What Is a Phase Change and What Energies Are Involved?

- A **phase** is any part of a system that looks uniform throughout. A **phase change** involves a change of matter from one physical state to another—that is, from a solid, liquid, or gaseous state to any one of the other two states.
- **Sublimation** is a change from a solid state directly to a gaseous state.
- **Heat of fusion** is the heat necessary to convert 1.0 g of any solid to a liquid.

- **Heat of vaporization** is the heat necessary to convert 1.0 g of any liquid to the gaseous state.
- A phase diagram allows the visualization of what happens to the phase of a substance when the temperature or pressure is changed.

- A phase diagram contains all the melting points, boiling points, and sublimation points where two phases coexist.
- A phase diagram also contains a unique triple point where all three phases coexist.

PROBLEMS

GOB
Chemistry ⚛ Now™

Assess your understanding of this chapter's topics with additional quizzing and conceptual-based problems at **http://now.brookscole.com/gob8** or on the CD.

A blue problem number indicates an applied problem.

■ denotes problems that are available on the GOB ChemistryNow website or CD and are assignable in OWL.

SECTION 6.3 What Are the Laws That Govern the Behavior of Gases?

6.12 A sample of gas has a volume of 6.20 L at 20°C at a pressure of 1.10 atm. What is its volume at the same temperature and at a pressure of 0.925 atm?

6.13 ■ Methane gas is compressed from 20 L to 2.5 L at a constant temperature. The final pressure is 12.2 atm. What was the original pressure?

6.14 A gas syringe at 20°C contains 20 mL of CO_2 gas. The pressure of the gas in the syringe is 1.0 atm. What is the pressure in the syringe at 20°C if the plunger is depressed to 10 mL?

6.15 Suppose that the pressure in an automobile tire is 2.30 atm at a temperature of 20°C. What will the pressure in the tire be if, after 10 miles of driving, the temperature of the tire increases to 47°C?

6.16 A sample of 23.0 L of NH_3 gas at 10.0°C is heated at constant pressure until it fills a volume of 50.0 L. What is the new temperature in °C?

6.17 If a sample of 4.17 L of ethane gas, C_2H_6, at 725°C is cooled to 175°C at constant pressure, what is the new volume?

6.18 A sample of SO_2 gas has a volume of 5.2 L. It is heated at constant pressure from 30°C to 90°C. What is its new volume?

6.19 A sample of B_2H_6 gas in a 35-mL container is at a pressure of 450 mm Hg and a temperature of 625°C. If the gas is allowed to cool at constant volume until the pressure is 375 mm Hg, what is the new temperature in °C?

6.20 A gas in a bulb as in Figure 6.3 registers a pressure of 833 mm Hg in the manometer in which the reference arm of the U-shaped tube (A) is sealed and evacuated. What will the difference in the mercury level be if the reference arm of the U-shaped tube is open to atmospheric pressure (760 mm Hg)?

6.21 In an autoclave, a constant amount of steam is generated at a constant volume. Under 1.00 atm pressure, the steam temperature is 100°C. What pressure setting should be used to obtain a 165°C steam temperature for the sterilization of surgical instruments?

6.22 A sample of the inhalation anesthetic gas Halothane, CH_2BrClF_3, in a 500-mL cylinder has a pressure of 2.3 atm at 0°C. What will be the pressure of the gas if its temperature is warmed to 37°C (body temperature)?

6.23 Complete this table:

V_1	T_1	P_1	V_2	T_2	P_2
546 L	43°C	6.5 atm	_____	65°C	1.9 atm
43 mL	−56°C	865 torr	_____	43°C	1.5 atm
4.2 L	234 K	0.87 atm	3.2 L	29°C	_____
1.3 L	25°C	740 mm Hg	_____	0°C	1.0 atm

6.24 Complete this table:

V_1	T_1	P_1	V_2	T_2	P_2
6.35 L	10°C	0.75 atm	_____	0°C	1.0 atm
75.6 L	0°C	1.0 atm	_____	35°C	735 torr
1.06 L	75°C	0.55 atm	3.2 L	0°C	_____

6.25 ■ A balloon filled with 1.2 L of helium at 25°C and 0.98 atm pressure is submerged in liquid nitrogen at −196°C. Calculate the final volume of the helium in the balloon.

6.26 ■ A balloon used for atmospheric research has a volume of 1×10^6 L. Assume that the balloon is filled with helium gas at STP and then allowed to ascend to an altitude of 10 km, where the pressure of the atmosphere is 243 mm Hg and the temperature is −33°C. What will the volume of the balloon be under these atmospheric conditions?

6.27 A gas occupies 56.44 L at 2.00 atm and 310 K. If the gas is compressed to 23.52 L and the temperature is lowered to 281 K, what is the new pressure?

6.28 A certain quantity of helium gas is at a temperature of 27°C and a pressure of 1.00 atm. What will the new temperature be if its volume is doubled at the same time that its pressure is decreased to one half of its original value?

6.29 ■ A sample of 30.0 mL of krypton gas, Kr, is at 756 mm Hg and 25.0°C. What is the new volume if the pressure is decreased to 325 mm Hg and the temperature is decreased to −12.5°C?

6.30 ■ A 26.4-mL sample of ethylene gas, C_2H_4, has a pressure of 2.50 atm at 2.5°C. If the volume is increased to 36.2 mL and the temperature is raised to 10°C, what is the new pressure?

SECTION 6.4 What Are Avogadro's Law and the Ideal Gas Law?

6.31 A sample of a gas at 77°C and 1.33 atm occupies a volume of 50.3 L.

(a) How many moles of the gas are present?

(b) Does your answer depend on knowing what gas it is?

6.32 ■ What is the volume in liters occupied by 1.21 g of Freon-12 gas, CCl_2F_2, at 0.980 atm and 35°C?

6.33 ■ An 8.00-g sample of a gas occupies 22.4 L at 2.00 atm and 273 K. What is the molecular weight of the gas?

6.34 ■ What volume is occupied by 5.8 g of propane gas, C_3H_8, at 23°C and 1.15 atm pressure?

6.35 Does the density of a gas increase, decrease, or stay the same as the pressure increases at constant temperature? As the temperature increases at constant pressure?

6.36 What volume in milliliters does 0.275 g of uranium hexafluoride gas, UF_6, gas occupy at its boiling point of 56°C at 365 torr?

6.37 A hyperbaric chamber has a volume of 200 L.

(a) How many moles of oxygen are needed to fill the chamber at room temperature (23°C) and 3.00 atm pressure?

(b) How many grams of oxygen are needed?

6.38 One gulp of air has a volume of 2 L at STP. If air contains 20.9% oxygen, how many molecules of oxygen are in one gulp?

6.39 An average pair of lungs has a volume of 5.5 L. If the air they contain is 21% oxygen, how many molecules of O_2 do the lungs contain at 1.1 atm and 37°C?

6.40 ■ Calculate the molecular weight of a gas if 3.30 g of the gas occupies 660 mL at 735 mm Hg and 27°C.

6.41 The three main components of dry air and the percentage of each are N_2 (78.08%), O_2 (20.95%), and Ar (0.93%).

(a) Calculate the mass of one mole of air.

(b) Given the mass of one mole of air, calculate the density of air in g/L at STP.

6.42 The ideal gas law can be used to calculate the density (mass ÷ volume = g/V) of a gas. Starting with the ideal gas law, $PV = nRT$, and the fact that n (number of moles of gas) = grams (g) ÷ molecular weight (MW), show that

$$\text{Density} = \frac{g}{V} = \frac{P \times MW}{RT}$$

6.43 Calculate the density in g/L of each of these gases at STP. Which gases are more dense than air? Which are less dense than air?

(a) SO_2 (b) CH_4 (c) H_2

(d) He   (e) CO_2

6.44 The density of Freon-12, CCl_2F_2, at STP is 4.99 g/L, which means that it is approximately four times more dense than air. Show how the kinetic molecular theory of gases accounts for the fact that, although Freon-12 is more dense than air, it nevertheless finds its way to the stratosphere, where it is implicated in the destruction of Earth's protective ozone layer.

6.45 The density of liquid octane, C_8H_{18}, is 0.7025 g/mL. If 1.00 mL of liquid octane is vaporized at 100°C and 725 torr, what volume does the vapor occupy?

6.46 How many molecules of CO are in 100 L of CO at STP?

6.47 The density of acetylene gas, C_2H_2, in a 4-L container at 0°C and 2 atm pressure is 0.02 g/mL. What would be the density of the gas under identical temperature and pressure if the container were partitioned into two 2-L compartments?

6.48 ■ Automobile air bags are inflated by nitrogen gas. When a significant collision occurs, an electronic sensor triggers the decomposition of sodium azide to form nitrogen gas and sodium metal. The nitrogen gas then inflates nylon bags, which protect the driver and front-seat passenger from impact with the dashboard and windshield. What volume of nitrogen gas measured at 1 atm and 27°C is formed by the decomposition of 100 g of sodium azide?

$$2NaN_3(s) \longrightarrow 2Na(s) + 3N_2(g)$$
Sodium azide

SECTION 6.5 What Is Dalton's Law of Partial Pressures?

6.49 ■ The three main components of dry air and the percentage of each are nitrogen (78.08%), oxygen (20.95%), and argon (0.93%).

(a) Calculate the partial pressure of each gas in a sample of dry air at 760 mm Hg.

(b) Calculate the total pressure exerted by these three gases combined.

6.50 ■ Air in the trachea contains oxygen (19.4%), carbon dioxide (0.4%), water vapor (6.2%), and nitrogen (74.0%). If the pressure in the trachea is assumed to be 1.0 atm, what are the partial pressures of these gases in this part of the body?

6.51 The partial pressures of a mixture of gases were as follows: oxygen, 210 mm Hg; nitrogen, 560 mm Hg; and carbon dioxide, 15 mm Hg. The total pressure of the gas mixture was 790 mm Hg. Was there another gas present in the mixture?

SECTION 6.6 What Is the Kinetic Molecular Theory?

6.52 Compare and contrast Dalton's atomic theory and the kinetic molecular theory.

SECTION 6.7 What Types of Attractive Forces Exist Between Molecules?

6.53 Which forces are stronger, intramolecular covalent bonds or intermolecular hydrogen bonds?

6.54 Under which condition does water vapor behave most ideally?
(a) 0.5 atm, 400 K   (b) 4 atm, 500 K
(c) 0.01 atm, 500 K

6.55 ■ Can water and dimethyl sulfoxide, $(CH_3)_2S=O$, form hydrogen bonds between them?

6.56 What kind of intermolecular interactions take place in (a) liquid CCl_4 and (b) liquid CO? Which will have the highest surface tension?

6.57 Ethanol, C_2H_5OH, and carbon dioxide, CO_2, have approximately the same molecular weight, yet carbon dioxide is a gas at STP and ethanol is a liquid. How do you account for this difference in physical property?

6.58 Can dipole–dipole interactions ever be weaker than London dispersion forces? Explain.

6.59 ■ Which compound has a higher boiling point: butane, C_4H_{10}, or hexane, C_6H_{14}?

SECTION 6.8 How Do We Describe the Behavior of Liquids at the Molecular Level?

6.60 The melting point of chloroethane, CH_3CH_2Cl, is −136°C and its boiling point is 12°C. Is chloroethane a gas, a liquid, or a solid at STP?

SECTION 6.9 What Are the Characteristics of the Various Types of Solids?

6.61 Which types of solids have the highest melting points? Which have the lowest melting points?

SECTION 6.10 What Is a Phase Change and What Energies Are Involved?

6.62 Calculate the specific heat (Section 1.9) of gaseous Freon-12, CCl_2F_2, if it requires 170 cal to change the temperature of 36.6 g of Freon-12 from 30°C to 50°C.

6.63 The heat of vaporization of liquid Freon-12, CCl_2F_2, is 4.71 kcal/mol. Calculate the energy required to vaporize 39.2 g of this compound. The molecular weight of Freon-12 is 120.9 amu.

6.64 The specific heat (Section 1.9) of mercury is 0.0332 cal/g · °C. Calculate the energy necessary to raise the temperature of one mole of liquid mercury by 36°C.

6.65 ■ Using Figure 6.13, estimate the vapor pressure of ethanol at (a) 30°C, (b) 40°C, and (c) 60°C.

6.66 CH_4 and H_2O have about the same molecular weights. Which has the higher vapor pressure at room temperature? Explain.

6.67 The normal boiling point of a substance depends on both the mass of the molecule and the attractive forces between molecules. Arrange the compounds in each set in order of increasing boiling point and explain your answer:
(a) HCl, HBr, HI   (b) O_2, HCl, H_2O_2

6.68 Refer to Figure 6.17. How many calories are required to bring one mole of ice at 0°C to a liquid state at room temperature (23°C)?

6.69 Compare the number of calories absorbed when 100 g of ice at 0°C is changed to liquid water at 37°C with the number of calories absorbed when 100 g of liquid water is warmed from 0°C to 37°C.

6.70 (a) How much energy is released when 10 g of steam at 100°C is condensed and cooled to body temperature (37°C)?
(b) How much energy is released when 100 g of liquid water at 100°C is cooled to body temperature (37°C)?
(c) Why are steam burns more painful than hot-water burns?

6.71 When iodine vapor hits a cold surface, iodine crystals form. Name the phase change that is the reverse of this condensation.

6.72 If a 156-g block of dry ice, CO_2, is sublimed at 25°C and 740 mm Hg, what volume does the gas occupy?

6.73 Trichlorofluoromethane (Freon-11, CCl_3F) as a spray is used to temporarily numb the skin around minor scrapes and bruises. It accomplishes this by reducing the temperature of the treated area, thereby numbing the nerve endings that perceive pain. Calculate the heat in kilocalories that can be removed from the skin by 1.00 mL of Freon-11. The density of Freon-11 is 1.49 g/mL, and its heat of vaporization is 6.42 kcal/mol.

6.74 Using the phase diagram of water (Figure 6.18), describe the process by which you can sublime 1 g of ice at −10°C and at 1 atm pressure to water vapor at the same temperature.

Chemical Connections

6.75 (Chemical Connections 6A) Which has lower entropy, a gas at 100°C or one at 200°C? Explain.

6.76 (Chemical Connections 6A) Which form of carbon presented in Figure 6.16 has the highest entropy?

6.77 (Chemical Connections 6B) What happens when a person lowers the diaphragm in his or her chest cavity?

6.78 (Chemical Connections 6C) In carbon monoxide poisoning, hemoglobin is incapable of transporting oxygen to the body's tissues. How does the oxygen get delivered to the cells when a patient is put into a hyperbaric chamber?

6.79 (Chemical Connections 6D) In a sphygmomanometer one listens to the first tapping sound as the constrictive pressure of the arm cuff is slowly released. What is the significance of this tapping sound?

6.80 (Chemical Connections 6E) Why is the damage by severe frostbite irreversible?

6.81 (Chemical Connections 6E) If you fill a glass bottle with water, cap it, and cool to $-10°C$, the bottle will crack. Explain.

6.82 (Chemical Connections 6F) In what way does supercritical CO_2 have some of the properties of a gas, and some of the properties of a liquid?

Additional Problems

6.83 Why is it difficult to compress a liquid or a solid?

6.84 Explain in terms of the kinetic molecular theory, what causes (a) the pressure of a gas and (b) the temperature of a gas.

6.85 The unit of pressure most commonly used for checking the inflation of automobile and bicycle tires is pounds per square inch (lb/in^2), abbreviated psi. The conversion factor between atm and psi is 1 atm = 14.7 psi. Suppose an automobile tire is filled to a pressure of 34 psi. What is the pressure in atm in the tire?

6.86 The gas in an aerosol can is at a pressure of 3.0 atm at 23°C. What will the pressure of the gas in the can be if the temperature is raised to 400°C?

6.87 Why do aerosol cans carry the warning "Do not incinerate"?

6.88 Under certain weather conditions (just before rain), the air becomes less dense. How does this change affect the barometric pressure reading?

6.89 An ideal gas occupies 387 mL at 275 mm Hg and 75°C. If the pressure changes to 1.36 atm and the temperature increases to 105°C, what is the new volume?

6.90 Which compound has greater intermolecular interactions, CO or CO_2?

6.91 On the basis of what you have learned about intermolecular forces, predict which liquid has the highest boiling point:
(a) Pentane, C_5H_{12}
(b) Chloroform, $CHCl_3$
(c) Water, H_2O

6.92 A 10-L gas cylinder is filled with N_2 to a pressure of 35 in. Hg. How many moles of N_2 do you have to add to your container to raise the pressure to 60 in. Hg? Assume a constant temperature of 27°C.

6.93 When filled, a typical tank for an outdoor grill contains 20 lb of LP (liquefied petroleum) gas, the major component of which is propane, C_3H_8. For this problem, assume that propane is the only substance present.
(a) How do you account for the fact that when propane is put under pressure, it can be liquefied?
(b) How many kilograms of propane does a full tank contain?
(c) How many moles of propane does a full tank contain?
(d) If the propane in a full tank were released into a flexible container, what volume would it occupy at STP?

6.94 Explain why gases are transparent.

6.95 ■ The density of a gas is 0.00300 g/cm^3 at 100°C and 1.00 atm. What is the mass of one mole of the gas?

6.96 The normal boiling point of hexane, C_6H_{14}, is 69°C, and that of pentane, C_5H_{12}, is 36°C. Predict which of these compounds has a higher vapor pressure at 20°C.

6.97 If 60.0 g of NH_3 occupies 35.1 L under a pressure of 77.2 in. Hg, what is the temperature of the gas, in °C?

6.98 Water is a liquid at STP. Hydrogen sulfide, H_2S, a heavier molecule, is a gas under the same conditions. Explain.

6.99 Why does the temperature of a liquid drop as a result of evaporation?

6.100 What volume of air (21% oxygen) measured at 25°C and 0.975 atm is required to completely oxidize 3.42 g of aluminum to aluminum oxide, Al_2O_3?

Tying It Together

6.101 Diving, particularly SCUBA (Self-Contained Underwater Breathing Apparatus) diving, subjects the body to increased pressure. Each 10 m (approximately 33 ft) of water exerts an additional pressure of 1 atm on the body.
(a) What is the pressure on the body at a depth of 100 ft?
(b) The partial pressure of nitrogen gas in air at 1 atm is 593 mm Hg. Assuming a SCUBA diver breathes compressed air, what is the partial pressure of nitrogen entering the lungs from a breathing tank at a depth of 100 ft?
(c) The partial pressure of oxygen gas in the air at 1 atm is 158 mm Hg. What is the partial pressure of oxygen in the air in the lungs at a depth of 100 ft?
(d) Why is it absolutely essential to exhale vigorously in a rapid ascent from a depth of 100 ft?

CHAPTER 7

Solutions and Colloids

GOB
Chemistry·Now™
Look for this logo in the chapter and go to GOB ChemistryNow at **http://now.brookscole.com/gob8** or on the CD for tutorials, simulations, and problems.

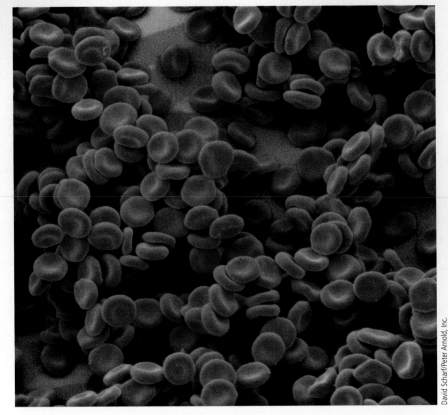

Human blood cells in an isotonic solution.

David Scharf/Peter Arnold, Inc.

Making a homogeneous solution. A green solid, nickel nitrate, is stirred into water, where it dissolves to form a homogeneous solution.

Charles D. Winters

7.1 | What Do We Need to Know as We Begin?

In Chapter 2, we discussed pure substances—compounds made of two or more elements in a fixed ratio. Such systems are the easiest to study, so it was convenient to begin with them. In our daily lives, however, we more frequently encounter mixtures—systems having more than one component. Air, smoke, sea water, milk, blood, and rocks, for example, are mixtures (Section 2.2C).

If a mixture is uniform throughout at the molecular level, we call it a homogeneous mixture or, more commonly, a solution. Air and sea water, for example, are both solutions. They are clear and transparent. In contrast, in most rocks, we can see distinct regions separated from each other by well-defined boundaries. Such rocks are heterogeneous mixtures. Another example is a mixture of sand and sugar. We can easily distinguish between the two components; the mixing does not occur at the molecular level (Figure 2.4). Thus mixtures are classified on the basis of how they look to the unaided eye.

Some systems, however, fall between homogeneous and heterogeneous mixtures. Cigarette smoke, milk, and blood plasma may look homogeneous,

192

Table 7.1 The Most Common Types of Solutions

Solute		Solvent	Appearance of Solution	Example
Gas	in	Liquid	Liquid	Carbonated water
Liquid	in	Liquid	Liquid	Wine
Solid	in	Liquid	Liquid	Salt water (saline solution)
Gas	in	Gas	Gas	Air
Solid	in	Solid	Solid	14-Carat gold

but they do not have the transparency of air or sea water. These mixtures are classified as colloidal dispersions (suspensions). We will deal with such systems in Section 7.7.

Although mixtures can contain many components, we will generally restrict our discussion here to two-component systems, with the understanding that everything we say can be extended to multicomponent systems.

7.2 | What Are the Most Common Types of Solutions?

When we think of a solution, we normally think of a liquid. Liquid solutions, such as sugar in water, are the most common kind, but there are also solutions that are gases or solids. In fact, all mixtures of gases are solutions. Because gas molecules are far apart from each other and much empty space separates them, two or more gases can mix with each other in any proportions. Because the mixing takes place at the molecular level, a true solution always forms; that is, there are no heterogeneous mixtures of gases.

With solids, we are at the other extreme. Whenever we mix solids, we get a heterogeneous mixture. Because even microscopic pieces of solid still contain many billions of particles (molecules, ions, or atoms), there is no way to achieve mixing at the molecular level. Homogeneous mixtures of solids (or **alloys**), such as brass, do exist, but we make them by melting the solids, mixing the molten components, and allowing the mixture to solidify.

Table 7.1 lists the five most common types of solutions. Examples of other types (gas in solid, liquid in gas, and so on) are also known but are much less important.

When a solution consists of a solid or a gas dissolved in a liquid, the liquid is called the **solvent**, and the solid or gas is called the **solute.** A solvent may have several solutes dissolved in it, even of different types. A common example is spring water, in which gases (carbon dioxide and oxygen) and solids (salts) are dissolved in the solvent, water.

When one liquid is dissolved in another, a question may arise regarding which is the solvent and which is the solute. In most cases, the one present in the greater amount is called the solvent, but no rigid rule applies.

7.3 | What Are the Distinguishing Characteristics of Solutions?

The following are some properties of solutions:

1. **The distribution of particles in a solution is uniform.**
   Every part of the solution has exactly the same composition and properties as every other part. That, in fact, is the definition of "homogeneous."

Beer is a solution in which a liquid (alcohol), a solid (malt), and a gas (CO_2) are dissolved in the solvent, water.

Mixtures can be homogenous, as with brass, which is a solid solution of copper and zinc. Alternatively, they can be heterogeneous, as with granite, which contains discrete regions of different minerals (feldspar, mica, and quartz.)

Alloys A homogeneous mixture of two metals

Many alloys are solid solutions. One example is stainless steel, which is mostly iron but also contains carbon, chromium, and other elements. (See also Chemical Connections 2E.)

We normally do not use the terms "solute" and "solvent" when talking about solutions of gases in gases or solids in solids.

CHEMICAL CONNECTIONS 7A

Acid Rain

The water vapor evaporated by the sun from oceans, lakes, and rivers condenses and forms clouds of water vapor that eventually fall as rain. The raindrops contain small amounts of CO_2, O_2, and N_2. The table shows that, of these gases, CO_2 is the most soluble in water. When CO_2 dissolves in water, it reacts with a water molecule to give carbonic acid, H_2CO_3.

$$CO_2(g) + H_2O(\ell) \longrightarrow H_2CO_3(aq)$$
$$\text{Carbonic acid}$$

The acidity caused by the CO_2 is not harmful; however, contaminants that result from industrial pollution may create a serious acid rain problem. Burning coal or oil that contains sulfur generates sulfur dioxide, SO_2, which has a high solubility in water. Sulfur dioxide in the air is oxidized to sulfur trioxide, SO_3. The reaction of sulfur dioxide with water gives sulfurous acid, and the reaction of sulfur trioxide with water gives sulfuric acid.

$$SO_2 + H_2O \longrightarrow H_2SO_3$$
$$\text{Sulfur dioxide} \qquad \text{Sulfurous acid}$$

$$SO_3 + H_2O \longrightarrow H_2SO_4$$
$$\text{Sulfur trioxide} \qquad \text{Sulfuric acid}$$

Smelting (melting or fusing an ore as part of the separation process) industries produce other soluble gases as well. In many parts of the world, especially those located downwind from heavily industrialized areas, the result is acid rain that pours down on forests and lakes. It damages vegetation and kills fish. Such is the situation in the eastern United States, in North Carolina, in the Adirondacks, and in parts of New England, as well as in eastern Canada, where acid rain has been observed with increasing frequency.

Trees killed by acid rain at Mt. Mitchell, North Carolina.

Will McIntyre/Photo Researchers, Inc.

Table 7A	Solubility of Some Gases in Water
Gas	Solubility (g/kg H_2O at 20°C and 1 atm)
O_2	0.0434
N_2	0.0190
CO_2	1.688
H_2S	3.846
SO_2	112.80
NO_2	0.0617

As a consequence, we cannot usually tell a solution from a pure solvent simply by looking at it. A glass of pure water looks the same as a glass of water containing dissolved salt or sugar. In some cases, we can tell by looking—for example, if the solution is colored and we know that the solvent is colorless.

2. **The components of a solution do not separate on standing.**
   A solution of vinegar (acetic acid in water), for example, will never separate.

3. **A solution cannot be separated into its components by filtration.**
   Both the solvent and the solute pass through a filter paper.

4. **For any given solute and solvent, it is possible to make solutions of many different compositions.**
   For example, we can easily make a solution of 1 g of glucose in 100 g of water, or 2 g, or 6 g, or 8.7 g, or any other amount up to the solubility limit (Section 7.4).

5. **Solutions are almost always transparent.**
   They may be colorless or colored, but we can usually see through them. Solid solutions are exceptions.

We use the word "clear" to mean transparent. A solution of copper sulfate in water is blue, but clear.

6. Solutions can be separated into pure components.

Common separation methods include distillation and chromatography, which we may learn about in the laboratory portion of this course. The separation of a solution into its components is a physical change, not a chemical one.

7.4 | What Factors Affect Solubility?

The **solubility** of a solid in a liquid is the maximum amount of the solid that will dissolve in a given amount of a particular solvent at a given temperature. Suppose we wish to make a solution of table salt (NaCl) in water. We take some water, add a few grams of salt, and stir. At first, we see the particles of salt suspended in the water. Soon, however, all the salt dissolves. Now let us add more salt and continue to stir. Again, the salt dissolves. Can we repeat this process indefinitely? The answer is no—there is a limit. The solubility of table salt is 36.2 g per 100 g of water at 30°C. If we add more salt than that amount, the excess solid will not dissolve but rather will remain suspended as long as we keep stirring; it will sink to the bottom after we stop stirring.

Solubility is a physical constant, like melting point or boiling point. Each solid has a different solubility in every liquid. Some solids have a very low solubility in a particular solvent; we often call these solids insoluble. Others have a much higher solubility; we call these soluble. Even for soluble solids however, there is always a solubility limit (see Section 5.6 for some useful solubility generalizations). The same is true for gases dissolved in liquids. Different gases have different solubilities in a solvent (see the table in Chemical Connections 7A). Some liquids are essentially insoluble in other liquids (gasoline in water), whereas others are soluble to a limit. For example, 100 g of water dissolves about 6 g of diethyl ether (another liquid). If we add more ether than that amount, we see two layers (Figure 7.1).

Some liquids, however, are completely soluble in other liquids, no matter how much is present. An example is ethanol, C_2H_6O, and water, which form a solution no matter what quantities of each are mixed. We say that water and ethanol are **miscible** in all proportions.

When a solvent contains all the solute it can hold at a given temperature, we call the solution **saturated.** Any solution containing a lesser amount of solute is **unsaturated.** If we add more solute to a saturated solution at constant temperature, it looks as if none of the additional solid dissolves, because the solution already holds all the solute that it can. Actually an equilibrium, similar to the one discussed in Section 6.8B, is at work in this situation. Some particles of the additional solute dissolve, whereas an equal quantity of dissolved solute comes out of solution. Thus, even though the concentration of dissolved solute does not change, the solute particles themselves are constantly going into and out of solution.

A **supersaturated** solution contains more solute in the solvent than it can normally hold at a given temperature under equilibrium conditions. A supersaturated solution is not stable; when disturbed in any way, such as by stirring or shaking, the excess solute precipitates—thus the solution returns to equilibrium and becomes merely saturated.

Whether a particular solute dissolves in a particular solvent depends on several factors, as discussed next.

A. Nature of the Solvent and the Solute

The more similar two compounds are, the more likely that one will be soluble in the other. Here the rule is "like dissolves like." This is not an absolute rule, but it does apply in most cases.

Figure 7.1 Diethyl ether and water form two layers. A separatory funnel permits the bottom layer to be drawn off.

We use the word "miscible" to refer to a liquid dissolving in a liquid.

Supersaturated solution A solution that contains more than the equilibrium amount of solute at a given temperature and pressure

Polar compounds dissolve in polar compounds because the positive end of the dipole of one molecule attracts the negative end of the dipole of the other molecule.

GOB
Chemistry•Now™
Click *Chemistry Interactive* to see **How a Change in Solubility Can Lead to Generation of Heat**

When we say "like," we mostly mean similar in terms of polarity. In other words, polar compounds dissolve in polar solvents, and nonpolar compounds dissolve in nonpolar solvents. For example, the liquids benzene (C_6H_6) and carbon tetrachloride (CCl_4) are nonpolar compounds. They dissolve in each other, and other nonpolar materials, such as gasoline, dissolve in them. In contrast, ionic compounds such as sodium chloride (NaCl) and polar compounds such as table sugar ($C_{12}H_{22}O_{11}$) are insoluble in these solvents.

The most important polar solvent is water. We have already seen that most ionic compounds are soluble in water, as are small covalent compounds that can form hydrogen bonds with water. It is worth noting that even polar molecules are usually insoluble in water if they cannot either react with water or form hydrogen bonds with water molecules. Water as a solvent is discussed in Section 7.6.

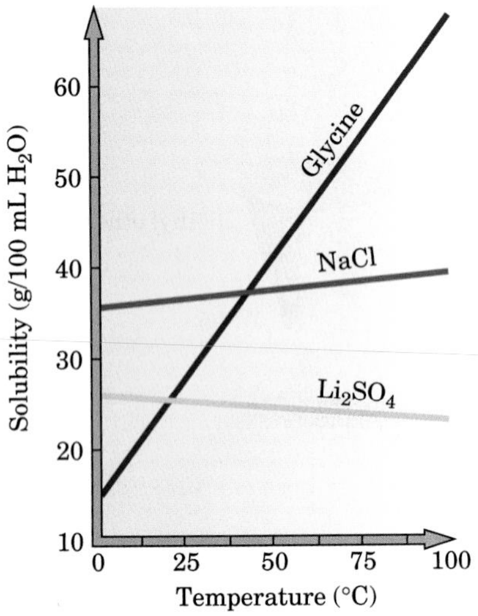

Figure 7.2 The solubilities of some solids in water as a function of temperature. The solubility of glycine increases rapidly, that of NaCl barely increases, and that of Li_2SO_4 decreases with increasing temperature.

B. Temperature

For most solids and liquids that dissolve in liquids, the rule is that solubility increases with increasing temperature. Sometimes the increase is great; at other times it is moderate. For a few substances, solubility even decreases with increasing temperature (Figure 7.2).

For example, the solubility of glycine, $H_2N—CH_2—COOH$, a white, crystalline solid and a polar building block of proteins, is 52.8 g in 100 g of water at 80°C but only 33.2 g at 30°C. If, for instance, we prepare a saturated solution of glycine in 100 g of water at 80°C, it will hold 52.8 g of glycine. If we then allow it to cool to 30°C where the solubility is 33.2 g, we might expect the excess glycine, 19.6 g, to precipitate from solution as crystals. It often does, but on many occasions it does not. The latter case is an example of a **supersaturated solution.** Even though the solution contains more glycine than the water can normally hold at 30°C, the excess glycine stays in solution because the molecules need a seed—a surface on which to begin crystallizing. If no such surface is available, no precipitate will form.

Supersaturated solutions are not indefinitely stable, however. If we shake or stir the solution, we may find that the excess solid precipitates at once (Figure 7.3). Another way to crystallize the excess solute is to add a crystal of the solute, a process called **seeding.** The seed crystal provides the surface onto which the solute molecules can converge.

For gases, solubility in liquids almost always decreases with increasing temperature. The effect of temperature on the solubility of gases in water can have important consequences for fish, for example. Oxygen is only slightly soluble in water, but fish need that oxygen to live. When the temperature of a body of water increases, perhaps because of the output from a nuclear power plant, the solubility of the oxygen decreases and may become so low that fish die. This situation is called thermal pollution.

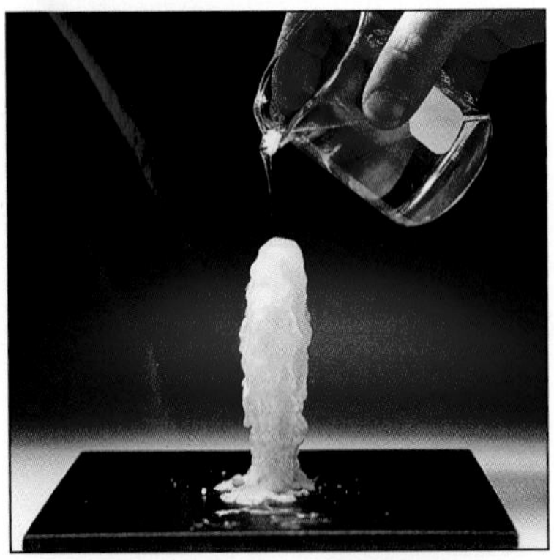
Charles D. Winters

Figure 7.3 When a supersaturated aqueous solution of sodium acetate ($CH_3COO^-Na^+$) is disturbed, the excess salt crystallizes rapidly.

C. Pressure

Pressure has little effect on the solubility of liquids or solids. For gases, however, **Henry's law** applies: The higher the pressure, the greater the solubility of a gas in a liquid. This concept is the basis of the hyperbaric medicine discussed in Chemical Connections 6C. When the pressure increases, more O_2 dissolves in the blood plasma and reaches tissues at higher than normal pressures (2 to 3 atm).

Henry's law also explains why a bottle of beer or a carbonated beverage foams when it is opened. The bottle is sealed under greater than 1 atm of pressure. When opened at 1 atm, the solubility of CO_2 in the liquid decreases. The excess CO_2 is released, forming bubbles, and the gas pushes out some of the liquid.

Henry's law The solubility of a gas in a liquid is directly proportional to the pressure

CHEMICAL CONNECTIONS 7B

The Bends

Deep-sea divers encounter high pressures (see Problem 6.101). For them to breathe properly under such conditions, oxygen must be supplied under pressure. At one time, this goal was achieved with compressed air. As pressure increases, the solubility of the gases in the blood increases. This is especially true for nitrogen, which constitutes almost 80% of our air.

When divers come up and the pressure on their bodies decreases, the solubility of nitrogen in their blood decreases as well. As a consequence, the previously dissolved nitrogen in blood and tissues starts to form small bubbles, especially in the veins. The formation of gas bubbles, called the **bends,** can hamper blood circulation. If this condition is allowed to develop uncontrolled, the resulting pulmonary embolism can prove fatal.

If the divers' ascent is gradual, the dissolved gases are removed by regular exhalation and diffusion through the skin. Divers use decompression chambers, where the high pressure is gradually reduced to normal pressure.

If decompression disease develops after a dive, patients are put into a hyperbaric chamber (see Chemical Connections 6C), where they breathe pure oxygen at 2.8 atm pressure. In the standard form of treatment, the pressure is reduced to 1 atm over a period of 6 hours.

Nitrogen also has a narcotic effect on divers when they breathe compressed air below 40 m. This "rapture of the deep" is similar to alcohol-induced intoxication.

Because of the problem caused by nitrogen, divers' tanks often hold a helium–oxygen mixture instead of air. The solubility of helium in blood is affected less by pressure than is the solubility of nitrogen.

Ascending too rapidly will cause dissolved nitrogen bubbles to be released and form bubbles in the blood.

Sudden decompression and ensuing bends are important not only in deep-sea diving but also in high-altitude flight, especially orbital flight.

7.5 | What Are the Most Common Units for Concentration?

GOB
Chemistry·❖·Now™
Click *Chemistry Interactive* to see how **Henry's Law** explains why soft drinks go flat

We can express the amount of a solute dissolved in a given quantity of solvent—that is, the **concentration** of the solution—in a number of ways. Some concentration units are better suited than others for some purposes. Sometimes qualitative terms are good enough. For example, we may say that a solution is dilute or concentrated. These terms give us little specific information about the concentration, but we know that a concentrated solution contains more solute than a dilute solution does.

For most purposes, however, we need quantitative concentrations. For example, a nurse must know how much glucose to give to a patient. Many methods of expressing concentration exist, but in this chapter we deal with just the three most important: percent concentration, molarity, and parts per million (ppm).

A. Percent Concentration

Chemists represent **percent concentration** in three ways. The most common is weight of solute per volume of solution (w/v):

$$\text{Weight/volume (w/v)}\% = \frac{\text{weight solute}}{\text{volume of solution}} \times 100$$

Percent concentration (% w/v)
The number of grams of solute in 100 mL of solution

If we dissolve 10 g of sucrose (table sugar) in enough water so that the total volume is 100 mL, the concentration is 10% w/v. Note that here we need to know the total volume of the solution, not the volume of the solvent.

EXAMPLE 7.1

The label on a bottle of vinegar says it contains 5.0% acetic acid, CH_3COOH. The bottle contains 240 mL of vinegar. How many grams of acetic acid are in the bottle?

Solution
We are given the volume of the solution and its weight/volume concentration. To find out how many grams of CH_3COOH are in this solution, we use the conversion factor 5.0 g of acetic acid in 100 mL of solution:

$$240 \text{ mL solution} \times \frac{5.0 \text{ g } CH_3COOH}{100 \text{ mL solution}} = 12 \text{ g } CH_3COOH$$

Problem 7.1
How would we make 250 mL of a 4.4% w/v KBr solution in water? Assume that a 250-mL volumetric flask is available.

EXAMPLE 7.2

If 6.0 g of NaCl is dissolved in enough water to make 300 mL of solution, what is the w/v percent of NaCl?

Solution
To calculate the w/v percent, we divide the weight of the solute by the volume of the solution and multiply by 100:

$$\frac{6.0 \text{ g NaCl}}{300 \text{ mL solution}} \times 100 = 2.0\% \text{ w/v}$$

Problem 7.2
If 7.7 g of lithium iodide, LiI, is dissolved in enough water to make 400 mL of solution, what is the w/v percent of LiI?

A second way to represent percent concentration is weight of solute per weight of solution (w/w):

$$\text{Weight/weight (w/w)}\% = \frac{\text{weight solute}}{\text{weight of solution}} \times 100$$

Calculations of w/w are essentially the same as w/v calculations, except that we use the weight of the solution instead of its volume. A volumetric flask is not used for these solutions. (Why not?)

Finally, we can represent percent concentration as volume of solute per volume of solution (v/v):

$$\text{Volume/volume (v/v)\%} = \frac{\text{volume solute}}{\text{volume of solution}} \times 100$$

The unit v/v is used only for solutions of liquids in liquids—most notably, alcoholic beverages. For example, 40% v/v ethanol in water means that 40 mL of ethanol has been added to enough water to make 100 mL of solution. This solution might also be called 80 proof, where proof of an alcoholic beverage is twice the v/v concentration.

A 40% v/v solution of ethanol in water is 80 proof. Proof is twice the percent concentration (v/v) of ethanol in water.

B. Molarity

For many purposes, it is easiest to express concentration by using the weight or volume percentage methods just discussed. When we want to focus on the number of molecules present, however, we need another way. For example, a 5% solution of glucose in water does not contain the same number of solute molecules as a 5% solution of ethanol in water. That is why chemists often use molarity. **Molarity (M),** is defined as the number of moles of solute dissolved in 1 L of solution. The units of molarity are moles per liter.

$$\text{Molarity } (M) = \frac{\text{moles solute } (n)}{\text{volume of solution (L)}}$$

Thus, in the same volume of solution, a 0.2-molar solution of glucose, $C_6H_{12}O_6$, in water contains the same number of molecules of solute as a 0.2-molar solution of ethanol, C_2H_6O, in water. In fact, this relationship holds true for equal volumes of any solution, as long as the molarities are the same.

We can prepare a solution of a given molarity in essentially the same way that we prepare a solution of given w/v concentration, except that we use moles instead of grams in our calculations. We can always find out how many moles of solute are in any volume of a solution of known molarity by using the following formula:

$$\text{Molarity} \times \text{volume in liters} = \text{number of moles}$$

$$\frac{\text{moles}}{\text{liters}} \times \text{liters} = \text{moles}$$

The solution is then prepared as shown in Figure 7.4.

EXAMPLE 7.3

How do we prepare 2.0 L of a 0.15 M aqueous solution of sodium hydroxide, NaOH?

Solution

We are given solid NaOH and want 2.0 L of a 0.15 M solution. First, we find out how many moles of NaOH will be in this solution:

$$\frac{0.15 \text{ mol NaOH}}{1 \text{ L}} \times 2.0 \text{ L} = 0.30 \text{ mol NaOH}$$

GOB
Chemistry ⚛ Now™
Click *Coached Problems* to try a problem calculating the **Amount of Solute Needed to Prepare a Solution of Known Molarity**

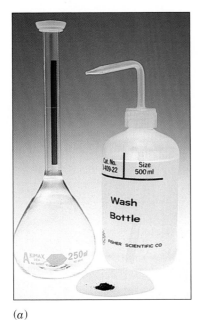

(a)

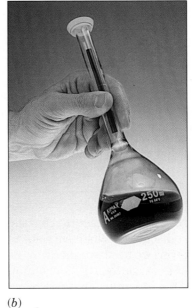

(b)

(c)

Figure 7.4 Preparation of 250 mL of 0.0100 M potassium permanganate solution. (a) A 250-mL volumetric flask. A 0.0100 M solution of $KMnO_4$ is made by adding enough water to 0.395 g (2.5×10^{-3} mol of $KMnO_4$, FW 158.03 g/mol) to make 0.250 L of solution. (b) 0.395 g of $KMnO_4$ is placed in a volumetric flask and dissolved in a small amount of water. (c) After dissolving is complete, sufficient water is added to fill the flask to the calibration mark.

To convert 0.30 mol of NaOH to grams of NaOH, we multiply by the molar mass of NaOH, which is 40.0 g/mol:

$$0.30 \text{ mol NaOH} \times \frac{40.0 \text{ g NaOH}}{1 \text{ mol NaOH}} = 12 \text{ g NaOH}$$

To prepare this solution, we place 12 g of NaOH in a 2-L volumetric flask, add some water, swirl until the solid dissolves, and then fill the flask with water to the 2-L mark.

Problem 7.3

How would we prepare 2.0 L of a 1.06 M aqueous solution of KCl?

Blood (left to right): serum, coagulated, and whole blood.

EXAMPLE 7.4

We dissolve 18.0 g of Li_2O (molar mass = 29.9 g/mol) in sufficient water to make 500 mL of solution. Calculate the molarity of the solution.

Solution

We are given 18.0 g Li_2O in 500 mL of water and want the molarity of this solution. We first calculate the number of moles of Li_2O in this solution. For this calculation, we use two conversion factors: molar mass of Li_2O = 29.9 g and 1000 mL = 1 L.

$$\frac{10.8 \text{ g Li}_2\text{O}}{500 \text{ mL}} \times \frac{1 \text{ mol Li}_2\text{O}}{29.9 \text{ g Li}_2\text{O}} \times \frac{1000 \text{ mL}}{1 \text{ L}} = 0.722 \text{ } M$$

Problem 7.4

If we dissolve 0.440 g of KSCN in enough water to make 340 mL of solution, what is the molarity of the solution?

EXAMPLE 7.5

The concentration of sodium chloride in blood serum is approximately 0.14 M. What volume of blood serum contains 2.0 g of NaCl?

Solution

We are given the concentration in moles per liter. We want the volume of blood that contains 2.0 g NaCl. To find the volume of blood, we use two conversion factors: the molar mass of NaCl is 55.8 g and the concentration of NaCl in blood is 0.14 M.

$$2.0 \text{ g } \cancel{\text{NaCl}} \times \frac{1 \text{ mol } \cancel{\text{NaCl}}}{55.8 \text{ g } \cancel{\text{NaCl}}} \times \frac{\text{L}}{0.14 \text{ mol } \cancel{\text{NaCl}}} = 0.24 \text{ L} = 240 \text{ mL}$$

Blood serum is the liquid part of the blood that remains after removal of the cellular particulates and fibrinogen.

Problem 7.5

If a 0.300 M glucose solution is available for intravenous infusion, how many milliliters are needed to deliver 10.0 g of glucose?

EXAMPLE 7.6

How many grams of HCl are in 225 mL of 6.00 M HCl?

Solution

We are given 225 mL of 6.00 M HCl and asked to find grams of HCl. We use two conversion factors: the molar mass of HCl = 36.5 g and 1000 mL = 1 L.

$$225 \text{ } \cancel{\text{mL}} \times \frac{1 \text{ } \cancel{\text{L}}}{1000 \text{ } \cancel{\text{mL}}} \times \frac{6.00 \text{ mol } \cancel{\text{HCl}}}{1 \text{ } \cancel{\text{L}}} \times \frac{36.5 \text{ g HCl}}{1 \text{ mol } \cancel{\text{HCl}}} = 49.3 \text{ g HCl}$$

Problem 7.6

A certain wine contains 0.010 M $NaHSO_3$ (sodium bisulfite) as a preservative. How many grams of sodium bisulfite must be added to a 100-gallon barrel of wine to reach this concentration? Assume no change in volume of wine upon addition of the sodium bisulfite.

C. Dilution

We frequently prepare solutions by diluting concentrated solutions rather than by weighing out pure solute (Figure 7.5). Because we add only solvent during dilution, the number of moles of solute remains unchanged. Before we dilute, the equation that applies is

$$M_1V_1 = \text{moles}$$

Figure 7.5 Making a solution by dilution from a concentrated one. Here 5.00 mL of potassium dichromate, $K_2Cr_2O_7$ is diluted to 500 mL. The result is dilution by a factor of 100.

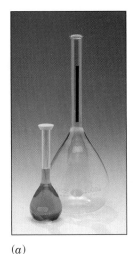  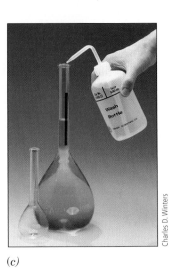

(a)　　　　　(b)　　　　　(c)

After we dilute, the volume and molarity have both changed and we have

$$M_2V_2 = \text{moles}$$

Because the number of moles of solute is the same both before and after, we can say that

We can use this handy equation for dilution problems.

$$M_1V_1 = M_2V_2$$

GOB
Chemistry⋅Now™

Click *Coached Problems* to try a problem calculating how much to dilute a stock solution to **Prepare a Specific Dilute Solution**

EXAMPLE 7.7

Suppose we have a bottle of concentrated acetic acid (6.0 M). How would we prepare 200 mL of a 3.5 M solution of acetic acid?

Solution
We are given $M_1 = 6.0\ M$ and asked to calculate V_1. We are also given $M_2 = 3.5\ M$ and $V_2 = 200$ mL.

$$M_1V_1 = M_2V_2$$

$$\frac{6.0\ \text{mol}}{1\ \text{L}} \times V_1 = \frac{3.5\ \text{mol}}{1\ \text{L}} \times 0.200\ \text{L}$$

Solving this equation for V_1 gives

$$V_1 = \frac{3.5\ \text{mol} \times 0.200\ \text{L}}{6.0\ \text{mol}} = 0.12\ \text{L}$$

To make this solution, we place 0.12 L, or 120 mL, of concentrated acetic acid in a 200-mL volumetric flask, add some water and mix, and then fill to the calibration mark with water.

Problem 7.7
We are given a solution of 12.0 M HCl and asked to make 300 mL of 0.600 M solution. How would we prepare it?

A similar equation can be used for dilution problems involving percent concentrations:

$$\%_1 V_1 = \%_2 V_2$$

EXAMPLE 7.8

Suppose we have a solution of 50% w/v NaOH on hand. How would we prepare 500 mL of a 0.50% w/v solution of NaOH?

Solution
We are given 50% w/v NaOH ($\%_1$) and asked to calculate V_1. We want 500 mL (V_2) of 0.50% w/v solution (V_2).

$$(50\%) \times V_1 = (0.50\%) \times 500 \text{ mL}$$

$$V_1 = \frac{0.50\% \times 500 \text{ mL}}{50\%} = 5.0 \text{ mL}$$

To prepare this solution, we add 5.0 mL of the concentrated solution to a 500-mL volumetric flask, then some water and mix, and finally fill to the mark with water. Note that this is a dilution by a factor of 100.

Problem 7.8

A concentrated solution of 15% w/v KOH solution is available. How would we prepare 20.0 mL of a 0.10% w/v KOH solution?

D. Parts per Million

Sometimes we need to deal with very dilute solutions—for example, 0.0001%. In such cases, it is more convenient to use **parts per million (ppm)** to express concentration. For example, if drinking water is polluted with lead ions to the extent of 1 ppm, it means that there is 1 mg of lead ions in 1 kg (1 L) of water. When reporting concentration in ppm, the units must be the same for both solute and solvent—for example, mg of solute per 10^6 mg solution, or g solute per g solution. Some solutions are so dilute that we use **parts per billion (ppb)** to express their concentrations.

$$\text{ppm} = \frac{\text{g solution}}{\text{g solvent}} \times 10^6$$

$$\text{ppb} = \frac{\text{g solution}}{\text{g solvent}} \times 10^9$$

EXAMPLE 7.9

Verify that 1 mg of lead in 1 kg of drinking water is equivalent to 1 ppm lead.

Solution
The units we are given are milligrams and kilograms. To report ppm, we must convert them to a common unit—say, grams. For this calculation we use two conversion factors: 1000 mg = 1 g and 1 kg = 1000 g. First we find the mass of lead in grams:

$$1 \text{ mg lead} \times \frac{1 \text{ g lead}}{1000 \text{ mg lead}} = 10^{-3} \text{ g lead}$$

Then we find the mass of the solution in grams:

$$1 \text{ kg solution} \times \frac{1000 \text{ g solution}}{1 \text{ kg solution}} = 10^3 \text{ g solution}$$

Finally, we use these values to calculate the concentration of lead in ppm:

$$\text{ppm} = \frac{10^{-3} \text{ g lead}}{10^3 \text{ g solution}} \times 10^6 = 1 \text{ ppm}$$

Problem 7.9

Sodium hydrogen sulfate, $NaHSO_4$, which dissolves in water to release H^+ ion, is used to adjust the pH of the water in swimming pools. Suppose we add 560 g of $NaHSO_4$ to a swimming pool that contains 4.5×10^5 L of water at 25°C. What is the Na^+ ion concentration in ppm?

Modern methods of analysis allow us to detect such minuscule concentrations. Some substances are harmful even at concentrations measured in ppb. One such substance is dioxin, an impurity in the 2,4,5-T herbicide sprayed by the United States as a defoliant in Vietnam.

7.6 | Why Is Water Such a Good Solvent?

Water covers about 75% of the Earth's surface in the form of oceans, ice caps, glaciers, lakes, and rivers. Water vapor is always present in the atmosphere. Life evolved in water, and without it life as we know it could not exist. The human body is about 60% water. This water is found both inside the cells of the body (intracellular) and outside the cells (extracellular). Most of the important chemical reactions in living tissue occur in aqueous solution; water serves as a solvent to transport reactants and products from one place in the body to another. Water is also itself a reactant or product in many biochemical reactions. The properties that make water such a good solvent are its polarity and its hydrogen-bonding capacity (Section 6.7C).

A. How Water Dissolves Ionic Compounds

We learned in Section 4.5 that ionic compounds in the solid state are composed of a regular array of ions. The crystal is held together by ionic bonds, which are electrostatic attractions between positive and negative ions. Water, of course, is a polar molecule. When a solid ionic compound is added to water, water molecules surround the ions at the surface of the crystal. The negative ions (anions) attract the positive ends of water molecules, and the positive ions (cations) attract the negative ends of water molecules (Figure 7.6). Each ion attracts two to four water molecules. When the combined force of attraction to water molecules is greater than the ionic bond that would keep the ion in the crystal, the ion will be completely dislodged. The ion removed from the crystal, is now surrounded by water molecules (Figure 7.7). Such ions are said to be **hydrated.** A more general term, covering all solvents, is **solvated.** The solvation layer—that is, the surrounding shell of solvent molecules—acts as a cushion. It prevents a solvated anion from colliding directly with a solvated cation, thereby keeping the solvated ions in solution.

Not all ionic solids are soluble in water. Some rules for predicting solubilities were given in Section 5.6.

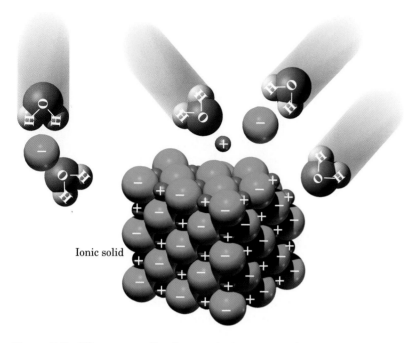

Figure 7.6 When water dissolves an ionic compound, water molecules remove anions and cations from the surface of an ionic solid.

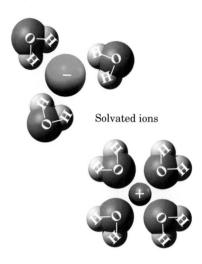

Solvated ions

Figure 7.7 Anions and cations solvated by water.

B. Solid Hydrates

The attraction between ions and water molecules is so strong in some cases that the water molecules are an integral part of the crystal structure of the solids. Water molecules in a crystal are called **water of hydration.** The substances that contain water in their crystals are themselves called **hydrates.** For example, gypsum and plaster of Paris are hydrates of calcium sulfate: Gypsum is calcium sulfate dihydrate, $CaSO_4 \cdot 2H_2O$, and plaster of Paris is calcium sulfate monohydrate, $(CaSO_4)_2 \cdot H_2O$. Some of these crystals hold on to their water tenaciously. To remove it, the crystals must be heated for some time at a high temperature. The crystal without its water is called **anhydrous.** In many cases, anhydrous crystals are so strongly attracted to water that they take it from the water vapor in the air. That is, some anhydrous crystals become hydrated upon standing in air. Crystals that do so are called **hygroscopic.**

Hydrated crystals often look different from the anhydrous forms. For example, copper sulfate pentahydrate, $CaSO_4 \cdot 5H_2O$, is blue, but the anhydrous form is white (Figure 7.8).

The difference between hydrated and anhydrous crystals can sometimes have an effect in the body. For example, the compound sodium urate exists as spherical crystals in the anhydrous form, but the crystals are needle-shaped in the monohydrate form (Figure 7.9). The deposition of sodium urate monohydrate in the joints (mostly in the big toe) causes gout.

C. Electrolytes

Ions in water migrate from one place to another, maintaining their charge along the way. As a consequence, solutions of ions conduct electricity. They can do so because the ions in the solution migrate independently of one another. As shown in Figure 7.10, cations migrate to the negative electrode, called the **cathode,** and anions migrate to the positive electrode, called the

Hygroscopic substance A substance able to absorb water vapor from the air

The dot in the formula $CaSO_4 \cdot 2H_2O$ indicates that H_2O is present in the crystal, but it is not covalently bonded to the Ca^{2+} or SO_4^{2-} ions.

Charles D. Winters

Figure 7.8 When blue hydrated copper(II) sulfate, $CuSO_4 \cdot 5H_2O$, is heated and the compound releases its water of hydration, it changes to white anhydrous copper(II) sulfate, $CuSO_4$.

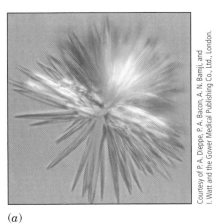

Courtesy of P. A. Deppe, P. A. Bacon, A. N. Bamji, and I. Watt and the Gower Medical Publishing Co., Ltd., London.

(a)

Origin of the Gout

Courtesy of National Library of Medicine

(b)

Figure 7.9 (a) The needle-shaped sodium urate monohydrate crystals that cause gout. (b) The pain of gout as depicted by a cartoonist.

anode. The movement of ions constitutes an electric current. The migration of ions completes the circuit initiated by the battery and can cause an electric bulb to light up (see also Chemical Connections 5B).

Substances that conduct an electric current when dissolved in water or when in the molten state are called **electrolytes.** Sodium chloride, for example, is an electrolyte. Hydrated Na^+ ions carry positive charges, and hydrated Cl^- ions carry negative charges; as a result, the bulb in Figure 7.10 lights brightly if these ions are present. Substances that do not conduct electricity are called **nonelectrolytes.** Distilled water, for example, is a nonelectrolyte. The lightbulb shown in Figure 7.10 does not light up if only distilled water is placed in the beaker. However, with tap water in the beaker, the bulb lights dimly. Tap water contains enough ions to carry elec-

Figure 7.10 Conductance by an electrolyte.

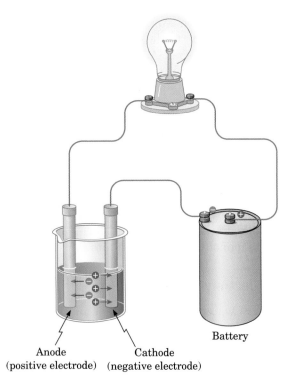

Anode
(positive electrode)

Cathode
(negative electrode)

Battery

CHEMICAL CONNECTIONS 7C

Hydrates and Air Pollution: The Decay of Buildings and Monuments

Many buildings and monuments in urban areas throughout the world are decaying, ruined by air pollution. The main culprit in this process is acid rain, an end product of air pollution. The stones most commonly used for buildings and monuments are limestone and marble, both of which are largely calcium carbonate. In the absence of polluted air, these stones can last for thousands of years. Thus many statues and buildings from ancient times (Babylonian, Egyptian, Greek, and others) survived until recently with little change. Indeed, they remain intact in many rural areas.

In urban areas, however, the air is polluted with SO_2 and SO_3, which come mostly from the combustion of coal and petroleum products containing small amounts of sulfur compounds as impurities (see Chemical Connections 7A). They react with the calcium carbonate at the surface of the stones to form calcium sulfate. When calcium sulfate interacts with water in the rain, it forms the dihydrate gypsum. The problem is that gypsum has a larger volume than the original marble or limestone, so it causes the surface of the stone to expand. This activity, in turn, results in flaking. Eventually, statues such as those in the Parthenon (in Athens, Greece) become noseless and later faceless.

Acid rain damage to stonework on the walls of York Minster.

tricity, but their concentration is so low that the solution conducts only a small amount of electricity.

As we see, electric conductance depends on the concentration of ions. The higher the ion concentration, the greater the electric conductance of the solution. Nevertheless, differences in electrolytes exist. If we take a 0.1 M aqueous solution of NaCl and compare it with a 0.1 M acetic acid (CH_3COOH) solution, we find that the NaCl solution lights a bulb brightly, but the acetic acid solution lights it only dimly. We might have expected the two solutions to behave similarly. They have the same concentration, 0.1 M, and each compound provides two ions, a cation and an anion (Na^+ and Cl^-; H^+ and CH_3COO^-). The reason they behave differently is that, whereas NaCl dissociates completely to two ions (each hydrated and each moving independently), in the case of CH_3COOH only a few molecules are dissociated into ions. Most of the acetic acid molecules do not dissociate, and undissociated molecules do not conduct electricity. Compounds that dissociate completely are called **strong electrolytes,** and those that dissociate into ions only partially are called **weak electrolytes.**

Electrolytes are important components of the body because they help to maintain the acid–base balance and the water balance. The most important cations in tissues of the human body are Na^+, K^+, Ca^{2+}, and Mg^{2+}. The most abundant anions in the body are bicarbonate, HCO_3^-; chloride, Cl^-; hydrogen phosphate, HPO_4^{2-}; and dihydrogen phosphate, $H_2PO_4^-$.

Sports drinks help to maintain the body's electrolytic balance.

D. How Water Dissolves Covalent Compounds

Water is a good solvent not only for ionic compounds but also for many covalent compounds. In a few cases, the covalent compounds dissolve because they react with water. An important example is the covalent compound HCl.

HCl is a gas (with a penetrating, choking odor) that attacks the mucous membranes of the eyes, nose, and throat. When dissolved in water, HCl molecules react with water to give ions:

H^+ does not exist in aqueous solution; it combines with a water molecule and forms a hydronium ion, H_3O^+.

$$HCl(g) + H_2O(\ell) \longrightarrow Cl^-(aq) + H_3O^+(aq)$$
Hydrogen   Hydronium ion
chloride

Another example is the gas sulfur trioxide, which reacts as follows:

$$SO_3(g) + 2H_2O(\ell) \longrightarrow H_3O^+(aq) + HSO_4^-(aq)$$
Sulfur   Hydronium
trioxide   ion

Because HCl and SO_3 are completely converted to ions in dilute aqueous solution, these solutions are ionic solutions and behave just as other electrolytes do (they conduct a current). Nevertheless, HCl and SO_3 are themselves covalent compounds, unlike salts such as NaCl.

Most covalent compounds that dissolve in water do not, in fact, react with water. They dissolve because the water molecules surround the entire covalent molecule and solvate it. For example, when methanol, CH_3OH, dissolves in water, the methanol molecules are solvated by the water molecules (Figure 7.11).

There is a simple way to predict which covalent compounds will dissolve in water and which will not. Covalent compounds will dissolve in water if they can form hydrogen bonds with water, provided that the solute molecules are fairly small. Hydrogen bonding is possible between two molecules if one of them contains an O or N atom and the other contains O—H or N—H bond. Every water molecule contains an O atom and O—H bonds. Therefore, water can form hydrogen bonds with any molecule that contains an O or N atom or an O—H or N—H bond. If these molecules are small enough, they will be soluble in water. How small? In general, they should have no more than three C atoms for each O or N atom.

For example, acetic acid, CH_3COOH, is soluble in water, but benzoic acid, C_6H_5COOH, is not. Similarly, ethanol, C_2H_5OH, is soluble in water, but dipropyl ether, $C_6H_{14}O$, is not. Table sugar, $C_{12}H_{22}O_{11}$ (Section 20.4A), is very soluble in water. Although it contains a large number of carbon atoms, it has so many oxygen atoms that it forms many hydrogen bonds with water molecules; thus this molecule is very well solvated.

Covalent molecules that do not contain O or N atoms are almost always insoluble in water. For example, methanol, CH_3OH, is infinitely soluble in water, but chloromethane, CH_3Cl, is not. The exception is the rare case where a covalent compound reacts with water—for instance, HCl.

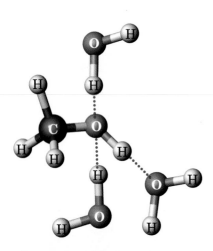

Figure 7.11 Solvation of a polar covalent compound by water. The dotted lines represent hydrogen bonds.

E. Water in the Body

Water is important in the body not only because it dissolves ionic substances as well as some covalent compounds, but also because it hydrates all polar molecules in the body. In this way, it serves as a vehicle to carry most of the organic compounds, nutrients, and fuels used by the body as well as waste material. Blood and urine are two examples of aqueous body fluids.

In addition, the hydration of macromolecules such as proteins, nucleic acids, and polysaccharides allows the proper motions within these molecules, which are necessary for such functions as enzyme activity (described in Chapter 23).

7.7 | What Are Colloids?

Up to now we have discussed only solutions. The maximum diameter of the solute particles in a true solution is about 1 nm. If the diameter of the solute particles exceeds this size, then we no longer have a true solution—we have a **colloid.** In a colloid (also called a colloidal dispersion or colloidal system), the diameter of the solute particles ranges from about 1 to 1000 nm. The term *colloid* has acquired a new name recently. In Chapter 6, we encountered the term *nanotube.* The "nano" part refers to dimensions in the nanometer (1 nm = 10^{-9} m) range, which is the size range of colloids. Thus, when we encounter terms such as "nanoparticle" or "nanoscience," they are equivalent to "colloidal particle" or "colloid science," although the former terms refer mostly to particles with well-defined geometrical shape (such as tubes), while the latter terms are more general.

Particles of this size usually have a very large surface area, which accounts for the two basic characteristics of colloidal systems:

1. They scatter light and therefore appear turbid, cloudy, or milky.
2. Although colloidal particles are large, they form stable dispersions— they do not form separate phases that settle out. As with true solutions, colloids can exist in a variety of phases (Table 7.2).

All colloids exhibit the following characteristic effect. When we shine light through a colloid and look at the system from a 90° angle, we see the pathway of the light without seeing the colloidal particles themselves (they are too small to see). Rather, we see flashes of the light scattered by the particles in the colloid (Figure 7.12). The **Tyndall effect** is due to light scattering of colloidal particles. Smoke, serum, and fog, to name a few examples, all exhibit the Tyndall effect. We are all familiar with the sunbeams that can be seen when sunlight passes through dusty air. This, too, is an example of the Tyndall effect. Again, we do not see the particles in dusty air, but only the light scattered by them.

Colloidal systems are stable. Mayonnaise, for example, stays emulsified and does not separate into oil and water. When the size of colloidal particles is larger than about 1000 nm, however, the system is unstable and separates into phases. Such systems are called **suspensions.**

For example, if we take a lump of soil and disperse it in water, we get a muddy suspension. The soil particles are anywhere from 10^3 to 10^9 nm in diameter. The muddy mixture scatters light and, therefore, appears turbid. It is not a stable system, however. If left alone, the soil particles soon settle to the bottom, with clear water found above the sediment. Therefore, soil in water is a suspension, not a colloidal system.

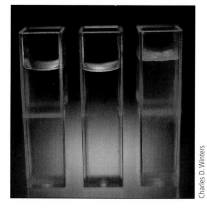

Figure 7.12 The Tyndall effect. A narrow beam of light from a laser is passed through a colloidal mixture (left). Then through a NaCl solution and finally through a colloidal mixture of gelatin and water (right). This illustrates the light-scattering ability of the colloid-sized particles.

Tyndall effect Light passing through and scattered by a colloid viewed at a right angle

Ordinary household dust particles, magnified 2200 times.

Table 7.2 Types of Colloidal Systems	
Type	**Example**
Gas in gas	None
Gas in liquid	Whipped cream
Gas in solid	Marshmallows
Liquid in gas	Clouds, fog
Liquid in liquid	Milk, mayonnaise
Liquid in solid	Cheese, butter
Solid in gas	Smoke
Solid in liquid	Jelly
Solid in solid	Dried paint

Table 7.3 Properties of Three Types of Mixtures

Property	Solutions	Colloids	Suspensions
Particle size (nm)	0.1–1.0	1–1000	>1000
Filterable with ordinary paper	No	No	Yes
Homogeneous	Yes	Borderline	No
Settles on standing	No	No	Yes
Behavior to light	Transparent	Tyndall effect	Translucent or opaque

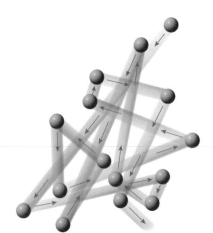

Figure 7.13 Brownian motion.

Freshly made wines are often cloudy because of colloidal particles (left). Removing the particles clarifies the wine (right).

Nanotubes, nanowires, and nanopores in composite coatings have unusual electronic and optical properties because of their enormous surface areas. For example, titanium oxide particles smaller than 20 nm are used to coat surfaces of plastics, glass, and other materials. These thin coatings have self-cleaning, antifogging, antifouling, and sterilizing properties.

Table 7.3 summarizes the properties of three types of mixtures: solutions, colloids, and suspensions.

What makes a colloidal dispersion stable? To answer this question, we must first realize that the colloidal particles are in constant motion. Just look at the dust particles dancing in a ray of sunlight that enters your room. Actually, we do not see the dust particles themselves; they are too small. Rather, we see flashes of scattered light. The motion of the dust particles dispersed in air is a random, chaotic motion. This motion of any colloidal particle suspended in a solvent is called **Brownian motion** (Figure 7.13).

The constant buffeting and collisions by solvent molecules cause the colloidal particles to move in random Brownian motion. (In the case of the dust particles, the solvent is air.) This ongoing motion creates favorable conditions for collisions between particles. When such large particles collide, they stick together, combine to give larger particles, and finally settle out of the solution. That is what happens in a suspension.

So why do colloidal particles remain in solution despite all the collisions due to their Brownian motion? Two reasons explain this phenomenon:

1. Most colloidal particles carry a large solvation layer. If the solvent is water, as in the case of protein molecules in the blood, the colloidal particles are surrounded by a large number of water molecules, which move together with the colloidal particles and cushion them. When two colloidal particles collide as a result of Brownian motion, they do not actually touch each other; instead, only the solvent layers collide. As a consequence, the particles do not stick together and thus stay in solution.

2. The large surface area of colloidal particles acquires charges from the solution. All colloids in a particular solution acquire the same kind of charge—for example, a negative charge. This development leaves a net positive charge in the solvent. When a charged colloidal particle encounters another colloidal particle, the two repel each other because of their like charges.

Thus the combined effects of the solvation layer and the surface charge keep colloidal particles in a stable dispersion. By taking advantage of these effects, chemists can either increase or decrease the stability of a colloidal system. If we want to get rid of a colloidal dispersion, we can remove the solvation layer, the surface charge, or both. For example, proteins in the blood form a colloidal dispersion. If we want to isolate a protein from blood, we may want to precipitate it. We can accomplish this task in two ways: by removing the hydration layer or by removing the surface charges. If we add solvents such as ethanol or acetone, each of which has great affinity for water, the water will be removed from the solvation layer of the protein, and then the unprotected protein molecules will stick together when they collide and form sediment. Similarly, by adding electrolytes such as NaCl to the

CHEMICAL CONNECTIONS 7D

Emulsions and Emulsifying Agents

Oil and water do not mix. Even when we stir them vigorously and the oil droplets become dispersed in the water, the two phases separate as soon as we stop stirring. There are, however, a number of stable colloidal systems made of oil and water, known as **emulsions**. For example, the oil droplets in milk are dispersed in an aqueous solution. This is possible because milk contains a protec-

tive colloid—the milk protein called casein. Casein molecules surround the oil droplets and, because they are polar and carry a charge, they protect and stabilize the oil droplets. Casein is thus an emulsifying agent.

Another emulsifying agent is egg yolk. This ingredient in mayonnaise coats the oil droplets and prevents them from separating.

---

solution, we can remove the charges from the surface of the proteins (by a mechanism too complicated to discuss here). Without their protective charges, two protein molecules will no longer repel each other. Instead, when they collide, they will stick together and precipitate from the solution.

Emulsion A system, such as fat in milk, consisting of a liquid with or without an emulsifying agent in an immiscible liquid, usually as droplets of larger than colloidal size

7.8 | What Is a Colligative Property?

A **colligative property** is any property of a solution that depends only on the number of solute particles dissolved in the solvent and not on the nature of the solute particles. Several colligative properties exist, including freezing-point depression and osmotic pressure. Of these two, osmotic pressure is the most important in biological systems.

Colligative property A property of a solution that depends only on the number of solute particles and not on the chemical identity of the solute

A. Freezing-Point Depression

One mole of any particle dissolved in 1000 g of water lowers the freezing point of the water by 1.86°C. The nature of the solute does not matter, only the number of particles.

Freezing-point depression The decrease in the freezing point of a liquid caused by adding a solute

$$\Delta T = \frac{1.86°C}{\text{mol}} \times \text{mol of particles}$$

This principle is used in a number of practical ways. In winter, we use salts (sodium chloride and calcium chloride) to melt snow and ice on our streets. The salts dissolve in the melting snow and ice, which lowers the freezing point of the water. Another application is the use of antifreeze in automobile radiators. Because water expands upon freezing (see Chemical Connections 6F), the ice formed in a car's cooling system when the outside temperature falls below 0°C can crack the engine block. The addition of antifreeze prevents this problem, because it makes the water freeze at a much lower temperature. The most common antifreeze is ethylene glycol, $C_2H_6O_2$.

Note that in preparing a solution for this purpose we do not use molarity. That is, we do not need to measure the total volume of the solution.

EXAMPLE 7.10

If we add 275 g ethylene glycol, $C_2H_6O_2$, a nondissociating molecular compound, per 1000 g of water in a car radiator, what will the freezing point of the solution be?

Solution

We are given 275 g of ethylene glycol (molar mass, 62.0 g) per 1000 g water and want the freezing point of the solution. We first need to calculate the

Salting lowers the freezing point of ice.

moles of ethylene glycol and then the freezing-point depression for this number of moles.

$$275 \text{ g } \cancel{C_2H_6O_2} \times \frac{1 \text{ mol } \cancel{C_2H_6O_2}}{62.0 \text{ g } \cancel{C_2H_6O_2}} \times \frac{1.86°C}{1 \text{ mol } \cancel{C_2H_6O_2}} = 8.26°C$$

The freezing point of the water will be lowered from 0°C to −8.26°C, and the radiator will not crack if the outside temperature remains above −8.26°C (17.18°F).

Problem 7.10

If we add 215 g of methanol to 1000 g of water, what will be the freezing point of the solution?

If a solute is ionic, then each mole of solute dissociates to more than one mole of particles. For example, if we dissolve one mole (58.5 g) of NaCl in 1000 g of water, the solution contains two moles of solute particles: one mole each of Na^+ and Cl^-. The freezing point of water will be lowered by twice 1.86°C—that is, by 3.72°C.

GOB
Chemistry‿·✦·‿Now™
Click *Coached Problems* to try a problem calculating the **Freezing Point** of a solution

EXAMPLE 7.11

What will be the freezing point of the solution if we dissolve one mole of potassium sulfate, K_2SO_4, in 1000 g of water?

Solution
One mole of K_2SO_4 dissociates to produce three moles of ions: two moles of K^+ and one mole of SO_4^{2-}. The freezing point will be lowered by $3 \times 1.86°C = 5.58°C$, and the solution will freeze at −5.58°C.

Problem 7.11

Which aqueous solution would have the lowest freezing point?
(a) 6.2 *M* NaCl
(b) 2.1 *M* $Al(NO_3)_3$
(c) 4.3 *M* K_2SO_3

Besides freezing-point depression, several other colligative properties exist, including vapor-pressure lowering, boiling-point elevation, and osmotic pressure. We discuss only the last of these because biologically it is the most important.

B. Osmotic Pressure

An osmotic membrane is a very selective semipermeable membrane that allows only solvent molecules, and nothing else, to pass through.

To understand osmotic pressure, let us consider the beaker shown in Figure 7.14(b). In this beaker, an osmotic semipermeable membrane separates the two compartments. A **semipermeable membrane** is a thin slice of some material, such as cellophane, that contains very tiny holes (far too small for us to see) that are big enough to let small solvent molecules pass through but not big enough to let large solute molecules pass. In the right compartment of the beaker is pure solvent—in this example, water. In the left compartment is a dispersion of starch (Section 20.5A) in water.

The starch molecules are too big to pass through the membrane and remain in the left compartment. The water molecules, however, easily go back and forth; as far as they are concerned, no membrane is present. Therefore, water molecules go from the right side to the left side because the concentration of water in the right compartment is higher (100%) than in the left compartment. Molecules will always diffuse from an area of higher concentration to an area of lower concentration. If no membrane separates the two solutions, the starch molecules would also follow this rule, moving from the higher concentration area (in this case, the left side) to the lower one (the right side). The membrane, of course, prevents such movement. However, it does not hinder the water molecules from moving into the left compartment. This passage of solvent molecules from the right (solvent or dilute solution) to the left (a more concentrated solution) across a semipermeable membrane is called **osmosis.** When a significant number of water molecules have moved from the right to the left side, the liquid level on the right side goes down and that on the left side goes up, as shown in Figure 7.14(b).

This process cannot continue indefinitely because gravity prevents the difference in levels from becoming too great. Eventually the process stops with the levels unequal. The levels can be made equal again if we apply an external pressure to the higher side. The amount of external pressure required to equalize the levels is called the **osmotic pressure.**

Although this discussion assumes that one compartment contains pure solvent, the same principle applies if both compartments contain solutions, as long as their concentrations are different. The solution of higher concentration always has a higher osmotic pressure than the one of lower concentration, which means that the flow of solvent always goes from the more dilute to the more concentrated side. Of course, the number of particles is the most important consideration. We must remember that, in ionic solutions, each mole of solute gives rise to more than one mole of particles. For

Osmotic pressure The amount of external pressure applied to the more concentrated solution to stop the passage of solvent molecules across a semipermeable membrane

GOB
Chemistry⚛Now™

Click *Chemistry Interactive* to see how **Osmotic Pressure** works on both the bulk and molecular scales

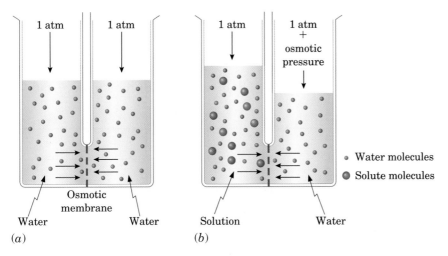

GOB
Chemistry⚛Now™

Active Figure 7.14 Osmotic pressure. (*a*) Two compartments separated by an osmotic semipermeable membrane. Each contains solvent molecules that can pass through the membrane. The liquid level on each side is the same. (*b*) The compartment on the right contains only solvent; the one on the left contains both solute and solvent. Solute molecules cannot pass through the membrane. In an effort to dilute the solution, more solvent molecules move from the right to the left compartment than vice versa, raising the liquid level on that side. **See a simulation based on this figure, and take a short quiz on the concepts at http://now.brookscole.com/gob8 or on the CD.**

Some ions are small but still do not go through the membrane because they are solvated by a shell of water molecules (see Figure 7.7).

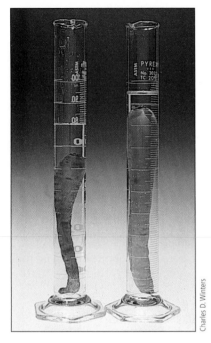

The effect of osmosis on a carrot. The carrot on the left is in a solution that contains a high concentration of NaCl. Water flowing out of the carrot has caused it to shrink. The carrot on the right, in pure water, is slightly swollen.

convenience in calculation, we define a new term, **osmolarity** (in osmol), as molarity (M) multiplied by the number of particles (i) produced by each formula unit of solute.

$$\text{Osmolarity} = M \times i$$

EXAMPLE 7.12

A 0.89% w/v NaCl solution is referred to as a physiological or isotonic saline solution because it has the same concentration of salts as normal human blood, although blood contains several salts and saline solution has only NaCl. What is the osmolarity of this solution?

Solution
We are given an 0.89% solution—that is, one that contains 0.89 g NaCl per 100 mL of solution. Because osmolarity is based on grams of solute per 1000 grams of solution, we calculate that this solution contains 8.9 g of NaCl per 1000 g of solution. Given this concentration, we can then calculate the molarity of the solution.

$$\frac{0.89 \text{ g NaCl}}{100 \text{ mL}} \times \frac{1000 \text{ mL}}{1 \text{ L}} \times \frac{1 \text{ mol NaCl}}{58.5 \text{ g NaCl}} = \frac{0.15 \text{ mol NaCl}}{1 \text{ L}} = 0.15 \ M$$

Each NaCl dissociates into two particles, Na^+ and Cl^-, in aqueous solutions. Therefore, the osmolarity is two times the molarity.

$$\text{Osmolarity} = 0.15 \times 2 = 0.30 \text{ osmol}$$

Problem 7.12
What is the osmolarity of a 3.3% w/v Na_3PO_4 solution?

As noted earlier, osmotic pressure is a colligative property. The osmotic pressure generated by a solution across a semipermeable membrane—the difference between the heights of the two columns in Figure 7.14(b)—

CHEMICAL CONNECTIONS 7E

Reverse Osmosis and Desalinization

In osmosis, the solvent flows spontaneously from the dilute solution compartment into the concentrated solution compartment. In reverse osmosis, the opposite happens. When we apply pressures greater than the osmotic pressure to the more concentrated solution, solvent flows from the more dilute solution to the more concentrated solution by a process we call **reverse osmosis.**

Reverse osmosis is used to make drinkable water from sea water or brackish water. In large plants in the Persian Gulf countries, for example, more than 100 atm pressure is applied to sea water containing 35,000 ppm salt. The water that passes through the semipermeable membrane under this pressure contains only 400 ppm salt—well within the limits set by the World Health Organization for drinkable water.

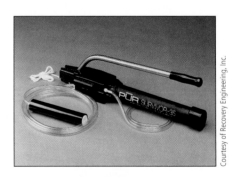

An emergency hand-operated water desalinator that works by reverse osmosis. It can produce 4.5 L of pure water per hour from sea water, which can save someone adrift at sea.

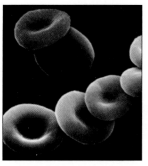

(a) Isotonic solution

(b) Hypertonic solution

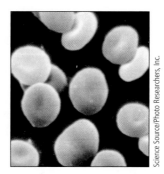

(c) Hypotonic solution

Figure 7.15 Red blood cells in solutions of different tonicity.

depends on the osmolarity of the solution. If the osmolarity increases by a factor of 2, the osmotic pressure will also increase by a factor of 2. Osmotic pressure is very important in biological organisms because cell membranes are semipermeable. Therefore, biological fluids must have the proper osmolarity. For example, red blood cells in the body are suspended in a medium called plasma, which must have the same osmolarity as the red blood cells. Two solutions with the same osmolarity are called **isotonic,** so plasma is said to be isotonic with red blood cells. As a consequence, no osmotic pressure is generated across the cell membrane.

What would happen if we suspended red blood cells in distilled water instead of in plasma? Inside the red blood cells, the osmolarity is approximately the same as in a physiological saline solution—0.30 osmol. Distilled water has zero osmolarity. As a consequence, water flows into the red blood cells. The volume of the cells increases, and the cells swell, as shown in Figure 7.15(c). The membrane cannot resist the osmotic pressure, and the red blood cells eventually burst, spilling their contents into the water. We call this process **hemolysis.**

Solutions in which the osmolarity (and hence osmotic pressure) is lower than that of suspended cells are called **hypotonic solutions.** Obviously, it is very important that we always use isotonic solutions and never hypotonic solutions in intravenous feeding and blood transfusion. Hypotonic solutions would simply kill the red blood cells by hemolysis.

Equally important, we should not use **hypertonic solutions.** A hypertonic solution has a greater osmolarity (and greater osmotic pressure) than the red blood cells. If red blood cells are placed in a hypertonic solution—for example, 0.5 osmol glucose solution—water flows from the cells into the glucose solution through the semipermeable cell membrane. This process, called **crenation,** shrivels the cells, as shown in Figure 7.15(b).

As already mentioned, 0.89% NaCl (physiological saline) is isotonic with red blood cells and is used in intravenous injections.

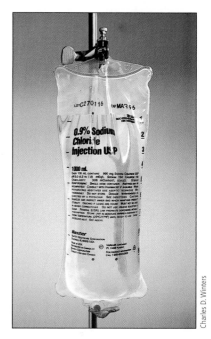

An isotonic saline solution.

A 5.5% glucose solution is also isotonic and is used in intravenous feeding.

EXAMPLE 7.13

Is a 0.50% w/v solution of KCl (a) hypertonic, (b) hypotonic, or (c) isotonic compared to red blood cells?

Solution
The 0.50% w/v solution of KCl contains 5.0 g KCl in 1.0 L of solution:

$$\frac{5.0 \text{ g KCl}}{1.0 \text{ L}} \times \frac{1.0 \text{ mol KCl}}{74.6 \text{ g KCl}} = \frac{0.067 \text{ mol KCl}}{1.0 \text{ L}} = 0.067\ M$$

A portable dialysis unit.

Dialysis A process in which a solution containing particles of different sizes is placed in a bag made of a semipermeable membrane. The bag is placed into a solvent or solution containing only small molecules. The solution in the bag reaches equilibrium with the solvent outside, allowing the small molecules to diffuse across the membrane but retaining the large molecules.

Because each KCl yields two particles, the osmolarity is $0.067 \times 2 = 0.13$ osmol; this is smaller than the osmolarity of the red blood cells, which is 0.30 osmol. Therefore, the KCl solution is hypotonic.

Problem 7.13

Which solution is isotonic compared to red blood cells: (a) 0.1 M Na_2SO_4, (b) 1.0 M Na_2SO_4, or (c) 0.2 M Na_2SO_4?

C. Dialysis

An osmotic semipermeable membrane allows only solvent and not solute molecules to pass. If, however, the openings in the membrane are somewhat larger, then small solute molecules can also get through, but large solute molecules, such as macromolecular and colloidal particles, cannot. This process is called **dialysis.**

For example, ribonucleic acids are important biological molecules that we will study in Chapter 25. When biochemists prepare ribonucleic acid solutions, they must remove small molecules, such as NaCl, from the solution to obtain a pure nucleic acid preparation. To do so, they place the nucleic acid solution in a dialysis bag (made of cellophane) of sufficient pore size to allow all the small molecules to diffuse and retain only the large nucleic acid

CHEMICAL CONNECTIONS 7F

Hemodialysis

The kidneys' main function is to remove toxic waste products from the blood. When the kidneys are not functioning properly, these waste products may threaten life. **Hemodialysis** is a process that performs the same filtration function.

In hemodialysis, the patient's blood circulates through a long tube of cellophane membrane suspended in an isotonic solution and then returns to the patient's vein. The cellophane membrane retains the large molecules (for example, proteins) but allows the small ones, including the toxic wastes, to pass through. In this way, dialysis removes wastes from the blood.

If the cellophane tube were suspended in distilled water, other small molecules and ions, such as Na^+ Cl^- and glucose, would also be removed from the blood. That is something we don't want to happen. The isotonic solution used in hemodialysis includes 0.6% NaCl, 0.04% KCl, 0.2% $NaHCO_3$, and 0.72% glucose (all w/v). It ensures that no glucose or Na^+ is lost from the blood.

A patient usually remains on an artificial kidney machine for four to seven hours. During this time, the isotonic bath is changed every two hours. Kidney machines allow people with kidney failure to lead a fairly normal life, although they must take these hemodialysis treatments regularly.

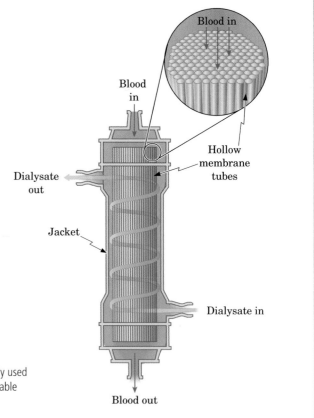

A schematic diagram of the hollow-fiber (or capillary) dialyzer, the most commonly used artificial kidney. The blood flows through small tubes constructed of a semipermeable membrane; these tubes are bathed in the dialyzing solution.

molecules. If the dialysis bag is suspended in flowing distilled water, all of the NaCl and small molecules will leave the bag. After a certain amount of time, the bag will contain only the pure nucleic acids dissolved in water.

Our kidneys work in much the same way. The millions of nephrons, or kidney cells, have very large surface areas in which the capillaries of the blood vessels come in contact with the nephrons. The kidneys serve as a gigantic filtering machine. The waste products of the blood dialyse out through semipermeable membranes in the glomeruli and enter collecting tubes that carry the urine to the ureter. Meanwhile, large protein molecules and cells are retained in the blood.

The glomeruli of the kidneys are fine capillary blood vessels in which the body's waste products are removed from the blood.

SUMMARY OF KEY QUESTIONS

SECTION 7.1 What Do We Need to Know as We Begin?

- Systems containing more than one component are **mixtures.**
- **Homogeneous mixtures** are uniform throughout.
- **Heterogeneous mixtures** exhibit well-defined boundaries between phases.

SECTION 7.2 What Are the Most Common Types of Solutions?

- The most common types of solutions are gas in liquid, liquid in liquid, solid in liquid, gas in gas, and solid in solid.
- When a solution consists of a solid or gas dissolved in a liquid, the liquid acts as the **solvent,** and the solid or gas is the **solute.** When one liquid is dissolved in another, the liquid present in greater amount is considered to be the solvent.

SECTION 7.4 What Factors Affect Solubility?

- The **solubility** of a substance is the maximum amount of the substance that dissolves in a given amount of solvent at a given temperature.
- "Like dissolves like" means that polar molecules are soluble in polar solvents and that nonpolar molecules are soluble in nonpolar solvents. The solubility of solids and liquids in liquids usually increases with increasing temperature; the solubility of gases in liquids usually decreases with increasing temperature.

SECTION 7.5 What Are the Most Common Units for Concentration?

- Percent concentration is given in either weight per unit volume of solution (w/v) or volume per unit volume of solution (v/v).
- Percent weight/volume (w/v) is the weight of solute per unit volume of solvent.
- Percent volume/volume (v/v) is the volume of solute per unit volume of solution (v/v).
- **Molarity** is the number of moles of solute in 1 L of solution.

SECTION 7.6 Why Is Water Such a Good Solvent?

- Water is the most important solvent, because it dissolves polar compounds and ions through hydrogen bonding and dipole–dipole interactions. Hydrated ions are surrounded by water molecules (as a solvation layer) that move together with the ion, cushioning it from collisions with other ions. Aqueous solutions of ions and molten salts are **electrolytes** and conduct electricity.

SECTION 7.7 What Are Colloids?

- Colloids exhibit a chaotic random motion, called **Brownian motion.** Colloids are stable mixtures despite the relatively large size of the colloidal particles (1 to 1000 nm). The stability results from the solvation layer that cushions the colloid's particles from direct collisions and from the electric charge on the surface of colloidal particles.

SECTION 7.8 What Is a Colligative Property?

- A **colligative property** is a property that depends only on the number of solute particles present.
- **Freezing-point depression** and **osmotic pressure** are two examples of colligative properties.
- Osmotic pressure operates across an osmotic semipermeable membrane that allows only solvent molecules to pass but screens out all other molecules. In osmotic pressure calculations, concentration is measured in **osmolarity,** which is the molarity of the solution multiplied by the number of particles produced by dissociation of the solute.
- Red blood cells in **hypotonic solution** swell and burst, a process called **hemolysis.**
- Red blood cells in **hypertonic solution** shrink, a process called **crenation.** Some semipermeable membranes allow small solute molecules to pass through along with solvent molecules.
- In **dialysis,** such membranes are used to separate large molecules from smaller ones.

PROBLEMS

A blue problem number indicates an applied problem.

■ denotes problems that are available on the GOB ChemistryNow website or CD and are assignable in OWL.

SECTION 7.2 What Are the Most Common Types of Solutions?

7.14 Vinegar is a homogeneous aqueous solution containing 6% acetic acid. Which is the solvent?

7.15 A solution is made by dissolving glucose in water. Which is the solvent and which is the solute?

7.16 In each of the following, tell whether the solutes and solvents are gases, liquids, or solids.
(a) Bronze (see Chemical Connections 2E)
(b) Cup of coffee
(c) Car exhaust
(d) Champagne

7.17 Give a familiar example of solutions of each of these types:
(a) Liquid in liquid
(b) Solid in liquid
(c) Gas in liquid
(d) Gas in gas

7.18 Are mixtures of gases true solutions or heterogeneous mixtures? Explain.

SECTION 7.4 What Factors Affect Solubility?

7.19 We dissolved 0.32 g of aspartic acid in 115.0 mL of water and obtained a clear solution. After two days standing at room temperature, we notice a white powder at the bottom of the beaker. What may have happened?

7.20 The solubility of a compound is 2.5 g in 100 mL of aqueous solution at 25°C. If we put 1.12 g of the compound in a 50-mL volumetric flask at 25°C and add sufficient water to fill it to the 50-mL mark, what kind of solution do we get—saturated or unsaturated? Explain.

7.21 To a separatory funnel with two layers—the non-polar diethyl ether and the polar water—is added a small amount of solid. After shaking the separatory funnel, in which layer will we find each of the following solids?
(a) NaCl
(b) Camphor, $C_{10}H_{16}O$
(c) KOH

7.22 On the basis of polarity and hydrogen bonding, which solute would be the most soluble in benzene, C_6H_6?
(a) CH_3OH (b) H_2O
(c) $CH_3CH_2CH_2CH_3$ (d) H_2SO_4

7.23 Suppose that we have a stain on an oil painting that we want to remove without damaging the painting. The stain is not water-insoluble. Knowing the polarities of the following solvents, which one would we try first and why?
(a) Benzene, C_6H_6
(b) Isopropyl (rubbing) alcohol, C_3H_7OH
(c) Hexane, C_6H_{14}

7.24 Which pairs of liquids are likely to be miscible?
(a) H_2O and CH_3OH
(b) H_2O and C_6H_6
(c) C_6H_{14} and CCl_4
(d) CCl_4 and CH_3OH

7.25 The solubility of aspartic acid in water is 0.500 g in 100 mL at 25°C. If we dissolve 0.251 g of aspartic acid in 50.0 mL of water at 50°C and let the solution cool to 25°C without stirring, shaking, or otherwise disturbing the solution, would the resulting solution be a saturated, unsaturated, or supersaturated solution? Explain.

7.26 Near a power plant, warm water is discharged into a river. Sometimes dead fish are observed in the area. Why do fish die in the warm water?

7.27 If a bottle of beer is allowed to stand for several hours after being opened, it becomes "flat" (it loses CO_2). Explain.

7.28 Would we expect the solubility of ammonia gas in water at 2 atm pressure to be (a) greater, (b) the same, or (c) smaller than at 0.5 atm pressure?

SECTION 7.5 What Are the Most Common Units for Concentration?

7.29 Verify the following statements.
(a) One part per million corresponds to one minute in two years, or a single penny in $10,000.
(b) One part per billion corresponds to one minute in 2000 years, or a single penny in $10 million.

7.30 ■ Describe how we would make the following solutions:
(a) 500.0 g of a 5.32% w/w H_2S solution in water
(b) 342.0 g of a 0.443% w/w benzene solution in toluene
(c) 12.5 g of a 34.2% w/w dimethyl sulfoxide solution in acetone

7.31 ■ Describe how we would make the following solutions:

(a) 280 mL of a 27% v/v solution of ethanol, C_2H_5OH, in water

(b) 435 mL of a 1.8% v/v solution of ethyl acetate, $C_4H_8O_2$, in water

(c) 1.65 L of an 8.00% v/v solution of benzene, C_6H_6, in chloroform, $CHCl_3$

7.32 Describe how we would make the following solutions:

(a) 250 mL of a 3.6% w/v solution of NaCl in water

(b) 625 mL of a 4.9% w/v solution of glycine, $C_2H_5NO_2$, in water

(c) 43.5 mL of a 13.7% w/v solution of Na_2SO_4 in water

(d) 518 mL of a 2.1% w/v solution of acetone, C_3H_6O, in water

7.33 Calculate the w/v percentage of each of these solutes:

(a) 623 mg of casein in 15.0 mL of milk

(b) 74 mg vitamin C in 250 mL of orange juice

(c) 3.25 g of sucrose in 186 mL of coffee

7.34 Describe how we would prepare 250 mL of 0.10 M NaOH from solid NaOH and water.

7.35 Assuming that the appropriate volumetric flasks are available, describe how we would make these solutions:

(a) 175 mL of a 1.14 M solution of NH_4Br in water

(b) 1.35 L of a 0.825 M solution of NaI in water

(c) 330 mL of a 0.16 M solution of ethanol, C_2H_5OH, in water

7.36 ■ What is the molarity of each solution?

(a) 47 g of KCl dissolved in enough water to give 375 mL of solution

(b) 82.6 g of sucrose, $C_{12}H_{22}O_{11}$, dissolved in enough water to give 725 mL of solution

(c) 9.3 g of $(NH_4)_2SO_4$ dissolved in enough water to give 2.35 L of solution

7.37 A teardrop with a volume of 0.5 mL contains 5.0 mg NaCl. What is the molarity of the NaCl in the teardrop?

7.38 ■ The concentration of stomach acid, HCl, is approximately 0.10 M. What volume of stomach acid contains 0.25 mg of HCl?

7.39 The label on a sparkling cider says it contains 22.0 g glucose ($C_6H_{12}O_6$), 190 mg K^+, and 4.00 mg Na^+ per serving of 240 mL cider. Calculate the molarities of these ingredients in the sparkling cider.

7.40 ■ If 3.18 g $BaCl_2$ is dissolved in enough solvent to make 500.0 mL of solution, what is the molarity?

7.41 ■ The label on a jar of jam says it contains 13 g of sucrose, $C_{12}H_{22}O_{11}$ per tablespoon (15 mL). What is the molarity of sucrose in the jam?

7.42 A particular toothpaste contains 0.17 g NaF in 75 mL toothpaste. What are the percent w/v and the molarity of NaF in the toothpaste?

7.43 A student has a bottle labeled 0.750% albumin solution. The bottle contains exactly 5.00 mL. How much water must the student add to make the concentration of albumin become 0.125%?

7.44 ■ How many grams of solute are present in each of the following aqueous solutions?

(a) 575 mL of a 2.00 M solution of HNO_3

(b) 1.65 L of a 0.286 M solution of alanine, $C_3H_7NO_2$

(c) 320 mL of a 0.0081 M solution of $CaSO_4$

7.45 A student has a stock solution of 30.0% w/v H_2O_2 (hydrogen peroxide). Describe how the student should prepare 250 mL of a 0.25% w/v H_2O_2 solution.

7.46 To make 5.0 L of a fruit punch that contains 10% v/v ethanol, how much 95% v/v ethanol must be mixed with how much fruit juice?

7.47 A pill weighing 325 mg contains the following. What is the concentration of each in ppm?

(a) 12.5 mg Captopril, a medication for high blood pressure

(b) 22 mg Mg^{2+}

(c) 0.27 mg Ca^{2+}

7.48 ■ One slice of enriched bread weighing 80 g contains 70 μg of folic acid. What is the concentration of folic acid in ppm and ppb?

7.49 Dioxin is considered to be poisonous in concentrations above 2 ppb. If a lake containing 1×10^7 L has been contaminated by 0.1 g of dioxin, did the concentration reach a dangerous level?

7.50 An industrial wastewater contains 3.60 ppb cadmium, Cd^{2+}. How many mg of Ca^{2+} could be recovered from a ton (1016 kg) of this wastewater?

7.51 According to the label on a piece of cheese, one serving of 28 g provides the following daily values: 2% of Fe, 6% of Ca, and 6% of vitamin A. The recommended daily allowances (RDA) of each of these nutrients are as follows: 15 mg Fe, 1200 mg Ca, and 0.800 mg vitamin A. Calculate the concentrations of each of these nutrients in the cheese in ppm.

SECTION 7.6 Why Is Water Such a Good Solvent?

7.52 Considering polarities, electronegativities, and similar concepts learned in Chapter 4, classify each of the following as a strong electrolyte, a weak electrolyte, or a nonelectrolyte.

(a) KCl   (b) C_2H_5OH (ethanol)   (c) NaOH

(d) HF   (e) $C_6H_{12}O_6$ (glucose)

7.53 Which of the following would produce the brightest light in the conductance apparatus shown in Figure 7.10?

(a) 0.1 M KCl   (b) 0.1 M $(NH_4)_3PO_4$

(c) 0.5 M sucrose

7.54 Ethanol is very soluble in water. Describe how water dissolves ethanol.

7.55 Predict which of these covalent compounds is soluble in water.
(a) C_2H_6 (b) CH_3OH
(c) HF   (d) NH_3
(e) CCl_4

SECTION 7.7 What Are Colloids?

7.56 A type of car tire is made of synthetic rubber in which carbon black particles of the size of 200–500 nm are randomly dispersed. Because carbon black absorbs light, we do not see any turbidity (that is, a Tyndall effect). Do we consider a tire to be a colloidal system and, if so, what kind? Explain.

7.57 On the basis of Tables 7.1 and 7.2, classify the following systems as homogeneous, heterogeneous, or colloidal mixtures.
(a) Physiological saline solution
(b) Orange juice
(c) A cloud
(d) Wet sand
(e) Suds
(f) Milk

7.58 Table 7.2 shows no examples of a gas-in-gas colloidal system. Considering the definition of a colloid, explain why.

7.59 A solution of protein is transparent at room temperature. When it is cooled to 10°C, it becomes turbid. What causes this change in appearance?

7.60 What gives nanotubes their unique optical and electrical properties?

SECTION 7.8 What Is a Colligative Property?

7.61 Calculate the freezing points of solutions made by dissolving one mole of each of the following ionic solutes in 1000 g of H_2O.
(a) NaCl   (b) $MgCl_2$
(c) $(NH_4)_2CO_3$ (d) $Al(HCO_3)_3$

7.62 ■ If we add 175 g of ethylene glycol, C_2H_6O, per 1000 g of water to a car radiator, what will be the freezing point of the solution?

7.63 Methanol, CH_3OH, is used as an antifreeze. How many grams of methanol do we need per 1000 g of water for an aqueous solution to stay liquid at −20°C?

7.64 ■ In winter, after a snowstorm, salt (NaCl) is spread to melt the ice on roads. How many grams of salt per 1000 g of ice is needed to make it liquid at −5°C?

7.65 A 4 M acetic acid (CH_3COOH) solution lowered the freezing point by 8°C; a 4 M KF solution yields a 15°C freezing-point depression. What can account for this difference?

Osmosis

7.66 In an apparatus using a semipermeable membrane, a 0.005 M glucose (small molecule) solution yielded an osmotic pressure of 10 mm Hg. What kind of osmotic pressure change would we expect if instead of a semipermeable membrane we used a dialysis membrane?

7.67 In each case, tell which side (if either) rises and why. The solvent is water.

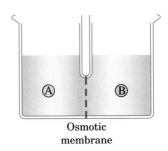

Osmotic membrane

	Ⓐ	Ⓑ
(a)	1% glucose	5% glucose
(b)	0.1 M glucose	0.5 M glucose
(c)	1 M NaCl	1 M glucose
(d)	1 M NaCl	1 M K_2SO_4
(e)	3% NaCl	3% NaI
(f)	1 M NaBr	1 M NaCl

7.68 An osmotic semipermeable membrane that allows only water to pass separates two compartments, A and B. Compartment A contains 0.9% NaCl, and compartment B contains 3% glycerol, $C_3H_8O_3$.
(a) In which compartment will the level of solution rise?
(b) Which compartment has the higher osmotic pressure (if either)?

7.69 Calculate the osmolarity of each of the following solutions.
(a) 0.39 M Na_2CO_3
(b) 0.62 M $Al(NO_3)_3$
(c) 4.2 M LiBr
(d) 0.009 M K_3PO_4

7.70 Two compartments are separated by a semipermeable osmotic membrane through which only water molecules can pass. Compartment A contains a 0.3 M KCl solution, and compartment B contains a 0.2 M Na_3PO_4 solution. Predict from which compartment the water will flow to the other compartment.

7.71 A 0.9% NaCl solution is isotonic with blood plasma. Which solution would crenate red blood cells?
(a) 0.3% NaCl
(b) 0.9 M glucose (MW 180)
(c) 0.9% glucose

Chemical Connections

7.72 (Chemical Connections 7A) Oxides of nitrogen (NO, NO_2, N_2O_3) are also responsible for acid rain. Which acids do we suppose can be formed from these oxides?

7.73 (Chemical Connections 7A) What makes normal rainwater slightly acidic?

7.74 (Chemical Connections 7B) Why do deep-sea divers use a helium–oxygen mixture in the tank instead of air?

7.75 (Chemical Connections 7B) What is nitrogen narcosis?

7.76 (Chemical Connections 7C) Write balanced equations (two steps) for the conversion of marble to gypsum dihydrate.

7.77 (Chemical Connections 7C) What is the chemical formula for the main component of limestone and marble?

7.78 (Chemical Connections 7D) What is the protective colloid in milk?

7.79 (Chemical Connections 7E) What is the minimum pressure on sea water that will force water to flow from the concentrated solution into the dilute solution?

7.80 (Chemical Connections 7E) The osmotic pressure generated across a semipermeable membrane by a solution is directly proportional to its osmolarity. Given the data in Chemical Connections 7E on the purification of sea water, estimate what pressure we need to apply to purify brackish water containing 5000 ppm salt by reverse osmosis.

7.81 (Chemical Connections 7F) A manufacturing error occurred in the isotonic solution used in hemodialysis. Instead of 0.2% $NaHCO_3$, 0.2% of $KHCO_3$ was added. Did this error change the labeled tonicity of the solution? If so, is the resulting solution hypotonic or hypertonic? Would such an error create an electrolyte imbalance in the patient's blood? Explain.

7.82 (Chemical Connections 7F) The artificial kidney machine uses a solution containing 0.6% w/v $NaCl$, 0.04% w/v KCl, 0.2% w/v $NaHCO_3$, and 0.72% w/v glucose. Show that this is an isotonic solution.

Additional Problems

7.83 When a cucumber is put into a saline solution to pickle it, the cucumber shrinks; when a prune is put into the same solution, the prune swells. Explain what happens in each case.

7.84 A solution of As_2O_3 has a molarity of $2 \times 10^{-5}\ M$. What is this concentration in ppm? (Assume that the density of the solution is 1.00 g/mL.)

7.85 Two bottles of water are carbonated, with CO_2 gas being added, under 2 atm pressure and then capped. One bottle is stored at room temperature; the other is stored in the refrigerator. When the bottle stored at room temperature is opened, large bubbles escape, along with a third of the water. The bottle stored in the refrigerator is opened without frothing or bubbles escaping. Explain.

7.86 Both methanol, CH_3OH, and ethylene glycol, $C_2H_6O_2$, are used as antifreeze. Which is more efficient—that is, which produces a lower freezing point if equal weights of each are added to the same weight of water?

7.87 We know that a 0.89% saline ($NaCl$) solution is isotonic with blood. In a real-life emergency, we run out of physiological saline solution and have only KCl as a salt and distilled water. Would it be acceptable to make a 0.89% aqueous KCl solution and use it for intravenous infusion? Explain.

7.88 Carbon dioxide and sulfur dioxide are soluble in water because they react with water. Write possible equations for these reactions.

7.89 A reagent label shows that it contains 0.05 ppm lead as a contaminant. How many grams of lead are present in 5.0 g of the reagent?

7.90 A concentrated nitric acid solution contains 35% HNO_3. How would we prepare 300 mL of 4.5% solution?

7.91 Which will have greater osmotic pressure:
(a) A 0.9% w/v $NaCl$ solution?
(b) A 25% w/v solution of a nondissociating dextran with a molecular weight of 15,000?

7.92 Government regulations permit a 6 ppb concentration of a certain pollutant. How many grams of pollutant are allowed in 1 ton (1016 kg) of water?

7.93 The average osmolarity of sea water is 1.18. How much pure water would have to be added to 1.0 mL of sea water for it to achieve the osmolarity of blood (0.30 osmol)?

7.94 A swimming pool containing 20,000 L of water is chlorinated to have a final Cl_2 concentration of 0.00500 M. What is the Cl_2 concentration in ppm? How many kilograms of Cl_2 were added to the swimming pool to reach this concentration?

Looking Ahead

7.95 Synovial fluid that exists in joints is a colloidal solution of hyaluronic acid (Section 20.6A) in water. When a biochemist wants to isolate hyaluronic acid from synovial fluid, he or she adds ethanol, C_2H_6O, to bring the solution to 65% ethanol. The hyaluronic acid precipitates upon standing. What makes the hyaluronic acid solution unstable and causes it to precipitate?

Challenge Problem

7.96 To ensure that tap water is safe to drink, the U.S. Environmental Protection Agency (EPA) proscribes regulations that limit the amount of certain contaminants in water provided for public water systems. MCL is the highest level of a contaminant that is allowed in drinking water. MCLs are set at very stringent levels. To understand the possible health effects described for many regulated constituents, a person would have to drink two liters of water every day at the MCL level for a lifetime to have a one-in-a-million chance of having the described health effect. More information about contaminants and potential health effects can be obtained by calling the EPA's Safe Drinking Water hotline at 800-426-4791.

If a person were to consume two liters of MCL water every day for a lifetime, (assume 72 years), how many grams of each contaminant would that person ingest over a lifetime?

Inorganic Contaminants	Maximum Contaminant Levels (MCL)*	Likely Sources of Contaminants
Arsenic	10	Erosion of natural deposits, runoff from orchards, runoff from glass and electronics production wastes
Barium	2	Discharge from drilling water, discharge from metal refineries, erosion of natural deposits
Chromium	100	Discharge from steel and pulp mills, erosion of natural deposits
Copper	1.3	Corrosion of household plumbing systems, erosion of natural deposits, leaching from wood preservatives
Fluoride	4	Erosion of natural deposits, water additive that promotes strong teeth, discharge from fertilizer and aluminum factories
Lead	15	Corrosion of household plumbing systems, erosion of natural deposits
Mercury	2	Erosion of natural deposits, discharge from refineries and factories, runoff from landfills and cropland
Nickel	100	Nickel occurs naturally in soils, ground water, and surface water, and is often used in electroplating, stainless steel, and alloy products
Nitrate	10 ppm[†]	Runoff from fertilizer use, leaching from septic tanks, sewage, erosion from natural deposits
Nitrite	1 ppm[†]	Runoff from fertilizer use, erosion from natural deposits

*Units of MCL are ppb (parts per billion) unless otherwise specified.
[†] Parts per million

Reaction Rates and Chemical Equilibrium

When magnesium burns in air, it creates a brilliant white light.

Charles D. Winters

In the course of several years, a few molecules of glucose and O_2 will react, but not enough for us to detect within a laboratory period.

8.1 | How Do We Measure Reaction Rates?

Some chemical reactions take place rapidly; others are very slow. For example, glucose and oxygen gas react with each other to form water and carbon dioxide:

$$C_6H_{12}O_6(s) + 6O_2(g) \longrightarrow 6CO_2(g) + 6H_2O(\ell)$$

Glucose

This reaction is extremely slow, however. A sample of glucose exposed to O_2 in the air shows no measurable change even after many years.

In contrast, consider what happens when you take one or two aspirin tablets for a slight headache. Very often, the pain disappears in half an hour or so. Thus the aspirin must have reacted with compounds in the body within that time.

Many reactions occur even faster. For example, if we add a solution of silver nitrate to a solution of sodium chloride (NaCl), a precipitate of silver chloride (AgCl) forms almost instantaneously.

Net ionic equation: $Ag^+(aq) + Cl^-(aq) \longrightarrow AgCl(s)$

> This is a net ionic equation, so it does not show spectator ions.

The precipitation of AgCl is essentially complete in considerably less than 1 s.

> **Chemical kinetics** The study of the rates of chemical reactions

The study of reaction rates is called **chemical kinetics.** The **rate of a reaction** is the change in concentration of a reactant (or product) per unit time. Every reaction has its own rate, which must be measured in the laboratory.

Consider the following reaction carried out in the solvent acetone:

> This is a net ionic equation, so it does not show spectator ions.

$$CH_3\!-\!Cl + I^- \xrightarrow{\text{Acetone}} CH_3\!-\!I + Cl^-$$
$$\text{Chloromethane} \qquad\qquad \text{Iodomethane}$$

To determine the reaction rate, we can measure the concentration of the product, iodomethane, in the acetone at periodic time intervals—say, every 10 min. For example, the concentration might increase from 0 to 0.12 mol/L over a period of 30 min. The rate of the reaction is the change in the concentration of iodomethane divided by the time interval:

> The rate could also be determined by following the decrease in concentration of CH_3Cl or of I^-, if that is more convenient.

$$\frac{(0.12 \text{ mol } CH_3I/L) - (0 \text{ mol } CH_3I/L)}{30 \text{ min}} = \frac{0.0040 \text{ mol } CH_3I/L}{\text{min}}$$

This unit is read "0.0040 mole per liter per minute." During each minute of the reaction, an average of 0.0040 mol of chloromethane is converted to iodomethane for each liter of solution.

The rate of a reaction is not constant over a long period of time. At the beginning, in most reactions, the change in concentration is directly proportional to time. This period is shown as the linear portion of the curve in Figure 8.1. The rate calculated during this period, called the **initial rate,** is constant during this time interval. Later, as the reactant is used up, the rate of reaction decreases.

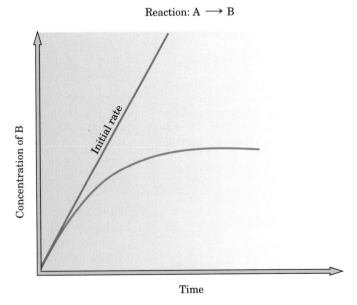

Reaction: A $\longrightarrow$ B

Concentration of B

Initial rate

Time

Figure 8.1   Changes in the concentration of B in the A → B system with respect to time. The rate (the change in concentration of B per unit time) is largest at the beginning of the reaction and gradually decreases until it reaches zero at the completion of the reaction.

EXAMPLE 8.1

Another way to determine the rate of the reaction of chloromethane with iodide ion is to measure the disappearance of I^- from the solution. Suppose that the concentration of I^- was 0.24 mol I^-/L at the start of the reaction. At the end of 20 min, the concentration dropped to 0.16 mol I^-/L. This difference is equal to a change in concentration of 0.08 mol I^-/L. What is the rate of reaction?

Solution

The rate of the reaction is

$$\frac{(0.16 \text{ mol } I^-/L) - (0.24 \text{ mol } I^-/L)}{20 \text{ min}} = \frac{-0.0040 \text{ mol } I^-/L}{\text{min}}$$

Because the stoichiometry of the components is $1:1$ in this reaction, we get the same numerical answer for the rate whether we monitor a reactant or a product. Note, however, that when we measure the concentration of a reactant that disappears with time, the rate of reaction is a negative number.

Problem 8.1

In the reaction

$$2HgO(s) \longrightarrow 2Hg(\ell) + O_2(g)$$

we measure the evolution of gas to determine the rate of reaction. At the beginning of the reaction (at 0 min), 0.020 L of O_2 is present. After 15 min, the volume of O_2 gas is 0.35 L. What is the rate of reaction?

The rates of chemical reactions—both the ones that we carry out in the laboratory and the ones that take place inside our bodies—are very important. A reaction that goes more slowly than we need may be useless, whereas a reaction that goes too fast may be dangerous. Ideally, we would like to know what causes the enormous variety in reaction rates. In the next three sections, we examine this question.

8.2 Why Do Some Molecular Collisions Result in Reaction Whereas Others Do Not?

For two molecules or ions to react with each other, they must first collide. As we saw in Chapter 6, molecules in gases and liquids are in constant motion and frequently collide with each other. If we want a reaction to take place between two compounds A and B, we allow them to mix if they are gases or dissolve them in a solvent if they are liquids. In either case, the constant motion of the molecules will lead to frequent collisions between molecules of A and B. In fact, we can even calculate how many such collisions will take place in a given period of time. Such calculations indicate that so many collisions occur between A and B molecules that most reactions should be over in considerably less than one second. Because the actual reactions generally proceed much more slowly, we must conclude that most collisions do not result in a reaction. Typically, when a molecule of A collides with a molecule of B, the two simply bounce apart without reacting. Every once in a while, though, molecules of A and B collide and react to form a new compound. A collision that results in a reaction is called an **effective collision.**

Effective Collision A collision between two molecules or ions that results in a chemical reaction

Figure 8.2 The energy of molecular collisions varies. (*a*) Two fast-moving molecules colliding head-on have a higher collision energy than (*b*) two slower-moving molecules colliding at an angle.

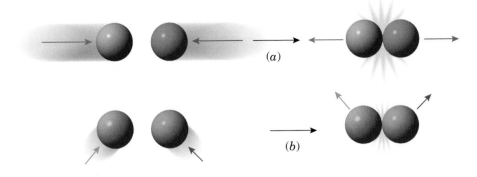

Why are some collisions effective whereas others are not? There are two main reasons:

1. In most cases, for a reaction to take place between A and B, one or more covalent bonds must be broken in A or B or both, and energy is required for this to happen. The energy comes from the collision between A and B. If the energy of the collision is large enough, bonds will break and a reaction will take place. If the collision energy is too low, the molecules will bounce apart without reacting. The minimum energy necessary for a reaction to occur is called the **activation energy.**

   The energy of any collision depends on the relative speeds (that is, on the relative kinetic energies) of the colliding objects and on their angle of approach. Much greater damage is done in a head-on collision of two cars both going 40 mi/h than in a collision in which a car going 20 mi/h sideswipes one going 10 mi/h. The same consideration applies with molecules, as Figure 8.2 shows.

2. Even if two molecules collide with an energy greater than the activation energy, a reaction may not take place if the molecules are not oriented properly when they collide. Consider, for example, the reaction between H_2O and HCl:

$$H_2O(\ell) + HCl(g) \longrightarrow H_3O^+(aq) + Cl^-(aq)$$

For this reaction to take place, the molecules must collide in such a way that the H of the HCl hits the O of the water, as shown in Figure 8.3(a). A

Activation energy The minimum energy necessary to cause a chemical reaction to occur

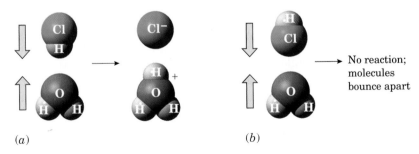

(*a*)   (*b*)

No reaction; molecules bounce apart

GOB
Chemistry⚛Now™
Active Figure 8.3   Molecules must be properly oriented for a reaction to take place. (*a*) HCl and H_2O molecules are oriented so that the H of HCl collides with the O of H_2O, and a reaction takes place. (*b*) No reaction takes place because Cl, and not H, collides with the O of H_2O. The colored arrows show the path of the molecules. **See a simulation based on this figure, and take a short quiz on the concepts at http://now.brookscole.com/gob8 or on the CD.**

collision in which the Cl hits the O, as shown in Figure 8.3(b), cannot lead to a reaction, even if sufficient energy is available.

Returning to the example given at the beginning of this chapter, we can now see why the reaction between glucose and O_2 is so slow. The O_2 molecules are constantly colliding with glucose molecules, but the percentage of effective collisions is extremely tiny at room temperature.

8.3 | What Is the Relationship Between Activation Energy and Reaction Rate?

Figure 8.4 shows a typical energy diagram for an exothermic reaction. The products have a lower energy than the reactants; we might, therefore, expect the reaction to take place rapidly. As the curve shows, however, the reactants cannot be converted to products without the necessary activation energy. The activation energy is like a hill. If we are in a mountainous region, we may find that the only way to go from one point to another is to climb over a hill. It is the same in a chemical reaction. Even though the products may have a lower energy than the reactants, the products cannot form unless the reactants "go over the hill" or over a high pass—that is, gain the necessary activation energy.

Let us look into this issue more closely. In a typical reaction, existing bonds are broken and new bonds form. For example, when H_2 reacts with N_2 to give NH_3, six covalent bonds (counting a triple bond as three bonds) must break, and six new covalent bonds must form.

$$3H{-}H \;+\; N{\equiv}N \longrightarrow 2H{-}N\Big\langle{\genfrac{}{}{0pt}{}{H}{H}}$$

Ammonia

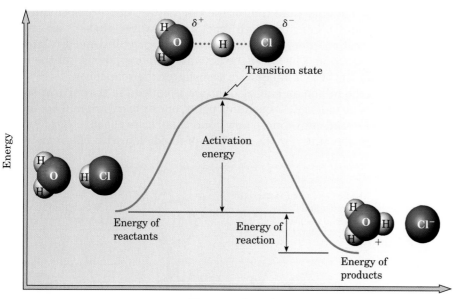

Figure 8.4   Energy diagram for the exothermic reaction

$$H_2O(\ell) + HCl(g) \longrightarrow H_3O^+(aq) + Cl^-(aq)$$

The energy of the reactants is greater than the energy of the products. The diagram shows the positions of all atoms before, at, and after the transition state.

Figure 8.5 Energy diagram for an endothermic reaction. The energy of the products is greater than that of the reactants.

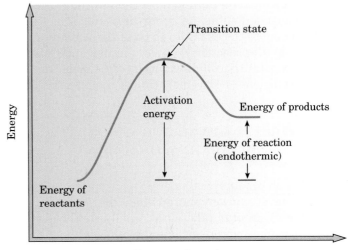

"Uphill" reactions are endothermic.

Breaking a bond requires an input of energy, but a bond forming releases energy. In a "downhill" reaction of the type shown in Figure 8.4, the amount of energy released in creating the new bonds is greater than that required to break the original bonds. In other words, the reaction is exothermic. Yet it may well have a substantial activation energy, or energy barrier, because, in most cases, at least one bond must break before any new bonds can form. Thus energy must be put into the system before we get any back. This is analogous to the following situation: Somebody offers to let you buy into a business from which, for an investment of $10,000, you could get an income of $40,000 per year, beginning in one year. In the long run, you would do very well. First, however, you need to put up the initial $10,000 (the activation energy) to start the business.

Every reaction has a different energy diagram. Sometimes, the energy of the products is higher than that of the reactants (Figure 8.5); that is, the reaction is ("uphill"). For almost all reactions, however, there is an energy "hill"—the activation energy. The activation energy is inversely related to the rate of the reaction. The lower the activation energy, the faster the reaction; the higher the activation energy, the slower the reaction.

The top of the hill on an energy diagram is called the **transition state.** When the reacting molecules reach this point, one or more original bonds are partially broken, and one or more new bonds may be in the process of formation. The transition state for the reaction of iodide ion with chloromethane

^{GOB}
Chemistry•♦•Now™
Click *Chemistry Interactive* to view
a **Reaction Transition State**

Figure 8.6 Transition state for the reaction of CH_3Cl with I^-. In the transition state, iodide ion, I^-, attacks the carbon of chloromethane from the side opposite the C—Cl bond. In this transition state, both chlorine and iodine have partial negative charges.

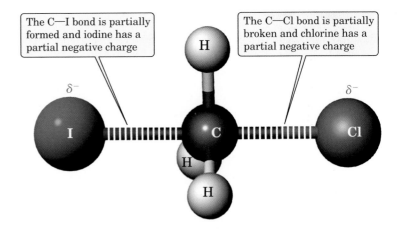

The C—I bond is partially formed and iodine has a partial negative charge

The C—Cl bond is partially broken and chlorine has a partial negative charge

occurs as an iodide ion collides with a molecule of chloromethane in such a way that the iodide ion hits the carbon atom (Figure 8.6).

The speed of a reaction is proportional to the probability of effective collisions. In a single-step reaction, the probability that two particles will collide is greater than the probability of a simultaneous collision of five particles. If you consider the net ionic reaction

$$H_2O_2 + 3I^- + 2H^+ \longrightarrow I_3^- + 2H_2O$$

it is highly unlikely that six reactant particles will collide simultaneously; thus this reaction should be slow. In reality, this reaction is very fast. This fact indicates that the reaction does not occur in one step but rather takes place in multiple steps. In each of those steps, the probability is high for collisions between two particles. Even a simple reaction such as

$$H_2(g) + Br_2(g) \longrightarrow 2HBr(g)$$

occurs in three steps:

$$\text{Step 1:} \quad Br_2 \xrightarrow{\text{slow}} 2Br\cdot$$

$$\text{Step 2:} \quad Br\cdot + H_2 \xrightarrow{\text{fast}} HBr + H\cdot$$

$$\text{Step 3:} \quad H\cdot + Br_2 \xrightarrow{\text{fast}} HBr + Br\cdot$$

The dot ($\cdot$) indicates the single unpaired electron in the atom. The overall rate of the reaction will be controlled by the slowest of the three steps, just as the slowest-moving car controls the flow of traffic on a street. In the preceding reaction, step 1 is the slowest, because it has the highest activation energy.

8.4 | How Can We Change the Rate of a Chemical Reaction?

In Section 8.2, we saw that reactions occur as a result of collisions between fast-moving molecules possessing a certain minimum energy (the activation energy). In this section, we examine some of the factors that affect activation energies and reaction rates.

A. Nature of the Reactants

In general, reactions that take place between ions in aqueous solution (Section 5.6) are extremely rapid, occurring almost instantaneously. Activation energies for these reactions are very low because usually no covalent bonds must be broken. As we might expect, reactions between covalent molecules, whether in aqueous solution or not, take place much more slowly. Many of these reactions require 15 min to 24 h or longer for most of the reactants to be converted to the products. Some reactions take a good deal longer, of course, but they are seldom useful.

B. Concentration

Consider the following reaction:

$$A + B \longrightarrow C + D$$

For reactions in the gas phase, an increase in pressure usually increases the rate.

Figure 8.7 The reaction of steel wool with oxygen. (*a*) When heated in air, steel wool glows but does not burn rapidly because the concentration of O_2 in the air is only about 20%. (*b*) When the glowing steel wool is put into 100% O_2, it burns vigorously.

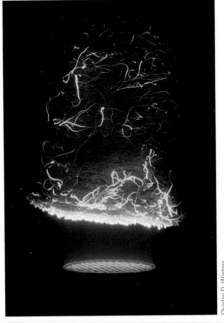

(*a*) (*b*)

In the case where one of the reactants is a solid, the rate is affected by the surface area of the solid. For this reason, a substance in powder form reacts faster than the same substance in the form of large chunks.

In most cases, the reaction rate increases when we increase the concentration of either or both reactants (Figure 8.7). For many reactions—though by no means all—a direct relationship exists between concentration and reaction rate; that is, when the concentration of a reactant is doubled, the reaction rate also doubles. This outcome is easily understandable on the basis of the collision theory. If we double the concentration of A, there are twice as many molecules of A in the same volume, so the molecules of B in that volume now collide with twice as many A molecules per second than before. Given that the reaction rate depends on the number of effective collisions per second, the rate doubles.

We can express the relationship between rate and concentration mathematically. For example, for the reaction

$$2H_2O_2(\ell) \longrightarrow 2H_2O(\ell) + O_2(g)$$

the rate was determined to be -0.01 mol H_2O_2/L/min at a constant temperature when the initial concentration of H_2O_2 was 1 mol/L. In other words, every minute 0.01 mol/L of hydrogen peroxide was used up. Researchers also found that every time the concentration of H_2O_2 was doubled, the rate also doubled. Thus the rate is directly proportional to the concentration of H_2O_2. We can write this relationship as

The brackets [ ] stand for the concentration of the chemical species whose formula is between the brackets.

$$\text{Rate} = k[H_2O_2]$$

Rate constant A proportionality constant, k, between the molar concentration of reactants and the rate of reaction; rate = k[compound]

where k is a constant, called the **rate constant.** Rate constants are usually calculated from the **initial rates of reaction** (Figure 8.1).

^{GOB}
Chemistry·⚛·Now™
Click *Coached Problems* to see **How Concentration Affects Reaction Rate**

EXAMPLE 8.2

Calculate the rate constant, k, for the reaction

$$2H_2O_2(\ell) \longrightarrow 2H_2O(\ell) + O_2(g)$$

using the rate and the initial concentration mentioned in the preceding discussion:

$$\frac{-0.01 \text{ mol } H_2O_2}{L \cdot \text{min}} \qquad [H_2O_2] = \frac{1 \text{ mol}}{L}$$

Solution

We start with the rate equation, solve it for k, and then insert the appropriate experimental values.

$$\text{Rate} = k[H_2O_2]$$

$$k = \frac{\text{Rate}}{[H_2O_2]}$$

$$= \frac{-0.01 \cancel{\text{ mol } H_2O_2}}{\cancel{L} \cdot \text{min}} \times \frac{\cancel{L}}{1 \cancel{\text{ mol } H_2O_2}}$$

$$= \frac{-0.01}{\text{min}}$$

Problem 8.2

Calculate the rate for the reaction in Example 8.2 when the initial concentration of H_2O_2 is 0.36 mol/L.

C. Temperature

GOB
Chemistry ⚛ Now™
Click *Coached Problems* to see **How Temperature and Activation Energy Affect Reaction Rate**

In virtually all cases, reaction rates increase with increasing temperature. A rule of thumb for many reactions is that every time the temperature goes up by 10°C, the rate of reaction doubles. This rule is far from exact, but it is not far from the truth in many cases. As you can see, this effect can be quite large. It says, for example, that if we run a reaction at 90°C instead of at

---

CHEMICAL CONNECTIONS 8A

Why High Fever Is Dangerous

Chemical Connections 1B points out that a sustained body temperature of 41.7°C (107°F) is invariably fatal. We can now see why a high fever is dangerous. Normal body temperature is 37°C (98.6°F), and all the many reactions in the body—including respiration, digestion, and the synthesis of various compounds—take place at that temperature. If an increase of 10°C causes the rates of most reactions to approximately double, then an increase of even 1°C makes them go significantly faster than normal.

Fever is a protective mechanism, and a small increase in temperature allows the body to kill germs faster by mobilizing the immune defense mechanism. This increase must be small, however: A rise of 1°C brings the temperature to 38°C (100.4°F); a rise of 3°C brings it to 40°C (104°F). A temperature higher than 104°F increases reaction rates to the danger point.

One can easily detect the increase in reaction rates when a patient has a high fever. The pulse rate increases and breathing becomes faster as the body attempts to supply increased amounts of oxygen for the accelerated reactions. A marathon runner, for example, may become overheated on a hot and humid day. After

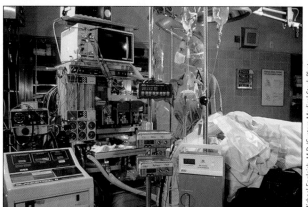

An operating table unit monitors a patient packed in ice.

Michael Engleish, M.D./Custom Medical Stock Photo

a time, perspiration can no longer cool his or her body effectively, and the runner may suffer hyperthermia or heat stroke, which, if not treated properly, can cause brain damage.

Figure 8.8 Distribution of kinetic energies (molecular velocities) at two temperatures. The kinetic energy on the x-axis designated E_a indicates the energy (molecular velocity) necessary to pass through the activation energy barrier. The shaded areas represent the fraction of molecules that have kinetic energies (molecular velocities) greater than the activation energy.

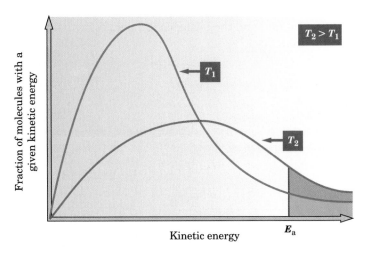

room temperature (20°C), the reaction will go about 128 times faster. There are seven 10° increments between 20°C and 90°C, and $2^7 = 128$. Put another way, if it takes 20 h to convert 100 g of reactant A to product C at 20°C, then it would take only 10 min at 90°C. Temperature, therefore, is a powerful tool that lets us increase the rates of reactions that are inconveniently slow. It also lets us decrease the rates of reactions that are inconveniently fast. For example, we might choose to run reactions at low temperatures because explosions might result or the reactions would otherwise be out of control at room temperature.

What causes reaction rates to increase with increasing temperature? Once again, we turn to collision theory. Here temperature has two effects:

1. In Section 6.6, we learned that temperature is related to the average kinetic energy of molecules. When the temperature increases, molecules move more rapidly, which means that they collide more frequently. More frequent collisions mean higher reaction rates. However, this factor is much less important than the second factor.

2. Recall from Section 8.2 that a reaction between two molecules takes place only if an effective collision occurs—a collision with an energy equal to or greater than the activation energy. When the temperature increases, not only is the average speed (kinetic energy) of the molecules greater, but there is also a different distribution of speeds. The number of very fast molecules increases much more than the number with the average speed (Figure 8.8). As a consequence, the number of effective collisions rises even more than the total number of collisions. Not only do more collisions take place, but the percentage of collisions that have an energy greater than the activation energy also rises. This factor is mainly responsible for the sharp increase in reaction rates with increasing temperature.

In this dish, chloride ion, Cl^-, acts as a catalyst for the decomposition of NH_4NO_3.

Charles D. Winters

Catalyst A substance that increases the rate of a chemical reaction by providing an alternative pathway with a lower activation energy

D. Presence of a Catalyst

Any substance that increases the rate of a reaction without itself being used up is called a **catalyst.** Many catalysts are known—some that increase the rate of only one reaction and others that can affect several reactions. Although we have seen that we can speed up reactions by increasing the temperature, in some cases they remain too slow even at the highest temperatures we can conveniently reach. In other cases, it is not feasible to increase the temperature—perhaps because other, unwanted reactions would be speeded up, too. In such cases, a catalyst, if we can find the right

CHEMICAL CONNECTIONS 8B

The Effects of Lowering Body Temperature

Like a significant increase in body temperature, a substantial decrease in body temperature below 37°C (98.6°F) can prove harmful because reaction rates are abnormally low. It is sometimes possible to take advantage of this effect. In some heart operations, for example, it is necessary to stop the flow of oxygen to the brain for a considerable time. At 37°C (98.6°F), the brain cannot survive without oxygen for longer than about 5 min without suffering permanent damage. When the patient's body temperature is deliberately lowered to about 28 to 30°C (82.4 to 86°F), however, the oxygen flow can be stopped for a considerable time without causing damage because reaction rates slow down. At 25.6°C (78°F), the body's oxygen consumption is reduced by 50%.

one for a given reaction, can prove very valuable. Many important industrial processes rely on catalysts (see Chemical Connections 8E), and virtually all reactions that take place in living organisms are catalyzed by enzymes (Chapter 22).

Catalysts work by allowing the reaction to take a different pathway, one with a lower activation energy. Without the catalyst, the reactants would have to get over the higher energy hill shown in Figure 8.9. The catalyst provides a lower hill. As we have seen, a lower activation energy means a higher reaction rate.

Each catalyst has its own way of providing an alternative pathway. Many catalysts provide a surface on which the reactants can meet. For example, the reaction between formaldehyde (CH₂O) and hydrogen (H₂) to give methanol (CH₃OH) goes so slowly without a catalyst that it is not practical, even if we increase the temperature to a reasonable level. If the mixture of gases is shaken with finely divided platinum metal, however, the reaction takes place at a convenient rate (Section 12.6D). The formaldehyde and hydrogen molecules meet each other on the surface of the platinum, where the proper bonds can be broken and new bonds form and the reaction can proceed:

Heterogeneous catalyst A catalyst in a separate phase from the reactants—for example, the solid platinum, Pt(s), in the reaction between CH₂O(g) and H₂(g)

Homogeneous catalyst A catalyst in the same phase as the reactants—for example, enzymes in body tissues

$$\underset{\text{Formaldehyde}}{\overset{H}{\underset{H}{>}}C=O + H_2} \xrightarrow{Pt} \underset{\text{Methanol}}{H-\overset{H}{\underset{H}{C}}-O-H}$$

We often write the catalyst over or under the arrow.

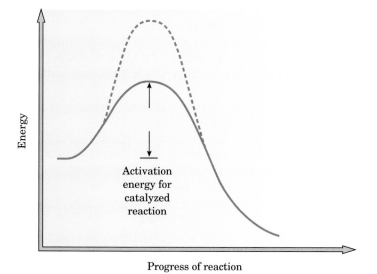

Figure 8.9 Energy diagram for a catalyzed reaction. The dashed line shows the energy curve for the uncatalyzed process. The catalyst provides an alternative pathway whose activation energy is lower.

CHEMICAL CONNECTIONS 8C

Timed-Release Medication

It is often desirable that a particular medicine act slowly and maintain its action evenly in the body for 24 h. We know that a solid in powder form reacts faster than the same weight in pill form because the powder has a greater surface area at which the reaction can take place. To slow the reaction and to have the drug be delivered evenly to the tissues, pharmaceutical companies coat beads of some of their drugs. The coating prevents the drug from reacting for a time. The thicker the coating, the longer it takes the drug to react. A drug with a smaller bead size has more surface area than a drug with a larger bead size; hence, drugs packaged in a smaller

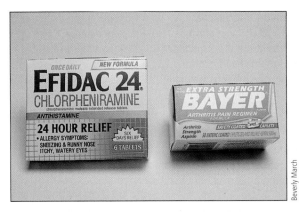

Two packages of timed-release medications.

bead size will react more rapidly. By combining the proper bead size with the proper amount of coating, the drug can be designed to deliver its effect over a 24-h period. In this way, the patient needs to take only one pill per day.

Coating can also prevent problems related to stomach irritation. For example, aspirin can cause stomach ulceration or bleeding in some people. Enteric (from the Greek *enteron*, which means affecting the intestines) coated aspirin tablets have a polymeric coat that is acid resistant. Such a drug does not dissolve until it reaches the intestines, where it causes no harm.

| 8.5 | What Does It Mean to Say That a Reaction Has Reached Equilibrium? |

Many reactions are irreversible. When a piece of paper is completely burned, the products are CO_2 and H_2O. Anyone who takes pure CO_2 and H_2O and tries to make them react to give paper and oxygen will not succeed.

A tree, of course, turns CO_2 and H_2O into wood and oxygen, and we, in sophisticated factories, make paper from the wood. These activities are not the same as directly combining CO_2, H_2O, and energy in a single process to get paper and oxygen, however. Therefore, we can certainly consider the burning of paper to be an irreversible reaction.

Other reactions are reversible. A **reversible reaction** can be made to go in either direction. For example, if we mix carbon monoxide with water in the gas phase at a high temperature, carbon dioxide and hydrogen are produced:

$$CO(g) + H_2O(g) \longrightarrow CO_2(g) + H_2(g)$$

If we desire, we can also make this reaction take place the other way. That is, we can mix carbon dioxide and hydrogen to get carbon monoxide and water vapor:

$$CO_2(g) + H_2(g) \longrightarrow CO(g) + H_2O(g)$$

Let us see what happens when we run a reversible reaction. We will add some carbon monoxide to water vapor in the gas phase. The two compounds begin to react at a certain rate (the forward reaction):

$$CO(g) + H_2O(g) \longrightarrow CO_2(g) + H_2(g)$$

As the reaction proceeds, the concentrations of CO and H_2O gradually decrease because both reactants are being used up. In turn, the rate of the reaction gradually decreases because it depends on the concentrations of the reactants (Section 8.4B).

But what is happening in the other direction? Before we added the carbon monoxide, no carbon dioxide or hydrogen was present. As soon as the forward reaction began, it produced small amounts of these substances, and we now have some CO_2 and H_2. These two compounds will now, of course, begin reacting with each other (the reverse reaction):

$$CO_2(g) + H_2(g) \longrightarrow CO(g) + H_2O(g)$$

At first, the reverse reaction is very slow. As the concentrations of H_2 and CO_2 (produced by the forward reaction) gradually increase, the rate of the reverse reaction also gradually increases.

We have a situation, then, in which the rate of the forward reaction gradually decreases, while the rate of the reverse reaction (which began at zero) gradually increases. Eventually the two rates become equal. At this point, the process is in **dynamic equilibrium** (or just **equilibrium**).

$$CO_2(g) + H_2(g) \underset{\text{reverse}}{\overset{\text{forward}}{\rightleftharpoons}} CO(g) + H_2O(g)$$

What happens in the reaction container once we reach equilibrium? If we measure the concentrations of the substances in the container, we find that no change in concentration takes place after equilibrium is reached (Figure 8.10). Whatever the concentrations of all the substances are at equilibrium, they remain the same forever unless something happens to disturb the equilibrium (as discussed in Section 8.8). This does not mean that all the concentrations must be the same—all of them can, in fact, be different and usually are—but it does mean that, whatever they are, they no longer change once equilibrium has been reached, no matter how long we wait.

Given that the concentrations of all the reactants and products no longer change, can we say that nothing is happening? No, we know that both reactions are occurring; all the molecules are constantly reacting—the CO and H_2O are being changed to CO_2 and H_2, and the CO_2 and H_2 are

GOB
Chemistry☀Now™
Click *Coached Problems* to see **How Reactants and Products Come to Equlibrium in a Chemical System**

Dynamic equilibrium A state in which the rate of the forward reaction equals the rate of the reverse reaction

We use a double arrow to indicate that a reaction is reversible.

Another way to look at this situation is to say that the concentration of carbon monoxide (and of the other three compounds) does not change at equilibrium, because it is being used up as fast as it is being formed.

Reaction A + B $\rightleftharpoons$ C + D

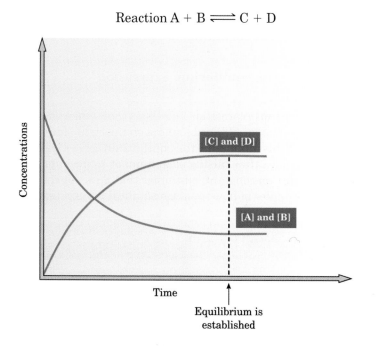

Figure 8.10 Changes in the concentrations of reactants (A and B) and products (C and D) as a system approaches equilibrium. Only A and B are present at the beginning of the reaction.

Figure 8.11 An equilibrium can be approached from either direction.

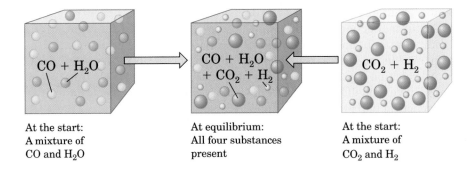

At the start:
A mixture of
CO and H_2O

At equilibrium:
All four substances
present

At the start:
A mixture of
CO_2 and H_2

being changed to CO and H_2O. Because the rates of the forward and reverse reactions are the same, however, none of the concentrations change.

In the example just discussed, we approached equilibrium by adding carbon monoxide to water vapor. Alternatively, we could have added carbon dioxide to hydrogen. In either case, we eventually get an equilibrium mixture containing the same four compounds (Figure 8.11).

It is not necessary to begin with equal amounts. We could, for example, take 10 moles of carbon monoxide and 0.2 mole of water vapor. We would still arrive at an equilibrium mixture of all four compounds.

8.6 | What Is an Equilibrium Constant and How Do We Use It?

Chemical equilibria can be treated by a simple mathematical expression. First, let us write the following reaction as the general equation for all reversible reactions:

$$aA + bB \rightleftharpoons cC + dD$$

In this equation, the capital letters stand for substances—CO_2, H_2O, CO, and H_2, for instance—and the lowercase letters are the coefficients of the balanced equation. The double arrow shows that the reaction is reversible. In general, any number of substances can be present on either side.

Once equilibrium is reached, the following equation is valid, where K is a constant called the **equilibrium constant:**

Equilibrium constant A value calculated from the equilibrium expression for a given reaction indicating in which direction the reaction goes

$$K = \frac{[C]^c[D]^d}{[A]^a[B]^b}$$ **The equilibrium expression**

Let us examine the equlibrium expression. It tells us that, when we multiply the equilibrium concentrations of the substances on the right side of the chemical equation and divide this product by the equilibrium concentrations of the substances on the left side (after raising each number to the appropriate power), we get the equilibrium constant, a number that does not change.

Let us look at several examples of how to set up equilibrium expressions.

EXAMPLE 8.3

Write the equilibrium expression for the reaction

$$CO(g) + H_2O(g) \rightleftharpoons CO_2(g) + H_2(g)$$

Solution

$$K = \frac{[CO_2][H_2]}{[CO][H_2O]}$$

This expression tells us that, at equilibrium, the concentration of carbon dioxide multiplied by the concentration of hydrogen and divided by the concentrations of water and carbon monoxide is a constant, K. Note that no exponent is written in this equation because all of the coefficients of the chemical equation are 1, and, by convention, an exponent of 1 is not written. Mathematically, it would be just as correct to write the left-side compounds on top, but the universal custom is to write them as shown here, with the products on top and the reactants on the bottom.

It is understood that the concentration of a species within brackets is always expressed in moles per liter.

_{GOB}
Chemistry•∴•Now™

Click *Coached Problems* to write some
Equilibrium Expressions

Problem 8.3

Write the equilibrium expression for the reaction

$$SO_3(g) + H_2O(\ell) \rightleftharpoons H_2SO_4(aq)$$

EXAMPLE 8.4

Write the equilibrium expression for the reaction

$$O_2(g) + 4ClO_2(g) \rightleftharpoons 2Cl_2O_5(g)$$

Solution

$$K = \frac{[Cl_2O_5]^2}{[O_2][ClO_2]^4}$$

In this case, the chemical equation has coefficients other than unity, so the equilibrium expression contains exponents.

Problem 8.4

Write the equilibrium expression for the reaction

$$2NH_3(g) \rightleftharpoons N_2(g) + 3H_2(g)$$

Now let us see how K is calculated.

EXAMPLE 8.5

Some H_2 is added to I_2 at 427°C and the following reaction is allowed to come to equilibrium:

$$H_2(g) + I_2(g) \rightleftharpoons 2HI(g)$$

When equilibrium is reached, the concentrations are $[I_2]$ = 0.42 mol/L, $[H_2]$ = 0.025 mol/L, and $[HI]$ = 0.76 mol/L. Calculate K at 427°C.

Solution

The equilibrium expression is

$$K = \frac{[HI]^2}{[I_2][H_2]}$$

Substituting the concentrations, we get

$$K = \frac{[0.76\ M]^2}{[0.42\ M][0.025\ M]} = 55$$

The equilibrium constant of this reaction has no units because the molarities cancel. Depending on the stoichiometry of the reaction, equilibrium constants may have different units, such as M, and so on.

Problem 8.5

What is the equilibrium constant for the following reaction? Equilibrium concentrations are given under the formula of each component.

$$PCl_3 + Cl_2 \rightleftharpoons PCl_5$$
$$1.66\ M \qquad 1.66\ M \qquad 1.66\ M$$

Example 8.5 shows us that the reaction between I_2 and H_2 to give HI has an equilibrium constant of 55. What does this value mean? At constant temperature, equilibrium constants remain the same no matter what concentrations we have. That is, at 427°C, if we begin by adding, say, 5 moles of H_2 to 5 moles of I_2, the forward and backward reactions will take place, and equilibrium will eventually be reached. At that point, the value of K will equal 55. If we begin at 427°C with different numbers of moles of H_2 and I_2, perhaps 7 moles of H_2 and 2 moles of I_2, once equilibrium is reached, the value of $[HI]^2/[I_2][H_2]$ will again be 55. It makes no difference what the initial concentrations of the three substances are. At 427°C, as long as all three substances are present and equilibrium has been reached, the concentrations of the three substances will adjust themselves so that the value of the equilibrium constant equals 55.

The equilibrium constant is different for every reaction. Some reactions have a large K; others have a small K. A reaction with a very large K proceeds almost to completion (to the right). For example, K for the following reaction is about 100,000,000, or 10^8 at 25°C:

$$N_2(g) + 3H_2(g) \rightleftharpoons 2NH_3(g)$$

The symbol $\rightleftharpoons$ means that the equilibrium lies far to the right.

This value of 10^8 for K means that, at equilibrium, $[NH_3]$ must be very large and $[N_2]$ and $[H_2]$ must be very small so that $[NH_3]^2/[N_2][H_2]^3 = 10^8$. Thus, if we add N_2 to H_2, we can be certain that, when equilibrium is reached, an essentially complete reaction has taken place.

On the other hand, a reaction such as the following, which has a very small K, hardly goes forward at all:

$$AgCl(s) \rightleftharpoons Ag^+(aq) + Cl^-(aq)$$

Equilibrium effects are most obvious in reactions with K values between 10^3 and 10^{-3}. In such cases, the reaction goes part of the way, and significant concentrations of all substances are present at equilibrium. An example is the reaction between carbon monoxide and water discussed in Section 8.5, for which K is equal to 10 at 600°C.

In dilute solutions, it is customary to omit the concentration of the solvent from the equilibrium expression. Consider the reaction between ammonia and water:

$$NH_3(aq) + H_2O(\ell) \rightleftharpoons NH_4^+(aq) + OH^-(aq)$$

If the concentration of ammonia is small, and consequently the concentrations of ammonium ion and hydroxide ion are small, the concentration of water molecules remains essentially the same. Because the molar concentration of water is effectively constant, we do not include it in the equilibrium expression:

$$K = \frac{[NH_4^+][OH^-]}{[NH_3]}$$

EXAMPLE 8.6

GOB
Chemistry•Now™
Click *Coached Problems* to try a problem calculating the **Equilibrium Constant** from concentrations at equilibrium

Calculate the equilibrium constant for the above reaction (a) with and (b) without the inclusion of water in the equilibrium expression. The equilibrium concentrations are as follows: $[NH_3] = 0.0100\ M$; $[NH_4^+] = 0.000400\ M$; $[OH^-] = 0.000400\ M$.

Solution

(a) Because molarity is based on 1 L, first we find the concentration of water in water—that is, how many moles of water are present in 1 L of water.

$$[H_2O] = \frac{1000\ g\ H_2O}{1\ L\ H_2O} \times \frac{1\ mol\ H_2O}{18.00\ g\ H_2O} = \frac{55.56\ mol\ H_2O}{1\ L\ H_2O}$$

$$= 55.56\ M$$

We then use this value and the concentration of the other species to calculate the equilibrium constant for this reaction.

$$K = \frac{[0.000400\ M][0.000400\ M]}{[0.0100\ M][55.56\ M]} = 2.88 \times 10^{-7}$$

(b) $$K = \frac{[0.000400\ M][0.000400\ M]}{[0.0100\ M]} = 1.60 \times 10^{-5}\ M$$

The inclusion of the concentration of the solvent, water, gives an equilibrium constant two magnitudes smaller than without it. The equilibrium constant without the inclusion of the solvent is the accepted one.

Problem 8.6

Ethyl acetate is a common solvent in many industrial products, ranging from nail enamel and remover to liquid cement for plastics. It is prepared by reacting acetic acid with ethanol in the presence of an acid catalyst, HCl. Note that this synthesis starts with acetic acid and pure ethanol. Water is one of the products and, therefore, its concentration must be included in the equilibrium constant. Write the equilibrium expressions for the reaction.

$$CH_3COOH(\ell) + C_2H_5OH(\ell) \overset{HCl}{\rightleftharpoons} CH_3COOC_2H_5(\ell) + H_2O(\ell)$$
Acetic acid　　Ethanol　　　　Ethyl acetate

HCl is a catalyst. It speeds up the attainment of equilibrium, but does not affect the equilibrium position.

The equilibrium constant for a given reaction remains the same no matter what happens to the concentrations, but the same is not true for changes in temperature. The value of K, however, does change when the temperature changes.

8.7 | How Long Does It Take for a Reaction to Reach Equilibrium?

As pointed out in Section 8.6, the equilibrium expression is valid only after equilibrium has been reached. Before that point, there is no equilibrium, and the equilibrium expression is not valid. But how long does it take for a reaction to reach equilibrium? There is no easy answer to this question. Some reactions, if the reactants are well mixed, reach equilibrium in less than one second; others will not get there even after millions of years.

There is no relationship between the rate of a reaction (how long it takes to reach equilibrium) and the value of K. It is possible to have a large K and a slow rate, as in the reaction between glucose and O_2 to give CO_2 and H_2O, which does not reach equilibrium for many years (Section 8.1), or a small K and a fast rate. In other reactions, the rate and K are both large or both small.

8.8 | What Is Le Chatelier's Principle?

Le Chatelier's principle A principle stating that when a stress is applied to a system in chemical equilibrium, the position of the equilibrium shifts in the direction that will relieve the applied stress

When a reaction reaches equilibrium, the forward and reverse reactions take place at the same rate, and the equilibrium concentration of the reaction mixture does not change as long as we don't do anything to the system. But what happens if we do? In 1888, Henri Le Chatelier (1850–1936) put forth the statement known as **Le Chatelier's principle:** If an external stress is applied to a system in equilibrium, the system reacts in such a way as to partially relieve that stress. Let us look at five types of stress that can be put on chemical equilibria: adding a reactant or product, removing a reactant or product, and changing the temperature.

A. Addition of a Reaction Component

Suppose that the reaction between acetic acid and ethanol has reached equilibrium:

$$\underset{\text{Acetic acid}}{CH_3COOH} + \underset{\text{Ethanol}}{C_2H_5OH} \underset{}{\overset{HCl}{\rightleftharpoons}} \underset{\text{Ethyl acetate}}{CH_3COOC_2H_5} + H_2O$$

This means that the reaction flask contains all four substances (plus the catalyst) and that their concentrations no longer change.

We now disturb the system by adding some acetic acid.

Adding CH_3COOH $\underset{\text{Acetic acid}}{CH_3\overset{\overset{\displaystyle O}{\|}}{C}OH} + \underset{\text{Ethanol}}{HOCH_2CH_3} \overset{HCl}{\rightleftharpoons} \underset{\text{Ethyl acetate}}{CH_3\overset{\overset{\displaystyle O}{\|}}{C}OCH_2CH_3} + H_2O$

→ Equilibrium shifts to formation of more products

The result is that the concentration of acetic acid suddenly increases, which increases the rate of the forward reaction. As a consequence, the concentrations of the products (ethyl acetate and water) begin to increase. At the same time, the concentrations of reactants decrease. Now, an increase in the concentrations of the products causes the rate of the reverse reaction to increase, but the rate of the forward reaction is decreasing, so eventually the two rates will be equal again and a new equilibrium will be established.

When that happens, the concentrations are once again constant, but they are not the same as they were before the addition of the acetic acid. The concentrations of ethyl acetate and water are higher now, and the concentration of ethanol is lower. The concentration of acetic acid is higher because we added some, but it is less than it was immediately after we made the addition.

When we add more of any component to a system in equilibrium, that addition constitutes a stress. The system relieves this stress by increasing the concentrations of the components on the other side of the equilibrium equation. We say that the equilibrium shifts in the opposite direction. The addition of acetic acid, on the left side of the equation, causes the rate of the forward reaction to increase and the reaction to move toward the right: More ethyl acetate and water form, and some of the acetic acid and ethanol are used up. The same thing happens if we add ethanol.

On the other hand, if we add water or ethyl acetate, the rate of the reverse reaction increases, and the reaction shifts to the left:

The tube on the left contains a saturated solution of silver acetate (Ag^+ ions and CH_3COO^- ions) in equilibrium with solid silver acetate. When more silver ions are added in the form of silver nitrate solution, the equilibrium shifts to the right, producing more silver acetate, as can be seen in the tube on the right.

$$Ag^+(aq) + CH_3COO^-(aq) \rightleftharpoons$$
$$CH_3COOAg(s)$$

$$\underset{\text{Acetic acid}}{CH_3COOH} + \underset{\text{Ethanol}}{C_2H_5OH} \underset{}{\overset{HCl}{\rightleftharpoons}} \underset{\text{Ethyl acetate}}{CH_3COOC_2H_5} + H_2O \qquad \text{Adding ethyl acetate}$$

⟵————————————— Equilibrium shifts toward
formation of reactants

We can summarize by saying that the addition of any component causes the equilibrium to shift to the opposite side.

EXAMPLE 8.7

When dinitrogen tetroxide, a colorless gas, is enclosed in a vessel, a color indicating the formation of brown nitrogen dioxide, soon appears (see Figure 8.12 later in this chapter). The intensity of the brown color indicates the amount of nitrogen dioxide formed. The equilibrium reaction is

$$\underset{\substack{\text{Dinitrogen}\\\text{tetroxide}\\\text{(colorless)}}}{N_2O_4(g)} \rightleftharpoons \underset{\substack{\text{Nitrogen}\\\text{dioxide}\\\text{(brown)}}}{2NO_2(g)}$$

When more N_2O_4 is added to the equilibrium mixture, the brownish color becomes darker. Explain what happened.

Solution
The darker color indicates that more nitrogen dioxide is formed. This happens because the addition of the reactant shifts the equilibrium to the right, forming more product.

Problem 8.7

What happens to the following equilibrium reaction when Br_2 gas is added to the equilibrium mixture?

$$2NOBr(g) \rightleftharpoons 2NO(g) + Br_2(g)$$

B. Removal of a Reaction Component

It is not always as easy to remove a component from a reaction mixture as it is to add one, but there are often ways to do it. The removal of a component, or even a decrease in its concentration, lowers the corresponding reaction rate and changes the position of the equilibrium. If we remove a reactant, the reaction shifts to the left, toward the side from which the reactant was removed. If we remove a product, the reaction shifts to the right, toward the side from which the product was removed.

In the case of the acetic acid–ethanol equilibrium, ethyl acetate has the lowest boiling point of the four components and can be removed by distillation. The equilibrium then shifts to that side so that more ethyl acetate is produced to compensate for the removal. The concentrations of acetic acid and ethanol decrease, and the concentration of water increases. The effect of removing a component is thus the opposite of adding one. The removal of a component causes the equilibrium to shift to the side from which the component was removed.

$$\underset{\text{Acetic acid}}{CH_3COOH} + \underset{\text{Ethanol}}{C_2H_5OH} \underset{HCl}{\rightleftharpoons} H_2O + \underset{\text{Ethyl acetate}}{CH_3COOC_2H_5} \quad \text{Removing ethyl acetate}$$

Equilibrium shifts toward ⟶
formation of more products

No matter what happens to the individual concentrations, the value of the equilibrium constant remains unchanged.

This headstone has been damaged by acid rain.

John D. Cunningham/Visuals Unlimited

EXAMPLE 8.8

The beautiful stone we know as marble is mostly calcium carbonate. When acid rain containing sulfuric acid attacks marble, the following equilibrium reaction can be written:

$$\underset{\substack{\text{Calcium}\\\text{carbonate}}}{CaCO_3(s)} + \underset{\substack{\text{Sulfuric}\\\text{acid}}}{H_2SO_4(aq)} \rightleftharpoons \underset{\substack{\text{Calcium}\\\text{sulfate}}}{CaSO_4(s)} + \underset{\substack{\text{Carbon}\\\text{dioxide}}}{CO_2(g)} + H_2O(\ell)$$

How does the fact that carbon dioxide is a gas influence the equilibrium?

Solution

The gaseous CO_2 diffuses away from the reaction site, meaning that this product is removed from the equilibrium mixture. The equilibrium shifts to the right, so that the statue continues eroding.

Problem 8.8

Consider the following equilibrium reaction for the decomposition of an aqueous solution of hydrogen peroxide:

$$2H_2O_2(aq) \rightleftharpoons 2H_2O(\ell) + O_2(g)$$

Hydrogen
peroxide

Oxygen has limited solubility in water (see the table in Chemical Connections 7A). What happens to the equilibrium after the solution becomes saturated with oxygen?

C. Change in Temperature

The effect of a change in temperature on a reaction that has reached equilibrium depends on whether the reaction is exothermic (gives off heat) or endothermic (requires heat). Let us look first at an exothermic reaction:

$$2H_2(g) + O_2(g) \rightleftharpoons 2H_2O(\ell) + 137,000 \text{ cal per mol } H_2O$$

If we consider heat to be a product of this reaction, then we can use Le Chatelier's principle and the same type of reasoning as we did before. An increase in temperature means that we are adding heat. Because heat is a product, its addition pushes the equilibrium to the opposite side. We can therefore say that, if this exothermic reaction is at equilibrium and we increase the temperature, the reaction goes to the left—the concentrations of H_2 and O_2 increase and that of H_2O decreases. This is true of all exothermic reactions.

- An increase in temperature drives an exothermic reaction toward the reactants (to the left).
- A decrease in temperature drives an exothermic reaction toward the products (to the right).

  For an endothermic reaction, of course, the opposite is true.

- An increase in temperature drives an endothermic reaction toward the products (to the right).
- A decrease in temperature drives an endothermic reaction toward the reactants (to the left).

  Recall from Section 8.4 that a change in temperature changes not only the position of equilibrium but also the value of K, the equilibrium constant.

 CHEMICAL CONNECTIONS 8D

Sunglasses and Le Chatelier's Principle

Heat is not the only form of energy that affects equilibria. The statements made in the text regarding endothermic or exothermic reactions can be generalized to reactions involving other forms of energy. A practical illustration of this generalization is the use of sunglasses with adjustable shading. The compound silver chloride, AgCl, is incorporated in the glasses. This compound, upon exposure to sunlight, produces metallic silver, Ag, and chlorine, Cl_2:

The more silver metal produced, the darker the glasses. At night, or when the wearer goes indoors, the reaction is reversed according to Le Chatelier's principle. In this case, the addition of energy in the form of sunlight drives the equilibrium to the right; its removal drives the equilibrium to the left.

$$\text{Light} + 2Ag^+ + 2Cl^- \rightleftharpoons 2Ag(s) + Cl_2$$

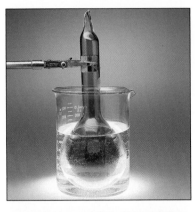

Figure 8.12 Effect of temperature on the N_2O_4—NO_2 system at equilibrium. (top) At 50°C, the deep brown color indicates the predominance of NO_2. (bottom) At 0°C, N_2O_4, which is colorless, predominates.

EXAMPLE 8.9

The conversion of nitrogen dioxide to dinitrogen tetroxide is an exothermic reaction:

$$2NO_2(g) \rightleftharpoons N_2O_4(g) + 13{,}700 \text{ cal}$$

Nitrogen dioxide   Dinitrogen tetroxide
(brown)   (colorless)

In Figure 8.12 we see that the brown color is darker at 50°C than it is at 0°C. Explain.

Solution

To go from 0°C to 50°C, heat must be added. But heat is a product of this equilibrium reaction, as it is written in the question. The addition of heat, therefore, shifts the equilibrium to the left. This shift produces more $NO_2(g)$, leading to the darker brown color.

Problem 8.9

Consider the following equilibrium reaction:

$$A \rightleftharpoons B$$

Increasing the temperature results in an increase in the equilibrium concentration of B. Is the conversion of A to B an exothermic reaction or an endothermic reaction? Explain.

D. Change in Pressure

A change in pressure influences the equilibrium only if one or more components of the reaction mixture are gases. Consider the following equilibrium reaction:

$$N_2O_4(g) \rightleftharpoons 2NO_2(g)$$

Dinitrogen   Nitrogen
tetroxide   dioxide

In this equilibrium, we have one mole of gas as a reactant and two moles of gas as products. According to Le Chatelier's principle, an increase in pressure shifts the equilibrium in the direction that will decrease the moles in the gas phase and thus decrease the internal pressure. In the preceding reaction, the equilibrium will shift to the left.

- An increase in pressure shifts the reaction toward the side with fewer moles of gas.
- A decrease in pressure shifts the reaction toward the side with more moles of gas.

EXAMPLE 8.10

In the production of ammonia, both reactants and products are gases:

$$N_2(g) + 3H_2(g) \rightleftharpoons 2NH_3(g)$$

What kind of pressure change would increase the yield of ammonia?

Solution

There are four moles of gases on the left side and two moles on the right side. To increase the yield of ammonia, we must shift the equilibrium to the right. An increase in pressure shifts the equilibrium toward the side with fewer moles—that is, to the right. Thus an increase in pressure will increase the yield of ammonia.

Problem 8.10

What happens to the following equilibrium reaction when the pressure is increased?

$$O_2(g) + 4ClO_2(g) \rightleftharpoons 2Cl_2O_5(g)$$

E. The Effects of a Catalyst

As we saw in Section 8.4D, a catalyst increases the rate of a reaction without itself being changed. For a reversible reaction, catalysts always increase the rates of both the forward and reverse reactions to the same extent. Therefore, the addition of a catalyst has no effect on the position of equilibrium. However, adding a catalyst to a system not yet at equilibrium causes it to reach equilibrium faster than it would without the catalyst.

CHEMICAL CONNECTIONS 8E

The Haber Process

Both humans and other animals need proteins and other nitrogen-containing compounds to live. Ultimately, the nitrogen in these compounds comes from the plants that we eat. Although the atmosphere contains plenty of N_2, nature converts it to compounds usable by biological organisms in only one way: Certain bacteria have the ability to "fix" atmospheric nitrogen—that is, convert it to ammonia. Most of these bacteria live in the roots of certain plants such as clover, alfalfa, peas, and beans. However, the amount of nitrogen fixed by such bacteria each year is far less than the amount necessary to feed all the humans and animals in the world.

The world today can support its population only by using fertilizers made by artificial fixing, primarily the **Haber process,** which converts N_2 to NH_3.

$$N_2(g) + 3H_2(g) \rightleftharpoons 2NH_3(g) + 22 \text{ kcal}$$

Early workers who focused on the problem of fixing nitrogen were troubled by a conflict between equilibrium and rate. Because the synthesis of ammonia is an exothermic reaction, an increase in temperature drives the equilibrium to the left, so the best results (largest possible yield) should be obtained at low temperatures. At low temperatures, however, the rate is too slow to produce any meaningful amounts of NH_3. In 1908, Fritz Haber (1868–1934) solved this problem when he discovered a catalyst that permits the reaction to take place at a convenient rate at 500°C.

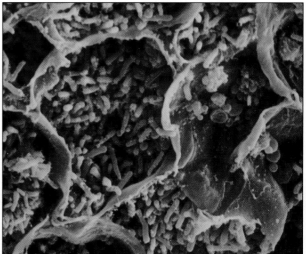

Ammonia is produced by bacteria in these root nodules.

The NH_3 produced by the Haber process is converted to fertilizers, which are used all over the world. Without these fertilizers, food production would diminish so much that widespread starvation would result.

SUMMARY OF KEY QUESTIONS

SECTION 8.1 How Do We Measure Reaction Rates?

- The **rate of a reaction** is the change in concentration of a reactant or a product per unit time. Some reactions are fast; others are slow.

SECTION 8.2 Why Do Some Molecular Collisions Result in Reaction Whereas Others Do Not?

- The rate of a reaction depends on the number of **effective collisions**—that is, collisions that lead to a reaction.
- The energy necessary for a reaction to take place is the **activation energy.** Effective collisions have (1) more than the activation energy required for the reaction to proceed forward and (2) the proper orientation in space of the colliding particles.

SECTION 8.3 What Is the Relationship Between Activation Energy and Reaction Rate?

- The lower the activation energy, the faster the reaction.
- An energy diagram shows the progress of a reaction.
- The position at the top of the curve in an energy diagram is called the **transition state.**

SECTION 8.4 How Can We Change the Rate of a Chemical Reaction?

- Reaction rates generally increase with increasing concentration and temperature; they also depend on the nature of the reactants.
- The rates of some reactions can be increased by adding a **catalyst,** a substance that provides an alternative pathway with a lower activation energy.
- A rate constant gives the relationship between the rate of the reaction and the concentrations of the reactants at a constant temperature.

SECTION 8.5 What Does It Mean to Say That a Reaction Has Reached Equilibrium?

- Many reactions are reversible and eventually reach equilibrium.
- At **equilibrium,** the forward and reverse reactions take place at equal rates, and concentrations do not change.

SECTION 8.6 What Is an Equilibrium Constant and How Do We Use It?

- Every equilibrium has an **equilibrium expression** and an **equilibrium constant,** K, which does not change when concentrations change but does change when temperature changes.

SECTION 8.7 How Long Does It Take for a Reaction to Reach Equilibrium?

- There is no necessary relationship between the value of the equilibrium constant, K, and the rate at which equilibrium is reached.

SECTION 8.8 What Is Le Chatelier's Principle?

- **Le Chatelier's principle** tells us what happens when we put stress on a system in equilibrium.
- The addition of a component causes the equilibrium to shift to the opposite side.
- The removal of a component causes the equilibrium to shift to the side from which the component is removed.
- Increasing the temperature drives an exothermic equilibrium to the side of the reactants; increasing the temperature drives an endothermic equilibrium to the side of the products.
- Addition of a catalyst has no effect on the position of equilibrium.

PROBLEMS

GOB
Chemistry⚛Now™

Assess your understanding of this chapter's topics with additional quizzing and conceptual-based problems at **http://now.brookscole.com/gob8** or on the CD.

A blue problem number indicates an applied problem.

■ denotes problems that are available on the GOB ChemistryNow website or CD and are assignable in OWL.

SECTION 8.1 How Do We Measure Reaction Rates?

8.11 Consider the following reaction:

$$CH_3\text{---}Cl \ + I^- \longrightarrow CH_3\text{---}I \ + Cl^-$$

Chloromethane   Iodomethane

Suppose we start the reaction with an initial concentration of 0.260 M. This concentration increases to 0.840 M over a period of 1 h 20 min. What is the rate of reaction?

SECTION 8.2 Why Do Some Molecular Collisions Result in Reaction Whereas Others Do Not?

8.12 Two kinds of gas molecules are reacted at a set temperature. The gases are blown into the reaction vessel from two tubes. In setup A, the two tubes are aligned parallel to each other; in setup B, they are 90° to each other; and in setup C, they are aligned against each other. Which setup would yield the most effective collisions?

8.13 Why are reactions between ions in aqueous solution generally much faster than reactions between covalent molecules?

SECTION 8.3 What Is the Relationship Between Activation Energy and Reaction Rate?

8.14 What is the likelihood that the following reaction occurs in a single step? Explain.

$$O_2(g) + 4ClO_2(g) \rightleftharpoons 2Cl_2O_5(g)$$

8.15 A certain reaction is exothermic by 9 kcal/mol and has an activation energy of 14 kcal/mol. Draw an energy diagram for this reaction, and label the transition state.

SECTION 8.4 How Can We Change the Rate of a Chemical Reaction?

8.16 A quart of milk quickly spoils if left at room temperature but keeps for several days in a refrigerator. Explain.

8.17 If a certain reaction takes 16 h to go to completion at 10°C, what temperature should we run it if we want it to go to completion in 1 h?

8.18 In most cases, when we run a reaction by mixing a fixed quantity of substance A with a fixed quantity of substance B, the rate of the reaction begins at a maximum and then decreases as time goes by. Explain.

8.19 If you were running a reaction and wanted it to go faster, what three things might you try to accomplish this goal?

8.20 What factors determine whether a reaction run at a given temperature will be fast or slow?

8.21 Explain how a catalyst increases the rate of a reaction.

8.22 If you add a piece of marble, $CaCO_3$, to a 6 M HCl solution at room temperature, you will see some bubbles form around the marble as gas slowly rises. If you crush another piece of marble and add it to the same solution at the same temperature, you will see vigorous gas formation, so much so that the solution appears to be boiling. Explain.

SECTION 8.5 What Does It Mean to Say That a Reaction Has Reached Equilibrium?

8.23 Burning a piece of paper is an irreversible reaction. Give some other examples of irreversible reactions.

8.24 Suppose the following reaction is at equilibrium:

$$PCl_3 + Cl_2 \rightleftharpoons PCl_5$$

(a) Are the equilibrium concentrations of PCl_3, Cl_2, and PCl_5 necessarily equal? Explain.

(b) Is the equilibrium concentration of PCl_3 necessarily equal to that of Cl_2? Explain.

SECTION 8.6 What is an Equilibrium Constant and How Do We Use It?

8.25 ■ Write equilibrium expressions for these reactions.
(a) $2H_2O_2 \rightleftharpoons 2H_2O + O_2$
(b) $2N_2O_5 \rightleftharpoons 2N_2O_4 + O_2$
(c) $6H_2O + 6CO_2 \rightleftharpoons C_6H_{12}O_6 + 6O_2$

8.26 Write the chemical equations corresponding to the following equilibrium expressions.

(a) $K = \dfrac{[H_2CO_3]}{[CO_2][H_2O]}$

(b) $K = \dfrac{[P_4][O_2]^5}{[P_4O_{10}]}$

(c) $K = \dfrac{[F_2]^3[PH_3]}{[HF]^3[PF_3]}$

8.27 ■ Consider the following equilibrium reaction. Under each species is its equilibrium concentration. Calculate the equilibrium constant for the reaction.

$$CO(g) + H_2O(g) \rightleftharpoons CO_2(g) + H_2(g)$$
$$0.933\ M \quad 0.720\ M \qquad 0.133\ M \quad 3.37\ M$$

8.28 When the following reaction reached equilibrium at 325 K, the equilibrium constant was found to be 172. When a sample was taken of the equilibrium mixture, it was found to contain 0.0714 M NO_2. What was the equilibrium concentration of N_2O_4?

$$2NO_2(g) \rightleftharpoons N_2O_4(g)$$

8.29 ■ The following reaction was allowed to reach equilibrium at 25°C. Under each component is its equilibrium concentration. Calculate the equilibrium constant, K, for this reaction.

$$2NOCl(g) \rightleftharpoons 2NO(g) + Cl_2(g)$$
$$2.6\ M \qquad 1.4\ M \quad 0.34\ M$$

8.30 Write the equilibrium expression for this reaction:

$$HNO_3(aq) + H_2O(\ell) \rightleftharpoons H_3O^+(aq) + NO_3^-(aq)$$

8.31 Here are equilibrium constants for several reactions. Which of them favor the formation of products and which favor the formation of reactants?

(a) 4.5×10^{-8} (b) 32
(c) 4.5   (d) 3.0×10^{-7}
(e) 0.0032

8.32 A particular reaction has an equilibrium constant of 1.13 under one set of conditions and an equilibrium constant of 1.72 under a different set of conditions. Which conditions would be more advantageous in an industrial process that sought to obtain the maximum amount of products? Explain.

SECTION 8.7 How Long Does It Take for a Reaction to Reach Equilibrium?

8.33 If a reaction is very exothermic—that is, if the products have a much lower energy than the reactants—can we be reasonably certain that it will take place rapidly?

8.34 If a reaction is very endothermic—that is, if the products have a much higher energy than the reactants—can we be reasonably certain that it will take place extremely slowly or not at all?

8.35 A reaction has a high rate constant but a small equilibrium constant. What does this mean in terms of producing an industrial product?

SECTION 8.8 What is Le Chatelier's Principle?

8.36 Complete the following table showing the effects of changing reaction conditions on the equilibrium and value of the equilibrium constant, K.

Change in Condition	How the Reacting System Changes to Achieve a New Equilibrium	Does the Value of K Increase or Decrease?
Addition of a reactant	Shift to product formation	Neither
Removal of a reactant		
Addition of a product		
Removal of a product		
Increasing pressure		

8.37 ■ Assume that the following exothermic reaction is at equilibrium:

$$H_2(g) + I_2(g) \rightleftharpoons 2HI(g)$$

Tell whether the position of equilibrium will shift to the right or the left if we

(a) Remove some HI
(b) Add some I_2
(c) Remove some I_2
(d) Increase the temperature
(e) Add a catalyst

8.38 The following reaction is endothermic:

$$3O_2(g) \rightleftharpoons 2O_3(g)$$

If the reaction is at equilibrium, tell whether the equilibrium will shift to the right or the left if we

(a) Remove some O_3
(b) Remove some O_2
(c) Add some O_3
(d) Decrease the temperature
(e) Add a catalyst
(f) Increase the pressure

8.39 The following reaction is exothermic: After it reaches equilibrium, we add a few drops of Br_2.

$$2NO(g) + Br_2(g) \rightleftharpoons 2NOBr(g)$$

(a) What will happen to the equilibrium?
(b) What will happen to the equilibrium constant?

8.40 Is there any change in conditions that changes the equilibrium constant, K, of a given reaction?

8.41 ■ The equilibrium constant at 1127°C for the following endothermic reaction is 571:

$$2H_2S(g) \rightleftharpoons 2H_2(g) + S_2(g)$$

If the mixture is at equilibrium, what happens to K if we

(a) Add some H_2S?
(b) Add some H_2?
(c) Lower the temperature to 1000°C?

Chemical Connections

8.42 (Chemical Connections 8A) In a bacterial infection, body temperature may rise to 101°F. Does this body defense kill the bacteria directly by heat or by another mechanism? If so, by which mechanism?

8.43 (Chemical Connections 8A and 8B) Why is a high fever dangerous? Why is a low body temperature dangerous?

8.44 (Chemical Connections 8B) Why do surgeons sometimes lower body temperatures during heart operations?

8.45 (Chemical Connections 8C) A painkiller—for example, Tylenol—can be purchased in two forms, each containing the same amount of drug. One form is a solid coated pill, and the other is a capsule that contains tiny beads and has the same coat. Which medication will act faster? Explain.

8.46 (Chemical Connections 8D) What reaction takes place when sunlight hits the compound silver chloride?

8.47 (Chemical Connections 8E) If the equilibrium for the Haber process is unfavorable at high temperatures, why do factories nevertheless use high temperatures?

Additional Problems

8.48 In the reaction between H_2 and Cl_2 to give HCl, a 10°C increase in temperature doubles the rate of reaction. If the rate of reaction at 15°C is 2.8 moles of HCl per liter per second, what are the rates at −5°C and at 45°C?

8.49 Draw an energy diagram for an exothermic reaction that yields 75 kcal/mol. The activation energy is 30 kcal/mol.

8.50 Draw a diagram similar to Figure 8.4. Draw a second line of the energy profile starting and ending at the same level as the first but having a smaller peak than the first line. Label them 1 and 2. What may have occurred to change the energy profile of a reaction from 1 to 2?

8.51 ■ For the reaction

$$2NOBr(g) \rightleftharpoons 2NO(g) + Br_2(g)$$

the rate of the reaction was −2.3 mol NOBr/L/h when the initial NOBr concentration was 6.2 mol NOBr/L. What is the rate constant of the reaction?

8.52 The equilibrium constant for the following reaction is 25:

$$2NOBr(g) \rightleftharpoons 2NO(g) + Br_2(g)$$

A measurement made on the equilibrium mixture found that the concentrations of NO and Br_2 were each 0.80 M. What is the concentration of NOBr at equilibrium?

8.53 In the following reaction, the concentration of N_2O_4 in mol/L was measured at the end of the times shown. What is the rate of the reaction?

$$N_2O_4(g) \rightleftharpoons 2NO_2(g)$$

Time (s)	[N_2O_4]
0	0.200
10	0.180
20	0.160
30	0.140

8.54 How could you increase the rate of a gaseous reaction without adding more reactants or a catalyst and without changing the temperature?

8.55 In an endothermic reaction, the activation energy is 10.0 kcal/mol. Is the activation energy of the reverse reaction also 10.0 kcal/mol, or would it be more or less? Explain with the aid of a diagram.

8.56 Write the reaction to which the following equilibrium expression applies:

$$K = \frac{[NO_2]^4[H_2O]^6}{[NH_3]^4[O_2]^7}$$

8.57 The rate for the following reaction at 300 K was found to be 0.22 M NO_2/min. What would be the approximate rate at 320 K?

$$N_2O_4(g) \rightleftharpoons 2NO_2(g)$$

8.58 Assume that two different reactions are taking place at the same temperature. In reaction A, two different spherical molecules collide to yield a product. In reaction B, the shape of the colliding molecules is rodlike. Each reaction has the same number of collisions per second and the same activation energy. Which reaction goes faster?

8.59 Is it possible for an endothermic reaction to have zero activation energy?

8.60 In the following reaction, the rate of appearance of I_2 is measured at the times shown. What is the rate of the reaction?

$$2HI(g) \rightleftharpoons H_2(g) + I_2(g)$$

Time (s)	[I_2]
0	0
10	0.30
20	0.60
30	0.90

8.61 (Chemical Connections 8D) You have a recipe to manufacture sunglasses: 3.5 g AgCl/kg glass. A new order comes in to manufacture sunglasses to be used in deserts like the Sahara. How would you change the recipe?

8.62 A reaction occurs in three steps which the following rate constants:

$$A \xrightarrow[\text{Step 1}]{k_1=0.3\,M} B \xrightarrow[\text{Step 2}]{k_2=0.05\,M} C \xrightarrow[\text{Step 3}]{k_3=4.5\,M} D$$

(a) Which step is the rate-determining step?

(b) Which step has the lowest activation energy?

Looking Ahead

8.63 As we shall see in Chapter 18, the reaction of a carboxylic acid with an alcohol in the presence of an acid catalyst to form an ester and water is an equilibrium reaction. An example is the reaction of acetic acid with ethanol in the presence of HCl to form ethyl acetate and water.

Adding CH_3COOH

$$CH_3\overset{\displaystyle O}{\overset{\|}{C}}OH + HOCH_2CH_3 \underset{}{\overset{HCl}{\rightleftharpoons}} CH_3\overset{\displaystyle O}{\overset{\|}{C}}OCH_2CH_3 + H_2O$$

Acetic acid   Ethanol   Ethyl acetate

Equilibrium shifts to formation of more products

	Initial	1.00 mol	1.00 mol	0 mol	0 mol
	At equilibrium	0.33 mol	——	——	——

(a) Given the stoichiometry of this reaction from inspection of the balanced equation, fill in the remaining three equilibrium concentrations.

(b) Calculate the equilibrium constant, K, for this reaction.

8.64 As we shall see in Chapter 25, there are two forms of glucose, designated alpha (α) and beta (β), which are in equilibrium in aqueous solution. The equilibrium constant for the reaction is 1.5 at 30°C.

$$\alpha\text{-D-glucose(aq)} \rightleftharpoons \beta\text{-D-glucose(aq)} \quad K = 1.5$$

(a) If you begin with a fresh 1.0 M solution of α-D-glucose in water, what will be its concentration when equilibrium is reached?

(b) Calculate the percentage of α-glucose and of β-glucose present at equilibrium in aqueous solution at 30°C.

Acids and Bases

Photo, Charles D. Winters; models, S. H. Young

Some foods and household products are very acidic while others are basic. From your prior experiences, can you tell which ones belong to which category?

GOB
Chemistry✦Now™

Look for this logo in the chapter and go to GOB ChemistryNow at **http://now.brookscole.com/gob8** or on the CD for tutorials, simulations, and problems.

9.1 | What Are Acids and Bases?

We frequently encounter acids and bases in our daily lives. Oranges, lemons, and vinegar are examples of acidic foods, and sulfuric acid is in our automobile batteries. As for bases, we take antacid tablets for heartburn and use household ammonia as a cleaning agent. What do these substances have in common? Why are acids and bases usually discussed together?

In 1884, a young Swedish chemist named Svante Arrhenius (1859–1927) answered the first question by proposing what was then a new definition of acids and bases. According to the Arrhenius definition, an **acid** is a substance that produces H_3O^+ ions in aqueous solution, and a **base** is a substance that produces OH^- ions in aqueous solution.

This definition of acid is a slight modification of the original Arrhenius definition, which stated that an acid produces hydrogen ions, H^+. Today we know that H^+ ions cannot exist in water. An H^+ ion is a bare proton, and a charge of $+1$ is too concentrated to exist on such a tiny particle (Section 4.2).

Hydronium ion The H_3O^+ ion

Therefore, an H^+ ion in water immediately combines with an H_2O molecule to give a **hydronium ion, H_3O^+.**

$$H^+(aq) + H_2O(\ell) \longrightarrow H_3O^+(aq)$$
Hydronium ion

Apart from this modification, the Arrhenius definitions of acid and base are still valid and useful today, as long as we are talking about aqueous solutions. Although we know that acidic aqueous solutions do not contain H^+ ions, we frequently use the terms "H^+" and "proton" when we really mean "H_3O^+." The three terms are generally used interchangeably.

When an acid dissolves in water, it reacts with the water to produce H_3O^+. For example, hydrogen chloride, HCl, in its pure state is a poisonous gas. When HCl dissolves in water, it reacts with a water molecule to give hydronium ion and chloride ion:

$$H_2O(\ell) + HCl(aq) \longrightarrow H_3O^+(aq) + Cl^-(aq)$$

Thus a bottle labeled aqueous "HCl" is actually not HCl at all, but rather an aqueous solution of H_3O^+ and Cl^- ions in water.

We can show the transfer of a proton from an acid to a base by using a curved arrow. First we write the Lewis structure of each reactant and product. Then we use curved arrows to show the change in position of electron pairs during the reaction. The tail of the curved arrow is located at the electron pair. The head of the curved arrow shows the new position of the electron pair.

In this equation, the curved arrow on the left shows that an unshared pair of electrons on oxygen forms a new covalent bond with hydrogen. The curved arrow on the right shows that the pair of electrons of the H—Cl bond is given entirely to chlorine to form a chloride ion. Thus, in the reaction of HCl with H_2O, a proton is transferred from HCl to H_2O and, in the process, an O—H bond forms and an H—Cl bond is broken.

With bases, the situation is slightly different. Many bases are metal hydroxides, such as KOH, NaOH, $Mg(OH)_2$, and $Ca(OH)_2$. When these ionic solids dissolve in water, their ions merely separate, and each ion is solvated by water molecules (Section 7.6A). For example,

$$NaOH(s) \xrightarrow{H_2O} Na^+(aq) + OH^-(aq)$$

Other bases are not hydroxides. Instead, they produce OH^- ions in water by reacting with water molecules. The most important example of this kind of base is ammonia, NH_3, a poisonous gas. When ammonia dissolves in water, it reacts with water to produce ammonium ions and hydroxide ions.

$$NH_3(aq) + H_2O(\ell) \rightleftharpoons NH_4^+(aq) + OH^-(aq)$$

As we will see in Section 9.2, ammonia is a weak base, and the position of the equilibrium for its reaction with water lies considerably toward the left. In a 1.0 M solution of NH_3 in water, for example, only about 4 molecules of

NH_3 out of every 1000 react with water to form NH_4^+ and OH^-. Thus, when ammonia is dissolved in water, it exists primarily as NH_3 molecules. Nevertheless, some OH^- ions are produced and, therefore, NH_3 is a base.

Bottles of NH_3 in water are sometimes labeled "ammonium hydroxide" or "NH_4OH," but this gives a false impression of what is really in the bottle. Most of the NH_3 molecules have not reacted with the water, so the bottle contains mostly NH_3 and H_2O and only a little NH_4^+ and OH^-.

We indicate how the reaction of ammonia with water takes place by using curved arrows to show the transfer of a proton from a water molecule to an ammonia molecule. Here, the curved arrow on the left shows that the unshared pair of electrons on nitrogen forms a new covalent bond with a hydrogen of a water molecule. At the same time as the new N—H bond forms, an O—H bond of a water molecule breaks and the pair of electrons forming the H—O bond moves entirely to oxygen, forming OH^-.

$$H-\overset{\overset{\displaystyle H}{|}}{\underset{\underset{\displaystyle H}{|}}{N}}\!:\,+\,H-\ddot{O}-H \longrightarrow H-\overset{\overset{\displaystyle H}{|}}{\underset{\underset{\displaystyle H}{|}}{\overset{+}{N}}}-H\;+\;\overset{-}{:}\ddot{O}-H$$

Thus ammonia produces an OH^- ion by taking H^+ from a water molecule and leaving OH^- behind.

GOB
Chemistry Now™
Click *Chemistry Interaction* to learn more about **Acid–Base Reactions**

9.2 | How Do We Define the Strength of Acids and Bases?

All acids are not equally strong. According to the Arrhenius definition, a **strong acid** is one that reacts completely or almost completely with water to form H_3O^+ ions. Table 9.1 gives the names and molecular formulas for six of the most common strong acids. They are strong acids because, when they dissolve in water, they dissociate completely to give H_3O^+ ions.

Weak acids produce a much smaller concentration of H_3O^+ ions. Acetic acid, for example, is a weak acid. In water it exists primarily as acetic acid molecules; only a few acetic acid molecules (4 out of every 1000) are converted to acetate ions.

$$CH_3COOH(aq) + H_2O(\ell) \rightleftharpoons CH_3COO^-(aq) + H_3O^+(aq)$$
Acetic acid   Acetate ion

There are four common **strong bases** (Table 9.1), all of which are metal hydroxides. They are strong bases because, when they dissolve in water,

Strong acid An acid that ionizes completely in aqueous solution

Weak acid An acid that is only partially ionized in aqueous solution

Strong base A base that ionizes completely in aqueous solution

Table 9.1   Strong Acids and Bases

Acid Formula	Name	Base Formula	Name
HCl	Hydrochloric acid	LiOH	Lithium hydroxide
HBr	Hydrobromic acid	NaOH	Sodium hydroxide
HI	Hydroiodic acid	KOH	Potassium hydroxide
HNO_3	Nitric acid	$Ba(OH)_2$	Barium hydroxide
H_2SO_4	Sulfuric acid		
$HClO_4$	Perchloric acid		

CHEMICAL CONNECTIONS 9A

Some Important Acids and Bases

STRONG ACIDS Sulfuric acid, H_2SO_4, is used in many industrial processes. In fact, sulfuric acid is one of the most widely produced single chemicals in the United States.

Hydrochloric acid, HCl, is an important acid in chemistry laboratories. Pure HCl is a gas, and the HCl in laboratories is an aqueous solution. HCl is the acid in the gastric fluid in your stomach, where it is secreted at a strength of about 5% w/v.

Nitric acid, HNO_3, is a strong oxidizing agent. A drop of it causes the skin to turn yellow because the acid reacts with skin proteins. A yellow color upon contact with nitric acid has long been a test for proteins.

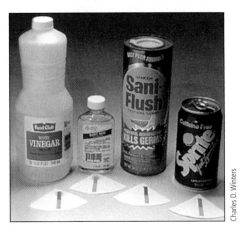

Weak acids are found in many common materials. In the foreground are strips of litmus paper that have been dipped into solutions of these materials. Acids turn litmus paper red.

Weak bases are also common in many household products. These cleaning agents all contain weak bases. Bases turn litmus paper blue.

WEAK ACIDS Acetic acid, CH_3COOH, is present in vinegar (about 5%). Pure acetic acid is called glacial acetic acid because of its melting point of 17°C, which means that it freezes on a moderately cold day.

Boric acid, H_3BO_3, is a solid. Solutions of boric acid in water were once used as antiseptics, especially for eyes. Boric acid is toxic when swallowed.

Phosphoric acid, H_3PO_4, is one of the strongest of the weak acids. The ions produced from it—$H_2PO_4^-$, HPO_4^{2-}, and PO_4^{3-}—are important in biochemistry (see also Section 27.3).

STRONG BASES Sodium hydroxide, NaOH, also called lye, is the most important of the strong bases. It is a solid whose aqueous

solutions are used in many industrial processes, including the manufacture of glass and soap. Potassium hydroxide, KOH, also a solid, is used for many of the same purposes as NaOH.

WEAK BASES Ammonia, NH_3, the most important weak base, is a gas with many industrial uses. One of its chief uses is for fertilizers. A 5% solution is sold in supermarkets as a cleaning agent, and weaker solutions are used as "spirits of ammonia" to revive people who have fainted.

Magnesium hydroxide, $Mg(OH)_2$, is a solid that is insoluble in water. A suspension of about 8% $Mg(OH)_2$ in water is called milk of magnesia and is used as a laxative. $Mg(OH)_2$ is also used to treat wastewater in metal-processing plants and as a flame retardant in plastics.

Weak base A base that is only partially ionized in aqueous solution

they ionize completely to give OH^- ions. Another base, $Mg(OH)_2$, dissociates almost completely once dissolved, but it is also very insoluble in water to begin with. As we saw in Section 9.1, ammonia is a **weak base** because the equilibrium for its reaction with water lies far to the left.

It is important to understand that the strength of an acid or a base is not related to its concentration. HCl is a strong acid, whether it is concentrated or dilute, because it dissociates completely in water to chloride ions and hydronium ions. Acetic acid is a weak acid, whether it is concentrated or dilute, because the equilibrium for its reaction with water lies far to the left. When acetic acid dissolves in water, most of it is present as undissociated CH_3COOH molecules.

$$HCl(aq) + H_2O(\ell) \longrightarrow Cl^-(aq) + H_3O^+(aq)$$

$$CH_3COOH(aq) + H_2O(\ell) \rightleftharpoons CH_3COO^-(aq) + H_3O^+(aq)$$

Acetic acid   Acetate ion

In Section 7.6C, we saw that electrolytes (substances that produce ions in aqueous solution) can be strong or weak. The strong acids and bases in Table 9.1 are strong electrolytes. Almost all other acids and bases are weak electrolytes.

9.3 | What Are Conjugate Acid–Base Pairs?

The Arrhenius definitions of acid and base are very useful in aqueous solutions. But what if water is not involved? In 1923, the Danish chemist Johannes Brønsted and the English chemist Thomas Lowry independently proposed the following definitions: An **acid** is a proton donor, a **base** is a proton acceptor, and an **acid–base reaction** is a proton transfer reaction. Furthermore, according to the Brønsted-Lowry definitions, any pair of molecules or ions that can be interconverted by transfer of a proton is called a **conjugate acid–base pair.** When an acid transfers a proton to a base, the acid is converted to its **conjugate base.** When a base accepts a proton, it is converted to its **conjugate acid.**

We can illustrate these relationships by examining the reaction between acetic acid and ammonia:

Conjugate acid–base pair

Conjugate acid–base pair

$$CH_3COOH + NH_3 \rightleftharpoons CH_3COO^- + NH_4^+$$

Acetic acid   Ammonia   Acetate   Ammonium
                          ion   ion

(Acid)   (Base)   (Conjugate   (Conjugate
                            base of   acid of
                          acetic acid)   ammonia)

> **Conjugate acid–base pair** A pair of molecules or ions that are related to one another by the gain or loss of a proton
>
> **Conjugate base** In the Brønsted-Lowry theory, a substance formed when an acid donates a proton to another molecule or ion
>
> **Conjugate acid** In the Brønsted-Lowry theory, a substance formed when a base accepts a proton

We can use curved arrows to show how this reaction takes place. The curved arrow on the right shows that the unshared pair of electrons on nitrogen becomes shared to form a new H—N bond. At the same time that the H—N bond forms, the O—H bond breaks and the electron pair of the O—H bond moves entirely to oxygen to form —O⁻ of the acetate ion. The result of these two electron-pair shifts is the transfer of a proton from an acetic acid molecule to an ammonia molecule:

Acetic acid   Ammonia   Acetate   Ammonium
(Proton donor)   (Proton acceptor)   ion   ion

A box of Arm & Hammer baking soda (sodium bicarbonate). Sodium bicarbonate is composed of Na^+ and HCO_3^-, the amphiprotic bicarbonate ion.

Table 9.2 gives examples of common acids and their conjugate bases. As you study the examples of conjugate acid–base pairs in Table 9.2, note the following points:

1. An acid can be positively charged, neutral, or negatively charged. Examples of these charge types are H_3O^+, H_2CO_3, and $H_2PO_4^-$, respectively.

2. A base can be negatively charged or neutral. Examples of these charge types are PO_4^{3-} and NH_3, respectively.

3. Acids are classified as monoprotic, diprotic, or triprotic depending on the number of protons each may give up. Examples of **monoprotic acids** include HCl, HNO_3, and CH_3COOH. Examples of **diprotic acids**

> **Monoprotic acid** An acid that can give up only one proton
>
> **Diprotic acid** An acid that can give up two protons

Table 9.2   Some Acids and Their Conjugate Bases

	Acid	Name	Conjugate Base	Name	
Strong Acids	HI	Hydroiodic acid	I^-	Iodide ion	Weak Bases
	HCl	Hydrochloric acid	Cl^-	Chloride ion	
	H_2SO_4	Sulfuric acid	HSO_4^-	Hydrogen sulfate ion	
	HNO_3	Nitric acid	NO_3^-	Nitrate ion	
	H_3O^+	Hydronium ion	H_2O	Water	
	HSO_4^-	Hydrogen sulfate ion	SO_4^{2-}	Sulfate ion	
	H_3PO_4	Phosphoric acid	$H_2PO_4^-$	Dihydrogen phosphate ion	
	CH_3COOH	Acetic acid	CH_3COO^-	Acetate ion	
	H_2CO_3	Carbonic acid	HCO_3^-	Bicarbonate ion	
	H_2S	Hydrogen sulfide	HS^-	Hydrogen sulfide ion	
	$H_2PO_4^-$	Dihydrogen phosphate ion	HPO_4^{2-}	Hydrogen phosphate ion	
	NH_4^+	Ammonium ion	NH_3	Ammonia	
	HCN	Hydrocyanic acid	CN^-	Cyanide ion	
	C_6H_5OH	Phenol	$C_6H_5O^-$	Phenoxide ion	
	HCO_3^-	Bicarbonate ion	CO_3^{2-}	Carbonate ion	
	HPO_4^{2-}	Hydrogen phosphate ion	PO_4^{3-}	Phosphate ion	Strong Bases
Weak Acids	H_2O	Water	OH^-	Hydroxide ion	
	C_2H_5OH	Ethanol	$C_2H_5O^-$	Ethoxide ion	

Triprotic acid An acid that can give up three protons

include H_2SO_4 and H_2CO_3. An example of a **triprotic acid** is H_3PO_4. Carbonic acid, for example, loses one proton to become bicarbonate ion, and then a second proton to become carbonate ion.

$$H_2CO_3 + H_2O \rightleftharpoons HCO_3^- + H_3O^+$$

Carbonic acid   Bicarbonate ion

$$HCO_3^- + H_2O \rightleftharpoons CO_3^{2-} + H_3O^+$$

Bicarbonate ion   Carbonate ion

4. Several molecules and ions appear in both the acid and conjugate base columns; that is, each can function as either an acid or a base. The bicarbonate ion, HCO_3^-, for example, can give up a proton to become CO_3^{2-} (in which case it is an acid) or it can accept a proton to become H_2CO_3 (in which case it is a base). A substance that can act as either an acid or a base is called **amphiprotic.** The most important amphiprotic substance in Table 9.2 is water, which can accept a proton to become H_3O^+ or lose a proton to become OH^-.

Amphiprotic A substance that can act as either an acid or a base

5. A substance cannot be a Brønsted-Lowry acid unless it contains a hydrogen atom, but not all hydrogen atoms can be given up. For example, acetic acid, CH_3COOH, has four hydrogens but is monoprotic; it gives up only one of them. Similarly, phenol, C_6H_5OH, gives up only one of its six hydrogens:

$$C_6H_5OH + H_2O \rightleftharpoons C_6H_5O^- + H_3O^+$$

Phenol   Phenoxide ion

This is because a hydrogen must be bonded to a strongly electronegative atom, such as oxygen or a halogen, to be acidic.

6. There is an inverse relationship between the strength of an acid and the strength of its conjugate base: The stronger the acid, the weaker its conjugate base. HI, for example, is the strongest acid listed in Table 9.2 and I^-, its conjugate base, is the weakest base. As another example, CH_3COOH (acetic acid) is a stronger acid than H_2CO_3 (carbonic acid); conversely, CH_3COO^- (acetate ion) is a weaker base than HCO_3^- (bicarbonate ion).

EXAMPLE 9.1

Show how the amphiprotic ion hydrogen sulfate, HSO_4^-, can react as both an acid and a base.

Solution
Hydrogen sulfate reacts like an acid in the equation shown below:

$$HSO_4^- + H_2O \rightleftharpoons H_3O^+ + SO_4^{2-}$$

It can react like a base in the equation shown below:

$$HSO_4^- + H_3O^+ \rightleftharpoons H_2O + H_2SO_4$$

Problem 9.1
Draw the acid and base reactions for the amphiprotic ion, HPO_4^{2-}.

GOB
Chemistry⚛Now™
Click *Chemistry Interactive* to learn more about **Acid–Base Conjugate Pairs**

9.4 | How Can We Tell the Position of Equilibrium in an Acid–Base Reaction?

We know that HCl reacts with H_2O according to the following equilibrium:

$$HCl + H_2O \rightleftharpoons Cl^- + H_3O^+$$

We also know that HCl is a strong acid, which means the position of this equilibrium lies very far to the right. In fact, this equilibrium lies so far to the right that out of every 10,000 HCl molecules dissolved in water, all but one react with water molecules to give Cl^- and H_3O^+.

For this reason, we usually write the acid reaction of HCl with a unidirectional arrow, as follows:

$$HCl + H_2O \longrightarrow Cl^- + H_3O^+$$

As we have also seen, acetic acid reacts with H_2O according to the following equilibrium:

$$\underset{\text{Acetic acid}}{CH_3COOH} + H_2O \rightleftharpoons \underset{\text{Acetate ion}}{CH_3COO^-} + H_3O^+$$

Acetic acid is a weak acid. Only a few acetic acid molecules react with water to give acetate ions and hydronium ions, and the major species present in equilibrium in aqueous solution is CH_3COOH and H_2O. The position of this equilibrium, therefore, lies very far to the left.

In these two acid–base reactions, water is the base. But what if we have a base other than water as the proton acceptor? How can we determine which are the major species present at equilibrium? That is, how can we determine if the position of equilibrium lies toward the left or toward the right?

As an example, let us examine the acid–base reaction between acetic acid and ammonia to form acetate ion and ammonium ion. As indicated by the question mark over the equilibrium arrow, we want to determine whether the position of this equilibrium lies toward the left or toward the right.

$$CH_3COOH + NH_3 \underset{}{\overset{?}{\rightleftharpoons}} CH_3COO^- + NH_4^+$$

| Acetic acid | Ammonia | Acetate ion | Ammonium ion |
| (Acid) | (Base) | (Conjugate base of CH_3COOH) | (Conjugate acid of NH_3) |

In this equilibrium there are two acids present: acetic acid and ammonium ion. There are also two bases present: ammonia and acetate ion. One way to analyze this equilibrium is to view it as a competition of the two bases, ammonia and acetate ion, for a proton. Which is the stronger base? The information we need to answer this question is found in Table 9.2. We first determine which conjugate acid is the stronger acid and then use this information along with the fact that the stronger the acid, the weaker its conjugate base. From Table 9.2, we see that CH_3COOH is the stronger acid, which means that CH_3COO^- is the weaker base. Conversely, NH_4^+ is the weaker acid, which means that NH_3 is the stronger base. We can now label the relative strengths of each acid and base in this equilibrium:

$$CH_3COOH + NH_3 \underset{}{\overset{?}{\rightleftharpoons}} CH_3COO^- + NH_4^+$$

| Acetic acid | Ammonia | Acetate ion | Ammonium ion |
| (Stronger acid) | (Stronger base) | (Weaker base) | (Weaker acid) |

In an acid–base reaction, the equilibrium position always favors reaction of the stronger acid and stronger base to form the weaker acid and

CHEMICAL CONNECTIONS 9B

Acid and Base Burns of the Cornea

The cornea is the outermost part of the eye. This transparent tissue is very sensitive to chemical burns, whether caused by acids or by bases. Acids and bases in small amounts and in low concentrations that would not seriously damage other tissues, such as skin, may cause severe corneal burns. If not treated promptly, these burns can lead to permanent loss of vision.

For acid splashed in the eyes, immediately wash the eyes with a steady stream of cold water. Quickly removing the acid is of utmost importance. Time should not be wasted looking for a solution of some mild base to neutralize it because removing the acid is more helpful than neutralizing it. The extent of the burn can be assessed after all the acid has been washed out.

Concentrated ammonia or sodium hydroxide of the "liquid plumber" type can also cause severe damage when splattered in the eyes. Again, immediately washing the eyes is of utmost importance; however, burns by bases can later develop ulcerations in which the healing wound deposits scar tissue that is not transparent, thereby impairing vision. For this reason, first aid is not sufficient for burns by bases, and a physician should be consulted immediately.

Charles D. Winters

Cleaning products like these contain bases. Care must be taken to make sure that they are not splashed into anyone's eyes.

Fortunately, the cornea is a tissue with no blood vessels and, therefore, can be transplanted without immunological rejection problems. Today, corneal grafts are common.

weaker base. Thus, at equilibrium, the major species present are the weaker acid and the weaker base. In the reaction between acetic acid and ammonia, therefore, the equilibrium lies to the right and the major species present are acetate ion and ammonium ion:

$$\text{CH}_3\text{COOH} \quad + \quad \text{NH}_3 \quad \rightleftharpoons \quad \text{CH}_3\text{COO}^- \quad + \quad \text{NH}_4^+$$

Acetic acid	Ammonia	Acetate ion	Ammonium ion
(Stronger acid)	(Stronger base)	(Weaker base)	(Weaker acid)

To summarize, we use the following four steps to determine the position of an acid–base equilibrium:

1. Identify the two acids in the equilibrium; one is on the left side of the equilibrium, and the other on the right side.
2. Using the information in Table 9.2, determine which acid is the stronger acid and which acid is the weaker acid.
3. Identify the stronger base and the weaker base. Remember that the stronger acid gives the weaker conjugate base and the weaker acid gives the stronger conjugate base.
4. The stronger acid and stronger base react to give the weaker acid and weaker base. The position of equilibrium, therefore, lies on the side of the weaker acid and weaker base.

EXAMPLE 9.2

For each acid–base equilibrium, label the stronger acid, the stronger base, the weaker acid, and the weaker base. Then predict whether the position of equilibrium lies toward the right or toward the left.

(a) $\text{H}_2\text{CO}_3 + \text{OH}^- \rightleftharpoons \text{HCO}_3^- + \text{H}_2\text{O}$

(b) $\text{HPO}_4^{2-} + \text{NH}_3 \rightleftharpoons \text{PO}_4^{3-} + \text{NH}_4^+$

Solution

Arrows connect the conjugate acid–base pairs, with the red arrows showing the stronger acid. The position of equilibrium in (a) lies toward the right. In (b) it lies toward the left.

(a) $\text{H}_2\text{CO}_3 + \text{OH}^- \rightleftharpoons \text{HCO}_3^- + \text{H}_2\text{O}$

Stronger acid	Stronger base	Weaker base	Weaker acid

(b) $\text{HPO}_4^{2-} + \text{NH}_3 \rightleftharpoons \text{PO}_4^{3-} + \text{NH}_4^+$

Weaker acid	Weaker base	Stronger base	Stronger acid

Problem 9.2

For each acid–base equilibrium, label the stronger acid, the stronger base, the weaker acid, and the weaker base. Then predict whether the position of equilibrium lies toward the right or the left.

(a) $\text{H}_3\text{O}^+ + \text{I}^- \rightleftharpoons \text{H}_2\text{O} + \text{HI}$

(b) $\text{CH}_3\text{COO}^- + \text{H}_2\text{S} \rightleftharpoons \text{CH}_3\text{COOH} + \text{HS}^-$

9.5 | How Do We Use Acid Ionization Constants?

In Section 9.2, we learned that acids vary in the extent to which they produce H_3O^+ when added to water. Because the ionizations of weak acids in water are all equilibria, we can use equilibrium constants (Section 8.6) to tell us quantitatively just how strong any weak acid is. The reaction that takes place when a weak acid, HA, is added to water is

$$HA + H_2O \rightleftharpoons A^- + H_3O^+$$

The equilibrium constant expression for this ionization is

$$K = \frac{[A^-][H_3O^+]}{[HA][H_2O]}$$

Notice that this expression contains the concentration of water. Because water is the solvent and its concentration changes very little when we add HA to it, we can treat the concentration of water, $[H_2O]$, as a constant equal to 1000 g/L or approximately 55.5 mol/L. We can then combine these two constants (K and $[H_2O]$) to define a new constant called an **acid ionization constant, K_a.**

Acid ionization constant (K_a)
An equilibrium constant for the ionization of an acid in aqueous solution to H_3O^+ and its conjugate base; also called an acid dissociation constant

$$K_a = K[H_2O] = \frac{[A^-][H_3O^+]}{[HA]}$$

The value of the acid ionization constant for acetic acid, for example, is 1.8×10^{-5}. Because acid ionization constants for weak acids are numbers with negative exponents, we often use an algebraic trick to turn them into numbers that are easier to use. To do so, we take the negative logarithm of the number. Acid strengths are therefore expressed as $-\log K_a$, which we call the pK_a. The "p" of anything is just the negative logarithm of that thing. The pK_a of acetic acid is 4.75. Table 9.3 gives names, molecular formulas, and values of K_a and pK_a for some weak acids. As you study the entries in this table, note the inverse relationship between the values of K_a and pK_a. The weaker the acid, the smaller its K_a, but the larger its pK_a.

pK_a is $-\log K_a$

One reason for the importance of K_a is that it immediately tells us how strong an acid is. For example, Table 9.3 shows us that although acetic acid, formic acid, and phenol are all weak acids, their strengths as acids are not

Table 9.3 K_a and pK_a Values for Some Weak Acids

Formula	Name	K_a	pK_a
H_3PO_4	Phosphoric acid	7.5×10^{-3}	2.12
HCOOH	Formic acid	1.8×10^{-4}	3.75
$CH_3CH(OH)COOH$	Lactic acid	1.4×10^{-4}	3.86
CH_3COOH	Acetic acid	1.8×10^{-5}	4.75
H_2CO_3	Carbonic acid	4.3×10^{-7}	6.37
$H_2PO_4^-$	Dihydrogen phosphate ion	6.2×10^{-8}	7.21
H_3BO_3	Boric acid	7.3×10^{-10}	9.14
NH_4^+	Ammonium ion	5.6×10^{-10}	9.25
HCN	Hydrocyanic acid	4.9×10^{-10}	9.31
C_6H_5OH	Phenol	1.3×10^{-10}	9.89
HCO_3^-	Bicarbonate ion	5.6×10^{-11}	10.25
HPO_4^{2-}	Hydrogen phosphate ion	2.2×10^{-13}	12.66

Increasing acid strength

the same. Formic acid, with a K_a of 1.8×10^{-4}, is stronger than acetic acid, whereas phenol, with a K_a of 1.3×10^{-10}, is much weaker than acetic acid. Phosphoric acid is the strongest of the weak acids. We can tell that an acid is classified as a weak acid by the fact that we list a pK_a for it, and the pK_a is a positive number. If we tried to take the negative logarithm of the K_a for a strong acid, we would get a negative number.

EXAMPLE 9.3

K_a for benzoic acid is 6.5×10^{-5}. What is the pK_a of this acid?

Solution
Take the logarithm of 6.5×10^{-5} on your scientific calculator. The answer is -4.19. Because pK_a is equal to $-\log K_a$, you must multiply this value by -1 to get pK_a. The pK_a of benzoic acid is 4.19.

Problem 9.3
K_a for hydrocyanic acid, HCN, is 4.9×10^{-10}. What is its pK_a?

EXAMPLE 9.4

Which is the stronger acid:
(a) Benzoic acid with a K_a of 6.5×10^{-5} or hydrocyanic acid with a K_a of 4.9×10^{-10}?
(b) Boric acid with a pK_a of 9.14 or carbonic acid with a pK_a of 6.37?

Solution
(a) Benzoic acid is the stronger acid, it has the larger K_a value.
(b) Carbonic acid is the stronger acid; it has the smaller pK_a value.

Problem 9.4
Which is the stronger acid:
(a) Carbonic acid, $pK_a = 6.37$, or ascorbic acid (vitamin C), $pK_a = 4.1$?
(b) Aspirin, $pK_a = 3.49$, or acetic acid, $pK_a = 4.75$?

All of these fruits and fruit drinks contain organic acids.

9.6 | What Are the Properties of Acids and Bases?

Today's chemists do not taste the substances they work with, but 200 years ago they routinely did so. That is how we know that acids taste sour and bases taste bitter. The sour taste of lemons, vinegar, and many other foods, for example, is due to the acids they contain.

A. Neutralization

The most important reaction of acids and bases is that they react with each other in a process called neutralization. This name is appropriate because, when a strong corrosive acid such as hydrochloric acid reacts with a strong corrosive base such as sodium hydroxide, the product (a solution of ordinary table salt in water) has neither acidic nor basic properties. We call such a solution neutral. Section 9.9 discusses neutralization reactions in detail.

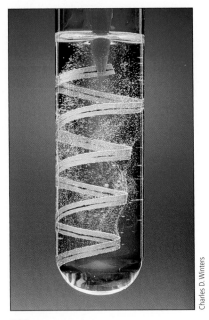

Charles D. Winters

GOB
Chemistry⚛Now™
Active Figure 9.1 A ribbon of
magnesium metal reacts with
aqueous HCl to give H₂ gas
and aqueous MgCl₂. **See a
simulation based on this
figure, and take a short quiz
on the concepts at http://
www.now.brookscole.com/
gob8 or on the CD.**

B. Reaction with Metals

Strong acids react with certain metals (called active metals) to produce hydrogen gas, H_2, and a salt. Hydrochloric acid, for example, reacts with magnesium metal to give the salt magnesium chloride and hydrogen gas (Figure 9.1).

$$Mg(s) + 2HCl(aq) \longrightarrow MgCl_2(aq) + H_2(g)$$

Magnesium   Hydrochloric   Magnesium   Hydrogen
acid   chloride

The reaction of an acid with an active metal to give a salt and hydrogen gas is a redox reaction (Section 5.7). The metal is oxidized to a metal ion and H^+ is reduced to H_2.

C. Reaction with Metal Hydroxides

Acids react with metal hydroxides to give a salt and water.

$$HCl(aq) + KOH(aq) \longrightarrow H_2O(\ell) + KCl(aq)$$

Hydrochloric   Potassium   Water   Potassium
acid   hydroxide   chloride

Both the acid and the metal hydroxide are ionized in aqueous solution. Furthermore, the salt formed is an ionic compound that is present in aqueous solution as anions and cations. Therefore, the actual equation for the reaction of HCl and KOH could be written showing all of the ions present (Section 5.6):

$$H_3O^+(aq) + Cl^-(aq) + K^+(aq) + OH^-(aq) \longrightarrow 2H_2O(\ell) + Cl^-(aq) + K^+(aq)$$

We usually simplify this equation by omitting the spectator ions (Section 5.6), which gives the following equation for the net ionic reaction of any strong acid and strong base to give a salt and water:

$$H_3O^+(aq) + OH^-(aq) \longrightarrow 2H_2O(\ell)$$

D. Reaction with Metal Oxides

Strong acids react with metal oxides to give water and a salt, as shown in the following net ionic equation:

$$2H_3O^+(aq) + CaO(s) \longrightarrow 3H_2O(\ell) + Ca^{2+}(aq)$$

Calcium
oxide

E. Reaction with Carbonates and Bicarbonates

When a strong acid is added to a carbonate such as sodium carbonate, bubbles of carbon dioxide gas are rapidly given off. The overall reaction is a summation of two reactions. In the first reaction, carbonate ion reacts with H_3O^+ to give carbonic acid. Almost immediately, in the second reaction, carbonic acid decomposes to carbon dioxide and water. The following equations show the individual reactions and then the overall reaction:

$$2H_3O^+(aq) + CO_3^{2-}(aq) \longrightarrow H_2CO_3(aq) + 2H_2O(\ell)$$
$$H_2CO_3(aq) \longrightarrow CO_2(g) + H_2O(\ell)$$

$$2H_3O^+(aq) + CO_3^{2-}(aq) \longrightarrow CO_2(g) + 3H_2O(\ell)$$

CHEMICAL CONNECTIONS 9C

Drugstore Antacids

Stomach fluid is normally quite acidic because of its HCl content. At some time, you probably have gotten "heartburn" caused by excess stomach acidity. To relieve your discomfort, you may have taken an antacid, which, as the name implies, is a substance that neutralizes acids—in other words, a base.

The word "antacid" is a medical term, not one used by chemists. It is, however, found on the labels of many medications available in drugstores and supermarkets. Almost all of them use bases such as $CaCO_3$, $Mg(OH)_2$, $Al(OH)_3$, and $NaHCO_3$ to decrease the acidity of the stomach.

Also in drugstores and supermarkets are nonprescription drugs labeled "acid reducers." Among these brands are Zantac, Tagamet, Pepcid, and Axid. Instead of neutralizing acidity, these compounds reduce the secretion of acid into the stomach. In larger doses (sold only with a prescription), some of these drugs are used in the treatment of stomach ulcers.

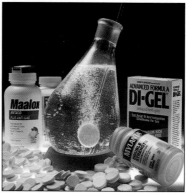

Commercial remedies for excess stomach acid.

Strong acids also react with bicarbonates such as potassium bicarbonate to give carbon dioxide and water:

$$H_3O^+(aq) + HCO_3^-(aq) \longrightarrow H_2CO_3(aq) + H_2O(\ell)$$
$$\underline{H_2CO_3(aq) \longrightarrow CO_2(g) + H_2O(\ell)}$$
$$H_3O^+(aq) + HCO_3^-(aq) \longrightarrow CO_2(g) + 2H_2O(\ell)$$

To generalize, any acid stronger than carbonic acid will react with carbonate or bicarbonate ion to give CO_2 gas.

The production of CO_2 is what makes bread doughs and cake batters rise. The earliest method used to generate CO_2 for this purpose involved the addition of yeast, which catalyzes the fermentation of carbohydrates to produce carbon dioxide and ethanol (Chapter 28):

$$C_6H_{12}O_6 \xrightarrow{\text{Yeast}} 2CO_2 + 2C_2H_5OH$$
$$\text{Glucose} \qquad\qquad \text{Ethanol}$$

The production of CO_2 by fermentation, however, is slow. Sometimes it is desirable to have its production take place more rapidly, in which case bakers use the reaction of $NaHCO_3$ (sodium bicarbonate, also called **baking soda**) and a weak acid. But which weak acid? Vinegar (a 5% solution of acetic acid in water) would work, but it has a potential disadvantage—it imparts a particular flavor to foods. For a weak acid that imparts little or no flavor, bakers use either sodium dihydrogen phosphate, NaH_2PO_4, or potassium dihydrogen phosphate, KH_2PO_4. The two salts do not react when they are dry but, when mixed with water in a dough or batter, they react quite rapidly to produce CO_2. The production of CO_2 is even more rapid in an oven!

$$H_2PO_4^-(aq) + H_2O(\ell) \rightleftharpoons HPO_4^{2-}(aq) + H_3O^+(aq)$$
$$\underline{HCO_3^-(aq) + H_3O^+(aq) \longrightarrow CO_2(g) + 2H_2O(\ell)}$$
$$H_2PO_4^-(aq) + HCO_3^-(aq) \longrightarrow HPO_4^{2-}(aq) + CO_2(g) + H_2O(\ell)$$

Baking powder contains a weak acid, either sodium or potassium dihydrogen phosphate, and sodium or potassium bicarbonate. When they are mixed with water, they react to produce the bubbles of CO_2 seen in this picture.

F. Reaction with Ammonia and Amines

Any acid stronger than NH_4^+ (Table 9.2) is strong enough to react with NH_3 to form a salt. In the following reaction, the salt formed is ammonium chloride, NH_4Cl, which is shown as it would be ionized in aqueous solution:

$$HCl(aq) + NH_3(aq) \longrightarrow NH_4^+(aq) + Cl^-(aq)$$

In Chapter 16 we will meet a family of compounds called amines, which are similar to ammonia except that one or more of the three hydrogen atoms of ammonia are replaced by carbon groups. A typical amine is methylamine, CH_3NH_2. The base strength of most amines is similar to that of NH_3, which means that amines also react with acids to form salts. The salt formed in the reaction of methylamine with HCl is methylammonium chloride, shown here as it would be ionized in aqueous solution:

$$\underset{\text{Methylamine}}{HCl(aq) + CH_3NH_2(aq)} \longrightarrow \underset{\substack{\text{Methylammonium} \\ \text{ion}}}{CH_3NH_3^+(aq)} + Cl^-(aq)$$

The reaction of ammonia and amines with acids to form salts is very important in the chemistry of the body, as we will see in later chapters.

9.7 | What Are the Acidic and Basic Properties of Pure Water?

We have seen that an acid produces H_3O^+ ions in water and that a base produces OH^- ions. Suppose that we have absolutely pure water, with no added acid or base. Surprisingly enough, even pure water contains a very small number of H_3O^+ and OH^- ions. They are formed by the transfer of a proton from one molecule of water (the proton donor) to another (the proton acceptor).

$$\underset{\text{Acid}}{H_2O} + \underset{\text{Base}}{H_2O} \rightleftharpoons \underset{\substack{\text{Conjugate} \\ \text{base of } H_2O}}{OH^-} + \underset{\substack{\text{Conjugate} \\ \text{acid of } H_2O}}{H_3O^+}$$

What is the extent of this reaction? We know from the information in Table 9.2 that, in this equilibrium, H_3O^+ is the stronger acid and OH^- is the stronger base. Therefore, as shown by the arrows, the equilibrium for this reaction lies far to the left. We shall soon see exactly how far, but first let us write the equilibrium expression:

$$K = \frac{[H_3O^+][OH^-]}{[H_2O]^2}$$

Because the degree of self-ionization of water is so slight, we can treat the concentration of water, $[H_2O]$, as a constant equal to 1000 g/L or approximately 55.5 mol/L, just as we did in Section 9.5 in developing K_a for a weak acid. We can then combine these two constants (K and $[H_2O]^2$) to define a new constant called the **ion product of water**, K_w. In pure water at room temperature, K_w has a value of 1.0×10^{-14}.

$$K_w = K[H_2O]^2 = [H_3O^+][OH^-]$$

$$K_w = 1.0 \times 10^{-14}$$

K_w is the ion product of water, also called the water constant, and is equal to 1×10^{-14}.

In pure water, H_3O^+ and OH^- form in equal amounts (see the balanced equation for the self-ionization of water), so their concentrations must be equal. That is, in pure water,

$$\left.\begin{array}{l} [H_3O^+] = 1.0 \times 10^{-7} \text{ mol/L} \\ [OH^-] = 1.0 \times 10^{-7} \text{ mol/L} \end{array}\right\} \text{ In pure water}$$

These are very small concentrations, not enough to make pure water a conductor of electricity. Pure water is not an electrolyte (Section 7.6C).

The equation for the ionization of water is important because it applies not only to pure water but also to any water solution. The product of $[H_3O^+]$ and $[OH^-]$ in any aqueous solution is equal to 1.0×10^{-14}. If, for example, we add 0.010 mol of HCl to 1 L of pure water, it reacts completely to give H_3O^+ ions and Cl^- ions. The concentration of H_3O^+ will be 0.010 M, or 1.0×10^{-2} M. This means that $[OH^-]$ must be $1.0 \times 10^{-14}/1.0 \times 10^{-2} = 1.0 \times 10^{-12}$ M.

EXAMPLE 9.5

The $[OH^-]$ of an aqueous solution is 1.0×10^{-4} M. What is its $[H_3O^+]$?

Solution
We substitute into the equation:

$$[H_3O^+][OH^-] = 1.0 \times 10^{-14}$$

$$[H_3O^+] = \frac{1.0 \times 10^{-14}}{1.0 \times 10^{-4}} = 1.0 \times 10^{-10} \text{ } M$$

Problem 9.5
The $[OH^-]$ of an aqueous solution is 1.0×10^{-12} M. What is its $[H_3O^+]$?

Aqueous solutions can have a very high $[H_3O^+]$ but the $[OH^-]$ must then be very low, and vice versa. Any solution with a $[H_3O^+]$ greater than 1.0×10^{-7} M is acidic. In such solutions, of necessity $[OH^-]$ must be less than 1.0×10^{-7} M. The higher the $[H_3O^+]$, the more acidic the solution. Similarly, any solution with an $[OH^-]$ greater than 1.0×10^{-7} M is basic. Pure water, in which $[H_3O^+]$ and $[OH^-]$ are equal (they are both 1.0×10^{-7} M), is neutral—that is, neither acidic nor basic.

GOB
Chemistry••Now™

Click *Chemistry Interactive* to learn more about the **Self-Ionization of Water**

HOW TO ...

Use Logs and Antilogs

When dealing with acids, bases, and buffers, we often have to use common or base 10 logarithms (logs). To most people, a logarithm is just a button they push on a calculator. Here we describe briefly how to handle logs and antilogs.

1. What is a logarithm and how is it calculated?
A common logarithm is the power to which you raise 10 to get another number. For example, the log of 100 is 2, since you must raise 10 to the second power to get 100.

$$\log 100 = 2 \quad \text{since} \quad 10^2 = 100$$

Other examples are

$$\log 1000 = 3 \quad \text{since} \quad 10^3 = 1000$$
$$\log 10 = 1 \quad \text{since} \quad 10^1 = 10$$
$$\log 1 = 0 \quad \text{since} \quad 10^0 = 0$$
$$\log 0.1 = -1 \quad \text{since} \quad 10^{-1} = 0.1$$

The common logarithm of a number other than a simple power is usually obtained from a calculator by entering the number and then pressing log. For example,

$$\log 52 = 1.72$$
$$\log 4.5 = 0.653$$
$$\log 0.25 = -0.602$$

Try it now. Enter 100 and then press log. Did you get 2? If so you did it right. Try again with 52. Enter 52 and press log. Did you get 1.72 (rounded to two decimal places)?

2. What are antilogarithms (antilogs)?
An antilog is the reverse of a log. It is also called the inverse log. If you take 10 and raise it to a power, you are taking an antilog. For example,

$$\text{antilog } 5 = 100,000$$

because taking the antilog of 5 means raising 10 to the power of 5 or

$$10^5 = 100,000$$

Try it now on your calculator. What is the antilog of 3? Enter 3 on your calculator. Press INV (inverse) or 2ndF (second function), and then press log. The answer should be 1000.

3. What is the Difference between antilog and −log?
There is a huge and very important difference. Antilog 3 means that we take 10 and raise it to the power of 3, so we get 1000. In contrast, −log 3 means that we take the log of 3, which equals 0.477, and take the negative of it. Thus −log 3 equals −0.48. For example,

$$\text{antilog } 2 = 100$$
$$-\log 2 = -0.30$$

In Section 9.8, we will use negative logs to calculate pH. The pH equals −log [H⁺]. Thus, if we know that [H⁺] is 0.01 *M,* to find the pH we enter 0.01 into our calculator and press log. That gives an answer of −2. Then we take the negative of that value to give a pH of 2.

In the last example, what answer would we have gotten if we had taken the antilog instead of the negative log? We would have gotten what we started with: 0.01. Why? Because all we calculated was antilog log 0.01. If we take the antilog of the log, we have not done anything at all.

9.8 | What Are pH and pOH?

Because hydronium ion concentrations for most solutions are numbers with negative exponents, these concentrations are more conveniently expressed as pH, where

$$pH = -\log [H_3O^+]$$

similarly to how we expressed pK_a values in Section 9.5.

In Section 9.7, we saw that a solution is acidic if its $[H_3O^+]$ is greater than 1.0×10^{-7}, and that it is basic if its $[H_3O^+]$ is less than 1.0×10^{-7}. We can now state the definitions of acidic and basic solutions in terms of pH.

A solution is acidic if its pH is less than 7.0
A solution is basic if its pH is greater than 7.0
A solution is neutral if its pH is equal to 7.0

The pH of this soft drink is 3.12. Soft drinks are often quite acidic.

Charles D. Winters

EXAMPLE 9.6

(a) The $[H_3O^+]$ of a certain liquid detergent is 1.4×10^{-9} M. What is its pH? Is this solution acidic, basic, or neutral?
(b) The pH of black coffee is 5.3. What is its $[H_3O^+]$? Is it acidic, basic, or neutral?

Solution

(a) On your calculator, take the log of 1.4×10^{-9}. The answer is -8.85. Multiply this value by -1 to give the pH of 8.85. This solution is basic.
(b) Enter 5.3 into your calculator and then press the +/- key to change the sign to minus and give -5.3. Then take the antilog of this number. The $[H_3O^+]$ of black coffee is 5×10^{-6}. This solution is acidic.

Problem 9.6

(a) The $[H_3O^+]$ of an acidic solution is 3.5×10^{-3} M. What is its pH?
(b) The pH of tomato juice is 4.1. What is its $[H_3O^+]$? Is this solution acidic, basic, or neutral?

Just as pH is a convenient way to designate the concentration of H_3O^+, pOH is a convenient way to designate the concentration of OH^-.

$$pOH = -\log [OH^-]$$

As we saw in the previous section, in aqueous solutions, the ion product of water, K_w, is 1×10^{-14}, which is equal to the product of the concentration of H^+ and OH^-:

$$K_w = 1 \times 10^{-14} = [H^+][OH^-]$$

By taking the logarithm of both sides, and the fact that $-\log(1 \times 10^{-14}) = 14$, we can rewrite this equation as shown below:

$$14 = pH + pOH$$

Thus, once we know the pH of a solution, we can easily calculate the pOH.

EXAMPLE 9.7

The $[OH^-]$ of a strongly basic solution is 1.0×10^{-2}. What are the pOH and pH of this solution?

Solution
The pOH is $-\log 1.0 \times 10^{-2}$ or 2, and the pH is $14 - 2 = 12$.

Problem 9.7

The $[OH^-]$ of a solution is 1.0×10^{-4} M. What are the pOH and pH of this solution?

The pH of three household substances. The colors of the acid–base indicators in the flasks show that vinegar is more acidic than club soda, and the cleaner is basic.

All fluids in the human body are aqueous; that is, the only solvent present is water. Consequently, all body fluids have a pH value. Some of them have a narrow pH range; others have a wide pH range. The pH of blood, for example, must be between 7.35 and 7.45 (slightly basic). If it goes outside these limits, illness and even death may result (Chemical Connections 9D). In contrast, the pH of urine can vary from 5.5 to 7.5. Table 9.4 gives pH values for some common materials.

One thing you must remember when you see a pH value is that, because pH is a logarithmic scale, an increase (or decrease) of one pH unit means a tenfold decrease (or increase) in the $[H_3O^+]$. For example, a pH of 3 does not sound very different from a pH of 4. The first, however, means a $[H_3O^+]$ of 10^{-3} M, whereas the second means a $[H_3O^+]$ of 10^{-4} M. The $[H_3O^+]$ of the pH 3 solution is ten times the $[H_3O^+]$ of the pH 4 solution.

There are two ways to measure the pH of an aqueous solution. One way is to use pH paper, which is made by soaking plain paper with a mixture of pH indicators. A pH **indicator** is a substance that changes color at a certain pH. When we place a drop of solution on this paper, the paper turns a certain color. To determine the pH, we compare the color of the paper with the colors on a chart supplied with the paper.

Strips of paper impregnated with indicator are used to find an approximate pH.

Table 9.4 pH Values of Some Common Materials

Material	pH	Material	pH
Battery acid	0.5	Saliva	6.5–7.5
Gastric juice	1.0–3.0	Pure water	7.0
Lemon juice	2.2–2.4	Blood	7.35–7.45
Vinegar	2.4–3.4	Bile	6.8–7.0
Tomato juice	4.0–4.4	Pancreatic fluid	7.8–8.0
Carbonated beverages	4.0–5.0	Sea water	8.0–9.0
Black coffee	5.0–5.1	Soap	8.0–10.0
Urine	5.5–7.5	Milk of magnesia	10.5
Rain (unpolluted)	6.2	Household ammonia	11.7
Milk	6.3–6.6	Lye (1.0 M NaOH)	14.0

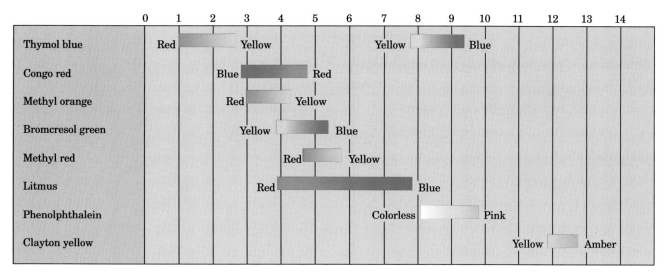

Figure 9.2 Some acid–base indicators. Note that some indicators have two color changes.

One example of an acid–base indicator is the compound methyl orange. When a drop of methyl orange is added to an aqueous solution with a pH of 3.2 or lower, this indicator turns red and the entire solution becomes red. When added to an aqueous solution with a pH of 4.4 or higher, this indicator turns yellow. These particular limits and colors apply only to methyl orange. Other indicators have other limits and colors (Figure 9.2)

The second way of determining pH is more accurate and more precise. In this method, we use a pH meter (Figure 9.3). We dip the electrode of the pH meter into the solution whose pH is to be measured, and then read the pH on a dial. The most commonly used pH meters read pH to the nearest hundredth of a unit. It should be mentioned that the accuracy of a pH meter, like that of any instrument, depends on correct calibration.

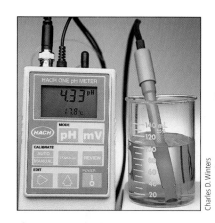

Figure 9.3 A pH meter can rapidly and accurately measure the pH of an aqueous solution.

Charles D. Winters

GOB
Chemistry Now™
Click *Coached Problems* to learn more about the **pH Scale**

9.9 | How Do We Use Titrations to Calculate Concentration?

Laboratories, whether medical, academic, or industrial, are frequently asked to determine the exact concentration of a particular substance in solution, such as the concentration of acetic acid in a given sample of vinegar, or the concentrations of iron, calcium, and magnesium ions in a sample of "hard" water. Determinations of solution concentrations can be made using an analytical technique called a **titration.**

In a titration, we react a known volume of a solution of known concentration with a known volume of a solution of unknown concentration. The solution of unknown concentration may contain an acid (such as stomach acid), a base (such as ammonia), an ion (such as Fe^{2+} ion), or any other substance whose concentration we are asked to determine. If we know the titration volumes and the mole ratio in which the solutes react, we can then calculate the concentration of the second solution.

Titrations must meet several requirements:

Titration An analytical procedure whereby we react a known volume of a solution of known concentration with a known volume of a solution of unknown concentration

1. We must know the equation for the reaction so that we can determine the stoichiometric ratio of reactants to use in our calculations.

2. The reaction must be rapid and complete.

Equivalence point The point at which there is an equal amount of acid and base in a neutralization reaction

3. When the reactants have combined exactly, there must be a clear-cut change in some measurable property of the reaction mixture. We call the point at which the reactants combine exactly the **equivalence point** of the titration.

4. We must have accurate measurements of the amount of each reactant.

Let us apply these requirements to the titration of a solution of sulfuric acid of known concentration with a solution of sodium hydroxide of unknown concentration. We know the balanced equation for this acid–base reaction, so requirement 1 is met.

$$2NaOH(aq) \ + \ H_2SO_4(aq) \ \longrightarrow \ Na_2SO_4(aq) + 2H_2O(\ell)$$

(Concentration not known)   (Concentration known)

Sodium hydroxide ionizes in water to form sodium ions and hydroxide ions; sulfuric acid ionizes to form hydronium ions and sulfate ions. The reaction between hydroxide and hydronium ions is rapid and complete, so requirement 2 is met.

To meet requirement 3, we must be able to observe a clear-cut change in some measurable property of the reaction mixture at the equivalence point. For acid–base titrations, we use the sudden pH change that occurs at this point. Suppose we add the sodium hydroxide solution slowly. As it is added, it reacts with hydronium ions to form water. As long as any unreacted hydronium ions are present, the solution is acidic. When the number of hydroxide ions added exactly equals the original number of hydronium ions, the solution becomes neutral. Then, as soon as any extra hydroxide ions are added, the solution becomes basic. We can observe this sudden change in pH by reading a pH meter.

Another way to observe the change in pH at the equivalence point is to use an acid–base indicator (Section 9.8). Such an indicator changes color when the solution changes pH. Phenolphthalein, for example, is colorless in acid solution and pink in basic solution. If this indicator is added to the original sulfuric acid solution, the solution remains colorless as long as excess hydronium ions are present. After enough sodium hydroxide solution has been added to react with all of the hydronium ions, the next drop of base provides excess hydroxide ions, and the solution turns pink (Figure 9.4). Thus we have a clear-cut indication of the equivalence point. The point at which an indicator changes color is called the **end point** of the titration. It is convenient if the end point and the equivalence point are the same, but there are many pH indicators whose end points are not at pH 7.

To meet requirement 4, which is that the volume of each solution used must be known, we use volumetric glassware such as volumetric flasks, burets, and pipets.

Data for a typical acid–base titration are given in Example 9.8. Note that the experiment is run in triplicate, a standard procedure for checking the precision of a titration.

EXAMPLE 9.8

Following are data for the titration of 0.108 M H_2SO_4 with a solution of NaOH of unknown concentration. What is the concentration of the NaOH solution?

	Volume of 0.108 M H$_2$SO$_4$	Volume of NaOH
Trial I	25.0 mL	33.48 mL
Trial II	25.0 mL	33.46 mL
Trial III	25.0 mL	33.50 mL

Solution

From the balanced equation for this acid–base reaction, we know the stoichiometry: Two moles of NaOH react with one mole of H$_2$SO$_4$. From the three trials, we calculate that the average volume of the NaOH required for complete reaction is 33.48 mL. Because the units of molarity are moles/liter, we must convert volumes of reactants from milliliters to liters. We can then use the factor-label method (Section 1.5) to calculate the molarity of the NaOH solution. What we wish to calculate is the number of moles of NaOH per liter of NaOH.

$$\frac{\text{mol NaOH}}{\text{L NaOH}} = \frac{0.108 \text{ mol H}_2\text{SO}_4}{1 \text{ L H}_2\text{SO}_4} \times \frac{0.0250 \text{ L H}_2\text{SO}_4}{0.03348 \text{ L NaOH}} \times \frac{2 \text{ mol NaOH}}{1 \text{ mol H}_2\text{SO}_4}$$

$$= \frac{0.161 \text{ mol NaOH}}{\text{L NaOH}} = 0.161 \; M$$

Problem 9.8

Calculate the concentration of an acetic acid solution using the following data. Three 25.0-mL samples of acetic acid were titrated to a phenolphthalein end point with 0.121 M NaOH. The volumes of NaOH were 19.96 mL, 19.73 mL, and 19.79 mL.

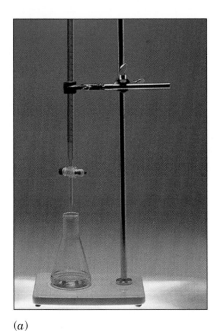
(a)

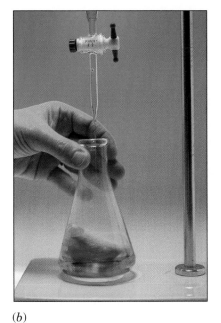
(b)

(c)

Charles D. Winters

Figure 9.4 An acid–base titration. (a) An acid of known concentration is in the Erlenmeyer flask. (b) When a base is added from the buret, the acid is neutralized. (c) The end point is reached when the color of the indicator changes from colorless to pink.

It is important to understand that a titration is not a method for determining the acidity (or basicity) of a solution. If we want to do that, we must measure the sample's pH, which is the only measurement of solution acidity or basicity. Rather, titration is a method for determining the total acid or base concentration of a solution, which is not the same as the acidity. For example, a 0.1 M solution of HCl in water has a pH of 1, but a 0.1 M solution of acetic acid has a pH of 2.9. These two solutions have the same concentration of acid and each neutralizes the same volume of NaOH solution, but they have very different acidities.

9.10 | What Are Buffers?

Buffer A solution that resists change in pH when limited amounts of an acid or a base are added to it; an aqueous solution containing a weak acid and its conjugate base

As noted earlier, the body must keep the pH of blood between 7.35 and 7.45. Yet we frequently eat acidic foods such as oranges, lemons, sauerkraut, and tomatoes, and doing so eventually adds considerable quantities of H_3O^+ to the blood. Despite these additions of acidic or basic substances, the body manages to keep the pH of blood remarkably constant. The body manages this feat by using buffers. A **buffer** is a solution whose pH changes very little when small amounts of H_3O^+ or OH^- ions are added to it. In a sense, a pH buffer is an acid or base "shock absorber."

The most common buffers consist of approximately equal molar amounts of a weak acid and a salt of the weak acid. Put another way, they consist of approximately equal amounts of a weak acid and its conjugate base. For example, if we dissolve 1.0 mol of acetic acid (a weak acid) and 1.0 mol of its conjugate base (in the form of CH_3COONa, sodium acetate) in 1.0 L of water, we have a good buffer solution. The equilibrium present in this buffer solution is

$$\underset{\substack{\text{Acetic acid} \\ \text{(A weak acid)}}}{\overset{\overset{\text{Added as}}{\overset{|}{CH_3COOH}}}{CH_3COOH}} + H_2O \rightleftharpoons \underset{\substack{\text{Acetate ion} \\ \text{(Conjugate base} \\ \text{of a weak acid)}}}{\overset{\overset{\text{Added as}}{\overset{|}{CH_3COO^-Na^+}}}{CH_3COO^-}} + H_3O^+$$

A. How Do Buffers Work?

A buffer resists any change in pH upon the addition of small quantities of acid or base. To see how, we will use an acetic acid–sodium acetate buffer as an example. If a strong acid such as HCl is added to this buffer solution, the added H_3O^+ ions react with CH_3COO^- ions and are removed from solution.

$$\underset{\substack{\text{Acetate ion} \\ \text{(Conjugate base} \\ \text{of a weak acid)}}}{CH_3COO^-} + H_3O^+ \longrightarrow \underset{\substack{\text{Acetic acid} \\ \text{(A weak acid)}}}{CH_3COOH} + H_2O$$

There is a slight increase in the concentration of CH_3COOH as well as a slight decrease in the concentration of CH_3COO^-, but there is no appreciable change in pH. We say that this solution is buffered because it resists a change in pH upon the addition of small quantities of a strong acid.

If NaOH or another strong base is added to the buffer solution, the added OH^- ions react with CH_3COOH molecules and are removed from solution:

$$CH_3COOH + OH^- \longrightarrow CH_3COO^- + H_2O$$

Acetic acid   Acetate ion
(A weak acid)   (Conjugate base
         of a weak acid)

Here there is a slight decrease in the concentration of CH_3COOH as well as a slight increase in the concentration of CH_3COO^-, but, again, there is no appreciable change in pH.

The important point about this or any other buffer solution is that when the conjugate base of the weak acid removes H_3O^+, it is converted to the undissociated weak acid. Because a substantial amount of weak acid is already present, there is no appreciable change in its concentration and, because H_3O^+ ions are removed from solution, there is no appreciable change in pH. By the same token, when the weak acid removes OH^- ions from solution, it is converted to its conjugate base. Because OH^- ions are removed from solution, there is no appreciable change in pH.

The effect of a buffer can be quite powerful. Addition of either dilute HCl or NaOH to pure water, for example, causes a dramatic change in pH (Figure 9.5).

When HCl or NaOH is added to a phosphate buffer, the results are quite different. Suppose we have a phosphate buffer solution of pH 7.21 prepared by dissolving 0.10 mol NaH_2PO_4 (a weak acid) and 0.10 mol Na_2HPO_4 (its conjugate base) in enough water to make 1.00 L of solution. If we add 0.010 mol of HCl to 1.0 L of this solution, the pH decreases to only 7.12. If we add 0.01 mol of NaOH, the pH increases to only 7.30.

Phosphate buffer (pH 7.21) + 0.010 mol HCl   pH 7.21 $\longrightarrow$ 7.12

Phosphate buffer (pH 7.21) + 0.010 mol NaOH   pH 7.21 $\longrightarrow$ 7.30

Figure 9.6 shows the effect of adding acid to a buffer solution.

B. Buffer pH

In the previous example, the pH of the buffer containing equal molar amounts of $H_2PO_4^-$ and HPO_4^{2-} is 7.21. From Table 9.3, we see that 7.21 is the pK_a of the acid $H_2PO_4^-$. This is not a coincidence. If we make a buffer

GOB
Chemistry ❖ Now™

Click *Chemistry Interactive* to learn more about **Buffers**

(a) pH 7.00

(b) pH 2.00

(c) pH 12.00

Charles D. Winters

Figure 9.5 The addition of HCl and NaOH to pure water. (a) The pH of pure water is 7.0. (b) The addition of 0.01 mol of HCl to 1 L of pure water causes the pH to decrease to 2. (c) The addition of 0.010 mol of NaOH to 1 L of pure water causes the pH to increase to 12.

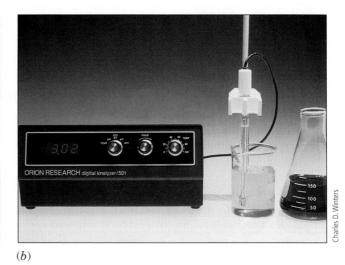

(a)   (b)

Figure 9.6 Buffer solutions. The solution in the Erlenmeyer flask on the right in both (a) and (b) is a buffer of pH 7.40, the same pH as human blood. The buffer solution also contains bromcresol green, an acid–base indicator that is blue at pH 7.40 (see Figure 9.2). (a) The beaker contains some of the pH 7.40 buffer and the bromcresol green indicator to which has been added 5 mL of 0.1 M HCl. After the addition of the HCl, the pH of the buffer solution drops only 0.65 unit to 6.75. (b) The beaker contains pure water and bromcresol green indicator to which has been added 5 mL of 0.10 M HCl. After the addition of the HCl, the pH of the unbuffered solution drops to 3.02.

solution by mixing equimolar concentrations of any weak acid and its conjugate base, the pH of the solution will equal the pK_a of the weak acid.

This fact allows us to prepare buffer solutions to maintain almost any pH. For example, if we want to maintain a pH of 9.14, we could make a buffer solution from boric acid, H_3BO_3, and sodium dihydrogen borate, NaH_2BO_3, the sodium salt of its conjugate base (see Table 9.3).

EXAMPLE 9.9

What is the pH of buffer solution containing equimolar quantities of
(a) H_3PO_4 and NaH_2PO_4?   (b) H_2CO_3 and $NaHCO_3$?

Solution
Because we are adding equimolar quantities of a weak acid and its conjugate base, the pH is equal to the pK_a of the weak acid, which we find in Table 9.3:
(a) pH = 2.12   (b) pH = 6.37

Problem 9.9
What is the pH of a buffer solution containing equimolar quantities of
(a) NH_4Cl and NH_3?   (b) CH_3COOH and CH_3COONa?

C. Buffer Capacity

Buffer capacity The extent to which a buffer solution can prevent a significant change in pH of a solution upon addition of a strong acid or a strong base

Buffer capacity is the amount of hydronium or hydroxide ions that a buffer can absorb without a significant change in its pH. We have already mentioned that a pH buffer is an acid–base "shock absorber." We now ask what makes one solution a better acid–base shock absorber than another solution. The capacity of a pH buffer depends on both its pH relative to its pK_a and its concentration.

pH:	The closer the pH of the buffer is to the pK_a of the weak acid, the greater the buffer capacity.
Concentration:	The greater the concentration of the weak acid and its conjugate base, the greater the buffer capacity.

An effective buffer has a pH equal to the pK_a of the weak acid ± 1. For acetic acid, for example, the pK_a is 4.75. Therefore, a solution of acetic acid and sodium acetate functions as an effective buffer within the pH range of approximately 3.75–5.75. The most effective buffer is one with equal concentrations of the weak acid and its salt—that is, one in which the pH of the buffer solution equals the pK_a of the weak acid.

Buffer capacity also depends on concentration. The greater the concentration of the weak acid and its conjugate base, the greater the buffer capacity. We could make a buffer solution by dissolving 1.0 mol each of CH_3COONa and CH_3COOH in 1 L of H_2O, or we could use only 0.10 mol of each. Both solutions have the same pH of 4.75. However, the former has a buffer capacity ten times that of the latter. If we add 0.2 mol of HCl to the former solution, it performs the way we expect—the pH drops to 4.57. If we add 0.2 mol of HCl to the latter solution, however, the pH drops to 1.0 because the buffer has been swamped out. That is, the amount of H_3O^+ added has exceeded the buffer capacity. The first 0.10 mol of HCl completely neutralizes essentially all the CH_3COO^- present. After that, the solution contains only CH_3COOH and is no longer a buffer, so the second 0.10 mol of HCl decreases the pH to 1.0.

D. Blood Buffers

The average pH of human blood is 7.4. Any change larger than 0.10 pH unit in either direction may cause illness. If the pH goes below 6.8 or above 7.8, death may result. To hold the pH of the blood close to 7.4, the body uses three buffer systems: carbonate, phosphate, and proteins (proteins are discussed in Chapter 22).

The most important of these systems is the carbonate buffer. The weak acid of this buffer is carbonic acid, H_2CO_3; the conjugate base is the bicarbonate ion, HCO_3^-. The pK_a of H_2CO_3 is 6.37 (from Table 9.3). Because the pH of an equal mixture of a weak acid and its salt is equal to the pK_a of the weak acid, a buffer with equal concentrations of H_2CO_3 and HCO_3^- has a pH of 6.37.

Blood, however, has a pH of 7.4. The carbonate buffer can maintain this pH only if $[H_2CO_3]$ and $[HCO_3^-]$ are not equal. In fact, the necessary $[HCO_3^-]/[H_2CO_3]$ ratio is about 10:1. The normal concentrations of these species in blood are about 0.025 M HCO_3^- and 0.0025 M H_2CO_3. This buffer works because any added H_3O^+ is neutralized by the HCO_3^- and any added OH^- is neutralized by the H_2CO_3.

The fact that the $[HCO_3^-]/[H_2CO_3]$ ratio is 10:1 means that this system is a better buffer for acids, which lower the ratio and thus improve buffer efficiency, than for bases, which raise the ratio and decrease buffer capacity. This is in harmony with the actual functioning of the body because, under normal conditions, larger amounts of acidic than basic substances enter the blood. The 10:1 ratio is easily maintained under normal conditions, because the body can very quickly increase or decrease the amount of CO_2 entering the blood.

The second most important buffering system of the blood is a phosphate buffer made up of hydrogen phosphate ion, HPO_4^{2-}, and dihydrogen phosphate ion, $H_2PO_4^-$. In this case, a 1.6:1 $[HPO_4^{2-}]/[H_2PO_4^-]$ ratio is necessary to maintain a pH of 7.4. This ratio is well within the limits of good buffering action.

9.11 | How Do We Calculate the pH of a Buffer?

Suppose we want to make a phosphate buffer solution of pH 7.00. The weak acid with a pK_a closest to this desired pH is $H_2PO_4^-$; it has a pK_a of 7.21. If we use equal concentrations of NaH_2PO_4 and Na_2HPO_4, however, we will have a buffer of pH 7.21. We want a phosphate buffer that is slightly more acidic than 7.21, so it would seem reasonable to use more of the weak acid, $H_2PO_4^-$, and less of its conjugate base, HPO_4^{2-}. But what proportions of these two salts do we use? Fortunately, we can calculate these proportions using the **Henderson-Hasselbalch** equation.

The Henderson-Hasselbalch equation is a mathematical relationship between pH, the pK_a of a weak acid, and the concentrations of the weak acid and its conjugate base. The equation is derived in the following way. Assume that we are dealing with weak acid, HA, and its conjugate base, A^-.

$$HA + H_2O \rightleftharpoons A^- + H_3O^+$$

$$K_a = \frac{[A^-][H_3O^+]}{[HA]}$$

Taking the logarithm of this equation gives

$$\log K_a = \log [H_3O^+] + \log \frac{[A^-]}{[HA]}$$

Rearranging terms gives us a new expression, in which $-\log K_a$ is, by definition, pK_a, and $-\log [H_3O^+]$ is, by definition, pH. Making these substitutions gives the Henderson-Hasselbalch equation.

$$-\log [H_3O^+] = -\log K_a + \log \frac{[A^-]}{[HA]}$$

$$pH = pK_a + \log \frac{[A^-]}{[HA]} \quad \text{Henderson-Hasselbalch Equation}$$

The Henderson-Hasselbalch equation gives us a convenient way to calculate the pH of a buffer when the concentrations of the weak acid and its conjugate base are not equal.

EXAMPLE 9.10

What is the pH of a phosphate buffer solution containing 1.0 mol/L of sodium dihydrogen phosphate, NaH_2PO_4, and 0.50 mol/L of sodium hydrogen phosphate, Na_2HPO_4?

Solution

The weak acid in this problem is $H_2PO_4^-$; its ionization produces HPO_4^{2-}. The pK_a of this acid is 7.21 (from Table 9.3). Under the weak acid and its conjugate base are shown their concentrations.

$$H_2PO_4^- + H_2O \rightleftharpoons HPO_4^{2-} + H_3O^+ \quad pK_a = 7.21$$
$$\text{1.0 mol/L} \qquad\qquad \text{0.50 mol/L}$$

Substituting these values in the Henderson Hasselbalch equation gives a pH of 6.91.

$$pH = 7.21 + \log \frac{0.50}{1.0}$$

$$= 7.21 - 0.30 = 6.91$$

Problem 9.10

What is the pH of a hydrocyanic acid buffer solution containing 0.25 mol/L of hydrocyanic acid, HCN, and 0.50 mol/L of cyanide ion, CN^-? See Table 9.3 for the pK_a of hydrocyanic acid.

CHEMICAL CONNECTIONS 9D

Respiratory and Metabolic Acidosis

The pH of blood is normally between 7.35 and 7.45. If the pH goes lower than that level, the condition is called **acidosis.** Acidosis leads to depression of the nervous system. Mild acidosis can result in dizziness, disorientation, or fainting; a more severe case can cause coma. If the acidosis persists for a sufficient period of time, or if the pH gets too far away from 7.35 to 7.45, death may result.

Acidosis has several causes. One type, called **respiratory acidosis,** results from difficulty in breathing (hypoventilation). An obstruction in the windpipe or diseases such as pneumonia, emphysema, asthma, or congestive heart failure may diminish the amount of oxygen that reaches the tissues and the amount of CO_2 that leaves the body through the lungs. You can even produce mild acidosis by holding your breath. If you have ever tried to see how long you could swim underwater in a pool without surfacing, you will have noticed a deep burning sensation in all your muscles when you finally came up for air. The pH of the blood decreases because the CO_2, unable to escape fast enough, remains in the blood, where it lowers the $[HCO_3^-]/[H_2CO_3]$ ratio. Rapid breathing as a result of physical exertion is more about getting rid of CO_2 than it is about breathing in O_2.

Acidosis caused by other factors is called **metabolic acidosis.** Two causes of this condition are starvation (or fasting) and heavy exercise. When the body doesn't get enough food, it burns its own fat, and the products of this reaction are acidic compounds that enter the blood. This problem sometimes happens to people on fad diets. Heavy exercise causes the muscles to produce excessive amounts of lactic acid, which makes muscles feel tired and sore. The lowering of the blood pH due to lactic acid is also what leads to the rapid breathing, dizziness, and nausea that athletes feel at the end of a sprint. In addition, metabolic acidosis is caused by a number of metabolic irregularities. For example, the disease diabetes mellitus produces acidic compounds called ketone bodies (Section 28.6).

Both types of acidosis can be related. When cells are deprived of oxygen, respiratory acidosis results. These cells are unable to produce the energy they need through aerobic (*oxygen-requiring*) pathways that we will learn about in Chapters 27 and 28. To survive, the cells must use the anaerobic (*without oxygen*) pathway called

These U.S. runners have just won the gold medal in the 4 × 400 m relay race at the 1996 Olympic Games. The buildup of lactic acid and lowered blood pH has caused severe muscle pain and breathlessness.

glycolysis. This pathway has lactic acid as an end product, leading to metabolic acidosis. The lactic acid is the body's way of buying time and keeping the cells alive and functioning a little longer. Eventually the lack of oxygen, called an oxygen debt, must be repaid, and the lactic acid must be cleared out. In extreme cases, the oxygen debt is too great, and the individual can die. This was the case of a famous cyclist, Tom Simpson, who died on the slopes of Mont Ventoux during the 1967 Tour de France. Under the influence of amphetamines, he rode so hard that he built up a fatal oxygen debt.

Returning to the problem posed at the beginning of this section, how do we calculate the proportions of NaH_2PO_4 and Na_2HPO_4 needed to make up a phosphate buffer of pH 7.00? We know that the pK_a of $H_2PO_4^-$ is 7.21 and that the buffer we wish to prepare has a pH of 7.00. We can substitute these two values in the Henderson-Hasselbalch equation as follows:

$$7.00 = 7.21 + \log \frac{[HPO_4^{2-}]}{[H_2PO_4^-]}$$

Rearranging and solving gives

$$\log \frac{[HPO_4^{2-}]}{[H_2PO_4^-]} = 7.00 - 7.21 = -0.21$$

$$\frac{[HPO_4^{2-}]}{[H_2PO_4^-]} = \frac{0.62}{1}$$

Thus, to prepare a phosphate buffer of pH 7.00, we can use 0.62 mol of Na_2HPO_4 and 1.0 mol of NaH_2PO_4. Alternatively, we can use any other amounts of these two salts, as long as their mole ratio is 0.62 : 1.0.

| 9.12 | What Are TRIS, HEPES, and These Buffers with the Strange Names? |

GOB
Chemistry⋅🞁⋅Now™
Click *Coached Problems* to learn more about calculating the **pH of Buffer Solutions**

The original buffers used in the lab were made from simple weak acids and bases, such as acetic acid, phosphoric acid, and citric acid. It was eventually discovered that many of these buffers had limitations. For example, they often changed their pH too much if the solution was diluted or if the temperature changed. They often permeated cells in solution, thereby changing the chemistry of the interior of the cell. To overcome these shortcomings, a scientist named N. E. Good developed a series of buffers that consist of zwitterions, molecules with both positive and negative charges. Zwitterions do not readily permeate cell membranes. Zwitterionic buffers also are more resistant to concentration and temperature changes.

Most of the common synthetic buffers used today have complicated formulas, such as 3-[*N*-morpholino]propanesulfonic acid, which we abbreviate MOPS. Table 9.5 gives a few examples.

CHEMICAL CONNECTIONS 9E

Alkalosis and the Sprinter's Trick

Reduced pH is not the only irregularity that can occur in the blood. The pH may also be elevated, a condition called **alkalosis** (blood pH higher than 7.45). It leads to overstimulation of the nervous system, muscle cramps, dizziness, and convulsions. It arises from rapid or heavy breathing, called hyperventilation, which may be caused by fever, infection, the action of certain drugs, or even hysteria. In this case, the excessive loss of CO_2 raises both the ratio of $[HCO_3^-]/[H_2CO_3]$ and the pH.

Athletes who compete in short-distance races that take about a minute to finish have learned how to use hyperventilation to their advantage. By hyperventilating right before the start, they force extra CO_2 out of their lungs. This causes more H_2CO_3 to dissociate into CO_2 and H_2O to replace the lost CO_2. In turn, the loss of the HA form of the bicarbonate blood buffer raises the pH of the blood. When an athlete starts an event with a slightly higher blood pH, he or she can absorb more lactic acid before the blood pH drops to the point where performance is impaired. Of course, the timing of this hyperventilation must be perfect. If the athlete artificially raises blood pH and then the race does not start quickly, the same effects of dizziness will occur.

Table 9.5   Acid and Base Forms of Some Useful Biochemical Buffers

Acid Form		Base Form	pK_a
TRIS—H⁺ (protonated form) $(HOCH_2)_3CNH_3^+$	N—*tris*[hydroxymethyl]aminomethane (TRIS) ⇌	TRIS (free amine) $(HOCH_2)_3CNH_2$	8.3
⁻TES—H⁺ (zwitterionic form) $(HOCH_2)_3\overset{+}{C}NH_2CH_2CH_2SO_3^-$	N—*tris*[hydroxymethyl]methyl-2-aminoethane sulfonate (TES) ⇌	⁻TES (anionic form) $(HOCH_2)_3CNHCH_2CH_2SO_3^-$	7.55
⁻HEPES—H⁺ (zwitterionic form) $HOCH_2CH_2\overset{+}{N}\underset{H}{\bigcirc}NCH_2CH_2SO_3^-$	N—2—hydroxyethylpiperazine-N′-2-ethane sulfonate (HEPES) ⇌	⁻HEPES (anionic form) $HOCH_2CH_2N\bigcirc NCH_2CH_2SO_3^-$	7.55
⁻MOPS—H⁺ (zwitterionic form) $O\bigcirc\underset{H}{\overset{+}{N}}CH_2CH_2CH_2SO_3^-$	3—[N—morpholino]propane-sulfonic acid (MOPS) ⇌	⁻MOPS (anionic form) $O\bigcirc NCH_2CH_2CH_2SO_3^-$	7.2
²⁻PIPES—H⁺ (protonated dianion) $^-O_3SCH_2CH_2N\underset{H}{\bigcirc}\overset{+}{N}CH_2CH_2SO_3^-$	Piperazine—N,N′-*bis*[2-ethanesulfonic acid] (PIPES) ⇌	²⁻PIPES (dianion) $^-O_3SCH_2CH_2N\bigcirc NCH_2CH_2SO_3^-$	6.8

The important thing to remember is that you don't really need to know the structure of these odd-sounding buffers to use them correctly. The important considerations are the pK_a of the buffer and the concentration you want to have. The Henderson-Hasselbalch equation works just fine whether or not you know the structure of the compound in question.

EXAMPLE 9.11

What is the pH of a solution if you mix 100 mL of 0.2 *M* HEPES in the acid form with 200 mL of 0.2 *M* HEPES in the basic form?

Solution

First we must find the pK_a, which we see from Table 9.5 is 7.55. Then we must calculate the ratio of the conjugate base to the acid. The formula calls for the concentration, but in this situation, the ratio of the concentrations will be the same as the ratio of the moles, which will be the same as the ratio of the volumes, because both solutions had the same starting concentration of 0.2. Thus, we can see that the ratio of base to acid is 2 : 1 because we added twice the volume of base.

$$pH = pK_a + \log([A^-]/[HA]) = 7.55 + \log(2) = 7.85$$

Notice that we did not have to know anything about the structure of HEPES to work out this example.

Problem 9.11

What is the pH of a solution made by mixing 0.2 mol of TRIS acid and 0.05 mol of TRIS base in 500 mL of water?

SUMMARY OF KEY QUESTIONS

SECTION 9.1 What Are Acids and Bases?

- By the **Arrhenius definitions,** acids are substances that produce H_3O^+ ions in aqueous solution.
- Bases are substances that produce OH^- ions in aqueous solution.

SECTION 9.2 How Do We Define the Strength of Acids and Bases?

- A strong acid reacts completely or almost completely with water to form H_3O^+ ions.
- A strong base reacts completely or almost completely with water to form OH^- ions.

SECTION 9.3 What Are Conjugate Acid–Base Pairs?

- The **Brønsted-Lowry definitions** expand the definitions of acid and base to beyond water.
- An acid is a proton donor; a base is a proton acceptor.
- Every acid has a **conjugate base,** and every base has a **conjugate acid.** The stronger the acid, the weaker its conjugate base. Conversely, the stronger the base, the weaker its conjugate acid.
- An **amphiprotic substance,** such as water, can act as either an acid or a base.

SECTION 9.4 How Can We Tell the Position of Equilibrium in an Acid–Base Reaction?

- In an acid–base reaction, the position of equilibrium favors the reaction of the stronger acid and the stronger base to form the weaker acid and the weaker base.

SECTION 9.5 How Do We Use Acid Ionization Constants?

- The strength of a weak acid is expressed by its **ionization constant, K_a.**
- The larger the value of K_a, the stronger the acid. $pK_a = -\log [K_a]$.

SECTION 9.6 What Are the Properties of Acids and Bases?

- Acids react with metals, metal hydroxides, and metal oxides to give **salts,** which are ionic compounds made up of cations from the base and anions from the acid.
- Acids also react with carbonates, bicarbonates, ammonia, and amines to give salts.

SECTION 9.7 What Are the Acidic and Basic Properties of Pure Water?

- In pure water, a small percentage of molecules undergo self-ionization:

$$H_2O + H_2O \rightleftharpoons H_3O^+ + OH^-$$

- As a result, pure water has a concentration of $10^{-7}\,M$ for H_3O^+ and $10^{-7}\,M$ for OH^-.
- The **ion product of water, K_w,** is equal to 1.0×10^{-14}. $pK_w = 14$.

SECTION 9.8 What Are pH and pOH?

- Hydronium ion concentrations are generally expressed in **pH** units, with $pH = -\log [H_3O^+]$.
- **pOH** $= -\log [OH^-]$.
- Solutions with pH less than 7 are acidic; those with pH greater than 7 are basic. A **neutral solution** has a pH of 7.
- The pH of an aqueous solution is measured with an acid–base indicator or with a pH meter.

SECTION 9.9 How Do We Use Titrations to Calculate Concentration?

- We can measure the concentration of aqueous solutions of acids and bases using **titration.** In an acid–base titration, a base of known concentration is added to an acid of unknown concentration (or vice versa) until an equivalence point is reached, at which point the acid or base being titrated is completely neutralized.

SECTION 9.10 What Are Buffers?

- A **buffer** does not change its pH very much when either hydronium ions or hydroxide ions are added to it.
- Buffer solutions consist of approximately equal concentrations of a weak acid and its conjugate base.
- The **buffer capacity** depends on both its pH relative to its pK_a and its concentration. The most effective buffer solutions have a pH equal to the pK_a of the weak acid. The greater the concentration of the weak acid and its conjugate base, the greater the buffer capacity.
- The most important buffers for blood are bicarbonate and phosphate.

SECTION 9.11 How Do We Calculate the pH of a Buffer?

- The **Henderson-Hasselbalch** equation is a mathematical relationship between pH, the pK_a of a weak acid, and the concentrations of the weak acid and its conjugate base:

$$pH = pK_a + \log \frac{[A^-]}{[HA]}$$

SECTION 9.12 What Are TRIS, HEPES, and These Buffers with the Strange Names?

- Many modern buffers have been designed, and their names are often abbreviated.
- These buffers have qualities useful to scientists, such as not crossing membranes and resisting pH change with dilution or temperature change.
- You do not have to understand the structure of these buffers to use them. The important things to know are the molecular weight and the pK_a of the weak acid form of the buffer.

PROBLEMS

A blue problem number indicates an applied problem.

■ denotes problems that are available on the GOB ChemistryNow website or CD and are assignable in OWL.

SECTION 9.1 What Are Acids and Bases?

9.12 Define (a) an Arrhenius acid and (b) an Arrhenius base.

9.13 Write an equation for the reaction that takes place when each acid is added to water. For a diprotic or triprotic acid, consider only its first ionization.
(a) HNO_3 (b) HBr (c) H_2SO_3
(d) H_2SO_4 (e) HCO_3^- (f) H_3BO_3

9.14 Write an equation for the reaction that takes place when each base is added to water.
(a) $LiOH$ (b) $(CH_3)_2NH$

SECTION 9.2 How Do We Define the Strength of Acids and Bases?

9.15 ■ For each of the following, tell whether the acid is strong or weak.
(a) Acetic acid (b) HCl
(c) H_3PO_4 (d) H_2SO_4
(e) HCN (f) H_2CO_3

9.16 ■ For each of the following, tell whether the base is strong or weak.
(a) $NaOH$ (b) Sodium acetate
(c) KOH (d) Ammonia
(e) Water

9.17 If an acid has a pK_a of 2.1, is it strong or weak?

SECTION 9.3 What Are Conjugate Acid–Base Pairs?

9.18 Which of these acids are monoprotic, which are diprotic, and which are triprotic? Which are amphiprotic?
(a) $H_2PO_4^-$ (b) HBO_3^{2-} (c) $HClO_4$ (d) C_2H_5OH
(e) HSO_3^- (f) HS^- (g) H_2CO_3

9.19 Define (a) a Brønsted-Lowry acid and (b) a Brønsted-Lowry base.

9.20 Write the formula for the conjugate base of each acid.
(a) H_2SO_4 (b) H_3BO_3 (c) HI (d) H_3O^+
(e) NH_4^+ (f) HPO_4^{2-}

9.21 Write the formula for the conjugate base of each acid.
(a) $H_2PO_4^-$ (b) H_2S
(c) HCO_3^- (d) CH_3CH_2OH
(e) H_2O

9.22 ■ Write the formula for the conjugate acid of each base.
(a) OH^- (b) HS^- (c) NH_3
(d) $C_6H_5O^-$ (e) CO_3^{2-} (f) HCO_3^-

9.23 Write the formula for the conjugate acid of each base.
(a) H_2O (b) HPO_4^{2-} (c) CH_3NH_2
(d) PO_4^{3-} (e) HBO_3^{2-}

SECTION 9.4 How Can We Tell the Position of Equilibrium in an Acid–Base Reaction?

9.24 For each equilibrium, label the stronger acid, stronger base, weaker acid, and weaker base. For which reaction(s) does the position of equilibrium lie toward the right? For which does it lie toward the left?
(a) $H_3PO_4 + OH^- \rightleftharpoons H_2PO_4^- + H_2O$
(b) $H_2O + Cl^- \rightleftharpoons HCl + OH^-$
(c) $HCO_3^- + OH^- \rightleftharpoons CO_3^{2-} + H_2O$

9.25 ■ For each equilibrium, label the stronger acid, stronger base, weaker acid, and weaker base. For which reaction(s) does the position of equilibrium lie toward the right? For which does it lie toward the left?
(a) $C_6H_5OH + C_2H_5O^- \rightleftharpoons C_6H_5O^- + C_2H_5OH$
(b) $HCO_3^- + H_2O \rightleftharpoons H_2CO_3 + OH^-$
(c) $CH_3COOH + H_2PO_4^- \rightleftharpoons CH_3COO^- + H_3PO_4$

9.26 Will carbon dioxide be evolved as a gas when sodium bicarbonate is added to an aqueous solution of each compound? Explain.
(a) Sulfuric acid
(b) Ethanol, C_2H_5OH
(c) Ammonium chloride, NH_4Cl

SECTION 9.5 How Do We Use Acid Ionization Constants?

9.27 Which has the larger numerical value?
(a) The pK_a of a strong acid or the pK_a of a weak acid
(b) The K_a of a strong acid or the K_a of a weak acid

9.28 ■ In each pair, select the stronger acid.
(a) Pyruvic acid ($pK_a = 2.49$) or lactic acid ($pK_a = 3.08$)
(b) Citric acid ($pK_a = 3.08$) or phosphoric acid ($pK_a = 2.10$)
(c) Benzoic acid ($K_a = 6.5 \times 10^{-5}$) or lactic acid ($K_a = 8.4 \times 10^{-4}$)
(d) Carbonic acid ($K_a = 4.3 \times 10^{-7}$) or boric acid ($K_a = 7.3 \times 10^{-10}$)

9.29 Which solution will be more acidic; that is, which will have a lower pH?
(a) $0.10\ M\ CH_3COOH$ or $0.10\ M\ HCl$
(b) $0.10\ M\ CH_3COOH$ or $0.10\ M\ H_3PO_4$
(c) $0.010\ M\ H_2CO_3$ or $0.010\ M\ NaHCO_3$
(d) $0.10\ M\ NaH_2PO_4$ or $0.10\ M\ Na_2HPO_4$
(e) $0.10\ M$ aspirin ($pK_a = 3.47$) or $0.10\ M$ acetic acid

9.30 Which solution will be more acidic; that is, which will have a lower pH?

(a) 0.10 M C_6H_5OH (phenol) or 0.10 M C_2H_5OH (ethanol)

(b) 0.10 M NH_3 or 0.10 M NH_4Cl

(c) 0.10 M $NaCl$ or 0.10 M NH_4Cl

(d) 0.10 M $CH_3CH(OH)COOH$ (lactic acid) or 0.10 M CH_3COOH

(e) 0.10 M ascorbic acid (vitamin C, $pK_a = 4.1$) or 0.10 M acetic acid

SECTION 9.6 What Are the Properties of Acids and Bases?

9.31 Write an equation for the reaction of HCl with each compound. Which are acid–base reactions? Which are redox reactions?

(a) Na_2CO_3 (b) Mg (c) NaOH (d) Fe_2O_3

(e) NH_3 (f) CH_3NH_2 (g) $NaHCO_3$

9.32 When a solution of sodium hydroxide is added to a solution of ammonium carbonate and is heated, ammonia gas, NH_3, is released. Write a net ionic equation for this reaction. Both NaOH and $(NH_4)_2CO_3$ exist as dissociated ions in aqueous solution.

SECTION 9.7 What Are the Acidic and Basic Properties of Pure Water?

9.33 Given the following values of $[H_3O^+]$, calculate the corresponding value of $[OH^-]$ for each solution.

(a) $10^{-11}\ M$ (b) $10^{-4}\ M$ (c) $10^{-7}\ M$ (d) $10\ M$

9.34 Given the following values of $[OH^-]$, calculate the corresponding value of $[H_3O^+]$ for each solution.

(a) $10^{-10}\ M$ (b) $10^{-2}\ M$ (c) $10^{-7}\ M$ (d) $10\ M$

SECTION 9.8 What Are pH and pOH?

9.35 What is the pH of each solution, given the following values of $[H_3O^+]$? Which solutions are acidic, which are basic, and which are neutral?

(a) $10^{-8}\ M$ (b) $10^{-10}\ M$ (c) $10^{-2}\ M$

(d) $10^0\ M$ (e) $10^{-7}\ M$

9.36 What is the pH and pOH of each solution given the following values of $[OH^-]$? Which solutions are acidic, which are basic, and which are neutral?

(a) $10^{-3}\ M$ (b) $10^{-1}\ M$ (c) $10^{-5}\ M$ (d) $10^{-7}\ M$

9.37 What is the pH of each solution, given the following values of $[H_3O^+]$? Which solutions are acidic, which are basic, and which are neutral?

(a) $3.0 \times 10^{-9}\ M$ (b) $6.0 \times 10^{-2}\ M$

(c) $8.0 \times 10^{-12}\ M$ (d) $5.0 \times 10^{-7}\ M$

9.38 Which is more acidic, a beer with $[H_3O^+] = 3.16 \times 10^{-5}$ or a wine with $[H_3O^+] = 5.01 \times 10^{-4}$?

9.39 ■ What is the $[OH^-]$ and pOH of each solution?

(a) 0.10 M KOH, pH = 13.0

(b) 0.10 M Na_2CO_3, pH = 11.6

(c) 0.10 M Na_3PO_4, pH = 12.0

(d) 0.10 M $NaHCO_3$, pH = 8.4

SECTION 9.9 How Do We Use Titrations to Calculate Concentration?

9.40 What is the purpose of an acid–base titration?

9.41 What is the molarity of a solution made by dissolving 12.7 g of HCl in enough water to make 1.00 L of solution?

9.42 What is the molarity of a solution made by dissolving 3.4 g of $Ba(OH)_2$ in enough water to make 450 mL of solution? Assume that $Ba(OH)_2$ ionizes completely in water to Ba^{2+} and OH^- ions.

9.43 Describe how you would prepare each of the following solutions (in each case assume that you have the solid bases).

(a) 400.0 mL of 0.75 M NaOH

(b) 1.0 L of 0.071 M $Ba(OH)_2$

9.44 If 25.0 mL of an aqueous solution of H_2SO_4 requires 19.7 mL of 0.72 M NaOH to reach the end point, what is the molarity of the H_2SO_4 solution?

9.45 A sample of 27.0 mL of 0.310 M NaOH is titrated with 0.740 M H_2SO_4. How many milliliters of the H_2SO_4 solution are required to reach the end point?

9.46 A 0.300 M solution of H_2SO_4 was used to titrate 10.00 mL of an unknown base; 15.00 mL of acid was required to neutralize the basic solution. What was the molarity of the base?

9.47 A solution of an unknown base was titrated with 0.150 M HCl, and 22.0 mL of acid was needed to reach the end point of the titration. How many moles of the unknown base were in the solution?

9.48 The usual concentration of HCO_3^- ions in blood plasma is approximately 24 millimoles per liter (mmol/L). How would you make up 1.00 L of a solution containing this concentration of HCO_3^- ions?

9.49 What is the end point of a titration?

9.50 Why does a titration not tell us the acidity or basicity of a solution?

SECTION 9.10 What Are Buffers?

9.51 Write equations to show what happens when, to a buffer solution containing equimolar amounts of CH_3COOH and CH_3COO^-, we add

(a) H_3O^+ (b) OH^-

9.52 Write equations to show what happens when, to a buffer solution containing equimolar amounts of HPO_4^{2-} and $H_2PO_4^-$, we add

(a) H_3O^+ (b) OH^-

9.53 We commonly refer to a buffer as consisting of approximately equal molar amounts of a weak acid and its conjugate base—for example, CH_3COOH and CH_3COO^-. Is it also possible to have a buffer consisting of approximately equal molar amounts of a weak base and its conjugate acid? Explain.

9.54 What is meant by buffer capacity?

9.55 How can you change the pH of a buffer? How can you change the capacity of a buffer?

9.56 What is the connection between buffer action and Le Chatelier's principle?

9.57 Give two examples of a situation where you would want a buffer to have unequal amounts of the conjugate acid and the conjugate base.

SECTION 9.11 How Do We Calculate the pH of a Buffer?

9.58 What is the pH of a buffer solution made by dissolving 0.10 mol of formic acid, HCOOH, and 0.10 mol of sodium formate, HCOONa, in 1 L of water?

9.59 The pH of a solution made by dissolving 1.0 mol of propanoic acid and 1.0 mol of sodium propanoate in 1.0 L of water is 4.85.
   (a) What would the pH be if we used 0.10 mol of each (in 1 L of water) instead of 1.0 mol?
   (b) With respect to buffer capacity, how would the two solutions differ?

9.60 Show that when the concentration of the weak acid, [HA], in an acid–base buffer equals that of the conjugate base of the weak acid, [A$^-$], the pH of the buffer solution is equal to the pK_a of the weak acid.

9.61 Calculate the pH of an aqueous solution containing the following:
   (a) 0.80 M lactic acid and 0.40 M lactate ion
   (b) 0.30 M NH$_3$ and 1.50 M NH$_4^+$

9.62 The pH of 0.10 M HCl is 1.0. When 0.10 mol of sodium acetate, CH$_3$COONa, is added to this solution, its pH changes to 2.9. Explain why the pH changes, and why it changes to this particular value.

9.63 If you have 100 mL of a 0.1 M buffer made of NaH$_2$PO$_4$ and Na$_2$HPO$_4$ that is at pH 6.8, and you add 10 mL of 1 M HCl, will you still have a usable buffer?

SECTION 9.12 What Are TRIS, HEPES, and These Buffers with the Strange Names?

9.64 Write an equation showing the reaction of TRIS in the acid form with sodium hydroxide (do not write out the chemical formula for TRIS).

9.65 What is the pH of a solution that is 0.1 M in TRIS in the acid form and 0.05 M in TRIS in the basic form?

9.66 Explain why you do not need to know the chemical formula of a buffer compound to use it.

9.67 If you have a HEPES buffer at pH 4.75, will it be a usable buffer? Why or why not?

9.68 Which of the compounds listed in Table 9.5 would be the most effective for making a buffer at pH 8.15? Why?

Chemical Connections

9.69 (Chemical Connections 9A) Which weak base is used as a flame retardant in plastics?

9.70 (Chemical Connections 9B) What is the most important immediate first aid in any chemical burn of the eyes?

9.71 (Chemical Connections 9B) With respect to corneal burns, are strong acids or strong bases more dangerous?

9.72 (Chemical Connections 9C) Name the most common bases used in over-the-counter antacids.

9.73 (Chemical Connections 9D) What causes (a) respiratory acidosis and (b) metabolic acidosis?

9.74 (Chemical Connections 9E) Explain how the sprinter's trick works. Why would an athlete want to raise the pH of his or her blood?

9.75 (Chemical Connections 9E) Another form of the sprinter's trick is to drink a sodium bicarbonate shake before the event. What would be the purpose of doing so? Give the relevant equations.

Additional Problems

9.76 4-Methylphenol, CH$_3$C$_6$H$_4$OH (pK_a = 10.26), is only slightly soluble in water, but its sodium salt, CH$_3$C$_6$H$_4$O$^-$Na$^+$, is quite soluble in water. In which of the following solutions will 4-methylphenol dissolve more readily than in pure water?
   (a) Aqueous NaOH   (b) Aqueous NaHCO$_3$
   (c) Aqueous NH$_3$

9.77 Benzoic acid, C$_6$H$_5$COOH (pK_a = 4.19), is only slightly soluble in water, but its sodium salt, C$_6$H$_5$COO$^-$Na$^+$, is quite soluble in water. In which of the following solutions will benzoic acid dissolve more readily than in pure water?
   (a) Aqueous NaOH   (b) Aqueous NaHCO$_3$
   (c) Aqueous Na$_2$CO$_3$

9.78 Assume that you have a dilute solution of HCl (0.10 M) and a concentrated solution of acetic acid (5.0 M). Which solution is more acidic? Explain.

9.79 Which of the two solutions from Problem 9.78 would take a greater amount of NaOH to hit a phenolphthalein end point? Explain.

9.80 If the [OH$^-$] of a solution is 1×10^{-14},
   (a) What is the pH of the solution?
   (b) What is the [H$_3$O$^+$]?

9.81 What is the molarity of a solution made by dissolving 0.583 g of the diprotic acid oxalic acid, H$_2$C$_2$O$_4$, in enough water to make 1.75 L of solution?

9.82 Following are three organic acids and the pK_a of each: butanoic acid, 4.82; barbituric acid, 5.00; and lactic acid, 3.85.
   (a) What is the K_a of each acid?
   (b) Which of the three is the strongest acid and which is the weakest?
   (c) What information would you need to predict which one of the three acids would require the most NaOH to reach a phenolphthalein end point?

9.83 The pK_a value of barbituric acid is 5.0. If the H_3O^+ and barbiturate ion concentrations are each 0.0030 M, what is the concentration of the undissociated barbituric acid?

9.84 If pure water self-ionizes to give H_3O^+ and OH^- ions, why doesn't pure water conduct an electric current?

9.85 Can an aqueous solution have a pH of zero? Explain your answer using aqueous HCl as your example.

9.86 If an acid, HA, dissolves in water such that the K_a is 1000, what is the pK_a of that acid? Is this scenario possible?

9.87 A scale of K_b values for bases could be set up in a manner similar to that for the K_a scale for acids. However, this setup is generally considered unnecessary. Explain.

9.88 Do a 1.0 M CH_3COOH solution and a 1.0 M HCl solution have the same pH? Explain.

9.89 Do a 1.0 M CH_3COOH solution and a 1.0 M HCl solution require the same amount of 1.0 M NaOH to hit a titration end point? Explain.

9.90 Suppose you wish to make a buffer whose pH is 8.21. You have available 1 L of 0.100 M NaH_2PO_4 and solid Na_2HPO_4. How many grams of the solid Na_2HPO_4 must be added to the stock solution to accomplish this task? (Assume that the volume remains 1 L.)

9.91 In the past, boric acid was used to rinse an inflamed eye. How would you make up 1 L of a $H_3BO_3/H_2BO_3^-$ buffer solution that has a pH of 8.40?

9.92 Suppose you want to make a CH_3COOH/CH_3COO^- buffer solution with a pH of 5.60. The acetic acid concentration is to be 0.10 M. What should the acetate ion concentration be?

9.93 For an acid–base reaction, one way to determine the position of equilibrium is to say that the larger of the equilibrium arrow pair points to the acid with the higher value of pK_a. For example,

$$CH_3COOH + HCO_3^- \rightleftharpoons CH_3COO^- + H_2CO_3$$
$$pK_a = 4.75 \qquad\qquad\qquad\qquad pK_a = 6.37$$

Explain why this rule works.

9.94 When a solution prepared by dissolving 4.00 g of an unknown acid in 1.00 L of water is titrated with 0.600 M NaOH, 38.7 mL of the NaOH solution is needed to neutralize the acid. What was the molarity of the acid solution?

9.95 Write equations to show what happens when, to a buffer solution containing equal amounts of HCOOH and $HCOO^-$, we add

(a) H_3O^+ (b) OH^-

9.96 If we add 0.10 mol of NH_3 to 0.50 mol of HCl dissolved in enough water to make 1.0 L of solution, what happens to the NH_3? Will any NH_3 remain? Explain.

9.97 Suppose you have an aqueous solution prepared by dissolving 0.050 mol of NaH_2PO_4 in 1 L of water. This solution is not a buffer, but suppose you want to make it into one. How many moles of solid Na_2HPO_4 must you add to this aqueous solution to make it into

(a) A buffer of pH 7.21
(b) A buffer of pH 6.21
(c) A buffer of pH 8.21

9.98 The pH of a 0.10 M solution of acetic acid is 2.93. When 0.10 mol of sodium acetate, CH_3COONa, is added to this solution, its pH changes to 4.74. Explain why the pH changes, and why it changes to this particular value.

9.99 Suppose you have a phosphate buffer of pH 7.21. If you add more solid NaH_2PO_4 to this buffer, would you expect the pH of the buffer to increase, decrease, or remain unchanged? Explain.

9.100 Suppose you have a bicarbonate buffer containing carbonic acid, H_2CO_3, and sodium bicarbonate, $NaHCO_3$, and that the pH of the buffer is 6.37. If you add more solid $NaHCO_3$ to this buffer solution, would you expect its pH to increase, decrease, or remain unchanged? Explain.

9.101 A student pulls a bottle of TRIS off of a shelf and notes that the bottle says, "TRIS (basic form), $pK_a = 8.3$." The student tells you that if you add 0.1 mol of this compound to 100 mL of water, the pH will be 8.3. Is the student correct? Explain.

Looking Ahead

9.102 Unless under pressure, carbonic acid in aqueous solution breaks down into carbon dioxide and water, and carbon dioxide is evolved as bubbles of gas. Write an equation for the conversion of carbonic acid to carbon dioxide and water.

9.103 Following are pH ranges for several human biological materials. From the pH at the midpoint of each range, calculate the corresponding $[H_3O^+]$. Which materials are acidic, which are basic, and which are neutral?

(a) Milk, pH 6.6–7.6
(b) Gastric contents, pH 1.0–3.0
(c) Spinal fluid, pH 7.3–7.5
(d) Saliva, pH 6.5–7.5
(e) Urine, pH 4.8–8.4
(f) Blood plasma, pH 7.35–7.45
(g) Feces, pH 4.6–8.4
(h) Bile, pH 6.8–7.0

9.104 What is the ratio of $HPO_4^{2-}/H_2PO_4^-$ in a phosphate buffer of pH 7.40 (the average pH of human blood plasma)?

9.105 What is the ratio of $HPO_4^{2-}/H_2PO_4^-$ in a phosphate buffer of pH 7.9 (the pH of human pancreatic fluid)?

Exponential Notation

The **exponential notation** system is based on powers of 10 (see table). For example, if we multiply $10 \times 10 \times 10 = 1000$, we express this as 10^3. The 3 in this expression is called the **exponent** or the **power,** and it indicates how many times we multiplied 10 by itself and how many zeros follow the 1.

There are also negative powers of 10. For example, 10^{-3} means 1 divided by 10^3:

$$10^{-3} = \frac{1}{10^3} = \frac{1}{1000} = 0.001$$

Numbers are frequently expressed like this: 6.4×10^3. In a number of this type, 6.4 is the **coefficient** and 3 is the exponent, or power of 10. This number means exactly what it says:

$$6.4 \times 10^3 = 6.4 \times 1000 = 6400$$

Similarly, we can have coefficients with negative exponents:

$$2.7 \times 10^{-5} = 2.7 \times \frac{1}{10^5} = 2.7 \times 0.00001 = 0.000027$$

For numbers greater than 10 in exponential notation, we proceed as follows: *Move the decimal point to the left,* to just after the first digit. The (positive) exponent is equal to the number of places we moved the decimal point.

Exponential notation is also called scientific notation.

For example, 10^6 means a one followed by six zeros, or 1,000,000, and 10^2 means 100.

APP. I.1	Examples of Exponential Notation
	$10,000 = 10^4$
	$1000 = 10^3$
	$100 = 10^2$
	$10 = 10^1$
	$1 = 10^0$
	$0.1 = 10^{-1}$
	$0.01 = 10^{-2}$
	$0.001 = 10^{-3}$

EXAMPLE

$$3\,7\,5\,0\,0 = 3.75 \times 10^4 \qquad \text{4 because we went four places to the left}$$

Four places to the left

Coefficient

$$628 = 6.28 \times 10^2$$

Two places to the left

Coefficient

$$859,600,000,000 = 8.596 \times 10^{11}$$

Eleven places to the left

Coefficient

We don't really have to place the decimal point after the first digit, but by doing so we get a coefficient between 1 and 10, and that is the custom.

Using exponential notation, we can say that there are 2.95×10^{22} copper atoms in a copper penny. For large numbers, the exponent is always *positive*. Note that we do not usually write out the zeros at the end of the number.

For small numbers (less than 1), we move the decimal point *to the right,* to just after the first nonzero digit, and use a *negative exponent.*

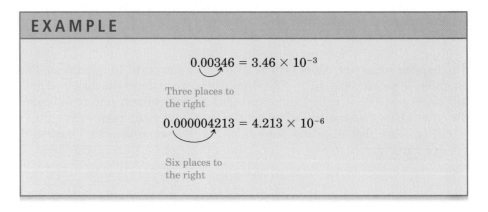

EXAMPLE

$$0.00346 = 3.46 \times 10^{-3}$$

Three places to
the right

$$0.000004213 = 4.213 \times 10^{-6}$$

Six places to
the right

In exponential notation, a copper atom weighs 2.3×10^{-25} pounds.

To convert exponential notation into fully written-out numbers, we do the same thing backward.

EXAMPLE

Write out in full: (a) 8.16×10^7 (b) 3.44×10^{-4}

Solution

(a) $8.16 \times 10^7 = 81,600,000$

Seven places to the right
(add enough zeros)

(b) $3.44 \times 10^{-4} = 0.000344$

Four places to the left

When scientists add, subtract, multiply, and divide, they are always careful to express their answers with the proper number of digits, called significant figures. This method is described in Appendix II.

A. Adding and Subtracting Numbers in Exponential Notation

We are allowed to add or subtract numbers expressed in exponential notation *only if they have the same exponent.* All we do is add or subtract the coefficients and leave the exponent as it is.

EXAMPLE

Add 3.6×10^{-3} and 9.1×10^{-3}.

Solution

$$
\begin{aligned}
3.6 &\times 10^{-3} \\
+ \quad 9.1 &\times 10^{-3} \\
\hline
12.7 &\times 10^{-3}
\end{aligned}
$$

The answer could also be written in other, equally valid ways:

$$12.7 \times 10^{-3} = 0.0127 = 1.27 \times 10^{-2}$$

When it is necessary to add or subtract two numbers that have different exponents, we first must change them so that the exponents are the same.

A calculator with exponential notation changes the exponent automatically.

EXAMPLE

Add 1.95×10^{-2} and 2.8×10^{-3}.

Solution
To add these two numbers, we make both exponents -2. Thus, $2.8 \times 10^{-3} = 0.28 \times 10^{-2}$. Now we can add:

$$
\begin{array}{r}
1.95 \times 10^{-2} \\
+\ 0.28 \times 10^{-2} \\
\hline
2.23 \times 10^{-2}
\end{array}
$$

B. Multiplying and Dividing Numbers in Exponential Notation

To multiply numbers in exponential notation, we first multiply the coefficients in the usual way and then algebraically *add* the exponents.

EXAMPLE

Multiply 7.40×10^5 by 3.12×10^9.

Solution

$$7.40 \times 3.12 = 23.1$$

Add exponents:

$$10^5 \times 10^9 = 10^{5+9} = 10^{14}$$

Answer:

$$23.1 \times 10^{14} = 2.31 \times 10^{15}$$

EXAMPLE

Multiply 4.6×10^{-7} by 9.2×10^4

Solution

$$4.6 \times 9.2 = 42$$

Add exponents:

$$10^{-7} \times 10^4 = 10^{-7+4} = 10^{-3}$$

Answer:

$$42 \times 10^{-3} = 4.2 \times 10^{-2}$$

To divide numbers expressed in exponential notation, the process is reversed. We first divide the coefficients and then algebraically *subtract* the exponents.

EXAMPLE

Divide: $\dfrac{6.4 \times 10^8}{2.57 \times 10^{10}}$

Solution

$$6.4 \div 2.57 = 2.5$$

Subtract exponents:

$$10^8 \div 10^{10} = 10^{8-10} = 10^{-2}$$

Answer:

$$2.5 \times 10^{-2}$$

EXAMPLE

Divide: $\dfrac{1.62 \times 10^{-4}}{7.94 \times 10^7}$

Solution

$$1.62 \div 7.94 = 0.204$$

Subtract exponents:

$$10^{-4} \div 10^7 = 10^{-4-7} = 10^{-11}$$

Answer:

$$0.204 \times 10^{-11} = 2.04 \times 10^{-12}$$

Scientific calculators do these calculations automatically. All that is necessary is to enter the first number, press $+$, $-$, $\times$, or $\div$, enter the second number, and press $=$. (The method for entering numbers of this form varies; consult the instructions that come with the calculator.) Many scientific calculators also have a key that will automatically convert a number such as 0.00047 to its scientific notation form (4.7×10^{-4}), and vice versa. For problems relating to exponential notation, see Chapter 1, Problems 1.17 through 1.24.

Significant Figures

If you measure the volume of a liquid in a graduated cylinder, you might find that it is 36 mL, to the nearest milliliter, but you cannot tell if it is 36.2, or 35.6, or 36.0 mL because this measuring instrument does not give the last digit with any certainty. A buret gives more digits, and if you use one you should be able to say, for instance, that the volume is 36.3 mL and not 36.4 mL. But even with a buret, you could not say whether the volume is 36.32 or 36.33 mL. For that, you would need an instrument that gives still more digits. This example should show you that *no measured number can ever be known exactly*. No matter how good the measuring instrument, there is always a limit to the number of digits it can measure with certainty.

We define the number of **significant figures** as the number of digits of a measured number that have uncertainty only in the last digit.

What do we mean by this definition? Assume that you are weighing a small object on a laboratory balance that can weigh to the nearest 0.1 g, and you find that the object weighs 16 g. Because the balance weighs to the nearest 0.1 g, you can be sure that the object does not weigh 16.1 g or 15.9 g. In this case, you would write the weight as 16.0 g. To a scientist, there is a difference between 16 g and 16.0 g. Writing 16 g says that you don't know the digit after the 6. Writing 16.0 g says that you do know it: It is 0. However, you don't know the digit after that. Several rules govern the use of significant figures in reporting measured numbers.

A. Determining the Number of Significant Figures

1. Nonzero digits are always significant.

For example, 233.1 m has four significant figures; 2.3 g has two significant figures.

2. Zeros at the beginning of a number are never significant.

For example, 0.0055 L has two significant figures; 0.3456 g has four significant figures.

3. Zeros between nonzero digits are always significant.

For example, 2.045 kcal has four significant figures; 8.0506 g has five significant figures.

4. Zeros at the end of a number that contains a decimal point are always significant.

For example, 3.00 L has three significant figures; 0.0450 mm has three significant figures.

5. Zeros at the end of a number that contains no decimal point may or may not be significant.

We cannot tell whether they are significant without knowing something about the number. This is the ambiguous case. If you know that a certain small business made a profit of $36,000 last year, you can be sure that the 3 and 6 are significant, but what about the rest? The profit might have been $36,126 or $35,786.53, or maybe even exactly $36,000. We just don't know because it is customary to round off such numbers. On the other hand, if the profit were reported as $36,000.00, then all seven digits would be significant.

In science, to get around the ambiguous case we use exponential notation (Section 1.3). Suppose a measurement comes out to be 2500 g. If we made the measurement, we of course know whether the two zeros are significant, but we need to tell others. If these digits are *not* significant, we write our number as 2.5×10^3. If one zero is significant, we write 2.50×10^3. If both zeros are significant, we write 2.500×10^3. Since we now have a decimal point, all the digits shown are significant.

B. Multiplying and Dividing

The rule in multiplication and division is that the final answer should have the *same* number of significant figures as there are in the number with the *fewest* significant figures.

EXAMPLE

Do the following multiplications and divisions:
(a) 3.6×4.27
(b) 0.004×217.38
(c) $\dfrac{42.1}{3.695}$
(d) $\dfrac{0.30652 \times 138}{2.1}$

Solution
(a) 15 (3.6 has two significant figures)
(b) 0.9 (0.004 has one significant figure)
(c) 11.4 (42.1 has three significant figures)
(d) 2.0×10^1 (2.1 has two significant figures)

C. Adding and Subtracting

In addition and subtraction, the rule is completely different. The number of significant figures in each number doesn't matter. The answer is given to the *same number of decimal places* as the term with the fewest decimal places.

EXAMPLE

Add or subtract:

(a) 320.084
   80.47
  200.23
   20.0
  620.8

(b) 61.4532
  13.7
  22
  0.003
  97

(c) 14.26
 −1.05041
 13.21

Solution
In each case, we add or subtract in the normal way but then round off so that the only digits that appear in the answer are those in the columns in which every digit is significant.

D. Rounding Off

When we have too many significant figures in our answer, it is necessary to round off. In this book we have used the rule that if *the first digit dropped* is 5, 6, 7, 8, or 9, we raise *the last digit kept* to the next number; otherwise, we do not.

EXAMPLE

In each case, drop the last two digits:
(a) 33.679   (b) 2.4715   (c) 1.1145   (d) 0.001309   (e) 3.52

Solution
(a) $33.679 = 33.7$
(b) $2.4715 = 2.47$
(c) $1.1145 = 1.11$
(d) $0.001309 = 0.0013$
(e) $3.52 = 4$

E. Counted or Defined Numbers

All of the preceding rules apply to *measured* numbers and **not** to any numbers that are *counted* or *defined*. Counted and defined numbers are known exactly. For example, a triangle is defined as having 3 sides, not 3.1 or 2.9. Here, we treat the number 3 as if it has an infinite number of zeros following the decimal point.

EXAMPLE

Multiply 53.692 (a measured number) $\times$ 6 (a counted number).

Solution

$$322.15$$

Because 6 is a counted number, we know it exactly, and 53.692 is the number with the fewest significant figures. All we really are doing is adding 53.692 six times.

For problems relating to significant figures, see Chapter 1, Problems 1.25 to 1.30.

Answers

Chapter 1 Matter, Energy, and Measurement

1.1 multiplication (a) 4.69×10^5 (b) 2.8×10^{-15}; division (a) 2.00×10^{18} (b) 1.37×10^5

1.2 (a) 147°F (b) 8.3°C

1.3 109 kg

1.4 13.8 km

1.5 743 mph

1.6 78.5 g

1.7 2.43 g/mL

1.8 1.016 g/mL

1.9 48×10^3 cal = 48 kcal

1.10 46°C

1.11 0.0430 cal/g·deg

1.13 (a) Matter is anything that has mass and takes up space. (b) Chemistry is the science that studies matter.

1.15 Dr. X's claim that the extract cured diabetes would be classified as (c) a hypothesis. No evidence had been provided to prove or disprove the claim.

1.17 (a) 3.51×10^{-1} (b) 6.021×10^2 (c) 1.28×10^{-4} (d) 6.28122×10^5

1.19 (a) 6.65×10^{17} (b) 1.2×10^1 (c) 3.89×10^{-16} (d) 3.5×10^{-23}

1.21 (a) 1.3×10^5 (b) 9.40×10^4 (c) 5.137×10^{-3}

1.23 4.45×10^6

1.25 (a) 2 (b) 5 (c) 5 (d) 5 (e) 3 (f) 3 (g) 2

1.27 (a) 92 (b) 7.3 (c) 0.68 (d) 0.0032 (e) 5.9

1.29 (a) 1.53 (b) 2.2 (c) 0.00048

1.31 330 min = 5.6 h

1.33 (a) 20 mm (b) 1 inch (c) 1 mile

1.35 Weight would change slightly. Mass is independent of location, but weight is a force exerted by a body influenced by gravity. The influence of the Earth's gravity decreases with increasing distance from sea level.

1.37 (a) 77°F, 298 K (b) 104°F, 313 K (c) 482°F, 523 K, (d) −459°F, 0 K

1.39 (a) 0.0964 L (b) 27.5 cm (c) 4.57×10^4 g (d) 4.75 m (e) 21.64 mL (f) 3.29×10^3 cc (g) 44 mL (h) 0.711 kg (i) 63.7 cc (j) 7.3×10^4 mg (k) 8.34×10^4 mm (l) 0.361 g

1.41 50 mi/h

1.43 solids and liquids

1.45 No, melting is a physical change.

1.47 bottom: manganese; top: sodium acetate; middle: calcium chloride

1.49 1.023 g/mL

1.51 water

1.53 One should raise the temperature of water to 4°C. During this temperature change, the density of the crystals decreases, while the density of water increases. This brings the less dense crystals to the surface of the more dense water.

1.55 The motion of the wheels of the car generates kinetic energy, which is stored in your battery as potential energy.

1.57 0.34 cal/g·C°

1.59 334 mg

1.61 The body shivers. Further temperature lowering results in unconsciousness and then death.

1.63 Methanol, because its higher specific heat allows it to retain the heat longer.

1.65 0.732

1.67 kinetic: (b), (d), (e); potential: (a), (c)

1.69 the European car

1.71 kinetic energy

1.73 The largest is 41 g. The smallest is 4.1310×10^{-8} kg.

1.75 10.9 h

1.77 The heavy water. When converting the specific heat given in J/g·°C to cal/g·°C, one finds that the specific heat of heavy water is 1.008 cal/g·°C, which is somewhat greater than that of ordinary water.

1.79 (a) 1.57 g/mL (b) 1.25 g/mL

1.81 two

1.83 60 J would raise the temperature by 4.5°C; thus the final temperature will be 24.5°C.

1.85 Weigh the solid urea on a balance, and measure the liquid with a graduated cylinder.

1.87 New medications would consist of the same elements, and many of the fundamental patterns would be similar. The differences would arise in the specific patterns that will be discussed in Chapters 10–20.

1.89 Diethyl ether is less dense than water and insoluble in it. Put the water sample and the diethyl ether in the separatory funnel. The contaminant will dissolve in the diethyl ether, leaving the water sample purified.

Chapter 2 Atoms

2.1 (a) $NaClO_3$ (b) AlF_3

2.2 (a) The mass number is 31.
(b) The mass number is 222.

2.3 (a) The element is phosphorus (P); its symbol is $^{31}_{15}P$.
(b) The element is radon (Rn); its symbol is $^{222}_{86}Rn$.

2.4 (a) The atomic number of mercury (Hg) is 80; that of lead (Pb) is 82.
(b) An atom of Hg has 80 protons; an atom of Pb has 82 protons.
(c) The mass number of this isotope of Hg is 200; the mass number of this isotope of Pb is 202.
(d) The symbols of these isotopes are $^{200}_{80}Hg$ and $^{202}_{82}Pb$.

2.5 The atomic number of iodine (I) is 53. The number of neutrons in each isotope is 72 for iodine-125 and 78 for iodine-131. The symbols for these two isotopes are $^{125}_{53}I$ and $^{131}_{53}I$, respectively.

2.6 Lithium-7 is the more abundant isotope.

2.7 The element is aluminum (Al). Its Lewis dot structure shows three valence electrons.

$$\ddot{A}l\cdot$$

2.9 (a) element (b) compound (c) mixture
(d) mixture (e) mixture (f) element
(g) elemen (h) mixture (i) mixture
(j) mixture (k) compound (l) mixture

2.11 (a) bohrium (Bh, 107) (b) curium (Cm, 96)
(c) einsteinium (Es, 99) (d) fermium (Fm, 100)
(e) lawrencium (Lr, 103) (f) meitnerium (Mt, 109)
(g) mendelevium (Md, 101) (h) nobelium (No, 102)
(i) rutherfordium (Rf, 104) (j) seaborgium (Sg, 106)

2.13 The four elements named for planets are mercury (Hg, 80), uranium (U, 92), neptunium (Np, 93), and plutonium (Pu, 94).

2.15 (a) $NaHCO_3$ (b) C_2H_6O (c) $KMnO_4$
2.17 the law of conservation of mass
2.19 H_2O: H = 11.2%, O = 88.8%; H_2O_2: H = 5.9%, O = 94.1%
2.21 The statement is true in the sense that the number of protons (the atomic number) determines the identity of the atom.
2.23 (a) The element is titanium-48. Its symbol is $^{48}_{22}Ti$.
(b) The element is osmium-190. Its symbol is $^{190}_{76}Os$.
(c) The element is selenium-79. Its symbol is $^{79}_{34}Se$.
(d) The element is plutonium-244. Its symbol is $^{244}_{94}Pu$.
2.25 Each would still be the same element because the number of protons has not changed.
2.27 Radon (Rn) has an atomic number of 86, so each isotope has 86 protons.
(a) Radon-210 has $210 - 86 = 124$ neutrons.
(b) Radon-218 has $218 - 86 = 132$ neutrons.
(c) Radon-222 has $222 - 86 = 136$ neutrons.
2.29 Two more neutrons: tin-120; symbol $^{120}_{50}Sn$;
three more neutrons: tin-121; symbol $^{121}_{50}Sn$;
six more neutrons: tin-124; symbol $^{124}_{50}Sn$
2.31 (a) An ion is an atom with an unequal number of protons and electrons.
(b) Isotopes are atoms with the same number of protons, but a different number of neutrons in their nuclei.
2.33 Rounded to four significant figures, the calculated value is 12.01 amu. The value given in the Periodic Table is 12.011 amu.

$$\left(\frac{98.90}{100} \times 12.000\right) + \left(\frac{1.10}{100} \times 13.003\right) = 11.87 + 0.143 = 12.01$$

2.35 Carbon-11 has 6 protons, 6 electrons, and 5 neutrons.
2.37 Americium-241 (Am) has atomic number 95. This isotope has 95 protons, 95 electrons, and $241 - 95 = 146$ neutrons.
2.39 In Period 3, there are three metals (Na, Mg, Al), one metalloid (Si), and four nonmetals (P, S, Cl, Ar).
2.41 Periods 1, 2, and 3 contain more nonmetals than metals. Periods 4, 5, 6, and 7 contain more metals than nonmetals.
2.43 (a) Pd, (c) Co, (d) Ce, and (f) Cr are transition metals.
2.45 (a) Argon is a nonmetal. (b) Boron is a metalloid.
(c) Lead is a metal. (d) Arsenic is a metalloid.
(e) Potassium is a metal. (f) Silicon is a metalloid.
(g) Iodine is a nonmetal. (h) Antimony is a metalloid.
(i) Vanadium is a metal. (j) Sulfur is a nonmetal.
(k) Nitrogen is a nonmetal.
2.47 The group number tells the number of electrons in the valence shell of the element in the group.
2.49 (a) Li (3): $1s^22s^1$ (b) Ne (10): $1s^22s^22p^6$
(c) Be (4): $1s^22s^2$ (d) C (6): $1s^22s^22p^2$
(e) Mg (12): $1s^22s^22p^63s^2$
2.51 (a) He (2): $1s^2$ (b) Na (11): $1s^22s^22p^63s^1$
(c) Cl (17): $1s^22s^22p^63s^23p^5$ (d) P (15): $1s^22s^22p^63s^23p^3$
(e) H (1): $1s^1$
2.53 In all three parts of this problem, the outer-shell electron configurations are the same. The only difference is the number of the valence shell being filled.
2.55 The element might be in Group 2A, whose members have two valence electrons. It might also be helium in Group 8A.
2.57 The properties are similar because all of them have similar outer-shell electron configurations. They are not identical because each has a different number of filled inner shells.

2.59 Ionization energy generally increases from left to right within a period in the Periodic Table and from bottom to top within a column:
(a) K, Na, Li (b) C, N, Ne (c) C, O, F (d) Br, Cl, F
2.61 Following are the ground-state electron configurations of the Mg atom, Mg^+, Mg^{2+}, and Mg^{3+}.

	Mg $\longrightarrow$ Mg^+ + e^- IE = 738 kJ/mol	
Electron configuration	$1s^22s^22p^63s^2$	$1s^22s^22p^63s^1$

	Mg^+ $\longrightarrow$ Mg^{2+} + e^- IE = 1450 kJ/mol	
Electron configuration	$1s^22s^22p^63s^1$	$1s^22s^22p^6$

	Mg^{2+} $\longrightarrow$ Mg^{3+} + e^- IE = 7734 kJ/mol	
Electron configuration	$1s^22s^22p^6$	$1s^22s^22p^5$

The first electron is removed from the $3s$ orbital. The removal of each subsequent electron requires more energy because, after the first electron is removed, each subsequent electron is removed from a positive ion, which strongly attracts the extranuclear electrons. The third ionization energy is especially large because the electron is removed from the filled second principal energy level, meaning that it is removed from an ion that has the same electron configuration as neon.
2.63 The most abundant elements by weight (a) in the Earth's crust are oxygen and silicon, and (b) in the human body are oxygen and carbon.
2.65 Calcium is an essential element in human bones and teeth. Because strontium behaves chemically much like calcium, strontium-90 gets into our bones and teeth and gives off radioactivity for many years directly into our bodies.
2.67 Copper can be made harder by hammering it.
2.69 (a) metals (b) nonmetals (c) metals
(d) nonmetals (e) metals (f) metals
2.71 (a) Phosphorus-32 has 15 protons, 15 electrons, and $32 - 15 = 17$ neutrons.
(b) Molybdenum-98 has 42 protons, 42 electrons, and $98 - 42 = 56$ neutrons.
(c) Calcium-44 has 20 protons, 20 electrons, and $44 - 20 = 24$ neutrons.
(d) Hydrogen-3 has 1 proton, 1 electron, and $3 - 1 = 2$ neutrons.
(e) Gadolinium-158 has 64 protons, 64 electrons, and $158 - 64 = 94$ neutrons.
(f) Bismuth-212 has 83 protons, 83 electrons, and $212 - 83 = 129$ neutrons.
2.73 For elements with atomic numbers less than that of iron (Fe), the number of neutrons is close to the number of protons. Elements with atomic numbers greater than that of Fe have more neutrons than protons. Therefore, heavy elements have more neutrons than protons.
2.75 Rounded to three significant figures, the atomic weight of naturally occurring boron is 10.8. The value given in the Periodic Table is 10.811.

$$\left(\frac{19.9}{100} \times 10.013\right) + \left(\frac{80.1}{100} \times 11.009\right)$$

$$= 1.993 + 8.818 = 10.811 = 10.81$$

2.77 It would require 6.0×10^{21} protons to equal the mass of 1×10^{-2} g of salt.

$$\frac{1.0 \times 10^{-2}\ g}{1.67 \times 10^{-24}\ g/proton} = 6.0 \times 10^{21}\ protons$$

2.79 The abundances are 23.5% for rubidium-87 and 76.5% for rubidium-85.

2.81 Predict that xenon (Xe) has the highest ionization energy.

2.83 Element 118 will be in Group 8A. Expect it to be a gas that forms either no compounds or very few compounds.

Chapter 3   Nuclear Chemistry

3.1 $^{139}_{53}I \longrightarrow {}^{139}_{54}Xe + {}^{0}_{-1}e$

3.2 $^{223}_{90}Th \longrightarrow {}^{4}_{2}He + {}^{219}_{88}Ra$

3.3 $^{74}_{33}As \longrightarrow {}^{0}_{+1}e + {}^{74}_{32}Ge$

3.4 $^{201}_{81}Tl + {}^{0}_{-1}e \longrightarrow {}^{201}_{80}Hg + {}^{0}_{0}\gamma$

3.5   Barium-122 (10 g) has decayed through 5 half-lives, leaving 0.31 g.

$10.0\,g \longrightarrow 5.0\,g \longrightarrow 2.5\,g \longrightarrow 1.25\,g \longrightarrow 0.625\,g \longrightarrow 0.31\,g$

3.6   1.5 mL

3.7 3.3×10^{-3} mCi

3.9 $5.2 \times 10^{9}/s$

3.11 Red light has a frequency of $4.6 \times 10^{14}/s$.

3.13 (a) $^{19}_{9}F$ (b) $^{32}_{15}P$ (c) $^{87}_{37}Rb$

3.15 Predict that boron-10 is the most stable isotope because it has an equal number of neutrons and protons in its nucleus.

3.17 Samarium-151 decays by beta emission to europium-151.

$^{151}_{62}Sm \longrightarrow {}^{151}_{63}Eu + {}^{0}_{-1}e$

3.19 The new nucleus is vandium-51.

$^{51}_{24}Cr + {}^{0}_{-1}e \longrightarrow {}^{51}_{23}V$

3.21 The bombarding nucleus was neon-28.

$^{248}_{96}Cm + {}^{28}_{10}Ne \longrightarrow {}^{116}_{51}Sb + {}^{160}_{55}Cs$

3.23 (a) $^{10}_{4}Be \longrightarrow {}^{10}_{5}B + {}^{0}_{-1}e$ (beta emission)

(b) $^{151}_{63}Eu^{*} \longrightarrow {}^{151}_{63}Eu + \gamma$ (gamma emission)

(c) $^{195}_{81}Tl \longrightarrow {}^{195}_{80}Hg + {}^{0}_{+1}e$ (positron emission)

(d) $^{239}_{94}Pu \longrightarrow {}^{235}_{92}U + {}^{4}_{2}He$ (alpha emission)

3.25 Gamma emission does not result in transmutation.

3.27 $^{239}_{94}Pu + {}^{4}_{2}He \longrightarrow {}^{240}_{95}Am + 2{}^{1}_{0}n + {}^{1}_{1}H$

3.29 After three half-lives, the percentage remaining will be $\frac{1}{2} \times \frac{1}{2} \times \frac{1}{2} = \frac{1}{8}$ or 12.5%.

3.31 No, the conversion of Ra to Ra^{2+} involves loss of valence electrons, which is not a nuclear process and, therefore, does not involve a change in radioactivity.

3.33 $50.0\,mg \longrightarrow 25.0\,mg \longrightarrow 12.5\,mg$
$\longrightarrow 6.25\,mg \longrightarrow 3.12\,mg$;

4 half-lives in 60 min = 60 min/4 = 15 min

3.35 Gamma radiation has the greatest penetrating power; therefore, it requires the largest amount of shielding.

3.37 3.0×10^{1} m = 30 m

3.39 (a) amount of radiation absorbed from the radiation source   (b) effective dose absorbed by humans or tissue (c) effective energy delivered   (d) intensity of radiation (e) amount of radiation absorbed by tissues from the radiation source   (f) intensity of radiation   (g) effective dose absorbed by humans or tissues

3.41 Alpha particles have so little penetrating power that they are stopped by the thin skin on the hand. If they get into the lungs, however, the thin membranes offer little resistance to them, and they then damage the cells of the lungs.

3.43 Alpha particles are the most damaging to tissue.

3.45 Iodine-131, which is concentrated in the thyroid, where the radiation can induce thyroid cancer.

3.47 (a) Cobalt-60 is used for (4) cancer therapy.
(b) Thallium-201 is used in (1) heart scans and exercise stress tests.
(c) Tritium is used to (2) measure the water content of the body
(d) Mercury-197 is used for (3) kidney scans.

3.49 Use curium-248 as the target nucleus.

$^{248}_{96}Cm + {}^{4}_{2}He \longrightarrow {}^{249}_{97}Bk + 2{}^{1}_{0}n + {}^{1}_{1}H$

3.51 The new element is the sought-after element 118.

$^{208}_{82}Pb + {}^{86}_{36}Kr \longrightarrow {}^{290}_{118}X + 4{}^{1}_{0}n$

3.53 The assumption of a constant carbon-14 to carbon-12 ratio rests on two assumptions: (1) that carbon-14 is continually generated in the upper atmosphere by the production and decay of nitrogen-14,

$^{14}_{7}N + {}^{1}_{0}n \longrightarrow {}^{14}_{6}C + {}^{1}_{1}H$

and (2) that carbon-14 is incorporated into carbon dioxide, CO_2, and other carbon compounds are then distributed worldwide as part of the carbon cycle. The continual formation of carbon-14; transfer of the isotope within the oceans, atmosphere, and biosphere; and the decay of living matter keep the supply of carbon-14 constant.

3.55 a bit more than 0.1 (or 10%) of the half-life of carbon-14

3.57 Radon-122 decays by alpha emission to polonium-218.

$^{222}_{86}Rn \longrightarrow {}^{218}_{84}Po + {}^{4}_{2}He$

3.59

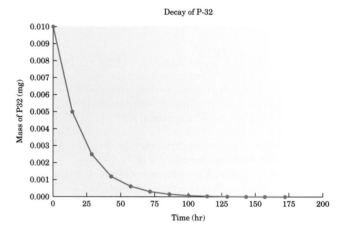

Decay of P-32

3.61 Neon-19 decays to fluorine-19 and sodium-20 decays to neon-20.

$^{19}_{10}Ne \longrightarrow {}^{19}_{9}F + {}^{0}_{+1}e$
$^{20}_{11}Na \longrightarrow {}^{20}_{10}Ne + {}^{0}_{+1}e$

3.63 Yes. Both the curie and the becquerel have units of disintegrations/second, a measurement of radiation intensity.

3.65 (a) naturally occurring sources = 82%
(b) diagnostic medical sources = 15%
(c) nuclear power plants = 0.1%

3.67 X rays will cause more ionization than radar waves because X rays have higher energy than radar waves.

3.69 The decay product is neptunium-237. 1000/432 = 2.3 half-lives. $\frac{1}{2} \times \frac{1}{2} = \frac{1}{4}$, so somewhat less than 25% of the original americium will remain after 1000 years.

3.71 One sievert is 100 rem. This dose is sufficient to cause radiation sickness but not certain death.

3.73 (a) Radioactive elements are constantly decaying to other isotopes and other elements that are now mixed in with the original isotope.
(b) Beta emission results from the decay of a neutron in the nucleus to a proton (the increase in atomic number) and an electron (the beta particle).

3.75 Oxygen-16 is stable because it has an equal number of protons and neutrons. The other isotopes are unstable because the numbers of protons and neutrons are unequal. In this case, the greater the neutron/proton ratio, the shorter the half-life of the isotope.

3.77 The new element is darmstadtium-266.

$$^{208}_{82}\text{Pb} + ^{64}_{28}\text{Ni} \longrightarrow ^{266}_{110}\text{Ds} + 6^{1}_{0}\text{n}$$

3.79 Boron-10 absorbs a neutron to become boron-11, which in turn decays by alpha emission to lithium-7.

$$^{10}_{5}\text{B} + ^{1}_{0}\text{n} \longrightarrow ^{11}_{5}\text{B}$$
$$^{11}_{5}\text{B} \longrightarrow ^{7}_{3}\text{Li} + ^{4}_{2}\text{He}$$

Chapter 4   Chemical Bonds

4.1 By losing two electrons, Mg acquires a complete octet. By gaining two electrons, sulfur acquires a complete octet.
(a) Mg (12 electrons): $1s^2 2s^2 2p^6 3s^2 \longrightarrow \text{Mg}^{2+}$
(10 electrons): $1s^2 2s^2 2p^6 + 2e^-$
(b) S (16 electrons): $1s^2 2s^2 2p^6 3s^2 3p^4 + 2e^- \longrightarrow \text{S}^{2-}$
(18 electrons): $1s^2 2s^2 2p^6 3s^2 3p^6$
4.2 Each pair of elements is in the same column (group) of the Periodic Table and electronegativity increases from bottom to top within a column.
(a) Li > K   (b) N > P   (c) C > Si
4.3 (a) KCl   (b) CaF$_2$ (c) Fe$_2$O$_3$
4.4 (a) magnesium oxide   (b) barium iodide
(c) potassium chloride
4.5 (a) MgCl$_2$ (b) Al$_2$O$_3$ (c) LiI
4.6 (a) iron(II) oxide, ferrous oxide
(b) iron(III) oxide, ferric oxide
4.7 (a) potassium hydrogen phosphate
(b) aluminum sulfate
(c) iron(II) carbonate, ferrous carbonate
4.8 (a) S—H (2.5 − 2.1 = 0.4); nonpolar covalent
(b) P—H (2.1 − 2.1 = 0.0); nonpolar covalent
(c) C—F (4.0 − 2.5 = 1.5); polar covalent
(d) C—Cl (3.0 − 2.5 = 0.5); polar covalent

4.9 (a) $\overset{\delta+}{\text{C}}$—$\overset{\delta-}{\text{N}}$ (b) $\overset{\delta+}{\text{N}}$—$\overset{\delta-}{\text{O}}$ (c) $\overset{\delta+}{\text{C}}$—$\overset{\delta-}{\text{Cl}}$

4.10 (a)   (b)

(c) H—C≡N:

4.12 (a) nitrogen dioxide
(b) phosphorus tribromide
(c) sulfur dichloride
(d) boron trifluoride

4.13 (a)

(b)

(c)

4.14 (a) A valid set of contributing structures.
(b) Not a valid set of contributing structures because the central carbon on the right has five bonds to it and, therefore, 10 electrons in its valence shell. The valence shell of carbon can contain only eight valence electrons.
4.15 Given are three-dimensional structures showing all unshared electron pairs and all bond angles.

(a)   (b)

(c)

4.16 (a) CH$_3$Cl contains a polar C—Cl bond and is a polar molecule.
(b) HCN contains a polar C—N bond and is a polar molecule.
(c) C$_2$H$_6$ contains no polar bonds and is not a polar molecule.

4.17 (a) A lithium atom has the electron configuration $1s^2 2s^1$. When Li loses its single 2s electron, it forms Li$^+$, which has the electron configuration $1s^2$. This configuration is the same as that of helium, the noble gas nearest Li in atomic number.
(b) Chlorine must gain one electron to attain an electron configuration that is the same as that of argon, the noble gas nearest it in atomic number.
(c) Phosphorus must gain three electrons to attain an electron configuration that is the same as that of argon, the noble gas nearest it in atomic number.
(d) Aluminum must lose three electrons to attain an electron configuration that is the same as that of neon, the noble gas nearest it in atomic number.
(e) Strontium must lose two electrons to attain an electron configuration that is the same as that of krypton, the noble gas nearest it in atomic number.
(f) Sulfur must gain two electrons to attain the electron configuration that is the same as that of argon, the noble gas nearest it in atomic number.
(g) Silicon must gain four electrons to attain an electron configuration that is the same as that of argon, the noble gas nearest it in atomic number, or it must lose four electrons to attain an electron configuration that is the same as that of neon.
(h) An oxygen atom has the electron configuration $1s^2 2s^2 2p^4$. When O gains two electrons, it forms O^{2-}, which has the electron configuration $1s^2 2s^2 2p^6$. This configuration is the same as that of neon, the noble gas nearest oxygen in atomic number.
4.19 (a) H $1s^1$ + $1e^-$ $\longrightarrow$ H$^-$ $1s^2$
       (an electron configuration the same as that of helium)
(b) Al $1s^2 2s^2 2p^6 3s^2 3p^1$ $\longrightarrow$ Al^{3+} $1s^2 2s^2 2p^6$ + $3e^-$
       (an electron configuration the same as that of neon)

4.21 Li⁻ is not a stable ion because it has an unfilled second shell.

4.23 The only stable ion in this set is (f) Cs⁺.

4.25 No. Copper is a transition metal so the octet rule does not apply. Transition metals can expand their octets using d orbitals.

4.27 Electronegativity increases going up a column (group) of the Periodic Table because valence electrons are in shells closer to the electropositive nucleus. The decreasing distance of the valence electrons from the positively charged nucleus causes the valence electrons to experience an increasing force of attraction.

4.29 (a) F   (b) O   (c) N   (d) F

4.31 The C—O bond is the most polar; the C—C bond is the least polar.

4.33 (a) C—Br is nonpolar covalent.
(b) S—Cl is polar covalent.
(c) C—P is nonpolar covalent.

4.35 (a) NaBr   (b) Na_2O (c) $AlCl_3$ (d) $BaCl_2$ (e) MgO

4.37 Sodium chloride in the solid state has each Na⁺ ion surrounded by six Cl⁻ ions and each Cl⁻ ion surrounded by six Na⁺ ions.

4.39 (a) $Fe(OH)_3$ (b) $BaCl_2$ (c) $Ca_3(PO_4)_2$ (d) $NaMnO_4$

4.41 (a) and (b) are incorrect; the correct formulas are (a) $(NH_4)_3PO_4$ and (b) $BaCO_3$. (c) and (d) are correct.

4.43 KCl and $KHCO_3$

4.45 (a) sulfite ion   (b) nitrate ion   (c) carbonate ion
(d) ammonium ion and hydroxide ion
(e) hydrogen phosphate ion

4.47 (a) sodium fluoride   (b) magnesium sulfide
(c) aluminum oxide   (d) barium chloride
(e) calcium hydrogen sulfite (calcium bisulfite)
(f) potassium iodide   (g) strontium phosphate
(h) iron(II) hydroxide (ferrous hydroxide)
(i) sodium dihydrogen phosphate
(j) lead(II) acetate (plumbous acetate)
(k) barium hydride   (l) ammonium hydrogen phosphate

4.49 (a) NH_4HSO_3 (b) $Mg(C_2H_3O_2)_2$ (c) $Sr(H_2PO_4)_2$
(d) Ag_2CO_3 (e) $SrCl_2$ (f) $Ba(MnO_4)_2$

4.51 (a) A single bond is a bond in which two atoms share one pair of electrons.
(b) A double bond is a bond in which two atoms share two pairs of electrons.
(c) A triple bond is a bond in which two atoms share three pairs of electrons.

4.53 Following are Lewis structures for each compound.

4.55 Following the compound is its number of valence electrons.
(a) NH_3, 8   (b) C_3H_6, 18   (c) $C_2H_4O_2$, 24
(d) C_2H_6O, 20   (e) CCl_4, 32   (f) HNO_2, 18
(g) CCl_2F_2, 32   (h) O_2, 12

4.57 A bromine atom contains seven electrons in its valence shell. A bromine molecule contains two bromine atoms bonded by a single covalent bond and with three lone pairs of electrons on each bromine atom. A bromide ion is a bromine atom that has gained one electron in its valence shell and has a complete octet and a charge of −1.

4.59 Hydrogen has the electron configuration $1s^1$. Hydrogen's valence shell has only the $1s$ orbital, which can hold a maximum of two electrons.

4.61 Nitrogen has five valence electrons. By sharing three more electrons with another atom or atoms, nitrogen can achieve an outer-shell electron configuration that is the same as that of neon, the noble gas nearest it in atomic number. The three shared pairs of electrons may be in the form of three single bonds, one double bond and one single bond, or one triple bond. With each of these bonding combinations, there is one unshared pair of electrons on nitrogen.

4.63 Oxygen has six valence electrons. By sharing two electrons with another atom or atoms, oxygen can achieve an outer-shell electron configuration that is the same as that of neon, the noble gas nearest it in atomic number. The two shared pairs of electrons may be in the form of one double bond or two single bonds. With either of these bonding combinations, there are two unshared pairs of electrons on oxygen.

4.65 O^{6+} has a charge too concentrated for such a small ion. It would take a tremendous amount of energy to form such a small, highly charged species as O^{6+}.

4.67 (a) BF_3 has only six electrons in the valence shell of boron. Thus it does not obey the octet rule.
(b) CF_2 does not obey the octet rule because carbon has only four electrons in its valence shell.
(c) BeF_2 does not obey the octet rule because beryllium has only four electrons in its valence shell.
(d) C_2H_4 obeys the octet rule.
(e) CH_3 does not obey the octet rule because carbon has only seven electrons in its valence shell.
(f) N_2 obeys the octet rule.
(g) NO does not obey the octet rule. The Lewis structures that can be drawn for this molecule show either nitrogen or oxygen with only seven electrons in its valence shell.

4.69 (a) The Lewis structure for the bicarbonate ion, HCO_3^-, must show 24 valence electrons.

4.71 (a) An N_2O molecule has 16 valence electrons.

(c) The given structure places 10 electrons in the valence shell of the central nitrogen, which is not possible. The valence shell of nitrogen contains $2s$ and $2p$ orbitals that can hold a maximum of 8 valence electrons.

4.73 (a) H_2O has 8 valence electrons, and H_2O_2 has 14 valence electrons.

(b)

$$H-\ddot{O}-H \qquad H-\ddot{O}-\ddot{O}-H$$

Water   Hydrogen peroxide

(c) Predict bond angles of 109.5° about each oxygen atom.

4.75 The shape of each molecule and approximate bond angles about each central atom are as follows:
(a) tetrahedral, 109.5° (b) pyramidal, 109.5°
(c) tetrahedral, 109.5° (d) bent, 120°
(e) trigonal planar, 120° (f) tetrahedral, 109.5°
(g) pyramidal, 109.5° (h) pyramidal, 109.5°

4.77 The difference in polarity arises because of their differences in shapes. CO_2 is a linear molecule, and SO_2 is a bent molecule.

(a) $\ddot{O}=C=\ddot{O}$ (b) $:\overset{\ddots}{O}=\overset{\overset{\ddot{S}}{\|}}{}=O:$

4.79 Yes, it is possible for a molecule to have polar bonds and yet no permanent dipole. This result occurs when the individual polar bonds act in equal but opposite directions, as in CO_2.

4.81 Use differences in electronegativity to predict bond polarity.
(a) nonpolar covalent (b) nonpolar covalent
(c) polar covalent (d) ionic (e) nonpolar covalent
(f) polar covalent (g) nonpolar covalent (h) ionic

4.83 calcium dihydrogen phosphate, calcium phosphate, and calcium carbonate

4.85 barium sulfate is used to visualize the gastrointestinal tract by x-ray examination.

4.87 Ca^{2+} is the main metal ion present in bone and tooth enamel.

4.89 Argon already has an octet with eight valence electrons in its outer shell; therefore, (a) it does not donate or accept electrons to form ions, and (b) it does not need to form covalent bonds by sharing electrons.

4.91 The two possibilities for a structure are square pyramidal and trigonal pyramidal.

Square pyramidal   Trigonal bipyramidal

The square pyramidal structure contains eight F—F 90° bonding electron pair repulsions. These repulsions are minimized in a trigonal bipyramidal structure, where there are only six F—F 90° bonding electron-pair repulsions. The VSEPR theory predicts molecules like PF_5 would adopt the least strained configuration, a trigonal bipyramidal structure.

4.93 ClO_2 has 19 valence electrons. In a Lewis structure, either chlorine or one of the oxygens must have only seven valence electrons. In the following structure, the odd electron is placed on chlorine, the less electronegative element.

$$\ddot{O}=\dot{C}l=\ddot{O}$$

4.95 The compound is zinc oxide, ZnO.

4.97 Lead(IV) oxide, PbO_2, and lead(IV) carbonate, $Pb(CO_3)_2$, are used as white pigments in paints.

4.99 Fe^{2+}

4.101 (a) $CaSO_3$ (b) $Ca(HSO_3)_2$ (c) $Ca(OH)_2$
(d) $CaHPO_4$

4.103 Perchloroethylene has four polar covalent C—Cl bonds, but it is not a polar compound. The molecule lacks a dipole because the polar covalent C—Cl bonds act in equal, but opposite directions.

4.105 (a) Following is a Lewis structure for tetrafluoroethylene.

(b) All bond angles are predicted to be 120°.
(c) Tetrafluoroethylene has four polar covalent C—F bonds but is a nonpolar molecule, because, as in Problem 4.103, the polar covalent bonds act in equal, but opposite directions.

Chapter 5   Chemical Reactions

5.1 (a) $C_{13}H_{18}O_2 = 206$ amu (b) $Ba_3(PO_4)_2 = 602$ amu

5.2 1500 g water is 83 mol water.

5.3 2.84 mol Na_2S is 222 g Na_2S.

5.4 In 2.5 mol of glucose, $C_6H_{12}O_6$, there are 15 mol C atoms, 30 mol H atoms, and 15 mol O atoms.

5.5 0.062 g $CuNO_3$ contains 4.9×10^{-4} mol Cu^+.

5.6 235 g H_2O contains 7.86×10^{24} molecules H_2O.

5.7 The balanced equation is

$$6CO_2(g) + 6H_2O(\ell) \xrightarrow{\text{Photosynthesis}} C_6H_{12}O_6(aq) + 6O_2(g)$$

5.8 The balanced equation is
$$2C_6H_{14}(g) + 19O_2(g) \longrightarrow 12CO_2(g) + 14H_2O(g)$$

5.9 The balanced equation is
$$3K_2C_2O_4(aq) + Ca_3(AsO_4)_2(s)$$
$$\longrightarrow 2K_3AsO_4(aq) + 3CaC_2O_4(s)$$

5.10 (a) The balanced equation is

$$2Al_2O_3(s) \xrightarrow{\text{Electrolysis}} 4Al(s) + 3O_2(g)$$

(b) It requires 51 g of Al_2O_3 to prepare 27 g of Al.

5.11 It requires 16.6 mol of CO to produce 16.6 mol of acetic acid.

5.12 334 g of ethanol is produced.

5.13 (a) C (0.50 mol) is the limiting reagent and H_2 (1.04 mol) is in slight excess.
(b) 8.0 g (0.50 mol) CH_4 is produced.

5.14 The percent yield is 81.00%.

5.15 The net ionic equation is
$Cu^{2+}(aq) + S^{2-}(aq) \longrightarrow CuS(s)$.

5.16 (a) Ni^{2+} gains two electrons, so it is reduced. Cr loses two electrons, so it is oxidized. Ni^{2+} is the oxidizing agent and Cr is the reducing agent.

(b) CH_2O gains hydrogens, so it is reduced. H_2 gains oxygen in being converted to CH_3OH, so it is oxidized. CH_2O is the oxidizing agent and H_2 is the reducing agent.

5.17 (a) KCl = 74.6 amu   (b) Na_3PO_4 = 163.9 amu
(c) $Fe(OH)_2$ = 89.9 amu

5.19 (a) $C_{12}H_{22}O_{11}$ = 342.3 amu   (b) $C_2H_5NO_2$ = 75.1 amu
(c) $C_{14}H_9Cl_5$ = 354.5 amu

5.21 (a) 81.4 g NO_2 (b) 50. g C_3H_8O (c) 1.30×10^3 g UF_6
(d) 62.7 g $C_6H_{12}O_6$ (d) 8.6 g $C_6H_8O_6$

5.23 (a) 6.56 mol S^{2-} ions   (b) 24.96 mol Mg^{2+} ions
(c) 0.86 mol acetate ions, CH_3COO^-

5.25 the same; that is, 2:1

5.27 (a) 2.9 mol TNT = 1.7×10^{24} TNT molecules
(b) 0.0500 g H_2O = 1.67×10^{21} H_2O molecules
(c) 3.1×10^{-3} g aspirin = 1.0×10^{21} aspirin molecules

5.29 1.1×10^{-19} grams per molecule.

5.31 (a) $H_2 + I_2 \longrightarrow 2$ HI
(b) $4Al + 3O_2 \longrightarrow 2Al_2O_3$
(c) $2Na + Cl_2 \longrightarrow 2NaCl$
(d) $2Al + 6HBr \longrightarrow 2AlBr_3 + 3H_2$
(e) $4P + 5O_2 \longrightarrow 2P_2O_5$

5.33 $CaCO_3(s) \xrightarrow{\text{Heat}} CaO(s) + CO_2(g)$

5.35 $4Fe(s) + 3O_2(g) \longrightarrow 2Fe_2O_3(s)$

5.37 $(NH_4)_2CO_3(s) \longrightarrow 2NH_3(g) + CO_2(g) + H_2O(\ell)$

5.39 $2Al(s) + 6HCl(aq) \longrightarrow 2AlCl_3(aq) + 3H_2(g)$

5.41 (a) 0.67 mol N_2 required
(b) 0.67 mol N_2O_3 produced
(c) 12 mol O_2 required

5.43 319 g of Cl_2 required

5.45 (a) The balanced equation is

$$2NaClO_2(aq) + Cl_2(g) \longrightarrow 2ClO_2(g) + 2NaCl(aq)$$

(b) 4.10 kg of ClO_2

5.47 7.5 g CO_2 required

5.49 0.13 g C needed

5.51 26 g of salicylic acid required

5.53 The theoretical yield is 12 g of ethyl chloride. The percentage yield in this problem is 68%.

5.55 (a) spectator ion: an ion that does not take part in a chemical reaction
(b) net ionic equation: a balanced equation with spectator ions removed
(c) aqueous solution: a solution using water as the solvent

5.57 (a) The spectator ions are Na^+ and Cl^-.
(b) $Sr^{2+}(aq) + CO_3^{2-}(aq) \longrightarrow SrCO_3(s)$

5.59 The net ionic equation is

$$Pb^{2+}(aq) + 2Cl^-(aq) \longrightarrow PbCl_2(s)$$

5.61 $NH_4^+(aq) + OH^-(aq) \longrightarrow NH_3(g) + H_2O(\ell)$

5.63 (a) $MgCl_2$ (soluble)
(b) $CaCO_3$ (insoluble)
(c) Na_2SO_3 (soluble)
(d) NH_4NO_3 (soluble)
(e) $Pb(OH)_2$ (insoluble)

5.65 No. In oxidation there is a loss of electrons, and there must be some species to accept those electrons—that is, some species that is reduced.

5.67 (a) C_7H_{14} is oxidized and O_2 is reduced.
(b) O_2 is the oxidizing agent, and C_7H_{14} is the reducing agent.

5.69 An exothermic chemical reaction or process releases heat as a product.
An endothermic chemical reaction or process absorbs heat as a reactant.

5.71 19.6 kcal

5.73 The heat liberated is 670/180 = 3.72 kcal/g of glucose. Therefore, metabolism of 15.0 grams of glucose will liberate 15.0 g × 3.72 kcal/g = 55.8 kcal.

5.75 (a) The synthesis of starch is endothermic.
(b) 26.4 kcal

5.77 Fluoride reacts with $Ca_{10}(PO_4)_6(OH)_2$ in the enamel by exchanging the F^- ions for OH^- ions, forming $Ca_{10}(PO_4)_6F_2$, which is less soluble under the acidic conditions found in the mouth.

5.79 Oxidation occurs at the anode, where Fe $\longrightarrow Fe^{2+}$ + $2e^-$. Reduction occurs at the cathode, where Zn^{2+} + $2e^- \longrightarrow$ Zn.

5.81 $N_2O_5(g) + H_2O(\ell) \longrightarrow 2HNO_3(aq)$

5.83 (a) Fe_2O_3 loses oxygen; it is reduced. CO gains oxygen; it is oxidized.
(b) 38.4 mol Fe requires 19.2 mol Fe_2O_3.
(c) 1.61×10^3 g CO is required.

5.85 $3Cd^{2+}(aq) + 2PO_4^{3-}(aq) \longrightarrow Cd_3(PO_4)_2(s)$

5.87 894 amu

5.89 (a) $Pb(NO_3)_2$ is the limiting reagent.
(b) 82.6% $PbCl_2$

5.91 (a) $C_5H_{12}(g) + 8O_2(g) \longrightarrow 5CO_2(g) + 6H_2O(g)$
(b) Pentane is oxidized and oxygen is reduced.
(c) Oxygen is the oxidizing agent and pentane is the reducing agent.

5.93 (a) $CH_4(g) + 2O_2(g) \longrightarrow CO_2(g)$
   Methane

$$+ 2H_2O(g) + 213 \text{ kcal/mol}$$

$$C_3H_8(g) + 5O_2(g) \longrightarrow 3CO_2(g)$$
   Propane

$$+ 4H_2O(g) + 530 \text{ kcal/mol}$$

(b) On the basis of kcal/mol, propane (530 kcal/mol) is a better source of heat energy than methane (213 kcal/mol).
(c) On the basis of kcal/gram, methane (13.3 kcal/g) is a better source of heat energy than propane (12.0 kcal/g).

Chapter 6   Gases, Liquids, and Solids

6.1   0.41 atm
6.2   16.4 atm
6.3   0.053 atm
6.4   4.84 atm
6.5   0.422 mol Ne
6.6   9.91 g He
6.7   0.107 atm H_2O vapor
6.8   (a) Yes, there can be hydrogen bonding between molecules of water and methanol.
(b) No, C—H bonds cannot form hydrogen bonds.
6.9   83 g H_2O can be vaporized.
6.10 Heat required to heat 1.0 g of iron to melting = 230 cal
6.11 According to the phase diagram of water (Figure 6.18), the vapor will condense to liquid water and then freeze at 0°. After all is frozen, the temperature will drop to −30°C.
6.13 1.5 atm CH_4
6.15 2.51 atm of air in the tire
6.17 1.87 L of ethane gas upon cooling
6.19 748 K (475°C)
6.21 1.17 atm

6.23

V_1	T_1	P_1	V_2	T_2	P_2
546 L	43°C	6.5 atm	**2.0 × 10³ mL**	65°C	1.9 atm
43 mL	−56°C	865 torr	**48 mL**	43°C	1.5 atm
4.2 L	234 K	0.87 atm	3.2 L	29°C	**1.5 atm**
1.3 L	25°C	740 mm Hg	**1.2 L**	0°C	1.0 atm

6.25 0.31 L is the balloon's final volume.
6.27 4.35 atm
6.29 61.0 mL
6.31 (a) 2.33 mol
(b) No. The only information that you need to know about the gas to solve this problem is that it is an ideal gas.
6.33 4.00 g/mol
6.35 Density increases as pressure increases and decreases as temperature increases.
6.37 (a) 24.7 mol O_2 (b) 790 g O_2
6.39 One lung volume of air (to two significant figures) contains 1.2 L (0.050 mol) of O_2, which is 3.0×10^{23} molecules of O_2.
6.41 (a) The mass of 1 mol of air (to two significant figures) is 29 g.
(b) The density of air is 1.29 g/L.
6.43 (a) SO_2 = 2.86 g/L
(b) CH_4 = 0.715 g/L
(c) H_2 = 0.0899 g/L
(d) He = 0.178 g/L
(e) CO_2 = 1.96 g/L
Gas comparison: SO_2 and CO_2 are more dense than air, and He, H_2, and CH_4 are less dense than air.
6.45 0.197 L
6.47 The densities would be the same. The density of a substance does not depend on its quantity.
6.49 (a) P_{N_2} = 593.4 mm Hg
P_{O_2} = 159.2 mm Hg
P_{Ar} = 7.1 mm Hg
$\overline{P_{total}}$ = 759.7 mm Hg or 760 mm Hg
(b) The total pressure exerted by the components is the sum of their partial pressures: 760. mm Hg (1.00 atm).
6.51 Yes. The partial pressures given in the problem total 785 mm Hg and the total pressure given is 790 mm Hg. The difference is 5 mm Hg. Therefore, there must be another gas present.
6.53 Intramolecular covalent bonds are stronger than intermolecular hydrogen bonds.
6.55 yes
6.57 Ethanol is a polar molecule and engages in intermolecular hydrogen bonding through its —OH group. Carbon dioxide is a nonpolar molecule, and the only forces of attraction between its molecules are weak London dispersion forces. The stronger hydrogen bonds require more energy (higher temperature) to break before vaporizing.
6.59 Hexane has the higher boiling point.
6.61 Ionic and network solids have the highest melting points. Molecular solids have the lowest melting points.
6.63 1.53 kcal to vaporize 39.2 g CF_2Cl_2
6.65 (a) approximately 90 mm Hg
(b) approximately 120 mm Hg
(c) approximately 330 mm Hg at 60°C

6.67 Boiling points are HCl = 84.9°C, HBr = −67°C, and HI = −35.4°C.
(a) HCl < HBr < HI; HCl is the most polar of the three acids, and hydrogen bonding would be strongest between molecules of HCl. The increasing size of each molecule increases the intermolecular London dispersion forces. London dispersion forces are the more important factor in determining the boiling points of this group of compounds.
(b) O_2 < HCl < H_2O_2; O_2 has only weak London dispersion forces between its molecules. HCl is a polar molecule with stronger dipole–dipole interactions between its molecules. H_2O_2 has the strongest intermolecular forces (hydrogen bonding) between its molecules.
6.69 The difference between heating water from 0°C to 37°C and heating ice from 0°C to 37°C is the heat of fusion of ice. 11,700 (1.2) kcal is required to heat ice from 0°C to 37°C. 3700 (3.7 kcal) is required to heat water from 0°C to 37°C.
6.71 sublimation
6.73 6.96×10^{-2} kcal
6.75 When the temperature of a substance increases, so does its entropy. Therefore, a gas at 100°C has a lower entropy than the same gas at 200°C.
6.77 When the diaphragm is lowered, the volume of the chest cavity increases, lowering the pressure in the lungs relative to the atmospheric pressure. Air at atmospheric pressure then rushes into the lungs, beginning the breathing process.
6.79 The first tapping sound one hears is the systolic pressure, which occurs when the sphygmomanometer pressure matches the blood pressure when the ventricle contracts, pushing blood into the arm.
6.81 When water freezes, it expands (water is one of the few substances that expands on freezing) and will crack the bottle when the ice expansion exceeds the volume of the bottle.
6.83 It is difficult to compress liquids and solids because their molecules are already very close together and there is very little empty space between them.
6.85 2.3 atm
6.87 Aerosol cans already contain gases under high pressure. Gay-Lussac's law predicts that the pressure inside the can will increase with increasing temperature, with the potential of explosive rupture of the can, causing injury.
6.89 112 mL
6.91 In order of increasing boiling point:
C_5H_{12} < $CHCl_3$ < H_2O
6.93 (a) When a gas is compressed, its molecules are forced closer together, at which point intermolecular forces are able to draw the molecules close enough to stick together and to form a liquid.
(b) 9.1 kg propane
(c) 2.1×10^2 mol propane
(d) 4.6×10^3 L propane
6.95 The density of the gas is 3.00 g/L and its molar mass is 91.9 g/mol.
6.97 313 K (40°C)
6.99 The temperature of a liquid decreases during evaporation because the molecules with higher kinetic energy leave the liquid, which decreases the average kinetic energy of those molecules remaining in the liquid. The temperature of the liquid is directly proportional to the average kinetic energy of the molecules in the liquid state. Therefore the temperature decreases as the average kinetic energy decreases.

6.101 (a) The pressure on the body is 4 atm.
(b) The partial pressure of N_2 entering the lungs is 3.1 atm.
(c) The partial pressure of O_2 entering the lungs is 0.83 atm.
(d) At 100 feet, the partial pressure of N_2 in the blood and fatty tissue is significantly increased. It takes time to release this N_2 by transfer to the blood and then to the lungs for exhalation. If a diver rises too quickly, too much N_2 remains in the blood and fatty tissue, affecting the nervous system. In addition, if bubbles of N_2 form in blood vessels, they can impede the flow of blood, which reduces the flow of O_2 to tissues.

Chapter 7 Solutions and Colloids

7.1 To 11 g of KBr, add a quantity of water sufficient to dissolve the KBr. Following dissolution of the KBr, add water to the 250 mL mark, stopper, and mix.
7.2 1.9% w/v
7.3 Place 158 g (2.12 mol) of KCl in a 2-L volumetric flask, add some water, swirl until the solid has dissolved, and then fill the flask with water to the 2.0 L mark.
7.4 0.0133 M KSCN
7.5 185 mL of glucose solution
7.6 Add 3.9×10^2 g $NaHSO_3$ to a 100-gallon barrel.
7.7 Place 50–100 mL of water in a 300-mL flask, add 15.0 mL of 12.0 M HCl, swirl until completely mixed, and then fill the flask with water to the 300 mL mark.
7.8 Place 0.13 mL of the 15% KOH solution in a 20-mL volumetric flask, add some water, swirl until completely dissolved, and then fill the flask with water to the 20 mL mark.
7.9 The Na^+ ion concentration is 0.24 ppm Na^+.
7.10 $-12.5°C$
7.11 Solution (c), 4.3 M K_2SO_3, has the highest concentration of solute particles and, therefore, has the lowest freezing point.
7.12 A Na_3PO_4 molecule gives 3 Na^+ ions and 1 PO_4^{3-} ion for a total of 4 solute particles. This solution is 0.81 osmol.
7.13 Solution (a) has the same osmolarity as red blood cells and, therefore, is isotonic compared to red blood cells.
7.15 Glucose is being dissolved; therefore, it is the solute. Water is dissolving the glucose; therefore, water is the solvent.
7.17 (a) wine (ethanol in water)
(b) saline solution (NaCl dissolved in water)
(c) carbonated water (CO_2 dissolved in water)
(d) air (O_2 and N_2)
7.19 One possible explanation is that the prepared aspartic acid solution was unsaturated. Over two days, some of the solvent (water) may have evaporated and the solution became supersaturated, precipitating the excess aspartic acid as a white solid.
7.21 (a) NaCl (an ionic solid) will dissolve in the polar water layer.
(b) Camphor (a nonpolar molecule) will dissolve in the nonpolar diethyl ether layer.
(c) KOH (an ionic solid) will dissolve in the polar water layer.
7.23 Isopropyl alcohol would be a good first choice. The oil base in the paint is nonpolar. Both benzene and hexane are nonpolar solvents and may dissolve the paint, destroying the painting.
7.25 The solubility of aspartic acid at 25°C in 50.0 mL of water is 0.250 g of solute. Assuming that no precipitation

occurs, the cooled solution will contain 0.251 g of aspartic acid in 50.0 mL of water and will be supersaturated by 0.001 g of aspartic acid.
7.27 According to Henry's law, the solubility of a gas in a liquid is directly proportional to the pressure. A closed bottle of a carbonated beverage is under excess CO_2 pressure. After the bottle is opened, the excess CO_2 pressure is released and the CO_2 escapes from solution as bubbles of gas.

7.29 (a) $\dfrac{1 \text{ min}}{1.05 \times 10^6 \text{ min}} \times 10^6 = 1$ ppm

$\dfrac{1 \text{ p}}{1.05 \times 10^6 \text{ p}} \times 10^6 = 1$ ppm

(b) $\dfrac{1 \text{ min}}{1.05 \times 10^9 \text{ min}} \times 10^9 = 1$ ppb

$\dfrac{1 \text{ p}}{1.05 \times 10^9 \text{ p}} \times 10^9 = 1$ ppm

7.31 (a) 76 mL of ethanol is dissolved in 204 mL of water to give 280 mL of solution.
(b) 7.8 mL of ethyl acetate is dissolved in 427 mL of water to give 435 mL of solution.
(c) 0.13 L of benzene is dissolved in 1.52 L of chloroform to give 1.65 L of solution.
7.33 (a) 4.15% w/v casein
(b) 0.030% w/v vitamin C
(c) 1.75% w/v sucrose
7.35 (a) Place 19.5 g of NH_4Br into a 175-mL volumetric flask, add some water, swirl to mix completely, and then fill the flask with water to the 175 mL mark.
(b) Place 167 g of NaI in a 1.35-L volumetric flask, add some water, swirl to mix completely, and then fill the flask with water to the 1.35 L mark.
(c) Place 2.4 g of ethanol in a 330-mL volumetric flask, add some water, swirl to mix completely, and then fill the flask with water to the 330 mL mark.
7.37 0.2 M NaCl
7.39 (a) 0.509 M glucose   **(b)** 0.0202 M K^+
(c) 7.25×10^{-4} M Na^+
7.41 2.5 M sucrose
7.43 The total volume of the diluted solution will be 30.0 mL. Start with 5.0 mL of solution and add 25.0 mL of water to reach a final volume of 30.0 mL.
7.45 Place 2.1 mL of 30.0% w/v H_2O_2 into a 250-mL volumetric flask, add some water, swirl to mix completely, and fill the flask with water to the 250 mL mark.
7.47 (a) 3.85×10^4 ppm Captopril
(b) 6.8×10^4 ppm Mg^{2+} **(c)** 8.3×10^2 ppm Ca^{2+}
7.49 Dioxin concentration = 0.01 ppb dioxin.
No, the dioxin level in the lake did not reach a dangerous level.
7.51 (a) 10 ppm Fe or 1×10^1 ppm
(b) 3×10^3 ppm Ca
(c) 2 ppm vitamin A
7.53 (b) 0.1 M $(NH_4)_3PO_4$
7.55 The polar covalent compounds (b) CH_3OH, (c) HF, and (d) NH_3 dissolve in water by forming hydrogen bonds with water molecules.
7.57 (a) homogeneous **(b)** heterogeneous **(c)** colloidal
(d) heterogeneous **(e)** colloidal **(f)** colloidal
7.59 As the temperature of the solution decreases, the protein molecules aggregate and form a colloidal mixture. The turbid appearance is the result of the Tyndall effect.
7.61 (a) $-3.72°C$ **(b)** $-5.58°C$ **(c)** $-5.58°C$ **(d)** $-7.44°C$

7.63 3.4×10^2 g CH_3OH

7.65 Acetic acid is a weak acid and, therefore, not completely dissociated into ions. KF is a strong electrolyte and ionizes completely in aqueous solution, thus doubling the effect on the freezing-point depression compared to acetic acid.

7.67 Assume that the first entry is column A, and that the second entry is column B. In each case, the side with the greater osmolarity rises.
(a) B (b) B (c) A (d) B (e) A (f) same

7.69 (a) 1.2 osmol (b) 2.5 osmol (c) 8.4 osmol
(d) 0.04 osmol

7.71 Red blood cells will undergo crenation (shrink) in a hypertonic solution. A 0.9% NaCl solution is 0.3 osmol. Solution (b) is 0.9 osmol (hypertonic) and will crenate red blood cells.

7.73 Carbon dioxide (CO_2) dissolves in rainwater to form a dilute solution of carbonic acid (H_2CO_3), which is a weak acid.

7.75 Nitrogen dissolved in the blood can lead to a narcotic effect referred to as "rapture of the deep," which is similar to alcohol-induced intoxication.

7.77 The main component of limestone and marble is calcium carbonate, $CaCO_3$.

7.79 The minimum pressure required for reverse osmosis in the desalinization of sea water exceeds 100 atm (the osmotic pressure of sea water).

7.81 Yes, the change in composition made a change in the tonicity. The error in replacing $NaHCO_3$ with $KHCO_3$ resulted in a hypotonic solution and an electrolyte imbalance by reducing the number of ions (osmolarity) in solution.

7.83 When a cucumber is placed in a saline solution, the osmolarity of the saline solution is greater than that of the water in the cucumber, so water moves from the cucumber to the saline solution and the cucumber shrinks. When a prune (a partially dehydrated plum) is placed in the same solution, it expands because the osmolarity inside the prune is greater than that of the saline solution, so water moves from the saline solution to inside the prune, causing the prune to expand.

7.85 The solubility of a gas in a solvent is directly proportional to the pressure (Henry's law) of the gas and is inversely proportional to the temperature. The dissolved carbon dioxide formed a saturated solution in water when bottled under 2 atm pressure. When the bottles are opened at atmospheric pressure, the gas becomes less soluble. The carbon dioxide becomes supersaturated in water at room temperature and 1 atm, and thus escapes as bubbles and frothing. In the other bottle, the solution of carbon dioxide in water is unsaturated at a lower temperature and does not lose carbon dioxide as readily.

7.87 No, it would not be acceptable to use an 0.89% KCl solution for intravenous infusions because it will not be isotonic with blood. KCl has a higher molecular weight than NaCl; consequently, its osmolarity will be smaller.

7.89 3×10^{-7} g Pb

7.91 (a) 0.9% w/v NaCl has the greater osmotic pressure by a factor of 18 times.

7.93 2.9 mL of pure water added to 1.0 mL of sea water gives a solution with the same osmolarity as blood.

7.95 The ethanol molecules displace water molecules from the solvation layer of the hyaluronic acid, allowing the hyaluronic acid molecules to stick together upon collision and form aggregates that precipitate.

Chapter 8   Reaction Rates and Chemical Equilibrium

8.1 rate of O_2 formation = 0.022 L O_2/min

8.2 rate = 4×10^{-3} mol H_2O_2/L · min for disappearance of H_2O_2

8.3 $K = \dfrac{[H_2SO_4]}{[SO_3][H_2O]}$

8.4 $K = \dfrac{[N_2][H_2]^3}{[NH_3]^2}$

8.5 $K = 0.602\ M^{-1}$

8.6 $K = \dfrac{[CH_3COOCH_2CH_3][H_2O]}{[CH_3COOH][HOCH_2CH_3]}$

8.7 Le Chatelier's principle predicts that adding Br_2 (a product) will shift the equilibrium to the left—that is, toward the formation of more NOBr(g).

8.8 Because oxygen's solubility in water is exceeded, oxygen bubbles out of the solution, driving the equilibrium toward the right.

8.9 If the equilibrium shifts to the right with the addition of heat, heat must have been a reactant, and the reaction is endothermic.

8.10 The equilibrium in a reaction where there is an increase in pressure favors the side with fewer moles of gas. Therefore, this equilibrium shifts to the right.

8.11 rate of formation of $CH_3I = 7.3 \times 10^{-3}\ M\ CH_3I$/min

8.13 Reactions involving ions in aqueous solution of ions are faster because they do not require bond breaking and have low activation energies. In addition, the attractive force between positive and negative ions provides energy to drive the reaction. Reactions between covalent compounds require the breaking of covalent bonds and have higher activation energies and, therefore, slower reaction rates.

8.15 The activation energy for the reverse reaction will be 14 + 9 = 23 kcal/mol.

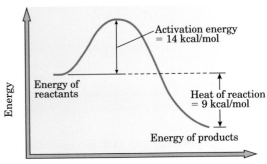

Progress of reaction

8.17 A general rule for the effect of temperature on the rate of reaction states that for every temperature increase of 10°C, the reaction rate doubles. In this case, a reaction temperature of 50°C would predict completion of the reaction in 1 h.

8.19 You might (a) increase the temperature, (b) increase the concentration of reactants, or (c) add a catalyst.

8.21 A catalyst increases the rate of a reaction by providing an alternative reaction pathway with lower activation energy.

8.23 Other examples of irreversible reactions include digesting a piece of candy, rusting of iron, exploding TNT, and the reaction of Na or K metal with water.

8.25 (a) $K = [H_2O]^2[O_2]/[H_2O_2]^2$
(b) $K = [N_2O_4]^2[O_2]/[N_2O_5]^2$
(c) $K = [C_6H_{12}O_6][O_2]^6/[H_2O]^6[CO_2]^6$

8.27 $K = 0.667$

8.29 $K = 0.099\ M$

8.31 Products are favored in (b) and (c). Reactants are favored in (a), (d), and (e).

8.33 No. The rate of reaction is independent of the energy difference between products and reactants—that is, it is independent of the heat of reaction.

8.35 The reaction reaches equilibrium quickly, but the position of equilibrium favors the reactants; therefore, it would not be a very good industrial process.

8.37 (a) right   (b) right   (c) left   (d) left   (e) no shift

8.39 (a) Adding Br_2 (a reactant) will shift the equilibrium to the right.
(b) The equilibrium constant will remain the same.

8.41 (a) no change   (b) no change   (c) smaller

8.43 As temperatures increase, the rates of most chemical processes increase. A high body temperature is dangerous because metabolic processes (including digestion, respiration, and biosynthesis of essential compounds) take place at a faster rate than is safe for the body. As temperatures decrease, so do the rates of most chemical reactions. As body temperature decreases below normal, the vital chemical reactions will slow to rates slower than is safe for the body.

8.45 The capsule with the tiny beads will act faster than the solid coated-pill form. The small bead size increases the drug's surface area, allowing the drug to react faster and deliver its therapeutic effects more quickly.

8.47 The addition of heat is used to increase the rate of reaction. The addition of a catalyst permits the reaction to take place at a more convenient temperature.

8.49 The following energy diagram can be drawn for this exothermic reaction.

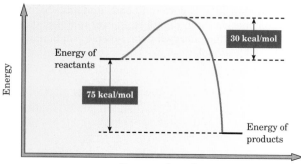

8.51 rate = 0.37/h

8.53 rate = 2.0×10^{-3} mol N_2O_4/L · s for disappearance of reactants

8.55 The activation energy of the reverse reaction will be 10.0 kcal/mol − energy of reaction.

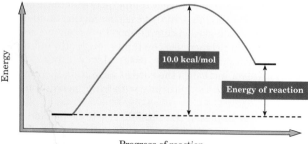

8.57 The temperature increase is 20°C, and the reaction rate would be predicted to double twice. The rate of reaction at 320 K is predicted to be 0.88 M/min.

8.59 No. An endothermic reaction must have an energy of activation greater than zero. By definition, an endothermic reaction is one in which the products have a greater energy than the reactants.

8.61 Assuming that there is an excess of AgCl from the previous recipe, the recipe does not need to be changed. The desert conditions add nothing that would affect the coating process.

8.63

(a)
$$\underset{\substack{\text{Initial} \quad 1.00\ \text{mol} \quad\quad 1.00\ \text{mol} \\ \text{At equilibrium} \quad 0.33\ \text{mol} \quad\quad \textbf{0.33 mol}}}{\overset{\overset{\displaystyle O}{\displaystyle \|}}{CH_3COH} + HOCH_2CH_3}$$

$$\underset{\substack{0\ \text{mol} \quad\quad\quad 0\ \text{mol} \\ \textbf{0.67 mol} \quad\quad \textbf{0.67 mol}}}{\rightleftharpoons \overset{\overset{\displaystyle O}{\displaystyle \|}}{CH_3COCH_2CH_3} + H_2O}$$

(b) $K = 4.1$

Chapter 9   Acids and Bases

9.1 acid reaction: $HPO_4^{2-} + H_2O \rightleftharpoons PO_4^{3-} + H_3O^+$; base reaction: $HPO_4^{2-} + H_2O \rightleftharpoons H_2PO_4^- + OH^-$

9.2 (a) toward the left;

$$\underset{\substack{\text{Weaker} \\ \text{acid}}}{H_3O^+} + \underset{\substack{\text{Weaker} \\ \text{base}}}{I^-} \rightleftharpoons \underset{\substack{\text{Stronger} \\ \text{base}}}{H_2O} + \underset{\substack{\text{Stronger} \\ \text{acid}}}{HI}$$

(b) toward the right;

$$\underset{\substack{\text{Weaker} \\ \text{base}}}{CH_3COO^-} + \underset{\substack{\text{Weaker} \\ \text{acid}}}{H_2S} \rightleftharpoons \underset{\substack{\text{Stronger} \\ \text{acid}}}{CH_3COOH} + \underset{\substack{\text{Stronger} \\ \text{base}}}{HS^-}$$

9.3 pK_a is 9.31

9.4 (a) ascorbic acid   (b) aspirin

9.5 1.0×10^{-2}

9.6 (a) 2.46   (b) 7.8×10^{-5}, acidic

9.7 pOH = 4, pH = 10

9.8 0.0960 M

9.9 (a) 9.25   (b) 4.74

9.10 9.61

9.11 7.7

9.13 (a) $HNO_3(aq) + H_2O(\ell) \longrightarrow NO_3^-(aq) + H_3O^+(aq)$
(b) $HBr(aq) + H_2O(\ell) \longrightarrow Br^-(aq) + H_3O^+(aq)$
(c) $H_2SO_3(aq) + H_2O(\ell) \longrightarrow HSO_3^-(aq) + H_3O^+(aq)$
(d) $H_2SO_4(aq) + H_2O(\ell) \longrightarrow HSO_4^-(aq) + H_3O^+(aq)$
(e) $HCO_3^-(aq) + H_2O(\ell) \longrightarrow CO_3^{2-}(aq) + H_3O^+(aq)$
(f) $H_3BO_3(aq) + H_2O(\ell) \longrightarrow H_2BO_3^-(aq) + H_3O^+(aq)$

9.15 (a) weak   (b) strong   (c) weak   (d) strong
(e) weak   (f) weak

9.17 weak

9.19 (a) A Brønsted-Lowry acid is a proton donor.
(b) A Brønsted-Lowry base is a proton acceptor.

9.21 (a) HPO_4^{2-} (b) HS^- (c) CO_3^{2-}
(d) $CH_3CH_2O^-$ (e) OH^-

9.23 (a) H_3O^+ (b) $H_2PO_4^-$ (c) $CH_3NH_3^+$
(d) HPO_4^{2-} (e) $H_2BO_3^-$

9.25 The equilibrium favors the side with the weaker acid–weaker base combination. Equilibria (b) and (c) lie to the left; equilibrium (a) lies to the right.

(a) $C_6H_5OH + C_2H_5O^- \rightleftharpoons C_6H_5O^- + C_2H_5OH$

      Stronger   Stronger   Weaker   Weaker
       acid   base   base   acid

(b) $HCO_3^- + H_2O \rightleftharpoons H_2CO_3 + OH^-$

    Weaker   Weaker   Stronger   Stronger
     base   acid   acid   base

(c) $CH_3COOH + H_2PO_4^- \rightleftharpoons CH_3COO^- + H_3PO_4$

    Weaker   Weaker   Stronger   Stronger
     acid   base   base   acid

9.27 (a) the pK_a of a weak acid (b) the K_a of a strong acid
9.29 (a) 0.10 M HCl (b) 0.10 M H_3PO_4 (c) 0.010 M
H_2CO_3 (d) 0.10 M NaH_2PO_4 (e) 0.10 M aspirin
9.31 Only (b) is a redox reaction. The others are acid–base
reactions.
(a) $Na_2CO_3 + 2HCl \longrightarrow 2NaCl + CO_2 + H_2O$
(b) $Mg + 2HCl \longrightarrow MgCl_2 + H_2$
(c) $NaOH + HCl \longrightarrow NaCl + H_2O$
(d) $Fe_2O_3 + 6HCl \longrightarrow 2FeCl_3 + 3H_2O$
(e) $NH_3 + HCl \longrightarrow NH_4Cl$
(f) $CH_3NH_2 + HCl \longrightarrow CH_3NH_3Cl$
(g) $NaHCO_3 + HCl \longrightarrow NaCl + H_2O + CO_2$
9.33 (a) $10^{-3} M$ (b) $10^{-10} M$ (c) $10^{-7} M$ (d) $10^{-15} M$
9.35 (a) pH = 8 (basic) (b) pH = 10 (basic) (c) pH = 2
(acidic) (d) pH = 0 (acidic) (e) pH = 7 (neutral)
9.37 (a) pH = 8.5 (basic) (b) pH = 1.2 (acidic)
(c) pH = 11.1 (basic) (d) pH = 6.3 (acidic)
9.39 (a) pOH = 1.0, $[OH^-]$ = 0.10 M
(b) pOH = 2.4, $[OH^-]$ = $4.0 \times 10^{-3} M$
(c) pOH = 2.0, $[OH^-]$ = $1.0 \times 10^{-2} M$
(d) pOH = 5.6, $[OH^-]$ = $2.5 \times 10^{-6} M$
9.41 0.348 M
9.43 (a) 12 g of NaOH diluted to 400 mL of solution:

$$400 \text{ mL sol} \left(\frac{1 \text{ L sol}}{1000 \text{ mL sol}} \right) \left(\frac{0.75 \text{ mol NaOH}}{1 \text{ L sol}} \right)$$

$$\times \left(\frac{40.0 \text{ g NaOH}}{1 \text{ mol NaOH}} \right) = 12 \text{ g NaOH}$$

(b) 12 g of $Ba(OH)_2$ diluted to 1.0 L of solution:

$$\left(\frac{0.071 \text{ mol } Ba(OH)_2}{1 \text{ L sol}} \right) \left(\frac{171.4 \text{ } Ba(OH)_2}{1 \text{ mol } Ba(OH)_2} \right) = 12 \text{ g } Ba(OH)_2$$

9.45 5.66 mL
9.47 3.30×10^{-3} mol
9.49 The point at which the observed change occurs during
a titration. It is usually so close to the equivalence point
that the difference between the two becomes insignificant.
9.51 (a)
$H_3O^+ + CH_3COO^- \rightleftharpoons CH_3COOH + H_2O$ (removal of H_3O^+)
(b)
$HO^- + CH_3COOH \rightleftharpoons CH_3COO^- + H_2O$ (removal of OH^-)
9.53 Yes, the conjugate acid becomes the weak acid and the
weak base becomes the conjugate base.
9.55 The pH of a buffer can be changed by altering the
weak acid/conjugate base ratio, according to the Henderson-
Hasselbalch equation. The buffer capacity can be changed
without a change in pH by increasing or decreasing the
amount of weak acid/conjugate base mixture while keeping
the ratio of the two constant.
9.57 This would occur in a couple of cases. One is very common: You are using a buffer, such as Tris with a pK_a of 8.3,
but you do not want the solution to have a pH of 8.3. If you
wanted a pH of 8.0, for example, you would need unequal

amounts of the conjugate acid and base, with there being
more conjugate acid. Another case might be a situation
where you are performing a reaction that you know will
generate H^+ but you want the pH to be stable. In that situation, you might start with a buffer that was initially set
to have more of the conjugate base so that it could absorb
more of the H^+ that you know will be produced.
9.59 (a) According to the Henderson-Hasselbalch equation,
no change in pH will be observed as long as the weak
acid/conjugate base ratio remains the same.
(b) The buffer capacity increases with increasing amounts
of weak acid/conjugate base concentrations; therefore,
1.0-mol amounts of each diluted to 1 L would have a
greater buffer capacity than 0.1 mol of each diluted to 1 L.
9.61 (a) 3.55 (b) 8.55
9.63 no
9.65 8.0
9.67 No. Hepes has a pK_a of 7.55, which means it is a
usable buffer between pH 6.55 and 8.55.
9.69 $Mg(OH)_2$ is a weak base used in flame-retardant
plastics.
9.71 Strong bases are more harmful to the cornea because
the healing of the wounds can deposit nontransparent scar
tissue that impairs vision.
9.73 (a) Respiratory acidosis is caused by hypoventilation,
which occurs due to a variety of breathing difficulties,
such as a windpipe obstruction, asthma, or pneumonia.
(b) Metabolic acidosis is caused by starvation or heavy
exercise.
9.75 Sodium bicarbonate is the weak base form of one of
the blood buffers. It tends to raise the pH of blood, which
is the purpose of the sprinter's trick, so that the person
can absorb more H^+ during the event. By putting $NaHCO_3$
into the system, the following reaction will occur:
$HCO_3^- + H^+ \rightleftharpoons H_2CO_3$. The loss of H^+ means that the
blood pH will rise.
9.77 (a) Benzoic acid is soluble in aqueous NaOH.
$C_6H_5COOH + NaOH \rightleftharpoons C_6H_5COO^- + H_2O$
$pK_a = 4.19$ $pK_a = 15.56$
(b) Benzoic acid is soluble in aqueous $NaHCO_3$.
$C_6H_5COOH + NaHCO_3 \rightleftharpoons CH_3C_6H_4O^- + H_2CO_3$
$pK_a = 4.19$ $pK_a = 6.37$
(c) Benzoic acid is soluble in aqueous Na_2CO_3.
$C_6H_5COOH + CO_3^{2-} \rightleftharpoons CH_3C_6H_4O^- + HCO_3^-$
$pK_a = 4.19$ $pK_a = 10.25$
9.79 The strength of an acid is not important to the
amount of NaOH that would be required to hit a phenolphthalein endpoint. Therefore, the more concentrated acid,
the acetic acid, would require more NaOH.
9.81 3.70×10^{-3}
9.83 0.9 M
9.85 Yes, a pH of 0 is possible. A 1.0 M solution of HCl
has $[H_3O^+]$ = 1.0 M. pH = $-\log[H_3O^+]$ = $-\log[1.0 \, M]$ = 0
9.87 The qualitative relationship between acids and their
conjugate bases states that the stronger the acid, the
weaker its conjugate base. This can be quantified in the
equation $K_b \times K_a = K_w$ or $K_b = 1.0 \times 10^{-14}/K_a$, where K_b
is the base dissociation equilibrium constant for the conju-
gate base, K_a is the acid dissociation equilibruim constant
for the acid, and K_w is the ionization equilibrium constant
for water.
9.89 Yes. The strength of the acid is irrelevant. Both acetic
acid and HCl have one H^+ to give up, so equal moles of
either will require equal moles of NaOH to titrate to an
end point.

9.91 need 0.182 mol of $H_2BO_3^-$ and 1.00 mol of H_3BO_3 in 1.00 L solution

9.93 An equilibrium will favor the side of the weaker acid/weaker base. The larger the pK_a value, the weaker the acid.

9.95 (a) $HCOO^- + H_3O^+ \rightleftharpoons HCOOH + H_2O$
(b) $HCOOH + HO^- \rightleftharpoons HCOO^- + H_2O$

9.97 (a) 0.050 mol   (b) 0.0050 mol   (c) 0.50 mol

9.99 According to the Henderson-Hasselbalch equation,

$$pH = 7.21 + \log \frac{[HPO_4^{2-}]}{[H_2PO_4^-]}$$

As the concentration of $H_2PO_4^-$ increases, the $\log \frac{[HPO_4^{2-}]}{[H_2PO_4^-]}$ becomes negative, lowering the pH and becoming more acidic.

9.101 No. A buffer will have a pH equal to its pK_a only if equimolar amounts of the conjugate acid and base forms are present. If this is the basic form of Tris, then just putting any amount of it into water will give a pH much higher than the pK_a value.

9.103 (a) pH = 7.1, $[H_3O^+] = 7.9 \times 10^{-8}\ M$, basic
(b) pH = 2.0, $[H_3O^+] = 7.9 \times 10^{-2}\ M$, acidic
(c) pH = 7.4, $[H_3O^+] = 4.0 \times 10^{-8}\ M$, basic
(d) pH = 7.0, $[H_3O^+] = 1.0 \times 10^{-7}\ M$, neutral
(e) pH = 6.6, $[H_3O^+] = 2.5 \times 10^{-7}\ M$, acidic
(f) pH = 7.4, $[H_3O^+] = 4.0 \times 10^{-8}\ M$, basic
(g) pH = 6.5, $[H_3O^+] = 3.2 \times 10^{-7}\ M$, acidic
(h) pH = 6.9, $[H_3O^+] = 1.3 \times 10^{-7}\ M$, acidic

9.105 4.9:1, or 5:1 to one significant figure

Chapter 10   Organic Chemistry

10.1 Following are Lewis structures showing all bond angles.

(a) H—C—C—O—H   CH₃CH₂OH

(b) H—C—C=C—H

10.2 Of the four alcohols with the molecular formula $C_4H_{10}O$, two are 1°, one is 2°, and one is 3°. For the Lewis structures of the 3° alcohol and one of the 1° alcohols, some C—CH₃ bonds are drawn longer to avoid crowding in the formulas.

(a) H—C—C—C—C—O—H   CH₃CH₂CH₂CH₂OH
Primary (1°)

(b) H—C—C—C—C—H   CH₃CH₂CHCH₃
Secondary (2°)

(c) H—C—C—C—O—H   CH₃CHCH₂OH
Primary (1°)

(d) H—C—C—OH   CH₃COH
Tertiary (3°)

10.3 The three secondary (2°) amines with the molecular formula $C_4H_{11}N$ are

$CH_3CH_2CH_2NHCH_3$ $CH_3CHNHCH_3$ $CH_3CH_2NHCH_2CH_3$

10.4 The three ketones with the molecular formula $C_5H_{10}O$ are

$CH_3CH_2CH_2CCH_3$ $CH_3CH_2CCH_2CH_3$ CH_3CCHCH_3

10.5 The two carboxylic acids with the molecular formula $C_4H_8O_2$ are

$CH_3CH_2CH_2COH$ CH_3CHCOH

10.6 The four esters with the molecular formula $C_4H_8O_2$ are

$HCOCH_2CH_2CH_3$ (1) $HCOCHCH_3$ (2)

$CH_3COCH_2CH_3$ (3) $CH_3CH_2COCH_3$ (4)

10.7 Assuming each is pure, there is no differences in chemical or physical properties.

10.9 Wöhler heated ammonium chloride and silver cyanate, both inorganic compounds, and obtained urea, an organic compound.

10.11 Among the textile fibers, think of natural fibers such as cotton, wool, and silk. Think also of synthetic textile fibers such as Nylon, Dacron polyester, and polypropylene.

Glossary

Absolute zero (*Section 1.4*) The lowest possible temperature; the zero point of the Kelvin temperature scale.

Acetal (*Section 17.4C*) A molecule containing two —OR groups bonded to the same carbon.

Achiral (*Section 15.1*) An object that lacks chirality; an object that is superposable on its mirror image.

Acid (*Section 9.1*) An Arrhenius acid is a substance that ionizes in aqueous solution to give a hydronium ion, H_3O^+, and an anion.

Acid–base reaction (*Section 9.3*) A proton-transfer reaction.

Acid ionization constant (K_a) (*Section 9.5*) An equilibrium constant for the ionization of an acid in aqueous solution to H_3O^+ and its conjugate base. K_a is also called an **acid dissociation constant**.

Acid rain (*Chemical Connections 7A*) Rain with acids other than carbonic acid dissolved in it.

Acidosis (*Chemical Connections 9D*) A condition in which the pH of blood is lower than 7.35.

Acquired immunity (*Section 31.1*) The second line of defense that vertebrates have against invading organisms.

Activating receptor (*Section 31.7*) A receptor on a cell of the innate immune system that triggers activation of the immune cell in response to a foreign antigen.

Activation energy (*Section 8.2*) The minimum energy necessary to cause a chemical reaction.

Actual yield (*Section 5.5C*) The mass of product formed in a chemical reaction.

Acyl group (*Section 18.3A*) An RCO— group.

Adaptive immunity (*Section 31.1*) Acquired immunity with specificity and memory.

Adhesion molecules (*Section 31.5*) Various protein molecules that help to bind an antigen to the T-cell receptor.

Advanced glycation end products (*Section 22.7*) A chemical product of sugars and proteins linking together to produce an imine.

Affinity maturation (*Section 31.4*) The process of mutation of T cells and B cells in response to an antigen.

AIDS (*Section 31.8*) *A*cquired *i*mmune *d*eficiency *s*yndrome. The disease caused by the human immunodeficiency virus, which attacks and depletes T cells.

Alcohol (*Section 10.3A*) A compound containing an —OH (hydroxyl) group bonded to a tetrahedral carbon atom.

Aldehyde (*Section 10.3C*) A compound containing a carbonyl group bonded to a hydrogen; a —CHO group.

Aliphatic amine (*Section 16.1*) An amine in which nitrogen is bonded only to alkyl groups.

Aliphatic hydrocarbon (*Section 11.1*) An alkane.

Alkaloid (*Chemical Connections 16B*) A basic nitrogen-containing compound of plant origin, many of which have physiological activity when administered to humans.

Alkalosis (*Chemical Connections 9E*) A condition in which the pH of blood is greater than 7.45.

Alkane (*Section 11.1*) A saturated hydrocarbon whose carbon atoms are arranged in an open chain—that is, not arranged in a ring.

Alkene (*Section 12.1*) An unsaturated hydrocarbon that contains a carbon–carbon double bond.

Alkyl group (*Section 11.3A*) A group derived by removing a hydrogen atom from an alkane; given the symbol R—.

Alkyne (*Section 12.1*) An unsaturated hydrocarbon that contains a carbon–carbon triple bond.

Allosteric proteins (*Chemical Connections 22G*) Proteins that exhibit a behavior where binding of one molecule at one site changes the ability of the protein to bind another molecule at a different site.

Alloys (*Section 7.2*) Homogeneous mixtures of metals.

Alpha (α-) amino acid (*Section 22.2*) An amino acid in which the amino group is bonded to the carbon atom next to the —COOH carbon.

Alpha helix (*Section 22.9*) A type of repeating secondary structure of a protein in which the chain adopts a helical conformation and the structure is held together by hydrogen bonds from the peptide backbone N—H to the backbone C=O four amino acids farther up the chain.

Alpha particle (α) (*Section 3. 2*) A helium nucleus, He^{2+}, ^4_2He.

Amino acid (*Section 22.1*) An organic compound containing an amino group and a carboxyl group.

Amino group (*Section 10.3B*) An —NH_2 group.

Amorphous solid (*Section 6.9*) A solid whose atoms, molecules, or ions are not in an orderly arrangement.

Amphiprotic (*Section 9.3*) A substance that can act as either an acid or a base.

Amphoteric (*Section 9.3*) An alternative for amphiprotic.

Amylase (*Section 30.3*) An enzyme that catalyzes the hydrolysis of α-1, 4-glycosidic bonds in dietary starches.

Aneuploid cell (*Chemical Connections 31F*) A cell with the wrong number of chromosomes.

Anion (*Section 4.2*) An ion with a negative electric charge.

Anode (*Chemical Connections 5B*) The negatively charged electrode.

Antibody (*Section 31.1*) A defense glycoprotein synthesized by the immune system of vertebrates that interacts with an antigen. It is also called an immunoglobulin.

Antigen (*Sections 31.1, 31.3*) A substance foreign to the body that triggers an immune response.

Antigen-presenting cells (**APCs**) (*Section 31.2*) Cells that cleave foreign molecules and present them on their surfaces for binding to T cells or B cells.

Aqueous solution (*Section 5.6*) A solution in which the solvent is water.

Ar— (*Section 13.1*) The symbol used for an aryl group.

Arene (*Section 13.1*) A compound containing one or more benzene rings.

Aromatic amine (*Section 16.1*) An amine in which nitrogen is bonded to one or more aromatic rings.

Aromatic compound (*Section 13.1*) A term used to classify benzene and its derivatives.

Aromatic sextet (*Section 13.1B*) The closed loop of six electrons (two from the second bond of each double bond) characteristic of a benzene ring.

Aryl group (*Section 13.1*) A group derived from an arene by removal of a hydrogen atom. Given the symbol Ar—.

Autoxidation (*Section 13.4C*) The reaction of a C—H group with oxygen, O_2, to form a hydroperoxide, R—OOH.

Avogadro's law (*Section 6.4*) Equal volumes of gases at the same temperature and pressure contain the same number of molecules.

Avogadro's number (*Section 5.3*) 6.02×10^{23} formula units per mole; the amount of any substance that contains the same number of formula units as the number of atoms in 12 g of carbon-12.

Axial position (*Section 11.5B*) A position on a chair conformation of a cyclohexane ring that extends from the ring parallel to the imaginary axis of the ring.

B cell (*Section 31.1*) A type of lymphocyte that is produced in and matures in the bone marrow. B cells produce antibody molecules.

Basal caloric requirement (*Section 30.2*) The caloric requirement for an individual at rest, usually given in Cal/day.

Base (*Section 9.1*) An Arrhenius base is a substance that ionizes in aqueous solution to give hydroxide (OH^-) ions and an cation.

Becquerel (Bq) (*Section 3.5A*) A measure of radioactive decay, equal to one disintegration per second.

Beta (β-) pleated sheet (*Section 22.9*) A type of secondary protein structure in which the backbone of two protein chains in the same or different molecules is held together by hydrogen bonds.

Beta particle (β) (*Section 3. 2*) An electron, $_{-1}^{0}\beta$.

Binary compound (*Section 4.6A*) A compound containing two elements.

Boiling point (*Section 6.8C*) The temperature at which the vapor pressure of a liquid is equal to the atmospheric pressure.

Bond angle (*Section 4.10*) The angle between two atoms bonded to a central atom.

Bonding electrons (*Section 4.7C*) Valence electrons involved in forming a covalent bond—that is, shared electrons.

Boyle's Law (*Section 6.3A*) The volume of a gas at constant temperature is inversely proportional to the pressure applied to the gas.

Brønsted-Lowry acid (*Section 9.3*) A proton donor.

Brønsted-Lowry base (*Section 9.3*) A proton acceptor.

Brownian motion (*Section 7.8*) The random motion of colloidal-size particles.

Buffer (*Section 9.10*) A solution that resists change in pH when limited amounts of an acid or a base are added to it; an aqueous solution containing a weak acid and its conjugate base.

Buffer capacity (*Section 9.10*) The extent to which a buffer solution can prevent a significant change in the pH of a solution upon addition of an acid or a base.

Calorie (*Section 1.9*) The amount of heat necessary to raise the temperature of 1 g of liquid water by 1°C.

Carbocation (*Section 12.6A*) A species containing a carbon atom with only three bonds to it and bearing a positive charge.

Carbonyl group (*Section 10.3C*) A C=O group.

Carboxyl group (*Section 10.3D*) A —COOH group.

Carboxylic acid (*Section 10.3D*) A compound containing a —COOH group.

Catalyst (*Section 8.4D*) A substance that increases the rate of a chemical reaction by providing an alternative pathway with a lower activation energy.

Cathode (*Chemical Connections 5B*) The positively charged electrode.

Cation (*Section 4.2*) An ion with a positive electric charge.

Cell reprogramming (*Chemical Connections 31F*) A technique used in whole-mammal cloning, in which a somatic cell is reprogrammed to behave like a fertilized egg.

Celsius scale (°C) (*Section 1.4*) A temperature scale based on 0° as the freezing point of water and 100° as the normal boiling point of water.

Chain reaction, nuclear (*Section 3.9*) A nuclear reaction that results from fusion of a nucleus with another particle (most commonly a neutron) followed by decay of the fused nucleus to smaller nuclei and more neutrons. The newly formed neutrons continue the process and result in a chain reaction.

Chair conformation (*Section 11.5B*) The most stable conformation of a cyclohexane ring; all bond angles are approximately 109.5°.

Chaperones (*Section 22.10*) Protein molecules that help other proteins to fold into the biologically active conformation and enable partially denatured proteins to regain their biologically active conformation.

Charles's law (*Section 6.3B*) The volume of a gas at constant pressure is directly proportional to the temperature in kelvins.

Chemical change (*Section 1.1*) Chemical reaction.

Chemical equation (*Section 5.4*) A representation using chemical formulas of the process that occurs when reactants are converted to products.

Chemical equilibrium (*Section 8.5*) A state in which the rate of the forward reaction equals the rate of the reverse reaction.

Chemical kinetics (*Section 8.1*) The study of the rates of chemical reactions.

Chemical property (*Section 1.1*) A chemical reaction that a substance undergoes.

Chemical reaction (*Section 1.1*) As substances are used up, others appear in their place.

Chemistry (*Section 1.1*) The science that deals with matter.

Chemokine (*Section 31.6*) A chemotactic cytokine that facilitates the migration of leukocytes from the blood vessels to the site of injury or inflammation.

Chiral (*Section 15.1*) From the Greek *cheir*, meaning "hand"; an object that is not superposable on its mirror image.

Cis (*Section 11.6*) A prefix meaning "on the same side."

Cis-trans isomers (*Section 11.6*) Isomers that have the same (1) molecular formula (2) order of attachment (connectivity) of their atoms (3) but a different arrangement of their atoms in space due to the presence of either a ring or a carbon–carbon double bond.

Cluster determinant (*Section 31.5*) A set of membrane proteins on T cells that help the binding of antigens to the T-cell receptors.

Coefficient (*Section 5.4*) A number placed in front of a chemical entity in a balanced chemical equation.

Colligative property (*Section 7.8*) A property of a solution that depends only on the number of solute particles and not on the chemical identity of the solute particles.

Colloid (*Section 7.7*) A two-part mixture in which the suspended solute particles range from 1 to 1000 nm in size.

Combined gas law (*Section 6.3C*) The pressure, volume, and temperature in kelvins of two samples of the same gas are related by the equation $P_1V_1/T_1 = P_2V_2/T_2$.

Combustion (*Section 5.4*) Burning in air.

Complete protein (*Section 30.5*) A protein source that contains sufficient quantities of all amino acids required for normal growth and development.

Condensation (*Section 6.7*) The change of a substance from the vapor or gaseous state to the liquid state.

Configuration (*Section 11.6*) The arrangement of atoms about a stereocenter—that is, the relative arrangements of the parts of a molecule in space.

Conformation (*Section 11.5A*) Any three-dimensional arrangement of atoms in a molecule that results from rotation about a single bond.

Conjugate acid (*Section 9.3*) In the Brønsted-Lowry theory, a substance formed when a base accepts a proton.

Conjugate acid–base pair (*Section 9.3*) A pair of molecules or ions that are related to one another by the gain or loss of a proton.

Conjugate base (*Section 9.3*) In the Brønsted-Lowry theory, a substance formed when an acid donates a proton to another molecule or ion.

Conjugated protein (*Section 22.11*) A protein that contains a nonprotein part, such as the heme part of hemoglobin.

Constitutional isomers (*Section 11.2*) Compounds with the same molecular formula but a different order of attachment (connectivity) of their atoms.

Contributing structure (*Section 4.8B*) Representations of a molecule or ion that differ only in the distribution of valence electrons.

Conversion factor (*Section 1.5*) A ratio of two different units.

Cosmic rays (*Section 3.6*) High-energy particles, mainly protons, from outer space bombarding the Earth.

Covalent bond (*Section 4.4A*) A bond resulting from the sharing of electrons between two atoms.

Crystallization (*Section 6.9*) The formation of a solid from a liquid.

C-terminus (*Section 22.6*) The amino acid at the end of a peptide chain that has a free carboxyl group.

Curie (Ci) (*Section 3.5A*) A measure of radioactive decay equal to 3.7×10^{10} disintegrations per second.

Cyclic ether (*Section 14.3A*) An ether in which the ether oxygen is one of the atoms of a ring.

Cycloalkane (*Section 11.4*) A saturated hydrocarbon that contains carbon atoms bonded to form a ring.

Cystine (*Section 22.4*) A dimer of cysteine in which the two amino acids are covalently bonded by disulfide bond between their side chain —SH groups.

Cytokine (*Section 31.6*) A glycoprotein that traffics between cells and alters the function of a target cell.

Daily Values (*Section 30.1*) The values recommended by the Food and Drug Administration for key nutrients in the diet.

Dalton's Law (*Section 6.5*) The pressure of a mixture of gases is equal to the sum of the partial pressures of each gas in the mixture.

Debranching enzyme (*Section 30.3*) The enzyme that catalyzes the hydrolysis of the 1,6-glycosidic bonds in starch and glycogen.

Decarboxylation (*Section 18.5E*) The loss of CO_2 from a carboxyl (—COOH) group.

Decay, nuclear (*Section 3.3B*) The change of a radioactive nucleus of one element into the nucleus of another element.

Dehydration (*Section 14.2B*) The elimination of a molecule of water from an alcohol. An OH is removed from one carbon, and an H is removed from an adjacent carbon.

Denaturation (*Section 22.12*) The loss of the secondary, tertiary, and quaternary structure of a protein by a chemical or physical agent that leaves the primary structure intact.

Dendritic cells (*Sections 31.1, 31.2*) Important cells in the innate immune system that are often the first cells to defend against invaders.

Density (*Section 1.7*) The ratio of mass to volume for a substance.

Detergent (*Section 18.4D*) A synthetic soap. The most common are the linear alkylbenzene sulfonic acids (LAS).

Dextrorotatory (*Section 15.4B*) The clockwise (to the right) rotation of the plane of polarized light in a polarimeter.

Dialysis (*Section 7.8C*) A process in which a solution containing particles of different sizes is placed in a bag made of a semipermeable membrane. The bag is placed into a solvent or solution containing only small molecules. The solution in the bag reaches equilibrium with the solvent outside, allowing the small molecules to diffuse across the membrane but retaining the large molecules.

Diastereomers (*Section 15.3A*) Stereoisomers that are not mirror images of each other.

Diet faddism (*Section 30.1*) An exaggerated belief in the effects of nutrition upon health and disease.

Dietary Reference Intake (DRI) (*Section 30.1*) The current numerical system for reporting nutrient requirements; an average daily requirement for nutrients published by the U.S. Food and Drug Administration.

Digestion (*Section 30.1*) The process in which the body breaks down large molecules into smaller ones that can then be absorbed and metabolized.

Diol (*Section 14.2B*) A compound containing two —OH (hydroxyl) groups.

Dipeptide (*Section 22.6*) A peptide with two amino acids.

Dipole (*Section 4.7B*) A chemical species in which there is a separation of charge; there is a positive pole in one part of the species and a negative pole in another part.

Dipole–dipole attraction (*Section 6.7B*) The attraction between the positive end of one dipole and the negative end of another dipole in the same or different molecule.

Diprotic acid (*Section 9.3*) An acid that can give up two protons.

Discriminatory curtailment diet (*Section 30.1*) A diet that avoids certain food ingredients that are considered harmful to the health of an individual—for example, low-sodium diets for people with high blood pressure.

Disulfide (*Section 14.4D*) A compound containing an —S—S— group.

Double bond (*Section 4.7B*) A bond formed by sharing two pairs of electrons; represented by two lines between the two bonded atoms.

Double-headed arrow (*Section 4.8A*) A symbol used to show that the structures on either side of it are resonance contributing structures.

Dynamic equilibrium (*Section 8.5*) A state in which the rate of the forward reaction equals the rate of the reverse reaction.

Effective collision (*Section 8.2*) A collision between two molecules or ions that results in a chemical reaction.

EGF (*Section 31.6*) Epidermal growth factor; a cytokine that stimulates epidermal cells during healing of wounds.

Electrolyte (*Section 7.4C*) A substance that, when dissolved in water, produces a solution that conducts electricity.

Electromagnetic spectrum (*Section 3.2*) The array of electromagnetic phenomena by wavelength.

Electron capture (*Section 3.3F*) A reaction in which a nucleus captures an extranuclear electron and then undergoes a nuclear decay.

Electron volt (eV) (*Section 3.2*) A non-SI energy unit frequently used in nuclear chemistry. $1.0 \text{ eV} = 1.60 \times 10^{-19}$ J.

Electronegativity (*Section 4.4B*) A measure of an atom's attraction for the electrons it shares in a chemical bond with another atom.

Embryonal carcinoma cell (*Chemical Connections 31F*) A cell that is multipotent and is derived from carcinomas.

Embryonic stem cell (*Chemical Connections 31F*) Stem cells derived from embryonic tissue. Embryonic tissue is the richest source of stem cells.

Emulsion (*Section 7.7*) A system, such as fat in milk, consisting of a liquid with or without an emulsifying agent in an immiscible liquid, usually as droplets larger than colloidal size.

Enantiomers (*Section 15.1*) Stereoisomers that are nonsuperposable mirror images; refers to a relationship between pairs of objects.

End point (*Section 9.9*) The point in a titration where a visible change occurs.

Endothermic reaction (*Section 5.8*) A chemical reaction that absorbs heat.

Energy (*Section 1.8*) The capacity to do work. The SI base unit is the joule (J).

Enol (*Section 17.5*) A molecule containing an —OH group bonded to a carbon of a carbon–carbon double bond.

Epigenetics (*Chemical Connections 31F*) The study of heritable processes that alter gene expression without altering the actual DNA.

Epitope (*Section 31.3*) The smallest number of amino acids on an antigen that elicits an immune response.

Equatorial position (*Section 11.3B*) A position on a chair conformation of a cyclohexane ring that extends from the ring roughly perpendicular to the imaginary axis of the ring.

Equilibrium (*Section 6.8B*) A condition in which two opposing physical forces are equal.

Equilibrium constant (*Section 8.6*) A value calculated from the equilibrium expression for a given reaction indicating in which direction the reaction goes.

Equivalence point (*Section 9.9*) The point in an acid–base titration at which there is an equal amount of acid and base.

Ergogenic aid (*Chemical Connections 30E*) A substance that can be consumed to enhance athletic performance.

Essential amino acid (*Section 30.5*) An amino acid that the body cannot synthesize in the required amounts and so must be obtained in the diet.

Essential fatty acid (*Section 30.4*) A fatty acid required in the diet.

Ester (*Section 18.5D*) A compound in which the OH of a carboxyl group, RCOOH, is replaced by an —OR' group; RCOOR'.

Ether (*Section 14.3A*) A compound containing an oxygen atom bonded to two carbon atoms.

Exothermic reaction (*Section 5.8*) A chemical reaction that gives off heat.

Exponential notation (*Section 1.3*) The expression of a number in base 10.

Extended helix (*Section 22.9*) A type of helix found in collagen, caused by a repeating sequence.

External innate immunity (*Section 31.1*) The innate protection against foreign invaders characteristic of the skin barrier, tears, and mucus.

Fact (*Section 1.2*) A statement based on experience.

Fatty acid (*Section 18.4A*) A long, unbranched chain carboxylic acid, most commonly with 10–20 carbon atoms, derived from animal fats, vegetable oils, or the phospholipids of biological membranes. The hydrocarbon chain may be saturated or unsaturated. In most unsaturated fatty acids, the *cis* isomer predominates. *Trans* isomers are rare.

Fiber (*Section 30.1*) The cellulosic, non-nutrient component in our food.

Fibrous protein (*Section 22.1*) A protein used for structural purposes. Fibrous proteins are insoluble in water and have a high percentage of secondary structures, such as alpha helices and/or beta-pleated sheets.

Fischer esterification (*Section 18.5D*) The process of forming an ester by refluxing a carboxylic acid and an alcohol in the presence of an acid catalyst, commonly sulfuric acid.

Fission, nuclear (*Section 3.9*) The fragmentation of a heavier nucleus into two or more smaller nuclei.

Formula weight (FW) (*Section 5.2*) The sum of the atomic weights of all atoms is a compound's formula expressed in atomic mass units (amu). Formula weight can be used for both ionic and molecular compounds.

Freezing-point depression (*Section 7.8*) The decrease in the freezing point of a liquid caused by adding a solute.

Frequency (ν) (*Section 3.2*) The number of wave crests that pass a given point per unit of time.

Functional group (*Section 10.3*) An atom or group of atoms within a molecule that shows a characteristic set of physical and chemical properties.

Fusion, nuclear (*Section 3.8*) The combining of two or more nuclei to form a heavier nucleus.

Gamma ray (γ) (*Section 3.2*) A form of electromagnetic radiation characterized by very short wavelength and very high energy.

Gas (*Section 1.6*) A physical state of matter in which there is no definite volume or shape.

Gay-Lussac's law (*Section 6.3C*) The pressure of a gas at constant volume is directly proportional to its temperature in kelvins.

Geiger-Müller counter (*Section 3.5*) An instrument for measuring ionizing radiation.

Globular protein (*Section 22.1*) Protein that is used mainly for nonstructural purposes and is largely soluble in water.

Glycol (*Section 14.1B*) A compound with hydroxyl (—OH) groups on adjacent carbons.

Gp120 (*Section 31.5*) A 120,000-molecular-weight glycoprotein on the surface of the human immunodeficiency virus that binds strongly to the CD4 molecules on T cells.

Gray (Gy) (*Section 3.6*) The SI unit of the amount of radiation absorbed from a source. 1 Gy = 100 rad.

Haber process (*Chemical Connections 8E*) An industrial process by which H_2 and N_2 are converted to NH_3.

Half-life, of a radioisotope (*Section 3.4*) The time it takes for one half of a sample of radioactive material to decay.

HDPE (*Section 12.7C*) *High-density polyethylene.*

Heat of combustion (*Section 5.8*) The heat given off in a combustion reaction.

Heat of reaction (*Section 5.8*) The heat given off or absorbed in a chemical reaction.

Helper T cells (*Section 31.2*) A type of T cell that helps in the response of the acquired immune system against invaders but does not kill infected cells directly.

Hemiacetal (*Section 17.4C*) A molecule containing a carbon bonded to one —OH and one —OR group; the product of adding one molecule of alcohol to the carbonyl group of an aldehyde or ketone.

Henderson-Hasselbalch equation (*Section 9.11*) A mathematical relationship between pH, the pK_a of a weak acid, HA, and the concentrations of the weak acid and its conjugate base.

$$pH = pK_a + \frac{\log [A^-]}{[HA]}$$

Henry's law (*Section 7.4C*) The solubility of a gas in a liquid is directly proportional to the pressure of the gas above the liquid.

Heterocyclic aliphatic amine (*Section 16.1*) A heterocyclic amine in which nitrogen is bonded only to alkyl groups.

Heterocyclic amine (*Section 16.1*) An amine in which nitrogen is one of the atoms of a ring.

Heterocyclic aromatic amine (*Section 16.1*) An amine in which nitrogen is one of the atoms of an aromatic ring.

Heterogeneous catalyst (*Section 8.4D*) A catalyst in a separate phase from the reactants—for example, the solid platinum, Pt(s), in the reaction between CO(g) and H_2(g).

Highly active antiretroviral therapy (HAART) (*Section 31.8*) An aggressive treatment against AIDS involving the use of several different drugs.

HIV (*Sections 31.4, 31.8*) Human immunodeficiency virus.

Homogeneous catalyst (*Section 8.4D*) A catalyst in the same phase as the reactants—for example, enzymes in body tissues.

Hybridoma (*Section 31.4*) A combination of a myleoma cell with a B cell to produce monoclonal antibodies.

Hydration (*Section 12.7C*) Addition of water.

Hydrobromination (*Section 12.6A*) The addition of HBr to the carbon–carbon double bond of an alkene.

Hydrocarbon (*Section 11.1*) A compound that contains only carbon and hydrogen atoms.

Hydrogen bond (*Section 6.7C*) A noncovalent force of attraction between the partial positive charge on a hydrogen atom bonded to an atom of high electronegativity, most commonly oxygen or nitrogen, and the partial negative charge on a nearby oxygen or nitrogen.

Hydrogenation (*Section 12.6B*) Addition of hydrogen atoms to a double or triple bond using H_2 in the presence of a transition metal catalyst, most commonly Ni, Pd, or Pt. Also called catalytic reduction or catalytic hydrogenation.

Hydronium ion (*Section 9.1*) The H_3O^+ ion.

Hydrophobic interaction (*Section 22.10*) Interaction by London dispersion forces between hydrophobic groups.

Hydroxyl group (*Section 10.3A*) An —OH group bonded to a tetrahedral carbon atom.

Hygroscopic substance (*Section 7.6B*) A compound able to absorb water vapor from the air.

Hypothermia (*Chemical Connections 1B*) Having a body temperature lower than normal.

Hypothesis (*Section 1.2*) A statement that is proposed, without actual proof, to explain certain facts and their relationship.

Ideal gas law (*Section 6.4*) $PV = nRT$.

Immunogen (*Section 31.3*) Another term for antigen.

Immunoglobulin (*Section 31.4*) An antibody protein generated against and capable of binding specifically to an antigen.

Immunoglobulin superfamily (*Section 31.1*) A family of molecules based on a similar structure that includes the immunoglobulins, T-cell receptors, and other membrane proteins that are involved in cell communications. All molecules in this class have a certain portion that can react with antigens.

Indicator, acid–base (*Section 9.8*) A substance that changes color within a given pH range.

Inhibitory receptor (*Section 31.7*) A receptor on the surface of a cell of the innate immune system that recognizes antigens on healthy cells and prevents activation of the immune system.

Innate immunity (*Section 31.1*) The first line of defense against foreign invaders, which includes skin resistance to penetration, tears, mucus, and nonspecific macrophages that engulf bacteria.

Interleukin (*Section 31.6*) A cytokine that controls and coordinates the action of leukocytes.

Internal innate immunity (*Section 31.1*) The type of innate immunity that is used once a pathogen has already penetrated a tissue.

International System of Units (SI) (*Section 1.4*) A system of units of measurement based in part on the metric system.

Intramolecular hydrogen bonds (*Section 22.9*) Hydrogen bonds that exist within a given molecule, such as those holding an α-helix together in a protein.

Ion product of water, K_w (*Section 9.7*) The concentration of H_3O^+ multiplied by the concentration of OH^-; $[H_3O^+][OH^-] = 1 \times 10^{-14}$.

Ionic bond (*Section 4.4A*) A chemical bond resulting from the attraction between a positive ion and a negative ion.

Ionic compound (*Section 4.5A*) A compound formed by the combination of positive and negative ions.

Ionizing radiation (*Section 3.5*) Radiation that causes one or more electrons to be ejected from an atom or molecule, thereby producing positive ions.

Isoelectric point (*Section 22.3*) The pH at which a molecule has no net charge; abbreviated pI.

Isotonic (*Section 7.8B*) Solutions of the same osmolarity.

Joule (J) (*Section 1.9*) The SI base unit for heat; 1 J is 4.184 cal.

Kelvin scale (K) (*Section 1.4*) The SI base unit for temperature.

Ketone (*Section 10.3C*) A compound containing a carbonyl group bonded to two carbons.

Ketone body (*Chemical Connections 18C*) One of several ketone-based molecules—for example, acetone, 3-hydroxybutanoic acid (β-hydroxybutyric acid) and acetoacetic acid (3-oxobutanoic acid) produced in the liver during over-utilization of fatty acids when the supply of carbohydrates is limited.

Killer T cell (*Section 31.2*) A T cell that kills invading foreign cells by cell-to-cell contact. Also called cytotoxic T cell.

Kinetic energy (*Section 1.8*) The energy of motion; energy that is in the process of doing work.

Kwashiorkor (*Section 30.5*) A disease caused by insufficient protein intake and characterized by a swollen stomach, skin discoloration, and retarded growth.

Law of conservation of energy (*Section 1.8*) Energy can be neither created nor destroyed.

LDPE (*Section 12.7B*) Low-density polyethylene.

Le Chatelier's principle (*Section 8.8*) When a stress is applied to a system in chemical equilibrium, the position of the equilibrium shifts in the direction that will relieve the applied stress.

Leukocytes (*Section 31.2*) White blood cells, which are the principal parts of the acquired immunity system and act via phagocytosis or antibody production.

Levorotatory (*Section 15.4B*) The counterclockwise rotation of the plane of polarized light in a polarimeter.

Lewis structure (*Section 4.7B*) A formula for a molecule or ion showing all pairs of bonding electrons as single, double, or triple lines, and all nonbonding (unshared) electrons as pairs of Lewis dots.

Limiting reagent (*Section 5.5B*) The reactant that is consumed, leaving an excess of another reagent or reagents unreacted.

Line-angle formula (*Section 11.1*) An abbreviated way to draw structural formulas in which each vertex and line terminus represents a carbon atom and each line represents a bond.

Lipase (*Section 30.4*) An enzyme that catalyzes the hydrolysis of an ester bond between a fatty acid and glycerol.

Liquid state (*Section 1.6*) A physical state of matter in which there is a definite volume but no specific shape.

London dispersion forces (*Section 6.7A*) Extremely weak attractive forces between atoms or molecules caused by the electrostatic attraction between temporary induced dipoles.

Lymphocyte (*Sections 31.1, 31.2*) A white blood cell that spends most of its time in the lymphatic tissues. Those that mature in the bone marrow are B cells. Those that mature in the thymus are T cells.

Lymphoid organs (*Section 31.2*) The main organs of the immune system, such as the lymph nodes, spleen, and thymus, which are connected together by lymphatic capillary vessels.

Macrophage (*Sections 31.1, 31.2*) An amoeboid white blood cell that moves through tissue fibers, engulfing dead cells and bacteria by phagocytosis, and then displays some of the engulfed antigens on its surface.

Magnetic resonance imaging (MRI) (*Chemical Connections 3C*) The detection of the flip of a nuclear spin from being aligned with an external magnetic field to being against it when the nucleus is irradiated with radio-frequency radiation.

Major histocompatibility complex (MHC) (*Sections 31.2, 31.3*) A transmembrane protein complex that brings the epitope of an antigen to the surface of the infected cell to be presented to the T cells.

Marasmus (*Section 30.2*) Another term for chronic starvation, whereby the individual does not have adequate caloric intake. It is characterized by arrested growth, muscle wasting, anemia, and general weakness.

Markovnikov's rule (*Section 12.6A*) In the addition of HX or H_2O to an alkene, hydrogen adds to the carbon of the double bond having the greater number of hydrogens.

Mass (*Section 1.4*) The quantity of matter in an object; the SI base unit is the kilogram; often referred to as weight.

Matter (*Section 1.1*) Anything that has mass and takes up space.

Memory cell (*Section 31.2*) A type of T cell that stays in the blood after an infection is over and acts as a quick line of defense if the same antigen is encountered again.

Mercaptan (*Section 14.4A*) A common name for any molecule containing an —SH group.

Meta (m) (*Section 13.2B*) Refers to groups occupying the 1 and 3 positions on a benzene ring.

Metabolic acidosis (*Chemical Connections 9D*) The lowering of the blood pH due to metabolic effects such as starvation or intense exercise.

Meter (*Section 1.4*) The SI base unit of length.

Metric system (*Section 1.4*) A system in which measurements of parameter are related by powers of 10.

Mineral in diet (*Section 30.6*) An inorganic ion that is required for structure and metabolism, such as Ca^{2+}, Fe^{2+}, and Mg^{2+}.

Mirror image (*Section 15.1*) The reflection of an object in a mirror.

Molar mass (*Section 5.3*) The mass of one mole of a substance expressed in grams; the formula weight of a compound expressed in grams.

Molarity (*Section 7.5*) The number of moles of solute dissolved in 1 L of solution.

Mole (mol) (*Section 5.3*) The formula weight of a substance expressed in grams.

Molecular weight (MW) (*Section 5.2*) The sum of the atomic weights of all atoms in a molecular compound expressed in atomic mass units (amu).

Monoclonal antibody (*Section 31.4*) An antibody produced by clones of a single B cell specific to a single epitope.

Monomer (*Section 12.7A*) From the Greek *mono*, "single," and *meros*, "part"; the simplest nonredundant unit from which a polymer is synthesized.

Monoprotic acid (*Section 9.3*) An acid that can give up only one proton.

Multiclonal antibodies (*Chemical Connections 31B*) The type of antibodies found in the serum after a vertebrate is exposed to an antigen.

Multipotent stem cell (*Chemical Connections 31F*) A stem cell capable of differentiating into many, but not all, cell types.

Natural killer cell (*Sections 31.1, 31.2*) A cell of the innate immune system that attacks infected or cancerous cells.

Net ionic equation (*Section 5.6*) A chemical equation that does not contain spectator ions.

Neutralizing antibody (*Section 31.8*) A type of antibody that completely destroys its target antigen.

Nonbonding electrons (*Section 4.7C*) Valence electrons not involved in forming covalent bonds—that is, unshared electrons.

Nonpolar covalent bond (*Section 4.7B*) A covalent bond between two atoms whose difference in electronegativity is less than 0.5.

Normal boiling point (*Section 6.8C*) The temperature at which a liquid boils under a pressure of 1 atm.

N-terminus (*Section 22.6*) The amino acid at the end of a peptide chain that has a free amino group.

Nuclear fission (*Section 3.9*) The process of splitting a nucleus into smaller nuclei.

Nuclear fusion (*Section 3.8*) Joining together atomic nuclei to form a heavier nucleus than the starting nuclei.

Nuclear reaction (*Section 3.3A*) A reaction that changes an atomic nucleus (usually to the nucleus of another element.)

Nutrient (*Section 30.1*) Components of food and drink that provide energy, replacement, and growth.

Obesity (*Section 30.2*) Accumulation of body fat beyond the norm.

Octet rule (*Section 4.2*) When undergoing chemical reactions, atoms of Group 1A–7A elements tend to gain, lose, or share electrons to achieve an election configuration having eight valence electrons.

Optically active (*Section 15.4A*) Showing that a compound rotates the plane of polarized light.

Organic chemistry (*Section 10.1*) The study of the compounds of carbon.

Ortho (o) (*Section 13.2B*) Refers to groups occupying the 1 and 2 positions on a benzene ring.

Osmolarity (*Section 7.8B*) Molarity multiplied by the number of particles produced in solution by each formula unit of solute.

Osmotic pressure (*Section 7.8B*) The amount of external pressure applied to the more concentrated solution to stop the passage of solvent molecules into it from across a semipermeable membrane.

Oxidation (*Section 5.7*) The loss of electrons; the gain of oxygen atoms or the loss of hydrogen atoms.

Oxidizing agent (*Section 5.7*) An entity that accepts electrons in an oxidation–reduction reaction.

Oxonium ion (*Section 12.6B*) An ion in which oxygen is bonded to three other atoms and bears a positive charge.

Para (p) (*Section 13.2B*) Refers to groups occupying the 1 and 4 positions on a benzene ring.

Parenteral nutrition (*Chemical Connections 29A*) The technical term for intravenous feeding.

Partial pressure (*Section 6.5*) The pressure that a gas in a mixture of gases would exert if it were alone in the container.

Peptide (*Section 22.6*) A short chain of amino acids linked via peptide bonds.

Peptide backbone (*Section 22.7*) The repeating pattern of peptide bonds in a polypeptide or protein.

Peptide bond (*Section 22.6*) An amide bond that links two amino acids.

Peptide linkage (*Section 22.6*) Another term for peptide bond.

Percent concentration (% w/v) (*Section 7.5*) The number of grams of solute in 100 mL of solution.

Percent yield (*Section 5.5C*) The actual yield divided by the theoretical yield times 100.

Perforin (*Section 31.2*) A protein produced by killer T cells that punches holes in the membrane of target cells.

Peroxide (*Section 12.7A*) A compound that contains an —O—O— bond—for example, hydrogen peroxide, H—O—O—H.

pH (*Section 9.8*) The negative logarithm of the hydronium ion concentration; $pH = -\log[H_3O^+]$

Phagocytosis (*Section 31.4*) The process by which large particulates, including bacteria, are pulled inside a white cell called a phagocyte.

Phase change (*Section 6.10*) A change from one physical state (gas, liquid, or solid) to another.

Phenol (*Section 13.4*) A compound that contains an —OH group bonded to a benzene ring.

Phenyl group (*Section 13.2*) C_6H_5—, the aryl group derived by removing a hydrogen atom from benzene.

Pheromone (*Chemical Connections 12B*) A chemical secreted by an organism to influence the behavior of another member of the same species.

Photon (*Section 3.2*) The smallest unit of electromagnetic radiation.

Physical change (*Section 1.1*) A change in matter in which it does not lose its identity.

Physical property (*Section 1.1*) Characteristics of a substance that are not chemical properties; those properties that are not a result of a chemical change.

Plane-polarized light (*Section 15.4A*) Light vibrating in only parallel planes.

Plasma cell (*Section 31.2*) A cell derived from a B cell that has been exposed to an antigen.

Plastic (*Chemical Connections 12D*) A polymer that can be molded when hot and that retains its shape when cooled.

Pluripotent stem cell (*Chemical Connections 31F*) A stem cell that is capable of developing into every cell type.

pOH (*Section 9.8*) The negative logarithm of the hydroxide ion concentration; $pOH = -log[OH^-]$

Polar covalent bond (*Section 4.7C*) A covalent bond between two atoms whose difference in electronegativity is between 0.5 and 1.9.

Polarimeter (*Section 15.4B*) An instrument for measuring the ability of a compound to rotate the plane of polarized light.

Polyatomic ion (*Section 4.3C*) An ion that contains more than one atom.

Polymer (*Section 12.7A*) From the Greek *poly*, "many," and *meros*, "parts"; any long-chain molecule synthesized by bonding together many single parts called monomers.

Polynuclear aromatic hydrocarbon (*Section 13.2D*) A hydrocarbon containing two or more benzene rings, each of which shares two carbon atoms with another benzene ring.

Polypeptide (*Section 22.6*) A long chain of amino acids bonded via peptide bonds.

Positive cooperativity (*Chemical Connections 22G*) A type of allosterism where binding of one molecule of a protein makes it easier to bind another of the same molecule.

Positron ($\beta+$) (*Section 3.3D*) A particle with the mass of an electron but a charge of $+1$, $_{+1}^{0}\beta$.

Positron emission tomography (PET) (*Section 3.7A*) The detection of positron-emitting isotopes in different tissues and organs; a medical imaging technique.

Potential energy (*Section 1.8*) Energy that is being stored; energy that is available for later use.

Pressure (*Section 6.2*) The force per unit area exerted against a surface.

Primary (1°) alcohol (*Section 10.3A*) An alcohol in which the carbon atom bearing the —OH group is bonded to only one other carbon group, a —CH_2OH group

Primary (1°) amine (*Section 10.3B*) An amine in which nitrogen is bonded to one carbon group and two hydrogens, a —CH_2NH_2 group.

Primary structure, of proteins (*Section 22.8*) The order of amino acids in a peptide, polypeptide, or protein.

Progenitor cells (*Chemical Connections 31F*) Another term for stem cells.

Prosthetic group (*Section 22.11*) The non-amino-acid part of a conjugated protein.

Protein (*Section 22.1*) A long chain of amino acids linked via peptide bonds. There must usually be 30 to 50 amino acids in a chain before it is considered a protein.

Protein complementation (*Section 30.5*) A diet that combines proteins of varied sources to arrive at a complete protein.

Protein microarray (*Chemical Connection 22F*) An automated technique used to study proteomics that is based on having thousands of protein samples imprinted on a chip.

Proteomics (*Chemical Connections 22F*) The collective knowledge of all the proteins and peptides of a cell or a tissue and their functions.

Quaternary structure The organization of a protein that has multiple polypeptide chains, or subunits; refers principally to the way the multiple chains interact.

R— (*Section 11.3A*) A symbol used to represent an alkyl group.

R- (*Section 15.2*) From the Latin *rectus*, meaning "straight, correct"; used in the *R,S* system to show that, when the lowest-priority group is away from you, the order of priority of groups on a stereocenter is clockwise.

R,S system (*Section 15.2*) A set of rules for specifying configuration about a stereocenter.

Racemic mixture (*Section 15.1*) A mixture of equal amounts of two enantiomers.

Rad (*Section 3.5*) Radiation *a*bsorbed *d*ose. The SI unit is the gray (Gy).

Radiation, nuclear (*Section 3.3*) Radiation emitted from a nucleus during nuclear decay. Includes alpha particles, beta particles, gamma rays, and positrons.

Radical (*Chemical Connections 3C*) An atom or molecule with one or more unpaired electrons.

Radioactive (*Section 3.2*) Refers to a substance that emits radiation during nuclear decay.

Radioactive dating (*Chemical Connections 3A*) The process of establishing the age of a substance by analyzing radioisotope abundance as compared with a current amount.

Radioactive isotope (*Section 3.3*) A radiation-emitting isotope of an element.

Radioactivity (*Section 3.2*) Another name for nuclear radiation. Includes alpha particles, beta particles, gamma rays, and positrons.

Random coils (*Section 22.9*) Proteins that do not exhibit any repeated pattern.

Rate constant (*Section 8.4B*) A proportionality constant, k, between the molar concentrations of reactants and the rate of reaction; $rate = k[compound]$.

Reaction mechanism (*Section 12.6A*) A step-by-step description of how a chemical reaction occurs.

Recommended Daily Allowance (RDA) (*Section 30.1*) *also* **Recommended Dietary Allowance**; an average daily requirement for nutrients published by the U.S. Food and Drug Administration.

Redox reaction (*Section 5.7*) An oxidation–reduction reaction.

Reducing agent (*Section 5.7*) An entity that donates electrons in an oxidation–reduction reaction.

Reduction (*Section 5.7*) The gain of electrons; the loss of oxygen atoms or the gain of hydrogen atoms.

Regioselective reaction (*Section 12.6A*) A reaction in which one direction of bond forming or bond breaking occurs in preference to all other directions.

Rem (*Section 3.6*) *R*oentgen *e*quivalent for *m*an; a biological measure of radiation.

Residue (*Section 22.6*) Another term for an amino acid in a peptide chain.

Resonance (*Section 4.8*) A theory that many molecules and ions are best represented as hybrids of two or more Lewis contributing structures.

Resonance hybrid (*Section 13.1B*) A molecule best described as a composite of two or more Lewis structures.

Respiratory acidosis (*Chemical Connections 9D*) The lowering of the blood pH due to difficulty in breathing.

Retrovaccination (*Section 31.8*) A process whereby scientists have an antibody they want to use and try to develop molecules to elicit it.

Roentgen (R) (*Section 3.6*) The amount of radiation that produces ions having 2.58×10^{-4} coulomb per kilogram.

s- (*Section 15.2*) From the Latin *sinister*, meaning "left"; used in the *R,S* system to show that, when the lowest-priority group is away from you, the order of priority of groups on a stereocenter is counter-clockwise.

Saturated hydrocarbon (*Section 11.1*) A hydrocarbon that contains only carbon–carbon single bonds.

Scientific method (*Section 1.2*) A method of acquiring knowledge by testing theories.

Scintillation counter (*Section 3.5A*) An instrument containing a phosphor that emits light on exposure to ionizing radiation.

Secondary (2°) alcohol (*Section 10.3A*) An alcohol in which the carbon atom bearing the —OH group is bonded to two other carbon groups.

Secondary (2°) amine (*Section 10.3B*) An amine in which nitrogen is bonded to two carbons groups and one hydrogen.

Secondary structure, of proteins (*Section 22.9*) Repeating structures within polypeptides that are based solely on interactions of the peptide backbone. Examples are the alpha helix and the beta-pleated sheet.

SI (*Section 1.4*) International System of Units.

Side chains (*Section 22.7*) The part of an amino acid that varies one from the other. The side chain is attached to the alpha carbon, and the nature of the side chain determines the characteristics of the amino acid.

Sievert (Sv) (*Section 3.6*) A biological measure of radiation. One sievert is the value of 100 rem.

Single bond (*Section 4.7C*) A bond formed by sharing one pair of electrons; represented by a single line between two bonded atoms.

Small nuclear RNA (*Section 25.4*) Small RNA molecules (100–200 nucleotides) located in the nucleus that are distinct from tRNA and rRNA.

Soap (*Section 18.4B*) A sodium or potassium salt of a fatty acid.

Solid (*Section 1.6*) A physical state of matter in which there is a definite volume and shape.

Solubility (*Section 7.4*) The maximum amount of solute that can be dissolved in a solute at a specific temperature and pressure.

Solute (*Section 7.2*) The substance or substances that are dissolved in a solvent to produce a solution.

Solvent (*Section 7.2*) The fraction of a solution in which other components are dissolved.

Specific gravity (*Section 1.7*) The density of a substance compared to water as a standard.

Specific heat (*Section 1.9*) The amount of heat (calories) necessary to raise the temperature of 1 g of a substance by 1°C.

Specificity (*Section 31.1*) A characteristic of acquired immunity based on the fact that cells make specific antibodies to a wide range of pathogens.

Spectator ion (*Section 5.6*) An ion that appears unchanged on both sides of a chemical equation.

Standard temperature and pressure (STP) (*Section 6.4*) One atmosphere pressure and 0°C (273 K).

Step-growth polymerization (*Section 18.8*) A polymerization in which chain growth occurs in a stepwise manner between difunctional monomers—as, for example, between adipic acid and hexamethyl-enediamine to form nylon-66.

Stereocenter (*Section 15.1*) An atom, most commonly a tetrahedral carbon atom, at which exchange of two groups produces a stereoisomer.

Stereoisomers (*Section 11.6*) Isomers that have the same connectivity (the same order of attachment of their atoms) but different orientations of their atoms in space.

Stoichiometry (*Section 5.5A*) The mass relationships in a chemical reaction.

Strong acid (*Section 9.2*) An acid that ionizes completely in aqueous solution.

Strong base (*Section 9.2*) A base that ionizes completely in aqueous solution.

Structural formula (*Section 4.7C*) A formula showing how atoms in a molecule or ion are bonded to each other. Similar to a Lewis structure except that a structural formula shows only bonding pairs of electrons.

Sublimation (*Section 6.10*) A phase change from the solid state directly to the vapor state.

Supersaturated solution (*Section 7.4*) A solution in which the solvent has dissolved an amount of solute beyond the maximum amount at a specific temperature and pressure.

Surface presentation (*Section 31.1*) The process whereby a portion of an antigen from a foreign pathogen that infected a cell is brought to the surface of the cell.

Surface tension (*Section 6.8A*) The layer on the surface of a liquid produced by uneven intermolecular attractions at its surface.

T cell (*Section 31.1*) A type of lymphoid cell that matures in the thymus and that reacts with antigens via bound receptors on its cell surface. T cells can differentiate into memory T cells or killer T cells.

Tautomers (*Section 17.5*) Constitutional isomers that differ in the location of an H atom and a double bond relative to an O or N atom.

T-cell receptor (*Section 31.1*) A glycoprotein of the immunoglobulin superfamily on the surface of T cells that interacts with the epitope presented by MHC.

T-cell receptor complex (*Section 31.5*) The combination of T-cell receptors, antigens, and cluster determinants (CD) that is involved in the T cell's ability to bind antigen.

Temperature (*Section 1.9*) The measure of the amount of heat in a substance. Measurement is made in a temperature scale (°F, °C, or K); K is the SI base unit.

Terpene (*Section 12.5*) A compound whose carbon skeleton can be divided into two or more units identical to the carbon skeleton of isoprene.

Tertiary = (3°) alcohol (*Section 10.3A*) An alcohol in which the carbon atom bearing the —OH group is bonded to three other carbon groups.

Tertiary (3°) amine (*Section 10.3B*) An amine in which nitrogen is bonded to three carbon groups.

Tertiary structure The overall conformation of a polypeptide chain, including the interactions of the side chains and the position of every atom in the polypeptide.

Theoretical yield (*Section 5.5C*) The mass of product that should be formed in a chemical reaction according to the stoichiometry of the balanced equation.

Theory (*Section 1.2*) A hypothesis that is supported by evidence; a hypothesis that has passed tests.

Thiol (*Section 14.4A*) A compound containing an —SH (sulfhydryl) group bonded to a tetrahedral carbon atom.

Tissue necrosis factor (TNF) (*Section 31.6*) A type of cytokine produced by T cells and macrophages that has the ability to lyse susceptible tumor cells.

Titration (*Section 9.9*) An analytical procedure whereby we react a known volume of a solution of known concentration with a known volume of a solution of unknown concentration.

Trans (*Section 11.6*) A prefix meaning "across from."

Transmutation (*Section 3.3B*) Changing one element into another element.

Transuranium element (*Section 3.8*) An element with an atomic number greater than that of uranium; that is, one with an atomic number greater than 92.

Triple bond (*Section 4.7C*) A bond formed by sharing three pairs of electrons; represented by three lines between the two bonded atoms.

Triple helix (*Section 22.11*) The collagen triple helix is composed of three peptide chains. Each chain is itself a left-handed helix. These chains are twisted around each other in a right-handed helix.

Triprotic acid (*Section 9.3*) An acid that can give up three protons.

Tyndall effect (*Section 7.7*) Light passing through and scattered by a colloid viewed at a right angle.

Universal gas constant (R) (*Section 6.4*) $0.0821 \text{ L} \cdot \text{atm} \cdot \text{mol}^{-1} \cdot K^{-1}$.

Vapor (*Section 6.8B*) A gas.

Vapor pressure (*Section 6.8B*) The pressure of gas in equilibrium with its liquid form in a closed container.

Vitamin (*Section 30.6*) An organic substance required in small quantities in the diet of most species, which generally functions as a cofactor in important metabolic reactions.

Volume (*Section 1.4*) The space that a substance occupies; the base SI unit is the cubic meter (m^3).

VSEPR model (*Section 4.10*) Valence-shell electron-pair repulsion model.

Wavelength (λ) (*Section 3.2*) The distance from the crest of one wave to the crest of the next.

Weak acid (*Section 9.2*) An acid that is only partially ionized in aqueous solution.

Weak base (*Section 9.2*) A base that is only partially ionized in aqueous solution.

Weight (*Section 1.4*) The result of a mass acted upon by gravity; the base unit of measure is a gram (g).

X ray (*Section 3.2*) A type of electromagnetic radiation with a wavelength shorter than ultraviolet light but longer than gamma rays.

Zwitterion (*Section 22.3*) A molecule that has equal numbers of positive and negative charges, giving it a net charge of zero.

Credits

Text and Illustrations

This page constitutes an extension of the copyright page. We have made every effort to trace the ownership of all copyrighted material and to secure permission from copyright holders. In the event of any question arising as to the use of any material, we will be pleased to make the necessary corrections in future printings. Thanks are due to the following authors, publishers, and agents for permission to use the material indicated.

Chapter 21 **p. 529:** From Biochemistry by Lubert Stryer © 1975, 1981, 1988, 1995 by Lubert Stryer; © 2002 by W. H. Freeman and Company. Used with permission of W. H. Freeman and Company.

Chapter 24 **p. 614:** Courtesy of Anthony Tu, Colorado State University.

Chapter 25 **p. 644:** Courtesy of Dr. Sung-Hou Kim. 644: From Biochemistry, 2nd ed., by Lubert Stryer. Copyright 1981 by W. H. Freeman and Company. All rights reserved. Used with permission of W. H. Freeman and Company.

Chapter 26 **p. 675:** Illustration by Irving Geis, from Scientific American, Jan. 1963. Rights owned by Howard Hughes Medical Institute. Not to be reproduced without permission. **p. 681:** Scientific American 292 (4) 2005, p. 61.

Photographs

pp. v-xii: Charles D. Winters.

Chapter 1 **p. 1:** James Balog/Stone/Getty Images. 2: National Library of Medicine. **p. 3:** Charles D. Winters. **p. 3:** Charles D. Winters. **p. 3:** Charles D. Winters **p. 3:** National Library of Medicine. **p. 7:** © 2003 Richard Megna/Fundamental Photographs, NYC. **p. 7:** © 1992 Kip Peticolas/Fundamental Photographs, NYC. **p. 9:** Photographer's Choice/Getty Images. **p. 10:** Courtesy of Brinkmann Instruments, Co. **p. 10:** Courtesy of Brinkmann Instruments, Co. **p. 10:** Charles D. Winters **p. 16:** Charles D. Winters. **p. 16:** Charles D. Winters. **p. 16:** Charles D. Winters. **p. 17:** Ken Graham/Stone/Getty Images. **p. 19:** Eric Lars Baleke/Black Star. **p. 20:** courtesy of Shell Solar Industries.

Chapter 2 **p. 29:** IBMRL/Visuals Unlimited, Inc. **p. 33:** Charles D. Winters. **p. 33:** Ken Eward/Science Source/Photo Researchers, Inc. **p. 33:** Charles D. Winters. **p. 33:** Charles D. Winters. **p. 33:** Charles D. Winters. **p. 40:** Courtesy Roger Freedman & Paul Hansma, University of California. Santa Barbara. **p. 41:** NASA. **p. 41:** E.F. Smith Memorial Collection, Special Collection Department, Van Pelt Library, University of Pennsylvania. **p. 42:** Charles D. Winters. **p. 42:** Charles D. Winters. **p. 42:** Charles D. Winters. **p. 44:** Charles D. Winters. **p. 44:** Charles D. Winters. **p. 44:** Charles D. Winters. **p. 45:** Werner Forman/Art Resource, NY. **p. 44:** Charles D. Winters.

Chapter 3 **p. 63:** NASA. **p. 73:** Sci-Vu/Visuals Unlimited. **p. 73:** © Corbis Sygma. **p. 73:** © Bettmann/Corbis. **p. 74:** Charles D. Winters. **p. 77:** Klaus Guldbrandsen/Science Photo Library/Photo Researchers, Inc. **p. 78:** Charles D. Winters. **p. 79:** CNRI/SPL/Photo Researchers, Inc. **p. 80:** CRC Handbook in Clinical Lab Science. **p. 80:** CRC Handbook in Clinical Lab Science. **p. 80:** CRC Handbook in Clinical Lab Science. **p. 82:** Dr. Peter T. Fox, Washington University, School of Medicine. **p. 81:** Beverly March/courtesty of Long Island Jewish Hospital. **p. 85:** Courtesy of Public Service Electric & Gas Co. **p. 87:** US Dept Energy.

Chapter 4 **p. 93:** Charles D. Winters. **p. 96:** Charles D. Winters. **p. 96:** Charles D. Winters. **p. 96:** Charles D. Winters. **p. 96:** Charles D. Winters. **p. 98:** Norian Corp, Cupertino, CA. **p. 104:** Charles D. Winters. **p. 112:** Charles D. Winters. **p. 116:** Charles D. Winters. **p. 116:** Charles D. Winters. **p. 116:** Charles D. Winters. **p. 118:** Arthur C. Smith, III/Grant Heilman Photography. **p. 126:** Charles D. Winters.

Chapter 5 **p. 129:** © Joseph Nettis/Photo Researches, Inc. **p. 132:** Charles D. Winters. **p. 132:** Charles D. Winters. **p. 135:** Charles D. Winters. **p. 136:** © Jeff J. Daly/Visuals Unlimited, Inc. **p. 141:** AT&T Bell Labs. **p. 146:** Charles Steele. **p. 146:** Beverly March. **p. 147:** Beverly March. **p. 147:** Beverly March. **p. 147:** Charles D. Winters. **p. 148:** Charles D. Winters. **p. 148:** Beverly March. **p. 148:** Beverly March. **p. 149:** Charles D. Winters. **p. 151:** Russell D. Curtis/Photo Researchers. **p. 152:** © Jeff Greenberg/Visuals Unlimited. **p. 152:** Charles D. Winters. **p. 152:** Charles D. Winters. **p. 153:** Yoav Levy, Phototake, NYC. **p. 153:** Charles D. Winters.

Chapter 6 **p. 160:** © Vince Streano/Corbis. **p. 164:** Greg Gawlowski/Dembinsky Photo Associates. **p. 165:** Custom Medical Stock Photo. **p. 168:** Charles D. Winters. **p. 168:** Gregory G Dimijian/Photo Researchers, Inc. **p. 175:** Hermann Eisenbeiss/Photo Researchers, Inc. **p. 180:** Mehau Kulyk/Science Photo Library/Photo Researchers, Inc. **p. 181:** Beverly March. **p. 181:** Beverly March. **p. 181:** Beverly March. **p. 181:** Beverly March. **p. 183:** Charles D. Winters. **p. 184:** Charles D. Winters.

Chapter 7 **p. 192:** David Scharf/Peter Arnold, Inc. **p. 192:** Charles D. Winters. **p. 193:** Beverly March. **p. 193:** Charles D. Winters. **p. 194:** Will McIntyre/Photo Researchers, Inc. **p. 196:** Charles D. Winters. **p. 197:** Brian Parker/Tom Stack and Assoc. **p. 200:** Charles D. Winters. **p. 200:** Charles D. Winters. **p. 200:** Charles D. Winters. **p. 200:** Stan Elems/Visuals Unlimited. **p. 202:** Charles D. Winters. **p. 202:** Charles D. Winters. **p. 202:** Charles D. Winters. **p. 205:** Charles D. Winters. **p. 206:** Courtesy of P.A. Dieppe, P.A. Bacon, A.N. Bamji, and I Watt and the Gower Medical Publishing Co., Ltd., London. **p. 206:** National Library of Medicine. **p. 207:** Martin Bond/Science Photo Library/Photo Researchers, Inc. **p. 207:** George Semple. **p. 209:** Charles D. Winters. **p. 209:** David Scharf/Peter Arnold, Inc. **p. 210:** NALCO Chemical Company. **p. 212:** Charles D. Winters. **p. 214:** Charles D. Winters. **p. 214:** Courtesy of Recovery Engineering, Inc. **p. 215:** Science Source/Photo Reseachers, Inc. **p. 215:** Science Source/Photo Reseachers, Inc. **p. 215:** Charles D. Winters. **p. 216:** SIU/Photo Researchers, Inc.

Chapter 8 **p. 223:** Charles D. Winters. **p. 230:** Charles D. Winters. **p. 230:** Leon Lewandowski. **p. 231:** Michael Engleish, M.D./Custom Medical Stock Photo. **p. 232:** Charles D. Winters. **p. 234:** Beverly March. **p. 241:** Charles D. Winters. **p. 242:** John D. Cunningham/Visuals Unlimited. **p. 244:** Charles D. Winters. **p. 244:** Charles D. Winters. **p. 245:** C.P. Vance/Visuals Unlimited.

Chapter 9 **p. 251:** Charles D. Winters. **p. 254:** Charles D. Winters. **p. 254:** Charles D. Winters. **p. 255:** Charles D. Winters. **p. 259:** Charles D. Winters. **p. 261:** Charles D. Winters. **p. 263:** Charles D. Winters. **p. 263:** Charles D. Winters. **p. 267:** Charles D. Winters. **p. 268:** Charles D. Winters. **p. 268:** Charles D. Winters. **p. 277:** © RB-GM-J.O. Atlanta/Liaison Agency/Getty Images. **p. 262:** Charles D. Winters. **p. 269:** Charles D. Winters. **p. 271:** Charles D. Winters. **p. 271:** Charles D. Winters. **p. 271:** Charles D. Winters. **p. 273:** Charles D. Winters. **p. 273:** Charles D. Winters. **p. 273:** Charles D. Winters. **p. 274:** Charles D. Winters. **p. 274:** Charles D. Winters.

Chapter 10 **p. 285:** Tom and Pat Leeson, Photo Researchers, Inc. **p. 288:** Pete K. Ziminiski/Visuals Unlimited. **p. 289:** George Semple. **p. 294:** Charles D. Winters.

Chapter 11 **p. 302:** J.L. Bohin/Photo Researchers, Inc. **p. 304:** Charles D. Winters. **p. 315:** Tim Rock/Animals/Animals. **p. 319:** Charles D. Winters. **p. 323:** Ashland Oil Co. **p. 324:** Charles D. Winters.

Chapter 12 **p. 330:** Charles D. Winters. **p. 337:** David Sieren/Visuals Unlimited. **p. 340:** Don Suzio. **p. 349:** Beverly March. **p. 349:** Charles D. Winters. **p. 349:** Beverly March. **p. 349:** Charles D. Winters. **p. 348:** The Stock Market/Corbis. **p. 351:** Charles D. Winters.

Chapter 13 **p. 358:** Douglas Brown. **p. 362:** US Dept of Agriculture. **p. 366:** Charles D. Winters. **p. 366:** John D. Cunningham/Visuals Unlimited. **p. 367:** Charles D. Winters. **p. 368:** Chuck Pefley/Stone/Getty Image.

Chapter 14 **p. 374:** Earl Robber/Photo Researchers, Inc. **p. 377:** Charles D. Winters. **p. 376:** Charles D. Winters. **p. 376:** The Bettmann Archive/Corbis. **p. 386:** Boston Medical Library in the Francis A. Countway Lib of Medicine. **p. 387:** Steven J. Krasemann/Photo Researchers, Inc. **p. 389:** D. Young/Tom Stack and Associates.

Chapter 15 **p. 396:** Lester Lefkowitz/Stone/Getty Images. **p. 399:** Charles D. Winters. **p. 399:** Charles D. Winters. **p. 398:** Charles D. Winters. **p. 398:** Charles D. Winters. **p. 412:** Wiliam Brown.

Chapter 16 **p. 417:** Jack Ballard/Visuals Unlimited. **p. 419:** Inga Spence/Visuals Unlimited. **p. 422:** Charles D. Winters. **p. 426:** Beverly March. **p. 433:** Tom McHugh/Photo Researchers, Inc.

Chapter 17 **p. 434:** Charles D. Winters. **p. 440:** Charles D. Winters.

Chapter 18 **p. 452:** Charles D. Winters. **p. 453:** Ted Nelson/Dembinsky Photo Associates. **p. 463:** Charles D. Winters.

Chapter 19 **p. 474:** SCIMAT/Science Source/Photo Researchers, Inc. **p. 487:** Charles D. Winters. **p. 487:** Charles D. Winters.

Chapter 20 **p. 493:** Charles D. Winters. **p. 497:** Claire Paxton and Jacqui Farrow/Science Photo Library/Photo Researchers, Inc. **p. 502:** Charles D. Winters. **p. 505:** Gregory Smolin. **p. 505:** © Martin Dohrn/SPL/Photo Researchers, Inc. **p. 508:** Larry Mulvehill/Photo Researchers, Inc.

Chapter 21 **p. 521:** Doug Perrine/TCL/Getty Images. **p. 525:** Charles D. Winters. **p. 534:** Drs. P. G. Bullogh and V. J. Vigorita and the Gower Med Publ Co. **p. 533:** Carlina Biological Supply Co/Phototake, NYC. **p. 540:** Jed Jacobson/AllSport USA/Getty Images.

Chapter 22 **p. 551:** Hans Strand/Stone/Getty Images. **p. 567:** G.W. Willis/Visuals Unlimited. **p. 578:** © Gideon Mendel/Corbis. **p. 579:** Charles D. Winters. **p. 578:** Larry Mulvehill/Photo Researchers.

Chapter 23 **p. 584:** Vertex Pharmaceuticals, Inc. **p. 594:** Vertex Pharmaceuticals, Inc.

Index

Index page numbers in **boldface** refer to boldface terms in the text. Page numbers in *italics* refer to figures. Tables are indicated by a *t* following the page number. Boxed material is indicated by *b* following the page number.

Chapter 1 Matter, Energy, and Measurement

1.1 Multiplication: (a) 4.68×10^5 (b) 2.8×10^{-15}
     Division: (a) 1.94×10^{18} (b) 1.36×10^5

1.3 $241 \ \cancel{lb} \left(\dfrac{453.6 \ \cancel{g}}{1 \ \cancel{lb}} \right) \left(\dfrac{1 \ kg}{1000 \ \cancel{g}} \right) = 109 \ kg$

1.5 $\dfrac{332 \ \cancel{m}}{\cancel{s}} \left(\dfrac{1 \ \cancel{km}}{1000 \ \cancel{m}} \right) \left(\dfrac{1 \ mi}{1.609 \ \cancel{km}} \right) \left(\dfrac{60 \ \cancel{s}}{1 \ \cancel{min}} \right) \left(\dfrac{60 \ \cancel{min}}{1 \ hr} \right) = 743 \ mi/hr$

1.7 $d = m/V = \dfrac{56.8 \ g}{23.4 \ mL} = 2.43 \ g/mL$

1.9 Amount of heat $= SH \times m \times (T_2 - T_1) = \dfrac{1.0 \ cal}{\cancel{g} \cdot \cancel{°C}} (731 \ \cancel{g})(74 - 8)\cancel{°C} = 4.8 \times 10^4 \ cal$

1.11 $SH = \dfrac{\text{Amount of heat}}{m \times (T_2 - T_1)} = \dfrac{88.2 \ cal}{(13.4 \ g)(176 - 23)°C} = 0.0430 \ cal/g \cdot °C$

1.13 (a) Matter is anything that has mass and takes up space.
     (b) Chemistry is the science that studies matter.

1.15 Dr. X's claim that the extract cured diabetes would be classified as a (c) hypothesis. No
     evidence had been provided to prove or disprove the claim.

1.17 (a) 3.51×10^{-1} (b) 6.021×10^2 (c) 1.28×10^{-4} (d) 6.28122×10^5

1.19 (a) 6.48×10^7 (b) 1.6×10^5 (c) 4.69×10^5 (d) 2.8×10^{-15}

1.21 (a) 1.3×10^5 (b) 9.40×10^4 (c) 5.137×10^{-3}

1.23 4.45×10^6

1.25 (a) 2   (b) 5   (c) 5   (d) 5
     (e) 3   (f) 3   (g) 2

1.27 (a) 92   (b) 7.3   (c) 0.68   (d) 0.0032   (e) 5.9

1.29 (a) 1.53   (b) 2.2   (c) 0.00048

1

1.31 Answers rounded to two significant figures:

$$20 \text{ ks} \left(\frac{1000 \text{ s}}{1 \text{ ks}} \right) \left(\frac{1 \text{ min}}{60 \text{ s}} \right) = 330 \text{ min}$$

$$20 \text{ ks} \left(\frac{1000 \text{ s}}{1 \text{ ks}} \right) \left(\frac{1 \text{ min}}{60 \text{ s}} \right) \left(\frac{1 \text{ hr}}{60 \text{ min}} \right) = 5.6 \text{ hr}$$

1.33 (a) 20 mm   (b) 1 inch   (c) 1 mile

1.35 (b) Weight would change slightly. Mass is independent of location, but weight is a force exerted by a body influenced by gravity. The influence of the Earth's gravity decreases with increasing distance from sea level.

1.37 Temperature conversions: $^\circ F = \frac{9}{5} \, ^\circ C + 32$ and $K = 273 + \, ^\circ C$

(a) $^\circ F = \frac{9}{5} \, 25^\circ C + 32 = \underline{77^\circ F}$ and $K = 273 + 25^\circ C = \underline{298 \text{ K}}$

(b) $^\circ F = \frac{9}{5} \, 40^\circ C + 32 = \underline{104^\circ F}$ and $K = 273 + 40^\circ C = \underline{313 \text{ K}}$

(c) $^\circ F = \frac{9}{5} \, 250^\circ C + 32 = \underline{482^\circ F}$ and $K = 273 + 250^\circ C = \underline{523 \text{ K}}$

(d) $^\circ F = \frac{9}{5} \, (-273)^\circ C + 32 = \underline{-459^\circ F}$ and $K = 273 + (-273)^\circ C = \underline{0 \text{ K}}$

1.39 Metric unit conversions:

(a) $96.4 \text{ mL} \left(\frac{1 \text{ L}}{1000 \text{ mL}} \right) = 0.0964 \text{ L}$ (b) $275 \text{ mm} \left(\frac{1 \text{ cm}}{10 \text{ mm}} \right) = 27.5 \text{ cm}$

(c) $45.7 \text{ kg} \left(\frac{1000 \text{ g}}{1 \text{ kg}} \right) = 4.57 \times 10^4 \text{ g}$ (d) $475 \text{ cm} \left(\frac{1 \text{ m}}{100 \text{ cm}} \right) = 4.75 \text{ m}$

(e) $21.64 \text{ cc} \left(\frac{1 \text{ mL}}{1 \text{ cc}} \right) = 21.64 \text{ mL}$ (f) $3.29 \text{ L} \left(\frac{1000 \text{ cc}}{1 \text{ L}} \right) = 3.29 \times 10^3 \text{ cc}$

(g) $0.044 \text{ L} \left(\frac{1000 \text{ mL}}{1 \text{ L}} \right) = 44 \text{ mL}$ (h) $711 \text{ g} \left(\frac{1 \text{ kg}}{1000 \text{ g}} \right) = 0.711 \text{ kg}$

(i) $63.7 \text{ mL} \left(\frac{1 \text{ cc}}{1 \text{ mL}} \right) = 63.7 \text{ cc}$

(j) $0.073 \ \cancel{kg} \left(\dfrac{1000 \ g}{1 \ \cancel{kg}} \right) \left(\dfrac{1000 \ mg}{1 \ g} \right) = 7.3 \times 10^4 \ mg$

(k) $83.4 \ \cancel{m} \left(\dfrac{1000 \ mm}{1 \ \cancel{m}} \right) = 8.34 \times 10^4 \ mm$ \qquad (l) $361 \ \cancel{mg} \left(\dfrac{1 \ g}{1000 \ \cancel{mg}} \right) = 0.361 \ g$

<u>1.41</u> Speed limit $= \left(\dfrac{80 \ \cancel{km}}{hr} \right) \left(\dfrac{1 \ mi}{1.609 \ \cancel{km}} \right) = 50 \ mph$

<u>1.43</u> Liquids and solids have definite volumes.

<u>1.45</u> Melting is a physical change, not a chemical change; therefore, when a substance melts from a solid to a liquid, its chemical nature does not change.

<u>1.47</u> Manganese (d = 7.21 g/mL) is more dense than the liquid (d = 2.15 g/mL) therefore it will sink. Sodium acetate (d = 1.528 g/mL) is less dense than the liquid; therefore it will float on the liquid. Calcium chloride (d = 2.15 g/mL) has a density equal to that of the liquid; therefore it will stay in the middle of the liquid.

<u>1.49</u> $d_{urine \ sample} = m/V = \left(\dfrac{342.6 \ g}{335.0 \ \cancel{cc}} \right) \left(\dfrac{1 \ \cancel{cc}}{1 \ mL} \right) = 1.023 \ g/mL$

<u>1.51</u> Water (d = 1.0 g/cc) will be the top layer in the mixture because its density is lower than dichloromethane (d = 1.33 g/cc).

<u>1.53</u> Water reaches its maximum density at 4°C; therefore, by warming the water from 2°C to 4°C, the lighter crystals will float on the water with an increased density at 4°C.

<u>1.55</u> While driving your car, the car's <u>kinetic energy</u> (energy of motion) is converted by the alternator to electrical energy, which charges the battery, storing <u>potential energy</u>.

<u>1.57</u> $SH_{unknown} = \dfrac{Heat}{m \times (T_2 - T_1)}$

$SH_{unknown} = \dfrac{2750 \ cal}{168 \ g \ (74° - 26°)°C} = 0.34 \ cal / g \cdot °C$

1.59 Drug dose$_{135lb}$ = 135 lb-man $\left(\dfrac{445 \text{ mg drug}}{180 \text{ lb-man}} \right)$ = 334 mg drug

1.61 The body first reacts to hypothermia by shivering. Further temperature lowering results in unconsciousness and later, followed by death.

1.63 Methanol would make a more effective cold compress because its higher specific heat allows it to retain the heat longer per mass unit.

1.65 $d_{brain} = \dfrac{1 \text{ lb}}{620 \text{ mL}} \left(\dfrac{453.6 \text{ g}}{1 \text{ lb}} \right) = 0.732 \text{ g/mL}$

Specific gravity$_{brain} = \dfrac{d_{brain}}{d_{H_2O}} = \dfrac{0.732 \text{ g/mL}}{1 \text{ g/mL}} = 0.732$

1.67 (a) Potential energy   (b) Kinetic energy   (c) Potential energy
      (d) Kinetic energy   (e) Kinetic energy

1.69 Convert European car's fuel efficiency of 22 km/L into mi/gal, then compare:

Fuel efficiency$_{European} = \dfrac{22 \text{ km}}{L} \left(\dfrac{1 \text{ mi}}{1.609 \text{ km}} \right) \left(\dfrac{3.785 \text{ L}}{1 \text{ gal}} \right) = 52 \text{ mi/gal}$

The European car is more fuel efficient by 12 miles per gallon

1.71 Shivering generates kinetic energy.

1.73 Convert each quantity into a common unit (grams): (a) is the largest and (d) is the smallest.
      (a) 41 g

(b) $3 \times 10^3 \text{ mg} \left(\dfrac{1 \text{ g}}{1000 \text{ mg}} \right) = 3 \text{ g}$

(c) $8.2 \times 10^6 \text{ μg} \left(\dfrac{1 \text{ g}}{10^6 \text{ μg}} \right) = 8.2 \text{ g}$

(d) $4.1310 \times 10^{-8} \text{ kg} \left(\dfrac{1000 \text{ g}}{1 \text{ kg}} \right) = 4.1310 \times 10^{-5} \text{ g}$

1.75 Travel time $= 1490 \text{ mi} \left(\dfrac{1.609 \text{ km}}{1 \text{ mi}} \right) \left(\dfrac{1 \text{ hr}}{220 \text{ km}} \right) = 10.9 \text{ hr}$

1.77 SH (water) = 1.000 cal/g · °C = 4.184 J/g · °C
SH (heavy water) = 4.217 J/g · °C
Heat = SH x m x ΔT: According to the equation, the heat required to raise the temperature of a substance is directly proportional to the specific heat of that substance. Heavy water, having the higher specific heat, will require more energy to heat 10 g by 10°C.

1.79 1.00 mL of butter = 0.860 g and 1.00 mL of sand = 2.28 g

(a) $d_{mixture} = \dfrac{3.14 \text{ g mixture}}{2.00 \text{ mL}} = 1.57 \text{ g/mL}$

(b) First calculate the volumes of sand and butter, which totals 1.60 mL

$$V_{sand} = 1.00 \text{ g sand} \left(\dfrac{1.00 \text{ mL sand}}{2.28 \text{ g sand}} \right) = 0.439 \text{ mL}$$

$$V_{butter} = 1.00 \text{ g butter} \left(\dfrac{1.00 \text{ mL butter}}{0.860 \text{ g butter}} \right) = 1.16 \text{ mL}$$

$$d_{mixture} = \dfrac{2.00 \text{ g}}{1.60 \text{ mL}} = 1.25 \text{ g/mL}$$

1.81 The final answer will be reported to two significant digits because the temperature is reported in two significant figures (the least accurate of the quantities used in the calculation)

$$SH_{unk} = \dfrac{\text{Heat}}{m \times (T_2 - T_1)} = \dfrac{3.200 \text{ kcal}}{(92.15 \text{ g})(45°C)} = 7.7 \times 10^{-4} \text{ kcal} / \text{g} \cdot °C = 0.77 \text{ cal} / \text{g} \cdot °C$$

1.83 $T_2 = \dfrac{\text{Heat}}{SH \times m} + T_1$

$$T_2 = \dfrac{60.0 \text{ J}}{(10.0 \text{ g})(1.339 \text{ J/g} \cdot °C)} + 20.0°C = 24.5°C$$

1.85 Quantities of solids are most easily measured by their masses; therefore, the mass of urea is measured using a balance. Quantities of liquids are easily measured by their volumes and masses. The volume of pure ethanol can be measured using a volumetric pipette or graduated cylinder. The advantage of measuring the volume of ethanol is that the mass of ethanol can be calculated using its volume and density.

1.87 New medications are going to mimic natural molecules involved in biochemical processes, therefore, the new medicines would be expected to have similar characteristics to the natural biomolecules.

1.89 The contaminate can be removed from water using a technique called a liquid-liquid extraction. By adding diethyl ether to the aqueous sample in a separatory funnel, two layers are formed, with the less dense water-immiscible diethyl ether floating on top of the water layer. After mixing the two layers, the contaminant will dissolve in the upper diethyl ether layer. The lower aqueous layer is removed and the diethyl ether evaporated to isolate the contaminant.

Chapter 2 Atoms

2.1 (a) $NaClO_3$ (b) AlF_3

2.3 (a) The element has 15 protons, making it phosphorus (P); its symbol is $^{31}_{15}P$.

  (b) The element has 86 protons, making it radon (Rn); its symbol is $^{222}_{86}Rn$.

2.5 The atomic number of iodine (I) is 53. The number of neutrons in each isotope is 125 - 53 = 72 for iodine-125 and 131 - 53 = 78 for iodine-131. The symbols for these two isotopes are $^{125}_{53}I$ and $^{131}_{53}I$.

2.7 This element has 13 electrons and, therefore, 13 protons. The element with atomic number 13 is Aluminum (Al).

$\dot{A}l:$

2.9 (a) Oxygen - an element
  (c) Sea water - a mixture
  (e) Air - a mixture
  (g) Diamond - an element
  (i) Gasoline - a mixture
  (k) Carbon dioxide - a compound

  (b) Table salt - a compound
  (d) Wine - a mixture
  (f) Silver - an element
  (h) A pebble - a mixture
  (j) Milk - a mixture
  (l) Bronze - a mixture

2.11 Given here is the element, its symbol, and its atomic number:
  (a) Bohrium (Bh, 107)
  (c) Einsteinium (Es, 99)
  (e) Lawrencium (Lr, 103)
  (g) Mendelevium (Md, 101)
  (i) Rutherfordium (Rf, 104)

  (b) Curium (Cm, 96)
  (d) Fermium (Fm, 100)
  (f) Meitnerium (Mt, 109)
  (h) Nobelium (No, 102)
  (j) Seaborgium (Sg, 106)

2.13 The four elements named for planets are mercury (Hg, 80), uranium (U, 92) neptunium (Np, 93), and plutonium (Pu, 94).

2.15 (a) $NaHCO_3$ (b) C_2H_6O (c) $KMnO_4$

2.17 The law of conservation of mass

2.19 Mass percent of H and O in:
  H_2O: 18.0 g/mol   H: 11.2%   O: 88.8%
  H_2O_2: 34.0 g/mol   H: 5.93%   O: 94.1%

2.21 The statement is true in the sense that the number of protons (the atomic number) determines the identity of the element.

2.23 (a) The element with 22 protons is titanium (Ti).
      (b) The element with 76 protons is osmium (Os).
      (c) The element with 34 protons is selenium (Se).
      (d) The element with 94 protons is plutonium (Pu).

2.25 Each would still be the same element because the number of protons has not changed.

2.27 Radon (Rn) has an atomic number of 86, so each isotope has 86 protons. The number of neutrons is mass number - atomic number.
      (a) Radon-210 has 210 - 86 = 124 neutrons
      (b) Radon-218 has 218 - 86 = 132 neutrons
      (c) Radon-222 has 222 - 86 = 136 neutrons

2.29 Two more neutrons: tin-120
      Three more neutrons: tin-121
      Four more neutrons: tin 124

2.31 (a) An ion is an atom with an unequal number of protons and electrons.
      (b) Isotopes are atoms with the same number of protons in their nuclei but a different number of neutrons.

2.33 Rounded to three significant figures, the calculated value is 12.0 amu. The value given in the Periodic Table is 12.011 amu.

$$\left(\frac{98.90}{100} \times 12.000 \text{ amu} \right) + \left(\frac{1.10}{100} \times 13.000 \text{ amu} \right) = 12.011 \text{ amu}$$

2.35 Carbon-11 has 6 protons, 6 electrons, and 5 neutrons.

2.37 Americium-241 (Am) has atomic number 95. This isotope has 91 protons, 91 electrons and 241 - 95 = 146 neutrons.

2.39 In period 3, there are three metals (Na, Mg, and Al), one metalloid (Si) and four nonmetals (P, S, Cl, and Ar).

2.41 Periods 1 - 3 contain more nonmetals than metals. Periods 4 -7 contain more metals than nonmetals.

2.43 Palladium (Pd), cobalt (Co), and chromium (Cr) are transition elements. Cerium (Ce) is an inner transition element and K and Br are main group elements.

2.45 (a) Argon is a nonmetal (b) Boron is a metalloid
(c) Lead is a metal (d) Arsenic is a metalloid
(e) Potassium is a metal (f) Silicon is a metalloid
(g) Iodine is a nonmetal (h) Antimony is a metalloid
(i) Vanadium is a metal (j) Sulfur is a nonmetal
(k) Nitrogen is a nonmetal

2.47 The group number tells the number of electrons in the valence shell of the element.

2.49 (a) Li(3): $1s^2 2s^1$ (b) Ne(10): $1s^2 2s^2 2p^6$ (c) Be(4): $1s^2 2s^2$
(d) C(6): $1s^2 2s^2 2p^2$ (e) Mg(12): $1s^2 2s^2 2p^6 3s^2$

2.51 (a) He(2): $1s^2$ (b) Na(11): $1s^2 2s^2 2p^6 3s^1$ (c) Cl(17): $1s^2 2s^2 2p^6 3s^2 3p^5$
(d) P(15): $1s^2 2s^2 2p^6 3s^2 3p^3$ (e) H(1): $1s^1$

2.53 In (a), (b), and (c); the outer-shell electron configurations are the same. The only difference is the number of the valence shell being filled.

2.55 The element might be in Group 2A, all of which have two valence electrons. It might also be helium.

2.57 The properties are similar because all of them have the same outer-shell electron configuration. They are not identical because each has a different number of filled inner shells.

2.59 Ionization energy generally increases from left to right within a period in the Periodic Table and from bottom to top within column:
(a) K, Na, Li (b) C, N, Ne (c) C, O, F (d) Br, Cl, F

2.61 Following are the ground-state electron configurations of Mg atom, Mg^+, Mg^{2+}, and Mg^{3+}.

Electron configuration $Mg \longrightarrow Mg^+ + e^-$ IE = 738 kJ/mol
$1s^2 2s^2 2p^6 3s^2$ $1s^2 2s^2 2p^6 3s^1$

Electron configuration $Mg^+ \longrightarrow Mg^{2+} + e^-$ IE = 1450 kJ/mol
$1s^2 2s^2 2p^6 3s^1$ $1s^2 2s^2 2p^6$

Electron configuration $Mg^{2+} \longrightarrow Mg^{3+} + e^-$ IE = 7734 kJ/mol
$1s^2 2s^2 2p^6$ $1s^2 2s^2 2p^5$

The first electron is removed from the 2s orbital. The removal of each subsequent electron requires more energy because, after the first electron is removed, each subsequent electron is removed from a positive ion, which strongly attracts the remaining electrons. The third ionization energy is especially large because the electron is removed from the filled second principal energy level, meaning that it is removed from an ion that has the same electron configuration as neon.

2.63 The most abundant elements by weight (a) in the Earth's crust are oxygen and silicon, and (b) in the human body they are oxygen and carbon.

2.65 Calcium is an essential element in human bones and teeth. Because strontium behaves chemically much like calcium, strontium-90 gets into our bones and teeth and gives off radioactivity for many years directly into our bodies.

2.67 Copper can be made harder by hammering it.

2.69 (a) Metals   (b) Nonmetals   (c) Metals
   (d) Nonmetals (e) Metals   (f) Metals

2.71 (a) Phosporous-32 has 15 protons, 15 electrons, and 32 - 15 = 17 neutrons.
  (b) Molybdenum-98 has 42 protons, 42 electrons, and 98 - 42 = 56 neutrons.
  (c) Calcium-44 has 20 protons, 20 electrons, and 44 - 20 = 24 neutrons.
  (d) Hydrogen-3 has 1 proton, 1 electron, and 3 - 1 = 2 neutrons.
  (e) Gadolinium-158 has 64 protons, 64 electrons, and 158 - 64 = 94 neutrons.
  (f) Bismuth-212 has 83 protons, 83 electrons, and 212 - 83 = 129 neutrons.

2.73 Isotopes of elements from 37 to 53 contain more neutrons than protons.

2.75 Rounded to three significant figures, the atomic weight of naturally occurring boron is 10.8. The value given in the Periodic Table is 10.811.

$$\left(\frac{19.9}{100} \times 10.013 \text{ amu} \right) + \left(\frac{80.1}{100} \times 11.009 \text{ amu} \right) = 10.811 \text{ amu}$$

2.77 It would take 6.0×10^{21} protons to equal the mass of a grain of salt.

$$\frac{1.0 \times 10^{-2} \text{ g NaCl}}{1.67 \times 10^{-24} \text{ g/proton}} = 6.0 \times 10^{21} \text{ protons}$$

2.79 Assume the isotope mass is equal to the isotope mass number. By using these relationships, the solution is reached as follows:

$$\frac{\%\ ^{85}\text{Rb}}{100} + \frac{\%\ ^{87}\text{Rb}}{100} = 1 \qquad \text{or} \qquad \frac{\%\ ^{85}\text{Rb}}{100} = 1 - \frac{\%\ ^{87}\text{Rb}}{100}$$

$$\left(\frac{\%\ ^{85}\text{Rb}}{100} \times 85\right) + \left(\frac{\%\ ^{87}\text{Rb}}{100} \times 87\right) = 85.47$$

$$\left[\left(1 - \frac{\%\ ^{87}\text{Rb}}{100}\right) \times 85\right] + \left(\frac{\%\ ^{87}\text{Rb}}{100} \times 87\right) = 85.47$$

$$85 - \left(\frac{\%\ ^{87}\text{Rb}}{100} \times 85\right) + \left(\frac{\%\ ^{87}\text{Rb}}{100} \times 87\right) = 85.47$$

$$2 \times \frac{\%\ ^{85}\text{Rb}}{100} = 85.47 - 85$$

$$^{87}\text{Rb} = 23.5\%$$

$$^{85}\text{Rb} = 100 - 23.5 = 76.5\%$$

2.81 Xenon (Xe) will have the highest ionization energy. Ionization energy increases from left to right going across the periodic table.

2.83 Element 118 will be in Group 8A. Expect it to be a gas that forms either no compounds or form very few compounds.

Chapter 3 Nuclear Chemistry

3.1 $^{139}_{53}I \rightarrow ^{0}_{-1}e + ^{139}_{54}Xe$

3.3 $^{74}_{33}As \rightarrow ^{0}_{+1}e + ^{74}_{32}Ge$

3.5 Barium-122 (10 g) has decayed through 5 half-lives, leaving 0.31 g:
$10 \text{ g} \rightarrow 5.0 \text{ g} \rightarrow 2.5 \text{ g} \rightarrow 1.25 \text{ g} \rightarrow 0.625 \text{ g} \rightarrow 0.31 \text{ g}$

3.7 The intensity of any radiation decreases with the square of the distance: $\dfrac{I_1}{I_2} = \dfrac{d_2^2}{d_1^2}$

$$\frac{300 \text{ mCi}}{I_2} = \frac{(3.0 \text{ m})^2}{(0.01 \text{ m})^2}$$

$$I_2 = \frac{(300 \text{ mCi})(0.01 \text{ m})^2}{(3.0 \text{ m})^2} = 3.3 \times 10^{-3} \text{ mCi}$$

3.9 $f = \dfrac{c}{\lambda} = \dfrac{3.0 \times 10^{10} \text{ cm/s}}{5.8 \text{ cm}} = 5.2 \times 10^9 \text{/s}$

3.11 $f = \dfrac{c}{\lambda} = \dfrac{3.0 \times 10^8 \text{ m/s}}{650 \text{ nm}}\left(\dfrac{10^9 \text{ nm}}{1 \text{ m}}\right) = 4.6 \times 10^{14} \text{/s}$

3.13 (a) $^{19}_{9}F$ (b) $^{32}_{15}P$ (c) $^{87}_{37}Rb$

3.15 For the lighter elements up to calcium, the stable isotopes have equal numbers of protons and neutrons. Boron-10 is the most stable isotope because of an equal number of protons and neutrons in the nucleus.

3.17 $^{151}_{62}Sm \rightarrow ^{0}_{-1}e + ^{151}_{63}Eu$

3.19 $^{51}_{24}Cr + ^{0}_{-1}e \rightarrow ^{51}_{23}V$

3.21 $^{248}_{96}Cm + ^{28}_{10}X \rightarrow ^{116}_{51}Sb + ^{160}_{55}Cs$
The bombarding nucleus is $^{28}_{10}Ne$.

12

3.23 (a) $^{10}_{4}\text{Be} \rightarrow \, ^{0}_{-1}\text{e} + \, ^{10}_{5}\text{B}$ Beta emission

(b) $^{151}_{63}\text{Eu*} \rightarrow \gamma + \, ^{151}_{63}\text{Eu}$ Gamma emission

(c) $^{195}_{81}\text{Tl} \rightarrow \, ^{0}_{+1}\text{e} + \, ^{195}_{80}\text{Hg}$ Positron emission

(d) $^{239}_{94}\text{Pu} \rightarrow \, ^{4}_{2}\text{He} + \, ^{235}_{92}\text{U}$ Alpha emission

3.25 Gamma emission does not result in transmutation.

3.27 $^{239}_{94}\text{Pu} + \, ^{4}_{2}\text{He} \rightarrow \, ^{240}_{95}\text{Am} + \, ^{1}_{1}\text{p} + 2\,^{1}_{0}\text{n}$

3.29 After three half-lives: $1/2 \times 1/2 \times 1/2 = 1/8$ or 12.5% of the original amount remains.

3.31 No, the conversion of Ra to Ra^{2+} involves the loss of valence electrons, which is not a nuclear process and does not involve a change in radioactivity.

3.33 50.0 mg $\rightarrow$ 25.0 mg $\rightarrow$ 12.5 mg $\rightarrow$ 6.25 mg $\rightarrow$ 3.12 mg
Four half-lives in 60 minutes: half-life = 60 min/4 = 15 minutes

3.35 Gamma radiation has the greatest penetrating power; therefore it requires the largest amount of shielding.

3.37 It would be best to stand at least 30 meters away if you wish to be subjected to no more than 0.20mCi.

$$\frac{I_1}{I_2} = \frac{d_2^{\,2}}{d_1^{\,2}}$$

$$d_2 = \sqrt{\frac{d_1^{\,2} I_1}{I_2}} = \sqrt{\frac{(1.0 \text{ m})^2 (175 \text{ mCi})}{(0.20 \text{ mCi})}} = 3.0 \times 10^1 \text{ m}$$

3.39 (a) Amount of radiation absorbed by tissues
(b) Effective dose absorbed by humans
(c) Effective does delivered
(d) Intensity of radiation
(e) Amount of radiation absorbed by tissues
(f) Intensity of radiation
(g) Effective dose absorbed by humans

3.41 Alpha particles have so little penetrating power that they cannot penetrate the thick layer of skin on the hand. If they get into the lung, the thin membranes offer little resistance to the particles, which then damage the cells of the lung.

3.43 Alpha particles are the most damaging to tissue.

3.45 Iodine-131 is concentrated in the thyroid; therefore it would be expected to induce thyroid cancer.

3.47 (a) Cobalt-60 is used for (4) cancer therapy.
(b) Thallium-201 is used in (1) heart scans and exercise stress tests.
(c) Tritium is used for (2) measuring water content of the body.
(d) Mercury-197 is used for (3) kidney scans.

3.49 $^{248}_{96}\text{Cm} + \,^{4}_{2}\text{He} \rightarrow 2\,^{1}_{0}\text{n} + \,^{1}_{1}\text{H} + \,^{249}_{97}\text{Bk}$

3.51 $^{208}_{82}\text{Pb} + \,^{86}_{36}\text{Kr} \rightarrow 4\,^{1}_{0}\text{n} + \,^{290}_{118}Unknown$

3.53 The lifetime of a plant is short relative to the slow radioactive decay of carbon-14 to carbon-12; therefore the change in carbon-14 to carbon-12 ratio is negligible over the lifetime of a plant.

3.55 2006 – 1350 = 656 years (if the experiment was run in the year 2006)
656 years/5730 = 0.114 half-lives

3.57 Radon-222 produced polonium-218 by alpha emission:
$^{222}_{86}\text{Rn} \rightarrow \,^{4}_{2}\text{He} + \,^{218}_{84}\text{Po}$

3.59 The decay of a radioactive isotope is an exponential curve:

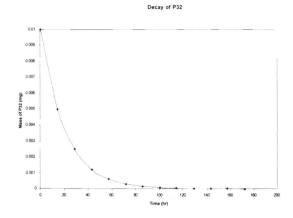

3.61 $^{19}_{10}\text{Ne} \rightarrow \,^{0}_{+1}\text{e} + \,^{19}_{9}\text{F}$
$^{20}_{11}\text{Na} \rightarrow \,^{0}_{+1}\text{e} + \,^{20}_{10}\text{Ne}$

3.63 Both the curie and the becquerel have units of disintegrations/second, a measurement of radiation intensity.

3.65 (a) $\dfrac{294 \text{ mrem/yr}}{359 \text{ mrem/yr}} \times 100 = 82\%$

(b) $\dfrac{39 \text{ mrem/yr}}{359 \text{ mrem/yr}} \times 100 = 11\%$

(c) $\dfrac{0.5 \text{ mrem/yr}}{359 \text{ mrem/yr}} \times 100 = 0.1\%$

3.67 X-rays will cause more ionization than radar because X-rays are higher energy.

3.69 $1000/475 \sim 2$ half-lives: $1/2 \times 1/2 = 1/4$ so 25% of the original americium will be around after 1000 years.

3.71 One sievert is equal to 100 rem. This is a sufficient dose to cause radiation sickness but not certain death.

3.73 (a) Radioactive elements are constantly decaying to other isotopes and elements mixed in with the original isotopes.
(b) Beta emissions result from the decay of a neutron in the nucleus to a proton (the increase in atomic number) and an electron (beta particle).

3.75 Oxygen-16 is stable because it has an equal number of protons and neutrons. The others are unstable because the numbers of protons and neutrons are unequal. In this case, the greater the difference in numbers of protons and neutrons, the faster the isotope decays.

3.77 $^{208}_{82}\text{Pb} + ^{64}_{28}\text{Ni} \rightarrow 6\,^{1}_{0}\text{n} + ^{266}_{110}\text{X}$

The new element is Darmstadtium: $^{266}_{110}\text{Ds}$

3.79 Lithium-7 and He-4 are produced when boron control rods absorb neutrons.

$^{10}_{5}\text{B} + ^{1}_{0}\text{n} \rightarrow ^{11}_{5}\text{B}$

$^{11}_{5}\text{B} \rightarrow ^{4}_{2}\text{He} + ^{7}_{3}\text{Li}$

Chapter 4 Chemical Bonds

4.1 (a) Magnesium (Mg) atom with two valance electrons, loses both electrons to form a Mg^{2+} ion with a Neon (Ne) electron configuration.

(b) Sulfur (S) atom with six valance electrons gains two electrons to give a sulfide ion (S^{2-}) with an eight valance electron octet of an argon electron configuration.

4.3 (a) KCl   (b) CaF_2 (c) Fe_2O_3

4.5 (a) $MgCl_2$ (b) Al_2O_3 (c) LiI

4.7 (a) Potassium hydrogen phosphate   (b) Aluminum sulfate
     (c) Iron (II) carbonate or Ferrous carbonate

4.9 (a) $\overset{\delta+\ \ \delta-}{C-N}$ (b) $\overset{\delta+\ \ \delta-}{N-O}$ (c) $\overset{\delta+\ \ \delta-}{C-Cl}$

4.11 Lewis structures:

(a) methane   H–C–H with H above and below (CH4)

(b) ethene $H_2C=CH_2$

(c) carbon dioxide   :O=C=O:

(d) acetylene   H–C≡C–H

4.13 Contributing structures:

(a)   (b)   (c)

4.15 Given are three-dimensional structures showing all unshared electron pairs.

(a) 109.5°   (b) 109.5°, 109.5°   (c) 109.5°, 109.5°, 120°

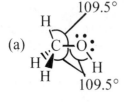

16

4.17 (a) By losing one electron, Li becomes Li^+, a helium electron configuration.
   Li: $1s^2 2s^1 \rightarrow Li^+$: $1s^2$ (filled s shell)

   (b) By gaining one electron, Cl becomes Cl^-, an argon electron configuration.
   Cl $1s^2 2s^2 2p^6 3s^2 3p^5 \rightarrow Cl^-$: $1s^2 2s^2 2p^6 3s^2 3p^6$ (octet)

   (c) By gaining three electrons, P becomes P^{3-}, an argon electron configuration.
   P $1s^2 2s^2 2p^6 3s^2 3p^3 \rightarrow P^{3-}$: $1s^2 2s^2 2p^6 3s^2 3p^6$ (octet)

   (d) By losing three electrons, Al becomes Al^{3+}, a neon electron configuration.
   Al: $1s^2 2s^2 2p^6 3s^2 3p^1 \rightarrow Al^{3+}$: $1s^2 2s^2 2p^6$ (octet)

   (e) By losing two electrons, Sr becomes Sr^{2+}, a krypton electron configuration.
   Sr: $1s^2 2s^2 2p^6 3s^2 3p^6 4s^2 3d^{10} 4p^6 5s^2 \rightarrow$ Sr: $1s^2 2s^2 2p^6 3s^2 3p^6 4s^2 3d^{10} 4p^6$ (octet)

   (f) By gaining two electrons, S becomes S^{2-}, an argon electron configuration.
   S: $1s^2 2s^2 2p^6 3s^2 3p^4 \rightarrow S^{2-}$: $1s^2 2s^2 2p^6 3s^2 3p^6$ (octet)

   (g) By gaining four electrons, Si becomes Si^{4-}, an argon electron configuration.
   Si: $1s^2 2s^2 2p^6 3s^2 3p^2 \rightarrow Si^{4-}$: $1s^2 2s^2 2p^6 3s^2 3p^6$ (octet)
   or by losing four electrons, Si becomes Si^{4+}, a neon electron configuration.
   Si: $1s^2 2s^2 2p^6 3s^2 3p^2 \rightarrow Si^{4+}$: $1s^2 2s^2 2p^6$ (octet)

   (h) By gaining two electrons, O becomes O^{2-}, a neon electron configuration
   O: $1s^2 2s^2 2p^4 \rightarrow O^{2-}$: $1s^2 2s^2 2p^6$ (octet)

4.19 (a) H: $1s^1$ + 1 electron $\rightarrow$ H: $1s^2$ (filled $1s$ shell)
   (b) Al: $1s^2 2s^2 2p^6 3s^2 3p^1 \rightarrow Al^{3+}$: $1s^2 2s^2 2p^6$ (octet) + 3 electrons

4.21 Li^- is not stable because it has an unfilled 2nd shell.

4.23 Only (f) Cs+ will be stable because it has a Nobel gas valance shell. The other ions have a partially filled shell or a charge that is too high.

4.25 No. Copper is a transition metal so the octet rule does not apply. Transition metals can expand their octet into the $3d$-orbitals.

4.27 Electronegativity increases going up a column of the Periodic Table because valence electrons are in shells closer to the electropositive nucleus. The decreasing distance of the valence electrons from the positively charged nucleus put the valence electrons under increasing pull.

4.29 (a) F occurs above Cl in the Periodic Table, therefore it is more electronegative.
   (b) O occurs above S in the Periodic Table, therefore it is more electronegative.
   (c) N occurs to the right of C in the Periodic Table, therefore it is more electronegative.
   (d) F occurs to the right of C in the Periodic Table, therefore it is more electronegative.

4.31 The most polar bond occurs with the greatest electronegativity difference between atoms. Bond polarity in decreasing order: C-O bond > C-N bond > C-C bond.

4.33 Use the difference in electronegativity to determine the character of the bond.
(a) C-Br (2.8-2.5 = 0.3); nonpolar covalent   (b) S-Cl (3.0-2.5 = 0.5); polar covalent
(c) C-P (2.5-2.1 = 0.4); nonpolar covalent

4.35 (a) NaBr   (b) Na_2O (c) $AlCl_3$ (d) $BaCl_2$ (e) MgO

4.37 Sodium chloride in the solid state has is a Na^+ ion surrounded by six Cl^- anions and each Cl^- anion surrounded by six Na+ ions.

4.39 (a) $Fe(OH)_3$ (b) $BaCl_2$ (c) $Ca_3(PO_4)_2$ (d) $NaMnO_4$

4.41 (a) The formula, $(NH_4)_2PO_4$, is incorrect. The correct formula is: $(NH_4)_3PO_4$.
(b) The formula, Ba_2CO_3, is incorrect. The correct formula is $BaCO_3$.
(c) The formula for aluminum sulfide, Al_2S_3 is correct.
(d) The formula for magnesium sulfide, MgS is correct.

4.43 KCl (potassium chloride) and $KHCO_3$ (potassium bicarbonate)

4.45 (a) SO_3^{2-} = sulfite   (b) NO_3^- = nitrate   (c) CO_3^{2-} = carbonate
(d) OH^- = hydroxide(e) HPO_4^{2-} = hydrogen phosphate

4.47 (a) Sodium fluoride   (b) Magnesium sulfide   (c) Aluminum oxide
(d) Barium chloride   (e) Calcium hydrogen sulfite (Calcium bisulfite)
(f) Potassium iodide   (g) Strontium phosphate
(h) Iron(II) hydroxide (Ferrous hydroxide)   (i) Sodium dihydrogen phosphate
(j) Lead(II) acetate (Plumbous acetate)   (k) Barium hydride
(l) Ammonium hydrogen phosphate

4.49 (a) NH_4HSO_3 (b) $Mg(C_2H_3O_2)_2$ (c) $Sr(H_2PO_4)_2$
(d) Ag_2CO_3 (e) $SrCl_2$ (f) $Ba(MnO_4)_2$

4.51 (a) A single bond results when one electron pair is shared between two atoms.
(b) A double bond results when two electron pairs are shared between two atoms.
(c) A triple bond results when three electron pairs are shared between two atoms.

4.53 Lewis structures for the following compounds:

(a)

(b) H–C≡C–H

(c)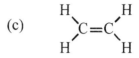

(d)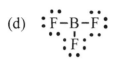

(e)

$$\ddot{O}=C\begin{smallmatrix}H\\ \\H\end{smallmatrix}$$

(f)

4.55 Total number of valence electrons for each compound:
(a) NH_3 has 8   (b) C_3H_6 has 18   (c) $C_2H_4O_2$ has 24
(d) C_2H_6O has 20   (e) CCl_4 has 32   (f) HNO_2 has 18
(g) CCl_2F_2 has 32   (h) O_2 has 12

4.57 A bromine atom contains seven electrons in its valence shell. A bromine molecule contains two bromine atoms bonded by a single bond. A bromide ion is a bromine atom that has gained one electron in its valence shell; it has a complete octet and a charge of -1.

(a) :Br·   (b) :Br–Br: (c) :Br:⁻

4.59 Hydrogen has the electron configuration $1s^1$. Hydrogen's valence shell has only a $1s$ orbital, which can hold only two electrons.

4.61 Nitrogen has five valence electrons. By sharing three more electrons with another atom(s), nitrogen can achieve the outer-shell electron configuration of neon, the noble gas nearest to it in atomic number. The three shared pairs of electrons may be in the form of three single bonds, one double bond and one single bond, or one triple bond. With any of these combinations, there is one unshared pair of electrons on nitrogen.

4.63 Oxygen has six valence electrons. By sharing two electrons with another atom(s), oxygen can achieve the outer-shell electron configuration of neon, the Noble gas nearest to it in atomic number. The two shared pairs of electrons may be in the form of a double bond or two single bonds. With either of these configurations, there are two unshared pairs of electrons on the oxygen.

4.65 O^{6+} has a charge too concentrated for a small ion.

4.67 (a) BF_3 has six valence electrons around the boron, thus does not obey octet rule.

(b) CF_2: does not obey the octet rule because carbon has 4 electrons around it.

(c) BeF_2: does not obey the octet rule because Be has 4 electrons around it.

(d) $H_2C=CH_2$ obeys the octet rule

(e) CH_3 does not obey the octet rule because carbon has 6 electrons around it.

(f) N_2 obeys the octet rule.

(g) NO does not obey the octet rule. Lewis structures drawn for the compound show either a nitrogen or an oxygen atom with 7 electrons.

4.69 Contributing structures for the bicarbonate ion:

4.71 (a) There are 16 valence electrons present in N_2O.

(b) The two contributing structures can be represented as follows:

(c) Valid contributing structures must have the same number of valence electrons. The proposed structure has only 14 valance electrons where N_2O must have 16 valence electrons.

4.73 (a) H_2O has 8 valence electrons, and H_2O_2 has 14 valence electrons.

(c) Predicted bond angles of 109.5° about each oxygen atom.

4.75 Shape of the each molecule and approximate bond angles about its central atom:

(a) Tetrahedral, 109.5°   (b) Pyramidal, 109.5°   (c) Tetrahedral, 109.5°

(d) Bent, 120°   (e) Trigonal planar, 120°   (f) Tetrahedral, 109.5°

(g) Pyramidal, 109.5°   (h) Pyramidal, 109.5°

4.77 The differences are in their shapes. Because CO_2 is a linear molecule, it is nonpolar. SO_2 is a bent molecule, therefore it is polar.

4.79 Yes, it is possible to have a molecule to have polar bonds, yet no dipole. This occurs when the individual polar bonds act in equal but opposite directions, as in CO_2.

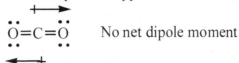

No net dipole moment

4.81 Use differences in electronegativity to predict the polarity of the bond.
(a) Nonpolar covalent (b) Polar covalent (c) Polar covalent (d) Ionic
(e) Polar covalent (f) Polar covalent (g) Nonpolar covalent (h) Ionic

4.83 Calcium dihydrogen phosphate, calcium phosphate, and calcium carbonate.

4.85 Barium sulfate is used to visualize the gastrointestinal tract by X-ray examination.

4.87 Calcium (Ca^{2+}) is the main metal ion present in bone and tooth enamel

4.89 Argon already has an octet with eight valence electrons in its outer shell, therefore (a) it does not donate or accept electrons to form ions and (b) it doesn't need to form covalent bonds by sharing electrons.

4.91 The two possibilities for a structure are square pyramidal and trigonal bipyramidal.

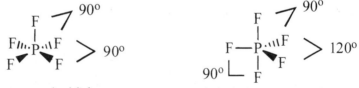

Square pyrimidal

Trigonal bipyrimidal

The square pyramidal structure contains eight F-F 90° bonding electron pair repulsions. These repulsions are minimized in a trigonal bipyramidal structure, where there are only six F-F 90° bonding electron pair repulsions. The VSEPR theory would then predict molecules like PF_5 would adopt the least strained configuration, a trigonal bipyramidal structure.

4.93 (a) ClO_2 has 19 valence electrons. In the Lewis structure, either the chlorine atom or one of the oxygen atoms must have only seven valence electrons. In the following Lewis structure, the odd electron is placed on the chlorine, which is the least electronegative element of the two atoms.
(b) Lewis structure of ClO_2:

$$\overset{\cdot\cdot}{\underset{\cdot\cdot}{O}}=\overset{\cdot\cdot}{\underset{\cdot}{Cl}}=\overset{\cdot\cdot}{\underset{\cdot\cdot}{O}}$$

4.95 Zinc oxide, ZnO, is present in sun blocking agents and helps reflect sunlight away from the skin.

4.97 Lead(IV) oxide, PbO_2, and lead(IV) carbonate, $Pb(CO_3)_2$, were used as pigments in paint.

4.99 Fe(II) is utilized in over-the-counter iron supplements.

4.101 (a) $CaSO_3$ (b) $Ca(HSO_3)_2$ (c) $Ca(OH)_2$ (d) $CaHPO_4$

4.103 Perchloroethylene does possess four polar covalent C-Cl bonds, but is not a polar compound. The molecule lacks a dipole because the polar covalent C-Cl bonds act in equal, but opposite directions.

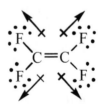

4.105 (a) Following is a Lewis structure for tetrafluoroethylene.
       (b) All bond angles are predicted to be 120°.
       (c) Tetrafluoroethylene has four polar covalent C-F bonds, but is a nonpolar molecule, because like in problem 4.103, the polar covalent C-F bonds act in equal, but opposite directions.

5.1   (a) Ibuprofen, $C_{13}H_{18}O_2$
        C 13 x 12.0 amu = 156 amu
        H 18 x 1.00 amu = 18.0 amu
        <u>O 2 x 16.0 amu =   32.0 amu</u>
        $C_{13}H_{18}O_2$ = 206 amu

      (b) Barium Phosphate, $Ba_3(PO_4)_2$
        Ba 3 x 137 amu = 411 amu
        P   2 x 31.0 amu = 62.0 amu
        <u>O   8 x 16.0 amu = 128 amu</u>
        $Ba_3(PO_4)_2$ = 601 amu

5.3 $2.84 \; \cancel{mol \, Na_2S} \left(\dfrac{87.1 \text{ g } Na_2S}{1 \; \cancel{mol \, Na_2S}} \right) = 222 \text{ g } Na_2S$

5.5   Moles of Cu(I) ions:

$$0.062 \; \cancel{g \, CuNO_3} \left(\frac{1 \, mol \, \cancel{CuNO_3}}{125.5 \; \cancel{g \, CuNO_3}} \right) \left(\frac{1 \, mol \, Cu^+ \, ions}{1 \, mol \, \cancel{CuNO_3}} \right) = 4.9 \times 10^{-4} \text{ mol } Cu^-$$

5.7   Balance: $CO_2(g) + H_2O(l) \longrightarrow C_6H_{12}O_6(aq) + O_2(g)$
       Step 1: Balance carbons with a coefficient of 6 in front of CO_2

           $6CO_2(g) + H_2O(l) \longrightarrow C_6H_{12}O_6(aq) + O_2(g)$

       Step 2: Balance hydrogen with a coefficient of 6 in front of H_2O

           $6CO_2(g) + 6H_2O(l) \longrightarrow C_6H_{12}O_6(aq) + O_2(g)$

       Step 3: Last step, balance oxygen with a coefficient of 6 in front of O_2

       Balanced equation: $6CO_2(g) + 6H_2O(l) \xrightarrow{\text{photosynthesis}} C_6H_{12}O_6(aq) + 6O_2(g)$

5.9   Balance the equation: $K_2C_2O_4(aq) + Ca_3(AsO_4)_2(s) \longrightarrow K_3AsO_4(aq) + CaC_2O_4(s)$
       Step 1: First balance the most complicated $AsO4$ with a 2 in front of K_3AsO_4

          $K_2C_2O_4(aq) + Ca_3(AsO_4)_2(s) \longrightarrow 2K_3AsO_4(aq) + CaC_2O_4(s)$

       Step 2: Next, balance the potassium by placing a 3 in front of $K_2C_2O_4$

          $3K_2C_2O_4(aq) + Ca_3(AsO_4)_2(s) \longrightarrow 2K_3AsO_4(aq) + CaC_2O_4(s)$

       Step 3: Now balance C_2O_4 and Ca with a coefficient of 3 in front of CaC_2O_4
       Balanced equation:

          $3K_2C_2O_4(aq) + Ca_3(AsO_4)_2(s) \longrightarrow 2K_3AsO_4(aq) + 3CaC_2O_4(s)$

5.11 Using the balanced equation: $CH_3OH(g) + CO(g) \longrightarrow CH_3COOH(l)$,
the molar ratio of CO required to produce CH_3COOH is 1:1; therefore 16.6 moles of CO is required to produce 16.6 moles of CH_3COOH.

5.13 6.0 g carbon = 0.50 mol of carbon   2.1 g H_2 = 1.1 mol H_2

Mass of H_2 required = $6.0 \ \text{g C} \left(\dfrac{1 \ \text{mol C}}{12.0 \ \text{g C}} \right) \left(\dfrac{2 \ \text{mol } H_2}{1 \ \text{mol C}} \right) \left(\dfrac{2.0 \ \text{g}}{1 \ \text{mol } H_2} \right) = 2.0 \ \text{g } H_2$

Mass of C required = $2.1 \ \text{g } H_2 \left(\dfrac{1 \ \text{mol } H_2}{2.0 \ \text{g } H_2} \right) \left(\dfrac{1 \ \text{mol C}}{2 \ \text{mol } H_2} \right) \left(\dfrac{12.0 \ \text{g C}}{1 \ \text{mol C}} \right) = 6.2 \ \text{g C}$

(a) H_2 is in excess and C is the limiting reagent.
(b) 8.0 grams of CH_4 are produced.

$6.0 \ \text{g C} \left(\dfrac{1 \ \text{mol C}}{12.0 \ \text{g C}} \right) \left(\dfrac{1 \ \text{mol } CH_4}{1 \ \text{mol C}} \right) \left(\dfrac{16.0 \ \text{g } CH_4}{1 \ \text{mol } CH_4} \right) = 8.0 \ \text{g } CH_4 \text{ produced}$

5.15 Overall chemical reaction: $CuCl_2(aq) + K_2S(aq) \rightarrow CuS(s) + 2KCl(aq)$
Step 1: Write an equation involving all of the chemical species participating in the chemical reaction.
$Cu^{2+}(aq) + 2Cl^-(aq) + 2K^+(aq) + S^{2-}(aq) \rightarrow CuS(s) + 2K^+(aq) + 2Cl^-(aq)$

Step 2: Cross out the aqueous ions that appear on both sides of the equation.
$Cu^{2+}(aq) + 2Cl^-(aq) + 2K^+(aq) + S^{2-}(aq) \rightarrow CuS(s) + 2K^+(aq) + 2Cl^-(aq)$

Net ionic equation: $Cu^{2+}(aq) + S^{2-}(aq) \rightarrow CuS(s)$
The net ionic equation shows the chemical species that actually undergo a chemical change. The ions that appear on both sides of the equation do not change, therefore are considered spectator ions.

5.17 (a) KCl = 74.6 amu   (b) Na_3PO_4 = 164.0 amu   (c) $Fe(OH)_2$ = 89.9 amu

5.19 (a) $C_{12}H_{22}O_{11}$ = 342.3 amu   (b) $C_2H_5NO_2$ = 75.1 amu   (c) $C_{14}H_9Cl_5$ = 354.5 amu

5.21 (a) $1.77 \ \text{mol } NO_2 \left(\dfrac{46.0 \ \text{g } NO_2}{1 \ \text{mol } NO_2} \right) = 81.4 \ \text{g } NO_2$

(b) 0.84 mol C_3H_8O $\left(\dfrac{60.1 \text{ g } C_3H_8O}{1 \text{ mol } C_3H_8O} \right)$ = 50 g C_3H_8O

(c) 3.69 mol UF_6 $\left(\dfrac{352.0 \text{ g } UF_6}{1 \text{ mol } UF_6} \right)$ = 1.30×10^3 g UF_6

(d) 0.348 mol $C_6H_{12}O_6$ $\left(\dfrac{180.2 \text{ g } C_6H_{12}O_6}{1 \text{ mol } C_6H_{12}O_6} \right)$ = 62.7 g $C_6H_{12}O_6$

(e) 4.9×10^{-2} mol $C_6H_8O_6$ $\left(\dfrac{176.1 \text{ g } C_6H_8O_6}{1 \text{ mol } C_6H_8O_6} \right)$ = 8.6 g $C_6H_8O_6$

5.23 (a) 6.56 mol Na_2S $\left(\dfrac{1 \text{ mol } S^{2-} \text{ ions}}{1 \text{ mol } Na_2S} \right)$ = 6.56 mol S^{2-} ions

(b) 8.320 mol $Mg_3(PO_4)_2$ $\left(\dfrac{3 \text{ mol } Mg^{2+} \text{ ions}}{1 \text{ mol } Mg_3(PO_4)_2} \right)$ = 24.96 mol Mg^{2+} ions

(c) 0.43 mol $Ca(CH_3COO)_2$ $\left(\dfrac{2 \text{ mol } CH_3COO^- \text{ ions}}{1 \text{ mol } Ca(CH_3COO)_2} \right)$ = 0.86 mol CH_3COO^- ions

5.25 The same; that is, just 2:1.

5.27 (a) 2.9 mol TNT $\left(\dfrac{6.02 \times 10^{23} \text{ molecules TNT}}{1 \text{ mol TNT}} \right)$ = 1.7×10^{24} molecules of TNT

(b) 5.00×10^{-2} g H_2O $\left(\dfrac{1 \text{ mol } H_2O}{18.0 \text{ g } H_2O} \right)$ = 2.78×10^{-3} mol H_2O

2.78×10^{-3} mol H_2O $\left(\dfrac{6.02 \times 10^{23} \text{ molec. } H_2O}{1 \text{ mol } H_2O} \right)$ = 1.67×10^{21} molecules H_2O

(c) 3.1×10^{-1} g $C_9H_8O_4$ $\left(\dfrac{1 \text{ mol } C_9H_8O_4}{180 \text{ g } C_9H_8O_4} \right)$ $= 1.7 \times 10^{-3}$ mol $C_9H_8O_4$

1.7×10^{-3} mol $C_9H_8O_4$ $\left(\dfrac{6.02 \times 10^{23} \text{ molec}}{1 \text{ mol } C_9H_8O_4} \right)$ $= 1.0 \times 10^{21}$ molec $C_9H_8O_4$

<u>5.29</u> $\left(\dfrac{68,000 \text{ amu}}{1 \text{ mol hemoglobin}} \right)\left(\dfrac{1 \text{ mol hemoglobin}}{6.02 \times 10^{23} \text{ molecules}} \right) = 1.1 \times 10^{-19}$ amu/molecule

<u>5.31</u> The following are balanced equations:

(a) $H_2 + I_2 \rightarrow 2HI$

(b) $4Al + 3O_2 \rightarrow 2Al_2O_3$

(c) $2Na + Cl_2 \rightarrow 2NaCl$

(d) $2Al + 6HBr \rightarrow 2AlBr_3 + 3H_2$

(e) $4P + 5O_2 \rightarrow 2P_2O_5$

<u>5.33</u> $CaCO_3(s) \xrightarrow{\text{heat}} CaO(s) + CO_2(g)$

<u>5.35</u> $4Fe(s) + 3O_2(g) \rightarrow 2Fe_2O_3(s)$

<u>5.37</u> $(NH_4)_2CO_3(s) \rightarrow 2NH_3(g) + CO_2(g) + H_2O(l)$

<u>5.39</u> $2Al(s) + 3HCl(aq) \rightarrow 2AlCl_3(aq) + 3H_2(g)$

<u>5.41</u> Using the balanced equation: $2N_2(g) + 3O_2(g) \rightarrow 2N_2O_3(g)$

(a) 1 mol O_2 $\left(\dfrac{2 \text{ mol } N_2}{3 \text{ mol } O_2} \right)$ $= 0.67$ mol N_2 required

(b) 1 mol O_2 $\left(\dfrac{2 \text{ } N_2O_3}{3 \text{ mol } O_2} \right)$ $= 0.67$ mol N_2O_3 produced

(c) 8 mol N_2O_3 $\left(\dfrac{3 \text{ mol } O_2}{2 \text{ mol } N_2O_3} \right)$ $= 12$ mol O_2 required

26

5.43 Using the balanced equation: $CH_4(g) + 3Cl_2(l) \rightarrow CHCl_3(g) + 3HCl(g)$

$$1.50 \ \text{mol CHCl}_3 \left(\frac{3 \ \text{mol Cl}_2}{1 \ \text{mol CHCl}_3} \right) \left(\frac{70.9 \ \text{g Cl}_2}{1 \ \text{mol Cl}_2} \right) = 319 \ \text{g Cl}_2 \ \text{needed}$$

5.45 (a) Balanced equation: $2NaClO_2(aq) + Cl_2(g) \rightarrow 2ClO_2(g) + 2NaCl(aq)$
      (b) 4.1 kg ClO_2

$$5.50 \ \text{kg NaClO}_2 \left(\frac{1000 \ \text{g NaClO}_2}{1 \ \text{kg NaClO}_2} \right) \left(\frac{1 \ \text{mol NaClO}_2}{90.4 \ \text{g NaClO}_2} \right) = 60.8 \ \text{mol NaClO}_2$$

$$60.8 \ \text{mol NaClO}_2 \left(\frac{2 \ \text{mol ClO}_2}{2 \ \text{mol NaClO}_2} \right) \left(\frac{67.5 \ \text{g ClO}_2}{1 \ \text{mol ClO}_2} \right) \left(\frac{1 \ \text{kg}}{1000 \ \text{g}} \right) = 4.10 \ \text{kg ClO}_2$$

5.47 Using the balanced equation: $6CO_2(g) + 6H_2O(l) \rightarrow C_6H_{12}O_6(aq) + 6O_2(g)$

$$5.1 \ \text{g Glucose} \left(\frac{1 \ \text{mol Glucose}}{180 \ \text{g Glucose}} \right) \left(\frac{6 \ \text{mol CO}_2}{1 \ \text{mol Glucose}} \right) \left(\frac{44.0 \ \text{g CO}_2}{1 \ \text{mol CO}_2} \right) = 7.5 \ \text{g CO}_2$$

5.49 Using the balanced equation in problem #5.48

$$0.58 \ \text{g Fe}_2O_3 \left(\frac{1 \ \text{mol Fe}_2O_3}{159.7 \ \text{g Fe}_2O_3} \right) \left(\frac{6 \ \text{mol C}}{2 \ \text{mol Fe}_2O_3} \right) \left(\frac{12.0 \ \text{g C}}{1 \ \text{mol C}} \right) = 0.13 \ \text{g C needed}$$

5.51 $$25.0 \ \text{g Asp actual yield} \left(\frac{100 \ \text{g Asp}}{75 \ \text{g Asp actual yield}} \right) \left(\frac{1 \ \text{mol Asp}}{180 \ \text{g Asp}} \right) = 0.185 \ \text{mol Asp}$$

$$0.185 \ \text{mol Asp} \left(\frac{1 \ \text{mol SA}}{1 \ \text{mol Asp}} \right) \left(\frac{138 \text{g SA}}{1 \ \text{mol SA}} \right) = 25.6 \ \text{g SA}$$

You will need to use 25.6 g salicylic acid to get 25.0 g of aspirin after a 75% yield.

5.53 Using the balanced equation: $CH_3CH_3(g) + Cl_2(g) \rightarrow CH_3CH_2Cl(l) + HCl(g)$

Theoretical yield of ethyl chloride:

$$5.6 \text{ g Ethane} \left(\frac{1 \text{ mol Ethane}}{30.1 \text{ g Ethane}} \right)\left(\frac{1 \text{ mol } CH_3CH_2Cl}{1 \text{ mol Ethane}} \right)\left(\frac{64.5 \text{ g } CH_3CH_2Cl}{1 \text{ mol } CH_3CH_2Cl} \right) = 12 \text{ g}$$

Actual yield of $CH_3CH_2Cl = 8.2$ g   % yield $= \dfrac{\text{Actual yield}}{\text{Theoretical yield}} \times 100$

$$\% \text{ Yield of } CH_3CH_2Cl = \frac{8.2 \text{ g } CH_3CH_2Cl}{12 \text{ g } CH_3CH_2Cl} \times 100 = 68\%$$

5.55 (a) Spectator ion: an ion that does not take part in a chemical reaction
(b) Net ionic equation: a balanced equation showing only the ions that react
(c) Aqueous solution: a solution using water as a solvent

5.57 (a) The spectator ions are Na^+ and Cl^-.

(b) $2Na^+(aq) + CO_3^{2-}(aq) + Sr^{2+}(aq) + 2Cl^-(aq) \rightarrow SrCO_3(s) + 2Na^+(aq) + 2Cl^-(aq)$

Balanced net ionic equation: $CO_3^{2-}(aq) + Sr^{2+}(aq) \rightarrow SrCO_3(s)$

5.59 $Pb^{2+}(aq) + 2NO_3^-(aq) + 2NH_4^+(aq) + 2Cl^-(aq) \rightarrow$

$$PbCl_2(s) + 2NO_3^-(aq) + 2NH_4^+(aq)$$

Balanced net ionic equation: $Pb^{2+}(aq) + 2Cl^-(aq) \rightarrow PbCl_2(s)$

5.61 $2Na^+(aq) + 2OH^-(aq) + 2NH_4^+(aq) + CO_3^{2-}(aq) \rightarrow$

$$2NH_3(g) + 2H_2O(l) + 2Na^+(aq) + CO_3^{2-}(aq)$$

Balanced net ionic equation: $NH_4^+(aq) + OH^-(aq) \rightarrow NH_3(g) + H_2O(l)$

5.63 (a) $MgCl_2$ (soluble): most compounds containing Cl^- are soluble
(b) $CaCO_3$ (insoluble): most compounds containing CO_3^{2-} are insoluble
(c) Na_2SO_4 (soluble): all compounds containing Na^+ are soluble
(d) NH_4NO_3 (soluble): all compounds containing NO_3^- and NH_4^+ are soluble
(e) $Pb(OH)_2$ (insoluble): most compounds containing OH^- are insoluble

5.65 No, one species gains electrons and the other loses electrons. Electrons cannot be destroyed, but transferred from one chemical species to another.

5.67 (a) C_7H_{12} is oxidized (the carbons gain oxygen going to CO_2) and O_2 is reduced.
(b) O_2 is the oxidizing agent and C_7H_{12} is the reducing agent.

5.69 An exothermic chemical reaction or process releases heat as a product.
An endothermic chemical reaction or process absorbs heat as a reactant.

5.71 19.6 kcal are given off.

5.73 $15.0 \text{ g Glucose} \left(\dfrac{1 \text{ mol Glucose}}{180 \text{ g Glucose}} \right) \left(\dfrac{670 \text{ kcal}}{1 \text{ mol Glucose}} \right) = 55.8$ kcal of heat evolved

5.75 (a) The synthesis of starch is endothermic.
(b) 26.4 kcal

$6.32 \text{ g starch} \left(\dfrac{10^{-3} \text{ kg starch}}{1 \text{ g starch}} \right) \left(\dfrac{4178 \text{ kcal}}{1.00 \text{ kg starch}} \right) = 26.4$ kcal heat required

5.77 Fluoride reacts with the $Ca_{10}(PO_4)_6(OH)_2$ in enamel, by exchanging the OH- ions with F⁻,
forming a less soluble $Ca_{10}(PO_4)_6F_2$ under the acidic conditions found in the mouth.

5.79 Oxidation occurs at the anode, where $Fe^0 \longrightarrow Fe^{2+}$
Reduction occurs at the cathode, where $Zn^{2+} \longrightarrow Zn^0$

5.81 $N_2O_5(g) + 2H_2O(l) \rightarrow 2HNO_3(aq)$

5.83 (a) Fe_2O_3 loses oxygen; it is reduced. CO gains oxygen: it is oxidized.

(b) $38.4 \text{ mol Fe} \left(\dfrac{1 \text{ mol Fe}_2O_3}{2 \text{ mol Fe}} \right) = 19.2$ mol Fe_2O_3 needed

(c) $38.4 \text{ mol Fe} \left(\dfrac{3 \text{ mol CO}}{2 \text{ mol Fe}} \right) \left(\dfrac{28.01 \text{ g CO}}{1 \text{ mol CO}} \right) = 1.61 \times 10^3$ g CO required

5.85 The spectator ions are Na^+ and NO_3^-.

$6Na^+(aq) + 2PO_4^{3-}(aq) + 3Cd^{2+}(aq) + 6NO_3^-(aq) \rightarrow$

$Cd_3(PO_4)_2(s) + 6NO_3^-(aq) + 6Na^+(aq)$

Balanced net ionic equation: $3Cd^{2+}(aq) + 2PO_4^{3-}(aq) \rightarrow Cd_3(PO_4)_2(s)$

5.87 $MW_{chlorophyll} = \dfrac{24.305 \text{ g Mg /mol}}{0.0272 \text{ g Mg /1 g chlorophyll}} = 893$ amu

5.89 8.00 g $Pb(NO_3)_2$ added to 2.67 g $AlCl_3$ yielded 5.55g $PbCl_2$

Mass of aluminum chloride required based on 8.00 g $Pb(NO_3)_2$:

$$8.00 \text{ g Pb(NO}_3)_2 \left(\frac{1 \text{ mol Pb(NO}_3)_2}{331.2 \text{ g Pb(NO}_3)_2} \right) \left(\frac{2 \text{ mol AlCl}_3}{3 \text{ mol Pb(NO}_3)_2} \right) = 1.61 \times 10^{-2} \text{ mol AlCl}_3$$

$$1.61 \times 10^{-2} \text{ mol AlCl}_3 \left(\frac{133.3 \text{ g AlCl}_3}{1 \text{ mol AlCl}_3} \right) = 2.15 \text{ g AlCl}_3 \text{ needed}$$

Mass of lead(II) nitrate required based on 2.67 g $AlCl_3$:

$$2.67 \text{ g AlCl}_3 \left(\frac{1 \text{ mol AlCl}_3}{133.3 \text{ g AlCl}_3} \right) \left(\frac{3 \text{ mol Pb(NO}_3)_2}{2 \text{ mol AlCl}_3} \right) = 3.00 \times 10^{-2} \text{ mol of Pb(NO}_3)_2$$

$$3.00 \times 10^{-2} \text{ mol Pb(NO}_3)_2 \left(\frac{331.2 \text{ g Pb(NO}_3)_2}{1 \text{ mol Pb(NO}_3)_2} \right) = 9.94 \text{ g Pb(NO}_3)_2 \text{ needed}$$

(a) $Pb(NO_3)_2$ is the limiting reagent.

(b) Actual yield of $PbCl_2$:

$$8.00 \text{ g Pb(NO}_3)_2 \left(\frac{1 \text{ mol Pb(NO}_3)_2}{331.2 \text{ g Pb(NO}_3)_2} \right) \left(\frac{3 \text{ mol PbCl}_2}{3 \text{ mol Pb(NO}_3)_2} \right) = 2.42 \times 10^{-2} \text{ mol PbCl}_2$$

$$2.42 \times 10^{-2} \text{ mol PbCl}_2 \left(\frac{278.1 \text{ g PbCl}_2}{1 \text{ mol PbCl}_2} \right) = 6.73 \text{ g PbCl}_2$$

$$\% \text{ Yield} = \frac{\text{Actual yield}}{\text{Theoretical yield}} = \frac{5.55 \text{g PbCl}_2}{6.73 \text{ g PbCl}_2} \times 100 = 82.5\% \text{ PbCl}_2$$

5.91 (a) $C_5H_{12}(g) + 8O_2(g) \rightarrow 5CO_2(g) + 6H_2O(g)$

(b) Pentane is oxidized and oxygen is reduced.

(c) Oxygen is the oxidizing agent and pentane is the reducing agent.

<u>5.93</u> (a) The balanced combustion reactions are listed below:

$$CH_4(g) + 2O_2(g) \rightarrow CO_2(g) + 2H_2O(g) \quad + 213 \text{ kcal/mol}$$

$$C_3H_8(g) + 5O_2(g) \rightarrow 3CO_2(g) + 4H_2O(g) + 530 \text{ kcal/mol}$$

(b) Propane releases more energy per mole (530 kcal/mol).

(c) Methane releases more energy per gram than propane.

$$\text{Methane heat of combustion (kcal/g)} = \frac{213 \text{ kcal/mol}}{16.0 \text{ g/mol}} = 13.3 \text{ kcal/g}$$

$$\text{Propane heat of combustion (kcal/g)} = \frac{530 \text{ kcal/mol}}{44.1 \text{ g/mol}} = 12.0 \text{ kcal/g}$$

<u>6.1</u> $P_2 = \dfrac{P_1 V_1}{V_2} = \dfrac{(0.70\ \text{atm})(3.8\ \cancel{L})}{6.5\ \cancel{L}} = 0.41\ \text{atm}$

<u>6.3</u> $P_2 = \dfrac{P_1 V_1 T_2}{T_1 V_2} = \dfrac{(0.92\ \text{atm})(20.5\ \cancel{L})(285\ \cancel{K})}{(296\ \cancel{K})(340.6\ \cancel{L})} = 0.053\ \text{atm}$

$P = \dfrac{nRT}{V} = \dfrac{(2.00\ \cancel{\text{mol}})(0.0821\ \cancel{L}\cdot\text{atm}\cdot\cancel{\text{mol}^{-1}}\cdot\cancel{K}^{-1})(295\ \cancel{K})}{10\ \cancel{L}} = 4.84\ \text{atm}$

<u>6.5</u>   Ideal Gas Law: $PV = nRT$

$n = \dfrac{PV}{RT} = \dfrac{(1.05\ \cancel{\text{atm}})(10.0\ \cancel{L})}{(0.0821\ \cancel{L}\cdot\cancel{\text{atm}}\cdot\text{mol}^{-1}\cdot\cancel{K}^{-1})(303\ \cancel{K})} = 0.422\ \text{mol Ne}$

<u>6.7</u>   Dalton's Law of Partial Pressures:
  Total pressure $(P_T) = P_{N_2} + P_{H_2O}$

$P_{H_2O} = P_T - P_{N_2} = 2.015\ \text{atm} - 1.908\ \text{atm} = 0.107\ \text{atm of } H_2O\ \text{vapor}$

<u>6.9</u>   Heat of vaporization of water = 540 cal/g

$45.0\ \cancel{\text{kcal}}\left(\dfrac{1000\ \cancel{\text{cal}}}{1\ \cancel{\text{kcal}}}\right)\left(\dfrac{1\ \text{g } H_2O}{540\ \cancel{\text{cal}}}\right) = 83.3\ \text{g } H_2O\ \text{vaporized}$

<u>6.11</u> According to the phase diagram of water (figure 5.18), the vapor will undergo reverse sublimation and form a solid.

<u>6.13</u> Boyle's Law:

At constant temperature, $\left(\dfrac{P_1 V_1}{\cancel{T_1}}\right) = \left(\dfrac{P_2 V_2}{\cancel{T_2}}\right)$ reduces to $P_1 V_1 = P_2 V_2$

$P_1 = \dfrac{P_2 V_2}{V_1} = \dfrac{(12.2\ \text{atm})(2.5\ \cancel{L})}{20\ \cancel{L}} = 1.5\ \text{atm } CH_4$

6.15 Gay-Lussac's Law: The tire is at constant volume.

At constant volume, $\left(\dfrac{P_1 \cancel{V_1}}{T_1}\right) = \left(\dfrac{P_2 \cancel{V_2}}{T_2}\right)$ reduces to $\dfrac{P_1}{T_1} = \dfrac{P_2}{T_2}$

$P_2 = \dfrac{P_1 T_2}{T_1} = \dfrac{(2.30 \text{ atm})(\cancel{320 \text{ K}})}{293 \cancel{K}} = 2.51$ atm of air in the tire

6.17 Charles's Law:

At constant presure, $\left(\dfrac{\cancel{P_1} V_1}{T_1}\right) = \left(\dfrac{\cancel{P_2} V_2}{T_2}\right)$ reduces to $\dfrac{V_1}{T_1} = \dfrac{V_2}{T_2}$

$V_2 = \dfrac{V_1 T_2}{T_1} = \dfrac{(4.17 \text{ L})(448 \cancel{K})}{998 \cancel{K}} = 1.87$ L of ethane gas upon cooling

6.19 Gay-Lussac's Law:

At constant volume, $\left(\dfrac{P_1 \cancel{V_1}}{T_1}\right) = \left(\dfrac{P_2 \cancel{V_2}}{T_2}\right)$ reduces to $\dfrac{P_1}{T_1} = \dfrac{P_2}{T_2}$

$T_2 = \dfrac{P_2 T_1}{P_1} = \dfrac{(375 \text{ mm Hg})(898 \text{ K})}{450 \text{ mm Hg}} = 748$ K (475°C)

6.21 Gay-Lussac's Law:

At constant volume, $\left(\dfrac{P_1 \cancel{V_1}}{T_1}\right) = \left(\dfrac{P_2 \cancel{V_2}}{T_2}\right)$ reduces to $\dfrac{P_1}{T_1} = \dfrac{P_2}{T_2}$

$P_2 = \dfrac{P_1 T_2}{T_1} = \dfrac{(1.00 \text{ atm})(438 \cancel{K})}{373 \cancel{K}} = 1.17$ atm

6.23 Complete this table: Use the $\dfrac{P_1 V_1}{T_1} = \dfrac{P_2 V_2}{T_2}$ equation.

V₁	T₁	P₁	V₂	T₂	P₂
546 L	43°C	6.5 atm	**1198 L**	65°C	1.9 atm
43 mL	-56°C	865 torr	**48 mL**	43°C	1.5 atm
4.2 L	234 K	0.87 atm	3.2 L	29°C	**1.5 atm**
1.3 L	25°C	740 mm Hg	**1.2 L**	0°C	1.0 atm

Chapter 6 Gases, Liquids, and Solids

6.25 Charles's Law: atmospheric pressure acting on balloon is constant

$$V_2 = \frac{V_1 T_2}{T_1} = \frac{(1.2\ L)(77\ K)}{298\ K} = 0.31\ L\ \text{balloon's final volume}$$

6.27 $P_2 = \frac{P_1 V_1 T_2}{T_1 V_2} = \frac{(56.44\ L)(2.00\ atm)(281\ K)}{(310\ K)(23.52\ L)} = 4.35\ atm$

6.29 $V_2 = \frac{P_1 V_1 T_2}{T_1 P_2} = \frac{(756\ mm\ Hg)(30.0\ mL)(260.5\ K)}{(298\ K)(325\ mm\ Hg)} = 61.0\ mL$

6.31 (a) $n = \frac{PV}{RT} = \frac{(1.33\ atm)(50.3\ L)}{(0.0821\ L \cdot atm \cdot mol^{-1} \cdot K^{-1})(350\ K)} = 2.33\ mol$

(b) The only information that we need to know about the gas is that it is an ideal gas.

6.33 Using the PV=nRT Gas Law equation, the following equation is derived:

$$MW = \frac{(mass)RT}{PV} = \frac{(8.00\ g)(0.0821\ L \cdot atm \cdot mol^{-1} \cdot K^{-1})(273\ K)}{(2.00\ atm)(22.4\ L)} = 4.00\ g/mol$$

6.35 Using the PV=nRT equation, we can derive:

$$\frac{mass}{V} = density = \frac{P(MW)}{RT}$$

(a) At constant T, equation reduces to density = (constant) x (pressure), therefore, the density increases as pressure increases.

(b) At constant P, the equation reduces to density = (constant)(1/T), therefore, density decreases with increasing T.

6.37 Using the PV = nRT equation:

(a) $n = \frac{PV}{RT} = \frac{(3.00\ atm)(200\ L)}{(0.0821\ L \cdot atm \cdot mol^{-1} \cdot K^{-1})(296\ K)} = 24.7\ mol\ O_2$

(b) Mass of $O_2 = 24.7\ mol\ O_2 \left(\frac{32.0\ g\ O_2}{1\ mol\ O_2} \right) = 790\ g\ O_2$

34

$\underline{6.39}$ 5.5 $\cancel{\text{L air}}\left(\dfrac{0.21 \text{ L O}_2}{1 \ \cancel{\text{L air}}}\right) = 1.16 \text{ L O}_2$

$$\text{Moles of O}_2 = n = \frac{PV}{RT} = \frac{(1.1 \ \cancel{\text{atm}})(5.5 \ \cancel{\text{L}})}{(0.0821 \ \cancel{\text{L}} \bullet \cancel{\text{atm}} \bullet \text{mol}^{-1} \bullet \cancel{\text{K}^{-1}})(310 \ \cancel{\text{K}})} = 0.238 \text{ mol O}_2$$

$0.238 \ \cancel{\text{mol O}_2}\left(\dfrac{6.02 \times 10^{23} \text{ molecules O}_2}{1 \ \cancel{\text{mol O}_2}}\right) = 1.4 \times 10^{23} \text{ molecules O}_2$

$\underline{6.41}$ 1.0000 mole air = 0.7808 mol N_2 + 0.2095 mol O_2 + 0.0093 mol Ar
1.000 mole of air =

$0.7808 \text{ mol}_{N_2}\left(\dfrac{28.01 \text{ g N}_2}{1 \text{ mol N}_2}\right) + 0.2095 \text{ mol}_{O_2}\left(\dfrac{32.00 \text{ g O}_2}{1 \text{ mol O}_2}\right) + 0.0093 \text{ mol}_{Ar}\left(\dfrac{39.95 \text{ g Ar}}{1 \text{ mol Ar}}\right)$

(a)   1.000 mole of air = 28.95 g/mol

(b) $d(\text{g/L})_{air} = \left(\dfrac{28.95 \text{ g air}}{1 \ \cancel{\text{mol air}}}\right)\left(\dfrac{1 \ \cancel{\text{mol air}}}{22.4 \text{ L}}\right) = 1.29 \text{ g/L}$

$\underline{6.43}$ (a) $d_{SO_2} = \left(\dfrac{64.1 \text{ g}}{1 \ \cancel{\text{mol SO}_2}}\right)\left(\dfrac{1 \ \cancel{\text{mol SO}_2}}{22.4 \text{ L}}\right) = 2.86 \text{ g/L}$

(b) $d_{CH_4} = \left(\dfrac{16.0 \text{ g}}{1 \ \cancel{\text{mol CH}_4}}\right)\left(\dfrac{1 \ \cancel{\text{mol CH}_4}}{22.4 \text{ L}}\right) = 0.714 \text{ g/L}$

(c) $d_{H_2} = \left(\dfrac{2.02 \text{ g}}{1 \ \cancel{\text{mol H}_2}}\right)\left(\dfrac{1 \ \cancel{\text{mol H}_2}}{22.4 \text{ L}}\right) = 0.0902 \text{ g/L}$

(d) $d_{He} = \left(\dfrac{4.00 \text{ g}}{1 \ \cancel{\text{mol H}_2}}\right)\left(\dfrac{1 \ \cancel{\text{mol He}}}{22.4 \text{ L}}\right) = 0.179 \text{ g/L}$

(e) $d_{CO_2} = \left(\dfrac{44.0 \text{ g}}{1 \ \cancel{\text{mol CO}_2}}\right)\left(\dfrac{1 \ \cancel{\text{mol CO}_2}}{22.4 \text{ L}}\right) = 1.96 \text{ g/L}$

Gas comparison: SO_2 and CO_2 are denser than air; He, H_2 and CH_4 are less dense than air.

6.45 1.00 mL of octane (d = 0.7025 g/mL)

$$\text{Mass of octane} = 1.00 \text{ mL Octane} \left(\frac{0.7025 \text{ g Octane}}{1 \text{ mL Octane}} \right) = 0.7025 \text{ g Octane}$$

$$V_{Octane} = \frac{nRT}{P} = \frac{\left(\frac{0.7025 \text{ g}}{114.2 \text{ g} \cdot \text{mol}^{-1}} \right) \left(0.0821 \text{ L} \cdot \text{atm} \cdot \text{mol}^{-1} \cdot \text{K}^{-1} \right) \left(373 \text{ K} \right)}{\left(725 \text{ torr} \right) \left(\frac{1.00 \text{ atm}}{760 \text{ torr}} \right)} = 0.197 \text{ L}$$

6.47 The densities would be the same. The density of a substance does not depend on its quantity.

6.49 (a) $P_T = P_{N2} + P_{O2} + P_{Ar}$

$P_{N_2} = (0.7808)(760 \text{ mm Hg}) = 594 \text{ mm Hg}$

$P_{O_2} = (0.2095)(760 \text{ mm Hg}) = 159 \text{ mm Hg}$

$P_{Ar} = (0.0093)(760 \text{ mm Hg}) = 7 \text{ mm Hg}$

$P_T = 760 \text{ mm Hg}$

(b) The total pressure exerted by the components is the sum of their partial pressures: 760 mm Hg (1.00 atm)

6.51 The total pressure should be the sum of its partial pressures.

$P_{N_2} = 560 \text{ mm Hg}$

$P_{O_2} = 210 \text{ mm Hg}$

$P_{CO_2} = 15 \text{ mm Hg}$

Partial Pressure Sum: 785 mm Hg $P_T = 790 \text{ mm Hg}$

Difference of 5 mm Hg, therefore, there must be another gas present.

6.53 Covalent bonds are stronger than hydrogen bonds. Covalent bonds involve the sharing of electrons, where hydrogen bonds involve weaker electrostatic interactions.

6.55 Yes, the water OH can hydrogen bond (the hydrogen bond donor) with the oxygen lone pair on the S=O (the hydrogen bond acceptor).

$$H_3C \quad \cdots \cdots H - O - H$$
$$S=O$$
$$H_3C$$

6.57 Ethanol is a polar molecule and engages in intermolecular hydrogen bonding. Carbon dioxide is a nonpolar molecule and has only weak intermolecular London dispersion forces. The stronger hydrogen bonding intermolecular forces require more energy and higher temperatures to break before boiling.

6.59 Hexane has a higher boiling point. It is a larger molecule than butane, thus hexane has larger London dispersion forces to overcome before boiling.

6.61 Ionic compounds (salts) have the highest melting points because they require the greatest amount of energy to exceed the strongest of intermolecular forces (170-970 kcal/mol). An example includes sodium chloride (m.p. 801 $^{\circ}$C). Nonpolar compounds have lowest melting points because London dispersion forces are the weakest of the intermolecular forces and require the least amount of energy to break (0.01-2 kcal/mol). An example of a nonpolar compound is naphthalene ($C_{10}H_8$, m.p. 80 $^{\circ}$C).

6.63 $39.2 \text{ g } CF_2Cl_2 \left(\dfrac{1 \text{ mol } CF_2Cl_2}{120.9 \text{ g } CF_2Cl_2} \right) \left(\dfrac{4.71 \text{ kcal}}{1 \text{ mol } CF_2Cl_2} \right) = 1.53 \text{ kcal to vaporize the } CF_2Cl_2$

6.65 (a) ~90 mm Hg   (b) ~120 mm Hg   (c) ~490 mm Hg

6.67 (a) HCl < HBr < HI
Increasing size of molecule increases London dispersion forces.

(b) O_2 < HCl < H_2O_2
O_2 has only weak London dispersion forces to overcome for boiling, where HCl is a polar molecule with stronger dipole-dipole attractions to overcome for boiling. H_2O_2 has the strongest intermolecular forces (hydrogen bonding) to exceed for boiling to occur.

<u>6.69</u> The difference between heating water from 0°C to 37°C and heating ice from 0°C to 37°C is the heat of fusion.

<u>The energy required to heat ice from 0°C to 37°C:</u>

$$100 \text{ g } H_2O\left(\frac{1.0 \text{ cal}}{\text{g} \cdot {}^\circ\text{C}}\right)\left(37^\circ\text{C}\right) + 100 \text{ g } H_2O\left(\frac{80 \text{ cal}}{\text{g}}\right) = 11700 \text{ cal (12 kcal)}$$

<u>The energy required to heat liquid water from 0°C to 37°C:</u>

$$100 \text{ g } H_2O\left(\frac{1.0 \text{ cal}}{\text{g} \cdot {}^\circ\text{C}}\right)\left(37^\circ\text{C}\right) = 3700 \text{ cal (3.7 kcal)}$$

<u>6.71</u> Sublimation is the conversion of a solid to gas, bypassing the liquid phase.

<u>6.73</u> $1.00 \text{ mL Freon-11}\left(\dfrac{1.49 \text{ g Freon-11}}{1 \text{ mL Freon-11}}\right)\left(\dfrac{1 \text{ mol Freon-11}}{137.4 \text{ g Freon-11}}\right) = 1.08 \times 10^{-2} \text{ mol Freon-11}$

$$1.08 \times 10^{-2} \text{ mol Freon-11}\left(\frac{6.42 \text{ kcal}}{1 \text{ mol Freon-11}}\right) = 6.94 \times 10^{-2} \text{ kcal}$$

<u>6.75</u> When the temperature of a substance increases, so does its entropy, therefore, a gas at 100°C has lower entropy than at 200°C.

<u>6.77</u> When a person lowers their diaphragm, the volume of the chest cavity increases, thus lowering the pressure in the lungs relative to atmospheric pressure. Air at atmospheric pressure then rushes into the lungs, beginning the breathing process.

<u>6.79</u> The first tapping sound one hears is the systolic pressure, which occurs when the sphygmomanometer pressure matches the blood pressure when the ventricle contracts, pushing blood into the arm.

<u>6.81</u> When water freezes, it expands (one of the few substances that expands upon freezing) and will break the bottle when the ice expansion exceeds the volume of the bottle.

<u>6.83</u> It is difficult to compress liquids and solids because their molecules or atoms are already very close together and there is very little empty space between them.

<u>6.85</u> Conversion of psi to atm of an average tire pressure of 34 psi:

$$34 \text{ psi}\left(\frac{1 \text{ atm}}{14.7 \text{ psi}}\right) = 2.3 \text{ atm}$$

6.87 Aerosol cans already contain gases under high pressures. Gay-Lussac's Law predicts that the pressure inside the can will increase with increasing temperature, with the potential of the can explosively rupturing and causing injury.

6.89 $V_2 = \dfrac{P_1 V_1 T_2}{T_1 P_2} = \dfrac{\left(275 \; \text{mm Hg}\right)\left(\dfrac{1 \; \text{atm}}{760 \; \text{mm Hg}}\right)(387 \; \text{mL})(378 \; \text{K})}{(348 \; \text{K})(1.36 \; \text{atm})} = 112 \; \text{mL}$

6.91 Boiling point order:
H_2O (H-bonding) > $CHCl_3$ (dipole-dipole) > C_5H_{12} (London dispersion forces)

6.93 (a) As a gas is compressed under pressure, the molecules are forced closer together and the intermolecular forces pull the molecules together, forming a liquid.

(b) $20 \; \text{lbs propane} \left(\dfrac{1 \; \text{kg}}{2.205 \; \text{lb of propane}}\right) = 9.1 \; \text{kg}$

(c) $9.1 \; \text{kg propane} \left(\dfrac{1000 \; \text{g propane}}{1 \; \text{kg propane}}\right)\left(\dfrac{1 \; \text{mole propane}}{44.1 \; \text{g propane}}\right) = 2.1 \times 10^2 \; \text{moles of propane}$

(d) $210 \; \text{mol propane} \left(\dfrac{22.4 \; \text{L propane}}{1 \; \text{mol propane}}\right) = 4.7 \times 10^3 \; \text{L propane}$

6.95 $d \; (\text{g/L}) = \left(\dfrac{0.00300 \text{g}}{\text{cm}^3}\right)\left(\dfrac{1000 \; \text{cm}^3}{\text{L}}\right) = 3.00 \; \text{g/L}$

$MW = \dfrac{\text{massRT}}{VP} = \dfrac{(3.00\text{g})(0.0821 \; \text{L·atm·mol}^{-1}\text{·K}^{-1})(373 \; \text{K})}{(1.00 \; \text{L})(1.00 \; \text{atm})} = 91.9 \; \text{g/mol}$

6.97 Use the PV = nRT equation after converting some of the units:

$$\text{Mol of NH}_3 = 60.0 \text{ g NH}_3 \left(\frac{1 \text{ mol NH}_3}{17.0 \text{ g NH}_3} \right) = 3.52 \text{ mol NH}_3$$

$$P \text{ (in atm)} = 77.2 \text{ inch Hg} \left(\frac{25.4 \text{ mm Hg}}{1 \text{ inch Hg}} \right) \left(\frac{1 \text{ atm}}{760 \text{ mm Hg}} \right) = 2.58 \text{ atm}$$

$$T = \frac{PV}{nR} = \frac{(2.58 \text{ atm})(35.1 \text{ L})}{(3.52 \text{ mol})(0.0821 \text{ L·atm·mol}^{-1} \text{·K}^{-1})} = 313 \text{ K} (40°C)$$

6.99 The temperature of a liquid drops during evaporation because the molecules with higher kinetic energy leave the liquid as a gas, decreasing the average kinetic energy of the liquid. The temperature of the liquid is directly proportional to its average kinetic energy, therefore, the temperature decreases as the average kinetic energy decreases.

6.101 (a) Pressure on body $= 100 \text{ ft} \left(\frac{1 \text{ atm}}{33 \text{ ft}} \right) = 3.0 \text{ atm}$

(b) At 1.00 atm, $P_{N2} = 593$ mm Hg (0.780 atm) and thus makes up 78.0% of the gas mixture, which does not change at the depth of 100 feet. At a depth of 100 feet, the total pressure on the lungs, which is equalized by pressure of air delivered by the SCUBA tank, is 3.0 atm.

$$P_{N_2} \text{ (at 100 ft)} = 3.0 \text{ atm total pressure} \left(\frac{0.78 \text{ atm } P_{N_2}}{1 \text{ atm total pressure}} \right) = 2.34 \text{ atm } P_{N_2}$$

(c) At 2 atm, $P_{O2} = 158$ mm Hg (0.208 atm) and thus makes up 20.8% of the gas mixture at 2 atm, which does not change at the depth of 100 feet. At a depth of 100 feet, the total pressure on the lungs, which is equalized by pressure of air delivered by the SCUBA tank, is 3.0 atm.

$$P_{O_2} \text{ (at 100 ft)} = 3.0 \text{ atm total pressure} \left(\frac{0.21 \text{ atm } P_{O_2}}{1 \text{ atm total pressure}} \right) = 0.63 \text{ atm } P_{O_2}$$

(d) As a diver ascends from 100 ft, the external pressure on the lungs decreases, therefore the volume of gasses in the lungs increases. If the diver does not exhale vigorously during a rapid ascent, the diver's lungs could over-inflate due to expanding gasses in the lungs, causing injury.

7.1 4.4% w/v KBr solution = 4.4 g KBr in 100 mL of solution

$$250 \text{ mL solution}\left(\frac{4.4 \text{ g KBr}}{100 \text{ mL solution}}\right) = 11 \text{ g KBr}$$

Add enough water to 11 g KBr to make 250 mL of solution

7.3 First, calculate the number of moles and mass of KCl that are needed:
Moles = M x V.

$$\text{Moles of KCl} = \left(\frac{1.06 \text{ mol KCl}}{1 \text{ L sol}}\right)(2.0 \text{ L sol}) = 2.12 \text{ mol KCl}$$

$$\text{Mass of KCl} = 2.12 \text{ mol KCl}\left(\frac{74.6 \text{ g KCl}}{1 \text{ mol KCl}}\right) = 158 \text{ g KCl}$$

Place 158 g of KCl into a 2-L volumetric flask, add some water, swirl until the solid has dissolved, and then fill the flask with water to the 2.0-L mark.

7.5 First, convert grams of glucose into moles of glucose, then convert moles of glucose into mL of solution:

$$\text{Moles of glucose} = 10.0 \text{ g glucose}\left(\frac{1 \text{ mol glucose}}{180 \text{ g glucose}}\right) = 0.0556 \text{ mol glucose}$$

$$0.0556 \text{ mol glucose}\left(\frac{1 \text{ L sol}}{0.300 \text{ mol glucose}}\right)\left(\frac{1000 \text{ mL sol}}{1 \text{ L sol}}\right) = 185 \text{ mL glucose sol}$$

7.7 Use the $M_1V_1 = M_2V_2$ equation:

$$V_1 = \frac{(0.600 \text{ M HCl})(300 \text{ mL sol HCl})}{(12.0 \text{ M HCl})} = 15.0 \text{ mL}$$

Place 15.0 mL of a 12.0 M HCl solution into a 300-mL volumetric flask, add some water, swirl until completely mixed, and then fill the flask with water to the 300-mL mark.

7.9 First calculate the mass of Na^+ ion in the 560 g of $NaHSO_4$. Then determine the Na^+ ion concentration in the solution using ppm.

$$560 \text{ g NaHSO}_4 \left(\frac{1 \text{ mol NaHSO}_4}{120 \text{ g NaHSO}_4} \right) \left(\frac{1 \text{ mol Na}^+}{1 \text{ mol NaHSO}_4} \right) \left(\frac{23.0 \text{ g Na}^+}{1 \text{ mol Na}^+} \right) = 107 \text{ g Na}^+$$

$$[Na^+] = \frac{107 \text{ g Na}^+}{4.5 \times 10^5 \text{ L sol}} \left(\frac{1 \text{ L sol}}{1 \text{ kg sol}} \right) \left(\frac{1 \text{ kg sol}}{1000 \text{ g sol}} \right) \times 10^6 \text{ ppm} = 0.24 \text{ ppm Na}^+$$

7.11 Compare the number of moles of ions or molecules in each solution. The solution with the most ions or molecules in solution will have the lowest freezing point.

Solution	Particle solution
(a) 6.2 M NaCl	2 x 6.2 M = 12.4 M ions
(b) 2.1 M Al(NO$_3$)$_3$	4 x 2.1 M = 8.4 M ions
(c) 4.3 M K$_2$SO$_3$	3 x 4.3 M = 12.9 M ions

Solution (c) has the highest concentration of solute particles (ions), therefore it will have the lowest freezing point.

7.13 The osmolarity of red blood cells is 0.30 osmol:

Solution	Particle solution
(a) 0.1 M Na$_2$SO$_4$	3 x 0.1 M = 0.3 osmol
(b) 1.0 M Na$_2$SO$_4$	3 x 1.0 M = 3.0 osmol
(c) 0.2 M Na$_2$SO$_4$	3 x 0.2 M = 0.6 osmol

Solution (a) has the same osmolarity as red blood cells, therefore is isotonic compared to red blood cells.

7.15 Glucose is being dissolved, therefore it is the solute. Water is dissolving the glucose, therefore water is the solvent.

7.17 (a) Wine (ethanol in water)
(b) Saline solution (NaCl dissolved in water)
(c) Carbonated water (carbon dioxide dissolved in water)
(d) Air (oxygen and nitrogen)

7.19 The prepared aspartic acid solution was unsaturated. Over two days time, some of the solvent (water) may have evaporated and the solution became supersaturated, precipitating the excess aspartic acid as a white solid.

7.21 (a) Ionic NaCl will dissolve in the polar water layer.
(b) Nonpolar camphor will dissolve in the nonpolar diethyl ether layer.
(c) Ionic KOH will dissolve in the polar layer.

7.23 Isopropyl alcohol would be a good first choice. The oil base in the paint is nonpolar. Both benzene and hexane are nonpolar solvents and may dissolve the paint, thus destroying the painting.

7.25 The solubility of aspartic acid at 25°C in 50.0 mL water is 0.250 g of solute. The cooled solution of 0.251 g aspartic acid in 50.0 mL water will be supersaturated by 0.001 g of aspartic acid.

7.27 According to Henry's Law, the solubility of a gas in a liquid is directly proportional to pressure. A closed bottle of a carbonated beverage is under pressure. After the bottle is opened, the pressure is released and the carbon dioxide becomes less soluble and escapes.

7.29 (a) Both quantities are equivalent to one significant figure.

$$\frac{1 \text{ min}}{2 \text{ yr}} \left(\frac{1 \text{ yr}}{365 \text{ days}} \right) \left(\frac{1 \text{ day}}{24 \text{ hr}} \right) \left(\frac{1 \text{ hr}}{60 \text{ min}} \right) \times 10^6 \text{ ppm} = 0.95 \text{ ppm}$$

$$\frac{1 \text{ cent}}{10,000 \text{ dol}} \left(\frac{1 \text{ dol}}{100 \text{ cents}} \right) \times 10^6 \text{ ppm} = 1 \text{ ppm}$$

(b) Both quantities are equivalent to one significant figure.

$$\frac{1 \text{ min}}{2000 \text{ yr}} \left(\frac{1 \text{ yr}}{365 \text{ days}} \right) \left(\frac{1 \text{ day}}{24 \text{ hr}} \right) \left(\frac{1 \text{ hr}}{60 \text{ min}} \right) \times 10^9 \text{ ppb} = 0.95 \text{ ppb}$$

$$\frac{1 \text{ cent}}{10,000,000 \text{ dol}} \left(\frac{1 \text{ dol}}{100 \text{ cents}} \right) \times 10^9 \text{ ppb} = 1 \text{ ppb}$$

7.31 (a) Vol. of ethanol = 280 mL sol $\left(\frac{27 \text{ mL ethanol}}{100 \text{ mL sol}} \right)$ = 76 mL ethanol

76 mL ethanol dissolved in 204 mL water (to give 280 mL of solution)

(b) Vol. of ethyl acetate = 435 mL sol $\left(\frac{1.8 \text{ mL ethyl acetate}}{100 \text{ mL sol}} \right)$ = 7.8 mL ethyl acetate

8 mL ethyl acetate dissolved in 427 mL water (to give 435 mL of solution)

(c) Vol. of benzene = 1.65 L sol $\left(\frac{1000 \text{ mL sol}}{1 \text{ L sol}} \right) \left(\frac{8.00 \text{ mL benzene}}{100 \text{ mL sol}} \right)$ = 132 mL benzene

0.13 L benzene dissolved in 1.52 L chloroform (to give 1.65 L of solution)

7.33 (a) % (w/v) = $\dfrac{623 \text{ mg casein}}{15.0 \text{ mL sol}}\left(\dfrac{1 \text{ g casein}}{1000 \text{ mg casein}}\right) \times 100\% = 4.15 \%$ w/v casein

(b) % (w/v) = $\dfrac{74 \text{ mg vit. C}}{250 \text{ mL sol}}\left(\dfrac{1 \text{ g vit. C}}{1000 \text{ mg vit. C}}\right) \times 100\% = 0.030 \%$ w/v vitamin C

(c) % (w/v) = $\dfrac{3.25 \text{ g sucrose}}{186 \text{ mL sol}} \times 100\% = 1.75 \%$ w/v sucrose

7.35 (a) $175 \text{ mL sol}\left(\dfrac{1 \text{ L sol}}{1000 \text{ mL sol}}\right)\left(\dfrac{1.14 \text{ mol NH}_4\text{Br}}{1 \text{ L solution}}\right)\left(\dfrac{97.9 \text{ g NH}_4\text{Br}}{1 \text{ mol NH}_4\text{Br}}\right) = 19.5 \text{ g NH}_4\text{Br}$

Place 19.5 g of NH_4Br into a 175-mL volumetric flask, add some water, swirl until completely dissolved, and then fill the flask with water to the 175-mL mark.

(b) $1.35 \text{ L sol}\left(\dfrac{0.825 \text{ mol NaI}}{1 \text{ L solution}}\right)\left(\dfrac{149.9 \text{ g NaI}}{1 \text{ mol NaI}}\right) = 167 \text{ g NaI}$

Place 167 g of NaI into a 1.35-L volumetric flask, add some water, swirl until completely dissolved, and then fill the flask with water to the 1.35-L mark.

(c) $330 \text{ mL sol}\left(\dfrac{1 \text{ L sol}}{1000 \text{ mL sol}}\right)\left(\dfrac{0.16 \text{ mol ethanol}}{1 \text{ L solution}}\right)\left(\dfrac{46.1 \text{ g ethanol}}{1 \text{ mol ethanol}}\right) = 2.4 \text{ g ethanol}$

Place 2.4 g of ethanol into a 330-mL volumetric flask, add some water, swirl until completely mixed, and then fill the flask with water to the 330-mL mark.

7.37 $M_{NaCl} = \dfrac{5.0 \text{ mg NaCl}}{0.5 \text{ mL sol}}\left(\dfrac{1 \text{ g NaCl}}{1000 \text{ mg NaCl}}\right)\left(\dfrac{1 \text{ mol NaCl}}{58.4 \text{ g NaCl}}\right)\left(\dfrac{1000 \text{ mL sol}}{1 \text{ L sol}}\right) = 0.2 \ M \text{ NaCl}$

7.39 $M_{glucose} = \dfrac{22.0 \text{ g glucose}}{240 \text{ mL sol}}\left(\dfrac{1 \text{ mol glucose}}{180 \text{ g glucose}}\right)\left(\dfrac{1000 \text{ mL sol}}{1 \text{ L sol}}\right) = 0.509 \ M \text{ glucose}$

$M_{K+} = \dfrac{190 \text{ mg K}^+}{240 \text{ mL sol}}\left(\dfrac{1 \text{ g}}{1000 \text{ mg}}\right)\left(\dfrac{1 \text{ mol K}^+}{39.1 \text{ g K}^+}\right)\left(\dfrac{1000 \text{ mL sol}}{1 \text{ L sol}}\right) = 0.0202 \ M \text{ K}^+$

$M_{Na+} = \dfrac{4.00 \text{ mg K}^+}{240 \text{ mL sol}}\left(\dfrac{1 \text{ g}}{1000 \text{ mg}}\right)\left(\dfrac{1 \text{ mol Na}^+}{23.0 \text{ g Na}^+}\right)\left(\dfrac{1000 \text{ mL sol}}{1 \text{ L sol}}\right) = 7.25 \times 10^{-4} \ M \text{ Na}^+$

7.41 $M_{sucrose} = \dfrac{13 \text{ g sucrose}}{15 \text{ mL sol}} \left(\dfrac{1 \text{ mol sucrose}}{342.3 \text{ g sucrose}} \right) \left(\dfrac{1000 \text{ mL sol}}{1 \text{ L sol}} \right) = 2.5 \; M$ sucrose

7.43 Use the $\%_1 V_1 = \%_2 V_2$ equation:

$$V_2 = \frac{\left(0.750\% \text{ w/v albumin}\right)\left(5.00 \text{ mL sol}\right)}{\left(0.125\% \text{ w/v albumin}\right)} = 30.0 \text{ mL}$$

The total volume of the dilution is 30.0 mL. Starting with a 5.00 mL solution, <u>25.0 mL of water must be added</u> to reach a final volume of 30.0 mL.

7.45 Use the $\%_1 V_1 = \%_2 V_2$ equation:

$$V_1 = \frac{\left(0.25\% \text{ w/v } H_2O_2\right)\left(250 \text{ mL sol}\right)}{\left(30.0\% \text{ w/v } H_2O_2\right)} = 2.1 \text{ mL } H_2O_2$$

Place 2.1 mL of 30.0% w/v H_2O_2 into a 250-mL volumetric flask, add some water, swirl until completely mixed, and then fill the flask with water to the 250-mL mark.

7.47 (a) $\dfrac{12.5 \text{ mg Captopril}}{325 \text{ mg pill}} \times 10^6 \text{ ppm} = 3.85 \times 10^4 \text{ ppm Captopril}$

(b) $\dfrac{22 \text{ mg Mg}^{2+}}{325 \text{ mg pill}} \times 10^6 \text{ ppm} = 6.8 \times 10^4 \text{ ppm Mg}^{2+}$

(c) $\dfrac{0.27 \text{ mg Ca}^{2+}}{325 \text{ mg pill}} \times 10^6 \text{ ppm} = 8.3 \times 10^2 \text{ ppm Ca}^{2+}$

7.49 Assume the density of the lake water to be 1.0 g/mL

$$1 \times 10^7 \text{ L water} \left(\frac{1000 \text{ mL water}}{1 \text{ L water}} \right) \left(\frac{1.0 \text{ g water}}{1.0 \text{ mL water}} \right) = 1 \times 10^{10} \text{ g water}$$

$$\frac{0.1 \text{ g dioxin}}{1 \times 10^{10} \text{ g water}} \times 10^9 \text{ ppb} = 0.01 \text{ ppb dioxin}$$

No, the dioxin level in the lake did not reach a dangerous level.

7.51 First, calculate the mass (in grams) of the nutrients in the cheese based on their percentages of daily allowances, then calculate concentration in ppm:

Iron: $(0.02)(15 \text{ mg Fe})\left(\dfrac{1 \text{ g Fe}}{1000 \text{ mg Fe}}\right) = 3 \times 10^{-4} \text{ g Fe}$

$$\dfrac{3 \times 10^{-4} \text{ g Fe}}{28 \text{ g cheese}} \times 10^6 \text{ ppm} = 10 \text{ ppm Fe}$$

Calcium: $(0.06)(1200 \text{ mg Ca})\left(\dfrac{1 \text{ g Ca}}{1000 \text{ mg Ca}}\right) = 7 \times 10^{-2} \text{ g Ca}$

$$\dfrac{7 \times 10^{-2} \text{ g Ca}}{28 \text{ g cheese}} \times 10^6 \text{ ppm} = 3 \times 10^3 \text{ ppm Ca}$$

Vitamin A: $(0.06)(0.800 \text{ mg Vit. A})\left(\dfrac{1 \text{ g}}{1000 \text{ mg Vit. A}}\right) = 5 \times 10^{-5} \text{ g Vitamin A}$

$$\dfrac{5 \times 10^{-5} \text{ g Vit. A}}{28 \text{ g cheese}} \times 10^6 \text{ ppm} = 2 \text{ ppm Vitamin A}$$

7.53 Both (a) 0.1 M KCl and (b) 0.1 M $(NH_4)_3PO_4$ will conduct electricity because they are strong electrolytes. A 0.1 M $(NH_4)_3PO_4$ solution (b) will have a greater conductivity than 0.1 M KCl because it has the largest concentration of dissociated ions (4 mole of ions dissociated per mole of $(NH_4)_3PO_4$, giving a 0.4 M solution of ions) compared to a 0.1 M KCl solution (2 mole of ions dissociated per mole of KCl, giving a 0.2 M solution of ions).

7.55 The polar compounds, (b), (c), and (d) will be soluble in water by forming hydrogen bonds with water.

7.57 (a) Homogeneous (b) Heterogeneous (c) Colloid
     (d) Heterogeneous (e) Colloid (f) Colloid

7.59 As the temperature of the solution decreased, the protein molecules must have aggregated and formed a colloidal mixture. The turbid appearance is the result of the Tyndall effect.

7.61 $\Delta T = (1.86°C/\text{mol})(\text{mole of particles in solution per 1000 g of water})$:

(a) $\Delta T = 1 \text{ mol NaCl}\left(\dfrac{2 \text{ mol particle}}{1 \text{ mol NaCl}}\right)\left(\dfrac{1.86°C}{\text{mol particle}}\right) = 3.72°C$ f.p. = -3.72°C

(b) $\Delta T = 1 \text{ mol } MgCl_2 \left(\dfrac{3 \text{ mol particle}}{1 \text{ mol } MgCl_2} \right) \left(\dfrac{1.86°C}{\text{mol particle}} \right) = 5.58°C$ f.p. = -5.58°C

(c) $\Delta T = 1 \text{ mol } (NH_4)_2CO_3 \left(\dfrac{3 \text{ mol particle}}{1 \text{ mol } (NH_4)_2CO_3} \right) \left(\dfrac{1.86°C}{\text{mol particle}} \right) = 5.58°C$

f.p. = -5.58°C

(d) $\Delta T = 1 \text{ mol } Al(HCO_3)_3 \left(\dfrac{4 \text{ mol particle}}{1 \text{ mol } Al(HCO_3)_3} \right) \left(\dfrac{1.86°C}{\text{mol particle}} \right) = 7.44°C$

f.p. = -7.44°C

7.63 Methanol is a non-electrolyte and does not dissociate. Use the following equation for freezing point depression while also converting to grams.

$$\text{Moles of } CH_3OH \text{ per } 1000 \text{ g } H_2O = \Delta T \left(\dfrac{1 \text{ mol particles}}{1.86°C} \right)$$

$$20°C \left(\dfrac{1 \text{ mol particles}}{1.86°C} \right) \left(\dfrac{1 \text{ mole } CH_3OH}{1 \text{ mol particles}} \right) \left(\dfrac{32.0 \text{ g } CH_3OH}{1 \text{ mol } CH_3OH} \right) = 344 \text{ g } CH_3OH$$

7.65 Acetic acid is a weak acid, therefore does not completely dissociate into ions. KF is a strong electrolyte, completely dissociating into two ions and doubling the effect on freezing point depression compared to acetic acid.

7.67 In each case, the side with the greater osmolarity rises.
(a) B   (b) B   (c) A   (d) B   (e) A   (f) same

7.69 (a) $\text{osmol}_{Na_2CO_3} = 0.39 \, M \times 3 \text{ particles} = 1.2 \text{ osmol}$

(b) $\text{osmol}_{Al(NO_3)_3} = 0.62 \, M \times 4 \text{ particles} = 2.5 \text{ osmol}$

(c) $\text{osmol}_{LiBr} = 4.2 \, M \times 2 \text{ particles} = 8.4 \text{ osmol}$

(d) $\text{osmol}_{K_3PO_4} = 0.009 \, M \times 4 \text{ particles} = 0.04 \text{ osmol}$

7.71 Cells in hypertonic solutions under crenation (shrink).

$$osmol_{NaCl} = \frac{0.9 \text{ g NaCl}}{100 \text{ mL sol}} \left(\frac{1000 \text{ mL sol}}{1 \text{ L sol}} \right) \left(\frac{1 \text{ mol NaCl}}{58.4 \text{ g NaCl}} \right) \left(\frac{2 \text{ mol particles}}{1 \text{ mol NaCl}} \right) = 0.3 \text{ osmol}$$

(a) $\dfrac{0.3 \text{ g NaCl}}{100 \text{ mL sol}} \left(\dfrac{1000 \text{ mL sol}}{1 \text{ L sol}} \right) \left(\dfrac{1 \text{ mol NaCl}}{58.4 \text{ g NaCl}} \right) \left(\dfrac{2 \text{ mol particles}}{1 \text{ mol NaCl}} \right) = 0.1 \text{ osmol NaCl}$

(b) $osmol_{glucose} = 0.9 \, M \times 1 \text{ particle} = 0.9 \text{ osmol}$

(c) $\dfrac{0.9 \text{ g glu}}{100 \text{ mL sol}} \left(\dfrac{1000 \text{ mL sol}}{1 \text{ L sol}} \right) \left(\dfrac{1 \text{ mol glu}}{180 \text{ g glu}} \right) \left(\dfrac{1 \text{ mol particles}}{1 \text{ mol glu}} \right) = 0.05 \text{ osmol glucose}$

Solution (b) has a concentration greater than the isotonic solution so it will crenate red blood cells.

7.73 Carbon dioxide (CO_2) dissolves in normal rainwater to form a dilute solution of carbonic acid (H_2CO_3), which is a weak acid.

7.75 Nitrogen dissolved in the blood can lead to nitrogen narcosis, a narcotic effect also referred to as "rapture of the deep", which is similar to alcohol-induced intoxication.

7.77 The main component of limestone and marble is calcium carbonate ($CaCO_3$).

7.79 The minimum pressure required for the reverse osmosis in the desalinization of seawater exceeds 100 atm (the osmotic pressure of sea water).

7.81 $\dfrac{0.2 \text{ g NaHCO}_3}{100 \text{ mL sol}} \left(\dfrac{1000 \text{ mL sol}}{1 \text{ L sol}} \right) \left(\dfrac{1 \text{ mol NaHCO}_3}{84.0 \text{ g NaHCO}_3} \right) \left(\dfrac{2 \text{ mol particles}}{1 \text{ mol NaHCO}_3} \right) = 0.05 \text{ osmol}$

$osmol_{NaHCO_3} = 0.05 \text{ osmol}$

$\dfrac{0.2 \text{ g KHCO}_3}{100 \text{ mL sol}} \left(\dfrac{1000 \text{ mL sol}}{1 \text{ L sol}} \right) \left(\dfrac{1 \text{ mol KHCO}_3}{100.1 \text{ g KHCO}_3} \right) \left(\dfrac{2 \text{ mol particles}}{1 \text{ mol KHCO}_3} \right) = 0.04 \text{ osmol}$

$osmol_{KHCO_3} = 0.04 \text{ osmol}$

Yes, the change made a change in the tonicity. The error in replacing $NaHCO_3$ with $KHCO_3$ resulted in a hypotonic solution and an electrolyte imbalance by reducing the number of ions (osmolarity) in solution.

7.83 When the cucumber is placed in a saline solution, the osmolarity of the saline is greater than the water in the cucumber, so water moves from the cucumber to the saline solution. When a prune (partially dehydrated plum) is placed in the same solution, it expands because the osmolarity inside the prune is greater than the saline solution, so the water moves from saline solution to inside the prune.

7.85 The solubility of a gas is directly proportional to the pressure (Henry's Law) and inversely proportional to the temperature. The dissolved carbon dioxide formed a saturated solution in water when bottled at 2 atm of pressure. When the bottles are opened at atmospheric pressure, the gas becomes less soluble in the water. The carbon dioxide becomes supersaturated in water at room temperature and 1 atm , thus escapes through bubbles and frothing. In the other bottle, the solution of carbon dioxide in water is unsaturated at lower temperatures and does not lose carbon dioxide.

7.87 No, it would not be acceptable to use a 0.89% KCl solution for intravenous infusions because it will not be isotonic with blood. KCl has a higher molecular weight than NaCl, consequently its osmolarity will be smaller.

$$\frac{0.89 \text{ g NaCl}}{100 \text{ mL sol}}\left(\frac{1000 \text{ mL sol}}{1 \text{ L sol}}\right)\left(\frac{1 \text{ mol NaCl}}{58.4 \text{ g NaCl}}\right)\left(\frac{2 \text{ mol particles}}{1 \text{ mol NaCl}}\right) = 0.30 \text{ osmol NaCl}$$

$$\frac{0.89 \text{ g KCl}}{100 \text{ mL sol}}\left(\frac{1000 \text{ mL sol}}{1 \text{ L sol}}\right)\left(\frac{1 \text{ mol KCl}}{74.6 \text{ g KCl}}\right)\left(\frac{2 \text{ mol particles}}{1 \text{ mol KCl}}\right) = 0.24 \text{ osmol KCl}$$

7.89 $5.0 \text{ g reagent}\left(\frac{0.05 \text{ g Pb}}{10^6 \text{ g reagent}}\right) = 3 \times 10^{-7} \text{ g Pb}$

7.91 $osmol_{NaCl} = \frac{0.9 \text{ g NaCl}}{100 \text{ mL sol}}\left(\frac{1000 \text{ mL sol}}{1 \text{ L sol}}\right)\left(\frac{1 \text{ mol NaCl}}{58.4 \text{ g NaCl}}\right)\left(\frac{2 \text{ mol particles}}{1 \text{ mol NaCl}}\right) = 0.3 \text{ osmol}$

$osmol_{dex} = \frac{25 \text{ g dex}}{100 \text{ mL sol}}\left(\frac{1000 \text{ mL sol}}{1 \text{ L sol}}\right)\left(\frac{1 \text{ mol dex}}{15,000 \text{ g dex}}\right)\left(\frac{1 \text{ mol particles}}{1 \text{ mol dex}}\right) = 0.017 \text{ osmol}$

The NaCl solution, solution (a), will have the greater osmotic pressure.

7.93 Use the $M_1V_1 = M_2V_2$ equation:

$$V_2 = \frac{M_1V_1}{M_2} = \frac{(1.18 \text{ osmol})(1.0 \text{ mL})}{0.30 \text{ osmol}} = 3.9 \text{ mL (final volume)}$$

3.9 mL - 1.0 mL = 2.9 mL of H_2O added to sea water (1.0 mL) to reach blood osmolarity

7.95 The ethanol displaced the water from the solvation layer of the hyaluronic acid and thus allowed hyaluronic acid molecules to stick together upon collision and aggregate.

<u>8.1</u>   The rate of the reaction is equal to the change in the amount of O_2 per unit time.

$$\text{Rate of } O_2 \text{ formation} = \frac{\left(0.35 \text{ L } O_2 - 0.020 \text{ L } O_2\right)}{15 \text{ min}} = 0.022 \text{ L } O_2/\text{min}$$

<u>8.3</u> $K = \dfrac{\left[H_2SO_4\right]}{\left[SO_3\right]\left[H_2O\right]}$

<u>8.5</u> $K = \dfrac{\left[PCl_5\right]}{\left[PCl_3\right]\left[Cl_2\right]} = \dfrac{\left[1.66 \, M\right]}{\left[1.66 \, M\right]\left[1.66 \, M\right]} = 0.602 \, M^{-1}$

<u>8.7</u>   Le Chatelier's principle would predict that the equilibrium would shift to the left by adding a product (Br_2).

<u>8.9</u>   If the equilibrium shifts right with the addition of heat, heat must have been a reactant and the reaction endothermic.

<u>8.11</u> Rate of CH_3I formation $= \dfrac{\left(0.840 \, M \text{ } CH_3I - 0.260 \, M \text{ } CH_3I\right)}{80 \text{ min}} = 7.25 \times 10^{-3} \, M \text{ } CH_3I/\text{min}$

<u>8.13</u> Reactions involving aqueous solution of ions require no bond breaking and are very fast because of low activation energies. Reactions between covalent molecules require covalent bonds to be broken, requiring higher activation energies, thus slower reaction rates.

<u>8.15</u> The following energy diagram can be drawn for an exothermic reaction:

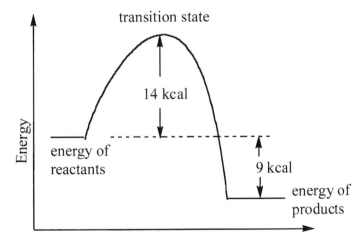

Progress of reaction

51

8.17 The general rule for temperature effect on reaction rates states that for every temperature increase of 10 °C, the reaction rate doubles.

Temperature: 10°C $\rightarrow$ 20°C $\rightarrow$ 30°C $\rightarrow$ 40°C $\rightarrow$ 50°C
Rate: 16 hr $\rightarrow$ 8 hr $\rightarrow$ 4 hr $\rightarrow$ 2 hr $\rightarrow$ 1 hr

A reaction temperature of 50 °C corresponds to a reaction completion time of 1 hr.

8.19 (1) Increase the temperature
(2) Increase the concentration of reactants
(3) Add a catalyst

8.21 A catalyst increases the rate by providing an alternate reaction pathway of lower activation energy.

8.23 Examples of irreversible reactions include: digesting a piece of candy, the rusting of iron, exploding TNT, and the reaction of sodium or potassium with water.

8.25 (a) $K = \dfrac{[H_2O]^2[O_2]}{[H_2O_2]^2}$

(b) $K = \dfrac{[N_2O_4]^2[O_2]}{[N_2O_5]^2}$

(c) $K = \dfrac{[C_6H_{12}O_6][O_2]^6}{[H_2O]^6[CO_2]^6}$

8.27 $K = \dfrac{[CO_2][H_2]}{[H_2O][CO]} = \dfrac{[0.133\ M][3.37\ M]}{[0.720\ M][0.933\ M]} = 0.667$

8.29 $K = \dfrac{[NO]^2[Cl_2]}{[NOCl_2]^2} = \dfrac{[1.4\ M]^2[0.34\ M]}{[2.6\ M]^2} = 0.099\ M$

8.31 When K > 1, equilibrium favors products; when K < 1, equilibrium favors reactants. Products are favored in (b) and (c). Reactants are favored in (a), (d), and (e)

8.33 No, the rate of reaction is independent of the energy difference between products and reactant. The rate of reaction is inversely proportional to the activation energy.

8.35 The reaction reaches equilibrium quickly, but the equilibrium favors the reactants (K < 1) and would not be a very good industrial process.

8.37 (a) Right   (b) Right   (c) Left   (d) Left   (e) No shift

8.39 (a) Adding Br_2 (a reactant), will shift the equilibrium to the right.
(b) The equilibrium constant will remain the same.

8.41 (a) No change   (b) No change   (c) Smaller
Equilibrium constants are independent of reactant and product concentrations. The K of an endothermic reaction will decrease with decreasing temperature

8.43 As temperatures increase, the rates of most chemical processes increase. A high body temperature is dangerous because metabolic processes (including digestion, respiration, and the biosynthesis of essential compounds) take place at a rate faster than what is safe for the body. As temperatures decrease, so do the rates of most chemical reactions. As body temperatures decrease below normal, the vital chemical reactions will slow down to rates slower than what is safe for the body.

8.45 The capsule with the tiny beads will act faster than the solid pill form. The small bead size increases the drug's surface area allowing the drug to react faster and deliver its therapeutic effects more quickly.

8.47 The addition of heat is used to increase the rate of reaction. The addition of a catalyst permits the reaction to take place at a convenient rate and temperature.

8.49 The following energy diagram can be drawn for an exothermic reaction:

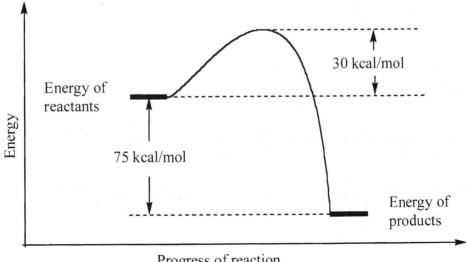

8.51 Rate = k[NOBr]

$$k = \frac{rate}{[NOBr]} = \frac{-2.3 \text{ mol NOBr/} \cancel{L} \cdot hr}{6.2 \text{ mol NOBr/} \cancel{L}} = -0.37/hr$$

8.53 Rate = $\frac{[0.180 \text{ mol/L } N_2O_4 - 0.200 \text{ mol/L } N_2O_4]}{10 \text{ s}}$ = -2.0 × 10^{-3} mol N_2O_4 / L · s

8.55 The activation energy of the reverse reaction will be:
      Ea = 10.0 kcal/mol – energy of reaction

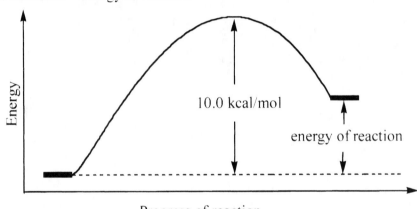

8.57 The temperature increase is 20°C, and the rate doubles twice. The rate of reaction at 320 K
      is 0.88 M/min.

8.59 Endothermic reactions must have an activation energy greater than zero. By definition,
      endothermic reactions occur where the products have a greater energy than the reactants.

8.61 Assuming that there is excess AgCl in the previous recipe, the new recipe does not need to
      change. The desert conditions add nothing that would affect an equilibrium initiated by
      light.

8.63 (a) At equilibrium: [Ethanol] = 0.33 mol and [Ethyl acetate] = [H_2O] = 0.67 mol.

      (b) $K_{eq} = \frac{[\text{Ethyl acetate}][H_2O]}{[\text{Acetic acid}][\text{Ethanol}]} = \frac{[0.33 \text{ mol}[0.33\text{mol}]}{[0.67 \text{ mol}][0.67\text{mol}]} = 0.24$

9.1   Acid reaction for HPO_4^{2-}:
$$HPO_4^{2-} + H_2O \rightleftharpoons H_3O^+ + PO_4^{3-}$$
Base reaction for HPO_4^{2-}:
$$HPO_4^{2-} + H_3O^+ \rightleftharpoons H_2O + H_2PO_4^{1-}$$

9.3 $pK_a = -\log K_a$
pK_a HCN $= -\log 4.9 \times 10^{-10} = 9.31$

9.5 $[H_3O^+][OH^-] = 1 \times 10^{-14}$
$$[H_3O^+] = \frac{1.0 \times 10^{-14}}{1.0 \times 10^{-12}} = 1.0 \times 10^{-2} \ M$$

9.7 $pH + pOH = 14$
$[OH^-] = 1.0 \times 10^{-4}$ $pOH = 4$
$[H_3O^+] = 1.0 \times 10^{-10}$ $pH = 10$

9.9   The pH of a buffer solution containing equimolar quantities of acid and conjugate base is equal to the pK_a of the weak acid.
(a) NH_4Cl and NH_3: pK_a $NH_4Cl = 9.25$
(b) CH_3COOH and CH_3COONa: pK_a $CH_3COOH = 4.75$

9.11 Use the Henderson-Hasselbalch Equation: $pH = pK_a + \log[A^-]/[HA]$ where:
$$pH = 8.3 + \log\left(\frac{0.05 \ mol}{0.2 \ mol}\right) = 7.7$$

The mole amount of TRIS acid and base was used instead of concentration because they are both dissolved in 500 mL of water, therefore, the amount of water cancels out. The TRIS buffer will have a pH of 8 (to one significant figure).

9.13 Listed below are the following acid ionization equilibrium equations:
(a) $HNO_3(aq) + H_2O(l) \rightleftharpoons H_3O^+(aq) + NO_3^-(aq)$

(b) $HBr(g) + H_2O(l) \rightleftharpoons H_3O^+(aq) + Br^-(aq)$

(c) $H_2SO_3(aq) + H_2O(l) \rightleftharpoons H_3O^+(aq) + HSO_3^-(aq)$

(d) $H_2SO_4(aq) + H_2O(l) \rightleftharpoons H_3O^+(aq) + HSO_4^-(aq)$

(e) $HCO_3^-(aq) + H_2O(l) \rightleftharpoons H_3O^+(aq) + CO_3^{2-}(aq)$

(f) $H_3BO_3(aq) + H_2O(l) \rightleftharpoons H_3O^+(aq) + H_2BO_3^-(aq)$

Chapter 9 Acids and Bases

<u>9.15</u> Acids (a), (c), (e), and (f) have pK_a's > 0, therefore do not ionize completely and are considered to be weak acids. Acids (b) and (d) have pK_a's < 0; therefore are ionized completely and are considered to be strong acids.

<u>9.17</u> Acids that have pK_a's > 0 do not ionize completely and are considered to be weak acids; therefore, an acid with a pK_a of 2.1 is a weak acid.

<u>9.19</u> (a) Brønsted-Lowry acids are considered proton donors.
(b) Brønsted-Lowry bases are considered proton acceptors.

<u>9.21</u> A conjugate base is the species that results after the acid lost its proton.
(a) HPO_4^{2-} (b) HS^- (c) CO_3^{2-}
(d) $CH_3CH_2O^-$ (e) OH^-

<u>9.23</u> A conjugate acid results from a base acquiring a proton from an acid:
(a) H_3O^+ (b) $H_2PO_4^-$ (c) $CH_3NH_3^+$
(d) HPO_4^{2-} (e) $H_2BO_3^-$

<u>9.25</u> The equilibrium favors the side with the weaker acid-weaker base.
Equilibria (b) and (c) favor the left, equilibrium (a) favors the right.

(a) C_6H_5OH + $C_2H_5O^-$ $\rightleftharpoons$ $C_6H_5O^-$ + C_2H_5OH
stronger acid   stronger base   weaker base   weaker acid

(b) HCO_3^- + H_2O $\rightleftharpoons$ H_2CO_3 + OH^-
weaker base   weaker acid   stronger acid   stronger base

(c) CH_3COOH + $H_2PO_4^-$ $\rightleftharpoons$ CH_3COO^- + H_3PO_4
weaker acid   weaker base   stronger base   stronger acid

<u>9.27</u> (a) Strong acids have smaller pK_a's, therefore weak acids have large pK_a's.
(b) Strong acids have large K_a's.

<u>9.29</u> At equal concentrations, pH decreases (becomes more acidic) as K_a increases.
(a) 0.10 M HCl   (b) 0.10 M H_3PO_4 (c) 0.010 M H_2CO_3
(d) 0.10 M NaH_2PO_4 (e) 0.10 M Aspirin

9.31 Only (b) Mg involves a redox reaction. The other reactions are acid-base reactions.

(a) Na_2CO_3 + 2HCl → CO_2 + 2NaCl + H_2O

(b) Mg + 2HCl → $MgCl_2$ + H_2

(c) NaOH + HCl → NaCl + H_2O

(d) Fe_2O_3 6HCl → $2FeCl_3$ + $3H_2O$

(e) NH_3 + HCl → NH_4Cl

(f) CH_3NH_2 + HCl → CH_3NH_3Cl

(g) $NaHCO_3$ + HCl → H_2CO_3 + NaCl → CO_2 + H_2O + NaCl

9.33 Using the equation: $[H_3O^+][OH^-] = 1.0 \times 10^{-14}\ M^2$

(a) $[OH^-] = 10^{-3}\ M$ (b) $[OH^-] = 10^{-10}\ M$

(c) $[OH^-] = 10^{-7}\ M$ (d) $[OH^-] = 10^{-15}\ M$

9.35 Using the equation: $pH = -\log[H_3O^+]$:

(a) pH = 8 (basic) (b) pH = 10 (basic) (c) pH = 2 (acidic)

(d) pH = 0 (acidic) (e) pH = 7 (neutral)

9.37 Using the equation: $pH = -\log[H_3O^+]$ and pH + pOH = 14.

(a) pH = 8.5 (basic) (b) pH = 1.2 (acidic)

(c) pH = 11 (basic) (d) pH = 6.3 (acidic)

9.39 Using the equation: $[OH^-] = 10^{-pOH}$ and pH + pOH = 14.

(a) pOH = 1.0, $[OH^-]$ = 0.10 M (b) pOH = 2.4, $[OH^-]$ = 4.0 x $10^{-3}\ M$

(c) pOH = 2.0, $[OH^-]$ = 1.0 x $10^{-2}\ M$ (d) pOH = 5.6, $[OH^-]$ = 2.5 x $10^{-6}\ M$

9.41 $M = \dfrac{mol}{L} = \left(\dfrac{12.7\ \text{g HCl}}{1.00\ \text{L sol}}\right)\left(\dfrac{1\ mol\ HCl}{36.5\ \text{g HCl}}\right) = 0.348\ M\ HCl$

9.43 (a) 12 g of NaOH diluted to 400 mL of solution:

$$400\ \text{mL sol}\left(\dfrac{1\ \text{L sol}}{1000\ \text{mL sol}}\right)\left(\dfrac{0.75\ \text{mol NaOH}}{1\ \text{L sol}}\right)\left(\dfrac{40.0\ g\ NaOH}{1\ \text{mol NaOH}}\right) = 12\ g\ NaOH$$

(b) 12 g of $Ba(OH)_2$ diluted to 1.0 L of solution:

$$\dfrac{0.071\ \text{mol Ba(OH)}_2}{1\ L\ sol}\left(\dfrac{171.4\ g\ Ba(OH)_2}{1\ \text{mol Ba(OH)}_2}\right) = 12\ g\ Ba(OH)_2$$

9.45 5.66 mL of 0.740 M H$_2$SO$_4$ are required to titrate 27.0 mL of 0.310 M NaOH.

$$27.0 \text{ mL NaOH sol} \left(\frac{1 \text{ L sol}}{1000 \text{ mL sol}} \right) \left(\frac{0.310 \text{ mol NaOH}}{1 \text{ L sol}} \right) = 8.37 \times 10^{-3} \text{ mol NaOH}$$

$$8.37 \times 10^{-3} \text{ mol NaOH} \left(\frac{1 \text{ mol H}_2\text{SO}_4}{2 \text{ mol NaOH}} \right) \left(\frac{1 \text{ L H}_2\text{SO}_4 \text{ sol}}{0.740 \text{ mol H}_2\text{SO}_4} \right) \left(\frac{1000 \text{ mL sol}}{1 \text{ L sol}} \right) = 5.66 \text{ mL}$$

9.47 Assuming that the base generates one mole of hydroxide per mole of base:

$$22.0 \text{ mL HCl sol} \left(\frac{0.150 \text{ mol HCl}}{1000 \text{ mL sol}} \right) \left(\frac{1 \text{ mol H}^+}{1 \text{ mol HCl}} \right) = 3.30 \times 10^{-3} \text{ mol H}^+$$

At the end point, 3.30×10^{-3} mol of H$^+$ added to 3.30×10^{-3} mol of the unknown base.

9.49 The point at which an indicator changes color is called the end point.

9.51 In the CH$_3$COOH/CH$_3$COO$^-$ buffer solution, the CH$_3$COO$^-$ is completely ionized while the CH$_3$COOH is only partially ionized.

(a) H$_3$O$^+$ + CH$_3$COO$^-$ $\rightleftharpoons$ CH$_3$COOH + H$_2$O (removal of H$_3$O$^+$)

(b) HO$^-$ + CH$_3$COOH $\rightleftharpoons$ CH$_3$COO$^-$ + H$_2$O (removal of OH$^-$)

9.53 Yes, the conjugate acid becomes the weak acid and the weak base becomes the conjugate base.

9.55 The pH of a buffer can be changed by altering the weak acid/conjugate base ratio according to the Henderson-Hasselbalch equation. The buffer capacity can be changed without change in pH by increasing or decreasing the amount of weak acid/conjugate base mixture while keeping the ratio of the two constant.

9.57 This would occur in a couple of cases. One is very common, which is where you are using a buffer, such as TRIS with a pKa of 8.3, but you do not want the solution to have a pH of 8.3. If you wanted a pH of 8.0, for example, you would have to have unequal amounts of the conjugate acid and base, with there being more conjugate acid. Another might be a situation where you are performing a reaction that you know will generate H$^+$ but you want the pH to be stable. In that situation, you might start with a buffer that was initially set to have more of the conjugate base so that it could absorb more of the H$^+$ that you know will be produced.

9.59 (a) According to the Henderson-Hasselbalch equation, no change in pH will be observed as long as the ratio of weak acid/conjugate base ratio remains the same.

(b) The buffer capacity increases with increasing amount of weak acid/conjugate base concentrations, therefore, 1.0 mol amounts of each diluted to 1 L would have a greater buffer capacity than 0.1 mol of each diluted to 1 L.

9.61 Using the Henderson-Hasselbalch Equation:

(a) $pH = pK_a + \log\dfrac{[\text{lactate}^-]}{[\text{lactic acid}]} = 3.85 + \log\dfrac{[0.40\ M]}{[0.80\ M]} = 3.5$

(b) $pH = pK_a + \log\dfrac{[NH_3]}{[NH_4^+]} = 9.25 + \log\dfrac{[0.30\ M]}{[1.50\ M]} = 8.6$

9.63 The 100 mL of 0.1 M phosphate buffer initially contains 0.01 moles of NaH_2PO_4 and Na_2HPO_4 components.

If the two components of the buffer are equal: $pH = 7.21 + \log\dfrac{[0.1M]}{[0.1M]} = 7.21$

A pH of 6.8 suggests that there is more of the acid (greater than 0.01 moles of NaH_2PO_4) than conjugate base (less than 0.01 moles of Na_2HPO_4). The addition of 10 mL of 1 M HCl (0.01 mol) will overwhelm the buffers' capacity to neutralize the additional acid.

9.65 $pH = pK_a + \log\dfrac{[\text{TRIS}]}{[\text{TRIS-H}]^+}$

$pH = 8.3 + \log\dfrac{[0.05M]}{[0.1M]} = 8.0$

9.67 No. HEPES has a pK_a of 7.55, which means it is a useable buffer between pH 6.55 and 8.55.

9.69 $Mg(OH)_2$ is a weak base used as a flame-retardant in plastics.

9.71 Both strong acids and strong bases are very harmful to the eyes, but strong bases are more harmful to the cornea because the healing of the wounds can deposit non-transparent scar tissue that impairs vision.

9.73 (a) Respiratory acidosis is caused by hypoventilation, which is caused by a variety of breathing difficulties, such as a windpipe obstruction, asthma, or pneumonia.

(b) Metabolic acidosis is caused by starvation or heavy exercise.

9.75 Sodium bicarbonate is the weak base form of one of the blood buffers. It will tend to raise the pH of the blood, which is the purpose of the sprinter's trick, so that the person can absorb more H$^+$ during the event. By putting NaHCO$_3$ into the system, the following reaction will occur:

$$HCO_3^-(aq) \ + \ H^+(aq) \ \rightleftharpoons \ H_2CO_3(aq)$$

The loss of the H$^+$ means that the blood pH will rise.

9.77 The equilibrium favors the side of the weaker acid/weaker base.
(a) Benzoic acid is soluble in aqueous NaOH.

$$C_6H_5COOH \ + \ NaOH \ \rightleftharpoons \ C_6H_5COO^- \ + \ H_2O$$

pK$_a$ = 4.19 \qquad\qquad\qquad\qquad pK$_a$ = 15.56

(b) Benzoic acid is soluble in aqueous NaHCO$_3$.

$$C_6H_5COOH \ + \ NaHCO_3 \ \rightleftharpoons \ CH_3C_6H_4O^- \ + \ H_2CO_3$$

pK$_a$ = 4.19 \qquad\qquad\qquad\qquad pK$_a$ = 6.37

(c) Benzoic acid is soluble in aqueous Na$_2$CO$_3$.

$$C_6H_5COOH \ + \ CO_3^{2-} \ \rightleftharpoons \ CH_3C_6H_4O^- \ + \ HCO_3^-$$

pK$_a$ = 4.19 \qquad\qquad\qquad\qquad pK$_a$ = 10.25

9.79 The strength of an acid is not important to the amount of NaOH that would be required to hit a phenolphthalein endpoint. Therefore, the more concentrated acid, the acetic acid, would require more NaOH.

9.81 The solution of oxalic acid is 3.70 x 10^{-3} M

$$\frac{0.583 \ g \ H_2C_2O_4}{1.75 \ L \ sol}\left(\frac{1 \ mol \ H_2C_2O_4}{90.04 \ g \ H_2C_2O_4}\right) = 3.70 \times 10^{-3} \ M \ oxalic \ acid$$

9.83 The concentration of barbituric acid equilibrates to 0.90 M.

$$K_a = \frac{[Barbiturate^-][H_3O^+]}{[Barbituric \ acid]} \qquad x = [H_3O^+] = [Barbiturate^-]$$

$$[Barbituric \ acid] = \frac{x^2}{K_a} = \frac{(0.0030)^2}{1.0 \times 10^{-5}} = 0.90 \ M$$

9.85 Yes, a pH = 0 is possible. A 1.0 M solution of HCl has a [H$_3$O$^+$] = 1.0 M.
pH = -log[H$_3$O$^+$] = -log[1.0 M] = 0

9.87 The qualitative relationship between acids and their conjugate bases states that the stronger the acid, the weaker its conjugate base. This can be quantified in the equation: $K_b \times K_a = K_w$ or $K_b = 1.0 \times 10^{-14}/K_a$ where K_b is the base dissociation equilibrium constant for the conjugate base, K_a is the acid dissociation equilibrium constant for the acid, and K_w is the ionization equilibrium constant for water.

9.89 Yes. The strength of the acid is irrelevant. Both acetic acid and HCl have one H^+ to give up, so equal moles of either will require equal moles of NaOH to titrate to an endpoint.

9.91 Using the Henderson-Hasselbalch equation:

$$\frac{[H_2BO_3^-]}{[H_3BO_3]} = 10^{pH - pKa} = 10^{8.40-9.14}$$

$$\frac{[H_2BO_3^-]}{[H_3BO_3]} = 0.182$$

Need 0.182 mol of $H_2BO_3^-$ and 1.00 mol of H_3BO_3 in 1.00 L of solution.

9.93 Equilibria favor the side of the weaker acid/weaker base. Large pK_a values correlate with weak acids and small pK_a values correlate with strong acids, therefore, equilibria favor the side with the largest pK_a values.

9.95 (a) $HCOO^- + H_3O^+ \rightleftharpoons HCOOH + H_2O$

(b) $HCOOH + HO^- \rightleftharpoons HCOO^- + H_2O$

9.97 Using the Henderson-Hasselbalch Equation:
(a) $[Na_2HPO_4] = [NaH_2PO_4]10^{pH - pKa} = [0.050M]10^{7.21-7.21} = 0.050\ M$
(b) $[Na_2HPO_4] = [NaH_2PO_4]10^{pH - pKa} = [0.050M]10^{6.21-7.21} = 0.0050\ M$
(c) $[Na_2HPO_4] = [NaH_2PO_4]10^{pH - pKa} = [0.050M]10^{8.21-7.21} = 0.50\ M$

9.99 According to the Henderson-Hasselbalch equation:

$$pH = 7.21 + \log\frac{[HPO_4^{2-}]}{[H_2PO_4^-]}$$

As the concentration of $H_2PO_4^-$ increases, the $\log\frac{[HPO_4^{2-}]}{[H_2PO_4^-]}$ becomes negative, thus lowering the pH and becoming more acidic.

9.101 No. A buffer will only have a pH equal to its pK_a if there are equimolar amounts of the conjugate acid and base forms. If this is the basic form of TRIS, then just putting any amount of that into water will give a pH much higher than the pK_a value.

9.103 (a) pH = 7.1, $[H_3O^+]$ = 7.9 x 10^{-8} M, basic
(b) pH = 2.0, $[H_3O^+]$ = 7.9 x 10^{-2} M, acidic
(c) pH = 7.4, $[H_3O^+]$ = 4.0 x 10^{-8} M, basic
(d) pH = 7.0, $[H_3O^+]$ = 1.0 x 10^{-7} M, neutral
(e) pH = 6.6, $[H_3O^+]$ = 2.5 x 10^{-7} M, acidic
(f) pH = 7.4, $[H_3O^+]$ = 4.0 x 10^{-8} M, basic
(g) pH = 6.5, $[H_3O^+]$ = 3.2 x 10^{-7} M, acidic
(h) pH = 6.9, $[H_3O^+]$ = 1.3 x 10^{-7} M, acidic

9.105 Using the Henderson-Hasselbalch equation:

$$7.9 = 7.21 + \log \frac{[HPO_4^{2-}]}{[H_2PO_4^-]}$$

$$\frac{[HPO_4^{2-}]}{[H_2PO_4^-]} = 10^{0.19} = 4.9$$

Some Important Organic Functional Groups

	Functional Group*	Example	IUPAC (Common) Name
Alcohol	$-\overset{\cdot\cdot}{\underset{\cdot\cdot}{O}}H$	CH_3CH_2OH	Ethanol (Ethyl alcohol)
Aldehyde	$-\overset{\displaystyle\overset{\cdot\cdot}{O}\cdot}{\underset{}{C}}-H$	$CH_3\overset{\displaystyle O}{\overset{\|}{C}}H$	Ethanal (Acetaldehyde)
Alkane		CH_3CH_3	Ethane
Alkene	$\overset{}{\underset{}{C}}=\overset{}{\underset{}{C}}$	$CH_2=CH_2$	Ethene (Ethylene)
Alkyne	$-C\equiv C-$	$HC\equiv CH$	Ethyne (Acetylene)
Amide	$-\overset{\displaystyle\overset{\cdot\cdot}{O}\cdot}{\underset{}{C}}-\overset{}{\underset{\|}{\overset{\cdot\cdot}{N}}}-$	$CH_3\overset{\displaystyle O}{\overset{\|}{C}}NH_2$	Ethanamide (Acetamide)
Amine	$-\overset{\cdot\cdot}{N}H_2$	$CH_3CH_2NH_2$	Ethanamine (Ethylamine)
Anhydride	$-\overset{\displaystyle\overset{\cdot\cdot}{O}\cdot}{\underset{}{C}}-\overset{\cdot\cdot}{\underset{\cdot\cdot}{O}}-\overset{\displaystyle\overset{\cdot\cdot}{O}\cdot}{\underset{}{C}}-$	$CH_3\overset{\displaystyle O}{\overset{\|}{C}}O\overset{\displaystyle O}{\overset{\|}{C}}CH_3$	Ethanoic anhydride (Acetic anhydride)
Arene			Benzene
Carboxylic acid	$-\overset{\displaystyle\overset{\cdot\cdot}{O}\cdot}{\underset{}{C}}-\overset{\cdot\cdot}{\underset{\cdot\cdot}{O}}H$	$CH_3\overset{\displaystyle O}{\overset{\|}{C}}OH$	Ethanoic acid (Acetic acid)
Disulfide	$-\overset{\cdot\cdot}{\underset{\cdot\cdot}{S}}-\overset{\cdot\cdot}{\underset{\cdot\cdot}{S}}-$	CH_3SSCH_3	Dimethyl disulfide
Ester	$-\overset{\displaystyle\overset{\cdot\cdot}{O}\cdot}{\underset{}{C}}-\overset{\cdot\cdot}{\underset{\cdot\cdot}{O}}-C-$	$CH_3\overset{\displaystyle O}{\overset{\|}{C}}OCH_3$	Methyl ethanoate (Methyl acetate)
Ether	$-\overset{\cdot\cdot}{\underset{\cdot\cdot}{O}}-$	$CH_3CH_2OCH_2CH_3$	Diethyl ether
Haloalkane (Alkyl halide)	$-\overset{\cdot\cdot}{\underset{\cdot\cdot}{X}}:$ X = F, Cl, Br, I	CH_3CH_2Cl	Chloroethane (Ethyl chloride)
Ketone	$-\overset{\displaystyle\overset{\cdot\cdot}{O}\cdot}{\underset{}{C}}-$	$CH_3\overset{\displaystyle O}{\overset{\|}{C}}CH_3$	Propanone (Acetone)
Phenol	$-\overset{\cdot\cdot}{\underset{\cdot\cdot}{O}}H$	$-OH$	Phenol
Sulfide	$-\overset{\cdot\cdot}{\underset{\cdot\cdot}{S}}-$	CH_3SCH_3	Dimethyl sulfide
Thiol	$-\overset{\cdot\cdot}{S}H$	CH_3CH_2SH	Ethanethiol (Ethyl mercaptan)